Slavery in
North Carolina,
1748–1775

Marvin L. Michael Kay and Lorin Lee Cary

Slavery

in North Carolina,

1748–1775

The

University

of North

Carolina

Press

Chapel Hill

and London

© 1995 The University of North Carolina Press

All rights reserved

Manufactured in the United States of America

The paper in this book meets the guidelines for permanence and durability of the Committee on Production Guidelines for Book Longevity of the Council on Library Resources.

Library of Congress Cataloging-in-Publication Data

Kay, Marvin L. Michael.

Slavery in North Carolina, 1748–1775 / Marvin L. Michael Kay and Lorin Lee Cary.

 p. cm.

 Includes bibliographical references and index.

 ISBN 0-8078-2197-7 (cloth: alk. paper)

 ISBN 0-8078-4819-0 (pbk.: alk. paper)

 1. Slavery—North Carolina—History—18th century. 2. North Carolina—History—Colonial period, ca. 1600–1775. I. Cary, Lorin Lee. II. Title.

E445.N8K39 1995   94-29751

306.3′62′0975609033   CIP

03 02 01 00 99 6 5 4 3 2

I want to thank my five children for their patience during these too many years of my working in the thickets of this research. And to my wife, Bettye Ruth, whose loving help saved me from being forever lost in the woods, I gratefully dedicate this book. And now she has died. And with her my soul.

—M.L.M.K.

My thanks to Marlene Cary—spouse, companion, friend—for her love and understanding; to my daughters, Elissa Stein and Michelle Wipf, for their patience with the process; and to Andy, Peggy, and Lauren Goldberg for support at several junctures.

I dedicate this book to my parents, Ruth and Harry. My mother, an artist, stimulated my creativity and encouraged an interest in history; my father, himself a researcher, taught the importance of inquiry and tolerance.

—L.L.C.

Where justice is denied, where poverty is enforced, where ignorance prevails, and where any one class is made to feel that society is in an organized conspiracy to oppress, rob, and degrade them, neither persons nor property will be safe.

—Frederick Douglass, speech delivered on the twenty-fourth anniversary
   of Emancipation in the District of Columbia,
   April 1886

A slave family was "driven in from the country, like swine for market. A poor wench clung to a little daughter and implored, with the most agonizing supplication, that they must not be separated. But alas, either the master or circumstances were inexorable—they were sold to different purchasers. The husband and the residue of the family were knocked off to the highest bidder."

—Elkanah Watson, description of a slave auction in Wilmington,
   North Carolina, 1778, in his *Memoirs*

Should you, my lord, while you peruse my song,
Wonder from whence my love of Freedom sprung,
Where flow these wishes for the common good,
By feeling hearts alone best understood,
I, young in life, by seeming cruel fate,
Was snatch'd from Afric's fancy'd happy seat:
What pangs excruciating must molest,
What sorrows labour in my parent's breast?
Steel'd was the soul and by no misery mov'd
That from a father seiz'd his babe belov'd:
Such, such my case. And can I then but pray
Others may never feel tyrannic sway?

—Phillis Wheatley,
   Poems on Various Subjects, Religious and Moral, 1773

"And we do hereby, by virtue of an Act of Assembly of this Province concerning Servants and Slaves, intimate and declare, if the said Jem does not surrender himself, and return home immediately after the Publication of these Presents, that any Person or Persons may kill and destroy said Slave, by such means as he or they shall think fit . . . without incurring any Penalty or Forfeiture thereby."

—Proclamation by two justices of the Craven County Court concerning a slave named Jem, believed to be "lurking about" his home plantation, *North Carolina Gazette* (New Bern), 12 May 1775

[Five slave] "conspirators, after their master was abed, went up to his room and with an handkerchief attempted to strangle him, which they thought they had effected, but in a little time after they left him, he recovered, and began to stir, on hearing which they went up and told him he must die, and that before they left the room; he begged very earnestly for his life, but one of them, his house wench, told him it was in vain, that as he had no mercy on them, he could expect none himself, and immediately threw him between two feather beds, and all got on him till he was stifled to death."

—An account of the murder of a wealthy Beaufort County slaveholder, Henry Ormond, which occurred sometime in July 1770, *Virginia Gazette* (Rind), 6 September 1770

Contents

Maps and Figures

Acknowledgments

Over the more than twenty years this book has been in process numerous persons have generously given of their time and talents. Many students have assisted in coding data for the computer and statistical analysis. We especially wish to thank Elissa Cary, Anita Gutin, Melisande Kay-Raining Bird, Tana Porter, and Frank Schubert. We also wish to thank Paula Ashton, secretary in the History Department of the University of Toledo, for her kind cooperation.

Many colleagues on the faculty at the University of Toledo have been helpful. Alfred A. Cave, in the History Department, graciously read and commented on our entire manuscript. Ronald Lora, also of the History Department, has read portions of this study. Theodore Natsoulas, Africanist in the History Department, has always generously donated his time, understanding of Africa, and library. Karl Vezner, former chairman of the Political Science Department, helped devise the formulas and computer programs necessary to construct "sex imbalance ratios," a new gauge we devised to aggregate gender imbalances among slaves on individual plantations. Calman Winegarden, former member of the Economics Department, developed the econometrics used in a collateral study to measure and explain inequities in the distribution of wealth in colonial North Carolina. Clement Idun, a former doctoral student, patiently taught us about the marital and familial institutions and practices that prevail in his native Ghana.

William D. Hoover, the chair of the Department of History for most of the time during which this project has been in the works, tirelessly supported our research. It was largely through Bill's efforts, together with those of Alfred A. Cave while he was Dean of Arts and Sciences, that we received considerable aid from the University of Toledo in the form of grants, sabbaticals, and released time. One such grant made it possible to present some of our findings at the Australia and New Zealand American Studies Association meeting at Newcastle, New South Wales, in 1988. An American Philosophical Society grant provided additional research moneys.

Several librarians at the Carlson Library, the University of Toledo, assisted with purchasing research materials, expediting interlibrary loans, and renewing piles of books. Special thanks go to the late John Morgan, whose assistance was especially valuable, Julia Baldwin, Mary T. Keil, and Leslie W. Sheridan.

Historians at other institutions who have read and commented on portions of this or collateral studies include the late Thomas D. Beatty, Ira Berlin,

Milton Cantor, Francine Cary, the late Philip Foner, Raymond Gavins, Gad Heuman, A. Leon Higginbotham, Rhys Isaac, Michael P. Johnson, Jackson Turner Main, the late Ernest S. Osgood, Herbert Shapiro, Donna J. Spindel, Richard Twombly, Peter H. Wood, and Alfred F. Young.

Members of the editorial staff at the University of North Carolina Press at Chapel Hill have done all that a press should do, and more, in seeing this manuscript through publication. We are especially grateful to Lewis Bateman for his quiet competence in guiding our manuscript through the evaluation process and for his aid thereafter. Special thanks must also go to Pamela Upton and Stevie Champion, who added immeasurably to the readability of the book through their professional editing.

We wish to thank for their kind cooperation the staffs at the Southern Historical Collection, University of North Carolina Library, Chapel Hill; North Carolina Collection, University of North Carolina Library, Chapel Hill; and Perkins Library, Duke University, Durham, North Carolina. But above all, we thank the staff at the North Carolina Department of Cultural Resources, Division of Archives and History, Raleigh, for putting up with us for these many years. The vast bulk of our research was done in this magnificent archive, and its staff rendered every service imaginable to us. George Stevenson gave special help to us in determining the density patterns of slaveholding in colonial North Carolina.

Anne S. Burnham, information writer for the *Northwest Ohio Quarterly*, University of Toledo, made life considerably easier by helping to proofread the book.

Louise A. Celley, our department secretary, has been essential to the successful completion of this manuscript. She typed it through innumerable transmogrifications, and in its final stages she worked closely and carefully with the University of North Carolina Press. We cannot overestimate the value of her services. We will always be in her debt.

Jeffrey J. Crow, Gary B. Nash, and William S. Price Jr. each critically evaluated the entire manuscript. Their appreciation of our effort has meant more than we can say. Their detailed critical comments helped make the book considerably better than it would have been. Probably obstinacy rather than good sense prevailed in the few cases we did not heed their suggestions. For this we take full responsibility, as we must do for all the defects that remain in this work.

Jeffrey Crow and William Price have worn other hats. Bill is director of the Division of Archives and History in Raleigh and Jeff is administrator of the Historical Publications Section of the archives. They skipper superb ships, and their friendship and aid through the years have been a blessing.

Last, it is impossible to thank adequately Marlene Cary and Bettye Ruth Bryan Kay for the help each has given to this study. Marlene listened to and read portions of drafts and offered suggestions and encouragement to Lorin through many years of research and writing. Bettye Ruth began her extraordinary contributions from the inception of the project by participating in archival research and note taking. Thereafter she typed a number of chapters, and with the touch of a gifted editor she corrected the manuscript through various drafts.

Bettye Ruth Bryan Kay died on 25 December 1996 after a courageous ten and one-half year struggle with breast cancer. Until the end she remained the magnificent, vital person she had always been—a loving, devoted mother and wife and an indefatigable proponent for labor, minority, and gender rights, peace, and social justice. Recognizing the inherent right of all human beings to experience a life of dignity made possible by a compassionate society, she conceived, brought into being, and became the first director of Bittersweet Farms, an internationally recognized care model for the autistic and the first residential farmstead community for autistic adults in North America. While being posthumously inducted into the Ohio Women's Hall of Fame on 21 October 1998, she was aptly described as a visionary committed to action. She truly more than equalled those Plato envisioned as persons of gold.

That this book could never have been written without Bettye Ruth is to state a simple fact. But it also illustrates how she was willing to find seemingly nonexistent time for causes on projects she believed in.

She is missed and loved, always.

Slavery in
North Carolina,
1748–1775

Introduction

      This study began amid an upsurge of interest in the history of slavery two decades ago. Scholars had become increasingly dissatisfied with a tendency to concentrate on antebellum slavery in the United States, and to infer from slavery at its mature apex the supposed essential qualities—or even the early history—of the institution in this country. More and more students of slavery urged that understanding slavery required an intensive look at the system over time and in various places. Thus colonial America became the frontier of slavery studies of our country, and an exciting burst of activity drew attention to a range of significant topics. These included the economics of specific slave systems, with stress on the slaves as laborers; the nature of the slave trade and the demographics of the slave and free populations; the laws and policies whites used to maximize production and profits, while maintaining security; and, perhaps most fascinating, the formation of a culture among the slaves—their developing institutions, behavioral and resistance patterns, art forms, value systems, and thought processes.[1]

Although the comprehension of slavery and of African Americans has changed substantially as a result of this scholarship, major gaps remain. Among the mainland southern colonies of British North America, the Chesapeake colonies and South Carolina have been studied extensively. Georgia has received considerably less scrutiny,[2] but North Carolina, except for the years of the American Revolution, has received the least attention.[3] Perhaps this is because its relatively late settlement and comparatively immature slave economy—based on the diversified production of tobacco, lumber products, naval stores, grains, and provisions—yielded the smallest slave population except for Maryland, the lowest proportion of blacks in its population, and the lowest density patterns among slaves of any southern colony.[4] Or perhaps it is because compared to its neighbors, there seemed to be a daunting paucity in the documentary record of slavery in colonial North Carolina.

Whatever the reasons for the neglect, our work tries to close the gap left in the literature and to see how slavery in North Carolina differed from, or more likely, paralleled slavery in other southern colonies. The attention is worthwhile, for North Carolina had one of the fastest-growing slave populations on the mainland. By midcentury, too, slaves in the coastal regions had become as concentrated on large plantations as they were in parts of tidewater Maryland and Virginia. And by the 1760s the concentration of slaves on large plantations in the Lower Cape Fear region paralleled concentrations in South Carolina's low country.[5]

Two interpretive perspectives unite this study. The first hinges on the fact that comparatively large numbers of Africans lived in the Carolinas and Georgia throughout the colonial era. As many as two-thirds of the adult slaves in North Carolina, for instance, were African at the outset of the period examined, 1748 to 1755, and during the years 1761 to the Revolution Africans still averaged about one-third of the adult population.[6] With this African presence and the slaves' (immigrants') habitual and unavoidable use of their African pasts to comprehend the myriad of details confronting them in their diaspora, African languages, institutions, values, and worldviews exerted a powerful hold on slaves and the cultures they shaped.[7] We illustrate this process primarily by discussing the slaves' resistance patterns, naming practices and languages, marriages and families, and religiosity.[8]

The second interpretive perspective flows from the first. In seeking to fathom the value system and worldview of slaves in North Carolina and their relationship to their masters, it is of little use to employ the Gramscian model of "cultural hegemony" with its emphasis on consent. Such a model may be a

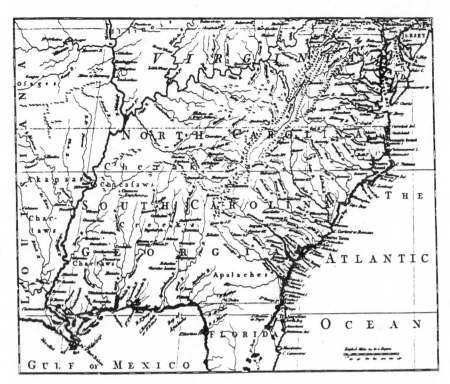

Map 1. The Southeastern Colonies, 1775
Source: "A Map of Virginia, North and South Carolina, Georgia, Maryland with Part of New Jersey &c." (Map Collection, North Carolina State Archives, Raleigh)

valuable conceptual tool for understanding labor in an industrializing country, to a lesser degree, eighteenth-century poor freemen or servants, and perhaps even slaves in a mature slave economy, but the requirements of slavery together with the characteristics of the slave population in colonial North Carolina preclude its application here.[9] The presence of so many Africans, for one thing, meant that many slaves would have had considerable difficulty understanding even a simplified version of English. They spoke a variety of African languages, plus pidgin-creole languages that they had constructed primarily to communicate among themselves. Linguistic differences were only one manifestation of the cultural chasm between European masters and African or even African American slaves. There was no substantial base of shared culture on which to build a hegemonic culture that embraced masters and slaves. Such a shared cultural base had to evolve through cultural diffusion, and in the colonial Carolinas and Georgia that process remained in its early stages (see Map 1).[10]

It would not have been easy for owners to convert such slaves to ruling-class values, then, even had that been the intention. And it often was not. Masters frequently preferred to withhold their culture from slaves rather than to convert them to it, particularly during the colonial era. Because slavery was in a formative state in much of the colonial South, certainly in North Carolina, masters focused primarily on establishing plantations, stocking them with slaves, and ensuring the essential power relationships necessary to maintain and extend the conditions of enslavement. Slaveowners used forceful, coercive, direct methods of control to implement this design, both co-optative and terroristic, the emphasis varying with time and circumstance. Their unbending quest to attain legal, political, and military dominance over their human chattels, in turn, made it impossible for the masters to embrace the modicum of reciprocity necessary to achieve cultural hegemony. Somewhat paradoxically, all this gave slaves the space to maintain and stress cultures that significantly incorporated their African heritages. And this considerable cultural autonomy, in turn, importantly freed slaves from depending on the masters' value system and definitions of moral behavior. Slaves, then, could use resistance techniques defined by their African cultures and social experiences in conjunction with, and as modified by, the possibilities available to them as well as their hopes and aspirations in thralldom.[11]

Chapter 1 sets the stage for this story. It focuses on North Carolina's developing slave economy during the eighteenth century, detailing how shifting patterns of the population in conjunction with a distinctive dependence on the production of a variety of goods—especially forest products, tobacco, grains, and provisions—largely determined the particular shape of slave labor in the colony.

Despite the rather distinctive productive roles played by slaves in colonial North Carolina, it is difficult to discern significant thematic differences between these slaves and those of other colonies that would not be erased by time and economic and demographic maturation. This runs counter to the findings of historians who have investigated other colonies. They have argued for the Chesapeake, for instance, that tobacco planters in the region presided directly over their labor-intensive slave plantations in paternalistic fashion, which, in turn, induced them to organize their slaves as gang labor.[12] On the other hand, wealthy rice planters in South Carolina's low country tended to flee to Charleston during the summer to escape the malarial fevers, thus delegating their authority over their slaves to overseers. Less motivated to implement a pervasive paternalism, these planters were willing to put a task system of slave labor into effect on rice plantations that supposedly lent themselves to this type of production.[13]

If the Chesapeake and low country regions were, indeed, so thematically defined, it is clear that the diversified slave economies in North Carolina or its particular regions lacked the homogeneity necessary to define its slave labor system along either task or gang labor lines. Thus, although planting tobacco achieved some significance in the counties of the northern tier of North Carolina, production levels never compared with those in the Chesapeake, and within the former tobacco was overshadowed by or shared a place with forest products, grains, provisions, and livestock. Similarly, North Carolina's Lower Cape Fear region resembled the South Carolina low country in its heavy concentration of slaves on large plantations, yet its dependence on rice was comparatively slight, the area substantially producing forest products such as naval stores, sawn lumber, shingles, and barrel staves.[14]

As one might predict from this, although there is evidence that the task system developed in colonial North Carolina, especially in the Lower Cape Fear region, it never became as definitive as it supposedly was in the low country of South Carolina. Moreover, evidence that slaves in North Carolina at times had gardens need not presuppose a task system because slaves involved in gang labor appear to have readily developed gardens. Finally, the large number of slaves in North Carolina who lived on small farms probably toiled within less formal arrangements than may be typified either as gang or task systems of labor. This last, more than likely, also occurred throughout much of the slave South.[15]

Regardless of the regional peculiarities of slave labor systems in the colonial South, it is certain that scholars have overemphasized paternalism in the Chesapeake in at least two ways. First, they have incorrectly tended to typify an entire region in the image of the Carters and the Byrds. Second, and related to the first, scholars have too often taken the pretentious and self-serving claims of these self-styled Hebrew patriarchs much too literally. Despite the hyperbole, for instance, masters never really accepted slaves as members of the slaveowners' families. Slaves assuredly were not misled. It would have been far too costly to their own families. They also were well aware, as were poorer free whites, servants, and, of course, the "patriarchs" themselves, that the latter's control significantly hinged on their precisely defining and implementing the distinctions and the relationships required by blood, class, color, and status.[16]

If regional and temporal studies of slavery during the colonial years have too often led to overly thematic and contrasting views of slavery, methodological correctives probably lie in two not entirely consistent directions. First, we must shorten our brush strokes. That is, richness of detail rather than broad renditions of thematic distinctiveness must establish both regional particularities *and* similarities, the latter frequently predominating. Paradoxically, however, detailed investigations of different slave economies and societies tend to increase our capacity to appreciate certain broad causal determinants that, in turn, induced shared cultural characteristics among slaves who produced a variety of crops in different regions. Thus the effects of the twin variables of time and economic and demographic maturation—growing slave populations, more densely settled, and more heavily concentrated on large plantations—transcend space and the production of different crops and define over time for each region changes in the possibilities available to slaves to reconstruct their African cultures in such realms as slave languages, names, marriages and families, and religiosity.[17]

To return to the organization of our book, Chapters 2 and 3 discuss the political power of affluent masters and the laws and policies they constructed to establish, maintain, and enhance their power and wealth. Slaveowning politicians shaped policies that integrated their varying methods of exploiting and controlling poorer free persons, servants, and slaves. Slaves received the harshest treatment, of course. Freed of the need to shape the ameliorating policies required in a quest to establish cultural hegemony, masters denied slaves the normative system of criminal justice used for whites that joined procedural due process with a tendency to temper justice with mercy. In its stead, wealthy slaveowners erected by statute and juridical practice a system of public criminal justice for slaves that denied elemental due process and subjected them to arbitrary and brutal sentences and punishments.

Masters on individual plantations dealt with slaves whose transgressions did not warrant court trials or peremptory public punishment. Normally more temperate than the public courts or authorities, individual plantation owners could balance terror with co-optation. Planter paternalism could thus work out both its fantasies and coldly realistic designs to help induce slaves to behave "properly." In this atmosphere masters granted slaves—the workers who made the plantation system go—some relief from the harshness of the public system of slave justice, as well as a degree of autonomy.

This discussion leads in Chapters 4 and 5 to analyses of slave resistance patterns, with running away largely handled in the latter chapter. We discuss resistance in its various facets in the context of "criminality," as masters viewed all noncompliant behavior. That is not the way slaves saw their actions. The absence of cultural hegemony helped to ensure that the cultural heritages of African slaves often remained normative and dominant in their daily lives. Christianity and the self-serving morality of the masters defined neither what slaves considered to be morally acceptable behavior nor often the behavior itself. Rather, the ethic slaves shaped essentially resulted from their African beliefs and practices in conjunction with the possibilities available to them, as well as their needs, hopes, and aspirations, and the utility to slaves of any contemplated act itself. In the context of forced bondage, where whip and noose were ever present and white laws and actions ubiquitously denied the slaves' humanity, slaves used whatever was at hand—from prayers to theft and running off, from the warmth and love of marital and familial ties to murder and rebellion. And all were morally acceptable behavior when used to relieve slaves from oppressive masters.

The final three chapters consider culture formation among the slaves beyond resistance patterns. Chapter 6 deals with naming patterns and languages, Chapter 7 with marriages and families, and Chapter 8 with religiosity. All stress that colonial slaves drew on their African heritages as they created a culture of their own. African names, or more likely their Anglicized derivatives, continued to be used by most slaves in colonial North Carolina and elsewhere. It is less clear that slaves continued to implement traditional African practices such as naming children after the day of the week they were born or their order of birth within a family. However much colonial slaves in North Carolina explicitly followed these naming practices, they still commonly gave their children day and positional names along with those derived from other African naming practices.

This last point argues that slaves controlled the naming process. Masters acquiesced to this fundamental way slaves achieved an identity because, if feasible, they wished to avoid the onus of denying to slaves this traditional, cherished power. Furthermore, names chosen from a large pool of African names ensured the diversity of slave names required by masters to avoid confusion. Finally, slaveowners ultimately acquiesced in the demands of slaves that they be allowed to control their own names and those of their children because such actions apparently did not affect their labor functions or the political hegemony of slaveowners.

The evidence also suggests that slaves from Delaware southward invented pidgin and creole languages largely from their African languages of origin. Although English words were incorporated along with some other European words, pidgin and creole languages were constructed and used by slaves principally to communicate among themselves, and relatively few whites apparently could speak or understand these languages. Whites and blacks talked to one another in English. Most colonial slaves, however, had little more than a workplace knowledge of English, and many lacked even this. Still others, as the runaway records reveal, acquired a capacity to speak standard English.

In no instance, except in the case of the criminal codes for slaves, were slaves defined as property more insistently, or, as a corollary, was their personhood denied more emphatically, than in the masters' delegitimization of slave marriages and families. The denial of de jure status stripped slaves of their lawful capacity to defend their marriages and families against external attack or disruption. De facto slave marriages and families, on the other hand, were accepted by masters, for it gave them added leverage to induce higher slave birthrates and more productive and better-disciplined slaves. Whatever the intentions of masters, slaves desperately tried to reconstruct marriages and families according to their traditional African beliefs and practices. They were increasingly successful as demographic factors became more propitious for the growth of slave marriages and families: greater numbers of slaves, greater numerical parity between male and female slaves, and increasingly heavy concentrations of slaves on larger plantations. Yet these changes occurred over time, and much of the African past was lost in the process because of the limited control slaves had over their lives, labor, and physical movement and because of their overriding poverty and lack of significant class and wealth distinctions or formal political power. These conditions ensured that slaves in colonial North Carolina could never successfully reconstruct polygynous marriages, lineages, or clans or participate in or be served by the colony's legal and political institutions.

Other African marital and familial forms and behavior remained significantly within the reach of slaves, however, especially as demographic conditions improved. Monogamous marriages, the prevailing though not the preferred marital form in eighteenth-century West and Central Africa, and consequent nuclear and extended families were increasingly descriptive of slave relationships. Indeed, it is probable that by the Revolution about half of the slaves in the colony lived in dual-headed households.

As for religion, most slaves in the southern mainland colonies, and certainly those in North Carolina, were denied the opportunity to learn about or were presented with limited versions of Christianity so that they would not be encouraged in hopes for freedom or equality. Still, the process of cultural diffusion is apparent among some colonial slaves as they blended their African religious beliefs with Christianity (primarily evangelical Christianity). But this process did not importantly affect the majority of slaves until the nineteenth century. Prior to this they primarily used their indigenous African beliefs and practices as their cosmological, ontological, and ethical guides to a sense of reality and identity, good order, and proper human behavior and relationships.

We often use a comparative approach in this examination of slavery in North Carolina from 1748 to 1775 in order to clarify the story, to identify broader implications, and to buttress statistics or other evidence obtained from too limited data. We gratefully acknowledge our debt to those scholars who have preceded us in attempting to track the story of slavery. But we pay homage to the African and African American slaves who left as legacies their struggles to recapture their pasts, to support their humanity, and to protect their posterity.

1

Slavery in North Carolina, 1748–1775

Demography, Production, Commerce, and Labor

By 1750 each colony in the various regions of British North America had gone through comparable stages of development: the invasion and conquest of Native American peoples and their lands; the replacement of indigenous populations by rapidly increasing numbers of European Americans and, in many areas, enslaved African Americans; the attempts by whites to achieve sufficiency in foodstuffs and other material necessities and to develop a viable export trade. Nonetheless, the results varied sharply with the southern colonies closest to the mercantilist ideal of plantation economies, producing staples needed by the mother country and absorbing British-manufactured goods. But historians have correctly stressed that the South was not a monolithic region. Varying blends of staples and complementary crops and differing rhythms of the slave trade, demographic configurations of the black and white populations, and African continuums yielded distinctive economies and produced varied slave societies over time and in the different colonial regions from Maryland south to Georgia.[1] Thus, colonial North Carolina contained fewer slaves and lacked as extensive a plantation economy and planter elite as did colonial Virginia and South Carolina.[2]

Partially responsible for North Carolina's slower rate of economic growth were the significant natural handicaps the colony was burdened with. Nature carved a jagged, dangerous, shoal-burdened and constantly changing coastline whose treacherous Capes Hatteras, Lookout, and Fear claimed countless vessels. Although numerous rivers flowed toward the ocean, with one exception they emptied into shallow sounds rather than deep harbors. Only the Cape Fear River fed directly into the ocean, and it had shoals at its mouth (see Maps 2, 3). Such hazards added to the cost of transportation and insurance and had implications for both urban growth and the direction of trade.[3]

Overwhelmingly rural throughout the colonial era, like other southern colonies, North Carolina was also plagued initially by poor roads. A rudimentary system of north-south roads evolved in the coastal plain and piedmont regions, but the flow of rivers from northwest to southeast slowed the development of east-west routes. This hindered trade with the backcountry, retarded the expansion of port towns, and reinforced the tendency for much of the province's early trade to flow southward to Charleston or north into Virginia and beyond. After 1750 the province made concerted efforts to develop overland links to meet the needs of the rapidly expanding backcountry. By the time of the Revolution, notwithstanding the persistent laments of travelers, roads in North Carolina compared favorably to those of other southern colonies. Improved transportation facilitated a rapid expansion of inland towns and aided the advance of such port towns as Edenton, New Bern, and Wilmington at the expense of others—Bath and Beaufort.[4]

The growth of this infrastructure both reflects and helps to explain why, by the late colonial period, North Carolina led all colonies in the production and export of naval stores and, having created a more diversified economy than other southern colonies, North Carolinia also came to export significant amounts of sawn lumber, shingles, barrel staves, Indian corn, wheat, livestock on the hoof, and meat and dairy products. Since perhaps more than one-half of the value of grain and livestock and a substantial proportion of the tobacco exports went overland to other colonies, and were thus counted there, it is impressive that the value of North Carolina's officially recorded exports still surpassed those of New Hampshire, Rhode Island, Connecticut, New Jersey, and Georgia for the years just before the Revolution.[5]

These developments, in turn, interplayed with such diverse factors as the

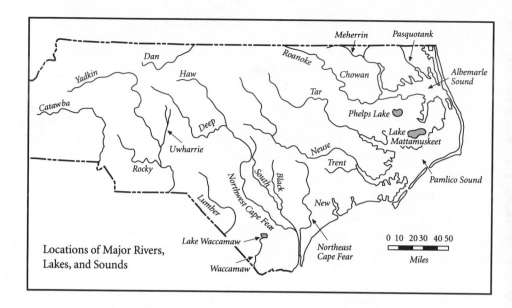

Locations of Major Rivers, Lakes, and Sounds

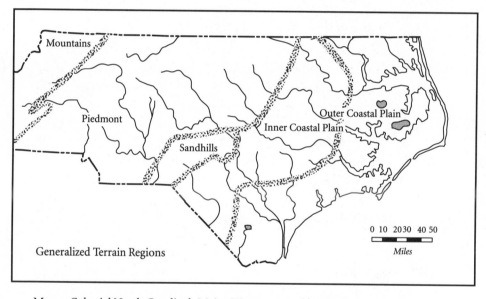

Generalized Terrain Regions

Map 2. Colonial North Carolina's Major Waterways and Regions
Source: Harry Roy Merrens, *Colonial North Carolina in the Eighteenth Century: A Study in Historical Geography* (Chapel Hill: University of North Carolina Press, 1964), 20, 37.

Map 3. Revolutionary North Carolina
Source: "A New and Accurate Map of North Carolina in North America," first published in *Universal Magazine* (London: J. Hinton, 1779). (Map Collection, North Carolina State Archives, Raleigh)

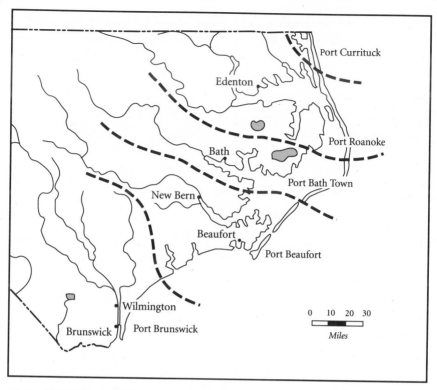

Map 4. The Ports of Colonial North Carolina
Source: Harry Roy Merrens, *Colonial North Carolina in the Eighteenth Century: A Study in Historical Geography* (Chapel Hill: University of North Carolina Press, 1964), 87. The assembly established customs districts, known as ports, in North Carolina early in the colonial period.

British mercantile system, population expansion, and the productive roles and services performed by those who toiled on, owned, and managed the colony's farms, workshops, and commercial establishments. British bounties encouraged the production of certain goods, most notably naval stores. The province itself sought to encourage trade, with varying degrees of success, by improving roads, bridges, waterways, and harbors, regulating inns and ferries, establishing warehouses to store goods and to facilitate credit and trade, and inspecting commodities to ensure the quality of exports. Individual merchants also frequently played decisive roles in encouraging commercial farming and in shaping the colony's trade. Usually clustered in the relatively small towns of North Carolina, and often agents of Scottish, English, or intercolonial mercantile houses, these merchants, together with local country store owners and itinerant traders, operated throughout the colony marketing local products while providing farmers with goods and credit.[6]

The process of European settlement and economic development began in North Carolina in the 1650s and 1660s, when the first white settlers entered the Albemarle region in the northeastern tip of the colony from Virginia. Assisted by their slaves, they prepared a variety of goods for export, among them tobacco, corn, wheat, and livestock products from cattle and hogs. This diversified farming, built on an extension southward of Virginia's economy and supplemented by fishing and whaling, had little impact on urban growth or the development of ancillary industries in the region. Still, Edenton was incorporated in 1722, having come into existence a few years before this, slowly growing into a settlement of about sixty houses in 1730, North Carolina's largest "urban center" at that time.

If North Carolina's towns remained throughout the colonial years comparatively small, merchants and stores in these towns functioned to aid the development of commercial farming. Nevertheless, many of the Albemarle region's exports, especially during the late seventeenth and early eighteenth centuries, were hauled or driven overland to Virginia's superior road and mercantile systems.[7]

Starting in the last decade of the seventeenth century, other white Virginians, some with their slaves, not only continued to move into the less-developed areas of the Albemarle region, but also went southward into the area watered by the Tar, Neuse, and Trent Rivers, all of which emptied into Pamlico Sound. By the early eighteenth century immigrants from France, Switzerland, and the Palatinate helped to swell the population of this Neuse-Pamlico region. Farmers first experimented with flax, hemp, and grapes, but, as in the Albemarle area, naval stores, wood products, Indian corn, provisions, livestock and its products, and tobacco came to be the mainstays of production. Limited urban settlements occurred even earlier in this area than in the Albemarle, with Bath chartered in 1706, Newbern in 1710, and Beaufort in 1715. Bath and Beaufort were ports of entry, or customs districts, but all three seaports handled the forest and agricultural products of the area (see Map 4).[8]

Whites, chiefly from South Carolina, began to settle the Cape Fear region in the southeastern tip of the colony in the 1720s. Slaveowners, they brought with them a penchant, fostered by British inducements, for naval stores and lumber production. Starting in 1705 Britain had paid substantial bounties on colonial naval stores—£6 a ton on hemp, £4 a ton on tar and pitch, £3 a ton on turpentine and rosin, and £1 a ton on masts, yards, and bowsprits. Although in 1713 Parliament extended these bounties until 1725, complaints about poorly prepared resinous products led to their revocation and to the subsequent plunge of colonial exports of tar and pitch. In 1729, the same year that North Carolina became a royal colony, Parliament restored reduced bounties on pitch (£1) and tar (£2 4s.). This reintroduction of bounties could not halt a permanent relocation of the naval stores industry. Major South Carolina planters turned to rice and indigo, labor-intensive yet highly profitable crops, as their principal exports and shunted other economic activities to the periphery of the plantation section. Although some Cape Fear planters also became involved with rice and indigo starting in the 1730s, naval stores and lumber products remained preeminent.[9]

Given the aggressively commercial orientation of Cape Fear planters, their early stress on slavery, and their heavy concentration on naval stores and lumber—products that required the exploitation of large areas of land and extensive processing, marketing, transportation, and storage facilities—it is not surprising that the Cape Fear region developed the largest slave plantations in North Carolina, comparable in their use of slave labor to those in the South Carolina low country, and that *two* seaports emerged on the lower Cape Fear River to handle the region's commerce. Although established in the early 1730s, eight years later than Brunswick (ca. 1725), Wilmington supplanted its neighbor because its location fifteen miles upstream at the confluence of the northwestern and northeastern branches of the Cape Fear River provided superior access to the interior. By 1754 Wilmington boasted seventy families to Brunswick's twenty, and by the outbreak of the Revolution it had become, together with Edenton, the largest urban settlement in the colony. Its population of around one thousand, however, was still only one-third as large as that of Savannah, Georgia, and one-sixth as large as that of Norfolk, Virginia.

By the 1730s settlement began to spread westward into the interior from the Albemarle, Neuse-Pamlico, and, to a limited degree, Lower Cape Fear regions as well as from other colonies, especially Virginia. Population growth in the four interior regions of the colony was impressive. There, by 1755, whites and blacks equaled 42,353 persons, or slightly more than half of the colony's total population of 83,945. The latter figure, in turn, amounted to a 48,000 person increase over the 30,000 whites and 6,000 blacks who lived in North Carolina in 1730—a per annum growth rate of 3.5 percent (see Tables 1.1–1.3).[10]

Despite this substantial population increase, the colony's commercial infrastructure and entrepreneurial activity lagged behind population growth. Regional urban centers did not develop in the province's newly populated and developing regions in the interior, and a poor east-west transportation system seems to have prevailed into the 1750s. Exports from the colony's ports also reflect the limited capacity of the mercantile community during the first half of the eighteenth century to move goods from the interior to the coast. In 1736 the official exports of the province totaled about one-tenth of South Carolina's. Despite the absence of other figures for the next two decades, the differential likely remained close to ten, for as late as 1768–72 it still equaled over six (see Table 1.9, Map 5).

Official records mask the colony's heavy dependence on neighbors to market its products abroad. But whatever their deficiencies, the extant records do point to the diversity of the province's exports, a characteristic that remained notable over time. In 1753, for instance, the colony shipped abroad about 100,000 pounds of tobacco, some 84,012 barrels of naval stores, and 62,000 bushels of corn, in addition to dairy products, beeswax, deerskins, peas, cattle hides, beef, and pork.[11]

The years after the onset of the French and Indian War witnessed an even more rapid surge of population than occurred from 1730 to 1755, changes that further reshaped North Carolina's demographic contours and profoundly affected its economy. The yearly population growth rate during the twelve years after 1755 soared to a startling 5.4 percent. The population of whites jumped from 65,000 to 124,000 persons, while the population of blacks grew even more rapidly, from 19,000 to 41,000. After 1767 the rate of population growth probably slowed to a bit over 4 percent because of the emigration of disgruntled farmers following the Regulator defeat in 1771. Still, the colony's population continued to mushroom, expanding about 40 percent to 230,000 during the eight years before the Revolution (Tables 1.1–1.3).[12]

All regions of the province grew rapidly after midcentury, but this occurred with heightened intensity as the population moved westward. In the Albemarle, Neuse-Pamlico, and Lower Cape Fear coastal regions, the total population rose by 29, 58, and 84 percent respectively between 1755 and 1767. In the interior Upper Cape Fear, Central Inner Plain–Piedmont, and Northern Inner Plain–Piedmont regions population totals jumped 125, 132, and 99 percent respectively. In the Western region, population soared by 229 percent (see Tables 1.1–1.2). The precipitous growth rates of the more westerly areas led to a significant redistribution in the colony's population: the three coastal regions' portion of North Carolina's total population dropped from nearly half in 1755 to less than one-third in 1767 (see Tables 1.1–1.2).

Placing the focus of this demographic analysis on race and ethnicity, natural increase and, to a lesser degree, immigration more than doubled North Carolina's white population to about 65,000 between 1730 and 1755, an annual growth rate of about 3 percent. Over the next twelve years the growth of the white population accelerated chiefly due to the increasing numbers of land-hungry settlers attracted to North Carolina from Virginia and other colonies to the north, especially Maryland and Pennsylvania. Streaming into the Northern Inner Plain–Piedmont and Western regions, they considerably outnumbered those migrating from North Carolina's more easterly counties. Unlike

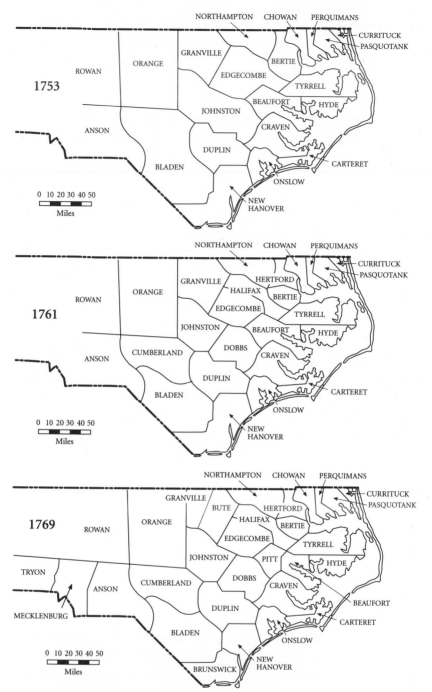

Map 5. North Carolina Counties, 1753, 1761, and 1769
Source: Harry Roy Merrens, *Colonial North Carolina in the Eighteenth Century: A Study in Historical Geography* (Chapel Hill: University of North Carolina Press, 1964), 72–73.

most earlier migrants, a majority of these newcomers from other colonies were not English. Waves of Scots-Irish and German migrants took up land in Orange, Anson, Rowan, and Mecklenburg Counties and probably dominated the latter two most western counties. In addition, Highland Scots, primarily in the 1760s and 1770s, came directly from Scotland to help populate the Upper Cape Fear River counties of Bladen and Cumberland and to settle as far west as Anson County. White numbers for the entire colony during the years 1755–67 significantly reflect the demographic impact of these migrations—increasing at an annual rate of growth of about 5.1 percent and numbering about 124,000 in 1767, for a net gain of 89 percent since 1755 (see Tables 1.2–1.3). Despite the emigration of disillusioned Regulators, the number of whites by 1775 still climbed to around 161,000.[13]

If economic opportunity and land attracted most white migrants, it was the white need for labor that primarily explains the increase in the black population. The earliest decade for which black population growth estimates may be calculated with any degree of confidence is the 1720s. During these years, expanding immigration to the sparsely populated province apparently accounted for most of the population growth calculated for both blacks and whites. Thus, from only about 4,370 whites and some 2,000 blacks in 1720, their respective numbers swelled in a decade to approximately 30,000 and 6,000, for yearly growth rates of 15 percent and 10 percent respectively.[14] After 1730 growth rates dropped sharply since they occurred within the context of relatively high population bases, but the black population began to increase more rapidly than did the white population because of the growing demand for slave labor and the probable increasing significance of the slave trade. North Carolina's black population tripled to about 19,000 between 1730 and 1755 for a per annum growth rate of just over 4 percent, as compared with a yearly increase of 3 percent for whites. Both populations grew even more rapidly into the sixties, with black numbers nearly doubling by 1767 to just under 41,000—augmenting 6.2 percent annually as compared with 5.1 percent for whites (see Tables 1.1–1.3). If the growth rate for blacks remained constant, they numbered approximately 66,000 by 1775, or just under 30 percent of the colony's population.

Although it is difficult to determine precisely what proportion of these increases stemmed from either natural increase or immigration, there is no doubt that, except for whites during the years 1730–55, immigration was an important factor. Historians have always recognized this for whites, but some have denied the even more obvious case for blacks. Yet except for 1730–55, when natural increase and immigration probably equally explain the increase in black numbers, immigration was the major factor motoring black popula-

New Bern, December 20, 1774.
Just imported in the SCHOONER HOPE,
Thomas Foster, Master, from AF-
RICA, a Parcel of likely healthy

SLAVES,

CONSISTING of Men, Women, and
Children, which are to be sold for Cash, or
Country Produce, by EDWARD BATCHELOR
& Co. at their Store at UNION POINT.

Slaves for sale. A significant portion of North Carolina's slaves were Africans. In this advertisement—first appearing in December 1774—New Bern merchant and slave dealer Edward Batchelor announces the arrival of a shipment of African slaves to be sold for cash or farm produce. (*North Carolina Gazette* [New Bern], 24 February 1775)

tion growth. The rates of increase were simply too sharp to be primarily explained by natural increase. If, as seems reasonable, about 2.5 percent of the per annum growth stemmed from natural increase, then some 11,000 blacks migrated to the colony during the years 1755–67.[15]

Extant port records suggest a vastly different story: less than 800 slaves are listed as being imported by sea routes during these twelve years. Yet evidence presented in contemporary newspapers suggests that port records severely understate the actual number of slaves who arrived in North Carolina via sea routes. For instance, according to a 1764 issue of the *North Carolina Magazine* 179 slaves entered Port Beaufort alone during the year beginning 1 October 1763 and ending 1 October 1764. Compared with this, a liberal reading of the port records has a total of 110 slaves entering *all* North Carolina's ports of entry during this period. Data are lacking to calculate the relative significance of each port of entry, but it is unlikely that Port Beaufort's share of the total exceeded, or even equaled, one-third. If this be true, multiplying the 180 slaves who entered Port Beaufort during this year by three suggests that around 540 slaves entered North Carolina via sea routes rather than the 110 listed in extant port records. Using this multiplier of five, in turn, and conservatively revising downward to 600 the total number of slaves listed in the port records as coming to North Carolina via sea routes during the years 1755–67, we arrive at an estimate of 3,000 slaves who reached North Carolina by sea during these years. Some 8,000 slaves, or over 70 percent of the 11,000 slave migrants to North Carolina, then, came over land routes during these twelve years.[16]

The extent to which North Carolinians relied on their provincial neighbors, both for white immigrants and for marketing services, makes it reasonable to assume that substantial numbers of slaves, both Africans and Creoles, traveled overland from Virginia and South Carolina either along with their migrating masters, or sent by absentee owners who remained at home, or, most likely, via an intercolonial slave trade. Governor George Burrington suggested as much 1 January 1733, when he groused that because the colony received so few slaves "directly from Affrica," North Carolinians had "to buy the refuse, refractory, and distemper'd Negroes brought in from other governments."[17] However askew his assessment of the quality of slaves brought from other colonies, or whatever the relative significance of the slave trade itself, Burrington undoubtedly was correct that sizable numbers of slaves came to North Carolina from other American colonies. This phenomenon, moreover, was also true of slaves arriving via sea routes, although in this case West Indians were the most significant reexporters.

Given the statistical insignificance of direct shipments of slaves from Africa to colonial North Carolina, it is impossible to calculate anything resembling precise estimates of the ethnic origins of the colony's slaves. Their provenance is made even murkier by the large numbers who came via overland routes.

In addition, North Carolina's planters made only occasional references to the slaves' tribal origins, usually in advertisements describing runaways as Angolans, Ibos, Mandingos, or Coramantees. South Carolina planters, by way of contrast, often mentioned the ethnicity of their slaves and apparently attempted to mold importation schedules to reflect the planters' preferences for slaves from particular tribes and regions. They could do this because Charleston was an important slave entrepôt and the bulk of entering slaves came directly from Africa. Because North Carolina planters had little control over the ethnicity of imported slaves, they understandably displayed less concern with the issue.

Given the flimsy evidence, we may, at best, hypothesize that since so many of North Carolina's slaves came from Virginia and South Carolina, their African origins roughly reflected those that prevailed among slaves in these colonies. Thus slaves living in North Carolina's northern counties perhaps most resembled Virginia's slaves and those living in the southern counties possibly had tribal backgrounds similar to those of South Carolina's slaves. This estimate would have to be revised if South Carolina and Virginia tended to get rid of less favored ethnic groups. We have no way of determining how frequently this last occurred.

Under the circumstances, it seems that any attempt to use a statistical analysis of the provenance of North Carolina's slaves as the underpinning for a discussion of the slaves' cultural characteristics would be too flawed to be of scholarly use. We consequently, in ensuing chapters, reverse the analytic procedure and attempt to determine the ethnicity of particular slaves in North Carolina through analyses of their peculiar cultural characteristics.[18]

Whatever the ethnic makeup of North Carolina's slave population, the maturation of slavery and its crucial role in the intensification of commercial farming in the province are both illustrated by the growth of slavery to prominence in almost all of the colony's regions during the years 1755–67. Only in the far western counties did slaves remain statistically insignificant—comprising less than 4 percent of this region's population in 1755 and remaining less than 8 percent in 1767. At the other end of the scale, Lower Cape Fear blacks comprised a lofty 62 percent of the population in both years. In the Upper Cape Fear, despite a 125 percent increase in absolute numbers, the black proportion of the total population declined slightly from 32 to 29 percent. The number of slaves, however, rose both absolutely and proportionately in all other regions of the colony: from one-eighth of the Central Inner Plain–Piedmont's population in 1755 to nearly one-fifth by 1767 and from about one-quarter of the Albemarle, Neuse-Pamlico, and Northern Inner Plain–Piedmont regions in 1755 to nearly 30 percent in each region in 1767. For North Carolina as a whole, blacks rose from slightly over 22 percent of the total population in 1755 to just under 25 percent in 1767 (see Tables 1.2–1.3). By 1775 blacks probably totaled close to 30 percent of the population.

As the black population increased, so did its density, a fact of some importance for slaves seeking to mold a viable culture and for masters intent on shaping a productive labor force. The number of blacks per square mile more than doubled between 1755 and 1767 (from .4 to .9) in the province as a whole, but there was considerable regional variation. Blacks were most densely settled in the Lower Cape Fear, their number per square mile rising from 1.4 in 1755 to 2.5 in 1767. At the other end of the scale, the density of the black population in the west was a sparse .03 in 1755 and rose to only .2 per square mile in 1767 (see Table 1.4). Yet even where blacks were most closely settled, rates remained slight compared to other provinces. In four contiguous tidewater counties on Maryland's lower Eastern Shore (totaling 1,662 square miles), for instance, the number of blacks per square mile increased from under 2 in 1704 to about 4 in 1730 and to over 9 by 1755.[19] These density figures were more than six times those for the Lower Cape Fear (1,989 square miles). The later settlement and development of North Carolina probably accounts for this difference, as does the Lower Cape Fear's dependence on forest industries, which required comparatively large plantations on which large numbers of slaves were more sparsely distributed than was the case in the mature tobacco-producing Chesapeake region.[20] Yet other regions in North Carolina, which were settled earlier than the Lower Cape Fear but well after the Maryland counties, produced considerable quantities of tobacco along with a diversity of other crops and forest products but had slave populations even more sparsely settled than in the Lower Cape Fear region.[21]

Because the number of slaves increased more rapidly than did the white population and their percentage of the total population rose or, as in the Lower Cape Fear, remained substantial, the proportion of blacks on large plantations was bound to increase in the colony at large given prevailing property distribution and inheritance patterns.[22] In fact, the concentration of slaves on units with ten or more slaves rose from 51 percent in 1748–55 to 62 percent in 1763–71, and those on plantations of twenty or more climbed from 19 to 29 percent (see Table 1.5). During the same period the number and size of extremely large slaveholdings also increased.

With some discrepancies, regional variations in the concentration of slaves on large plantations correlate most significantly with the proportion of whites and blacks in each region—the higher the percentage of blacks, the greater their concentration on large plantations (compare Tables 1.2 and 1.5). The heaviest concentration occurred in the Lower Cape Fear: there masters with ten or more slaves owned 88 percent of the slaves from 1748 to 1755 and 90 percent in the 1763–71 period, and those with twenty or more slaves owned 74 and 73 percent respectively during the two periods. Although the proportion of slaves living on large holdings was lower elsewhere, still, unlike the Lower Cape Fear, concentrations of slaves on larger plantations, especially those with twenty or more slaves, rapidly increased over time: from 7 to 32 percent in the Northern Inner Plain–Piedmont, from 9 to 21 percent in the Albemarle, from 14 to 20 percent in the Neuse-Pamlico, and from 37 to 48 percent in the Upper Cape Fear (see Table 1.5).

Given the comparatively low density of the North Carolina black population, the high proportion of slaves on large plantations in some areas of the province is surprising. In two Maryland tidewater counties and one such county in Virginia during the years 1741–50, an average of 55 percent of the slaves lived on plantations with eleven or more slaves and 24 percent lived on units with twenty-one or more slaves. From 1761 to 1770 the respective percentages were 72 and 43. In North Carolina's roughly comparable if less homogeneous three coastal regions—the Albemarle Sound, Neuse-Pamlico, and Lower Cape Fear—an average of 63 percent of the slaves lived on plantations with ten or more slaves during the years 1748–55, and 32 percent resided on plantations with twenty or more slaves. For 1763–71 the respective percentages were 66 and 38, figures similar to those for the Chesapeake.[23]

Perhaps more startling are the results of a comparison of the distribution of slaves in the South Carolina low country with the region in North Carolina where slaves were most heavily concentrated on large plantations, the Lower Cape Fear. During the years 1760–69, 88 percent of the low country's slaves lived on units with ten or more slaves, 75 percent on units with twenty or more, 40 percent on units with fifty or more, and 12 percent on units of one hundred or more. The distribution in the Lower Cape Fear region in North Carolina during the same period was much the same; indeed, slaves were even more heavily concentrated on the largest plantations. Seventy-five percent of the slaves lived on plantations with twenty or more slaves, and fully 46 and 21 percent respectively were owned by wealthy planters with fifty and one hundred or more slaves (see Table 1.6).[24]

These demographic patterns tell us quite a bit about the relationship of slavery to the growth of the North Carolina economy.[25] By the mid-1750s, the point at which North Carolina stood on the brink of a significant population explosion, slaves were most numerous, most densely settled, and most concentrated on large production units in the oldest regions of the colony. This was especially the case in the Lower Cape Fear region, whose commercially oriented economy both reflected and required a heavy reliance by whites on slave labor. These patterns tended to persist down to the Revolution, but the growing number of slaves, the rising proportion of blacks in the population, and the increasing concentration of slaves living on large plantations all came to typify the growth of slavery in the developing regions of the colony along with its maturation in the coastal area. Except in the most westerly counties, these tendencies were among the most important social and economic developments of the period. Economic expansion in North Carolina to the west relied on a growing labor force, and when whites could afford it they rapidly acquired more and more slaves to meet this need. Thus, by the eve of the Revolution the Albemarle Sound, the Neuse-Pamlico, and the Lower Cape Fear regions had been joined by the Upper Cape Fear and Northern Inner Plain–Piedmont regions in developing slave economies in which the proportion of slaves living on large plantations was comparable to distributive patterns in tidewater Maryland and Virginia.

All of this meant that the necessary critical mass of slaves and supporting demographic factors had unfolded that were preconditions for the effective transgenerational transmission of African cultures among the slaves. Slave populations, then, were great enough and their concentration on large units of production large enough to provide for substantial social contacts and the close personal relationships that helped slaves to transmit their African languages (and creole derivatives), names, marital and familial relationships, and religiosity over the years.

The varied trends of decreasing sex ratios in colonial North Carolina also reflect the province's late settlement, distinctive forms of economic maturation, and diverse regional development. By the early fifties sex ratios ranged between 137 and 163 males per 100 females in all regions of the province except in the Central Inner Plain–Piedmont, the Upper Cape Fear, and the west, where the ratios were even higher (see Table 1.7). Evidence uncovered by other investigators indicates that African slavers typically carried to Virginia about two male slaves for every female slave.[26] Probably a similar sex ratio existed among slaves brought directly from Africa to North Carolina. Because a large percentage of North Carolina's slave immigrants were both Creole and African-born slaves reexported from other colonies, however, the ratio of men to women among such slaves very likely was lower than that for slaves imported directly from Africa. This variable, in turn, beclouds the statistical role played by natural increase in explaining both growth-rate patterns among North Carolina's slaves and the interrelated factor of decreasing sex ratios.[27] Thus North Carolina's sex ratios, which averaged about 153 men per 100 women from 1751 to 1755, can possibly be explained largely by the immigration patterns peculiar to the colony.

It is nevertheless reasonable to assume that after 1755 natural increase, along with a fast-growing creole slave population, played an increasingly significant role in explaining the rapidly decreasing ratio of men to women among North Carolina's slave population. And this decrease occurred despite an increased flow of slaves into North Carolina from Africa and other colonies during these years. By the early 1760s (and probably sooner) the ratios of men to women had decreased in the different regions for which we have data to a range of from 106 to 134 men per 100 women. These ratios, roughly averaging 125, remained stable through the early 1770s (see Table 1.7). The ratios of men to women, as we will see in Chapter 7, were low enough after 1755 to enable large numbers of slaves to construct marital and familial patterns.

Estimates of sex ratios, in turn, offer a way to calculate the proportion of Africans in colonial North Carolina's slave population. Poor data prevent doing this directly, so we used the questionable technique of implementing a gauge constructed by Allan Kulikoff for the Chesapeake to compute the number of Africans in North Carolina.[28] Applied to North Carolina's sex ratios,

Kulikoff's formulas suggest that Africans made up about two-thirds of North Carolina's adult slave population between 1751 and 1755, when sex ratios averaged around 153, and about one-third during the last fifteen years of the colonial period, when sex ratios averaged about 125. These findings, without making undue claims for their precision, appear reasonable. They are consistent with North Carolina's relatively late settlement and maturation, comparable statistics for South Carolina—a colony of similar vintage—and our previous estimates on the comparative significance of immigration in explaining the growth of North Carolina's slave population. They are supported, too, by David Galenson's calculations that North Carolina's net black migration was high during the years 1750–70 and extraordinarily so during the 1760s, when it equaled 24,608, the highest for any British mainland or West Indian colony except Jamaica.[29]

Although estimated sex ratios help discern the importance of Africans in the population, they are a poor gauge of the actual gender imbalances confronting slaves on individual plantations in colonial North Carolina. Sex ratios equaled the optimum (least disparate) distribution of slaves for a specific region under review. For instance, if all slaves of the Albemarle Sound region during the years 1751–55 were distributed in accordance with the sex ratio, each plantation would have had male and female slaves at a ratio of 163 to 100 (see Table 1.7). This, of course, was not the case. Sex disparities varied considerably on individual plantations, many, indeed, having more female than male slaves. The obvious question, then, is, did the distributive patterns actually followed by slaveowners worsen sexual maldistribution to a significant degree? The answer is yes.[30]

Table 1.8 demonstrates that, despite significant regional variations, North Carolina's slaveowners maldistributed slaves by sex considerably beyond what one would predict from regional sex ratios. For instance, in the Albemarle Sound region the possible percentage of slaves who could not be paired because of sex ratios equaled only 6 percent, whereas the percentage who could not be paired because of the actual sexual maldistribution on the different units of production was 30 percent. The farther west one goes, the greater the actual sexual imbalances on particular plantations and the higher the proportion of slaves unable to marry other slaves on the home plantations because of a maldistribution of slaves by sex. In the three eastern regions from 30 to 39 percent of the slaves could not marry other slaves on their own plantations because of sex disparities; in the two middle regions about half could not, and in the west somewhat under two-thirds of the slaves could not. The many relatives slaves often had on the plantation on which they lived, in conjunction with incest taboos and exogamous marital practices, all increased the percentage of slaves unable to find mates on their own plantations. On the other hand, because interplantation marriages probably occurred with some frequency, they somewhat alleviated the problems caused by gender imbalances on particular plantations.

The maldistribution of slaves by sex reflects the fact that owners normally purchased slaves to meet productive rather than reproductive needs. This was in keeping with the comparative socioeconomic immaturity of North Carolina's slave system and the consequent need for slaveowners, in a period of rapid growth, to build their labor force as rapidly as possible. As demonstrated in later chapters, the slaveowners' need to satisfy the elemental requirements of an immature but fast-growing slave system colored their actions well beyond the actual purchase of slaves.

Meanwhile, although the enlarged role of slavery was of critical importance, the years after 1750 witnessed other signs of a maturing economy. As population ballooned and settlers established hundreds of new farms, considerable road, bridge, and town building and increasing numbers of merchants and country stores furthered the development of trade and communications. This growth, in turn, boosted the production of naval stores, lumber products, grains, and livestock and their by-products and helped to continue the expansion of tobacco production from the Northeast to the Northern and Central Inner Plain–Piedmont regions.[31]

Whereas the economic significance of towns rose during the fifties, sixties, and seventies, the number of seaport towns that played important commercial roles gradually declined. Three ports became dominant in late colonial North Carolina: Edenton, primarily serving the Albemarle Sound region and more westerly northern areas; New Bern, essentially serving the Neuse-Pamlico region and its interior; and Wilmington, serving the Lower and Upper Cape Fear regions and an expansive interior as far west and north as Hillsborough in Orange County and Salem and Salisbury in Rowan County.[32]

Midland towns, such as Halifax (formed in 1757), Cross Creek (late 1750s), Campbellton (1762), and Tarboro (1760), developed during the last quarter century of the colonial years to bring supplies, marketing services, and credit directly to the growing Central and Northern Inner Plain–Piedmont regions and to provide similar services for farmers and merchants in the Western region. In fulfilling these functions, the midland towns helped link the colony's regional economies as well as boosted intercolonial and British commercial contacts. Of the midland towns, Halifax and Cross Creek easily achieved first rank. The former, located in Halifax County, was connected commercially by roads with the west, its links to Hillsborough and environs being especially significant. Halifax also established commercial ties with Virginia and eastward with Edenton.[33]

Cross Creek may have come to play an even larger role than did Halifax. It was founded on a small stream of that name, one and one-half miles west of where the creek flowed into the Northwest Cape Fear River in Cumberland County. Goods from the interior, brought by wagons to Cross Creek, could continue an overland journey to Wilmington or could be taken by wagon a mile and a half to the Cape Fear Landing to be loaded on vessels for Wilmington. Since the early 1760s, for example, the bulk of the Moravians' considerable export trade had been destined for Charleston, South Carolina, but by 1775 most of the Moravians' wagons were making their way to Cross Creek. They carried deerskins, wheat, corn, butter, tallow, and hides, plus flour and meal produced in their mill and their own manufactured items such as pottery, candles, and leather goods.[34]

The increase in scale and networking of the operations of merchants in coastal and midland towns helped to stimulate the westward movement of commercial farming and towns—Hillsborough and Salisbury both began around 1754 and Salem and Charlotte in 1766. All of this, in turn, both aided and reflected the colony's growing dependence on slave labor, as the maturation of slave economies in the colonial South invariably was intertwined with the improvement of roads, river systems, and harbor facilities and the networking of interdependent towns where most of each colony's merchants and stores were located. In short, a combination of growth factors was significantly interconnected: a booming population, a heightened commitment to commercial activities and hence to the use of slave labor, the increased production of commodities from farm and forest, a rapidly developing commercial infrastructure, and burgeoning exports.[35]

Exports provide one available statistical gauge of North Carolina's developing commercial agriculture and forestry in the later colonial years. Records before 1750 are poor and those before 1768 erratic. Data for 1768–72, however, show that the value of the colony's exports grew faster during this four-year period than was the case for any other southern colony except Georgia, whose growth rate easily outdistanced North Carolina's. The percentage growth figures for Georgia, North Carolina, South Carolina, Virginia, and Maryland respectively equaled 102, 47, 43, 38, and 24 (see Table 1.9).[36]

Georgia was busily replicating South Carolina's earlier development from a frontier economy with a heavy emphasis on forest production, diversified agriculture, raising livestock, and hunting for deerskins to a staple-producing economy featuring rice complemented by indigo. North Carolina, on the other hand, although not still relying on the deerskin trade nearly as much as Georgia, remained heavily dependent on the export of forest products and tended to diversify its agricultural industry while continuing to focus on the production of beef and pork. This also meant that but for the Lower Cape Fear region with its stress on producing naval stores and lumber products for export, North Carolina's relatively greater tendency to produce a variety of agricultural, forest, and pastoral products led it to emphasize more than other colonies the servicing of intra- and intercolonial markets at the expense of transoceanic markets. Moreover, the faster growth rates of both Georgia's and North Carolina's exports significantly reflect the low base points used to calculate their growth rates. Accordingly, North Carolina's exports by sea for 1768–72 equaled only about 10 and 16 percent respectively of Virginia's and South Carolina's.[37]

Because much of North Carolina's produce was sent to Virginia or South Carolina for reexport, and these commodities simply were recorded as the latter two colonies' exports in the official figures, their recorded exports were thereby inflated whereas North Carolina's were understated. A rough if conservative effort to correct for these distortions suggests that North Carolina's exports equaled closer to £670,000 sterling in value, with Virginia's and South Carolina's respectively equaling about £3,290,000 and £1,880,000 sterling (see Table 1.9). This was hardly parity, but if such figures are used, North Carolina's listed exports for 1768–72, when compared with those of South Carolina and Virginia, equaled respectively 36 percent and 20 percent of their value, rather than the official figures of 16 and 10 percent.

Several examples illustrate the flow of exports over land. As late as 1771 as much North Carolina rice, almost entirely grown in the Lower Cape Fear, was exported via Charleston as was shipped out from the nearby downriver Port Brunswick (the seaports of Wilmington and Brunswick). This occurred, despite the extra time and costs required, to take advantage of the well-developed marketing facilities in Charleston. Similarly, although Ports Brunswick and Roanoke recorded exports of wheat and flour until the 1770s, these products normally went from the backcountry overland as flour to South Carolina and Virginia. And although Port Roanoke handled the bulk of North Carolina's tobacco exports, large quantities of the crop continued to be rolled or hauled overland to Virginia. If North Carolina shipped out substantial quantities of barreled beef and pork, as well as livestock products such as butter, cheese, lard, and tallow, these too went overland to Virginia and South Carolina. And finally, starting in the 1750s cattle drives extended as far north as Pennsylvania and New Jersey, and hogs were regularly driven into Virginia.[38]

The official figures do correctly show that the distribution of North Carolina's exports in the late colonial period differed from those that prevailed in both the upper and the lower South.[39] Most significant, unlike every other colony, even recently settled Georgia, forest products rather than a staple crop dominated North Carolina's exports. Tobacco accounted for 64 percent of Maryland's and 77 percent of Virginia's exports, for instance, while rice made up 65 percent of South Carolina's and 59 percent of Georgia's exports. By contrast, North Carolina's leading exports were naval stores (pitch, tar, and turpentine), which made up 40 percent of the value of all its exports, and wood products (pine boards, stavings, and headings), which comprised another 25 percent. No other southern colony produced these products so extensively. Second, although the dominant commodities of the upper and lower South, tobacco and rice respectively, were exported in considerably smaller quantities from North Carolina, tobacco, at least, played a significant role in North Carolina's economy, comprising 11 percent of the province's exports. Grains and grain products (corn, rice, wheat, bread, and flour) played an even greater role, totaling 13 percent of the value of all exports (see Table 1.9).[40]

Although North Carolina's trade lagged behind that of its southern neighbors and many of its colonists eked out little more than a near-subsistence living, the considerable growth of commercial agriculture frequently is masked by contemporary travel accounts that focus on some of the more visible signs of an undeveloped economy—the absence of intensive land use, the few plows, "poor" care of livestock, and so on. Domestic consumption of farm output may have exceeded exports to an even greater degree than was usually the case in the other southern mainland colonies, yet there seems little question that even in the more recently settled piedmont counties in North Carolina production for market animated an increasing number of farmers by the late colonial period.[41]

Initially few farms were fully commercialized, and the sale of crops and purchase of commodities represented a relatively small percentage of total income and expenditures. During this early stage of settlement, whether in the Albemarle in the early part of the century or in the west in the decades preceding the Revolution, several factors limited commercial production: the amount of available capital and labor, the state of agricultural technology, the need to clear land, the restricted size of markets, and, finally, the nature of transportation. As a result, most settlers, especially those primarily dependent on family labor and limited in their ability to hire or buy additional hands, diversified their efforts to spread labor demands across the year. They planted a variety of crops, raised livestock, and engaged in assorted handicrafts, rather than concentrating on a single staple crop that had highly seasonal labor requirements.[42]

Over time—quite rapidly in the Lower Cape Fear, where well-to-do migrants from South Carolina and the Albemarle Sound region brought considerable numbers of slaves with them to the large land grants they received—more and more settlers accumulated enough capital to intensify their commitment to commercial agriculture by purchasing or hiring indentured servants or slaves or hiring free labor. It is difficult to trace this process, but the demographic patterns already outlined point to the tendency for the slave system to spread steadily from the older to the newer regions of the province after midcentury.[43] As for indentured servitude, it seems always to have been an important source of labor in the colony. Servants had become less numerous than slaves sometime before 1748. Between then and the Revolution important regional and temporal variations developed, with servants relatively more numerous in the less economically mature regions and consequently comparatively less significant in the 1770s than in the 1750s. Still, servants represented an important source of labor into the late colonial era, perhaps equaling about 27 percent of the unfree population of the colony during the years 1755–69 (see Table 1.10).[44]

The spread of slavery, especially by purchase in the late colonial period, occurred despite a steady increase in the price of slaves. Between 1748 and 1754, an adult slave cost, on average, £32.17.10 in North Carolina currency—par being gauged as proclamation money, that is, at 4:3 with the British pound sterling. That price climbed to £55.13.3 between 1759 and 1764 and to £71.18.7 during the years 1764–72. There was no statistically significant difference between male and female prices when female slaves were relatively scarce before the 1760s, the sex ratio for the years 1751–55 equaling about 153. When the sex ratio fell to about 125 during the years 1761–72, the price differential between males and females slowly rose to an average of £5 between 1759 and 1764 and then rapidly to £22 for the years 1765–72. Although the average adult male sold for about £89 during the last period, artisans in their prime commanded prices up to £200 (see Table 1.11).[45] Many planters and farmers could not afford such a capital outlay. Their labor needs could be met by purchasing or hiring servants, or hiring slaves or free persons.

However frequent the incidence of hiring slaves for temporary service, there is little question that large numbers of North Carolinians, even small farmers, viewed slave ownership as desirable. It fulfilled a practical need, overcoming a pressing labor shortage that restricted economic activities. In the process, slave ownership appeared to be the path to wealth, or at least to comfort, and thus a key means of achieving upward social mobility and political power since both derived from wealth. Last, partially offsetting the high cost of slaves was the supposed undependability of free workers, especially if they were land owners or renters themselves.[46]

Such calculations had profound implications for slaves, whether African or Creole. Whatever other benefits whites derived from the enslavement of blacks, it was their functional worth as laborers that explained slavery. And slaves recognized this, as a conversation that William Attmore had with two slaves who rowed him across the Tar River in 1787 suggests. The Philadelphia merchant questioned Polydore, one of the rowers. "Where was you born, boy?" he asked. Polydore responded that he had been "born in Guinea" but did not reply immediately when Attmore wondered if he wanted to return to his country. The other slave answered for him. "He is fast," he said, "he can't go."[47] And that was so. They were held fast, bound against their will to labor in a strange land as slaves, more than likely until the grave released them.

Indeed, work was the key element of the new setting in which Africans found themselves and in which Creoles were born. It stood at the center of the system that held them fast. Whites defined the value of their slaves in terms of their capabilities as laborers. And work, in a fundamental manner, shaped the very pattern and rhythm of slaves' lives; it framed their world, providing both pain and, ironically, a means by which they could mold a sense of self-worth.

The conditions under which slaves worked varied substantially and hinged in part on the size of the unit on which they lived. Plantation size affected occupational structure and work organization, among other things. The larger the unit, the wider was the range of specialized jobs. The truly large units of the Cape Fear region, those with well over a hundred slaves, had the greatest occupational specialization. Slaves on such plantations worked in the forest cutting down or tapping the trees to produce lumber products or naval stores, followed these industrial processes to their conclusion, or labored in rice or cornfields; in these or collateral pursuits the vast majority served as field hands and semi-industrial laborers. A growing minority of male slaves, however, worked as artisans, domestic servants, drivers, boatmen, loaders, and teamsters. Some, enough to spark complaints in 1773 by whites in the job, worked as river pilots. A few served as slave drivers and helped to supervise the labor of the other slaves. Females who did not toil in the fields were almost all domestics, but some specialized as spinners and a few were industrial slaves or labored as weavers on large plantations.[48]

Detailed occupational breakdowns for slaves exist for only three large North Carolina plantations during the years 1770–1809. Using these data ensures an overestimate of skilled slaves among the colony's slaves, since the proportion of such slaves increased over time and was highest on large plantations. The percentage of slaves who worked at nonfield pursuits on these three plantations averaged about 10 percent. The proportion of males who were not field hands, largely artisans, nearly equaled 13 percent, whereas the figure for females was less than 8 percent, largely domestics (see Table 1.12). Estimates for the last twenty years of the colonial period are bound to be even less dependable, but our impression is that the average percentage of nonfield slaves was no more than 7 to 8 percent of the total number of slaves, with the male and female percentages respectively equaling a bit under 10 and 6 percent.

These percentages for North Carolina, while understandably lower than those for its more economically mature neighbors, still followed like trends and are roughly similar. For instance, in four southern Maryland counties an estimated 10 to 15 percent of the slave men and a smaller percentage of the women, as early as 1730, did not work as field hands.[49] In Prince Georges County, an area of concentrated slaveholding in southern Maryland, the proportion of males who toiled as agricultural field hands dropped from 90 to 82 percent between 1733 and 1776, and by the latter date roughly 3 to 5 percent of slave women were domestic servants.[50] In South Carolina, 11 percent of all slaves were not field hands between 1730 and 1779; the breakdowns for males and females were 16 and 4 percent respectively. Except for the 1750s, the percentage of nonfield hands rose slowly over time. By the 1760s, 12 percent of all slaves and 17 and 5 percent respectively of males and females had been exempted from field work.[51]

Only a minority of all North Carolina slaves lived on units large enough for such extensive specialization. By the end of the colonial period, a little over seven out of every ten slaves were owned by masters who had fewer than twenty slaves. James Auld of Halifax County exemplified the small planters with one to four slaves who owned roughly a quarter of all slaves in colonial North Carolina between 1748 and 1771 (see Table 1.5). In 1771 he produced thirty barrels of corn with the help of "one old Fellow" and his "house wench."[52] On such small farms and plantations the situation was akin to Harry Braverman's description of the "farming family": "The farming family combines its [agricultural] craft with the rude practice of a number of others, including those of the smith, mason, carpenter, butcher, miller, and baker."[53] In such a setting all slaves of working age toiled at a variety of tasks, and the master, who often worked alongside his slaves, handled discipline.

The composition of the workforce also shaped the work world of many slaves. Especially in the earlier settled or less economically mature areas where slaves formed a relatively small proportion of the total population, workforces tended to be both multiracial and multistatus. Black, white, red, mulatto, and mustee indentured servants, apprentices, and free workers often labored with slaves who were themselves diverse—Africans, African Americans, mulattoes, mustees, and some Indians. The mix of aspirations and expectations, the extent of cultural diffusion, and efforts to limit the pace of work inevitably took different shapes in such situations from those where blacks, many of them Africans, dominated the unfree labor force and made up a large proportion of the total population. This last was most clearly the case in the Lower Cape Fear region. Still, whatever the demographic characteristics of a region, diversity of experience was commonplace among slaves. They acquired new owners or were hired out. Adult male slaves worked alongside nonslaves from five to ten days a year on the roads, and a variety of slaves often labored with nonslaves off the home plantation on other specific tasks.[54]

White attitudes about work, which also affected slaves, varied substantially in the preindustrial and overwhelmingly rural society of colonial North Carolina. Although commercialization was on the rise, economic activities ranged from essentially subsistence farming to production for market, and some whites acted out an intense quest for economic advancement while others did not. Eighteenth-century observers frequently allude to such differences. John Brickell noted in the 1730s, for instance, that although most white workers were "indolent," some were "laborious, and equalize with the Negros in hard labor." Thirty years later Josiah Quincy wrote that because slaves were far less numerous than in South Carolina, "labour becomes more necessary, and he who has an interest of his own to serve, is a labourer in the field." Scotus Americanus implied a similar link between the absence of hardworking slaves and the diligence of whites when he claimed that recent immigrants, who seldom could afford to purchase more than a few slaves, tended to be "far more industrious" than those who had been in the colony for some time.[55]

If this remark hinted at an acquired laxity, other comments suggest that certain whites had reputations for industriousness. "The Germans are Loyal and Industrious," William Faris of Wilmington advised a friend, and because they were "not so ready to complain and be uneasy as many others," they made "choice servants." Johann Schoepf singled out the Moravians as "distinguished above the other inhabitants for their industry and diligence in agriculture and the crafts." Two Virginians who visited the Moravians in the early 1770s were equally impressed, but when told that the Moravians owned only two slaves they "were the more surprised to find that white people had done so much work."[56]

The Virginians' surprise reflected their assumptions about proper work arrangements and a commonplace lament about the work habits of whites in the colonial era.[57] White North Carolinians, despite evaluations to the contrary, early acquired an unenviable reputation for lax morals and habits. Observers cited various explanations for such attitudes and behavior, from the presence of runaway criminals, servants, and debtors, to the plenitude of natural resources and the mildness of the climate.[58]

Contemporaries also linked this alleged laxity with prevailing techniques of production. Observers familiar with the intensive and land-saving agricultural practices of England and Europe regarded colonial methods as crude, unscientific, and wasteful. The English author of *American Husbandry*, the most authoritative contemporary survey of agricultural conditions in the colonies, complained, for example, that North Carolinians were "spoiled for good husbandry by plenty of land." They failed to rotate or fertilize crops on a systematic basis, and they left fields unweeded. And North Carolinians, supposedly unlike Virginians, did not manage their tobacco "with any spirit." This generally "careless manner" characterized the handling of livestock as well. Cattle and hogs roamed free, and because there was an "almost total neglect of inclosure," they frequently trampled crops.[59]

Africans who entered this world confronted a situation not wholly unfamiliar, for their own concepts of time and labor meshed neatly with existing ideas and practices. In addition to specific skills, Africans brought with them a task-oriented conception of work close to that of other preindustrial peoples, including the European colonists. West Africans also shared with them a notion of time as dictated by the seasons, natural phenomena such as the phases of the moon, and the harvesting of particular crops. Work among all of these folk proceeded in spurts relating to specific tasks. "The work pattern was one of alternate bouts of intense labour and of idleness," E. P. Thompson has written, "wherever men were in control of their own working lives." The length of each work day and week varied in an irregular fashion but generally followed an annual cycle in which an individual's inclination to work or not figured importantly.[60] Thus, although Africans had to adjust to the seasonal patterns of particular crops or products, regulating life in this manner was a familiar practice. And Africans could see all about them examples of white workers who displayed irregular and lax work habits similar to their own. The chief difference, of course, was that slaves had far less opportunity to follow their own inclination to work or not than they had had in West African societies. They were no longer people "in control of their own working lives."

Although North Carolina planters and small farmers who held slaves were not steeped in the time-conscious mentality of later factory superintendents, they understood the central importance of slave labor in augmenting their wealth and ensuring their comfort, and they attempted to maximize the work slaves did. Generally speaking, they could do this by using either positive or negative incentives, either inducing their slaves to work hard, that is, or forcing them to do so and punishing them if they did not.

Direct evidence as to the extent of negative incentives is elusive but suggestive. When the wealthy planter James Murray casually remarked in a letter that close supervision was the key to exacting "steady work" from slaves, he pointed to the central role of the overseer on large production units: "I have made about 1000 lb. to my share this [year?], and might have made clear double that quantity had my overseer been good." Murray did not expand on how a "good" overseer might have doubled production, but the results of one approach used by a particularly harsh overseer are revealed by two slaves who made their way to their absentee owner, Penelope Dawson. Her overseer, they complained, beat them regularly, "just as much without fault as with one." After nearly killing one of them with a hoe on Saturday, he had "promised to give 4 hundred lashes on monday."[61] Such pathological cruelty might be unusual, but ads for runaways that describe punishment scars boldly laid bare the presence of the whip as a common instrument of discipline.[62]

Because harsh treatment could damage slave property, and because slaves engaged their masters in an ongoing dialogue regarding the proper amount of work that would be done, owners also sought to induce steady labor by using more positive motivational techniques.[63] The task system was one of these. It most significantly evolved in early-eighteenth-century rice cultivation in South Carolina and had become routine there by the Revolutionary era. A highly flexible measure of work, tasking was adaptable both to chores of varying difficulty and to slaves of different ages and physical capacities. It remained standard practice among slave field hands in coastal South Carolina and Georgia into the Civil War.[64]

It is impossible to determine to what degree a similar process existed in North Carolina prior to the Revolution, for the evidence is ambiguous. One would expect references to the task system to show up chiefly in materials relating to the Lower Cape Fear region, where some rice was grown and slaveholding patterns were closest to those in the South Carolina low country. Scotus Americanus, who seemingly observed work there, notes that slaves "generally" completed their assigned "daily tasks" by early afternoon and were then free to tend their own plots of land. If this was true, then the system worked as it was supposed to: slaves labored quickly and efficiently so as to get to their own work. Janet Schaw, another visitor to the region, provides the only other direct statement that we have located about plantation labor organization for North Carolina prior to the Revolution. She describes corn cultivation in a tantalizingly equivocal fashion: "a number of Negroes follow each other's tail the day long, and have a task assigned them."[65] Schaw may have witnessed the assertion of African collective work patterns superimposed on the individualistic tasking system of their masters, something that occurred in South Carolina.[66]

Although the comments of Schaw and Scotus Americanus hardly are conclusive even for the Cape Fear region, two other observations at least imply that tasking may have spread more widely by the late colonial period. James Millis, superintendent of an iron-making facility in Chatham County, mentions in a detailed letter written in 1777 that the "Dayly Task for a Negro Wood Cutter is a Cord, some can cut more but I never knew more than a Cord Required, if they Cut more, it is usual to pay them for it." Too much should not be made of this since so few slaves were employed in iron making. Yet the comment is suggestive, as is the clear evidence of direct money payments for work beyond a specified task.[67] A remark made by William Attmore, who visited the state a decade later, intimates that tasking had been used for some time in more commonplace slave assignments. Commenting on the sparsity of food available to North Carolina slaves, Attmore wrote that "they are allowed no Meat, they have the privilege sometimes of working a bit of Ground for themselves, out of such time as they gain when Task'd, or on Sundays."[68] If the offhand usage of "Task'd" suggests that the practice was not a novel one, the context argues its limited implementation among slaves who received a poor diet. The term is used ambiguously. One cannot be sure if Attmore was using *task'd* to define a chore assigned to a group (a gang) or to individuals. The former use of the term would hardly be unusual since certain tasks normally would be required of gangs of slaves who would thereby be held to "acceptable" levels of performance as would individual slaves within the gang.

Despite the many imponderables, it seems that the task system, as opposed to a system of gang labor, did play some role in organizing slave labor on colonial North Carolina's larger plantations. Even if this were not the case, it is clear that a number of slaves in the province worked on farms and plantations too small to have gangs, as slave gangs were employed either on Caribbean sugar plantations or on Chesapeake tobacco plantations (see Table 1.5). Their labor probably was integrated with the work habits of their owners, and tasking frequently would have been perfectly suited to the labor needs of small farms.

Whether slaves toiled by the task or gang systems, or some less formal arrangement, and whether they had cruel or "good" masters, they sometimes were allowed to have garden plots that they worked in their "own" time, as William Attmore noted in the mid-1780s.[69] Owners allowed this because the privilege might calm unrest created by bondage and thereby make for more productive labor. In addition, food grown on such garden plots supplemented rations supplied by masters and thus reduced the annual cost of slave upkeep. For slaves, there were understandable attractions. Even before 1740, John Brickell noted, these plots provided slaves with a "sufficient quantity of Tobacco for their own use, a part of which they may sell, and likewise on Sundays, they gather Snake-root, otherwise it would be excessive dear if the Christians were to gather it; with this and the Tobacco they buy Hats, and other Necessaries for themselves, as Linen, Bracelets, Ribbons, and several other Toys for their Wives and Mistresses." Nearly forty years later Janet Schaw described the dual functions of garden plots somewhat differently. "The allowance for a Negro is a quart of Indian corn pr. day," she observed, "and a little piece of land which they cultivate much better than their masters. There they rear hogs and poultry, sow calabashes, etc. and are better provided in every thing than the poorer white people among us."[70]

It is unclear how common slave gardens were or how typical were the productive plots described by Schaw for the Lower Cape Fear region, for other contemporaries who touch on the issue of slave conditions stress the meagerness of the rations masters supplied and do not mention how slaves might have supplemented them. The picture they paint is not a pleasant one. One visitor to the colony, Johann Schoepf, claimed that the daily rations were minimal fare for slaves other than house servants and that they rarely included meat or fish. Although "well-disposed masters" provided adequate clothing, he added, "those who have the largest droves keep them the worst, let them run naked mostly or in rags, and accustom them as much as possible to hunger, but exact of them steady work."[71] Masters no doubt varied in their treatment of slaves, yet it seems that slave maintenance was not a high priority. One measure of this inadvertently has been left behind in estate records. They reveal that guardians of orphan children commonly listed £3–4 North Carolina currency as the annual cost of maintaining slaves and that they spent two to three times more than that caring for white orphans.[72]

Masters often sought to find a balance between economy and care sufficient to ensure a productive labor force, for they well knew that their slaves had the capacity to resist or to define limits. Slaves understood how valuable their labor was and sometimes made it clear that a penurious policy could be as counterproductive as harsh punishment. Penelope Dawson learned this when one of her slaves came to her "with a grievous complaint of being starved" by her overseer. The slave warned her that "he was sure the Negroes would all leave the plantation" if conditions did not improve.[73] Yet there were limits to what slaves could do. Unlike Scottish Highlanders employed at an iron furnace in western North Carolina who, as we shall see, let their own needs dictate when they would work as hired hands, slaves normally could not just "leave the plantation" without repercussions. Masters could unilaterally and arbitrarily assert their authority; they could coerce, intimidate, and terrorize their human property. The threat to withhold labor, nonetheless, was one of the ways in which slaves could attempt to exert their will and assert their worth, but it was but one tactic in an ongoing struggle between master and slave about how much work should be done.[74]

Other stratagems used by slaves to lighten their workload included feigning illness, playing dumb, sabotaging property, and deliberately misunderstanding instructions. When James Auld noted in an offhand fashion that the slave carpenter he had hired for the year "proved tardy," he pointed to perhaps the most common technique.[75] As Johann David Schoepf learned while waiting for a boat in Edenton, slaves manipulated the opportunities for delay to the fullest. Once the boat arrived, the slaves put off ferrying him as long as possible. The head ferryman had fallen asleep, so Schoepf and several slaves "had to rouse him up, and then wait until he had called together a dozen negroes who were to look for two others whose business it was to tend the boat, which they only now began to make ready; more time lost." After finally reaching his destination, the punctilious Schoepf, by now beside himself, penned an acerbic postlude about the conditions that underlay this power struggle: "No people can be so greedy after holidays as the whites and blacks here and none with less reason, for at no time do they work so as to need a long rest. It is difficult to say which are the best creatures, the whites here or their blacks, or which have been formed by the others; but in either case the example is bad. The white men are all the time complaining that the blacks will not work, and they themselves do nothing. The white men complain further that they cannot trust the faithless blacks, and they set them a dubious model."[76]

Tactics such as those that so infuriated Schoepf were not unique to slaves in colonial North Carolina or to slaves in general. Workers of varying status in different times and places have always sought to impose limits on what they do, as new workers in any factory will attest. In the late nineteenth century, whether unionized or not, artisans commonly fixed "stints" or output quotas despite management's coercive attempts to speed up the process. Often formalized in union work rules, such practices persisted into the twentieth century. As "efficiency expert" Henry Gantt explained in 1919, "There is in every workroom a fashion, a habit of work, and the new worker follows that fashion, for it isn't respectable not to."[77] Shortly before the Civil War, Frederick Law Olmsted came across just such an instance in Virginia. A nonslaveholder who hired whites and free blacks as laborers, he observed, "has suffered a good deal from the demoralizing influence of adjacent slave labor, the men, after a few months' residence, inclining to follow the customs of the slaves with regard to the amount of work they should do in a day, or their careless mode of operation."[78]

A detailed letter written by James Millis, superintendent of the Chatham Furnace in 1777, provides a few clues about such "customs" among both whites and slaves in colonial North Carolina. Millis repeatedly complained of the performance of hired white hands. "Seven or Eight Highlanders . . . Employ'd in Digging Ore . . . went home to put their plantations in Order for a Crop," as did four others hired to cut wood. The white woodcutters, he lamented, "will only Cut when it Suits them, and leave their work often when you are in most Want, or Stand off from working at all purely to Enhance their wages." Millis requested additional slave labor to rectify this uncertain situation. Seventeen adult male slaves and three boys already worked at the forge and furnace, and Millis seemed generally pleased by their work. These slaves probably knew of Millis's problems with white labor, although the document does not divulge how this knowledge affected their own work performance. Millis's letter does suggest that at least one task performed by the slaves also had a set limit. A cord was the accepted daily quantity in wood cutting. If a slave cut more than that, he was paid for it.[79]

Whatever the exact arrangements worked out between masters and slaves, the work regimen still hinged on the seasons and the uncertain nature of the weather. This meant that the intensity of labor varied throughout the year depending on the particular tasks to be done. Slaves usually toiled six days a week, but during the hectic harvesting seasons their one day of rest also might be taken away.[80] Even the most arduous work could be interrupted by natural phenomena. In the spring of 1771, for instance, a flood destroyed nearly all of the winter wheat and freshly planted tobacco on Thomas Barker's plantation near Edenton, swept away most of the livestock, and left "scarce Corn . . . to feed the Negroes and the remains of the stock."[81]

Various other factors affected slave work life. Where Africans were numerous, as Peter Wood has so amply demonstrated for South Carolina, they undoubtedly exerted a great deal of influence on how work was done. In South Carolina, knowledgeable Africans and their descendants used their skills to enable the colony to develop early economies of diversified farming, open-range stock raising, the production of forest products, and, later, the manner in which rice was cultivated.[82] Such defining, or redefining, of colonial agriculture by African slaves, or their melding African customs with those of their European enslavers, undoubtedly also occurred in North Carolina in precisely the areas cited by Wood. The process by which this was achieved has been outlined above and below for North Carolina in discussions about the conjoining of African with European conceptions and practices of work such as the slaves' integrating African ironsmithing techniques with those of their colonial masters, or the slaves' combining African collective approaches to work with the individualistic tasking system of slaveowners.

Janet Schaw added yet another dimension to this story when she noted that slaves, far more than their masters, became skilled in putting to use the Native American flora they found about them. To illustrate her point, she sent a friend "a paper of their vegetable pins made from the prickly pear, also molds for buttons made from the calibash, which likewise serves to hold their victuals." Such slave accomplishments were considerably more complex and extensive than even the astute Schaw observed. Slaves were more capable than their owners of making use of local flora and fauna because of their African holistic incorporation of natural phenomena into their social, economic, religious, medical, and philosophical beliefs and practices. As an instance, they would incorporate local plants into their already vast store of botanical knowledge to help them develop herbs or potions both to cure illnesses and to deal with the causal agents of sickness. The slaves' capacity to unravel the mysteries of their new surroundings was further aided by their comparative receptivity to the lore of the Native Americans. The African cultures of the slaves bore closer resemblances to those of the Indians than did European cultures and were less burdened by dogma and arrogance.[83]

Elkanah Watson, while traveling through North Carolina to South Carolina in 1777, described a scene that encapsulates some of what we have just discussed. During his trip "four jolly, well-fed negroes" rowed him across Wingran Bay. "The evening was serene, the stars shone brightly," he recalled, "and the poor fellows amused us the whole way by singing their plaintive African songs in cadence with the oars."[84] The craft in which Watson and his companions traveled was probably a dugout canoe or a larger piragua, made of hollowed-out tree trunks joined together or engaged in the middle with planking, a type of boat known both to precontact Indians of the area and to West Africans, at least in its fundamental dugout mold. As in South Carolina, it was a common form of transportation and one that probably reflected how Africans, in employing skills that they brought with them into slavery, helped, along with Native Americans and whites, to shape life in the colonies. The songs Watson refers to but cannot understand, on the other hand, may well have been work chanties sung in any of a number of African tongues, but perhaps in the prevailing pidgin-creole language.[85]

As much is hidden as is revealed by Watson's intriguing observations. He never attempts to reconcile his paradoxical juxtaposition of "four jolly, well-fed negroes" with "poor fellows . . . singing their plaintive African songs." Nor do we know the lyrics, rhythms, harmonies, and melodies of the songs that were sung. The language or languages used similarly remain blurred beyond the encompassing terms *African* or *creole*. Yet though the mysteries remain, Africa pervades the scene on a moonlit bay in Carolina some two centuries ago as slaves set the "cadence with the oars" to the rhythms of "their plaintive

African songs." Such cadences had been and would be set countless times before and after this event by slaves performing and somewhat transforming their work routines.

If the slaves' African backgrounds helped to determine how they would toil, this occurred within the parameters established by the particular jobs, or set of discrete tasks, to which slaves were assigned. Thus, how agricultural workers toiled largely depended on which crops they cultivated. A field hand in the counties adjacent to Virginia and south into the Neuse-Pamlico regions, all of which stressed diversified farming and produced tobacco, grains, livestock, lumber, and naval stores, had to learn many skills that differed from those required of the slaves who concentrated on producing naval stores supplemented by lumber products and, to a lesser degree, rice in the Lower Cape Fear region. In addition, nonfield hands such as artisans, riverboatmen, teamsters, and domestics each had distinct work routines. Every crop and craft had a seasonal and work pattern or rhythm all its own, which in turn helped to mold slave life.

In most areas, even those that specialized in certain cash "crops," a variety of crops were planted or tended, and each had its unique annual calendar. In October or November as well as in March hands planted wheat, whereas in April they attended to Indian corn and tobacco. In early March slaves set out flax, harvesting it in early May. The corn and tobacco harvests came in September, except for late-planted corn in May, followed by the planting of turnips. The pattern was not identical in all regions, but in each the growing and harvesting schedules formed a distinct element of the year-round cycle. Alec Martin, a farmer near Salisbury in Rowan County, hinted at this rhythm when he wrote to a friend in Virginia. "The Crop is on the ground that must be gathered and disposed of before my Mother's Removal," he explained, "which cannot be till Spring."[86]

Crops not only had their own schedules, they each had to be handled in different ways that, in turn, became a part of the life of the slaves involved. Corn, for instance, had to be cultivated several times during the summer "to keep down the weeds." "To accomplish this," Janet Schaw observed, "a number of Negroes follow each other's tail the day long, and have a task assigned to them, and it will take twenty at least to do as much work as two horses with a man and a boy will perform."[87] Without realizing it, Schaw may have observed an adaptation of West African horticultural and collective work patterns. What she certainly did see, but also probably without full comprehension, was an example of slaves regulating the pace of their work. Not all slaves worked in groups such as this, where they could assert their collective solidarity, but since corn was grown throughout the colony almost all field hands at one time or another probably had to tend it.

Some crops required more attention than corn. Rice, concentrated in portions of the Lower Cape Fear region, was one. Various West Africans understood the intricacies of growing rice, a crop that required constant care in inherently unhealthy conditions. Slaves planted the rice seed in shallow trenches in low-lying areas in the early spring, using their feet, as had been done in Africa, to cover each seed. After the fields had been flooded and the delicate shoots reached a height of six to eight inches, slaves drained, rehoed, and reflooded the fields. They repeated this process several times throughout the summer, alternately hoeing the dry fields and wading through water to tend the plants. In September or October, when the rice was "ripe," the fields were drained, the rice reaped and stacked, then threshed, winnowed, "pounded," and packed. In December the cycle started over. Slaves burned or plowed under the stubble of the previous crop, prepared the earth for spring planting, and repaired irrigation ditches. The labor required to do all this, Schaw thought, "is only fit for slaves, and I think the hardest work I have seen them engaged in."[88]

Tobacco, although less arduous to cultivate than rice, was also a labor-intensive crop. Nonetheless, unlike rice or naval stores, tobacco could be profitably produced on farms with relatively few slaves. Grown principally in the northern tier of counties bordering Virginia, but also moving southward into the Neuse-Pamlico and the Central Inner Plain–Piedmont regions, tobacco was raised from seeds embedded in rich mold. When the young plants reached a height of four to five inches in May or June, they were transplanted into soil that had first been plowed and laced with manure. Slaves working with hoes formed little hills six to nine feet apart. Once the plants reached a height of one foot they had to be pruned, topped, and the bottom leaves cut off. Twice a week thereafter suckers had to be removed, the hills weeded, and the plant carefully gone over for worms. When the tobacco leaves began to brown in the late summer or early fall, they were cut and piled in stacks and then taken to a shed where they hung for about a month. After being stacked in piles again, this time for one to two weeks, the leaves were finally packed into hogsheads.[89]

As we have seen, however, the heaviest concentrated use of slave labor was not in the growing of agricultural commodities but in various nonagricultural pursuits, the most important being the production of lumber products and naval stores, North Carolina's principal exports. The Cape Fear region dominated the naval stores industry, but pitch, tar, and turpentine, as well as shingles, staves, and sawn lumber, were also significantly produced in the other coastal regions. When Bishop August Gottlieb Spangenburg visited Bertie and

Chowan Counties in the early 1750s, for instance, he reported them covered with pine forests and noted: "The people make tar, pitch, and turpentine, whenever they are near enough to a river to load the products on small boats and take it to a sloop or other small vessel."[90]

The economic appeal of naval stores production is easy to understand. Although arduous and time-consuming, the operations induced a number of related profitable activities that, in turn, complemented the crop cycle. Tar, for example, could be produced in the summer but was generally a "winter business" and thus provided year-round employment for slaves.[91] Nor was it expensive to produce tar, because the raw materials—dead trees, trees knocked down by the wind, and those previously "boxed" for turpentine—cost little if anything. The people, Schoepf claimed, "make money almost from nothing." Slaves did the bulk of the labor, and "the profit arising is so much greater because no establishment is necessary beyond the working hands themselves." Each working hand, he estimated, "what with these and other uses made of the forest, should bring in to his master one to two hundred pounds current a year."[92] Profits were substantial. One North Carolinian observed that "our naval stores [are] so high that those who have . . . negroes Employ them in Burning Tar."[93]

Contemporaries well understood the relationship between large-scale slave production and potential profits in naval stores. Edward Moseley, one of the early leaders of the colony, underscored this when he justified his request for a large tract of land on the grounds that he had "a considerable number of Slaves, and no Lightwood land for his Slaves to make Tar." And when James Murray advised Henry McCulloh about settling in the colony, he pointed to a similar relationship: "If you intend to do any business here a Cooper and a Craft that will carry about 100 barrels will be absolutely necessary. I have suffer'd much for want of them, and that want of Craft and negroes will be a great obstruction in securing the Quantity of Naval Stores at this time that otherwise I might do."[94] It was no coincidence, then, that naval stores production centered in key slaveholding areas. For example, even though Cumberland County was located in the midst of the belt of longleaf pines, the trees most desirable for naval stores, and adequate transportation to the coast was available, only small amounts of naval stores were produced there because few large slaveholdings existed in the county.[95]

Numerous contemporaries described the methods used to produce pitch, tar, and turpentine. In winter or early spring slaves "blazed" the pine trees by cutting diagonal slashes through the bark. Starting some time in April, the resinous sap, turpentine, would begin to flow down these cuts into "boxes" or bowls chopped into the base of the tree. Twice a month these bowls had to be "dipped" or "scraped" and the turpentine collected. Schoepf, who seems to have observed this process in person, gives the following description: "One man can readily care for 3000 boxes [two to four boxes per tree], and that number is generally assigned one negro, the negroes doing the most of the work. At the best and warmest season one negro can easily fill 15–20 barrels of turpentine per day. In rainy or cloudy weather the outflow is less, and nothing is done. It is reckoned that from 3000 boxes more than 100–120 barrels in the average should be obtained in a summer. For these 3000 boxes some 12–15 acres of forest should suffice, according as the trees stand close or far apart, and are strong or not."[96]

Gathering the turpentine was merely the first step. When distilled, turpentine yielded oil of turpentine and a thick resin that could be dried to powder form. Tar, essentially the same gum, was produced in a different way. A circular clay floor would be prepared that sloped toward a hole in the center. Split pine would be stacked on the floor, covered with earth, and then set afire through a hole at the top. The intensity of the fire could be controlled by poking holes through the earth to let in more air. As the pine burned, tar would be forced out of the logs and would flow through the hole in the floor into a barrel. The collected tar might then be boiled to produce another by-product, pitch.[97]

During the rest of the year Cape Fear slaves worked at other assignments besides those dealing with naval stores. Some grew rice and indigo, many more worked to prepare trees for lumber, others shaped shingles or barrel staves, hoops and ends, and almost all helped in the production of other crops both for export and subsistence while toiling at a variety of chores common to farming at that time.[98] The operations of one wealthy Cape Fear planter illustrate the multiplicity of economic tasks in which slaves engaged. When Janet Schaw visited John Rutherford's estate some thirty miles from Wilmington, the "vast number of Negroes employed in various works" impressed her considerably. Although Rutherford had some three hundred acres planted in corn and grains, he also operated a large sawmill, the "finest I ever met with." It could turn out three thousand boards or planks a day and, if necessary, double that number. The "immense" woods around the estate provided the required wood for lumber and a thriving subsidiary industry, the making of "staves, hoops and ends for barrels and casks for the West India trade." Not surprisingly, Rutherford had "a great number of his slaves bred coopers and carpenters."[99]

Few other North Carolina plantations rivaled Rutherford's in size and complexity, but whether on small or large units slaves followed what became well-established annual routines. They rotated from task to task through the year. A contemporary traveler in the tobacco counties noted, for instance, that "the whole culture of tobacco is over in the summer months; in the winter the negros are employed in sawing and butting timber, threshing corn, clearing new land, and preparing for tobacco."[100] The precise routine varied from region to region, yet in all cases a typical field hand would acquire familiarity with diverse agricultural techniques and, often, with rough carpentry and a variety of other skills.

The seasonal demands of a rural economy devoted to the production for market of lumber, naval stores, and agricultural produce largely dictated the year-round pattern of labor for artisans and other nonfield slaves. Domestic servants on large plantations probably were the least affected by such cycles, because the essential character of their work did not alter. If owned by wealthy planters, however, where they worked might vary during the course of the year. In the Cape Fear and Albemarle regions, especially, it was fairly common for well-to-do planters to reside in Wilmington or Edenton for a portion of the year and on their home plantations for the rest of the time. Domestics on smaller plantations, on the other hand, probably labored in the fields at least part of the time, especially during harvest seasons. Riverboatmen and artisans may also have helped with field work during harvest seasons and occasionally at other times, the nature of their work shifting in accordance with seasonal requirements. Thomas Pollock's slave Bowman, a gifted blacksmith, devoted most of his time between March and mid-July each year to making plows. Even such highly skilled slaves sometimes worked at other jobs. This happened to both Bowman and Charles, another slave blacksmith owned by Pollock. During part of one year the overseer in charge of the two set them to work building houses.[101] Pollock's dismay at what he considered a misuse of Bowman's and Charles's talents intimates that their experiences were atypical for slave artisans.

Fragmentary evidence leaves only a sketchy view of the routines followed by artisans, riverboatmen, and domestics. There is little question, however, that in many ways the employment conditions of nonfield slaves often were different from those of the slave majority. Artisans ordinarily worked alone or with one or two other slaves and, often, a white artisan. Bowman and Charles, for instance, worked with several different white blacksmiths in the late 1740s and early 1750s. Both slaves were trusted, relatively independent, and in time seem to have worked more or less on their own. "If Bowman should want Iron before I have an opportunity to send any to them," Pollock wrote on one occasion, "it will be well to buy at Mrs. Meads Store." In another letter Pollock used the phrase "his Shoop" when referring to Bowman. Neither Bowman nor Charles were free, as the terms of Pollock's contracts and his admonition to one white "to order Bowman to be verry careful" and not waste any iron make clear, yet their circumstances set them apart from field hands.[102]

The seventeen adult male slaves and three boys who worked at North Carolina's tiny Chatham Furnace also performed essential services with minimal white supervision. Aside from James Millis, the furnace supervisor, only two other whites, a collier and a stonecutter, labored at the works on a regular basis. Eleven or twelve white farmers from the neighborhood sporadically dug ore and cut wood. Thus slaves worked beside whites but nonetheless handled the main jobs at both the forge and the foundry, two distinct operations that were apparently separated by some distance. Four men and one boy worked at the forge. Sambo, a carpenter, worked at "mending" the forge. Mingo, assisted by Toney, a boy who led the oxen, carted coal there, while Cuffee kept the forge fired with coal. The forge also had its own mill, presumably a sawmill, and Old Peter was in charge of it. The furnace operations were more complex. The only blacksmith named by Millis was Julius, a slave, whose "smiter," or helper, was a slave named Sandy who "sometimes Stocks Coal." George was responsible for tending the furnace's sawmill and "keeping" the furnace when it was in blast. Doctor removed "Rubbish" from the furnace and made coal baskets. Jemmy and Peter worked "with the Stone Cutter helping him to get Hearth stone," Bristol and Tom toiled with the collier making charcoal, and Toney, Ceasar, Jacob, and Africa cut wood. Davy, also at the furnace, was "lame, and can't do any work." Although few direct clues exist as to precisely how the blacks and whites interacted, Millis relied on the slaves to run the bulk of his operations, and they did so largely without close supervision. Perhaps the slaves' adeptness may partially be explained by their African backgrounds and the significance of iron production in Africa. The close African connection is suggested by the names of many of the slaves employed in the ironworks.[103]

As a result of their distinctive work many riverboatmen, domestics, and personal servants may have had even more sustained contacts with whites than Bowman, Charles, or the Chatham Furnace slaves. Personal servants regularly traveled with their masters, as James Iredell's Peter did for over twenty years. Their chores as messengers also ensured that for much of each day they were frequently in contact with whites.[104] Richard Templeman revealed how dependent he had been on such a slave in a 1780 letter: "I am not without my misfortunes—I lost my Servant Jess who died a few days ago he was my dependence in taking care of my Covering horse &c. I have not another to suply his place and [am] altogether ignorant myself."[105]

Although field hands had fewer and less personal contacts with whites and were less privileged than artisans, domestics, and the like, their labor nonetheless could take them into the world beyond their own huts and plantations. Working on the average five to ten days per year on the county roads, they toiled with other slaves as well as with white and black servants and poor freemen who lived in the same road district. Some field hands were used as messengers, and many shared with nonfield slaves the varied experiences of being hired out.[106]

Hiring out slaves offered so many advantages to whites that it undoubtedly was as widespread in North Carolina as in all of the other southern colonies.[107] It made the slave labor supply more flexible; profited alike those who hired the slaves, the owners, and recent inheritors of slaves; and bound more closely the interests of slaveowners with those who owned no slaves. Masters could hire out surplus slaves during slack seasons, thereby maximizing profits while cutting upkeep costs. Small property owners, renters, tenants, and town dwellers, unable to purchase slaves, could hire them at reasonable rates. And the practice simplified the division of estates and the care of both minor heirs and those incapable of running an active plantation.

The case of young Elizabeth Hilliard of Edgecombe County illustrates how hiring out was supposed to work in settling estates. The two slaves left to her by her father in 1765 toiled as hired labor for twelve years. Sam, then ten, earned Elizabeth £2 in 1765, while four-year-old Davey brought in 18 shillings and 6 pence. Ten years later their combined wages netted Elizabeth £31.15.14 and by 1777 brought £45.8.6.[108] Yet hiring out for the benefit of minor heirs or widows did not always turn out so well, as Samuel Johnston Sr. disclosed. Discussing the problems arising from the division of an estate and the plight of the widow involved, Johnston wrote a friend that he had just received "an acct of the nigers names. Two men are as old as the North Star, two young wenches & a lazy boy, now if they were working negers she might have hird them here, so as to supply her selfe with necessaries, the want of which she complains of."[109]

Under ideal circumstances, hiring out "working negers" let owners maximize the profit they derived from their investment in human beings. Although plantation owners and farmers might devise work for most of their slaves year-round, the largest owners had extra slaves who could be spared. And in some semi-industrial situations, finding work for all hands could be difficult. For instance, in addition to the seventeen adult males and three boys of working age, the Chatham Furnace operators owned five adult women slaves, two young women, and at least eight children, presumably the wives and families of the male slaves. Only three females actually worked at the furnace. Because James Millis, the white superintendent, regarded the other women and children as an unwarranted economic burden, he hired them out. Milley and her two children went to Martin Kendreck "near the Forge," and Patty and her one child "to Malcolm Sinclair the collier at the Furnace." Whatever their chores, at least these five slaves would be close to their husbands and fathers. The remaining women and children were sent to more distant locations.[110]

Contracts for hiring out followed a legal form that only indirectly touched on the pain such separations might cause. An agreement between James Murray and James Hazel in 1744, for example, covered the hire of three slaves to Hazel for a three-year period in chiefly financial ways. Hazel agreed to pay £21 sterling or £28 proclamation money per year, in cash "or Merchantable Produce fitt for a british market," and to return the slaves at the end of three years. If any of them died or ran off in the interval, he would pay £500 old tenor (about £50 to £60 proclamation money or £37.10.0 to £45 sterling) for Glasgow and £400 old tenor for Kelso and Berwick. Hazel also agreed that if "any of them shall Receive any Damage by the Wilful abuse" of his overseer, then he would "allow for Such Damage at the Returning of the Said Slaves."[111]

If slaveowners saw that the contractual relationships governing hiring out essentially served their own investment needs, it should come as no surprise that the wages paid to slaves and free persons for comparable work were about the same. To have paid less for unfree labor primarily would have hurt owners, not the slaves. Thus during the years 1748–55 the pay for unskilled and semiskilled male workers, regardless of color or status, probably equaled about two shillings and six pence per diem. Remuneration rose a meager two pence by 1762, remaining at this level at least until 1772. The per diem wage rate paid to white skilled workers during the seventeen-year period, 1759–76, as a point of comparison, probably equaled slightly over five shillings. It should be noted that wage rates for comparable work calculated by the day were always considerably higher than those calculated on a monthly or yearly basis. This was so because daily rates did not include the cost of room and board, nor did they cover a variety of special expenses and risks assumed by the long-term hirers of unfree labor.[112]

The contractual format illustrated above did not change much over the years. "Whoever hired a negro," Schoepf observed in the early 1780s after seeing several slaves hired out in Wilmington, "gives on the spot a bond for the amount, to be paid at the end of term, even should the hired negro fall sick or run off in the meantime. The hirer must also pay the negro's head tax, feed him and clothe him. Hence a negro is capital put out at a very high interest, but because of elopement and death very unstable."[113]

The cryptic observation "because of elopement and death very unstable" hints at so much—how whites viewed blacks, what blacks endured when hired out. What multitude of sins against slaves and agonies suffered by them do these words reveal or conceal? Whatever the full story, hiring out still must have been a two-sided experience for slaves. It undoubtedly had benefits—increased social contacts, enhanced geographic knowledge, perhaps a chance to earn money, and sometimes greater freedom and a more varied routine. For skilled slaves allowed to hire their own time, the sense of quasi-freedom had to be strong. Yet the bulk of slaves who were hired out were unskilled hands, if our sample is an accurate reflection of reality, and they did not have a say in when they would be hired out or to whom. Surely then, what most concerned and affected the majority of slaves who were hired out was their forcible separation from spouses, families, and friends, and their frequently harsh or bleak experiences with new masters. They usually must have feared and detested being hired out.[114]

Despite the profitability for whites of hiring out slaves, we have no way of calculating how frequently it occurred or if its incidence increased more rapidly than the rate at which the slave population grew between 1748 and 1776. The sharp rise in slave prices during those years, however, would suggest a rapid increase. In any case, hiring out probably was of pervasive importance in the colony, for it made slavery more functional and profitable for whites. That it exacted a hardship upon most slaves hardly entered the whites' calculations.[115]

As the North Carolina economy grew and developed, especially after 1750, exports rose, a network of small urban centers and merchants emerged, and the demand for labor expanded significantly within the fast-growing white population. This need intensified the reliance of many North Carolinians on slavery and caused a dramatic increase in slave imports. Blacks came to number around 18,000 by 1755 and 41,000 by 1767, or respectively about 22 and 25 percent of the population. Although black numbers increased dramatically, the percentage of blacks in North Carolina's population, together with their density patterns, remained less than those in any other southern colony. Nonetheless, slaves became increasingly concentrated on larger plantations in North Carolina. The Lower Cape Fear region resembled the South Carolina low country in this respect, whereas distributive patterns in North Carolina's eastern counties as a whole corresponded to those in the Chesapeake. Such demographic trends, together with the high proportion of Africans in the slave population (about two-thirds during the years 1751–55 and about one-third from 1760 to the Revolution), helped to shape the contours of life for slaves. In the midst of bondage, with its harsh constraints and the insistent hegemonic and expropriative thrusts of masters, slaves still largely shaped from their African pasts vital resistance patterns, languages, religious beliefs and practices, and marriages and families.

We have already seen some of the ways slaves directly challenged the power of masters and their control over the distribution of goods produced by the slaves: withholding or threatening to withhold their labor, feigning illness, sabotaging property, deliberately misunderstanding instructions, and using a variety of other malingering techniques to put off, lessen, or avoid work. Slaves, however, also ran off, at times as maroons, and they committed thefts, assaults, arson, rapes, and murders, mostly against whites. But before examining at length the resistance among slaves along with their interior lives, we will, in the next two chapters, analyze how masters used their great powers in the political, juridical, military, and police spheres to structure a system of slavery that attempted to maximize slave production, discipline, and procreation and thereby planter profits and white security.

2

Power and the Law of Slavery

Although not the principal labor system in all regions of North Carolina in the generation before the American Revolution, slavery formed an important source of wealth, prestige, and power almost everywhere in the province. Here, as in other mainland British colonies, a traditional hierarchical English model—within the added but powerful definitions of slavery—shaped the basic outlines of the social structure. A wealthy upper class, the number of slaves each member owned varying with individual wealth and the economic maturity of particular regions, governed the colony in keeping with an ideology designed to bolster their firm hold on power. All major posts in government, that is those involved in making important decisions, went to members of the upper class; middle-rung positions, those with few discretionary powers but with some authority over subordinates, went to small and middling property holders. The poor performed the menial and lowest-status political tasks. Because political power correlated with the degree of importance of each office, the wealthy colonists who monopolized the major governmental posts could and did implement their class will with singular assiduity—usually with little effective resistance from within the political apparatus.[1]

Using British models such as provided by common law, but especially the mixed constitution (balanced government) with its strong sense of hierarchy and the balanced power of the estates, the North Carolina oligarchy, like the ruling classes in Britain and other colonies, theorized the necessary and organic conjunction of wealth, power, and status. The ruling class thus demanded proper deference to its "natural" and "God-given" prerogatives and proclaimed paternalistically that it represented all elements of society, even the lowest—propertyless freemen, women and children, apprentices, servants, and slaves.[2] When, for example, Colonel Edmund Fanning ran for reelection to the Assembly in 1770, at the height of the Regulator movement, his wealthy supporters stressed in a campaign statement that his "considerable" property ensured that "the interest of the public must be his interest." They branded those who questioned Fanning's "attachment to the welfare and interest of his constituents" both as "assassin[s] who . . . stab in the dark" and as "persons courting the voice of popularity."[3]

This paternalistic ruling-class claim that deference by others to its prerogatives would ensure benevolent rule paradoxically enabled it to pursue with self-interested avidity John Locke's dictum that "Government has no other end but the preservation of property."[4] Paternalism in eighteenth-century North Carolina, as in England, therefore, was not a powerful, internalized motivational force, a conscientious day-by-day attention to responsibilities to the lower class. Rather, in contrast to its earlier feudal character, it had become essentially a device by which the upper class sought to establish hegemony over the lower classes. To a large extent this involved what E. P. Thompson refers to as a "theatrical role," one in which the wealthy shrouded their actions, actions that filled their coffers and perpetuated their control over the lower classes, in highly visible pomp and overt acts of largess, mercy, or patronage.[5]

The members of North Carolina's ruling class did not have the wherewithal to clothe their acts with as much pomp and circumstance as did either their British or Virginia cousins. They also had to operate within the constraints imposed by a less mature economy in using other paternalistic co-optative techniques. But use them they did, with varying degrees of success, and the upper classes in England, Virginia, and North Carolina consequently often succeeded in receiving "a return in deference quite disproportionate to the outlay," thus making the poor accessories to their oppression.[6]

For paternalism to be effective, certainly in the case of this pale eighteenth-century version of the medieval original, it had to be supported by a "judicious" application of terror. Lord Shaftesbury, the enlightened rationalist and patron of John Locke, thus admonished, even as he attacked the church and Thomas Hobbes for making fear the binding mortar of the social order, that "the Mere Vulgar of Mankind. . . . Often stand in Need of Such a Rectifying Object as the Gallowes Before their Eyes."[7] Tyburn tree, "where criminals were hung," thus "stood at the heart" of the property-centered ideology of the English ruling oligarchy and profoundly shaped the nation's popular culture as well.[8] In North Carolina, the presence of slavery ensured that as the colonial slaveholding elite molded the laws that expressed its ideology and needs, it would transplant the fatal hanging tree and place it even more conspicuously at the center of the ceremony of power where it would bear strange fruit indeed.

To assert that terror was a necessary component of paternalism, therefore, is not to deny the presence of paternalism, but to delineate one of its major manifestations. Indeed, what seems to distinguish different examples of both European and American paternalism during the seventeenth and eighteenth centuries is not the presence or absence of terror—it always exists—but rather the extensiveness and intensity of its use as a conjunctive support of the more benevolent characteristics of paternalism. The obverse is also true; the exact qualities of the paternalistic ideology along with its institutional and behavioral traits, aside from the use of terror to complement the creed, varied in time and place.

In addition, affirming the presence of both paternalism and its supporting component, terror, in a wide variety of societies and polities does not argue that the lower or middle classes necessarily internalized significant portions of this prevailing (i.e., ruling-class) ideology. Nor does it deny that when internalization occurred, it varied over time and with changing circumstances. Neither does it question the possibility that various groups within the lower to middling portions of society reacted differently at any given moment to the cultural appeals of the ruling class. The specific application of a useful explanatory model that embraces ruling-class paternalism, therefore, is not self-evident. Rather, its precise nature only can be determined empirically.[9]

For instance, there undoubtedly were variations in how the poorer and middling farmers of various regions in North Carolina internalized the paternalistic ethos before, during, and after the Regulator years of the 1760s and 1770s. Farmers in Orange, Rowan, and Anson Counties overwhelmingly and enthusiastically embraced the Regulation—with its countervailing ideology that stressed class conflict, the rule of farmers, and greater democracy—and in fact comprised the bulk of the Regulator insurgency. The grievances, allegiances, and ideological commitments of farmers in other parts of the province remain obscured by the relative silence of the records.

If the Regulators were to convince farmers elsewhere of the legitimacy of their claims, they effectively had to deny the authority of the ruling class by demonstrating that its claim of paternalistic benevolence was a pretense to hide its avarice and lust for power. The Regulators followed this tack aggressively, depicting their rich opponents as expropriators of the fruits of "the people's" labor—"rich and powerful . . . designing Monsters in iniquity" who (practicing "every Fraud and . . . threats and menaces") parasitically were "dependent in their Fortunes, with great Expectations from others." Calling upon farmers to elect farmers, the Regulators saw this class solution to their problems as absolutely necessary because "the highest study" of the wealthy elected to office "is the Promotion of their wealth." They would consequently allow "the Interest of the Public, when it comes in Competition with their private Advantages . . . to sink." Repeatedly and forcefully made, these points resonated among farmers everywhere in the province given shared grievances. Still, the precise degree of commitment to the counterhegemonic creed of the Regulators by farmers who resided outside the core counties of the movement remains unclear.[10]

Perhaps Rhys Isaac presents a way out of the dilemma. He admits, in concluding his massive study of the institutional and cultural characteristics of Virginia, 1740–90, that he "can scarcely tell to what extent the hardhanded common planters internalized their roles as supporting cast in the staging of parish and county performances." Isaac, however, immediately qualifies this by noting that these farmers "had no positive, organized alternative until the appearance of New Light churches at mid-century. After that time the rapid growth of the Baptist and Methodist following among the lower ranks showed how readily weak attachment turned into active disaffection."[11] In similar fashion, North Carolina's farmers did not have an effective organized alternative to the institutions and values of the ruling class prior to the Regulators. The powerful countercultural attack by the Regulators, and the ready conversion of the vast majority of the people in Orange, Rowan, and Anson Counties to the movement, argue that these western farmers had only a weak attachment to many elements of ruling-class ideology during the years immediately preceding the Regulation. If this be true, it is reasonable to assume that the ideological claims of the ruling class had only limited appeal to small and middling farmers outside the three Regulator counties given many shared socioeconomic conditions and grievances with the Regulators.[12]

If limited extant data necessarily obscure this process among whites, the problem is even more severe for black slaves. Yet, as with whites, alternate, if indirect, methods may be used to determine whether slaves internalized the planters' paternalistic ideology, or, viewed more expansively, whether "cultural hegemony" is a useful conceptual model to explain culture formation among slaves.

Great planters with patriarchal affectations such as William Byrd II, Landon Carter, and Robert Carter of Virginia certainly had their counterparts in North Carolina. A variety of historians of Virginia have presented these nabobs as archetypes of patriarchs who closely defined slavery, including the precise ways their slaves became acculturated.[13] The ensuing chapters argue that a detailed review of slave culture formation reveals a different social reality. Slave cultural patterns primarily hinged on the traditions, beliefs, and actions of the slaves themselves. That is, slaves desperately attempted to challenge, alleviate, or accommodate themselves to the harsh constraints of thralldom by using, as much as possible, the traditional African beliefs and institutions that gave a sense of reality and credibility to their existences. This perspective makes it relatively simple to explain the absence in colonial North Carolina of evidence to support the notion that slaves developed an organic relationship with their masters out of the latter's paternalistic ideology. No such relationship existed.[14]

Rhys Isaac reaches a similar conclusion for Virginia. Summarizing the years 1740–70, he stresses that the Virginia gentry used an integrated official set of symbols to support its patriarchal claims to rule over a hierarchical and over-whelmingly rural society. These symbols "had served to shape the awareness of those Virginians who could be drawn or coerced into entering the consensus that was expressed in land boundaries, tobacco warehouses, courthouses, and churches. The Africans and Afro-Virginians, with their own ways of compre-hending the world, remained largely outside this system of persuasion, and the gentry orchestrators of the otherwise inclusive, compulsory community were clearly content that it should be so."[15]

This assertion may be further argued in a number of ways. For instance, use of the Gramscian model of cultural hegemony, with its emphasis on consent, to describe the value system and worldview of slaves—especially during the colonial period—is inconsistent with the requirements of slavery.[16] For slaves to accept the essentials of their exploiters' culture, freedom—with its oppor-tunities and rewards—had to be offered as well as the responsibilities of disci-plined labor. Such, of course, was not the case. Moreover, masters were often anxious to withhold their culture from slaves rather than to convert them to it. At no time was this more in evidence than during the colonial era. Given the formative state of slavery in much of the South—and certainly in North Caro-lina—masters primarily focused on establishing plantations, stocking them with slaves, and ensuring the essential power relationships necessary to maintain and extend the conditions of enslavement. Rather than even dreaming of achieving cultural hegemony to implement this, masters used forceful, coercive, direct methods of control, both co-optative and terroristic, the stress varying with time and circumstance.[17]

Martin Howard, a transplanted Rhode Islander recently arrived from England and now the chief justice of North Carolina, laid much of this bare in an impassioned charge to a grand jury late in 1771.[18] Condemning the unadorned and uninhibited use of terror as the distinguishing characteristic of the criminal justice system for slaves in the colony, Howard more specifically denounced the arbitrary and summary "justice" meted out by special slave courts that denied slaves due process and hastily delivered them to the hangman. In addition, he explicitly attacked the ease with which runaway slaves could be outlawed by order of two justices and then "hunted like a beast of the forest, and any person may kill or destroy him in what manner they please." "Surely," Howard remonstrated, if North Carolinians examined "our regulations relating to slaves by our acts of assembly, we shall find that we have power enough over them to satiate the hardness of our hearts without desiring anything more." Thus arguing the superfluousness, nay ridiculousness, of going beyond existent statutory law to establish either planter dominance or the slaves' subservience, Howard assailed grand juries for doing just that by refusing to return indictments of whites for murdering slaves as true bills. He condemned this "cruel and sanguinary opinion" that denied slaves any legal protection of their very lives as being "of a most pernicious nature, tending to a gross corruption both of the understanding, and the heart, and at the same time repugnant to law." In arguing that these views and behavior were "repugnant to law," he cited "the definition of murder as it is laid down in all the books. 'Murder is, when a man of sound mind and memory, and of the age of discretion, unlawfully killeth any Reasonable Creature, being under the kings peace.' So that we persuade ourselves, that a negro slave is a reasonable creature, it must be murder in any one that shall feloniously slay him."[19] Apparently the proof that Howard thought was self-evident either was rejected or ignored, for grand juries did not accept the primacy of common law in the absence of specific statutory direction to extend protections to slaves against white aggressions.

If, as Howard makes abundantly clear, the presence of terror often defined the landscape of slavery to such a degree as to make it highly unlikely that slaves would accept the culture of their persecutors, the elemental techniques used by slaveowners to co-opt their slaves also led away from significant steps toward acculturation. Increased allotments of food or clothing, a day off, the owners' acceptance of de facto slave marriages and families, and extending visiting privileges all aimed to shape external behavior rather than to effect the internalizing of the values of masters.

The inappropriateness of using cultural hegemony to explain the worldview and values of slaves becomes more evident by looking at the issue from the vantage point of the slaves. Comparatively large numbers of Africans lived in the Carolinas and Georgia through the Revolution. In North Carolina, the percentage of African-born people among the adult slave population ranged from about two-thirds during the years 1751–55 to one-third during the last fifteen years of the colonial period.[20] Many of these slaves would have had considerable difficulty understanding even a simplified version of English. They spoke a variety of African languages, plus pidgin-creole languages that they had constructed primarily to communicate among themselves. It consequently would not have been easy to convert them to ruling-class values.[21]

Linguistic differences were only one element of the cultural chasm between European masters and African slaves to be bridged before cultural hegemony could even be contemplated. There was no substantial base of shared culture on which to build cultural hegemony. This was evolving through gradual cultural diffusion, but in the colonial Carolinas and Georgia the process was still in its infancy. Thus, to postulate a hegemonic culture for colonial North Carolina that embraced masters and slaves is to be teleological with an anachronistic vengeance. Such a construct is made possible by ignoring or understating the powerful hold that African languages, institutions, values, and worldviews had on African slaves and their descendants.

Slaveowners, or the more affluent of them, engaged slaves in an elemental if frequently deadly dialogue that, nonetheless, often permitted slaves to implement many aspects of their African cultures while paradoxically linking freemen, servants, and slaves into an interconnected, hierarchical system of control and exploitation. Within this setup, less affluent farmers—either as landowners, tenants, or squatters—controlled much of the means of production, that is, farm lands and tools. Normally these farmers did not work directly for the landowning ruling class or others who complemented or serviced the planters' economic needs, such as merchants, lawyers, land speculators, and money lenders. Multiple economic interests as well as economic interdependence closely bound members of this composite ruling class to make them even more capable of withstanding challenges from below.

Although farmers performed few direct work services for this elite, the latter's control over the political and juridical apparatuses helped to ensure that the wealthy still expropriated a significant amount of the labor value produced by the poor and middling through interest, rents, land sales, court suits, regressive taxes, corrupt handling of public monies, and subsidies and favors granted to the wealthy. The last included offering lucrative building or service contracts; designating ruling-class lands as town sites, thus vastly increasing their value almost overnight; and granting favored treatment to the wealthy in the building and location of roads. Finally, the courts granted the elite a disproportionate share of the compensations paid to slaveowners for their executed slaves—payments made directly out of provincial monies raised through regressive taxes.[22]

Free artisans and laborers, comparatively few in number but crucial to the economy, not only were subjected to the same exploitation as farmers, but also frequently *did* have to perform direct labor services for others and thus had a portion of their labor value directly expropriated by their employers. Servants and slaves similarly had the surplus value they produced (value beyond the cost of providing "subsistence" to workers) directly expropriated by their employers (owners). However, unlike free workers, who sold their labor as a commodity in the marketplace to those who would hire them, the actual bodies of slaves and servants were purchased as commodities. They were then used as labor. They, therefore, existed for their owners both as a significant capital investment and as a source of labor.[23]

Despite similarities, servants differed from slaves in that the contractual relationship in which servitude was legally grounded created mutual obligations for masters and servants and ensured that the personhood of servants was to some degree protected by custom, law, and normal due process. Slaves, on the other hand, were legally defined almost completely by their chattel status. Indeed, if legal definitions fully described reality, only the most elemental survival needs limited the degree of their exploitation, and even these were in jeopardy.[24]

Although the distinct demands and exigencies of free and unfree labor systems required different patterns of manipulation, these diverse workers could sometimes be subjected to similar or identical forms of exploitation. The effects of such policies, however, hinged on the status of workers and the several designs of the ruling class. This is illustrated by the uncompensated labor on the roads required of all adult males sixteen to sixty years of age, regardless of status or color, for an average of five to ten days each year. For the roads to be built, slaves, servants, and freemen all had to be used as road hands. The slaveowning ruling class acquiesced only under the compulsion of necessity to use their slaves and servants, for road work was a tax on the owners of unfree male hands whose labor time on the roads was at least partially lost labor time for the owner. To the degree that this loss was made up by masters who implemented a work speedup, the laborers themselves bore the direct effects of the work tax.

Road service imposed a statistically measurable hardship on poor and middling freemen. In money terms, calculating a day's labor as equaling 2 shillings and 8 pence per day, the per annum road tax for each road hand amounted to from 13 shillings and 4 pence to £1.6.8. Despite the fact that masters had to send their adult male dependents (including servants and slaves) to work on the roads, this work tax was inequitable and ultimately regressive because poorer freemen suffered more from the loss of labor time than wealthier freemen and because a heavy dependence on this tax reached a greater proportion of the wealth of the poor than that of the affluent. The tax was also specifically regressive because the law exempted wealthy persons from working on road gangs, and most, in practice, did not make a commensurate contribution by other forms of more prestigious road service. Of considerably greater significance in defining the tax's regressivity is that provincial law exempted altogether a sizable proportion of the unfree plantation workforce from road service—male slaves twelve to sixteen years of age and all female slaves; all were considered full hands.[25]

Militia service, on the other hand, exemplifies how masters designed exploitative policies that fully took into account the diversity of the workforce. All adult male freemen and servants sixteen to sixty years of age had to serve in the militia an average of ten to twelve days annually. Slaves did not. The dangers involved in arming slaves coincided with the masters' desire not to lose the labor of their slaves during the days the militia was mustered each year. It was possible to exempt slaves because of the large number of servants and poor-to-middling white freemen available to serve as privates and noncommissioned officers. Militia service equaled in lost labor time for each serviceman a value of from £1.7.0 to £1.12.10 per year. The exemption of slaves from militia service ensured that the slaveowners would be spared this tax on their labor. It consequently was the colony's most regressive tax.[26]

What is particularly impressive here is how North Carolina's oligarchy wove both the patterns of exploitation and the exploited workers into an integrated system that essentially served the interests of the oligarchy. Militia and road service, for instance, benefited the wealthy in ways other than those just described. Although roads roughly met the transportation needs of the province as a whole, they especially enhanced the value of the property of the affluent. The militia protected the colony from external aggression but also disciplined and provided protection from servants, slaves, and dissident poor freemen within the province.[27]

This integrated system of exploitation extended to North Carolina's entire tax system, which incorporated high rates into a harshly regressive tax system.[28] The burdensome and grossly inequitable tax system, in turn, supported the colony's courts, militia, and police, which were used to protect the interests of the ruling class by keeping order among slaves, servants, and unreconstructed white freemen, like the Regulators, who challenged the status quo. Organically linked to all of this, both as an important subsidy to slaveowners, especially the wealthiest, and as an integral part of the colony's attempt, when necessary, to terrorize the slaves into an acceptance of their lot, was the practice of compensating masters for their executed slaves.[29] The tax and compensation systems, at little cost to the slaveowners, each was, in its turn, woven into a comprehensive slave policy that channeled the behavior and limited the movement, resistance, and power of slaves while maximizing slave productivity and the security of the white public.

North Carolina first enacted a slave code in 1715, at a time when slaves probably numbered around two thousand. The framers of this legislation drew on their experiences as owners of unfree labor and the precedents provided by statutes passed in other southern mainland colonies as well as in the West Indies. Even though slavery generally remained less developed in North Carolina than in its neighboring colonies, the province, prodded by the 1739 Stono Rebellion in South Carolina and increasing nervousness about its own slaves, built upon its earlier law to construct a far more elaborate slave code in 1741. This remained the basic slave code throughout the colonial period, although it was amended in 1753, 1758, and 1764.[30] Like other colonies, North Carolina, through these statutes and juridical and social definitions and practices, effectively limited enslavement to nonwhites and defined slaves as chattels, with almost no legal protections of their persons, whose permanent status passed from mother to child.

Yet, in truth, these so-called slave codes dealt with servants as well as slaves. Dealing with both groups in the same code made it simpler for the elite to define the two labor systems both in terms of their differences and their many similarities. Intertwining the two groups also reflected the ongoing economic significance of servants. As late as 1741, their numbers were still about half again as much as slaves (see Table 1.10). Linking slave and servant made sense, too, because the law defined slavery by what it was not, that is, freedom and indentured servitude, a contractually based and temporary form of bondage with the servants' rights, protections, obligations, and duties stipulated in the law.

Enslavement, then, was relegated to persons who could not demonstrate that they had "been free in any Christian Country, Island or Plantation, or Turk or Moor, in Amity with his Majesty." Clearly, black sub-Saharan Africans or, for that matter, Native Americans normally were not covered by such restrictions, and just as clearly it was the law's basic purpose to relegate slavery to these ethnic groups. Conversely, "Imported" or "Indented Christian Servants" were limited to bondage for a set term of years. The law of 1715 further required that master or mistress had to provide their Christian Servants with a "Competent Dyet, Clothing & Lodging." It adds that masters or mistresses could mete out only moderate punishments to these servants, who, in turn, could seek judicial remedies for mistreatment. Finally, when the indentures were up, servants were to receive freedom dues. Slaves pointedly always were omitted from receiving such rights, protections, or remedies. Their bondage was both permanent and complete.[31]

Laws concerning runaways illustrate both likenesses and dissimilarities in the treatment of slaves and servants. Running away was a social crime with political implications that challenged both the stability of upper-class institutions and particular policies. Masters may not have recognized runaways as "premature revolutionaries or reformers, forerunners of popular movements," but they did react severely to the heavy losses in property and labor and to the serious challenge to authority caused by the efforts of servants and slaves to flee.

One gauge of how seriously owners regarded flight by the unfree is the proportion of the two basic slave and servant codes devoted to the issue. Five of the twenty-one articles in the 1715 law pertained directly to or mentioned runaways, and when legislators reshaped and enlarged the code in 1741, they penned fifty-eight highly detailed articles, twenty-two of which were devoted to the problem.[32]

The colony's legislators early understood that the entire citizenry had to be enrolled to check running away and other dangerous behavior on the part of servants and slaves. The law of 1715 thus enjoined "all persons" to "use their utmost endeavours to apprehend all such Servants and Slaves as they conceive to be runaways" and advised that any slave or servant carrying a gun off the master's property without written permission was to be assumed a runaway and liable to arrest. In such cases, the statute provided for citizens' arrests with liberal payments to those who seized runaways, took them before a justice of the peace—who could "adjudge such Corporal Punishment . . . as he shall think fitt"—and then returned them to their owners. If the owners were unknown, the runaways were to be delivered to the provost marshal, an early civil officer whose duties were largely delegated to the county sheriffs in 1738. Owners of the runaways were to indemnify both the captors and the public for any expenses incurred. Those who harbored runaway servants and slaves "above one Night," on the other hand, were to be fined at the rate of ten shillings per day for each runaway plus whatever costs and damages occurred—all to be paid to the owners.[33]

Because whites feared runaway slaves more than fleeing servants, the preventative clauses dealing with slaves were more elaborate and severe than those devoted to servants. For instance, during the colonial period no laws specifically prevented servant movement off the masters' property. Servants were admonished to fulfill their contracts and be properly subordinate, and the 1715 law made it illegal for servants to "absent" themselves from their masters' service and forbade them from leaving their masters' property with a gun, unless performing a legal duty or obligation. The same law, by contrast, stipulated that all slaves—save those who wore livery, were personal slaves, or were accompanied by a "White servant"—had to carry tickets issued by their owners if they left the master's property.[34]

On the other hand, the temporary nature of servitude enabled masters to develop a deterrent to servants running away that was inappropriate for slaves. A clause in the 1715 law dealing with runaway servants compensated masters for both the loss of labor time and expenses. It added to the runaway servant's original term of servitude a block of time equal to twice the period the servant had run away, plus additional service equal in value to the charges and damages the master and public had incurred in finding the runaway. Legislators could not apply the same formula to slaves, who already served for life, but they did bar the manumission of "Runaways or Refractory Negroes."[35]

The framers of a 1729 statute revealed in yet another way how differently they regarded servants and slaves. Designed "for the better suppressing of Negroes travelling and Associating themselves together in great Numbers to the Terror and Damage of the white people," the law specified punishments for "any Negro or Negroes [who] shall presume to travel in the Night, or be found in the Quarters or Kitchens among other Persons' Negroes."[36] Runaway slaves who lurked about an inhabited area provoked even greater fear among whites. They obtained food, aid, and companionship from family, friends, or other slave collaborators and often burglarized, robbed, attacked, or in other ways threatened or did violence to whites. Hence the 1715 law bluntly authorized "any person or persons" to "kill any Runaway Slave that hath lyen out two months" and stipulated that "such person or persons shall not be called to answer for the same if he give Oath that he could not apprehend such Slave but was constrained to kill him."[37] This response underscores the use of terror by the ruling class in a society significantly dependent on unfree labor, especially slaves, and calls into question dated notions that North Carolina was a "progressive" exception to the brutal handling of slaves in the southern colonies.[38]

The 1741 "Act Concerning Servants and Slaves" laid out procedures essentially similar to but more elaborate and detailed than those outlined in the earlier act. It encouraged citizens to capture unfree runaways and return them to owners. Specified rewards were to be paid by the master or by church wardens who then collected from the master. If the runaway refused to divulge the master's name, or could not speak English, he or she was taken to a justice of the peace and then sent to the local jail. For a two-month period the sheriff was to advertise the runaway's description and then, if no one came forth to claim him or her, to transfer the prisoner to the provincial jail. In later years this probably meant, in practice, transferal to the public jail that served the superior court district in which the runaway had been captured. The law directed the keeper of this jail, normally the sheriff, to hire out the runaway after receiving permission to do so from the General Court (later the Superior Court), the nearest county court, or two justices from either of these courts. When the runaway was hired out, the jailer or sheriff was to place an iron collar stamped with the letters *PG*, for *Public Goal*, around his or her neck. Such runaways were hired out until claimed by their owners, who then became liable for all public charges and costs up to that time. In turn, the owners received all the funds that had accumulated from the hiring out of their runaway slaves or servants.[39]

The 1741 act also introduced or etched more sharply certain distinctions concerning the treatment of servants and slaves. Individuals who induced apprentices, servants, or slaves to leave their masters and those who harbored runaways "for any Space of Time whatsoever" now were to be fined £2 per offense and an additional five shillings for each twelve hours the runaway was absent from his or her master. Those who induced slaves to run off and who planned to ship them out of North Carolina were to be fined £25; if they actually transported such slaves out of the colony and were subsequently prosecuted and condemned, they were guilty of a felony. The 1741 law continued the penalty for servants who fled, but, as in the case of slaves, also subjected them to up to thirty-nine lashes "well laid on the bare back" when they were first brought before a justice of the peace. Yet the act also substantially expanded the protection available to "Christian Servants" in order to encourage them "to perform their Service with Fidelity and Cheerfulness." Meanwhile, the legal restrictions imposed on slaves intensified. As before, the law required that slaves off the master's property had to carry a written "Certificate of leave," but now it exempted only "negroes wearing Liveries" and stiffened the penalties for unauthorized armed slaves.[40]

The act also, even more specifically than did the statute of 1715, addressed the problem of slaves who "lurked about." Because "many Times Slaves run away and lie out hid and lurking in the Swamps, Woods and other Obscure Places, killing Cattle and Hogs, and committing other injuries to the Inhabitants in this Government," legislators now required any two justices of the peace to

CRAVEN COUNTY, ſſ.
By JOHN HAWKS, and LANCELOT GRAVE
BERRY, Eſquires, Two of his Majeſty's Juſtices
of the Peace for ſaid County.

WHEREAS Complaint hath been made to us,
by James Biggleſton, that a Negro Slave belonging to him, named JEM, about 28 Years of
Age, a ſtout likely Fellow, about 5 Feet 7 Inches
high, and is Country born; had on when he went
away, a light coloured milled Duffil Jacket and
Breeches, and check Shirt, hath run away from his
ſaid Maſter, and is ſuppoſed to be lurking about,
doing Acts of Felony in this Province.
    THESE are therefore in his Majeſty's Name, to
command the ſaid Slave forthwith to ſurrender himſelf, and return home to his ſaid Maſter. And we
do hereby command the Sheriff of the ſaid County of
Craven to make diligent Search after the above-
mentioned Slave, and him having found, to apprehend and ſecure, ſo that he may be conveyed to his
ſaid Maſter, or otherwiſe diſcharged as the Law di-
rects; and the ſaid Sheriff is hereby impowered to
raiſe and take with him ſuch Power of his County
as he ſhall think fit for apprehending the ſaid Slave.
And we do hereby, by Virtue of an Act of Aſſembly
of this Province concerning Servants and Slaves, intimate and declare, if the ſaid Jem doth not ſurrender himſelf, and return home immediately after the
Publication of theſe Preſents, that any Perſon or
Perſons may kill and deſtroy the ſaid Slave, by ſuch
Means as he or they ſhall think fit, without Impeachment or Accuſation of any Crime or Offence for ſo
doing, or without incurring any Penalty or Forfeiture thereby.
    GIVEN under our Hands and Seals, this 3d Day of
    May, 1775, and in the 15th Year of his Majeſ-
    ty's Reign.
                        JOHN HAWKS,
                        L. G. BERRY.
    N. B. The above Negro Slave is ſuppoſed to be
harboured or kept out by his Wife, named Rachel,
a Wench belonging to Mr. Iſaac Fonvielle, and it is
very poſſible he is lurking in the Neighbourhood of
his Plantation. Whoever will take Him up and
bring him to me, ſhall receive a Reward of three
Pounds for his Trouble.
                        JAMES BIGGLESTON.

Advertisement for a runaway slave. A slave's decision to flee involved the considerable risk of being outlawed. For instance, the justices in this advertisement believed that Jem was lurking about his home plantation, harbored by his wife who lived nearby. The two justices of the Craven County Court on 13 May 1775 proclaimed that if Jem did not return to his owner immediately after the publication of this proclamation, he was to be declared an outlaw and "any Person . . . may Kill and destroy the said Slave, by such means as he or they shall think fit" without being chargeable with any crime or subject to any penalty or damages. (*North Carolina Gazette* [New Bern], 12 May 1775)

issue a proclamation of outlawry. Posted in various public places, it both ordered "lying out" slaves to surrender themselves and empowered the sheriff "to take such Power with him as he shall think fit and necessary" and search out and apprehend the slave or slaves. If those named in the proclamation did not "immediately return home," then it was "lawful for any Person or Persons whatsoever to kill and destroy such Slave or Slaves by such Ways and Means as he or she shall think fit, without Accusation or Impeachment of any Crime for the same." And whereas the 1715 act both required the killer of such a slave to testify that capture had been impossible and provided compensation to the owner by a "pole-Tax on all Slaves" in the province, the 1741 law made compensation the responsibility of "the Public" and required virtually no justification by the slave's killer.[41] All whites through this act became legally sanctioned predators and slaves who were outlawed, their prey.

The increased detail, complexity, and often harshness of North Carolina's evolving codes for slaves and servants reflect the concern of slaveowners with the growing importance of unfree labor in the colony, but their concern did not end there. Authorities and masters alike assiduously attempted to implement the laws concerning runaways. References to runaways being hired out and having collars placed around their necks by court order pepper the legal records of the province.[42] And since compensating masters for killed slave runaways and outlaws encouraged anyone to kill criminal elements of a subordinate and despised portion of the population, sadistic killings of outlawed slave runaways abounded. The frequent choice by outlawed slaves of suicide rather than capture underlines this sadism, as does the practice of some masters to offer greater rewards for the return of their runaway slave's head than for the slave alive.[43]

Slaveowners attempted to prevent the loss of property and labor not only by limiting the ability of their unfree laborers to run away, but also by restricting manumission and the number of free blacks. Whites feared free blacks as a focal point for slave discontent and considered them a dangerous anomaly. Laws to inhibit manumission thus date to 1715. The slave code shaped that year both prohibited freeing "Runaways or Refractory Negroes" and restricted manumission to slaves who had performed "honest and Faithful service."[44] The 1741 statute strengthened the latter clause by stipulating that no slave could be freed "upon any Pretence whatsoever, except for meritorious Services, to be adjudged and allowed of by the County Court, and license thereupon first had and obtained."[45]

If masters still freed their slaves despite these obstacles, provincial laws attempted to ensure that such blacks left the colony quickly. The 1715 law required that manumitted blacks leave the province within six months after being freed, on pain of being sold by the precinct court for a term of five years to a purchaser who would then transport the ex-slave out of the province.[46] A 1723 statute continued the same penalties but added that former slaves who returned to the province after the six-month period were to be sold for seven years to the highest bidder. If, on being freed after seven years, the ex-slave still refused to leave the province, the penalty could be reimposed.[47] In 1741, because manumission for good cause required approval by the county court,

clauses to ensure the emigration of manumitted slaves were considered necessary only if masters somehow freed their slaves without court authorization.
Slaves so freed would be reenslaved if they did not leave the colony within six
months or if they returned after six months. Finally, a fine of £100 current
money was to be levied against persons convicted of harboring "such Negroes
or Slave set free."[48]

Nevertheless, slaves were manumitted and some remained, legally or illegally, in the province. The law of 1723 noted two subterfuges freed slaves used
to avoid leaving the province and thus remain with family, kin, and friends.
Some former slaves apparently briefly left the province during the six-month
grace period provided in the 1715 law, and others married whites.[49] How frequently such ruses worked is unclear; what is certain is that the price was high.
Beginning in 1723 North Carolina levied a discriminatory poll tax against all
free blacks, their white wives, and their progeny. A person one-eighth black
was identified as black. Accordingly, all "blacks," males and females (including
the white wives of free blacks), who were twelve years of age and older, were
deemed to be polls (taxables). Among whites, only males sixteen and older
were considered polls. Tax lists attest to the implementation of such legislation,
and this severe tax discrimination helps to explain why disproportionately
large numbers of free blacks were servants. Normally poor to begin with, they
were often forced into servitude to work off their tax delinquency. Originally
passed to prevent racial intermarriage, discriminatory tax laws ultimately hurt
all free blacks by making an already severely inequitable tax system especially
injurious to them.[50]

The Assembly also tried to halt interracial marriages by other means. The
1715 act regulating servants and slaves imposed a £50 fine on any white who
married a "Negro, Mulatto or Indyan Man or Woman" and a similar fine on
any minister, justice of the peace, or other person who performed the marriage
ceremony.[51] A 1741 act regulating marriages renewed both fines and now referred to interracial marriage as "an abominable Mixture" and the resulting
children as "spurious issue."[52]

Thus, one set of discriminatory or prohibitory laws begat similar legislation.
Some aimed to limit the manumission of slaves; others attempted to force the
emigration of freed slaves, or to prohibit interracial marriage, or to discrimi-
nate against those who managed to remain in the colony. From 1723, tax
discrimination represented the major device used to punish free blacks who
remained in the province.

In their eagerness to avert the loss of their human property, masters left no
gates open—including the pearly ones. Slaveholders who shaped the Fundamental Constitutions of 1669 explicitly asserted that conversion to Christianity

would not qualify a slave for freedom, and by 1741 the law limited manumission to slaves who had been approved by the county courts as having rendered "meritorious services" to their masters.[53] Although such laws should have assured masters that conversion did not equal freedom, doubts about what an Anglican minister in 1719 termed "this silly buckbear" persisted, and clerics repeatedly lamented planter resistance or apathy to their efforts "to increase the Kingdom of our Lord Jesus Christ."[54] Yet even after such fears ebbed after 1730, when the Crown sent instructions to Governor Burrington "to find out the best means to facilitate and encourage the conversion of Negroes and Indians to the Christian religion," few conversions occurred. Many masters feared that religious instruction would cut into labor time. Others were simply indifferent about the whole matter or fretted that conversion and the consequent egalitarian idea that we are all "brothers in Christ" would lead to "saucy," recalcitrant, or even rebellious slaves.[55]

Masters dreaded numbers of slaves armed with guns even more than those equipped with the armor of God. Although the elite had doubts concerning poor whites who bore arms, they could neither effectively disarm them nor afford to lose the firepower of freemen and servants in manning the police and militia forces of the colony. Thus freemen could legally bear arms and servants by law could carry weapons when they left their owner's property on official business. Slaves, on the other hand, rarely were allowed arms and were subjected to a varied list of repressive measures and severe punishments if found illegally armed.

Lawmakers barred slaves from militia service and in 1753 established a special constabulary, the searchers, to deal with the increasing problem of armed slaves roaming about in "divers Parts of this Province."[56] They also tightened the law of 1741, which had been "ineffectual" in limiting armed slaves to one per plantation, simply by requiring masters to issue certificates that were countersigned by the chairman of the county court.[57] Primarily wishing to beef up "the Remedy in the said Act," the law of 1753 also detailed that henceforth no slave was to have or carry a gun "in any Plantation where a Crop is not tended, nor more than one in any Plantation where there is a Crop tended, nor after [the] Crop is Housed." The master of a slave authorized by the county court to carry a gun had to post a bond to ensure the slave's "good and honest Behavior." Any person subsequently "injured" by the slave would receive the bond. If someone found a slave illegally possessing a gun, sword, or other weapon, the master had to pay that person twenty shillings and bear the expense of "any Punishment inflicted on the Slave" and forfeit "the Gun, Sword, or other Weapon" unless the owner or overseer could prove that the slave possessed such weapons "without their consent or knowledge."[58]

Slaves not only were to be disarmed but also were prevented from congregating together. Whites believed that assembled blacks were up to no good, and fears concerning them were especially rife in the towns. A 1765 Wilmington ordinance provided that if "any number of slaves exceeding three shall be seen together in the streets, alleys, Vacant lots, House or other parts within this Borrough, playing, Riotting, or Caballing on . . . Sunday, or on any other day, or in the night time of any Day, whereby the Inhabitants or any of them may be disturbed or mollested, the slave or slaves" were to be apprehended, taken to the mayor, recorder, or any alderman and then "Committed or whiped, or both." The same act imposed a ten o'clock curfew. The only slaves who could be out past that hour were those "having a Ticket, or a Lanthorn and Candle." All others were to be punished by whipping or imprisonment.[59] Town commissioners closed a loophole in this law in 1768 by applying the restrictions to individual slaves as well as to those in groups. Any slave or slaves "found playing or making a noise in The Streets so as to Disturb any . . . Inhabitants" were to be given "Thirty lashes on his or her bare back" unless their owners paid a five shilling fine.[60] Finally, in 1772 Wilmington authorities met "to prevent Riotting and Disturbances that often happen among the Negroes" in town. To do this they barred all slaves, even those who had their masters' permission, from trading at street stands, and they reenacted the 1765 ordinance prohibiting more than three slaves from "Playing, Rioting, or Caballing."[61] Despite the stated need to pass such severe ordinances, not one case of a slave violator of the laws dealing with curfews or unlawful assembly appears in the available records for Wilmington, including its Town Book, between 1765 and 1772.[62]

If a few trusted slaves on individual plantations were armed by apparently complacent masters or mistresses in order to keep their game larders full, this only reveals a small part of the slaveholders' sense of the social realities of slavery. Far more revealing were the enormous efforts expended by masters in criminal codes to ensure that slaves complied with all the ground rules of slavery.

3

The "Criminal Justice" System for Slaves

This chapter analyzes North Carolina's criminal codes for slaves, the special slave courts set up to implement these statutes and those limited aspects of common law that the legislature and courts deemed to be applicable to slaves, and the consequent brutal punishments meted out to slaves by courts bent on terrorizing them into submissiveness. A significant part of this process was to deny to the persons of slaves almost any legal protection from white attack. Precisely because the harsh criminal codes threatened their capital investment, masters sought to establish laws to compensate slaveowners for their executed slaves.

We have already discussed issues related to this agenda in considering how provincial law dealt with slaves who "stole themselves" and the especially revealing clauses concerning slaves who had been outlawed for "lurking about." We also summarized Chief Justice Martin Howard's assessment of the colony's criminal justice system for slaves. In denouncing an arrangement that denied to slaves the most elemental protections to their persons through either procedural due process or humane substantive justice, Howard typified the special slave courts as being comprised of "three justices and four freeholders" who "may despatch a negro slave into the other world, with very little ceremony, for a fault which the naked, half-starved wretch had, perhaps, been forced to commit, because of the rigor or covetousness of his master."[1]

The slave courts Howard condemns had been set up at least as early as 1715 and were continued in their essentials by the more expansive legislation of 1741. These statutes challenged the inviolability of procedural due process for slaves by granting the slave courts arbitrary authority to set up the judicial procedures they were to follow. Moreover, they were given plenary power to determine which slave crimes they would adjudicate and the sentences they would impose. The law of 1715 states this clearly: "Any slave . . . guilty of any Crime or Offense whatsoever the same shall be heard and determined by . . . [the special tribunal which] . . . shall have full power & authority & they are hereby required & commanded to Trye the same according to their best Judgment & Discretion . . . & to pass Judgment for life or Member or any other Corporal Punishment on such Offender & Cause Execution of the same Judgment to be made & done."[2]

Slave courts, then, were authorized to act arbitrarily and summarily, and the slaveowning judges used their power to pursue economic gain and social security. Facilitating this self-serving course was a clause in the law of 1715 that inverted the usual presumption of the innocence of the accused until proven guilty beyond a reasonable doubt. It directed the special slaves courts to try slaves "guilty of any crime or Offense." This volte-face of the usual presumption was continued in the slave law of 1741 and remained in effect throughout the colonial years.[3]

It is hardly surprising, then, that the slave courts eliminated almost all the procedural protections normally accorded the accused. Grand juries and trials before petty juries of their peers were denied to slaves. They also almost surely could not subpoena witnesses. Indeed, slave defendants rarely were allowed any witnesses. This was true despite the widespread use of witnesses by the prosecution and a statutory provision that slaves could have "credible Witnesses or such Testimony of Negroes, Mulattoes, or Indians, bond or free, with pregnant Circumstances."[4] We have uncovered only one slave trial in which a witness appeared for the defense—Sambo's 1761 trial in Pasquotank County. Jack Hall, a courageous free black, came forth as a witness for Sambo, who had pleaded innocent to the charge of preparing poison and conspiring to have it administered to the wife of a neighboring planter.[5] Nor do the records reveal that slaveowners or overseers availed themselves of their legal opportunity to testify on behalf of their slaves.[6]

A sample of sixty-nine surviving case summaries of slaves tried before special slave courts during the years 1748–72 divulges the unsurprising results of this criminal justice system. Two or perhaps three slaves were found innocent—2.9 to 4.3 percent of the total.[7] If this indicates, as recently urged by a historian working from similar statistics for the years 1715–85, that "indictment was not synonymous with conviction," one might still stress more convincingly the extraordinarily high conviction rate among slaves—some 96 to 97 percent.[8] By comparison, only 38 percent of the 3,041 charges against whites during the years 1670–1776 with known outcomes resulted in convictions. Slaves, though unaware of such statistics, undoubtedly fully understood the odds against their avoiding conviction; they could ill afford the luxury of sophistry.[9]

Donna Spindel, despite her inadequate recognition of how ruling-class needs weighted the scales of justice against poorer whites, still presents a persuasive explanation for the massive variations in conviction rates by distinguishing sharply between the two systems of justice set up in colonial North Carolina: one for slaves, "designed to produce absolute submission," and one for whites, "based on centuries of law and tradition, designed to protect individuals and society from errant behavior."[10] The sharp differences between white and slave systems of justice were, in turn, outgrowths of the specific societal roles and relationships that prevailed among the different classes of whites and between slaves and whites. Thus poorer whites were exploited in a class-driven society, but one in which the ruling class had to give some indication that it acted benevolently in service of the commonweal if its quest for cultural hegemony was to have any credibility. The prevailing system of criminal justice was a significant factor in helping to foster among the poorer whites a belief that they could use the law to serve their own interests.

Because cultural hegemony over slaves was not a goal actively pursued by the white ruling class, any pretense that the law equally served the interests of all persons would be dispensed with in setting up the criminal justice system for slaves. Rather, the law was reduced to a direct, unrelenting weapon to induce planter supremacy and slave subservience. Statutes thus created slave courts with close to plenary powers and gave public authorities peremptory power to kill certain slave transgressors when their crimes were deemed to be too heinous or dangerous to be dealt with by plantation justice. It was considered necessary to apply the full and, as slaveowners hoped, awesome power of state authority, a leviathan, to keep the "worst" passions or tendencies of slaves in check.

The necessity for establishing such a system of "justice" seemed to North Carolina whites to be dictated by a form of thralldom intent on achieving the slaves' total submission to their overlords' absolute control. Two seemingly paradoxical but substantially complementary institutional arrangements enabled the slave courts and the authorities to implement this savage ideal of slave criminal justice. First, individual masters were assured compensation out of the public treasury for each of their slaves who died as a result of punishments ordered by the slave courts, or who were peremptorily killed by the authorities (frequently any person in a position to render such a punishment) in accordance with statutory law—that is, outlaws, some runaways, and slaves killed while committing a crime or who died in jail. The compensation system enabled the authorities and slave courts to implement the slave criminal justice system to its harsh, logical limits without fear of financially burdening slaveowners.

Second, the public system of slave criminal justice was one part of a two-tiered arrangement that also included a system of private or plantation justice directly administered by individual slaveowners or their surrogates. This enabled masters to establish and implement a draconian public system of criminal justice while limiting the bloody results of this enterprise by circumscribing the number of slaves actually tried by slave courts or who were peremptorily dealt with by persons in authority. Many slaves charged with a variety of "transgressions" thus faced plantation rather than public justice.

The statistical effect of a private system of slave criminal justice on the number of cases handled by the public system is suggested by comparing the caseload in the slave courts with that of the regular court system that tried whites. Considerably more whites than slaves, per capita, were dealt with in their respective public criminal justice systems. Extrapolating for time and population differentials, the close to 4,500 criminal court actions against whites uncovered by Spindel for the years 1670–1776 and the close to 160 slave trials or their equivalents we have found for slaves from 1748 through 1772 suggest that whites probably had a three to four times greater chance than slaves to be tried before a public system of criminal justice.[11]

The private system of "plantation justice," which obviously played an important role in disciplining slaves, was an extralegal judicial system that was not directly provided for by statutory law. Indeed, the slave courts were granted jurisdiction over *all* slave crimes, whether misdemeanors or felonies, and had plenary power to mete out "appropriate" sentences and punishments. Yet, if the design of achieving absolute planter control over slaves required a judicial leviathan to deal with serious slave crimes, this selfsame absolutist thrust called for uninhibited planter control over slaves on each plantation. The paradox, such as it was, could not be adequately dealt with by statutory law. Rather, slaveholders in their day-to-day dealings with slaves roughly worked out the parameters of each system of slave justice. If an overlapping of jurisdiction remained, the consequences were not too disturbing, for the functional limits of each system were well known and accepted. After all, it was not as if the two systems resulted from the conflicting interests of competing groups or classes. To the contrary, slaveowners, especially the most affluent, crafted this two-tiered system because it seemingly best served their class needs and interests by establishing their uninhibited control over productive, nonthreatening, disciplined bondsmen.

More specifically, plantation justice was meant to keep slaves in line within the confines of each unit of production. Slaves accused of shoddy or unproductive work, intentional tool breaking or mistreatment of livestock, and malingering or saucy behavior would almost invariably be dealt with directly by the slaveowners or their surrogates. This was also true, as a rule, of slaves accused of stealing solely from their owners, even if the pilfered items were chickens or hogs. As for slaves who "stole themselves," they too, except when outlawed, usually were dealt with by their owners. In accordance with the provisions of statutory law, however, peace officers, individual magistrates, and what amounted to a deputized citizenry were often involved in the capture of runaways, and these authorities, as well as the slaves' owners, might be involved in the punishment of runaways.[12]

Slave crimes against other slaves, including theft, assault, or even rape, were usually dealt with by individual slaveowners, when the masters, indeed, recognized such crimes. The rape of a slave by another slave, for instance, was not considered a punishable crime. Only when slaves attacked or poisoned other slaves with the intent of committing murder or mayhem, or when slaves actually killed, maimed, or wounded other slaves, did slave-on-slave crimes reach the slave courts, and then only because valuable property had either been destroyed, damaged, or jeopardized, and the harmony, discipline, and productivity of the plantation had been disrupted.[13]

To avoid even the semblance of planter vulnerability, no statutory limitation was ever placed on the right of slaveowners to respond to any type of slave crime, although masters normally deferred to the broad jurisdiction of the slave courts over serious slave crimes. After all, large slaveholders, as legislators, had given these courts authority in the first place because they generally felt that the full power of the state had to be marshaled against slaves who committed serious crimes if proper order were to be maintained on the slave plantation. Further, to ensure compliance by individual masters to this policy, slaveowners would be compensated only for those slaves who died as a result of orders by slave courts or through the direct action of public authorities in accordance with statutory law. The latter allowed a deputized citizenry (including, of course, the owners of offending slaves) to kill outlawed slaves or to use, if need be, deadly force to capture or subdue runaways or slaves apprehended during the commission of other "crimes." Masters were compensated for slaves who died under such circumstances, while the persons actually killing the slaves would be neither chargeable with a crime nor subject to civil damages but rather would receive public payment for services rendered.

Last, to break down any remaining inhibitions among whites to use deadly force on slaves when the occasion seemed to warrant it, North Carolina passed no law before 1774 making it a crime to attack, wound, disable, maim, or kill a slave, including the willful, malicious murder of a slave. Chief Justice Howard vigorously reacted to this barbaric policy in a number of ways. On one occasion he publicly attacked the moral acuity of the colony's Whigs by asking them if any proper justification could be given to a slave who remonstrated: "You invoke Heaven and earth against a claim to take from you a trifling sum of money without your consent, or to try you without a jury, when you are charged with any crime; and are you so judicially hardened and reprobate as to take from us every right and privilege of humanity."[14]

Always trying to claim the high moral ground, the colony's Whigs had to be affected by Howard's gibes. But regardless of whether or not the "reform" law of 1774 was a direct Whiggish response to Howard's taunt, the statute roughly aligned legislation in North Carolina with the laws already in place in Virginia and Georgia. No longer would North Carolina be the only colony in British North America without *any* statutory restrictions on the murder of slaves.[15]

Yet the act of 1774 reflects both the reluctance of slaveowners in North Carolina to inhibit their "right" to treat their slaves in any manner they chose and the low appreciation owners continued to have for the personhood of a slave. Thus the title of the law, "An Act to Prevent the wilful and malicious killing of slaves," together with an overblown opening statement of the supposed intentions of the law contain more than a little deception and puffery. But whatever the inflated claims, the statute rapidly gets down to business. Although the willful and malicious murder of a white was always a capital crime, the statute of 1774 sentenced whites convicted of maliciously murdering their first slave to only twelve months' imprisonment. Whites had to be convicted of maliciously murdering a second slave before receiving a sentence of death without benefit of clergy. A succeeding clause carefully protected the property of the master by ensuring that the white murderer of the master's slave, if a first offender, would be imprisoned in the district jail of the owner until he had fully compensated the owner. The statute's final clause turned to another pressing matter, making certain, despite having made the willful murder of a slave a criminal act, that slaveowners, their surrogates, and public authorities, including a deputized citizenry, could use such physical force or correction as was necessary to keep slaves in "proper" check. Thus was born in North Carolina what William Wiecek has called the "notorious 'moderate correction' proviso": "That this Act shall not extend to any Person killing any Slave by virtue of any Act of Assembly in this Province, or to any Slave in the Act of Resistance to his lawful Owner or Master, or to any Slave dying under Moderate Correction."[16] Tracing the impact of this proviso takes us beyond the period under review, but the "moderate correction proviso" was superfluous in North Carolina *prior* to 1774 in the sense that before that year it was not a crime in the colony for any white to beat, wound, maim, or kill a slave.

After evaluating available evidence, it is nonetheless our view that plantation justice itself, contrary to the public system of slave justice, seems to have caused relatively few violent deaths during the decades preceding passage of the law of 1774 and that the corporal punishments directly meted out by slaveowners usually did not match the savage penalties almost invariably ordered by the slave courts or summarily implemented by public authorities in accordance with statutory law. This hardly argues the existence of a lenient system of plantation discipline and labor, or a system that offered many official avenues of relief from the normal demands of slavery. Rather, it simply acknowledges that the same economic interests that tended to moderate plantation justice contrastingly prompted the slave courts and public authorities to enforce the statutory law in draconian fashion while compensating slaveowners against any possible financial loss.[17]

Beyond the figures already presented concerning the far higher conviction rates for slaves than whites, the most convincing available statistical evidence of the extraordinarily heavy dependence on terror by the slave courts and public authorities to quell slave unrest lies in the disproportionate number of slaves executed in colonial North Carolina and the much harsher forms of execution and corporal punishment meted out to convicted slaves than to whites found guilty of the same crimes. According to Spindel, the number of whites sentenced to death during the years 1663–1776 equaled the comparatively low figure of 67, or 2.2 percent of all whites convicted of crimes by the county and higher courts. However, 21 of the 67 were saved from the gallows by benefit of clergy, 2 were pardoned, and another was deported in place of execution. Spindel suggests that probably many of the remaining 43 white felons were not executed, for she was able to find specific verification of the execution of only 2 of these convicted felons. Given the vagaries of how and why some records have survived whereas others have not, Spindel's willingness to assume, without further verification, that a number of the 43 white felons were spared by the authorities is probably unwarranted.[18]

By way of contrast, records reveal that at least 100 slaves were ordered to be executed or were killed by the authorities during the limited time span of 1748–72. Moreover, there is no evidence that capital punishment for slaves was ever voided by benefit of clergy, a pardon, or deportation. Precise confirmation exists that at least 86 of the 100 recorded slaves actually were executed by court order or were killed by the authorities while the slaves were in jail or when they were apprehended as runaways, outlaws, or persons committing crimes. Eighty-one of the 86 executions are confirmed in the Committee of Claims records that document compensations paid to the owners of slaves and the fees and charges paid to sheriffs and other authorities for carrying out the courts' death sentences.[19] The other 5 deaths are verified in court orders evaluating slaves who had already died under "correction." Dorcas, a female slave, was listed as being found dead in jail, and Harry had been "Burnt in the Publick Goal of this county." An unnamed "Negroe man cooper . . . was outlawed and killed in bringing home," and Belinda and York committed suicide rather than submit to the horrors dealt out to captured outlaws.[20]

The remaining 14 cases not confirmed in these ways are fewer in number than one would predict from the sets of missing Claims Committee records.[21] Also, in each of these 14 instances, significant details of the cases are documented, including the slaves' sentences, the names or titles of their executioners, and the prospective locales and dates of their executions.[22] With *no* data to the contrary, this is compelling evidence that all 100 slave deaths actually occurred. And this total is undoubtedly an underestimation given the loss of many trial and claims records.

Although less certitude exists that all 43 of the convicted white felons were actually executed, it is reasonable to assume that the executions did occur in order to establish a point of statistical comparison with slave deaths wrought by the public authorities. If this assumption somewhat inflates white numbers, missing records at least partially offset this tendency. Even if there still is some overestimation of white executions, the statistical effect of this would be to reinforce figures illustrating that relatively more slaves than whites were subjected to the death penalty.

Calculating, then, for 43 white executions spread over 114 years from 1663 to 1776, there was less than 1 white executed for every 100,000 whites during these years. By way of contrast, calculating for 100 slave executions over a span of 25 years, 1748–72, more than 13 slaves were executed for every 100,000 slaves—a rate more than 13 times greater than that for whites. If castrations are added to slave executions, as they should be, the revised figure for slaves is more than 15 slaves executed or castrated for every 100,000 slaves, or more than 15 times the rate of white executions.

Although the number of whites who were executed was cut back by granting some felons convicted of capital crimes benefit of clergy, pardons, or deportation, a far greater number charged with crimes were never convicted. Whites accused of a variety of crimes, including homicide, were discharged by grand juries, had their charges dismissed by judges, or were acquitted after a trial by jury. Thus, among the 3,041 charges against whites recorded during 1670–1775 whose outcomes are known, about 1,164 or 38 percent did not result in convictions. Also, judges who accepted the importance of a white being repentant for his or her crime and who were normally anxious to end the trial as promptly and expeditiously as possible, frequently responded positively to plea-bargaining whites willing to plead guilty to lesser charges.[23]

Slaves, on the other hand, rarely avoided conviction before the slave courts, or they were treated summarily according to statutory law by public authorities. Moreover, no slave convicted of a capital crime from 1748 to 1772 was ever granted benefit of clergy, pardoned, or deported. Last, fearful of blunting the terrorizing force of brutal punishments among slaves, the slave courts avoided plea bargaining. Indeed, to what end would they bargain with accused slaves? Slave trials were arbitrarily and summarily conducted. Plea-bargaining slaves, therefore, had little to offer the slave court except on those rare occasions when an accused slave could offer a quid pro quo. A plea of guilty to facilitate matters, under the circumstances just described, rarely fit the bill.[24]

One such exception occurred in a trial involving the murder of a wealthy Beaufort County slaveowner, Henry Ormond, by five slaves, four of whom were owned by Ormond and one by his neighboring relative, Wyriot Ormond. One of the conspirators, an unnamed male slave owned by Henry Ormond, escaped execution by confessing his role in the murder and giving testimony that was instrumental in breaking the case. Because this led to the execution of his four coconspirators, a spared life in the midst of a group execution was a limited enough stilling of the mailed fist to entice other prospective slave informers to perform like services. The unusual circumstances leading to the sparing of this slave's life is underlined by the fact that at least two but probably all four of the executed slaves also confessed.

Three of the slaves involved in Ormond's murder were females and two were males, but all were motivated by the hatred inspired by Ormond's maltreatment of his slaves. The killing of Ormond is graphically described in the *Virginia Gazette* of 6 September 1770. Sometime in July 1770 the slaves

> conspired against their master, and on the Sunday night he was said to have rode from home in quest of one of his slaves who was missing, the conspirators, after their master was abed, went up to his room and with an handkerchief attempted to strangle him, which they thought they had effected, but in a little time after they left him, he recovered, and began to stir, on hearing which they went up again, and told him he must die, and that before they left the room; he begged very earnestly for his life, but one of them, his house wench, told him it was in vain, that as he had no mercy on them, he could expect none himself, and immediately threw him between two feather beds, and all got on him till he was stifled to death.[25]

One of the convicted female slaves was sentenced to the torturous death of being burned at the stake. The unfortunate slave probably was Ormond's "house wench," because it was she who reportedly told Ormond that "it was in vain" to plead for his life; "as he had no mercy on them, he could expect none himself." Perhaps she and the others pled guilty precisely to avert such a punishment, believing that throwing themselves on the mercy of the court and avoiding a more lengthy trial might have this modest effect. In any case, although the surviving records are not precise about how the remaining three slaves were executed, it is almost certain that they were hanged.

While the slave court selected a variety of punishments for the convicted four slaves, the pocketbook interests of the owners and heirs of the executed slaves were well protected. Henry Ormond's heirs, accordingly, were granted £70 for Annis (probably the burned domestic), £20 for Phyllis, and £80 for Cuff. Wyriot Ormond received £65 for Lucy.[26]

As just seen, one factor encouraging slaves to plead guilty was to avoid especially grisly punishments. This may also have influenced Pompey to admit to his guilt of attempting to "Murther His said Master by Seiring Cutting and Wounding him etc." The court, "after considering the Matter Maturely and Deliberately was of Opinion that the Prisoner at the Bar was Guilty of Felony in such a Manner as to Deserve Death." This pro forma phraseology undoubtedly masked the court's alarm at the nature of the crime. Intent on administering a punishment with special admonitory impact on the slave population, it ordered that after death by hanging, Pompey's "Head shall be Severed from his Body, and Stuck up on a Stake Below the Cross Road." This was done on 24 October 1765. Although Pompey's confession may have influenced the court not to order a more painful execution, his being sentenced to decapitation after death undoubtedly appalled the convicted, helpless slave. At this point, however, the court turned to what it believed to be an equally weighty matter, the valuing of "the . . . said Negro Man Slave" at £60. As was almost always the case in slave trials, the Hertford County Court conducted its deliberations with dispatch. Pompey's trial lasted only a portion of a day, and all aspects of the sentencing were completed within five days. Promptness kept down the expenses of maintaining and guarding the prisoner, lessened the chances of escape from inadequate jails, and helped to create a sense of the inexorable quality of slave "justice."[27]

Simon also confessed to the charges leveled against him and gave evidence against a slave collaborator, but to no avail. On 22 September 1764 in Craven County he testified that Bob carried off the items they had burglarized from a store: "Two Pockett Books and Papers and . . . some ribbons and a pen knife." Despite the charge of burglary and probably because of the low value of the stolen goods—around 10 shillings in proclamation money—the court decided that the evidence was not "sufficient to take the life of the prisoner." It thereupon sentenced Bob to 150 lashes well laid on his bare back beginning the following Monday, with 50 lashes administered on each of three consecutive days. Simon not only received the same whipping, but also had both of his ears nailed to the whipping post and then cut off.[28]

Perhaps Simon was treated more harshly than Bob because he came from Pennsylvania and supposedly led the local slave astray. Still, neither Simon's confession nor his testimony before the court seem to have counted for much in his sentencing unless one argues that it saved his life. The trial and punishments once again took place promptly, slowed down only by the weekend and the three days it took to complete the whippings and mutilation.

The slave trials summarized above all involved unanimous court verdicts. This was typical in such proceedings because it was necessary for masters to present a united front against slave resistance. Yet, to prevent the possibility of slaves avoiding punishment in the rare event that unanimity did not prevail, statutory law provided that a simple majority could render both judgment and sentencing in each slave case. Nevertheless, we know of no case in which a slave's guilt was not decided by a unanimous court.

There was an instance of punishment being proscribed by a simple majority, however. On 2 August 1761 Sambo was sentenced to be castrated by a divided tribunal in Pasquotank County. He had been found guilty of preparing poison that was to be given to the wife of a neighboring wealthy planter and of being instrumental in carrying out the plan to use this "touck" to alter Mary Nash's personality. Just why a minority of the court voted against castration is not specified in this otherwise extraordinarily detailed trial record. The court minutes do suggest that, to ensure Sambo's conviction, torture and the threat of torture were used to extract testimony from David, Sambo's collaborator, and from other witnesses. Perhaps the minority also questioned whether poison was ever really given to Mary Nash, since there is no indication in the trial records or elsewhere that she had suffered any ill effects from her supposed "poisoning." In any case, such sentiments did not prevail, and the sheriff castrated Sambo sixteen days after the court majority sentenced him. Although Sambo survived the life-threatening mutilation, he had been evaluated during the trial, always part of the ritual of the sentencing of slaves to castration, "in case he dies under the opperation." Because of his age Sambo was valued at only £31 proclamation money.[29]

The relative harshness and cruelty of the punishments meted out to slaves in colonial North Carolina may be demonstrated statistically. All executed whites were hanged, although perhaps a few were decapitated after death and had their heads displayed on poles.[30] By contrast, among the fifty-six slaves whose mode of execution is known for the years 1748–72, about half suffered comparatively brutal if not sadistic executions. One was chained alive in a gibbet to die slowly and horribly. Six were burned, two were castrated and then hanged, five were hanged and decapitated with their heads displayed on poles, one was hanged and burned, twenty-four were hanged, three died or were killed in jail, one committed suicide in jail, two died as a result of castration, seven slaves, most having been outlawed, were shot or beaten to death when captured, and five outlawed runaways drowned themselves to avoid capture and sadistic treatment.[31]

White authorities reserved the most brutal punishments for outlawed runaways and those who committed murder, rape, or house burning. Thus Will, tried and convicted on 2 February 1768 for murdering both his master and his master's wife, Bryant and Mary Lee of New Hanover County, was hanged alive in a gibbet.[32] We can trace the charges against four of the six slaves executed by burning: two (one a female) had been convicted of murder and one of rape; one was an outlaw burned in jail by his captors.[33] Isaac, one of two slaves convicted of house burning, was one of the two slaves castrated prior to being hanged. The other slave so punished, Jimmy, had been convicted of a second felonious offense that is not specified in the records.[34]

The outlaw burned in jail by his captors illustrates just one of the frightful ways outlawed slaves were disposed of in accordance with the law. Cato, of Craven County, outlawed and charged with a "felony," on being apprehended sometime in April 1762 "was so Wounded and abused . . . that he soon after Dyed in gaol." Further in this successful motion to persuade the county court to evaluate Cato so his owner, "The Honorable Richard Spaight, Esq." could be compensated, it is mentioned that Cato's "skull was fractured" during the violent abuse he was subjected to after capture. Titus of New Hanover County was shot by his captors in 1764. Phyllis of New Hanover County in 1768 was "Shot in taking and died of her Wounds."[35] The records leave to our imaginations what happened to "a Negroe man cooper," also from New Hanover County, when in 1757 this skilled workman was "outlawed and killed in bringing home." Five other outlawed slaves were reported to have committed suicide in order to avoid capture.[36]

Only the treatment of Native Americans adds an important dimension to this scene. From May through November 1760 the province paid a party of volunteers £120 for twelve scalps. It evaluated each Indian at £10 per scalp. This equaled in value twenty panther pelts. Hunters, by law, were to be recompensed ten shillings a pelt by the county courts for exterminating these "vermin."[37]

The litany of terror that describes the punishments meted out to executed slaves carried over in the types of corporal punishments imposed by courts. Once again, the penalties inflicted on whites were considerably less severe than those reserved for slaves. No whites were legally castrated in colonial North Carolina, whereas nineteen slaves were. Slaves were branded on the face or forehead, whites only on the thumb. Whites received fewer lashes for the same crimes, and, during the period under review, we can find no whites who had their ears cut off—a frequent punishment for slaves. One white, "notorious felon" John Burnet, did have his hand amputated in December 1767—a self-defeating punishment for slaves.[38]

Setting aside for the moment consideration of the slaves who were castrated in accordance with court orders, we have uncovered the trial records of fifteen slaves who, during the years 1748–72, were sentenced to a variety of corporal punishments. Among the slaves in this limited sample, six were sentenced to varying numbers of "lashes well laid on the bare back"—one slave receiving the comparatively light sentence of 25 lashes, while two had to bear being lashed 150 times. Bob, convicted of hog stealing in 1763, received 25 lashes.[39] In a similar case in 1757, Moses received 50 lashes for stealing and killing a hog; his accomplice, Negro Tom, endured 20 lashes and had his right ear nailed to the whipping post and then cut off. For the same crime in 1748, Cato suffered 40 lashes and had both his ears alternately nailed to the whipping post and cut off.[40]

Phoebe, after being led with a halter around her neck to the public execution place in New Hanover County, received 50 lashes well laid on her bare back for the same unrecorded crime her collaborator, Mary, was executed for in 1757. Ben, of Pasquotank County, had to endure 50 lashes for receiving only a pint or a dram of whiskey from a white man and drinking it.[41]

A series of thefts brought even harsher punishments to other slaves. Andrew in 1762 was given 150 lashes (50 every other day) for stealing £20 from someone's room, and Bob and Simon, as previously recounted, each was sentenced to 150 lashes for burglary; Simon also had to bear having both his ears nailed to the whipping post and then cut off. Dublin in 1764 received 100 lashes and was branded on the cheek with the letter *R* for stealing a few undelineated articles and some clothing from various persons. Dick's punishment for burglarizing a store in 1764 in Cumberland County was 100 lashes and branding on the cheek with a "Red hot Iron Letter T." Tom received a lighter sentence in 1756 for breaking open a store and stealing goods, perhaps because he argued that a white man and another slave were the primary culprits in the theft. In any case, he was sentenced to 50 lashes and the loss of a third of his right ear after having it nailed to the whipping post. Ben, in 1759, lost half of his right ear and was given 50 lashes for robbing sundry goods, including a gun. Sippey was also convicted of stealing a gun and some wearing apparel; he was subjected to 50 lashes and having his right ear nailed to the whipping post and then cut off. Last, Seller received 75 lashes and had both his ears cut off for providing poison to a slave to give to his owner.[42]

As these sentences reveal, courts acted brutally, arbitrarily, and unpredictably. They were unconstrained even by laws specifically directing them to sentence slaves to particular punishments for specified crimes. In 1741, for example, the law stipulated that slaves convicted of hog stealing "suffer both . . . Ears to be Cut off, and be publickly whipt" for a first offense and "suffer death" for a second offense.[43] Yet, in three out of four cases that involved hog stealing, slaves were sentenced to lesser punishments than were required by law. Cato was the lone exception, receiving 40 lashes and having both of his ears cut off.

Slave courts were willing to disregard the law's directives concerning the punishment for hog stealing perhaps because of a prevailing feeling that the punishment was too severe for this common "crime," normally dealt with as a plantation matter. More significant, over the years a sense of autonomy was ingrained in the judges of the slave courts through their exercise of plenary legal authority in the vast sum of slave cases brought before them. Occasional narrowly constructed statutory limitations on the prerogatives of judges, therefore, were readily ignored. Yet, as we have seen, the arbitrariness of the slave courts normally produced brutally harsh sentencings. Indeed, the courts' plenary powers are a major factor in explaining the severe implementation of the criminal justice system for slaves.

The story of corporal punishment becomes most grim when castrations are considered. The actual implementation of this ghastly punishment ordered by the slave courts for nineteen slaves is verified by records that list the fees paid to the castrators for performing these "opperations."[44] The law of 1758 designated sheriffs to implement this punishment unless they chose to appoint a substitute. The twenty-shilling fee allotted by law for each castration was substantial, and fourteen of the nineteen sheriffs chose to administer the mutilations themselves. Castrating the slaves also better enabled the sheriffs to collect the additional sixty shillings paid to "defray the expense of the Cure of each Slave Castrated." Only two of the remaining slaves were castrated by "doctors," and three were castrated by other white males picked by the sheriffs. Of the two slaves who died as a result of castration, both had been castrated by sheriffs.[45]

Castrations are recorded only for the years 1755–67, but of these sixteen out of nineteen occurred from 1758 to 1764 when a law in effect made it compulsory to castrate rather than execute male slaves convicted of their first capital crime. (Female slaves were to be given other corporal punishments.) Excluded from this provision were slaves found guilty of murder or rape. All felonious second offenders would also be executed.[46]

We only know the crimes committed by five of the nineteen slaves sentenced to be castrated. Tom, owned by John DuBois, an upper-class slaveowner of New Hanover County, had been convicted of breaking into the house of a white man, Joshua Toomer, and stealing the property of yet another white man. He died in 1755 after "having both his stones cut out by the county sheriff." Two other slaves, Tom and Prymus, owned respectively by two members of the Craven County upper class, John Oliver, Esq., and John Beavers, Esq., were sentenced on 13 April 1761 to be castrated for conspiring to poison various slaves and actually poisoning one of them, Toby, owned by a master on a neighboring plantation. The sheriff of Craven County castrated both slaves; Prymus survived, but Tom died as a result of the mutilation. Sambo, who as we have seen was also charged with preparing and using poison, but against a white woman on a neighboring plantation, survived castration by Lemuel Sawyer, the sheriff of Pasquotank County, in 1761. One of the two slaves convicted of house burning during the years 1748–72, Isaac, owned by Peter Clear, a small slaveowner of Chowan County, was sentenced in 1764 to be castrated and then hanged for his crime. Joseph Blount, the county sheriff, performed the grisly punishment.[47]

The only case among these five that did not occur during the years castration was a compulsory punishment was that of Tom, who had broken into a white man's house and stolen the property of another white male. The slave courts in the other four cases could not arbitrarily choose execution over castration because the legislature would not confirm the slave court's order to compensate the owners of the executed slaves. To do so would negate the purpose of the law, which was to limit such payments because of the financial strains of the French and Indian War. On the other hand, it is true that some convicted "felonious" male slaves could have been sentenced during the years 1758–64 to other corporal punishments, but it is unlikely that this occurred frequently since the records for only two cases involving corporal punishments other than castration survive for the time the law was in effect, whereas sixteen castrations are recorded for these years. In any case, three of the remaining four slaves were castrated for crimes related to the preparation and use of poisons, and one was convicted of house burning.

Castration, then, was not limited as a punishment to any set group of crimes and certainly was not used as a specific deterrent in North Carolina to sexual crime. Indeed, between 1758 and 1764 statutory law mandated it as the sentence for male first offenders who committed any felony except rape or murder. Slaves guilty of the latter crimes continued to be executed. The punishment of castration, however, was reserved exclusively for slaves and sometimes was used as a method of torture prior to the execution of those who had committed crimes deemed by masters to be especially heinous. Thus Isaac was castrated and then hanged for house burning. Jimmy, of New Hanover County, convicted of an unspecified felony for the second time in 1762, was also castrated before he was hanged. Another New Hanover slave received the same punishment, although in his case castration followed death. Convicted of raping a white woman, Sarah Baucum, Phill was sentenced on 18 November 1743 to be "Hanged till he is dead on the nineteenth day of afsd. and then his private parts cut off and thrown in his face."[48] If castration rarely was used specifically to punish sexual crimes, its exclusive use on blacks and its application as a special device of torture or to work out the fantasies of white men are not without special meaning.

The treatment of the crime of rape in colonial North Carolina adds other dimensions to the way gender and race affected the manner in which society and the judiciary viewed alleged victims and the accused. Slave women simply were denied status as credible victims by both the regular and slave court systems, and consequently there are no cases on record in which either white or slave males were charged with the rape of slave women. Indeed, prior to 1774 whites were not considered to be legally chargeable with any offense against the person of a slave. But even if this were not true, the charge of rape would not have been entertained in a system in which the ownership of human chattels existed and the masters had the right to command the obedience of slaves and the right to control their bodies. Further limiting the possibility of such a charge were the inability of slaves to initiate court cases or to testify against whites and the presumption of the libidinous nature of slaves, in general, and the prurience of slave women, in particular.[49] These last two assumptions also influenced whites to refrain from prosecuting slave men for raping slave women. The thought of such a charge undoubtedly appeared ludicrous to whites, especially with thralldom's stress on slaves as chattels and the consequent delegitimation of slave marriages and families. In fact, slaveowners generally encouraged slave women to be prolific with little fastidiousness regarding who the fathers were, recognizing that progeny born as a result of any union, including rape, served the pocketbook interests of masters.[50] This is hardly to say that masters encouraged slave rapists, but simply that the raping of slaves by slaves was not prevented through the use of the slave courts. Deterrents to such rapes might well have been implemented by masters on individual slave plantations to prevent undue discord. More likely, the slave communities themselves provided their own deterrents. But these matters are not revealed in the slave records.

Neither do the records indicate that white women received much relief in the courts when they were raped by white men, as the latter rarely were charged with the crime and it is likely that no white male ever was convicted of rape in colonial North Carolina. Among the more than 4,100 white males prosecuted for crimes during the 113-year period from 1663 to 1776, only 9 were charged with rape. And of the nearly 2,750 white males charged with crimes with known outcomes to their cases, just under 40 percent were convicted; none of the 7 charged with rape was found guilty. The absurdly low number of accused white males testifies both to the short shrift all-white male juries and judges gave to the charge of rape and the doubtless reluctance of white females to present their grievances before such hostile courts. The absence of any known convictions of rape also gives witness to a view of women that perversely assumed that their supposed prurience invited rape.[51]

A complete reversal of these attitudes occurred, however, when the accused rapist of a white woman was a black slave. Between 1748 and 1772 three slaves were charged with this crime, and all were convicted and executed. We know how two of the three were killed. Cato of Chowan County, in a slave court held on 14 November 1766, was found guilty of "feloniously ravishing and carnally knowing a certain Elizabeth Hallow contrary to the kings peace." His sentence was to be "fastened to a stake and there being burnt untill he be dead." In a trial before a slave court in Duplin County on 1 May 1770, George was found guilty of the rape of Jane Rynchy and sentenced to death by hanging with his head then severed from his body and "Stuck up at the Forks of the Road."[52] As noted earlier, another slave convicted of rape in 1743 was sentenced to death by hanging, but immediately afterward "his private parts [were] cut off and thrown in his face." All known punishments for slaves convicted of raping white women were ferociously calculated to strike terror in the hearts of slaves, and the charge itself was tantamount to conviction and execution. The slave courts obviously did not stress the descendants of Eve the temptress in these decisions, but rather the seed of Cain and Ham—black, carnal, and murderous.[53]

Compensation laws were passed to ensure that harsh punishments were meted out to slaves, not only for rape but also for all "serious slave crimes." Thus masters inserted in the slave laws of 1715 and 1741 clauses that compensated slaveowners for the loss of slaves sentenced to death by the slave courts or who died as a result of punishments ordered by a court, or who were killed during apprehension as outlaws or runaways or while committing a crime. In the first two instances, the special court established to try slave offenders set the monetary value of slaves. In the latter three situations, the county court evaluated the deceased slaves. In all cases, the compensation awarded to owners or their assignees had to be approved by the Committee of Public Claims, a joint committee of both houses of the legislature that was actually controlled by the lower house. If sanctioned by the committee, the claim went to each of the houses for its endorsement and then to the governor for his signature. Officials on the provincial level rarely rejected or amended claims of this nature. For reasons that will be explained later, the legislature eventually limited the compensation for individual slaves to a maximum of £60 in 1758 and £80 in 1764. John Brickell, writing some two decades before these liberally estimated ceilings were introduced, accurately summed up the province's compensation system. When slaves were executed, he explained, "the Planters suffer little or nothing by it, for the Province is obliged to pay the full value they judge them worth to the Owner; this is the common Custom or Law in the Province, to prevent the Planters being ruined by the loss of their Slaves, whom they have purchased at so dear a rate."[54]

Slaveowners, however, compounded their gains from the compensation system by their methods of financing it. Both the policing of the slave community and the cost of compensations were funded by provincial rather than local tax revenues, forcing all taxpayers, including those who owned few or no slaves and those living in areas with sparse slave populations, to pay the cost of these twin pillars of social control. And because these services and compensations in support of slavery especially benefited the affluent slaveowners, they made an already highly regressive tax system even more so.[55]

More precisely, over 98 percent of the tax payments of colonial North Carolina came from a highly regressive tax system composed of direct work levies, fees, poll taxes, and duties on imported liquor. Work levies, that is, militia and road service, when converted into money value equaled at least 50 percent of the colony's tax load. These levies were severely regressive because they demanded from the poor a considerably greater proportion of their available labor time than was taken from the rich and their legal dependents. This regressivity was compounded by the fact that the poor could least afford the loss of labor time. Fees, which equaled about 23.5 percent of the tax load, were paid directly by individuals to officials for their services. They were regressive because they had to be paid on a wide variety of services required by large numbers of inhabitants. Liquor duties, comprising about 4.5 percent of the tax load, were also regressive because they were passed on to the large mass of consumers by the merchants. The poll (head) tax brought in revenues nearly as significant as those provided by fees, equaling about 20.5 percent of the colony's total receipts. This was levied on each head of a household in accordance with the total number of white males aged sixteen and over and black males and females twelve and over living in each respective household. This meant that the tax was heaviest for free blacks but was comparatively negligible for affluent westerners and those whose wealth derived from nonplanting pursuits that required relatively few slaves or servants. Although slaveholding planters paid relatively higher poll taxes than their western and mercantile peers, they were willing to do so because they received more money and services through compensations and the colony's system of policing slaves than they paid in poll taxes. Thus in 1767 the wealthiest 10 percent of North Carolina's population, as a group, paid in poll taxes about £1,350 while receiving in compensations for their executed slaves at least £1,000 and in services by the state to maintain slavery the equivalent of considerably more than £350.[56]

Slaveowning legislators further ensured that financial concerns would not deter harsh slave punishments by not placing any limits on compensations prior to 1758. Consequently, in the decade before 1758 compensation levels consistently exceeded the market price for slaves, with the gap between the two increasing with the onset of the French and Indian War. Masters of twenty-one executed slaves received on average £56.6.11, while prices for forty-three adult slaves averaged £32.17.10 (see Tables 3.1 and 1.11). More precisely taking the war into account, the total number of compensations rose from eleven during the seven-year period from 1748 to 1754 to twelve for the four years from 1755 to 1758, and the total cost of compensations increased even more dramatically, from £392.10.0 to £795.0.0. Calculating for time differentials between the two periods, the rate of yearly compensations for 1755–58 was three-and-a-half times greater than for the earlier years (see Table 3.1). To pay for these fast-rising compensation payments, but especially to finance the burgeoning war expenditures, provincial import duties on alcoholic beverages, for example, averaged about three times those of 1748–54, and the mean of poll taxes rose within the same time spans just less than five times.[57]

With such trends in mind and unable to reverse the rising war expenditures that were bending poorer freemen under the weight of fast-increasing regressive taxes, the ruling class momentarily restrained its cupidity by cutting public expenditures to finance the policing and disciplining of slaves. The law of 1758 used a variety of methods to do this, including two relatively minor cost-cutting techniques: denying compensations to owners of executed slaves who had either been purchased from "foreign parts" as known criminals or had been slaves allowed by their owners to hire themselves out. These clauses, as the preamble to the law suggests, primarily were meant to cut policing costs.[58]

The essential purpose of the law, however, is also stated in the preamble: "Whereas many great Charges have arisen to the Province . . . by the condemnation of Slaves to Death for capital Crimes, for want of a punishment adequate to the Crimes they have been guilty of; and by the High Valuation of Slaves condemned to Death or killed by Virtue of an Outlawry."[59] The law solved this problem with phraseology that in no way hinted that legislators were doing anything but establishing an "adequate" punishment to resolve a financial issue: "be it further Enacted by the Authority aforesaid" that castration would be substituted for execution for male first offenders of crimes other than for murder and rape. Then, with one eye on the need for fiscal restraint and the other on the cost of replacing slaves, the lawmakers set at £60 the maximum compensation for executed slaves, those who died after being castrated, or those "killed on outlawry, or in being apprehended when run away." This figure still ensured that owners would be compensated liberally, for, as we have seen, sale prices for *adult* slaves during the years 1748–58 had averaged only £32.17.10. Only four slaves in ninety-two recorded sales sold for more than £60 (see Table 1.11).[60]

While in force between 1759 and 1764 this act achieved its intended purpose of reducing the provincial outlay for compensations. Largely because of the new £60 assessment limit, mean compensations fell by £15.10.0 as compared to the level of 1755–58, while total yearly money compensations decreased from £198.15.0 to £110. This last reflected the dramatically altered pattern of public punishments for major slave crimes. During a period in which the slave population increased significantly, the number of annual compensated slave executions declined from twelve in the *four* years 1754–58 to thirteen in the *six* years 1759–64, or from an average of three per year to just over two (see Table 3.1). The declining rate of executions, however, was offset by a steep rise in castrations: sixteen slaves were castrated between 1759 and 1764, compared with one in the early war years and none during 1748–54.

The end of the war brought rising market price levels for slaves along with decreasing public expenditures and tax levels, ensuring that slaveowners would amend or scuttle the law of 1758 as soon as possible (see Table 1.11).[61] They did so in 1764 during the first Assembly session after the war. While raising the compensation maximum to £80, they repealed the clause in the 1758 statute that had substituted castration for execution as the compulsory punishment for most slave males convicted for the first time of "felonies."[62]

Once again, the maximum compensation was set to ensure that planters were well compensated for the loss of their property: about 91 percent of the slaves sold between 1759 and 1764 fetched a price of £80 or less. Although slave prices continued to climb between 1764 and 1772, average compensations and market prices for adult slaves during these years remained nearly equal, £70.13.10 and £71.18.7 respectively. A master whose slave had been executed normally could purchase an acceptable replacement with the money paid to him or her out of provincial revenues (see Tables 1.11 and 3.1).

It is mystifying how some historians profess to see in the repeal of the clause calling for compulsory castration evidence of some change for the better in planter morality.[63] If that were the case, one could plot a bizarre graph of the jagged development of planter morals in colonial North Carolina: from a high before 1758, to a low with the implementation of compulsory castration during the years 1758 to 1764, and once again to a high after 1764, when planters chose to have their slaves killed instead of castrated. Rather, the facts are that the castration clause had originally been enacted as an economy measure and once the pressure for fiscal restraint had passed, the clause was removed. Because slave criminality was not affected by changes in the type of punishment used, this was not a factor in repeal. Slaveowners apparently preferred to replace, out of public funds, male slaves found guilty of capital crimes, instead of dealing with embittered slaves following their castration.

The amendments of 1764, in any case, once again altered the pattern of punishments and compensations. Only two castrations occurred between 1765 and 1772, whereas executions quadrupled to fifty-two. The yearly average number of compensations more than doubled compared to the period 1755–58 and were three times the average for the years 1759–64. Moreover, annual compensations in cash exceeded those of 1759–64 by £359.10.0, an increase of nearly 327 percent (see Table 3.1).

The total financial cost of the compensation system was high. Recorded compensations totaled £5,523.10.0, about 21 to 25 percent of all claims (excluding remunerations to members and officials of the General Assembly) awarded by the Committee of Public Claims between 1748 and 1772 (see Table 3.1). And if committee expenditures for policing and disciplining slaves are added to compensations, the total outlay probably represented around 32 percent of all awarded provincial claims. Securing the "troublesome property," indeed, had a high public price tag.[64]

The cost to the public of maintaining slavery directly advantaged one class in particular: the large slaveholders who played the dominant role in provincial and county politics. They had designed the compensation system, and they benefited most from it. The compensations awarded members of the upper class in North Carolina averaged £4.1.11 more than those granted other masters during the period 1748–72. This disparity diminished over the years, probably because maximum compensation laws limited flexibility in evaluations. During the years 1748–54 and 1755–58, when such laws were not in effect, upper-class owners received respectively £5.2.6 and £7.5.9 more than other owners. After the laws were passed, the disparity dropped to £2.2.5 between 1759 and 1764 and to twelve shillings from 1765 to 1772. Using a different gauge, the proportion of compensations awarded to the upper class surpassed substantially what its slaveholdings warranted. Thus the leading slaveholders in the province, that is, the top 4 percent among the colony's heads of households, owned about 46.4 percent of the slaves in North Carolina but received 54.5 percent of the compensations for executed slaves paid out by the province (see Table 3.2).

Large planter control of the courts was not the sole cause of this distribution, for it is possible that slaves on larger plantations on the average had a higher labor value and had committed more crimes than those on smaller farms. But even if the compensations large planters received were entirely the result of social and economic forces beyond their control, the fact remains that the compensation system they constructed most significantly served their interests.

If the compensation system so carefully served the needs of all slaveholders, but especially those who were wealthy, and the poorer and middling freemen disproportionately footed the bill, the system also brought increased horrors to the slave community, as it was meant to do. We do not contend that terror was either the sum total of the masters' treatment of slaves or the full portion of the slaves' lives. We do argue, however, that the judicial procedures followed by the authorities and the slave courts in accordance with slave criminal law and the compensation system were meant to, and in fact did, ensure the implementation of a harsh system of public justice where death sentences and castrations and other severe corporal punishments were regularly meted out. Indeed, a design to maximize terror's impact on the slave population is evident as early as 1715, when the legislation of that year admonished slaveholders to see that condemned slaves normally "be publickly executed to the Terror of other Slaves."[65]

Almost nothing in this legal aggression on slaves protected them from acts of violence by masters or other whites. As Chief Justice Howard wrote in 1771, slaves "are degraded from every right of human nature" when life itself is forfeited to the "caprice of a white man should [he] be pleased to take it away from them."[66] The minutes of North Carolina's superior and county courts testify to the violence that emanated from this legal wasteland, for they record a number of instances where whites assaulted, maimed, and murdered slaves with no penalties assessed for these crimes. Yet grand juries did indict a few white perpetrators, who actually were tried before petty juries. In these cases, even when the question of guilt was not in doubt, the accused still escaped conviction or punishment for killing slaves because there was no relevant statute to try whites for aggressing on slaves and the prevailing belief was that neither common law nor natural law was directly applicable.

A case in point involved William Luten, tried late in November 1763 for manslaughter before the Edenton Superior Court. Sarah Lewis had given Luten permission to "correct" her "Negroe Woman Kate." When Kate

> resisted him . . . he with force and Arms . . . did beat strike beat and wound the sd. Negroe Woman Kate on . . . [13 August 1762] giving to her the several mortal Bruises in the Indictment Mentioned and that of those Mortal Wounds & Bruises she afterwards languished & died. . . . And if upon the whole matter the killing and Slaying the said Negroe Kate in manner & form afsd. be felony Then we find the sd. William Luten Guilty of the manslaughter of the said Kate in Manner & form as in the Indictment afsd. is charged But if the Killing and slaying the said Kate in manner afsd. be in Law no Felony then we do find that the said William Luten . . .

The minutes exasperatingly end here, for the next two pages are missing.[67]

Another case reflects similar confusion as to whether or not the murder of a slave was a felony, or indeed a crime at all. During a court session begun on 27 November 1771, the Wilmington District Superior Court tried Peter Lord for the murder of his "Negroe man slave." The jury agreed that the slave had hidden from Lord "for a few hours." Lord, on finding his slave hiding in a house (possibly on Lord's plantation), began chastising the slave with a knife, intending "to mark or cut the said Negroes ears and that one of the ears of the said Negroe was cut previous to the wound of which he died. We find the said wound was accidentally received by the Deceased in Struggling with the said Peter Lord and with the knife mentioned in the indictment then in the hand of the said Prisoner and that the said Negroe died of the said wound in a few hours after he received it. And whether this is murder, manslaughter, or homicide by misadventure, we pray the advice of the Court."[68] Lord and his securities posted a total of £1,000 bond to ensure his appearance at the next session of the superior court in May 1772. Although the court met at that time, and again in November 1772, there is no further record of his case.[69] The inescapable fact is that whites who assaulted, maimed, or killed slaves rarely were indicted and never were convicted of a crime against the person of a slave.

The master's property, on the other hand, was protected by the law against attack from other whites. Thus, amid clauses that nearly stripped slaves bare of all legal protections while compensating masters for their slaves killed under the auspices of such laws, the law of 1741 still intoned: "That nothing herein contained, shall be construed, deemed or taken, to defeat or bar the Action of any Person or Persons, whose Slave or Slaves shall happen to be killed by any other Person whosoever, contrary to the Directions and true Intent and Meaning of this Act; but that all and every Owner or Owners of such Slave or Slaves, shall and may bring his, her or their Action for Recovery of Damages for such Slave or Slaves so killed."[70]

Slaveowners made use of the clause, bringing civil suits for damages against other whites who illegally killed, maimed, or injured the owners' slaves. Thus James Luten on 20 May 1761 before the Edenton Superior Court brought charges against Drury Stokes for "Trespass" for beating his "Negro Slave." The court rendered judgment by default for Luten and awarded him seven shillings for damages plus costs but never charged Stokes with a crime against the slave.[71]

In another case, this adjudicated in the Chowan County Court during the July session of 1757, Charles Jordan filed a "Plea of Trespass" against William Winham for attacking two of Jordan's slaves, Frank and Jack, with "Force and Arms." Winham had "assaulted beat & bruised" Frank so that he "languished *whereby the said Plt was deprived of his Service & the Benefit of his Labour*" (emphasis added). Still not satiated, Winham on 25 April 1757 attacked Jack on Jordan's plantation and "did beat bruise & evilly intreat by Means of which beating & bruising the said Negro Man Servant languished from the said Twenty fifth Day of April untill the fifth Day of May . . . Whereby the said Plt totally lost the Service of the said Servant during the time aforesaid & other Injuries to the said plt the sd William then & there did against the Peace of our Soveriegn Lord the now King Whereupon the sd *Plaintiff saith he is injured & hath Damage to the Value of [space] Therefore Sues*."[72] The amount of the damages called for is not entered, and the disposition of the case is not revealed in other extant documents. The industrious Charles Jordan, however, also received approval from the Assembly in 1768 of his court-sanctioned 1765 claim of £80 "for a Negro Man Executed . . . for Felony."[73] The pain of slaves so often resulted in repeated financial gain to their owners.

The record in North Carolina was hardly better when it came to ensuring that masters fed, clothed, and housed their slaves adequately or to limiting the harshness of slave discipline. Servants had fairly substantial legal protections accorded them to minimize abuses and ensure minimal standards, but such was not the case for slaves. The courts were of little use to slaves as an instrument for rectifying harshly exploitative treatment since slaves could not appeal directly to the courts, nor could they even testify against whites. Legally they were completely dependent on whites, especially their owners or other individuals with official authority over them. Court actions were undertaken by owners only to protect their property, never to protect the person of slaves.[74] During the quarter century before the Revolution, the provincial legislature shaped only two limited and ineffectual clauses to protect the well-being of slaves. Both were included in a 1753 statute, one stipulating that before a master could be compensated for a slave killed under state authority, the owner, or a surrogate if the owner were unavailable, had to state that the deceased slave had been sufficiently clothed and had received at least one quart of corn per diem during the year preceding his conviction or death. As the slave trial records reveal, these declarations were simply pro forma. The second clause merely stated that owners of slaves who did not appear to have received such minimal treatment were liable to actions of trespass to recover damages and costs by owners of "Corn, Cattle, Hogs, or other Goods" stolen by the slaves of the delinquent owner.[75]

Both the inability and the unwillingness of the ruling class in colonial North Carolina to establish cultural hegemony over their slaves freed masters from having to pursue ameliorative policies that would prompt slaves to accept their owners' culture. Without such constraints, masters could deny to slaves the normative system of criminal justice used for whites, one that joined traditional procedural due process with a tendency to temper justice with mercy. In its place was installed a public system of criminal justice that set up special slave courts with near plenary powers to define arbitrarily their jurisdiction and judicial procedures and powers. And, as the laws intended, judicial terror was used to establish absolute control by the state and slaveowners over their slave chattels. Aiding in this quest to terrorize slaves were police officers and a deputized citizenry with peremptory power to kill slave outlaws or, indeed, any slave apprehended in a crime. In addition, prior to 1774 slaves had no legal protection for their person against white attacks.

Slaves received some relief from these statutory and juridical assaults through a de facto system of private slave justice that was administered on individual plantations and was made available to all slaves except those whose transgressions, it was felt, warranted public trials or peremptory public punishments. Normally more temperate in their punishments than the slave courts or public authorities, individual plantation owners balanced terror with co-optative techniques. Planter paternalism could here work out both its fantasies and its coldly realistic designs to help induce slaves to behave "properly." In this atmosphere masters granted slaves—the indispensable workers who made the plantation system go—enough space to ensure their viability as producers. This necessarily also provided the space for slaves to control significant areas of their personal lives. Indeed, the absence of cultural hegemony helped to ensure that the slaves' African cultural heritages frequently remained normative and dominant in their daily lives.

It was in this broader context that slaves directly resisted their enslavers. We must now analyze the forms of resistance they used and, as best we can, fathom their intentions and the values and ideology they used to comprehend and justify their behavior. Any proposal to discuss the inner lives of slaves, certainly colonial slaves for whom primary sources and folk materials are especially scarce, is bound to fall woefully short of the promise. Yet the enormous significance of the subject requires that a strenuous effort be made to reveal as much as possible.

4

"Criminal" Resistance Patterns, I

Despite significant variations among African cultures dispersed in a variety of American settings and the resulting regional and temporal differences among American slave ecologies and cultures, the emerging African American slave societies and cultures still shared much in common. For instance, slaves incorporated into their cosmologies a typically African holistic approach to understanding reality and structuring their lives. This ensured that however much slaves compartmentalized elements of their existences, they nonetheless integrated their experiences within models that stressed the intricate interrelationships that exist among institutions, roles, values, and behavior. Slaves thus interwove in complex, profound, if often hidden ways different patterns of resistance with a variety of methods of adjustment that historians commonly view as disparate slave responses to bondage, including murder, arson, sabotage, flight, and truancy, as well as a sustaining religiosity and powerful marital, familial, and communal ties.[1]

The Ormond case discussed in Chapter 3, for instance, illustrates that the mistreatments and punishments to which all slaves were subjected led them to respond in a variety of ways.[2] Each of their responses, from running away to murder, also contributed to the sense of injustice felt by other slaves on the Ormond plantation, as well as those who lived elsewhere and heard of the resistance. Even more intriguing is the blurred line that separates murder and insurrection illustrated by the case. What, indeed, distinguishes the murder of Ormond by five slaves, one from a neighboring plantation, from numerous examples of what are normally defined as minor or, for that matter, major slave insurrections? The action of the five slaves who murdered Ormond, and who refused to grant his pleas for mercy because he had always been merciless in his dealings with them, is similar, for example, to the plans of what are generally considered prospective if nascent insurrectionists in Chowan County during 1783. At that time the slave Grainge was tried and convicted for the "atrocious crime of endeavoring to stir up slaves for the diabolical purpose of murdering their masters and Mistresses." The point is that slaves murdering or planning to murder their owners or other whites was a starting point for many slave rebellions from Stono to Nat Turner. The particular situation had to grow in magnitude and organization to acquire attributes more recognizably political and insurrectionary. But the roots of such uprisings, including the basic consciousness that informed them, often lay buried within such cases as the murder of Henry Ormond.[3]

This argument rejects an overly thematic approach to resistance, which tends to categorize specific forms of lower-class resistance rigidly and almost irrevocably. In the latter view, many everyday forms of slave resistance—from foot-dragging, dissimulation, false compliance, feigned ignorance, sabotage, and petty pilfering, to the varied uses of "poison," house burning, rape, outlawry, and murder—have been classified, by definition, as individual or self-indulgent forms of resistance that necessarily lack sufficient organization or principled motivation to give the actions effective class and political content. By way of contrast are those slave actions that are organized and principled, and thereby significantly class and politically defined or motivated, most evidently insurrections and rebellions. The two modes of resistance, supposedly, are so different that there is no possibility of growth from one to the other by multiple repetition.[4]

Yet history frequently has witnessed the actions of "self-indulgent," "unorganized" draft dodgers, whose numbers increase over time, destroying or seriously weakening national war efforts and, at times, becoming a significant determinant in fomenting a revolution. A similar example, but closer to this study, is of slaves who ran away in increasing numbers, some to maroon settlements, resulting in escalating violence and perhaps slave rebellions. The absence of prior organization or defining principles among such slaves has not necessarily deterred such progressions from occurring.

The Stono Rebellion in South Carolina demonstrates both how murders could escalate into a full-scale rebellion and how running away could precipitate a rebellion and help to define the course of the uprising itself. Thus slaves in South Carolina during the 1730s in increasing numbers successfully ran off to seek refuge in a maroon haven near St. Augustine in Spanish Florida. With both tensions and slave expectations rising and with slaves receiving word of the onset of a long-anticipated war with Spain the very weekend of the rebellion, the pot boiled over on Sunday morning, 9 September 1739. Twenty runaway slaves gathered near the western branch of Stono River, about twenty miles from Charlestown, and shortly afterward began to murder whites and to collect small arms and ammunition. As the number of slave escapees increased to between 60 and 100, they marched ten miles through the countryside virtually unhindered, killing a total of 20 whites. With each success, slave spirits and expectations mounted. Standards were found and raised, shouts for liberty rang out, and stirring drumbeats aroused passions for rebellion. As the morning and afternoon hours passed, increasingly large numbers of runaways, committed to both escape to Florida and continued violence at home, had established the necessary organization and symbols of a rebellion.[5]

Although organization among the slaves had been minimal until Stono, running away and violent attacks on whites had been informed by political considerations long before the rebellion. This consciousness existed along with the self-serving, individualistic elements that were often central to running away or acts of violence perpetrated by individuals or small groups. Indeed, it was precisely the immediate rewards obtained from these personal forms of resistance together with the relative ease with which slaves could implement them that made them so attractive. Yet slaves who thieved, ran off, or assaulted or murdered whites to alleviate their own or their families' needs or to protect their person or institutions from white attack also, by definition, directly challenged the capacity of whites to define slave discipline, behavior, and production. Whites and slaves alike understood these political dimensions of slave criminality despite its individualistic or limited and unorganized features. Thus Henry Ormond's "house wench" called for reciprocity between masters and slaves when she bitterly urged the death of Ormond because "as he had no mercy on them, he could expect none himself." The slave court, in turn, fully aroused by the murder and its impact on the slave community, hanged three of the collaborators while burning alive a fourth, Annis, the domestic.[6]

Nevertheless, neither the Ormond murder nor any other set of inflammatory circumstances in colonial North Carolina resulted in a slave uprising. Just why becomes evident when we recognize that despite a more favorable demography in South Carolina for slave uprisings—blacks comprising two-thirds of the colony's population in 1740 and three-fifths in 1770—no further slave insurrections occurred in that colony after 1740. Wood argues that this was the case primarily because of the concerted efforts by white South Carolinians after their military crushed the Stono rebels to pass repressive legislation that severely limited slave autonomy.[7] If such measures succeeded in stifling slave uprisings in South Carolina after 1740, it is understandable why North Carolina's slaves—comprising less than a quarter of the colony's population and without much opportunity to escape to Spanish Florida, though still subjected to similar types of repression as were their brethren to the south—never rose up in rebellion.

Yet an opportunity reminiscent of the events leading to the Stono Rebellion occurred in New Hanover County in September 1767, when justices of the peace were alarmed to learn "that upwards of Twenty runaway Slaves in a body Arm'd . . . are now in this County." The county court promptly ordered "that the Sheriff do immediately raise the power of the County not to be less than Thirty Men well Arm'd to go in pursuit of the said runaway slaves and that the said Sheriff be impowered to Shoot to kill and destroy all such of the said runaway Slaves as shall not Surrender themselves." Because the records are silent beyond this, it is implausible that a bloody confrontation took place between the runaways and the *posse comitatus*. The fugitives probably either gave up peaceably or escaped northward to join the maroons in the Great Dismal Swamp. Less likely, they went to South Carolina's backcountry or to the Cherokee on the western frontier.[8]

Mention of the possibility of escape to South Carolina's backcountry raises the intriguing question of banditry among slaves, perhaps even social banditry. Eric Hobsbawm characterizes both sorts of bandits as poorer, country folk. He distinguishes between them by stressing that common bandits simply were criminal and venal—indiscriminately preying on the peasants and landless laborers together with whoever else might be available. Social bandits, however, managed to rise above victimizing the poor, somehow being "drawn by a dialectic of social demand and interdependence." Consequently, they came to act "as protectors, redistributors, and avengers."[9]

Banditry undoubtedly existed in the eighteenth-century colonial South, especially in South Carolina, whose fast-growing backcountry in the 1750s and 1760s still remained unorganized as counties or even as local juridical units. Wealthy low-country planters refused to allow counties or juridical units to be established in the west because they feared that this would limit their power to control the political apparatus of the province. The resulting vacuum of local organization helped to maintain the political and economic viability of numbers of backcountry hunters and marginal farmers who often relied on banditry to supplement their incomes. The more substantial farmers of the region, tied to the norms and values of commercial agriculture and the potentialities of slavery, were the primary victims of bandits. They organized into "Regulators" and used direct and violent action to protect themselves against these backcountry bandits and to force the colonial legislature's hand to create courts and counties in the west. The Regulators hoped that these reforms would not only end banditry in the west, but also break the political hegemony of the eastern planters.[10]

Probably many of South Carolina's bandits were social bandits. Illustrative of this was their class solidarity, at least to the degree that they chose their victims primarily from the ranks of the more affluent backcountry farmers. They consequently were not a dangerous class to themselves, and banditry induced a partial redistribution of wealth.

What of the slave runaways among these bandits, some reaching positions of leadership? Should they be understood solely within the framework of social banditry, that is, as part of a power conflict between two essentially white classes with one to some degree being racially integrated? Probably not. Runaway slave bandits certainly must be regarded as part of this picture, but to understand them requires that their special status as runaway *slaves* also be stressed. Thus slaves who ran off to join the backcountry bandit gangs directly challenged slavery itself along with the claims of slaveowners to hegemony. Slave bandits did so in the strongest terms—not only as runaways who declared their freedom with their feet, but also as maroon bandits who integrated with whites and who maintained their freedom by force of arms while redistributing white wealth through banditry. Last, they set an extremely bold example for other slaves and undoubtedly directly helped some to escape.

North Carolina's Regulator movement during the 1760s and early 1770s, on the other hand, was very different from that in South Carolina, offering few opportunities for social banditry. The well-organized western counties in North Carolina with their active courts, militias, shrievalties, and constabularies generally made the backcountry secure from all types of banditry. Indeed, the very strength of these institutions and the abuse of power and corruption of the county officials themselves led less affluent farmers in the backcountry to challenge the equity of the laws and the legitimacy of the officials. Although the Regulators employed diverse techniques—court suits, petitions, political campaigns, civil disobedience, violent interference with county and provincial officials, disruptions of the courts, and, ultimately, armed rebellion—social banditry, at most, played only a peripheral role in their resistance. Blacks, particularly runaway slaves, had precious few opportunities to participate in North Carolina's Regulator movement. In addition to the fact that the movement was concentrated where few slaves lived, the Regulators were openly contemptuous of black slaves, and there is no indication that the Regulators had any belief that such an alliance would serve their interests.[11]

If the Regulators in North Carolina presented no significant opportunities for potential slave resisters, the Great Dismal Swamp did offer a relatively safe haven for numbers of slave runaways. They escaped deep into its watery isolation, which stretched from Norfolk, Virginia, to Edenton in North Carolina's Albemarle Sound region.[12] J. F. D. Smyth noted in 1784 that runaways in the swamp were "perfectly safe, and with the greatest facility elude the most diligent search of their pursuers." He added that blacks had lived there "for twelve, twenty, or thirty years and upwards, subsisting . . . upon corn, hogs, and fowls."[13] If by chance they were discovered, Elkanah Watson observed in 1777, "they could not be approached with safety" because of their belligerence.[14] It would be surprising if such slaves did not attempt to enhance their subsistence livelihoods by raiding on whites, trading with other receptive whites, and establishing liaisons, economic or otherwise, with slaves in the vicinity of the swamp. To the degree that this occurred, along with their influencing other slaves to join them, either through direct contact or by example, we are dealing with elements of social banditry. The evidence is hardly as substantial as that available for South Carolina, yet the possibility is there.

If common forms of resistance at times led to or even helped to define slave rebellions or other comparatively large and complex types of resistance, the fact remains that the everyday problems confronting slaves normally called forth everyday forms of slave resistance. Slaves usually resisted in small groups or as individuals, often surreptitiously and anonymously, but invariably they used methods requiring little or no organization or overt coordination, from foot-dragging, dissimulation, false compliance, feigned ignorance, sabotage and petty pilfering, to more serious, often collaborative, forms of slave theft and the use of poison, to running away, house burning, rape, and murder. Such techniques challenged the authority and power of the slaveowners while bringing immediate, if at times all too short-lived, relief to slaves involved in elemental struggles with their owners for survival and power.

Slaves chose these forms of criminal resistance not only because of their availability, immediate rewards, and political aptness, but also because slaves, far more than other exploited colonial classes, had so few lawful options at their disposal. Similar to other poorer classes, slaves could not play direct roles in the parliamentary process; but unlike them, slaves were also denied access to the courts except as witnesses against one another or as defendants in the special slave courts that denied slaves all procedural due process while rendering distinctively harsh judgments and punishments. Thus stripped of political and juridical powers and protections and subjected to a public criminal justice system intent on terrorizing them into submission, slaves were forced to rely on their own resources for relief; frequently, for lack of other choices, they chose criminal expedients. These tendencies were further reinforced by the distinctiveness of slavery, which was permanently binding on slaves and their descendants, while it defined them essentially as property, thereby denying their personhood and the legitimacy of the slaves' institutions. Thus slave marriages and families, unlike those of servants, had no legal standing. Yet slaves established de facto marriages and families, and when masters threatened these vital institutions, slaves had to rely on their own devices to defend themselves. They chose behavior that more often than not was defined by the masters' law as criminal—from theft, running away, and the use of herbs and witchcraft, to assault and murder.

Even slave attempts to defend their elemental right to keep or choose a name for themselves or their children against the counterdemands of masters could result in major confrontations with criminal implications. The physical punishments endured by young Olaudah Equiano in his unsuccessful attempt to prevent his name from being changed by his master, for instance, undoubtedly would have been even more severe, and the owner's sense of the meaning of Olaudah's intransigence more ominous, if his resistance had persisted. Certainly this would have been the case if the slave had been older than eleven and capable of more telling resistance.[15]

It is fair to ask whether the peculiarly harsh conditions of enslavement, which confined the relief of slaves to criminal acts, played an even crueler trick on slaves by inducing them to turn their rage and frustrations inward, thus becoming a dangerous class to themselves and limiting the value of criminal acts as a tool of resistance against slaveowners. Both John Brickell and Janet Schaw witnessed such destructive behavior in North Carolina. Brickell wrote in 1737 that "an abundance" of slaves were "given to theft," especially from one another, but "sometimes" from whites as well. His assessment of whom the slaves stole from most frequently may have been correct concerning petty thefts, but another of his observations contradicts even this. "Rum, with which they entertain their Wives and Mistresses at night," he said, was the favorite target of slave thieves despite the fact that they were "often detected and punished for it."[16] If rum was their favorite target, so were whites—for they had the available supplies. Schaw, some forty years later, suggested that slave theft was directed against both fellow slaves and masters but stressed its effect on the latter when she noted that blacks "steal whatever they can come at, and even intercept the cows and milk them. They are indeed the constant plague of their Tyrants, whose severity or mildness is equally regarded by them in these matters."[17]

Slaves, then, undoubtedly pilfered small amounts of food and other items from one another as well as from whites to alleviate their hunger or to satisfy other material needs. Whatever moral and social strains this placed on the slave community, it appears that slaves normally did not go beyond petty theft in victimizing one another and, therefore, were not a dangerous class to themselves. With few exceptions, almost all major crimes committed by slaves were directed against whites. "Stealing themselves," sabotaging productivity, destroying livestock and other property, burning houses, and burglarizing or stealing by other means were all practiced by slaves as techniques to alleviate their wants and assuage their rage and hence were logically, and frequently, used against whites, who overwhelmingly owned the surplus property.

Nonetheless, slaves occasionally lashed out violently at their fellow slaves, perhaps using them as less dangerous surrogates for the true butt of slave anger and hatred, whites. Yet slaves, unlike some other abused classes, largely avoided this tragedy. Perhaps this was so partially because slaveowners would execute slaves who murdered other slaves, and there consequently was no rationale to shift their aggressions against their fellow slaves. In any case, twenty-one of the twenty-three (91.3 percent) slaves executed in colonial North Carolina for murder or attempted murder chose white victims, with fourteen of these (60.9 percent of the total) murdering their owners. Just one slave (4.1 percent) was put to death for trying to kill some of his fellow slaves along with his master, and another was executed for murdering a fellow slave. The only other slaves punished for murdering or attempting to murder slaves were two males who poisoned a slave (who survived) and were planning to poison others. Both were castrated, and one died as a result of the mutilation.[18]

Herbs and conjuring, as just intimated, were used by slaves against other slaves. This emanated from African practices where helpful magic was used to defeat destructive sorcery. Yet slaves only infrequently defended themselves against their fellow slaves in this fashion even though it was a traditional, legitimate method of self-defense. Rather, slaves usually applied herbal potions (poisons) in conjunction with conjuring to blunt the attacks of their white oppressors.[19]

Slaves, then, did not dissipate the effects of criminality as a tool of resistance by becoming a dangerous class to themselves. As the records amply show, they made effective use of everyday forms of criminality both to service individual needs and designs and to challenge the slaveowners' authority and power. Historians such as Eugene Genovese, however, still raise other questions about the utility but especially the morality of slave criminality. He argues that this form of resistance was destructive to the slaves' moral fiber while it had a harmful impact on African American society over the long term. Moreover, given his stress on the supposed effects of the masters' cultural hegemony on slaves, he concludes that slaves were unable to incorporate criminality into their prevailing moral code.[20]

Lawrence Levine, following the lead of modern criminologists like Gresham Sykes and David Matza, partially challenges Genovese by arguing that the slaves' practical set of values and norms of behavior, including criminal resistance activities, could be used to neutralize rather than replace their normative values because "norms may be violated without surrendering allegiance to them." This was so, Levine explains, because "most if not all norms in society are conditional rather than categorically imperative." Slaves thus could "rationalize their need to lie, cheat and steal without holding these actions up as models to be followed in all instances, without creating, that is, a counter morality."[21]

Alex Lichtenstein, in turn, makes use of Marxist criminologists to provide a theoretical framework for discussing Sykes and Matza's model. He posits that because neutralization theory "ignores structures of power and forms of struggle against oppression in societies based on class (or race) domination," it is not, in fact, a "technique" meant to deal with slave behavior and goals at odds with a normative morality, but rather a "mystification" of the process. This is so, more precisely, "because the 'cultural options available [to the oppressed] in an inequitable . . . society are designed to make opposition look like neutralizations rather than the critique of the frustrated and deprived.'" Moreover, depicting delinquent acts solely as "the neutral negation of societal norms avoids the essential ideological and material significance of theft: the fact that the mass of delinquents are literally involved in the practice of redistributing private property." Lichtenstein even more expansively concludes in a way similar to our previous summaries of the essential qualities of common forms of slave criminality by noting: "If theft was a focus of tension on the plantation, that tension is not found in the slaves' attempts to forge a contradictory neutralizing morality, but in the struggle between slaves and masters to define conflicting notions of authority, property and customary rights."[22]

Despite their significantly different evaluations of the impact of slave criminality on the lives of slaves and their systems of morality, Genovese, Levine, and Lichtenstein still discuss the effects of criminal behavior within the context of a prevailing hegemonic morality. Although Lichtenstein believes that slave theft was a "focus of tension" found in the "struggle between slaves and masters to define conflicting notions of authority, property, and customary rights," and that this struggle enabled slaves to construct a countermorality of theft, he nevertheless chides Genovese for not placing his sense of the planters' paternalistic hegemonic morality within the context of the clash between slaves and slaveowners to define some of the parameters of slavery. To do so, he further argues, would reject a "static model of paternalist master-slave relations" for one in which "theft served as a potential means with which slaves could redefine and extend the bounds of paternalism."[23]

Building upon this conceptualization of the dialectical conflict between masters and slaves, Lichtenstein emphasizes that slaves understood theft as a proper way to protect those traditional economic and social rights and customs that they believed could not be legitimately abrogated. Adding to this description of how the slaves understood and used a "moral economy," Lichtenstein states that it also may be described as the *process* in which specific acts such as bread riots, poaching, or stealing by the English poor, or sabotage, stealing, or murder by slaves in America, are used to avenge or correct abridgements of the traditional rights and practices of the oppressed classes.[24]

Lichtenstein, still closely following E. P. Thompson, the intellectual fount of analyses about moral economies of the poor, further emphasizes that "the existence of a moral economy is predicated upon the fact that the ruling class traditionally permits the exercise of customary economic rights similar to the workings of 'Genovese's paternalism' and clearly exemplified" among slaves by their gardens. "It is only when the existence of these rights appears to challenge the hegemony of the ruling class or blocks a reconsolidation of their power in new economic relationships that a struggle ensues" in which the masters try to redefine previously legitimate behavior as illegal and slaves have to resort to illegal acts, such as theft, to continue to operate effectively in traditional spheres of activity.[25]

We are in accord with Lichtenstein's rejection of both Genovese's and Levine's diverse arguments about why a hegemonic morality was able to continue to define the normative morality of slaves despite their use of countervailing measures such as lying, stealing, and deceit. Yet Lichtenstein's arguments for a countermorality of theft, placed squarely within the contextual framework of a dialectic between slaves and masters to determine the limits of a paternalistically defined hegemonic morality, runs directly counter to our evidence for colonial North Carolina. For, as we have urged in the previous chapters, with cultural hegemony neither possible nor consequently sought by colonial North Carolina's ruling class for their slaves, this also ruled out a hegemonic morality and necessarily transformed how ruling-class paternalism would be applied to slaves. Thus, rather than the ruling class being at least partially bound by the moral economies of the poor, as was true, except in times of fundamental change, in societies where cultural hegemony prevailed, slave masters in colonial North Carolina were free to apply a paternalism to their slaves that mechanistically balanced complementing co-optative and terroristic techniques.

Reciprocity between rulers and ruled was rendered meaningless by the unremitting claims by masters of their absolute power over slaves, who, in turn, were stripped of their legal rights and protections. Statutory laws divested slaves of almost all procedural due process in the courts; granted to the juridical and police forces dealing with slaves plenary, arbitrary, and summary powers; and almost entirely, if paradoxically, consigned the legal defense of slave "persons" to masters protecting their chattels. This being the case, the use of terror against slaves, especially as administered by the separate public system of criminal justice for slaves, grew as the occasions required, unimpeded by the limits normally set by a ruling class that felt the need to convince the ruled that the laws and the courts provided all classes with an unbiased system of law.

Rather than slaves using a moral economy to protect traditional values and customs within systems of law and governance that had both a sense of limits and reciprocity, slaves could only attempt to define customary rights and practices within a legal system that offered them no legal options or relief. Conflicts between masters and slaves, therefore, most readily developed into power struggles in which the only options available to slaves often were criminal options. It is not that this situation bore no resemblance to the one that confronted the eighteenth-century white American or English poor, but that it was one in which the power struggle frequently was stripped to its barest essentials.[26]

Unsurprisingly, in a situation where cultural hegemony was most noticeable by its absence, but where political and economic hegemony were unstintingly implemented, the cultural autonomy of both slaves and slaveowners was well established. The wealthy slaveowners accordingly used their powers to establish, as best they could, hegemonic cultural relationships with subordinate classes other than slaves, while politically and economically controlling and exploiting all subordinate classes, including slaves, in a virtuoso performance that deftly took into account the various characteristics of each. The slaves, on the other hand, used their cultural autonomy to build on their African past as much as ecological and political circumstances permitted.

Unrestrained by the tenets of a hegemonic morality whose values challenged the values related to criminal acts, and not curbed by fears or guilt that their criminal behavior resulted in their being a dangerous class to themselves, slaves followed both utilitarian and traditional means to help them choose the particular criminal acts that would enable them to achieve their personal goals and to challenge the power and authority of masters. Utilitarian factors, normally, are relatively easy for the contemporary investigator to fathom, but traditional reasons are more difficult to come by for they include African-derived customs and values. In any case, colonial slaves, rather than having to challenge or change a hegemonic morality of masters by establishing a countermorality largely based on everyday forms of criminality, had to choose and justify such criminal behavior in accordance with its utility and the slaves' African and African American values and codes of behavior.[27]

For instance, Sambo chose to administer a harmful, mind-bending drug, "touck," to a woman who was known to haze her slaves and who intended to purchase Sambo's daughter. His choice of such a drug or poison was grounded in African religious practices that integrated the use of magical, religious rituals with a highly sophisticated understanding and application of herbal "medicines." The surreptitiousness of the act, on the other hand, undoubtedly served Sambo's and his daughter's circumstances better than did direct and open violence, which almost certainly would have led to his death and to the severe punishment of his daughter. Verbal persuasion surely was beyond Sambo's power, and running off with his daughter probably was even less likely to succeed and more dangerous for his daughter than relying on his herbal and magical powers.

Sambo's goal, then, was to use these African-derived powers, acquired by him as a medicine man, to protect his daughter from the machinations of a woman (sorceress?) who was known for her mistreatment of slaves and who wished to purchase Sambo's daughter. Following the proper rituals, no doubt, he prepared and helped to administer to Mary Nash the potion or "poison" known as "touck." The conjuration supposedly would transform her mind-set and personality so that she would not purchase his daughter. It would also induce Nash to cease abusing her slaves, an outcome sought by Sambo's collaborator, David, a slave owned by Nash. As we know, they failed. David turned state's evidence, and Sambo was eventually castrated.[28] But slaves in colonial North Carolina and elsewhere continued to use poison or other forms of resistance despite severe punishments.

Although everyday forms of slave resistance normally involved little or no effective organization or overt coordination, the need for organization frequently was replaced by traditional or commonly held folk beliefs that gave to individual, unorganized, and uncoordinated actions a degree of communal comprehension and thereby political import. Sambo's actions undoubtedly resonated in the slave quarters, for slaves appreciated the value of medicine men and the use of touck to defend themselves against the aggressions or "sorcery" of whites.[29] They also doubtlessly knew that such actions hardly were considered base or criminal in Africa, but rather were a proper means of protection against evil. In this last, they did not differ from most other cultures that normally condone the use of destructive acts to defend oneself, one's family, and one's community or society from harm. Yet slave practices that threatened whites or their authority, whatever the derivation of such behavior, were inevitably defined by the ruling class as criminal.

Other African forms of resistance beyond the use of herbs and conjuration informed the criminal resistance patterns of slaves in the Americas. To detail this continuum, however, requires an intense investigation of the actual crimes of resistance traditionally practiced by oppressed groups in Africa. There is a dearth of evidence available to complete such a task since few Africanists have investigated the story, particularly for Africa before European conquests. Such studies that have been completed suggest that African peasants used banditry, theft, and murder to confront their precolonialist African exploiters as well as the Europeans and their surrogates or allies who followed. Thus Africans in the diaspora did not present a tabula rasa on which the experiences of slavery simply impressed themselves to enable the slaves to construct their resistance techniques. Rather, similar to other social and cultural development in the Americas, traditional African approaches to resistance informed slaves as to how they might respond to specific oppressions. Unfortunately, the precise ways in which these transferals occurred, except when slaves used African techniques of herbalism and witchcraft, remain obscured by the dearth of records and studies of African criminality.[30]

The preceding pages of this chapter have, among other things, served as a prelude and conceptual model to understand how and why everyday forms of criminality came to play *the dominant role* in slave resistance in the mainland colonies. With this in place, we may now more effectively discuss the details of criminality in colonial North Carolina. This discussion is divided into two parts. All forms of criminal resistance but running away are covered in the remainder of this chapter; the "crime of stealing oneself" will be considered in Chapter 5.

It is often difficult, at times impossible, to quantify certain aspects of slave criminality. Many "crimes" remained uncovered or if known went unrecorded. This was especially true of in-house "crimes" such as truancy, foot-dragging, work slowdowns, false compliance, feigned illness or ignorance, poor or sloppy work, sabotage, and theft. Indeed, only major crimes such as murder and attempted murder, rape, house burning, outlawry, the use of "poison," or major thefts of goods from whites other than the slaves' owners were routinely recorded. Even among these offenses, documentation is more readily available for cases resulting in capital punishment or castration than corporal punishments.

Nonetheless, it is still necessary to use the only available precise figures, those involving major offenses, to attempt to discern temporal trends in slave crime in North Carolina. Doing so, for instance, will provide the best clue as to whether slave crime was simply a manifestation of demography, or whether variables such as serious changes in the way slave offenders were punished or the occurrence of major political crises before the American Revolution discernibly affected how often slaves committed serious crimes.[31] Statistics reveal that the actual number of slaves executed or castrated within four time periods—1748–54 (13), 1755–58 (14), 1759–64 (28), 1765–72 (60)—corresponds almost exactly with the ratios one would calculate in accordance with population estimates for each of these periods: 14.9, 13.9, 27.7, 58.4 (see Figure 1). Thus neither changes in punishments nor political crises among whites during these years had perceptible effects on the incidence of major slave crimes.[32] Rather, slave criminal behavior remained constant, increasing in accordance with population growth.

Statistical breakdowns of the incidence of specific major slave crimes is made problematic by the difficulty of collecting data for slave thefts. A rough attempt is nonetheless made to extrapolate for the missing data in Table 4.1, yet the estimate for such slave thefts probably remains too low. In any case, data used to construct this table include all recorded executed and castrated slaves, those killed peremptorily by the authorities in accordance with statutory law, and all slaves sentenced by *slave courts* to other forms of corporal punishment. Table 4.1 reveals that slaves executed for murder or attempted murder equaled 25.6 percent of the slaves punished for crimes delineated in the records; another 3.3 percent were executed for rape and 10 percent for preparing and using "poison." Slaves convicted of crimes against property included the 30 percent punished for major thefts and the 8.9 percent for hog stealing. A total of 14.4 percent of slave "criminals" either were killed by the authorities without trial in accordance with statutory law or were outlawed slaves who committed suicide to avoid the grisly deaths they would have been subjected to after capture. The remaining 7.7 percent probably were slaves who, for the most part, were convicted for crimes against property (see Table 4.1).[33]

Except for Lettice, a "Negro Girl" who was convicted and executed for "murder" by a slave court in Perquimans County during February 1763, only adult slaves were tried by slave courts or were outlawed and either killed by the

Figure 1. Dates When Slaves Were Executed or Castrated, Delineated According to Time Periods

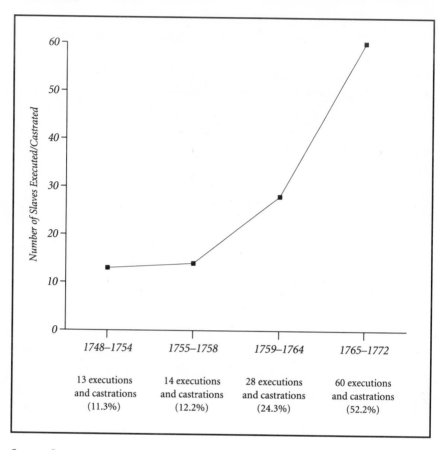

1748–1754	1755–1758	1759–1764	1765–1772
13 executions and castrations (11.3%)	14 executions and castrations (12.2%)	28 executions and castrations (24.3%)	60 executions and castrations (52.2%)

Sources: See note 18.

authorities or committed suicide during the years 1748–72. In addition, they were overwhelmingly male: 79 male slaves were executed, 15 were castrated, and 14 were subjected to other types of corporal punishment, or 90.7 percent of the total, with only 10 females executed and one whipped by court order. Among the slaves who perpetrated major crimes, however, males and females committed violent crimes with similarly proportionate frequency. Thus, among slaves whose crimes are listed in the records, 4 out of 8 executed female slaves were convicted of murder or murder-related crimes, and 25 out of 49 castrated or executed male slaves were convicted of such crimes.[34] Insufficient data prevent a determination of the geographic origins of the slaves who committed these crimes.[35]

Perhaps fairly reliable estimates, however, may be obtained about the occupations of the slaves punished for crimes in colonial North Carolina. It is reasonable to assume, since compensations played such a significant role in slave trials and punishments, that the occupations of these slaves would be listed to justify the evaluation of each slave. Following this logic, we have run across only 2 artisans and 1 domestic among the 130 slaves punished for crimes during the years 1748–72. Close to 98 percent of these slaves, therefore, possibly were field hands. If true, this may be explained by the comparative reluctance of both artisans and domestics to commit felonious crimes because of their preferred position in slave society and the hazardous nature of such criminality. They understood that their chances of escape after committing a major crime were remote and that apprehension invariably meant a severe punishment, most often, death. Field hands, however, were less inhibited by close contact with and knowledge of whites, and they were not held back by the fear of losing a superior social and economic situation. Because they also could not appeal to their owners as effectively as artisans or domestics for a redress of grievances, they were driven more often to the point of desperation. As a result, field hands were probably more prone than other slaves to commit whatever crime best served their immediate needs.[36]

Nearly one-quarter of the convicted slave felons (28 out of 115) operated in collaboration with others. Twelve out of the 29 slaves convicted of murder or murder-related crimes committed such crimes in groups of two or more, and 6 out of the 17 slaves who were sentenced to corporal punishments other than castration also collaborated. Of these, 2 stole sundry items and 2 stole a hog. The crimes committed by the other 2 slaves, who were women, are unknown. Last, 2 out of the 10 slaves executed or castrated for theft had acted together with 2 other slaves who managed to escape and thus evaded conviction.[37] A review of such collaboration is highly suggestive. First, and almost by definition, slaves intelligently planned their crimes and implemented them with resourcefulness and, at times, ruthlessness. Second, female slaves worked together in disproportionate numbers: 36.4 percent of the major crimes committed by females involved 2 or more collaborators, whereas 28.4 percent of the males leagued together. Third, collaborators from different plantations often directed their criminal activities not only against their owners, but also against the persons or property of other whites. In doing so they demonstrated their knowledge of the countryside and frequently their skill in handling boats and horses. And fourth, they recruited other slaves to aid them to avoid capture and to further their efforts.

Slave collaborators included the five slaves, three of them females, who murdered Henry Ormond. Four were owned by Ormond, and one lived on a nearby plantation owned by a relative. In another previously cited case, Sambo and David, who also lived on neighboring plantations, conspired in 1761 to poison David's mistress. In addition, Tom and Prymus, owned respectively by John Oliver and John Benners, conspired in 1761 to poison various slaves and actually poisoned one of them, Toby, who was owned by yet another master, Joseph Bell. Tom and Prymus's motives are not recorded, but their activities undoubtedly seriously disrupted at least three plantations and probably others. Both slaves were castrated; Prymus survived, but Tom died as a result of the savage punishment. In 1768 Robin, Jack, and Jemmy—all from the same plantation—were executed for murdering an unnamed victim, probably their Northampton County owner, Samuel Thomas. That same year two slaves in Bute County, Ned owned by John Thornton and Daniel owned by William Williamson, were hanged for poisoning Daniel's master.[38]

A capital case concerning slaves who collaborated in the theft of property involved Stephen, a slave owned by William Sparrel of Virginia, and Jack, a North Carolina slave owned by Edward Howeall. The pair broke into and burglarized several stores in Beaufort County on 27 and 28 November 1748. Prior to this, Jack had helped Stephen break out of jail at Bath Town by giving him "a piece of iron about eighteen inches in length" that enabled Stephen to spring "his hand cuffs" and the padlock on the door and then to escape through a hole in the floor outside his cell. Once Stephen was outside the jail, Jack carried him—his feet still shackled—to a canoe attached to a Mr. Caita's landing. They hid out at Jack's home plantation that night and the following day. But on the night of the twenty-eighth Jack broke into a blacksmith's shop to get a file to remove Stephen's shackles. Not finding one, the two slaves went to Charles Simpson's store in Bath Town, where, using a chisel and a tomahawk, they broke into the store and then a desk in the store to steal three bottles of rum, three jack knives, and sundry items. Still lacking a file, they went to yet another store to look for one but while attempting to break in they were apprehended. Jack escaped in the canoe, but the shackled Stephen was caught. In addition to the crimes cited above, Stephen was charged with having previously stolen a mare, saddle, and bridle from Thomas Lee of Tyrrell County. Finding him guilty of all the thefts, the slave tribunal on 13 December 1748 sentenced Stephen to be hanged.[39]

A similar case involved Tom and Manger, runaway slaves owned by William Mace Sr. of Edgecombe County. In 1758 the two committed a series of break-ins, burglaries, and possibly some robberies. Mace's son, who had been searching for the runaways, found them one evening in "Mr. Tool's" slave quarters. While passing the quarters, the younger Mace had noticed a light that was "put out on a Sudden." He went to the quarters and when the slaves ran away, he shot Tom in the head, killing him. Manger, however, escaped. The county court on 29 June 1758, after taking testimony concerning the slaves' criminal activities and the manner in which Tom died, got down to the crux of the matter, Tom's worth, and recommended to the Committee of Claims that Mace be compensated £50 proclamation money for his dead slave.[40]

In three other trials dealing with slave theft, all of which resulted in corporal punishments, further reference to collaboration appears. When a Cumberland County slave court on 29 October 1764 questioned Dick, "a negro slave" owned by Patrick Francis who was charged with "robbery & the murder of Mitchell Carroll," he confessed that he was "aiding and assisting in Carrying the Goods taken out of Mr. Tracerses Store." It is not clear who Dick aided and assisted, nor is it known what else Dick said. The court appears to have absolved him of the murder charge, however, for the punishment prescribed was not death. Instead, the court ordered that Dick "shall receive one hundred Lashes on his Bare Back well laid on & be Brdnd on the right cheek with a Red hot Iron Letter T."[41]

Evidence of slave collaboration is more specific in the other two trials. In one case, two slaves were accused of burglary—Bob, owned by Margaret Vail of Craven County, and Simon, whose master was Joseph Ridgway of Pennsylvania. Bob pleaded guilty, but the court examined Simon "as an Evidence agst . . . Bob" anyway, and it was his testimony on 29 December 1764 that detailed the crime. Simon, who did not explain how he and Bob met, confirmed that the two "did break open [during] the present month John Greens store and that Bob Did take out of the store Two Pockett Books with Papers and he took some Ribbons and a Penknife." The court concluded that this evidence was not "sufficient to take the life of the prisoner" and so ordered Bob to be "whipt" 50 lashes on each of three separate days, for a total of 150 lashes. Simon, perhaps because he was from outside the province, received no special dispensation for providing the court with the details of the crime. To the contrary, his punishment was even more brutal. The court ordered that he receive the same punishment meted out to Bob but provided further that he was to have "Both of his Ears nailed to the whiping post and have them cut off and afterwards to Remain in goal until he is sent to Philadelphia and all fees paid."[42]

The second case, the trial of "a Black Slave called Tom" on 2 September 1756, points to probable collaboration among slaves and whites. Tom, who was owned by William Turner Jr., first denied that he had broken into "the dwelling house of Caleb Trueblood" and stolen "Sundry goods and cash to the Value of Twenty Pounds." Then, for some reason he changed his story and confessed to the Pasquotank County Court that "he had been present on the Plantation of Caleb Trueblood" on the night of 28 August. With him, he said, were "Ezekial Chartwright and a Slave belonging to Solomon Pool, Junr. called

Moses." Chartwright's race is not mentioned, an omission that, given the use of two names, suggests that he was not a free black but white—perhaps one of the "idle and disorderly" whites who so incensed provincial legislators by their "dissolute" behavior. According to Tom, Chartwright and Moses "Broke open the said house and Stole from thence a Desk with money and that Ezekial Chartwright," who seems to have been in charge of the theft, "gave him some money and promised him more another time." The trial record makes no further mention of Chartwright and Moses. It ends abruptly with the sentence imposed on Tom. He was to "receive fifty Lashes well laid on his bear back and his right Ear nailed to the Whipping post and one third part of his Ear . . . Cutt off."[43]

Despite these various instances of collaboration, slaves committed most of their crimes individually. Such slaves also exhibited ingenuity and often deep feelings of alienation and hostility to enslavement. Who knows the particulars behind the raging fury of Dick, owned by "John Brevard, Esq." In December 1764 Dick wounded his owner in an effort to kill him. He also sought to kill "severall Negroes the property of Said Brevard." And when "Divers Subjects . . . did attempt to take him," he armed himself and resisted them until subdued. Dick was hanged, and his head was "chopped off and set up at the Forks of the Road that Leads to George Davison's as an example etc.—." To the slaves, the court rendered a grisly admonition; to the master, compensation for his executed slave amounted to £35 proclamation money.[44]

Such typically savage punishments did not end the needs or stem the fury, frustration, and desperation that kindled slave crime. It was indeed like a small but protracted war, albeit one in which whites, intent on regulating and exploiting their chattels, controlled the guns and also the mechanisms of power. Unequal as the contest was, whites hardly came through unscathed. Many were murdered, assaulted, robbed, burgled, or had their houses burned. They paid a price for their continued aggressions on blacks.

Thus Cain was executed for "feloniously shooting and killing John Green Senr" in Bladen County in 1749. Also in Bladen Cato was executed in 1753 for attacking Margaret Thompson with a knife "To the Great Danger of her Life." Peter was "executed for committing a rape" in Johnston County in 1758. Morrise was burned alive for murder in Duplin County in 1762, the same year that Cesar was executed for the murder of his master in Bertie County. Lettice, a "Negro Girl," was executed in 1763 for murder in Perquimans County. In 1764 Dick of Anson County was hanged for poisoning a slave on another plantation and Isaac was castrated and executed for house burning in Chowan County. The next year Pompey was hanged for attempting to murder his master Richard Yates of Hertford County "by Seiring, Cutting and Wounding him etc."

Afterward Pompey's "head . . . [was] severed from his Body, and Stuck up on a Stake Below the Cross Road at Mr. Ramsays'" as an example. Another Cato was charged in 1766 with "feloniously ravishing and carnally knowing a certain Elizabeth Hallow." Found guilty, he was sentenced to be "fastened to a stake there burnt untill he is dead." In the same year Rose was executed for burning a house in Halifax County. In 1767 Quash was hanged in Chowan County for murdering a slave, London, on another plantation; Dick was executed in Dobbs County for murder; Simon of Duplin County was put to death for the murder of Lewis Bell, a neighboring plantation owner; and Bacchus was executed for rape in Bertie County. Jonny and Quamino of New Hanover County were both charged in 1768 with robbing several people. Found guilty, they were hanged and decapitated—their heads being displayed at points near Wilmington. That same year Jack was also hanged for robbing several persons in New Hanover County.[45]

Will murdered both his master, Bryant Lee, and Lee's wife Mary in New Hanover County in 1768. For this he was hanged "alive in a Gibbet at the Gallows near Wilmington." The same year that Will agonized in his slow, torturous death, seven other slaves were put to death by the hangman's rope: Harry, Jemmy, and Isaac in Edenton, Chowan County; Jack and another Jemmy in Northampton County; and Ned and Daniel in Bute County. The following year, Jack was executed in New Hanover County, and Toney, also of New Hanover, was hanged for robbing his master, Francis Clayton. In 1769 Mrs. Elizabeth Blaning's slave, Will, very likely was murdered but perhaps committed suicide while in the Bladen County jail because of a supposed design to poison his mistress. Cuff, also in 1769, was hanged for poisoning and killing his owner, Benjamin Ward of Onslow County. During 1770 Ceasar, a Virginia slave, killed James Bond of Chowan County. He, too, was hanged. George, found guilty of raping Jane Rynchy, was hanged and his severed head "Stuck up at the Forks of the Road." And the next year Scip of Craven County was hanged for burglarizing the house of Mary Worsley and threatening her life. His master, James Coor, received £80 proclamation money in compensation.[46] It was indeed like a war—unfair as the odds may have been.

Although we have discussed slave theft in a number of different contexts, we have largely ignored minor thefts. Both minor and major thefts, however, should receive greater attention. This is true not only because thefts frequently occurred—as was also the case with minor crimes such as foot-dragging, work slowdowns, false compliance, feigned illness or ignorance, poor or sloppy work, tool breaking, and the abuse of livestock—but also because theft offered the most direct challenge to the ruling class's control over the distributive process and its power to define proper class relations.[47]

Attesting both to the frequency and the seriousness of theft are the comments by contemporary observers already cited plus the number of sugges-
tively phrased laws and ordinances passed in the province and towns.[48] Some
of the ordinances and statutes tried to deal with illegal trading between slaves
and whites, white-black criminal collusion being one of the ruling class's abiding fears. For example, the slave and servant code of 1741 forbade any freeman
to "buy, sell, trade, barter or borrow any Commodities . . . with, to or from any
Apprentice or Servant, . . . or with any slave . . . without the consent of the
Master, Mistress, or Owner" of such unfree persons on penalty of fines equal to
three times the value of the items traded (paid to the public) plus £6 proclamation money (paid to the owner of the unfree person traded with). If the
freeman could not pay these fines, he or she was to be sold by the county court
as a servant "for the same." Another clause of the same law stated that servants
who "imbezzel, purloin, willfully waste or shall trade, sell or barter" any property of their master or mistress were subject for each conviction to serve their
owners added time to their indentures equal to what the county court "shall
think reasonable."[49] In the case of the slaves, either the owners punished them
privately or they were tried and sentenced by the town commissioners or the
slave tribunals of the county. Capital punishment might result from the last
instance.

These clauses, then, dealt with the collateral questions of theft of goods by
slaves and servants and trading between unfree persons and free whites. The
latter was viewed as both a result and a cause of slave theft, hence the statutory
linking of slave trade and slave theft.

Town ordinances are a considerably richer source than provincial statutes
for reconstructing upper-class attempts to limit the capacity of slaves to trade
with whites. This is true because such transactions were most common in
towns, where markets, fairs, and traffic in goods were relatively significant.
Thus in 1765 the town of Wilmington passed an elaborate ordinance "for the
better regulation of Negroes and other slaves" that included extensive provisions to prevent all slaves from participating in commercial activities in the
town except those who were given a ticket written and signed by their masters
granting them the right to sell, purchase, or barter in the town markets. The
ticket was to include "the name of such slave or slaves, and to whom belonging
or under whose care or direction, together with the quality and quantity of
such provision or other effects sent by the said slave or slaves to Market." The
goods offered for sale by slaves who were discovered trading without a ticket
were to be confiscated and sold at public auction to the highest bidder. Moreover, free persons convicted of dealing with slaves without tickets were to be

fined £1.15.0 "for each and every such offense." Freemen unable to pay these fines were to be placed in the stocks for a maximum of six hours.[50]

Partially to prevent slaves from stealing and dealing on the black market, the town in the same year tightened ordinances governing both the hiring out of slaves and the practice of town slaves living apart from their masters. The 1765 ordinance prohibited masters from allowing any slave to hire himself or herself out for more than one day at a time. Masters had to give slaves who hired themselves out by the day tickets specifying the terms of hire, and employers who hired slaves without these tickets were subject to prohibitive fines. The ordinance also attempted to prevent slaves from receiving financial benefits from the hiring-out system. Moreover, under pain of a fine of £1.15.0 per offense, the ordinance prohibited any freeman from allowing a slave (except those imported for sale) to live in a residence the freeman controlled other than "the House, Outhouse or Tenement belonging to or in which the Master, Mistress or overseer of such slave or slaves generally live or reside when in Wilmington."[51]

These ordinances were not completely successful, as the passage of further legislation demonstrates. An act dated 22 January 1772 stated that all slaves who lived in houses separate from those of their owners had to leave such houses by 1 March or be subject to thirty-nine lashes on the bare back at the public whipping post. Whites who permitted slaves to continue living in such houses were to be fined five shillings for each day the slaves remained after 1 March. On the same day ordinances similar to those of 1765 were passed to prevent slaves from selling, purchasing, or bartering in the town markets and to limit the independence of hired-out slaves. The ordinances were tightened further in July 1772, when all slaves were prohibited from having commercial dealings with one another; even slaves with tickets were prohibited from "Trading or Traficking" at stands in the town streets. Thus all commercial dealings among slaves in the town were prohibited under penalty of thirty-nine lashes for each offense.[52]

Extensive Wilmington town records between 11 June 1772 and 8 November 1774 enable us to trace the number of slaves and freemen prosecuted for illicit trading. These prosecutions undoubtedly reveal only the tip of the iceberg of such illegal contacts. Within these dates 10 white persons in Wilmington were charged with illicitly selling rum to slaves; of these, 8 were found guilty. Fourteen slaves were involved in these charges, and 14 were found guilty. At the same time, 14 whites, 3 white-owned companies, and 1 free black were charged with illegally "trafficking" with slaves. Of these, 5 were found guilty, 4 were declared innocent, and the disposition of 8 cases (including those of the companies and the free black) is not known. Charged for the same illicit dealings were at least 18 slaves, of whom 4 were acquitted and 6 were found guilty. The disposition of 8 of the cases is unknown.[53]

Other provincial laws that dealt with theft only incidentally referred to slaves. In 1715, for example, the Assembly passed an act that dealt with the theft of "Boats, Canoes, and Pettiaguas from landings, or elsewhere." Calling such larcenies "so usual and common" as to cause considerable inconvenience to owners, the statute, though not primarily aiming at slaves, did specify punishments for slave offenders of up to twenty lashes unless their owners paid a fine of forty shillings (old tenor). If this suggests that some anxiety existed among masters that slaves might use stolen boats to escape, the anxiety persisted, for a law of 1741 raised to thirty-nine lashes the maximum punishment for slaves of masters who refused to pay a twenty-shilling (proclamation money) fine.[54] As we shall see, advertisements for runaways occasionally confirm that slaves stole river craft in their efforts to flee.[55]

Lawmakers were even more concerned about slaves stealing cattle and hogs. An act passed in 1741 moans that many "Wicked Men," who were "Too lazy to get their Living by honest Labour," made it "their Business to ride in the Woods and steal Cattle and Hogs, and alter and deface the Marks and Brands of others, and mismark and misbrand Horses, Cattle and Hogs, not marked or branded." It further complains that the "common Custom . . . of killing . . . Cattle and Hogs in the Woods" provided "great opportunities . . . to steal the Cattle and Hogs of other People." The list of villains includes slaves, and the harshness of the penalties imposed on "any Negro, Indian, or Mulatto slave" who killed or stole or misbranded or mismarked a horse, cow, or hog indicates that the lawmakers believed that slaves had engaged in such practices for some time. Convicted slaves were to "suffer both . . . Ears to be Cut off, and be publickly whipt" for a first offense and to "suffer death" for a second offense.[56]

A belief that slaves frequently stole livestock also appears to explain the inclusion in the colony's 1741 revised slave code of a clause that flatly barred slaves from owning hogs, cattle, or horses. Within six months "all Horses, Cattle and Hogs that . . . belong to any Slave, or [have] any Slave's Mark" were to be seized and sold to the benefit of the church wardens in the parish.[57] Hog killing and stealing, despite these laws, was a crime that only occasionally was punished publicly. Four separate cases appear in the records surveyed, hardly a dramatic number, and certainly not one that accurately reflects the incidence of such crimes, which were normally punished on plantations by the owners. Yet three of the cases tried before slave courts are worth reviewing as they provide a variety of insights into slave behavior, including the apparent need of slaves to supplement their diets through theft.

On 13 February 1748, seven years after the Assembly first specifically linked slaves to the problem of livestock theft, a Craven County court tried "a Certain Negro Man a Slave belonging to Roger Moore Esqr. named Cato" who had been charged with "Hog Stealing, etc." Asked whether or not he was guilty, Cato related the following. He had been "Grinding at the Mill" when "some sows" approached and began to eat corn. He took an "ax in his hands & threw it at him which killed the said Hog so he dresd it & put it up." The court then asked Cato if he thought the hog belonged to his mistress, and Cato said he thought so. A witness, Benjamin Brockett, testified, but the trial record does not indicate what he said. Apparently it did not help Cato's cause, for after a two-hour recess the court judged Cato guilty and ordered the sheriff to "take the said negro Cato to the Public Whipping Post & there to nail his Ears to the said Post & then cut off them." In addition, as the law provided, Cato was to be whipped. The court settled on forty lashes as an appropriate figure. Once this punishment had been meted out, Cato was to be returned to the jail until all fees had been paid. Then he was to be "delivered to his Owner."[58]

Nine years later, on 22 March 1757, two Pasquotank slaves went on trial for collaborating in the same offense. In this instance the two were owned by different masters: Moses by Sollomon Pool Jr. and "Negro Tom" by Ann Peggs, "Daughter of John Peggs Deceased." Moses and Tom were accused of "feloniously Killing and Stealing a Hogg belonging to Thomas Nicholson of [adjoining] Perquimans county." Under questioning, both slaves confessed. Tom admitted that he had "killed the Hog . . . and did bear him away." Moses's testimony, at least as recorded, was more extensive and more revealing, for it outlined the specific manner in which the two had caught and killed Nicholson's hog. Moses explained that "he went with Negro Tom to the Hogg pen of Mr. Nicholson's and that Negro Tom Throw'd corn on an old tree and whilst the Hogg was Eating the corn . . . Negro Tom killed the Hogg . . . and then Tom carreyed the Hog away with him." Although Moses portrayed himself as merely having accompanied Tom on this escapade, the court found both slaves guilty and ordered punishments that varied for the two as well as departed somewhat from those specified by the law of 1741. Tom was to be immediately taken to the whipping post and have his right ear nailed to it and then cut off. Then he was to receive twenty lashes. For his part in the crime, Moses was to be whipped fifty times.[59]

A third case occurred in Craven County on 12 October 1763. Bob, owned by the estate of William Brice, denied his guilt, but white witnesses convinced the court otherwise. John Smith related that when he had visited John Prinder's house, he saw a hog's head with "John Dunns mark" on it "brought out of the Prisoners wifes house." And James Newall swore that while visiting Captain

Prinder's house "he heard a hogg squile," whereupon "he took a gun and went toward where the hogg squiled and mett with the Prisoner in his wifes Potato Patch with an Ax in his hand." On Monday, Newall said, he "found a hoggs head in the Prisoners wifes house on a Shelf covered with a Bason." Bob apparently did not testify, but John Norwood related the slave's side of the story. Norwood told the court that on Monday morning Bob had come to him to say that "on that morning as he was going home he saw a fire and went towards it and saw a negroe at it." The Negro, according to Bob, "ran off . . . into a swamp," and when Bob approached he "found a Bagg of Shott and a hoggs head and part of a hoggs Shoulder at the fire." He took the shot to Norwood, to whom he may have been hired out, "and left the head at his wifes house." Perhaps the court found Bob's explanation plausible, for it ordered him taken to the public whipping post immediately and lashed "only" twenty-five times, a punishment considerably less severe than that called for by law.[60]

Many slaves chose escape as their method of alleviating their suffering, serving their interests and needs, and challenging the authority and power of their owners. We will discuss these slaves in detail in the next chapter.

5

"Criminal" Resistance Patterns, II

Slave Runaways

Running away represented perhaps the most significant of slave crimes. When slaves "stole themselves," they dramatically challenged the controls that masters had carefully crafted to regulate the lives, labor, and destinies of their human property. Slaves understood this even though they were threatened, constrained, and battered psychologically and physically and however different their individual reasons for flight might be. Running away, then, must be viewed as an act of resistance with significant political implications.[1] Masters recognized this in their obsessive reference to the problem in their laws, and slaves underscored it by their frequent escapes.[2]

Although the political implications of running away had significant ramifications among slaves throughout the Americas, variations in geography, demography, and the social and psychological makeup of individual slave populations affected specific runaway patterns. Some scholars have analyzed such factors for other mainland British colonies; none has done so for pre-Revolutionary North Carolina.[3] Our research attempts to fill part of this gap by examining the province's slave runaways for the years 1748–75. It compares runaways in North Carolina with those from neighboring Virginia and South Carolina both to clarify the North Carolina story and to buttress our statistics with those derived from more substantial samples.

Slaves who ran off to or formed maroon settlements best illustrate the importance of setting and the political dimensions of running away. At times these slaves settled among Indians or sought the security offered by other European powers such as the Spanish in Florida. Closer to both the Spanish and the Indians in Florida than were the slaves of North Carolina or Virginia, many slaves in South Carolina fled successfully southward to marronage, although not without numerous confrontations with whites. These possibilities and tensions, together with favorable demographic circumstances, tended to make slaves in South Carolina particularly receptive to open revolt. The Stono Rebellion of 1739 must be considered in this context.[4] North Carolina's less numerous and more sparsely settled slaves, on the other hand, had fewer chances to run off as maroons to the west among the unpredictable, often hostile, Cherokee.[5] Yet maroons from North Carolina did make their way to the Great Dismal Swamp, stretching southward from Norfolk, Virginia, to Edenton, Chowan County, in the Albemarle Sound region of North Carolina, which was an ideal hideout. Despite this, marronage remained less important in North Carolina than in South Carolina, and, conversely, this helped minimize the conditions necessary to spark a revolt.[6]

A dearth of records in North Carolina makes it difficult to understand why and how frequently its slaves actually ran off, their goals, destinations, choice of time, and the manner in which they escaped from slavery—individually, collaboratively, or as maroons. Quantification is especially problematic for maroons who only occasionally are noted in surviving documents. Some individual or group runaways certainly must have attempted to settle in maroon communities.

Newspapers are the richest source of information on runaways in every colony. Unfortunately, the surviving issues of newspapers in colonial North Carolina are scattered unevenly across the years, are not properly representative of the several regions in the province, and account for under 7 percent of the issues published between 1748 and 1775.[7] The practices followed by masters to recapture their runaways compound the problem. First, owners living closest to where the existing newspapers were published were most likely to advertise.[8] Second, owners tended to advertise as a last resort except when they lived near a newspaper and thought that their runaways were lurking about the neighborhood. Generally, owners relied first on their own devices and the services of the county courts to retrieve runaways.[9] Jacob Wilkinson of Wilmington typified this approach. In November 1766 he wrote Colonel Alexander McAllister that his "Negro Fellow Jack" had run off and was probably headed for Cumberland County. Wilkinson, who had purchased Jack there, urged McAllister to "Scheame so as to have him apprehended" and promised to pay the costs involved.[10] For these reasons it is impossible to extrapolate from the 134 cited runaways, just a small portion of the actual total, to determine approximately how many slaves actually ran off during this period.

Data deficiencies also prevent a quantitative determination of the effects of the growing Revolutionary crisis on runaway patterns in the colony. Because 30 percent of the runaways between 1748 and 1775 escaped during the last three years of the survey, for instance, it might be concluded that the crisis prompted slaves to run off in greater numbers. A more plausible explanation is that 37 percent of the extant North Carolina newspapers date from these same three years, 1773–75.[11]

Whatever diachronic trends actually occurred, the paucity of available data also hinders a social and psychological description of the runaways. The most detailed information appears in formal outlaw notices for 10 runaways and in advertisements placed by masters of 61 runaways. Newspaper notices for 39 captured fugitives and 1 advertisement placed by a sheriff about an escape contain much less information but are more detailed than the brief references to 23 other runaways that appear in county court minutes, records of the colony's Committee of Claims, private correspondence, an inventory, and a newspaper story.

Information most often included in these diverse sources concerns readily observable characteristics—sex, ability to speak English, and age, in that order. Masters and captors alike also noted traits such as family ties, scars, height, color, and demeanor and often commented in varying detail on motives for flight and possible destinations. Occupations were listed when they distinguished particular runaways from others and hence served as important clues to identification.[12] Occasionally, bits of detail about the runaways' perspectives also appear in these sources.

At times the notices cite African origins, but most often one must infer African nativity from a combination of characteristics such as scarification and the degree of facility in English. Masters noted origins other than African only when that information might lead to capture. For instance, a Virginia-raised slave might be thought to be headed for his home plantation. The origins of less than half of the runaways could be learned.[13]

Despite the limitations of the data, it is likely that the samples fairly accurately reflect for the years 1748 to 1775 the runaways' actual ages, sex distribution, occupations, and geographic origins. The ages of North Carolina runaways correspond with the pattern in other colonies: they were disproportionately young adults, twenty to thirty-five years of age. Forty-four (62 percent) of North Carolina's runaways were in this age category, although this population group comprised only about 30 percent of the colony's slave population. Slaves thirty-six and older ran away slightly more frequently than their percentage of the population would indicate: 24 percent of the runaways and 20 percent of the colony's slave population. At the other extreme, slaves under twenty comprised about 50 percent of the slave population but only 14 percent of runaways in North Carolina (see Table 5.1).[14]

The vast majority of slave runaways in North Carolina, 89 percent, were males. This finding parallels Lathan A. Windley's and Gerald W. Mullin's estimates for Virginia, but the computations of Windley, Philip D. Morgan, and Daniel C. Littlefield for males in South Carolina range from 7 to 11 percentage points less than was the case in the two more northern provinces (see Table 5.2). Despite these differences, and because male preponderance among runaways is far greater than sex ratios would suggest in all the surveyed colonies, other factors more substantially explain this disparity. Indeed, South Carolina with the highest sex ratios also had the lowest discrepancy between male and female runaways.[15]

Familial considerations influenced many runaway slaves, inducing some to flee in order to join spouses, families, or prospective mates. The death of an owner or a direct sale of slaves, both of which often led to the separation of spouses or, more likely, children from parents, significantly affected slave runaway patterns. The fact that over a third of the skilled slaves and 17 percent of the field-hand runaways had been owned by more than one master suggests the impact of such uprootings.[16]

Many owners acknowledged that slaves ran off to be with mates or families.[17] George Moore advised readers of the *Virginia Gazette*, for example, that Bristol, a field hand, "is supposed to have made his way for *Richmond* county, in VIRGINIA, where he has three brothers, whom the subscriber sold to Col. Tayloe, one of his Majesty's Council." Jacob Wilkinson of New Hanover wrote a friend in Cumberland County that his field hand, Jack, whom he had recently purchased, was "undoubtedly" headed in that direction, as "I was told When I bought him that he was about getting a molatto wench of Jeff Williams for a Wife." Five other North Carolina field hands fled, their masters indicated, chiefly for family reasons.[18] Another seventeen North Carolina field hands ran off as representatives of familial groups: three couples, a father and son, and two families consisting of four and five members respectively. Among field hands, therefore, at least one-fifth of the slaves who ran away probably did so to maintain family relationships. Yet this already high figure is clearly an underestimate. Given the masters' desire to pinpoint where the runaways might be, it was logical for them simply to designate where the slaves' previous owners lived without including information about the slaves' families. This practice apparently explains why, in the small available sample for nonfield slaves, advertisements for six of these runaways (35 percent of the sample) list information about the slaves' previous owners; in only one instance involving a domestic did the master imply that familial ties might have motivated flight.[19]

The importance of marriage and the family to slaves and the consequent large number of slaves who ran away to rejoin spouses and kin explain much of the predominance of males among runaways. Because husbands and fathers usually were the ones separated from their families, it was they who most often ran off to be reunited with wives and kin. The converse was also true; marital and familial obligations limited the number of female slaves who ran away.

Males also ran away in larger numbers because their experiences had tended to enhance their knowledge of the countryside, social sophistication, and marketable skills to a greater extent than was the case among females. Males probably were hired out more frequently, and only males worked on the roads and were boatmen, ferrymen, guides, porters, and teamsters. Particular job skills, especially artisanal, often made it easier for males to be hired as "free laborers" than for females, who, on the average, lacked such skills. Male field hands could even pass more readily as free blacks because employers were more inclined to hire them than female hands.

Although North Carolina's small runaway sample makes suspect an analysis of the frequency distribution of various occupations among the colony's runaways, our findings seem plausible when compared with those for colonies for which larger samples have been compiled. Field hands in North Carolina ran away in numbers slightly less than their proportion of the colony's slave population would suggest, comprising about 87 percent of the runaways and perhaps 90 percent of the slave population (see Tables 5.3–5.4). Although some of the sex-specific details in the two colonies differ, these figures closely parallel what occurred in South Carolina, where field slaves ran away in numbers about 1.5 percent less than one would predict from their proportion of the slave population (see Tables 5.5–5.6). Field slaves in the Carolinas fled in such large numbers, despite slender chances of success, perhaps because they were less cognizant of the full scope of white power, had fewer material advantages to lose than skilled slaves, and had fewer lawful alternatives to relieve harsh circumstances. Perhaps of greater significance, large numbers of field hands were Africans, who tended to run off with disproportionate frequency.

Relatively few domestics ran off in North Carolina, comprising 0.8 percent of the colony's runaways and 3.7 percent of the slave population. This ratio of about 1 to 5 is suspect because of the especially small sample involved. A much more substantial sample for South Carolina reveals that domestics ran away roughly in proportion to their percentage of that colony's slave population. Perhaps, then, too much should not be made of the discrepancy revealed by statistics about North Carolina.

It is essential that a sex-specific analysis be used for artisans because almost all were males, and it was preponderantly male slaves who ran off. In North Carolina, male artisans fled in slightly greater numbers (just under 11 percent of the male runaways) than their proportion of the male slave population (10 percent). A substantially smaller percentage ran off in South Carolina: there they totaled about 8 percent of the male runaways but 12.3 percent of the colony's male slave population.

Neither of these findings substantiate Gerald W. Mullin's arguments that acculturated slaves, especially those with skills, chose to flee in disproportionately large numbers because of greater chances of escaping successfully. Moreover, it is questionable whether his figures for Virginia's artisans and domestics, equaling respectively 14.8 and 7.8 percent of the slaves who ran away during the period 1736–1801 (see Table 5.7), actually support his contentions, for he does not estimate the size of the two groups in the colony's slave population. Indeed, given Virginia's comparative economic maturity and the fact that Mullin calculates occupational patterns for runaway male slaves only, it is quite possible that his reckoning for at least the runaway artisans is congruent with their running away in numbers commensurate with their proportion of the slave population. Such a conclusion is less likely for domestics who ran off; it is doubtful that they comprised as much as 8 percent of the male slave population.

An investigation of watermen who fled slavery adds to the element of doubt. North Carolina's statistics are again suspect because of the small sample. Since watermen were males, a sex-specific analysis is once more required, with only 1.3 percent of the colony's slaves reckoned as watermen in contrast with 2.5 percent of its runaways (see Tables 5.3–5.4). Findings for South Carolina are similar: the group comprised 1.7 percent of the male slave population but 4.3 percent of the colony's runaways (see Tables 5.5–5.6). Despite the absence of comparative figures about the percentage of slaves who were watermen in Virginia, Windley's and Mullin's percentages for these runaways, 5.2 and 7.5 respectively, are sufficiently high (especially in the latter case) to suggest that watermen there also ran off in disproportionately large numbers (see Table 5.7).

Special characteristics prompted watermen to run away in large numbers and to do so with relative success. Similar to artisans and domestics, they had the advantage of being relatively acculturated, and like artisans they could sell their skills on the free labor market more readily than most other slaves. Even so, because of their preferred jobs and status, all three groups—watermen, artisans, and domestics—had more to lose than did field slaves if they ran off. Although the very knowledge of whites by skilled slaves increased their capacity to escape successfully, it could paradoxically raise their level of apprehension. Skilled slaves understood precisely the power of whites and their willingness to use it. The special talents of watermen—their boating skills and especially their geographic sophistication—mitigated against those inhibitions, prompting them to run off with uncommon frequency. Last, there is some evidence to suggest a high incidence of Africans among watermen.[20] If this was so, it would compound the probability of watermen absconding because Africans tended to run off with disproportionate frequency.

African-born slaves in the Chesapeake declined from about one-third of the adult slave population in the 1750s to one-tenth in the 1770s. In North Carolina during these years the proportion dropped from two-thirds to one-third. In South Carolina Africans constituted about 45 percent of the adult slave population in the 1760s but rose to 49.1 percent in 1775. During the years 1730–74, Windley estimates that about 31.5 percent of Virginia's runaways were Africans, suggesting a comparatively high propensity for flight. Mullin presents a considerably lower estimate, 11 percent, which perhaps can only partially be explained by the different time span he reviews, 1736–1801 (see Table 5.7). The percentage of African runaways in North Carolina between 1748 and 1775, 54.1 percent, accords with the province's larger African slave population and the relative frequency with which Africans escaped (see Table 5.8).[21] Although estimates for South Carolina vary somewhat with the investigator and the time span studied—40.4 percent to 68.5 percent for the period 1732–87—the high percentages also tend to reflect the comparatively large number of Africans in the colony's slave population and their greater propensity than creole slaves to flee (see Table 5.9).[22]

Africans, then, despite their greater difficulties in traveling in a strange land, communicating, and passing as free, still ran off in relatively large numbers because of the especially wrenching separations and traumas they had experienced. Torn from their families, friends, and communities and shipped to a foreign continent, treated abusively and as objects, sold to masters who could not understand them, often isolated within the slave community, they reacted

Newbern, February 20, 1775.

ONE HUNDRED AND TEN POUNDS REWARD.

ABSENTED themselves very early on Sun-day Morning the 19th Instant, from the House of the Subscribers, Five newly imported Slaves, (Four Men and One Woman:) Two of the Men, named Kauchee and Boohum, are Six Feet One or Two Inches high, and about 30 Years of Age; another named Ji, is near Five Feet Nine Inches high, and about 25 Years of Age, has sore Eyes; and the Fourth, named Sambo Pool, is a short well set Fellow, aged 18 Years; the Woman, named Pig Miany, is of short Stature and elderly. The Fellows were uniformly clad in coarse green Cloth Jackets, brown Cloth Trowsers, a Blanket, and red Cloth Cap; and the Wench had on an emboss'd Flannel Petticoat and brown Cloth Cloak. As they are incapable of uttering a Word of English, have been extremely well fed, and very little worked, it is surmised they have been inveigled away by some infamously principled Person, of a fairer Complexion, but darker Disposition than theirs. Whoever, therefore, secures the said Negroes for their Owners, and the Person or Persons so inveigling them, or facilitating their Escape, provided that he or they be convicted thereof, shall receive the above-mentioned Reward of One Hundred and Ten Pounds, Proclamation Money, or Forty Shillings for each of the Slaves.

EDWARD BATCHELOR & Co.

. All Masters of Vessels, Boatmen, and others plying by Water, are forbid to give them Passage at their Peril.

Advertisements for runaway slaves. In the above notice, slave dealer Edward Batchelor offers a reward for the return of five of his newly arrived African slaves, who apparently escaped at the first opportunity. Although the five soon were recaptured, two of the males, Kauchee and Boohum, shortly fled again, as indicated by Batchelor's second announcement. (*North Carolina Gazette* [New Bern], 24 February 1775, 5 May 1775) predictably. If opportunities existed, they fled. When they did, they fell back on their African sense of communality and tended to run away in groups.

One-third of the North Carolina runaways, all of them field hands, escaped in groups, and 88 percent of the group runaways whose origins are known were African.[23] The presence of so many Africans among the group runaways accounts for the fact that few of these slaves had facility in English. Among the group runaways whose linguistic abilities could be determined, half spoke some English, fully 36 percent spoke none, and only 14 percent spoke good English (see Table 5.10).

The experience of five Africans, possibly shipmates, who fled from Edward Batchelor of Craven County illustrates both the limits confronting such Africans and their determination in the face of adversity. Kauchee, Boohum, Ji, and Sambo Pool, all males, and Peg Manny, an aged female, ran off early one Sunday morning in February 1775; none spoke English. Batchelor advertised for them the following day, an unusual step but one that produced immediate results. The five managed to travel only ten miles before being captured by William Gatling of Break Creek. But matters did not end there. Two months later two of the men, Kauchee and Boohum, fled again. In the interval William Gatling had purchased Peg Manny, perhaps with the reward money, and Batchelor thought that Kauchee and Boohum would be "lurking about" Gatling's farm.[24] The runaways' fate is unknown.

Most North Carolina runaways, 67.2 percent, including eleven identified as African-born field hands, fled alone (see Table 5.10). Caesar, an Angolan, and Jack, an African of unidentified tribal origin, probably were more experienced with whites even than the other Africans who escaped individually: both had had prior owners, Caesar in South Carolina and Jack in Pennsylvania. The other Africans had been in the colony long enough to learn some English, but they undoubtedly shared with those imported more recently the distinct disadvantage of unfamiliarity with white ways. Still, the Africans used their knowledge of the natural world to good advantage, if only temporarily. A Coromantee slave owned by John Dunn of Rowan County, for example, made his way to Wilmington, more than two hundred miles to the southeast, before he was captured in August 1759. Jikowife displayed similar abilities, escaping after being captured with a "*French* musket" in Chowan County near Mattacomack Creek in June 1774. Late that August he was recaptured in Hyde County, across Albemarle Sound. Quamino, the only individual runaway who clearly spoke no English, may have had more success. Only four feet, ten inches tall, this dynamic thirty-year-old African with filed teeth and country marks fled in August 1774 with "a Collar about his Neck with Two Prongs, marked P.G. [Public Gaol], and an iron on each leg." Ten months later Henry Young of Wilmington gave up hope that Quamino would falter in his bid for freedom and placed an advertisement in the *North Carolina Gazette*.[25]

The eleven African slaves who escaped as individuals comprised only a minority of such runaways. Two-thirds of runaway slaves whose origins could be traced were born in one of the mainland colonies of British North America. Moreover, fully 98.5 percent of the sixty-five slaves who ran off individually and whose ability to speak English could be determined had some facility with the language (see Table 5.10).

The national origins and language patterns that prevailed among runaway artisans reflect how slave artificers were selected to pursue their trades and their subsequent special characteristics as slaves. Chosen from those who apparently were best equipped to learn and benefit from their experiences, slave artisans tended to be young Creoles who handled English with relative skill and quite possibly had fathers or other relatives who already were artisans.[26] Thus the records reveal that even the youngest of the skilled nonfield runaways spoke English well. Eighteen-year-old George, for instance, was so proficient with the language that William Person described him as "a very artful Fellow" who would "impose upon any Person that will credit what he says," a lesson his master must have learned firsthand. Over time the varied work experiences of such slaves, who were often hired out, and their relative freedom to move from place to place further enhanced their command of English, their knowledge of geography, and their ability to deal with whites. Along the way they sometimes picked up other skills that would facilitate escape. Thomas Boman, for instance, could "read, write, and cypher."[27]

Understanding whites, language skills, and the consequent capacity to deceive whites obviously enlarged the chances of nonfield slaves for successful escape. Yet field hands often shared such qualities. Because about 75 to 85 percent of the slaves outside the Cape Fear region lived on units of less than twenty slaves during the years 1748–75, interracial contact must have been common.[28] Field hands also were hired out, worked on road gangs, or acquired experience with whites as a result of a change of owners. These diverse experiences help to account for the differences in the patterns among individual and group runaways. Only two of the twenty-one field hands identifiable as American-born fled in groups, both of them children who ran off with their parents.[29] The other nineteen, all of whom spoke English, ran off by themselves.

Why some field hands fled alone related not only to origin or facility with English but also to how they perceived their situations. As we have seen, at least seven fled to be with mates or families. Two others, both of whom spoke good English, fled after their masters died. One headed back to his home plantation, and the other, a middle-aged male who had been hired out, was thought to be "lurking about." Two young men, also believed to be "lurking about," fled at times of peak work. Two other males went "visiting" friends or relatives.[30] But seven of the field-hand runaways set out to pass for free, a goal that must have seemed easier to achieve as an individual.

This last cluster of field-hand runaways, all but one American-born, was unique in several respects. Included were one Negro born in Virginia, a mustee woman and man, a full-blooded male Indian, and a woman born in New England.[31] Because of their distinct backgrounds and experiences, they undoubtedly confronted the prospect of passing for free in a white-dominated world with a greater self-confidence than most field hands. Each of them had social and verbal skills similar to those of all nonfield-hand runaways. Like artisans, they had a better chance of succeeding than did the bulk of field-hand runaways. Not all eluded capture, of course, but their decision to run off and the methods they used to escape reflected a rational assessment of the risks involved balanced against their needs and talents.

Artisans normally were acculturated, but along with mariners, river boatmen, and other skilled slaves who were not field hands, they also possessed highly salable expertise. Because their success in passing as free workers hinged on not calling undue attention to themselves, all sixteen artisan runaways as well as all the river boatmen and sailors ran off as individuals (see Tables 5.3 and 5.10). Although information is not available for most runaways, many artisans and sailors made use of their special abilities by seeking sanctuary in the relative anonymity of towns and at considerable distances from their homes in order to ply their trades.[32]

In puzzling over the question of why some slaves chose to flee enslavement, it is not surprising that some white North Carolinians, despite overwhelming evidence to the contrary, doubted that slaves could plot their own escapes. Edward Batchelor, the merchant in New Bern, Craven County, for instance, announced with opaque if familiar certainty that the five "newly imported" slaves who escaped from him in February 1775 had not done so on their own. "As they are incapable of muttering a word of English, have [been] extremely well fed, and very little worked," he observed, "it is surmised they have been in-vegelied away by some infamously principled Persons, of a fairer Complexion, but darker Disposition than theirs." Robert Snow of Cape Fear lacked Batche-lor's gift with words but shared his unwillingness to attribute self-motivation to slaves. When London and Bess ran off in the fall of 1755, Snow concluded that they had been "decoyed away" by a former overseer.[33] However soothing such fantasies may have been to whites, slaves almost invariably determined for themselves when they would run off, under what circumstances they would do so, and what goals they would pursue. If often goaded by anger and despair, they nonetheless attempted to evaluate rationally their options and then plot the particularities of their escape.

In the process of calculating their odds, slaves considered the examples set by other slaves as well as fleeing indentured servants and apprentices. Several slaves fled from owners who also had runaway indentured servants. For in-stance, the Rowan County Court in August 1769 ordered Paul Crosby to serve former sheriff Francis Locke for four extra years after his indenture expired "for absenting himself 2 years." Two months after Crosby's sentencing, three of Locke's slaves also fled.[34] Perhaps the only relationship between these two escapes was a shared resentment of a disliked owner. But it would be strange if the behavior of one group did not affect that of the other. Even where such clear juxtapositions are not evident, slaves undoubtedly were well aware that servants regularly fled from their masters, that in some cases they were never captured, that others—like Crosby—managed to stay out for long periods of time, and that some who were caught fled again.[35] Servants probably were similarly aware of slave escapes.

If slave runaways by their actions compounded the burden of bondage felt by other slaves and heightened a sense of the possibility of escape, slaves still fled for specific reasons. Although they regularly sought freedom for its own sake, they also fled as males or females within the context of their occupa-tional backgrounds and as the situation provided. Calculating their particular chances, some slaves ran off hoping to obtain more negotiable economic rewards for their labor. Newly imported Africans fled the terrible traumas of slavery. Many slaves escaped to reestablish marital and familial ties, others to express discontent with changes of ownership. What prompted particular slaves varied, but they constantly assessed their situation and the opportunities available to them before deciding on a course of action, for the decision to flee was not an easy one. It involved considerable risk, and though often spawned by a desire to rejoin family or friends, it also frequently demanded departure from a familiar community peopled by friends and family.

At times the brutality of enslavement could offset all other considerations. Evidence of how individual masters mistreated their slaves appears in a number of newspaper advertisements. Referring with equanimity to marks left by punishments, owners revealed the cruelty to which they subjected their human chattel. Samuel Johnston, the noted Revolutionary leader, advertised that his field hand Frank was "branded on the left Buttock with a P," and another master wrote that Bess was "branded in the breast." In such cases the assumption that this information would be useful in identifying the runaways is a revealing commentary on a system designed to strip blacks of personal dignity.[36] Nor did highly prized skilled slaves, for whom larger rewards were tendered, escape such cruelties. Riverboatman Frank's back had "frequently undergone the Discipline of the Whip," as his wealthy master Richard Quince quipped.[37]

It is nonetheless unclear whether punishment prompted flight in every case. Any number of additional reasons could spark running away, which no amount of punishment could deter. Field hand Frank was an "old Offender and a great thief," who presumably had fled before. The master of Charles specified that the brands on his cheeks "were fresh given him by the Person of whom I bought him, and not cured when he left me," raising the possibility that Charles was not only "incorrigable" but that he also fled because of a desire to return "home" to relatives and friends—however brutal his past master.[38]

Bondage also produced psychological scars. Indeed, behind the decision to flee there sometimes lay a festering frustration born of an acute sense of self-worth and knowledge of the inherent limits of slavery. None of the riverboatmen cited displayed behaviors, such as stuttering, that could be interpreted as outward signs of inner turmoil, but Thomas Boman, a blacksmith, was "slow of Speech" and Rob, a cooper, had a "flaw of speech, as if he had an impedi-. ment."[39] It is possible that these "flaws" stemmed from physiological rather than psychological reasons. Other runaways, in any case, both field hands and artisans, bore expressions such as "an ill look," which could indicate buried hostility.[40] More open was Ned, a "good sawyer and hewer, and part of a carpenter" with a "very good sense," who retained a "bold look" even after repeated brandings before he fled from James Barnes of Halifax County in April 1768.[41]

Whatever inner conflicts existed, slaves often tried to conceal their animosities. Outward appearance and behavior could be deceptive. As numerous masters learned all too well, slaves could hide their innermost thoughts behind deferential, dissembling, even stuttering masks. The "Negro Wench" Joan, for instance, had "a smiling Countenance," "outlandish" Jack "a pleasant countenance," and a slave who called himself Tom Buck "an uncommon flippant Tongue, full of Complement."[42] All were runaways.

The timing of their departure is further evidence of how slaves rationally assessed their opportunities as runaways and often carefully planned their escape. Masters did not always specify when their slaves had absconded and generally took their time placing notices. But some observations can be drawn from the pattern evident for 58 slaves for whom escape dates were given (see Table 5.11). The most popular periods for running away were the harvesting season of September–November, when 23 slaves (40 percent) fled, followed by February–April, the months during which the slack season ended and spring planting began. Seventeen slaves, or 29 percent, ran off at this time. Another 15 fled during the four months of May to August, and only three ran during the winter months of December and January. No significant variation in the timing of escape set nonfield runaways apart from field hands who fled. Most North Carolina runaways thus timed their departure to avoid both work and bad weather. This pattern unaccountably differs somewhat from the timing of flight among both Virginia and South Carolina runaways (see Tables 5.11–5.12).[43]

What runaways wore and took with them often hinted at prior planning, but also reflected the varying conditions of slaves. Typically, skilled runaways were better clothed and equipped than other slaves who fled. Blacksmith Thomas Boman was unusual even among skilled slaves. He carried away with him "about fifty or sixty Pounds in Cash, and a grey Roan horse, Bridle and Saddle, a Pair of Money-Scales and Weights, and one Pair of Sheets, three Coats, one a Broad-Cloth or Sarge, one a Bear-Skin Cape Coat, of a grey Colour, one a Home-spun Coat, a Blue Jacket, and a great many other Cloaths."[44]

Some field hands, including Africans, wore more than the stock issue, dressed in finery, or carried extra clothing with them to guard against inclement weather and to disguise themselves.[45] Usually, field hands fled wearing only the seasonal issue of clothing. Thus Will wore "Negro Cottens" when he ran off in the spring, whereas Peter and Abraham, who fled in November, wore woolen jackets and trousers and osnaburg shirts. Most recent immigrants had the least clothing of all. This lack of clothing could mean that they discarded what they regarded as cumbersome garments, that they had not had time to accumulate clothes, or that their owners had provided them with a minimal amount of clothing, perhaps in the belief that it would hinder their escape. Two Africans captured in Craven County in July 1767 wore "nothing . . . but an old Negro cloth jacket, and a blue sailors jacket without sleeves"; four other Africans each had nothing on but a "striped Dutch blanket" when captured in October 1769.[46]

Whether they took little or considerable clothing, North Carolina runaways usually carried few other items. Quantities of goods would have attracted too much attention. Jemmy, an Ibo, and Jikowife, an African whose tribal origin is not indicated, were atypical: both fled with guns.[47] Wishing not to appear too unusual and lacking access to other forms of transportation, the overwhelming majority of runaways fled on foot. Only two slaves rode off on stolen horses, and apparently two Africans were the only ones who escaped by canoe.[48] Many runaways, whatever their occupation or origin, used the waterways as escape routes and as a means of sustenance. For instance, Sambo, who fled from a Moravian owner in Wachovia, "had wandered for several weeks in the wilderness along the Catawba River" and "had suffered much from hunger"; he was "willingly taken and brought back here." At least twelve other runaways were captured or sought to escape captors near rivers, lakes, or other bodies of water. Sam displayed considerably less willingness than Sambo when he was captured in Craven County: while being taken back to his Johnston County master, he "broke out of Custody . . . near the *South-West* bridge."[49]

The determination of slaves is also apparent when one considers their destinations. Thirty-six of the 100 runaways who were captured or for whom a destination was given tried to escape from the province, some doing so successfully. Included were 29 field hands and 7 nonfield slaves. Whatever their individual reasons for escape may have been, collectively these 36 runaways shared many characteristics. Fifteen can be identified as American-born, and they as well as 8 other slaves spoke English. The one identifiable African in this group had had two previous masters in South Carolina, and a West Indian–born slave had been owned in New York. Eleven of the 36 runaways who fled the colony left in groups, and all of them were captured—a family of 4 in South Carolina, a family of 5 in Williamsburg, and 2 males in Middlesex, Virginia.[50] In all, 16 of these runaways, or 46 percent of the 36, were actually captured outside of North Carolina.

The 64 runaways known to have remained in North Carolina stayed for various reasons and displayed no less resolution than those who crossed into neighboring colonies. Twelve were thought to be headed for or were actually captured in locations outside, sometimes at quite a distance from their home counties. The home counties were unknown of another 22 slaves who were apprehended in North Carolina. Finally, 10 of the 64 were thought to be "lurking about" their home plantations or seeking to get to other places within the same county. Whether they lived as outliers or were harbored by relatives and friends, those who stayed close by risked more than recapture. They might also be declared outlaws, which subjected them to summary execution. Eleven of the 18 runaways caught in their home counties either were killed or committed suicide.[51]

Although place of capture is not proof of where runaways intended to go, the 64 slaves who remained in North Carolina differed sharply from the 36 runaways who escaped from the province. All but 2 were field hands, and 17, all Africans, fled in groups. The others—including 7 Africans and 4 American-born slaves, 2 of them artisans—fled alone. Only 4 others, besides the American-born, spoke English well. Twelve spoke some English, and 14 could not speak it at all. Neither the origins of the remaining slaves nor their facility with English could be determined.

In all, 61 field hands and 3 artisans were captured or killed, 48 percent of the 134 North Carolina runaways examined. Twenty-four of the 33 African-born runaways, or 73 percent, were among those who failed in their bid for freedom. Among the 40 captured or killed field hands whose ability to speak English could be determined, only 5, or 9 percent, spoke it well. That Africans and those who spoke little or no English stood a poor chance of escaping is hardly surprising. Those slaves who could manipulate the language and their environment and most readily market their skills stood the best chance of eluding captors.[52]

Deciding whether to flee was a complex, often painful process for slaves confronted by severely limited options. This sense of limits could generate among some an immobilizing despair. For others the desire for freedom with perhaps its resulting or concomitant economic rewards, relief from harsh masters, or reunion or escape with friends or family could be stilled by neither the probable risks nor the demands and preachments of masters. Thus field hands, despite their poor odds of escape, ran away in rough proportion to their numbers in the population. And Africans, though ill-equipped to remain at large for long in the white-shaped world into which they had been thrust, still fled in disproportionately large numbers, mainly together.

Seeking to protect what was sacred and inviolable, including their memories and hopes, all of these slaves challenged their masters and slavery. The fact that they frequently ended up dead, jailed, whipped, or tortured only testifies to the strength of their dreams and their indomitable wills. These particular slaves attempted escape; others stole, assaulted, and killed. But all did so within the framework of the African American culture the slaves reconstituted from their African pasts and the harsh realities of thralldom. We now turn to three significant dimensions of that culture—the slaves' naming practices and linguistic development, their marriages and families, and their religiosity.

6

Slave Names and Languages

Africa profoundly affected the names of slaves and the languages they used to communicate with one another and with whites. Slaves were not unique in this respect; all ethnic and religious groups who have migrated to the Americas have tried to maintain their familiar folk traditions. Yet forcible removal from their homeland together with vicious, many-sided attacks on their culture both inhibited the slaves' ability to reconstruct their African pasts and heightened their need to do so.

Owners often denied their slaves access to important features of white folkways while attempting to destroy elements of the slaves' African culture in order to ensure their productivity and subservience. Thus colonial slaves long were denied access to Christianity while proselytizers often proffered limited versions of the creed so as not to encourage "false" hopes for freedom or equality among the slaves. Or again, masters delegitimated slave marriages and families while allowing slaves to develop de facto versions of these vital institutions. Slaveowners, therefore, could sell or otherwise alienate their chattel with no legal restrictions yet use slave marriages and families as levers to achieve more prolific, disciplined, and productive laborers. Throughout, slaves resisted these assaults by stubbornly adhering to African traditions while combating directly the attacks of their masters.

It was in this atmosphere that slaveowners as a rule acquiesced to demands by slaves that they be allowed to control their own names and those of their children. Owners tended to accede to slave claims in this area because this power, though of great significance to the slaves themselves, affected the political hegemony of the slaveowners in only minor ways. When slaves chose their own names they also met the need of owners that slave names be as diverse as possible on each plantation. Such diversity resulted from the varied ethnic backgrounds of the African slaves, each with its own large pool of names and varied naming practices, and the common use of multiple names. Allowing slaves to control their own names also relieved owners of the burden of developing a lexicon of slave names as well as of accepting the onus of needlessly destroying this important means of the slaves establishing their individual and social identities.[1]

The ceremonies associated with the naming of a child vary considerably among African ethnic groups, but among all they are important, joyous occasions used to congratulate the good fortune of parents on the birth of their children. The significance of the naming of a child is attested to by the widespread belief that a child is not a person until named. Accordingly, a name is not given until enough time has elapsed after birth to be reasonably optimistic about the child's survival. The naming ceremony brings the entire community together—from the youngest to the oldest—with ritualistic feasting and dancing to welcome a newcomer into a family and community within which the child, and the subsequent adult, will achieve fulfillment. Through this process an entire people's life is ritually reaffirmed, while the powers of deities and significant ancestors (the "living dead") are invoked to ensure a happy, healthy future for the child.[2]

Although slave names and naming practices differed among the ethnic traditions represented in the African diaspora, many groups shared customs— still used today—of naming children according to the day of the week on which they were born or their birth position in the family. It also has been common to give names that indicate the peculiar circumstances of the child's birth or its proximity in time and place to noteworthy events. Resemblances to deceased relatives, which might be understood in terms of reincarnation, the joy of the parents at their child's birth, or their fears, hopes, and aspirations for the child could also determine the choice of a name.

Traditionally, more than one name is given in the initial naming ceremony. For instance, seven to nine days after a Yoruban birth, the infant receives three names: a personal name, a praise name, and a name indicating the child's lineage. Thereafter other names are bestowed to celebrate rites of passage and the particular accomplishments of the person named, or names are given by significant others based on their sense of the individual's character and personality.[3]

Even though these African naming patterns, though perhaps not the accompanying ceremonies, continued in colonial North Carolina and elsewhere on the mainland, the names of slaves were frequently changed by their masters. Slaveowners transcribed imprecisely or Anglicized unfamiliar African names that they could not pronounce or spell. Despite these changes or distortions, slaves undoubtedly continued to pronounce their names correctly among themselves. Nevertheless, because of the slaveowners' monopoly over the written record, their transcriptions eventually altered the names that slaves actually used and passed on to their children.

Illustrative of this dialectical process is Joseph Hancock's advertisement for his runaway slave in the summer of 1774. The "Negro Fellow" who had run off was "named Buck," Hancock explained, but he "calls himself *Tom Buck*." Hancock went on to provide other details typical of runaway notices.[4] Especially noteworthy is that the fugitive was fifty years old, spoke "good *English*," and after years in the colony still insisted on calling himself *Tom Buck*. The insistence was neither capricious nor designed to deceive—otherwise he surely would have chosen a name unfamiliar to his master.[5]

Hancock's slave probably clung to "Tom Buck" because that was his African name. Or more precisely, it was Hancock's Anglicized version of the African name or names that "Tom Buck" represented. Assuming this to be correct, "Buck" could have been Hancock's shortened rendering of one of a number of African single names, including the Yoruban personal name, Taiwo (Tah'-ee-woh), "the first born of twins," or the Ngoni (Malawi) name of Thambo (Tham'-boh). Also distinct possibilities were a host of African words used as names over the years by slaves and their descendants, such as Taba (Tabbah), Tabu (Tahboo), Tamba (Tahmbah), Tambo (Tahmboh,), Tambu (Tahmboo), Tomba (Tohmbah), and Turnbu (Toornboo). Or perhaps Buck was Hancock's transformation of two African names. Tom could have been derived from any of the above names or a number of other homophones, and Buck, to cite just a few examples, could have been Hancock's version of the Ibo name, Ubaka, the Ibibio name, Ibak, or the common Akan name, Baako, which means first born.[6] Thus, since Africans often had several names, Hancock originally could have selected one of them, Buck, while the slave in question insisted on maintaining two of his African names.

On the other hand, Tambo (Tahmboh) or Tamba (Tahmbah) just as readily could have been transformed into Tom as Buck, but perhaps Hancock already owned one or more slaves named Tom and shied away from using the name again.[7] This is a strong possibility, as Tom was the fourth most common male slave name in our sample for colonial North Carolina (see Table 6.1).

The struggle between Tom Buck and Hancock effectively illustrates the possible respective roles played by slaves and slaveowners in the development of slave names in North Carolina, as well as in the other colonies. Yet it probably overdramatizes the story for most slaves; the masters' distorted versions of the slaves' true names usually went unchallenged because slaves normally continued to use their correct African names among themselves. As reasonable as this conjecture is, one may only guess at the ways in which the slaves privately parodied or vilified the masters' confounding of the slaves' true African names.

Unfortunately, there is no way to assess systematically the names actually used among the slaves themselves. The only surviving records of slave names are those left by slaveowners. If, however, a study of these available records, which necessarily minimize the African continuum, still reveals that Africa played the paramount role in determining slave names and naming practices, we may confidently expect that the slaves applied African traditions in even more pristine and consistent fashion among themselves.

Indeed, we will show that much of the evidence left by the owners argues that Africa played the dominant role in determining the names and naming practices used by slaves. But we must admit at the outset that this cannot be demonstrated conclusively because the statistical results obtained from the available data for colonial North Carolina, and elsewhere, are determined by assumptions about the origins of slave names. In other words, an unavoidable circularity of reasoning contaminates the statistical findings.

This problem can be illustrated by developing two disparate sets of statistical findings from data in North Carolina. The numerical and percentage breakdowns listed in Table 6.2 follow procedures essentially used by Darret B. and Anita Rutman in their attempt to demonstrate that the masters normally named their slaves and usually gave them common English names.[8] That is, in all cases where names could have both an African and non-African derivation, we follow the Rutmans' lead and list them in the appropriate non-African category. Thus popular slave names such as Ben, Bob, Cato, Ceasar, Charles, Dick, George, Jack, Jacob, Jim or Jimmy, Joe or Jo, London, Ned, Peter, Sam, Tobe, Tom, Will, Amy, Beck, Bess, Bet, Betty, Chloe, Dinah, Esther, Flora, Hannah, Jane, Jenny, Judy, Judith, Kate, Lucy, Moll, Nan, Nancy, Pegg, Penny, Phillis, Rose, Sarah, and Venus—all of which had numerous possible African derivations—were identified as either common Anglo-American, biblical, classical, or place names (see Tables 6.1–6.2).

In constructing Table 6.3 we reversed this procedure and now categorized such names according to our assumption that slaves substantially controlled the naming process and often continued to use African names themselves or chose them for their children. Each name that could have been derived from like-sounding African names, including all of those illustrated above, were so identified. With the use of this procedure, estimates of African-derived names rose from 12.7 percent (Table 6.2) to 89.5 percent (Table 6.3).

It is impossible either to reconcile or to correct these two sets of statistics. The disparities directly result from the different methods devised by scholars to categorize the names to be quantified, and it is these very methods of categorization that are under dispute. With both statistical agreement and precision beyond reach, we can only present the available evidence that supports our contention that the statistics that most closely mirror reality are those in Table 6.3. The figures reflect the heavy reliance of slaves on African names and naming practices, usually from debarkation onward.

Considerable data argue this point persuasively. To begin with, owners occasionally managed to transcribe African names precisely. Scholars, including the Rutmans, almost invariably agree that in such obvious cases of indisputable African derivation the slaves themselves chose these names from an African pool of names. Instances of this phenomenon in North Carolina are male slave names such as Quamee, Quamina, Quamino, Quash, and Sambo and the female name Quasheba.

More commonly, as in Tom Buck's case, owners misspelled, mispronounced, shortened, or Anglicized the African names of their slaves. Thus a host of slave names developed in addition to the Toms or Bucks that, while seemingly English, may be traced to African origins. The sheer frequency of such possibilities is in itself persuasive evidence of the significance of Africa in the naming of slaves in North Carolina and the other colonies. It is not difficult to envision how Africans named Adeben, Bem, Bena, Benda, Beni, Benin, Beng, or Kwabena could all become Ben or Benn; how Bilali, Bili, and Bilu could become Billy or Billico; and how Ba, Baba, Babo, Babu, Bawbi, Bawbaw, Bo, and Bobo could become Bob. Perhaps Cato derived from Kata, Kate, or Kaya; others named Sayr, Sese, Seka, Sise, or Sisi could be heard by some owners as Ceasar. Adikah, Dibi, Digbe, Diga, and Diji could all become Dick, and Kwa, Kwakko, Kwakou, and Quak would change to Jack. No doubt Djima, Jima, Jimba, and Njimbu often entered the world of slavery as Jim or Jimmy; George was the new name for Gowon, Jode, Yao, Yaw, and Yawo; and Joe or Jo could be derived from Ajo, Coujoe, Jojo, Kawjo, Kodjo, Kojo, Njoku, or Ojo. Kpeya, Kpia, Kpini,

Kpita, Kpinya, Paya, Pisa, Pisu, Pitipa, and perhaps many others could all become Peter, while many Sambas and Sambos would become Sams or Sampsons. Place names such as London and York perhaps not only represented the possible continuation of an African tradition of naming a child after an appropriate place (Lunda was a source of slaves in West Central Africa), but also were chosen because of London's closeness to Loma, Londi, Lowa, Lugna, Luma, Luna, and Lunda and York's similarity to one of the Fante versions of the day name for Thursday, Yorkoo.

Among females, Ama, Amadi, Amma, Ame, Ameni, and Ami could easily be transformed into Amy. Baka, Abeke, Be, Bek, Beka, Beke, Mbek, Mbeke, and Mgbeke could all become Beck or Rebecca. Bat, Bata, Bate, Bati, Beta, and Biti would change to Bet or Betty; Bese and Bise, to Bess; and Ehse, Esa, Ese, Esi, Esinam, Esiya, and Nsia, to Esther or Easter. Flawa or Fawlana could be understood as Flora, while Hana, Hanu, and Nana easily became the biblical Hannah. Ga, Gana, Gane, Gani, Gibi, Gini Kanwa, Janna, Jena, Jene, and Jinisa could readily be transformed into the numerous Janes, Jennys, and Ginnys, whereas perhaps Adioula, Adjua, Juba, and Jula remained Juba or became Juda, Jude, Judith, or Judy. Latsi, Lesa, Leshe, Lisa, Lulu, Lumusi, Luri, Lusa, Luce, and Lushinda frequently became or remained Lucy, Lucea, Lucinda, or Lulu, while Anang, Anani, Ananse, Gnana, Nana, Nena, Nene, and Neni could all become the popular slave names of Nan and Nancy. Pegba could become Peg; Kpeya, Panyin, Pendu, Pene, or Pinde would be called Penny, and Afiba, Afouba, Efia, Fiba, Fibea, and Fie—Febe or Phebe. Fila or Fili could readily change to Phyllis; and Omorose, Osa, Ose, Oseye, Oze, Rus, Rusa, Rowa, and Rushe, to Rose. Sara, Sare, Sari, Saria, Sareya, and Seriya easily became Sabeah, Sabia, Sabina, Saliena, or Sally, but above all, Sarah. Finally, Afena, Aminaba, Vema, Vena, and Venda are likely sources of the female slaves named Venice, Venis, or Venus (see Table 6.1).[9]

If our stress on slave control over the naming process and the dominant role that African heritage played in the slaves' choices of names is correct, this would help to explain why slaves rarely bore the names of their particular owners or those of their owners' immediate families. In only 3 percent of the North Carolina cases reviewed did slaves have the same name, or an abbreviated or diminutive form, as their actual owners or their owners' immediate families. The names shared even in such limited cases were primarily those most commonly used in the general slave and free populations.[10]

The frequent use of shortened versions or the diminutive forms of English names—a practice far more common among slaves than whites in colonial North Carolina or elsewhere—may best be explained by the African connection rather than a specific expression of planter paternalism or an attempt by masters to deride their slaves.[11] Thus names such as Joe or Jo were used more commonly among slaves than Joseph because they could be derived from African names more readily. Dick was frequently used but Richard never appeared in our sample because there were many African names that sounded like Dick, but none, as far as we are aware, from which to derive Richard. Similar reasons explain why Beck, Bess, Bet, and Betty were popular, whereas Elizabeth was never used among slaves in our sample. Conversely and tellingly, the frequent use of such full names as Amy, Hannah, Judith, Phillis, and Rose, along with George, James, John, and Peter—all of which could be derived from numerous African names—also helps to undercut the argument that slaves were given shortened, diminutive or "familial" forms of names either by masters intent on casting aspersion on them or by paternalistic masters who were thereby treating slaves as members of their families. Last, the limited use by slaves of such popular white names as Henry, Frederick, Andrew, and Alexander—no slaves in our sample have the last three names, and there are only two Henrys—can be explained by the fact that these names did not have close African counterparts (see Table 6.1).

Of course, some slaves were given African-sounding names according to the whim of their masters. But we venture to say that this did not occur frequently, for they had little reason to do so. Also, at times masters named slaves with no regard for the names they already had. Perhaps this explains some of the Hectors, Neptunes, and Valentines, or Grasiases, Clarindas, and Bridgetts. When this occurred, some slaves apparently resisted, making it even more likely that masters normally would bequeath names to their slaves in accordance with the slaves' wishes.

Olaudah Equiano, author of the most revealing eighteenth-century autobiographical account of slavery, is an example of a slave resisting, if unsuccessfully, the arbitrariness or whimsy of masters. He was given three different names after his enslavement, the last, Gustavas Vassa, literally being forced on him. This, we daresay, was the exception to the rule. After all, Olaudah was especially vulnerable to such treatment. Enslaved as a mere boy, he was isolated from his own family and people, the Ibo, and often from all other slaves during his first months of enslavement in Virginia and then aboard an English ship.[12]

Few North Carolina slaves during the colonial years used their substantial control over the naming process to choose biblical names. This situation both reflects and illustrates the fact that few slaves were deeply affected by Christianity at this time (see Tables 6.2–6.3), as most continued to adhere to the religious traditions of their African past. This tendency, in turn, undoubtedly reinforced the powerful African continuum exhibited in the naming process. But toward the end of the eighteenth century and thereafter, when more slaves seriously embraced Christianity, the use of biblical names by slaves increased.[13]

The evidence, in short, most consistently supports the view that eighteenth-century slaves in colonial North Carolina substantially controlled the naming process and that they usually kept or chose African names in accordance with their African experiences and memories. Whites, in turn, usually attempted to abide by these choices—recording names as they heard them, but often in the process transforming or perhaps shortening the African names into like-sounding English equivalents. Though masters at times snickered at some of the results—Ceasar, Venus, and Cato indeed!—the slaves still had approximations of their own names. And certainly the correct pronunciations frequently prevailed in the slave quarters among these first- and second-generation slaves.

If slaves in colonial North Carolina normally continued to use names derived in various ways from their African heritage, it is also likely that they chose these names in accordance with a variety of African naming practices. But this cannot be demonstrated directly. Extant data for North Carolina slaves, for instance, is insufficient to prove that slave day or positional names respectively corresponded with the day on which particular slaves were born or their birth sequence with regard to their siblings.[14]

Nevertheless, the large number of colonial slaves bearing African or like-sounding day and positional names suggests that the naming practices survived along with the actual names. The high proportion of Africans in the slave population, the frequent incidence of such naming practices among a variety of African ethnic groups that were enslaved in North Carolina, and the relative ease with which such concrete, straightforward naming practices could be continued by the slaves all facilitated this. Moreover, although ethnic variations occurred in the day and positional names actually used, the strong linguistic affinities of a large number of African slaves in North Carolina—such as those who were Asante, Fante, Twi, Ewe, Ga, and Fon, all Kra-speaking peoples who had lived in close proximity to one another in Ghana, Togo, and Dahomey—mitigated such differences. Tables 6.4–6.6 best illustrate these similarities.[15] As we have seen, masters also helped to reconcile differences by Anglicizing or otherwise homogenizing the slaves' names, with the changed versions gradually being accepted by the slaves themselves.

Even when different ethnic versions of particular African day or positional names varied too greatly to be reconciled with those used by other ethnic groups, as usually was the case, for instance, with the Ibo names in our sample, the diverse names still could be incorporated into a growing pool of slave names. This helped the slaves to maintain ethnic harmony while meeting the needs of their rapidly growing population. Masters welcomed such diversity because it maximized the number and variety of slave names and hence avoided the confusion produced by too many slaves having the same name.

However frequently slaves actually gave their children day names in accordance with the day on which they were born, the continuing use of day names among North Carolina's slaves during the years 1748–75 is significant. Of the 570 male slaves and 467 female slaves for whom we have records, 179 men (31.4 percent) and 81 women (17.3 percent) possibly used these names or their derivatives (see Tables 6.4–6.5). This equals a combined total of 260 out of 1,037 slaves, or 25.1 percent.

We must reemphasize, however, that we have not hereby demonstrated that one-quarter of colonial North Carolina's slaves actually named their children after the day of the week on which they were born. For as just noted, we lack direct evidence, one way or the other, to show this conclusively. Nor are we able even to quantify precisely the linkages between African day names and their English soundalikes. The figure of 25 percent is suggestive rather than definitive given the large margin of possible error. On the other hand, the specific number of day names would be increased along with clearer manifestations of their African purity if we were able to develop an aggregative analysis of the names slaves actually used among themselves. But even focusing on the recorded slave names, as we must, the total number of day names in our sample would still be larger if we had taken into account the complete pool of such names from *all* ethnic groups who helped to populate North Carolina rather than from select groups. In any case, the extraordinarily large number of slave names possibly derived from a limited ethnic pool of African day names is, in itself, indicative both of their significance and of the probable continuation of the African naming practice at least during the colonial years.

Another West African naming practice that apparently survived in North Carolina was the naming of children in accordance with their birth position in the family. Positional names, like day names, were commonly used by a variety of African ethnic groups living in areas that stretched from current Mali west to the coast and south and east to Nigeria—covering the entire geographic expanse of West Africa. Cultural groups that used positional names included the Mandingo of Guinea; the Mende of Sierra Leone; the Akan-speaking peoples of Ghana, including the Twi, Fante, and Asante; the Ewe and Fon of Ghana, Togo, and Dahomey; and the Hausa, Ibo, and Ibibio of Nigeria (see Tables 6.6–6.7).

Possibly 12.0 percent (56) of the female slaves and 10.4 percent (59) of the male slaves bore positional names. Subtracting from these totals the eighteen female and eight male slave names found on the two lists of day and positional names in our sample (thereby avoiding duplication), the percentage of colonial North Carolina slaves who bore names taken from either of these categories perhaps equaled somewhere around 24.5 percent for females, 40.9 percent for males, and 33.6 percent for both.

The numerous Joes (Jos and Josephs), Bens (Benns) or Bobs (Bobbs), Jacks (Jacobs), Georges, Toms, and Ceasars very likely were often named after African equivalents of children born on Monday, Tuesday, Wednesday, Thursday, Saturday, and Sunday. Dick (Dicke), the third most popular name for male slaves in colonial North Carolina, probably was frequently derived from Ewe and other African equivalents for first-born children, and the numerous Sams, Sambos, and Sampsons (Samsons) were sometimes continuations of the Hausa name, Sambo, for a second-born son. Daniel could have been derived from the African equivalents of children born on Friday and Sunday or a first-born child, and Adam from the homophonic equivalents of a child born on Monday or the fourth-born child. Among females, Judy and Judith were possibly derived from the African day names for Monday. The Venuses, Phebes, and Amys could respectively have been named after African children born on Tuesday, Friday, and Saturday. Nan, Nann, Nancy, Nance, or Nanny all could have come from the African equivalents of the fourth-born child, and the many Becks could have been named after either a child born on Sunday or a first-born child.

None of this denies that there were other possible African derivations for many of these names. For example, Mandingo, Temne, and Yoruban uses of Sisi may have provided additional African sources for Ceasar along with the Fante word for Sunday. Or the numerous Bobs besides being derived from the Fante name for Tuesday, Bobo, could also have come from Bobo, Ba, Boba, Babo, and Babu, which had a variety of meanings among ethnic groups from the Mandinka south to the Kimbundu and Kongo in Angola. Ibo names such as Dike or Diji with a variety of meanings could have been the source of Dick along with Adika, the Ewe name for first born or first-born son. And the Akan, Ewe, and Twi names for the trickster spider, Ananse, probably shared place with Akan names of Anan and Anani (fourth born) as the source for the numerous slaves named Nan, Nann, or Nancy. These along with many other possibilities are further evidence arguing that caution be used in evaluating the importance of day and positional names among the slaves in colonial North Carolina. Certainly, exact statistics will remain elusive.[16]

Despite the tenuousness of any statistical analysis that attempts to describe the derivation of slave names, it is still suggestive to note that twenty-nine male slaves (5.1 percent of the total) were given descriptive names, such as Boson (Boatswain), Duke, Shark, or Sharper, that perhaps continued the African practice of giving names in accordance with the alleged personality characteristics of a child or the achievement of a new occupation. Slaves named Boston, Essex, London, and York most obviously could have manifested the persistence of the common African practice of giving children place names, but such names also could have been derived from numerous other African naming practices and like-sounding African names. In any case, thirty-three male slaves (5.8 percent of the total) bore geographic names. Rarely were such descriptive or place names ever shared by whites.[17] Last, the twenty-four female slave names defined as Puritanical and descriptive in Table 6.2 (5.2 percent of the total) could have been derived, at least in part, from the African practice of bequeathing names in accordance with the supposed moral or personality traits of a child or the religious beliefs of a people. Nonetheless, Puritanical names occurred frequently among white females.

Slaves, therefore, chose their names from a large pool of African names and were influenced by African naming practices. In keeping with this reliance on an African past, slaves in colonial North Carolina seldom used surnames because they were not traditionally used in Africa.[18] Thus the gradual implementation of surnames by slaves probably emanated from acculturation. White opposition to slaves' having surnames, at the same time, hindered their capacity to make this change.

The earliest use of surnames that we have uncovered for North Carolina is by the slaves of John Walker of Wilmington during the first decade of the nineteenth century. Charity had seven children, all of them listed both by their first name and the surname "Short."[19] Given the fragmented documentary record and the inclination of masters to list only first names for slaves, it is probable that a more complete set of colonial records would reveal other and earlier possible origins of slave surnames. Among the 57 slaves on the Allen plantation in the Lower Cape Fear in 1761, for instance, two of Phebe's seven children bore the names Tom Cooper and Marcus Cooper. Other possibilities are exemplified by several of the 123 slaves on the Pollock plantation in the Neuse-Pamlico region. Included in a 1770 list are Old George, Old Emanuel, Young Emanuel, Young Todge, Young Jim, Big Emanuel, Mill Creek George, Smith George, Miller Jimmy, and Tom Cooper.[20] These examples suggest that some surnames probably flowed from a process involving both master and slave that was substantively akin to a similar development in England some centuries earlier.

Some remarks made by Elkanah Watson in 1777 take the question of linguistics beyond the names slaves used to the languages they spoke. En route from

North Carolina to South Carolina, "four jolly, well-fed negroes" rowed Watson across "Wingran Bay." While doing so, he recalled, "the poor fellows amused us the whole way by singing their plaintive African songs in cadence with the oars."[21] The songs Watson referred to but could not understand were work chanties that could have been sung in a number of African tongues, or perhaps in the prevailing pidgin-creole language.[22]

If the specific languages used by the four slaves on Wingran Bay remain obscured by time, so must precise versions of most of the languages actually spoken by the slaves in colonial North Carolina. This is because we only have a vague understanding of the ethnic backgrounds of the colony's slaves. Nor do we have significant examples of their actual speech patterns, whether African, pidgin creole, or English. Yet some understanding of the languages spoken by the slaves and the genesis of these tongues can be obtained by a careful analysis of available evidence.

For instance, if the evolution of slave names is one manifestation of the development of slave languages, we may employ our understanding of how names evolved as a model to describe how slave languages developed. Thus, similar to the genesis of names, it appears likely that slaves played the predominant role in the development of pidgin-creole languages in the colonies and that these languages were best understood and had greatest currency and utility within the slave quarters rather than as a means of communication between blacks and whites. In the ensuing pages we will attempt to demonstrate the validity of these assertions—primarily for North Carolina, but also for the other southern colonies from Delaware to Virginia. Few scholars can aid in this task, for only a handful have not rejected, played down, or ignored the evolution of pidgin-creole languages in these colonies.[23] We will not use the growth of Gullah in South Carolina to demonstrate how pidgin-creole languages unfolded elsewhere, for this is precisely what is in question—did such languages indeed develop north of South Carolina? But we will draw on the South Carolina story when necessary to illuminate the growth patterns and functions of pidgin-creole languages in other areas.[24]

A linguistic profile of slave runaways in colonial North Carolina suggests that there was a great need among the colony's slaves for a lingua franca even as late as 1748–75. During those years, 32.7 percent of slave runaways in North Carolina spoke "some" English and 13.9 percent spoke no English at all. Moreover, it is likely that most of the runaway slaves assessed as speaking "good" English simply could communicate adequately in the workplace. It, therefore, was urgent that slaves had other more sophisticated means of talking with one another.[25]

Some idea of the way they communicated may be obtained from the journals of travelers to America, especially the correspondence of Anglican missionaries interested in converting the slaves. Philip Reading, an Anglican minister in Delaware, in a letter of 1748, precisely describes the ways in which a pidgin-creole language functioned in that province. He observed that a significant obstacle to converting the slaves was the "difficulty of conversing with the majority of the Negroes themselves" for "they have a language peculiar to themselves, a wild confused medley of Negro and corrupt English which makes them unintelligible except to those who conversed with them for many years."[26] J. F. D. Smyth, an English visitor to the colonies at the beginning of the American Revolution, confirmed the existence of a pidgin-creole language in use among Virginia and North Carolina slaves at that late date when he noted that many slaves "speak a mixed dialect between the Guinea and the English."[27] Indeed, as late as the antebellum years some slaves in the North Carolina coastal region, and probably elsewhere in the state, still spoke a creole language. Dr. Edward Warren, who visited a plantation in Washington County in the Albemarle Sound area during this period, observed that there were many old "Guinea negroes" who spoke what he called an unintelligible "gibberish which was a medley of their original dialect and the English language."[28]

Other Anglican observers in the colonies in addition to Reading also stressed their difficulties in converting slaves because of language differences both among slaves and between slaves and whites. Joseph Ottolenghe, for instance, writing in 1754 from Savannah, Georgia, emphasized that proselytizers faced greater obstacles in converting blacks than the early Christians had in dealing with the "Catechumens." Early Christians, he argued,

> had none of those many Hindrancies, & great Difficulties which are to be met with in the Instruction of Negroes. The Formers understood the Language of the Instructors, & if not Persons were appointed skill'd in the Language of the Novices, whereas our Negroes are so Ignorant of the English Language, & none can be found to talk in their own, that it is great while before you can get them to understand what the Meaning of Words is, & yet that without such a knowledge Instructions would prove Vain, & the Ends proposed abortive, for how can a Proposition be believed, without first being understood? And how can it be understood if the Person to whom it is offer'd has no Idea even of the Sound of those Words which expressess the Proposition?[29]

In 1758 and 1759 Ottolenghe reiterated the problem.[30] That it was both widespread and long lived is indicated in a letter written by the Reverend James Marye Jr. in 1764 from Orange County, Virginia:

You must understand there are great Quantities of those Negroes imported here yearly from Africa, who have Languages peculiar to themselves, who are here many years before they understand English; & great Numbers there are that never do understand it, well Enough to reap any Benefit from what is said in Church which was my Reason for mentioning, as I did in some former Letter, that the distributing religious Tracts to the Owners would be a more probable Way of Success, as those being wrote in the most plain intelligible Style, they might by their Owners be made in Time to understand what was said to them.

But you must suppose it to be impossible for me to go from House to House, to instruct a thousand Negroes perhaps or more, some of which would take me a Week to make them understand one single Sentence.

The Number of Negroe Communicants is very small not exceeding half a Dozen in the Parish or there abouts. All that understand English, & that are but tolerably convenient to Church, bring their Children to be baptised.[31]

Although the relative and absolute number of American-born slaves increased over the years in the colonies, as did the slaves' facility with English, the continuation of the language problem until the end of the colonial period is indicated in an October 1770 letter written by a Bray Associate in London to "an American Planter." The Reverend John Waring tries to counter the planter's arguments against attempting to convert the slaves by contending:

But perhaps you will say, "the *Negroes* are utter Strangers to our Language, and we to theirs." But,

Do not many of the *Negroes*, who are grown Persons when imported, even of themselves attain so much of our Language, as to enable them to understand, and be understood in Things which concern the ordinary Business of Life? And if so,

May they not with a little Instruction, easily attain so much further Knowledge of it, as to enable them to understand the Things which concern the Welfare of their Souls? At least,

Might not some *few*, who are more capable and serious than the rest, having first learnt our Language, be taught the Principles of our Religion by themselves; and then be appointed to convey Instruction to their Fellow-Slaves of lower Capacities, in their own Language?[32]

These observations of contemporaries plus the statistics cited earlier concerning the linguistic characteristics of slave runaways in North Carolina demonstrate that substantial numbers of slaves throughout the southern colonies spoke little or no English up to the Revolution. Moreover, Smyth's, Reading's, and Warren's comments, taken together, describe widely spoken pidgin-creole languages in Delaware, Virginia, and North Carolina that were derived substantially from African languages and were comprised of words taken from both English and a variety of African tongues. Although not specified by these observers, it is probable, as suggested by various studies of slave linguistics, that the syntax of such tongues was primarily African.[33] This probably helps to explain why creole was comprehensible only to whites who had conversed in the language "for many years."[34] Together with Reading's and Smyth's observations that pidgin and creole were widely used by slaves, it also suggests that the languages had been primarily constructed and passed on by slaves and served mainly as a means of communication among the slaves themselves.

Ottolenghe's and Marye's letters stress the continued significance of African languages in Georgia and Virginia, whereas Waring leaves to our imagination which slave language or languages he is referring to. Evidence uncovered by other investigators demonstrates that a pidgin-creole language, similar to that of Gullah in South Carolina, developed in Georgia. This fact makes the Georgian Ottolenghe's failure to mention Gullah, while dwelling on the continued impact of African languages, even less compelling. In other words, there is the distinct possibility that Ottolenghe often failed to understand that what he heard was slaves speaking creole rather than African languages.[35]

Waring's letter suggests a collateral point already touched upon, that it is likely that the substantial number of slaves in the runaway records described as speaking "good English" actually spoke English in a manner that could satisfy few of the slaves' needs. Or as the Reverend Waring put it, their English could only express "the ordinary Business of Life."[36] Slaves with "some" or no English could not even do that. A majority of colonial slaves, certainly in the Carolinas and Georgia, could hardly be content to converse with one another, or even with slaves who had considerable facility in English, in a tongue that functionally and aesthetically served so many of them so poorly. A pidgin-creole language, on the other hand, had all the qualities needed: a highly functional, aesthetically pleasing language that could be learned and spoken readily by persons from diverse African heritages and that could be used as a primary means of communication by any slave—from those who spoke no English to those who spoke standard English.

Scholars who have argued that slaves at any given moment spoke a variety of languages are correct. Certainly this was true during the colonial years. Many slaves in colonial North Carolina continued to use their African tongue of origin as their primary language while gradually learning pidgin along with utilitarian English. Still others, both African and American born, came to speak the lingua franca, a creole language that gradually became more complex and useful than the original pidgin. Constructed from a variety of African languages that had many syntactical similarities and, to varying degrees, shared vocabularies, each creole language always remained in flux as fast-arriving slave immigrants from diverse cultures continued to infuse the language with new vitality. From the outset English words, and some from other European tongues, also helped form the pidgin-creole amalgam. The infusion of English continued over time as African Americans gradually became more proficient in English itself. Some American-born slaves carried this process to its logical conclusion in their use of standard English. Slaves, therefore, were a more linguistically diverse group than whites. It was they, far more than whites, who accommodated themselves to a polyglot ethnic situation by becoming multilingual and by inventing a new, complex creole language. Whites, characteristically, took all this as a sign of the slaves' brute incapacity to learn English, a rather bizarre criticism coming from a relatively mono-linguistic people.

Using their African heritage, slaves managed to maintain substantial control over their linguistic development and the names they bore. They often played similarly dominant roles in determining the particular ways they understood and structured other crucial social institutions and practices. Among these, none were more decisive in enabling slaves to protect their human viability against the onslaughts of enslavement than slave marriages and families. It is this story to which we turn in the next chapter.

7

Marriage and the Family

In 1806 Mourning Ivins, a free black woman, petitioned the Warren County Court to free her husband Nat. Mourning had married Nat "early in life," probably in the 1770s or early 1780s, while he was still a slave owned by William West, a shoemaker of modest means. In 1804 she had purchased her husband from West with money accumulated by her "sole care and industry." In a supporting statement to Mourning Ivins's petition, West described Nat Ivins as an "Engenus hand" and "an Extradanary Shewmaker"; he further noted that he had "Entrusted abundance of business in his hands and he proformed his duty Very faithfully to me." Mourning was proud and clear about her relationship with Nat. "By him She has Eight children [and] . . . Nat has ever conducted himself towards her as a faithful and affectionate husband—that in all circumstances as well in sickness and in health he has manifested to your memorialist & her children the most unceasing care and solicitude—that by his industry & attention he has enabled your memorialist

[to] support her children free from want and as respectably as any persons in their Condition." She urged the court to "free & emancipate" her husband lest on her death he "be reduced again to a state of slavery."[1]

The poignantly etched circumstances of Mourning's marriage to Nat were distinctive in their details, yet typical in their expression of the depth of feeling slaves normally felt for their spouses and children, as well as in the troubled and circumscribed nature of marriage and the family among the enslaved. Johann David Schoepf gave vivid testimony to these common slave feelings and experiences when he visited North Carolina in the early 1780s and witnessed an auction in Wilmington, New Hanover County. Describing the sale of a father and his fifteen-year-old son, both of them coopers, he reported: "The father was put up first, his anxiety lest his son fall to another purchaser and be separated from him was more painful than his fear of getting into the hands of a hard master. 'Who buys me,' he was continually calling out, 'must buy my son too,' and it happened as he desired, for his purchaser, if not from motives of humanity and pity, was for his own advantage obliged so to do." According to Schoepf, others were less fortunate: "often the husband is snatched from his wife, the children from their mother, if this better answers the purpose of buyer or seller, and no heed is given the doleful prayers with which they seek to prevent a separation."[2] Shoepf's account supports the observations of Elkanah Watson, who had attended a slave auction in Wilmington in 1778. In this instance a Negro family was "driven in from the country, like swine for market. A poor wench clung to a little daughter, and implored, with the most agonizing supplication, that they must not be separated. But alas, either the master or circumstances were inexorable—they were sold to different purchasers. The husband and the residue of the family were knocked off to the highest bidder."[3] A final example involved Sambo, a slave owned by Edward Williams of Pasquotank County, who was tried by a special slave court on 2 August 1761.[4] To prevent the sale of his daughter to "Mrs. Mary Nash," a woman known to maltreat slaves, Sambo had collaborated with David, owned by "Josiah Nash, Esqr.," Mary's husband, to have a mind altering "poison" (drug) administered to the woman. Sambo probably not only failed to protect his daughter, but he also was found guilty of the attempted "crime" and was ordered to be castrated by the county sheriff.[5]

These examples, scarcely unique in the history of enslavement in British North America, show several things. They suggest the distressing frequency with which slave sales or other devices broke up marriages and families and the terrible sense of loss experienced by slaves forcibly separated from their loved ones. They point to the harsh, at times brutal treatment of slaves by self-interested owners who operated within the legal system. And they reveal not merely the existence of marriages and families among slaves, but how centrally these institutions figured in their lives. Profoundly satisfying expressions of sexual, parental, and filial love, marriages and families were also intimately intertwined with the primal phases of the life cycle—birth, child rearing, inter-generational culture transmission, and death. Hardly surprising, then, were the frequent slave attempts to implement their sense of a moral society—a conceived right to defend traditional social patterns and values, in this case rooted in the needs of marriage and the family. Despite the frequent breakup of slave marriages and families by masters, slaves rejected the treatment ac-corded them. Whether or not they actively resisted, they typically construed such breakups as an abuse, an attack on cherished institutions that embodied the people they loved best—spouse, children, and siblings. Growing out of and incorporated within the needs and demands of slave marriages and families, therefore, were slave definitions regarding acceptable limits on treatment by masters.[6]

All of these citations vividly illustrate slaves' intense feelings about marriage and the family, but they do not reveal the process by which these institutions evolved. Slaves transported to North Carolina, or elsewhere, from a multi-plicity of African cultural heritages had experienced a succession of traumas: capture; separation from homelands, families, and friends; hideous conditions on forced marches and during the middle passage; and a series of slave sales. Nonetheless, once in America the slaves began the never-ending process of adjusting to their new environments, resisting engulfment by the masters' power and definitions, and conjunctly constructing African American cultures from their diverse African backgrounds as allowed, modified, or redefined by the possibilities and needs prescribed by enslavement.

In this process, African memories consisted not merely of recollections of times past; they encompassed the habitual ways slaves understood reality.[7] This holding onto their past would tend to be true for any immigrant group, but it would be evident especially when persons from traditional, kinship-defined societies lived against their will among, but significantly apart from, ascendant groups whose belief patterns, mores, practices, and institutions differed sub-stantially from their own and often were denied to them.

The degree of success slaves had in replicating their pasts hinged on the fortuitous concordance of a number of variables. For one thing, although Afri-cans came from divergent cultures with distinct practices, they often shared both underlying principles and particular cultural forms. Such equivalencies enabled numerous reconciliations or convergences among slaves, whether by the continuation of mutually inclusive behavioral practices, cultural syntheses, or the dominance of the customs and beliefs of particular ethnic groups.[8] Yet the specific reconstitution and development of marital and familial forms varied among the diverse regions in America and at different times within each region. This was so because treatment, labor demands, and epidemiological and demographic conditions—factors significantly determined by masters and the natural environment rather than by slaves—differed in time and place, as did the slaves' particular African backgrounds.

We look first at how West African and western Bantu marital practices fared in North Carolina. Nearly all of these societies have traditionally required a material consideration of the prospective groom and his family in order to legitimize and stabilize a marriage, to symbolize the worth of the woman, to compensate her family for the loss of a valuable member, and to help guarantee that the husband will treat her properly and fulfill his obligations. This can be paid to the prospective bride and her family in goods, in services, or in kind. If paid in goods such as cloth, currency, or livestock, it is called bride price, bride wealth, or bride gift. If the groom labors for the bride's parents, the consideration is called bride service. Payment in kind, exchange marriage, involves giving a woman of the groom's family to a relative of the bride in exchange for her. Bride price, however, predominates among these peoples and probably has done so in the past. It is often supplemented by bride service but seldom replaced by it. Exchange marriage is relatively uncommon.[9]

Eighteenth-century instances of West African bride wealth practices are briefly described in two narratives. The first one was written by Ayuba Suleiman Diallo, known to Europeans as Job ben Solomon. A Fulani Muslim, he resided in the Senegal River Valley in present-day Senegal or Guinea.[10] Covering the 1720s and 1730s, his account reveals Berber influences on the Fulani in that the bride's parents customarily transferred to her as a dowry the bride price they had received from her future husband's parents.[11] The author of the second narrative, written in the 1780s, was Olaudah Equiano (Gustavus Vassa), an Ibo who lived along the Niger River just north of its delta before he was sold to British slavers in 1756 at age eleven. His chronicle is often sketchy, as Equiano had to recall details of his childhood without having had contact with his compatriots for nearly three decades.[12] All that he notes about bride price is that the "parents of the bridegroom present gifts to those of the bride, whose property she is looked upon before marriage; but after it, she is esteemed the sole property of her husband."[13]

Much more detailed descriptions of bride price are found in a nineteenth-century compilation of various cultural characteristics of a group of slaves from Sierra Leone who had successfully mutinied and taken over a Spanish slaver, the *Amistad*. They eventually were captured by American naval personnel off Montauk Point, Long Island, and while a federal court in Connecticut during the 1830s was deciding whether to free the mutineers and return them to their African homes, a number of remarkable interviews were compiled. It is likely that the customs of these traditional folk, including that of bride wealth, had not significantly changed between the years we are investigating and the period of the *Amistad* mutiny. Moreover, there is no indication in the interviews that the practice of bride price varied among the more than six ethnic groups represented, as only one summation is given for all the tribes.[14] It notes:

> Matrimonial matters are managed somewhat after this manner. The gentleman calls upon the lady that pleases him and presents her some small gift; if she does not feel inclined to encourage his intentions, she refuses its acceptance and the matter is at an end. But if she receives it, thereby expressing satisfaction with the giver, she carries it after his departure to her parents; they hold a consultation, and if they approve, the suitor is made acquainted with the fact at a subsequent call; then or soon after he makes a present to the parents and takes the daughter. In case the parents are dissatisfied, it is the lady's duty to return the gift, and this closes the negotiation.[15]

Bride wealth in this description involves two gifts, one to the prospective bride, another, the major gift, to her parents. Either the prospective bride or her parents could end all negotiations by rejecting the first gift. Although acceptance by the bride's parents of the marriage was essential, there is no indication that either principal's family prearranged it or that any kin other than the parents of the prospective spouses were involved in these arrangements. Lineages are not mentioned.

Additional descriptions of bride wealth appear in two of the thirty-six biographical sketches appended to the general account. Neither reveals the ethnicity of the slaves. The only new information provided concerns the actual prestige goods paid for the wife and, in one instance, the role played by the prospective husband's mother. In neither case is a two-step process described. Explaining that "all have to pay for their wives" in his country, Ban observed, for instance, that he had paid for his wife "10 cloths, 1 goat, 1 gun, and plenty of mats; his mother made the cloth for him." Ngaboni stated that he had given "twenty clothes and one shawl for his wife."[16]

Perhaps the *Amistad* slaves had described more complex practices, including some ethnic variations in bride wealth, that were simplified or generalized in the process of translation and compilation.[17] Suggestive of this are the bride wealth customs of the present-day Yoruba in Nigeria, who reside about one thousand miles southwest of Sierra Leone. A recent study cites a number of details for the Yoruba that either did not exist in nineteenth-century Sierra

Leone or were omitted from the *Amistad* account. The Yoruban tribal oracle is consulted to help in the original decision by the bride's family, and at least four—and for some, five—types of gifts and many more actual payments are included in bride price. Most of the bride price is actually kept by the bride and used after marriage to help maintain her economic independence and to prevent her from being ill-used by her husband.[18]

Meyer Fortes stresses matrilineal descent in describing how the Asante observed the practice of bride wealth some fifty to seventy years ago. Asante bridegrooms and their matrilineages paid a variety of customary gifts to the bride, the head of her lineage, her parents, and her brothers. In addition, "offerings may have to be presented to gods (obosom) or medicines (suman) under whose protection the bride's parents have lived." The initial gift, *tiri nsa*, paid by the bridegroom's matrilineage to that of the bride (half of it to the bride's father), cemented the marriage, giving the husband exclusive sexual rights over his wife, legal paternity over all children born during the marriage, and the right to essential services from his wife. He was obliged to reciprocate by providing his spouse and children with food, clothing, and, if she had none, housing. He also had to give her sexual satisfaction, provide for her when she was ill, assume her debts, and obtain her consent before seeking another wife. Divorce could be granted if either partner did not live up to his or her responsibilities, especially those concerning sexual satisfaction and procreation.[19]

A. I. Richards depicts yet another pattern of bride wealth for the same time period, here for the Mayombe, a western Central Bantu people who reside in the lower Congo River region southwest of Brazzaville, about six hundred miles as the crow flies to the southeast of the Ibo. The Mayombe, like most central Bantu and the Asante, currently are matrilineal and probably followed this pattern during the eighteenth century as well. Marriage among the Mayombe is described by Richards as a relationship in which "a man acquires sex access to a woman, and certain clearly defined rights to her services and those of her adolescent children in return for a substantial payment in money or goods" and his assumption of some obligations in the upkeep of the children. Marriage payments made by the Mayombe are considerably greater than those of other Bantu-speaking people Richards discusses—perhaps equaling during the 1940s in cloth, beads, and money as much as an unskilled worker earned in thirty to forty months. The men of the bridegroom's matrilineage apparently provide the marriage payment, but Richards does not denote who, if anyone, receives the bride wealth in addition to the bride, nor if more than one payment is made. In case of divorce, the bride price is returned to the bridegroom and his matrilineage.[20]

Despite variations in West and Central African bride wealth customs, the numerous convergences of practices and underlying similarities in functions and meanings probably made either the acceptance of one tribal pattern, the implementation of various tribal practices, or a synthesis of customs by slaves from different African ethnic backgrounds relatively easy if other factors did not intervene. In North Carolina conditions did significantly interfere, as indicated by John Brickell's description in the 1730s of an abbreviated form of bride wealth in which he observed that no marriage took place if the woman rejected a small gift by the prospective spouse. The smallness of the gift continued the West African practice of varying the material value of bride wealth in accordance with the comparative wealth of the people involved. In case of a marital breakup, Brickell added, the wife returned the gift.[21]

Although Brickell may have missed some details of the slave practice in his unsympathetic rendering of bride wealth, it is almost certain that the slave institution of bride wealth had lost many of its normal African functions. There were several reasons for this: the masters' delegitimation and frequent breakup of slave marriages and families, the limited economic value of female slaves to their African American families, and, conversely, the poverty of male slaves and their limited capacity to make choices. Thus, although the African custom of bride wealth endured, it could not effectively fulfill its traditional functions such as to legitimize and stabilize marriages and families, represent the worth of a woman, compensate her family for the loss of a valuable member, or help to guarantee that the husband would treat his wife properly and fulfill his obligations. If many of the specific African functions of bride wealth did not survive the transatlantic crossing, neither did many of its numerous organic interrelationships with the prospective spouses' class, status, and wealth accumulation and the customary tribal forms of polygyny, lineages, living arrangements, inheritance, and religiosity. What probably remained was a remembered ceremony that slaves used to highlight, consummate, solemnize, and, as best they could under the circumstances, stabilize their marriages.

The West African practices of bride service and polygyny did not continue in North Carolina even in such attenuated forms. The limited control a man had over his labor probably ensured the discontinuance of bride service. Sex ratios in the province, despite decreasing from 153:100 to 125:100 during the last twenty-five years of the colonial period, were not conducive to polygyny's continuation (see Table 1.7). Also making it extremely difficult for slaves to practice polygyny were such factors as the restricted physical movement of slaves, their poverty, their low population density, and, compared with the West Indies, the limited numbers of slaves on large plantations.[22] Last, when mainland masters for self-interested reasons accepted de facto slave marriages, they probably tended to press slaves to implement monogamy because it coincided with the needs of most male slaves and thereby could be used by owners more efficiently than polygyny to promote slave harmony, discipline, and productivity. Although the owners delegitimized and willingly broke up slave marriages and families, they could pressure slaves to practice monogamy on moral grounds with no discernible trace of embarrassment.

For slaves, however, monogamous marriages represented something more than succumbing to the demands of demography, plantation discipline, and the values of masters. To understand this requires a closer look at African marriage patterns. Once again, the testimony of the *Amistad* slaves is valuable. These records confirm for various ethnic groups of Sierra Leone what was probably true among the vast majority of African societies: polygyny, although preferred, was hardly the exclusive or even the predominant nuptial form practiced at any given moment. Sixteen of the thirty-six interviewed *Amistad* mutineers were married, and of these only one, Fabanna, a middle-aged Mende slave, was polygynous. He had two wives. Of the fifteen monogamous slaves (seven Mende, one Nalu or Baule, one Temne, one Gbande, and five whose ethnicity is not known), eight were "middle-aged," perhaps around 30–35, and seven were younger adults, probably between 18 and 25 years of age.[23] Testimony concerning marital practices in eighteenth-century Sierra Leone corroborates the *Amistad* evidence. An English slave trader in 1788 reported that "tho polygamy is allowed in ye Country it is practiced only by the rich."[24] Such data stress a point long obvious to anthropologists; wherever polygyny has been or is the "preferred" marital form, monogomy is acceptable and probably common because of limits imposed by demographic and economic factors.[25]

Slaves coming from Africa, then, had experiences encompassing both polygyny and monogamy and thus need not have relied on their masters' example to institute monogamy. Indeed, most male slave imports, normally young adults who had not had time to accumulate much wealth, had practiced only monogamy in Africa prior to capture. When confronted by the severely limiting demographic and social conditions in America, they tended to replicate their monogamous but not their polygynous tribal experiences. Owners in the southern mainland colonies simply reinforced this tendency. Albemarle Sound slaveowners, Brickell observed, became involved in the marital arrangements of their slaves only to give permission for such unions or when no children had been born within a year. In the latter case planters might "oblige" slave women "to take a second, third, fourth, fifth, or more Husbands or Bed Fellows; a fruitful Woman amongst them being very much valued by the Planters, and a numerous Issue esteemed the greatest Riches in this Country."[26]

However common planter-induced serial monogamy was in North Carolina during the 1730s, plantation records for the second half of the eighteenth century do not support Brickell's suggestion that owners frequently broke up and reconstructed slave marriages to impel more prolific matches. The data do support his general contention that masters had a keen interest in slave fecundity and consequently acquiesced to slave attempts to implement monogamous marital arrangements.[27] Slaves did so informed by their memories and preferences within the constraints imposed by slavery.

Among these curbs none demarcated marital and familial possibilities for slaves more precisely than did the demands of demography. North Carolina's relatively late settlement and immature slave economy, with its diversified production of tobacco, lumber products, naval stores, grains, and provisions, is reflected demographically most precisely in the extremely low density patterns of its black population, by far the lowest in the South. Also, except for Maryland, North Carolina had the smallest slave population and the lowest proportion of blacks in its total population of any of the southern colonies. Nonetheless, North Carolina had one of the fastest-growing slave populations on the mainland. Moreover, by midcentury slaves in the coastal regions had come to be about as heavily concentrated on large plantations as were slaves in three surveyed tidewater counties in Maryland and Virginia. Even more surprisingly, during the 1760s the Lower Cape Fear region of North Carolina, where the colony's slaves were most heavily concentrated on large plantations, had aggregations similar to those that prevailed in the low country of South Carolina.[28]

Sex ratios and "sex imbalance ratios" (a new scale we have constructed to measure sex disparities) also reflect the relatively late but uneven regional development of the slave economies of North Carolina. A decrease in sex ratios in the province from about 153 during the years 1751–55 to approximately 125 between 1761 and the Revolution demonstrates the late maturation, but also the increasing opportunities for slaves in North Carolina to find mates and raise families.[29] Sex imbalance ratios, a surer guide than sex ratios to marital possibilities among slaves on individual plantations, suggest that the proportion of slaves who could not find spouses on individual plantations was considerably greater than the figures indicated by sex ratios. Viewed in the aggregate, sex imbalance ratios indicate, during the years 1748 to 1772, that at a maximum about one-third of the slaves living in the eastern counties could not find mates; one-half were so affected in the inner coastal plain and eastern piedmont counties and two-thirds in the western counties (see Tables 1.7–1.8).[30]

Although the use of sex imbalance ratios corrects downward overestimates of the demographic possibilities of slave marriages calculated from sex ratios, these figures still overstate the slaves' opportunities for marriage. This is true because marital possibilities calculated from sex imbalance ratios do not take into account the number of related slaves on each plantation who could not marry because of their incest taboos and exogamous tendencies. We consequently have felt it necessary to develop new algorithms to estimate more accurately for the years 1750–75 not only the proportion of slaves who were married, but also the number of children who lived with them in dual-headed nuclear family units, the number of children in single-headed families, and the number of slaves who lived on plantations where no visible family members were present (see Table 7.4).[31]

As illustrated in Tables 7.4–7.7, plantation size is the most significant indicator of marital and familial development among slaves. Thus, as was the case in other colonies, the dual-headed family in North Carolina from 1750 to 1775 probably was the most common familial form on estates with sixteen or more slaves; one-half to three-fifths of these slaves comprised such families in the colony. Slaves on smaller plantations in the province had fewer chances of living with both their parents, the incidence dropping to between one-fifth to one-quarter among slaves residing on estates with two to five slaves.

Analyzing all the slaves as a single cohort, most did not live in dual-headed families in the province during the years 1750–75. An average of from 35 to 43 percent of all slaves probably made up such families during the last twenty-five years of the colonial period. If, despite insufficient samples, we distributed the data summarized in Table 7.4 into time cohorts, we would find that dual-headed families increased 1.3 times from the 1750s to the 1760s and 1.4 times from the fifties to the seventies. Given such trends, it is possible that by 1775 about half the slaves in the province lived on plantations with their mothers and fathers. Yet throughout the period reviewed, some 36 to 44 percent of the slaves comprised single-headed families and close to 22 percent lived on plantations with no parents present. The dual-headed family among slaves on individual plantations, therefore, still was in the process of becoming the predominant institutional form in colonial North Carolina that it would be in the state during the nineteenth century.

Patterns of familial development similar to those that occurred over time for the entire province may be discerned for the various regions of North Carolina because of differences in maturation. Between 1750 and 1775 more than two times as many slaves comprised dual-headed families in the eastern regions of Albemarle Sound and Neuse-Pamlico than in the Western region (see Tables 7.5–7.6). Indeed, only about 17 to 21 percent of the western slaves lived on the same plantations as did both of their parents. The statistics for the east and the west, however, normally exhibit the same monotonic tendencies, that is, the larger the estate, the greater the proportion of slaves comprising dual-headed families.

This discussion of dual-headed families, it must be reiterated, refers to those that existed on individual plantations.[32] An unknown number of the heads of single-headed households had spouses living on separate farms or plantations, the children occasionally being divided between the parents but more likely living with the mother. In any case, the high percentages of single-headed families and unattached slaves on individual plantations in colonial North Carolina suggest that demographic factors prevented many slaves from marrying and forced others, adults and minors, to live apart from spouses and families either temporarily or permanently. Although factors beyond the control of slaves usually caused such separations, the willingness to consummate interplantation marriages and the ability to deal with living apart from loved ones depended in large part on whether the slaves could develop suitable compensatory social and psychological devices.

That slaves did this can be gleaned from Herbert Gutman's study of slave naming practices. Gutman argues that nineteenth-century slaves most frequently named children for fathers because they "were more likely to be separated from their children than mothers." The naming process thus "confirmed that dyadic tie and gave it an assured historical continuity that complemented the close contact that bound the child to its mother."[33] Available plantation records indicate that slaves in colonial North Carolina also tended to name their children after fathers more frequently than after mothers: 50 to 60 percent as compared with 16 to 20 percent.[34]

West and Central African customs directly helped slaves deal with the problem of living apart from spouse and family. This may be seen, for instance, in the residential patterns of the Asante and Fante of Ghana. Women on marrying traditionally go to live in their husbands' compounds, but when pregnant they return to their matrilineal households and remain there for three to four years, or until they wean the child. During lactation Asante and Fante women may not have sex, and the husband's sexual needs are satisfied by institutionally approved extramarital sexual liaisons and polygynous relationships. New marriages may also be consummated at this time. After weaning, the wife returns to her husband's compound and sexual intercourse resumes. The child, however, remains behind to be reared by the matrilineage under the primary authority of the oldest maternal uncle, the lineage providing both economic sustenance and eventual inheritance. Each succeeding pregnancy follows the same process. After menopause wives normally return to their matrilineal homes.

Although the Ga, also of Ghana, practice the same sex taboos as those of their Akan-speaking neighbors, their customs vary because they are patrilineal. Ga women customarily live in their own patrilineal family compounds after marriage. Husbands, who reside in their own familial homes, visit their spouses from time to time. Children stay with their mothers until weaned and then live with their fathers and their patrilineages.[35] A different residential pattern prevails among the Ibo of southeastern Nigeria, a patrilineal and patrilocal people; each co-wife lives with her children in a separate hut or apartment in her husband's compound. Finally, among the matrilineal Mayombe the basic domestic unit is a parental polygynous family located in the husband's village. This homestead in pre-European days also included the huts of slaves. Mayombe children remain in the homestead until they marry, when they settle elsewhere, the sons and their wives and children residing in the homestead presided over by their mother's oldest brother. Also living in this compound are the daughters' grown sons, unmarried and married, and the daughters' unmarried but adolescent daughters. In case of divorce the mother and her children immediately go to live in the compound presided over by the mother's senior brother.[36]

The precise practices may vary, but the fact remains that wives and children in West and Central Africa often have lived apart from their spouses and fathers. Such practices were sufficiently widespread to have influenced the attitudes of uprooted and enslaved Africans toward the idea of spouses and children living on separate plantations. Presumably this background made interplantation marriages and familial separations somewhat more palatable to slaves *who had reasonable access to their spouses, parents, and children.* This tendency would have had special force during the colonial era, when Africans and their mores and values were most significant. Even then, of course, slaves frequently had to draw on their memories without the presence of networking African institutions that gave meaning, identity, nurturance, support, security, and satisfaction to mothers, fathers, and children who formally lived apart. In time slaves partially bridged their institutional limitations with the development of extended families and significant communal ties.

Before further discussion of the growth of extended slave families, let us examine the interior life of the nuclear family itself. When did slave women commonly give birth to their first child? What was the typical interval between children, and how large were slave families in eighteenth-century North Carolina? Admittedly the samples available for the study of birthing patterns are imperfect. Considerably smaller than those used for our review of slave marriages and nuclear families, they also are drawn solely from data relating to slaves on larger plantations. Our analysis thus depends on the birthing experiences of slave women who had maximal demographic opportunities to marry and procreate, but we know of no way to correct for resulting statistical distortions.

Establishing the early age of slave women at primapartum is easier than explaining why they were so young. Many reasons have been given. John Brickell in the 1730s suggested that masters pushed young slave women to have children for the reason that "a fruitful Woman amongst them being very much valued by the Planters, and a numerous Issue esteemed the greatest Riches in this Country."[37] Some historians doubt that masters interfered in this fashion, arguing that if they had done so there would be a closer correspondence between the age when slave women actually began to bear children and the age at which they became biologically capable of doing so. Any gap between the two ages, indeed, is treated as prima facie evidence of insignificant planter interference.[38] It demands too much of the argument for effective planter intervention, however, to postulate that its validity depends on establishing the fact of complete dominance in the determination of when slave women would begin to bear children.

Several other conditions may have hastened childbearing among slave women. High sex ratios, for instance, normally created social pressures on females to begin childbearing at an early age because of the excessive number of mates available for women. West African beliefs presumably also influenced slave parents to bear children early and often. In traditional West and Central African societies children consummated and blessed marriages, gave parents status, respect, and sustenance as the life cycle progressed, and after death offered their parents' spirits proper ritualistic respect.[39]

If some needs prompted early birth, others could lead in the opposite direction. In the West Indies slave parents, fearful of their advancing years, often persuaded children to remain unmarried because of their economic contribution to the family.[40] A similar if considerably less-pronounced situation may have existed among mainland slaves. It is possible, too, that white childbearing practices affected slaves. White women, on average, began to bear children well beyond the onset of menarche. Slaves could have used this as a role model, one that reinforced and interrelated with their own inclinations to postpone sexual activity.[41] Moreover, white pressures on slave women to begin bearing children at an early age might have been somewhat tempered by the whites' own sexual behavior.

The full and undoubtedly complex answer to the conundrum remains elusive. Whatever the relative significance of each causal factor, the early age at which slave women began to bear children hardly rules out, and rather reinforces, arguments that planters effectively pressured slave women to begin bearing children early. Nowhere is this more evident than in colonial North Carolina. Trussell and Steckel estimate that menarche occurred among slave women, at the latest, by age fifteen and that early sexual intercourse would thereby probably have produced an average age at the birth of a first child of 16.6–17.0 years.[42] In our sample, seventeen was the approximate mean and median age at which North Carolina slave mothers born between 1766 and 1780 gave birth to their first child. The mean ages of mothers born during the years 1726–41 and 1781–92 were somewhat higher, about eighteen and nineteen respectively. Placing all the mothers within a single cohort, 1726–92, the mean and median ages equaled about eighteen, or on the average a year to eighteen months after they were biologically capable of bearing children (see Table 7.7).

Although slave women in neighboring colonies also began to give birth at an early age, they did so later than did slave mothers in North Carolina. Slave women on the Ball family plantations in the South Carolina low country during roughly the same years as in North Carolina on the average gave birth to their first child from one to two and one-half years after the age that prevailed among their North Carolina cousins. Their median age, however, varied from the same age to about one year older (see Table 7.8). In southern Maryland during the 1720s and 1730s, slave mothers on the average were about six months older at first conception than their counterparts in North Carolina (see Table 7.9).

Despite these differences, the following points may be made for all these provinces. First, slave women generally began to bear children at an early age although sometime after they were biologically capable of doing so. Second, a combination of factors probably determined their early age at primapartum: an African continuum, demography, African American sociocultural needs and characteristics, and white pressures and models. Third, as a result, from 1740 to the Revolution slave women at primapartum usually were considerably younger than white women in the colonies; in North Carolina the difference was approximately three years, a statistically significant variance.[43] Fourth, variations in the age of slaves at primapartum were pronounced *within* each of the colonies, although the range in North Carolina was less than elsewhere (see Tables 7.10–7.11). A sizable proportion of the slave women began to bear children at an extremely early age. In North Carolina among those mothers born from 1726 to 1792, only four (10 percent) gave birth to their first child after reaching twenty (none did so over age twenty-four). Thirty-one (77.5 percent) had their first child between fifteen and nineteen, and five (12.5 percent) gave birth before the age of fifteen (see Table 7.10).

If slave women tended to have their first child at an early age, childbearing among them often was interrupted or prematurely ended by demanding work regimens, the sickness and death of either spouse, and the forced separation of married slaves, either permanent or temporary, as a result of sale, estate breakups on the death of owners, the early bequething of slaves by owners to their children, the redistribution of slaves to different quarters, and hiring-out practices.[44]

In addition, and despite slave attempts to establish marriages and families at an early age, carryovers of West African birth control practices may also account for the relatively long birth intervals that came to prevail among eighteenth-century slaves. Cheryll Ann Cody rejects the statistical significance of such practices, for though accepting the persistence of West African modes of nursing, she denies their effectiveness as contraceptive techniques and flatly rejects the possibility that West African sex taboos continued among the Ball plantation slaves. Instead, she postulates that slave births occurred within the context of free fertility patterns as affected by plantation labor demands and epidemiological factors.[45] On the other hand, Joan Gundersen, in her study of colonial slave and white women living in a parish around Richmond, Virginia, argues that slave women continued, at least in part, both West African lactation practices and sex taboos. She uses this factor to help explain the exceptionally wide range of birth intervals that prevailed among slave women in her sample. The particularly high birth intervals that existed among our sample of North Carolina slave women, averaging five to eight months longer than Gundersen's Manakin slaves, is even more indicative of an African continuum (see Table 7.12).[46]

Birth intervals among North Carolina's slaves on the larger plantations were considerably higher than those that prevailed among slave women on the Ball plantations in South Carolina, in the Chesapeake region, and in the Richmond area of Virginia. In North Carolina birth intervals for the years 1725–60 and again for 1766–1808 averaged thirty-three and thirty-six months. The median figures are thirty-six and thirty-four. Differences between the average intervals among slave women in North Carolina and those in the other regional groupings thus ranged from five to ten months, and median differences equaled three to nine months (see Table 7.12).

The size of completed slave families in part reflects statistically the length of birth intervals among women who lived through their childbearing years and their age at primapartum. We have included as completed families the children of all mothers who lived to or beyond their forty-fifth year. Other investigators use variant gauges, a fact to be considered in reviewing the following comparative analysis. Estimates for mean and median completed family size in North Carolina for slave families begun during the years 1725–85 equal 8.4 and 8.5

respectively (see Table 7.13). These figures are much lower than those among slave families on the large plantations of the Ball family in coastal South Carolina, the mean and median size equaling 10.8 and 12.0 respectively (see Table 7.13). The composite mean completed size for an expansive eighteenth-century Chesapeake sample, however, is about 8.0, or comparable to that for North Carolina (see Table 7.14). Most slave families were considerably smaller than are indicated by figures for completed family size because of high mortality and morbidity rates, severe labor demands on slaves, and marital breakups.[47]

Thus far, we have only alluded to the importance and complexity of West and Central African familial units beyond nuclear families. We now must discuss in detail why and how familial groupings such as extended families, lineages, and clans either survived or succumbed to the ordeal of the transatlantic crossing to North Carolina. It is understandable that uprooted Africans would attempt strenuously to reconstruct extended families because of their past significance in Africa and the important functions they could perform for the slaves. Yet many of the elaborate structures and patterns within which extended families existed and were defined in African societies—for example, lineages, clans, and various interrelated political institutions—could not be rebuilt in North Carolina. Political institutions normally were well beyond the reach of slaves, and unilineages were dysfunctional since they traced ancestry and gave most of the significant social functions to either the familial line of the father, patrilineage, or to that of the mother, matrilineage. Such unilineal descent and organizational patterns were too luxurious for slaves who had to horde and use all members of the family to the fullest extent. Descent, therefore, came to be traced bilaterally, through both the maternal and paternal lines. Because clans were comprised of kin groups defined significantly by existing unilineages and affinal ties, they, too, could not be transplanted by the slaves.[48]

Evidences of bilaterally defined extended families among slaves are, however, frequently found in surviving plantation records. Of the fifty-seven slaves on the Allen plantation in the Lower Cape Fear county of New Hanover in 1761, for instance, thirty-six were members of five families, each consisting of three generations. John Walker of Wilmington, also in New Hanover County, left less detailed records about his slaves, but of the sixteen listed, ten were members of a single three-generation extended family.[49]

On Thomas Pollock's plantation in Craven County (Neuse-Pamlico region) in 1770, only 5 of 122 slaves seem to have had no relatives on the estate.[50] Forty-nine slaves were members of single-headed families, and another 60 were

Figure 2. Old George and Kate's Family on the Pollock Plantation, Craven County, Neuse-Pamlico Region, 27 March 1770

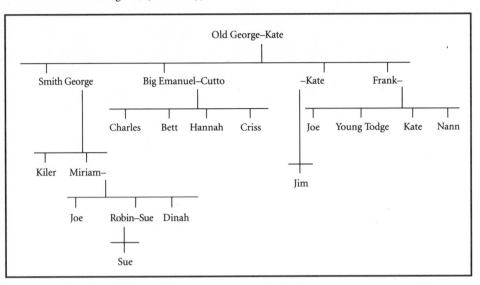

Source: "Lean by Thomas Pollock to Jacob Mitchell," Craven County, Pollock Papers, P.C. 31.1, North Carolina State Archives.

members of dual-headed families. Three of the slave families each had three generations, and, most remarkable, Old George and Kate's family spanned five generations. The great-great-grandparents, Old George and Kate, had four children, eleven grandchildren, four great-grandchildren, and one great-great-grandchild. The family of Old Emanuel and Jenny, who had eleven children, only encompassed two generations, but a comparative name analysis of this family and that of Old George and Kate suggests that the two were related in some way. Each family named one son Emanuel and another George, although in different rank orders, and two of Old Emanuel and Jenny's daughters had the same names as two of Old George and Kate's granddaughters, Bet (Beth) and Nanny (Nann) (see Figures 2, 3). Assuming that the two families were related, they not only represented 30 percent of the 122 slaves on the plantation, but also, in addition to the relationships already listed, comprised a network of uncles, aunts, nephews, nieces, and cousins. By 1770 extensive kinship lines clearly had developed among North Carolina slaves on large plantations in the east and probably on such estates everywhere in the province. Moreover, evidence and logic argue that kinship ties also reached beyond single plantations.[51]

Given the dearth of records, few of the functions performed by extended slave families in colonial North Carolina are known. One that was documented was the role assumed by some grandparents as effective heads of three-

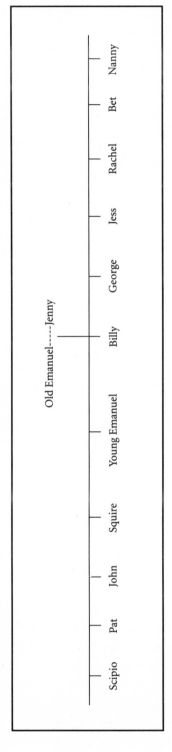

Figure 3. Old Emanuel and Jenny's Family on the Pollock Plantation, Craven County, Neuse-Pamlico Region, 27 March 1770

Old Emanuel----Jenny

Scipio   Pat   John   Squire   Young Emanuel   Billy   George   Jess   Rachel   Bet   Nanny

Source: See Figure 2.

generation families consisting of grandparents, their immediate families, and those grandchildren who were members of single-headed families. Additionally, older mothers or fathers at times lived with mature children. Grandparents assumed responsibilities for child rearing, then, at least occasionally, and both parents and children often gave and received support and nurturance throughout their lives.[52]

Equally evocative are slave naming practices. The extended family of Old George and Kate in conjunction with the family of Old Emanuel and Jenny, for example, illustrates that children were named not only after parents but also after grandparents, as well as uncles and aunts separated by two, three, or more generations (see Figures 2, 3). These naming patterns reveal, as Herbert Gutman notes, the existence of "self-conscious African-American slave kin networks" and suggest the significance of a wide variety of relatives.[53] The paucity of records conceals the actual roles and functions of such relations and relationships.

Increasing numbers of slaves in North Carolina in the course of the last two and one-half decades of the colonial era drew on their African pasts to build monogamous marriages and nuclear and extended families. By the Revolution perhaps one-half of the colony's slaves constituted dual-headed nuclear families on individual plantations. Other African marital and familial elements such as bride service, polygyny, lineages, and clans never gained a recognizable foothold in the colony. Still others like bride price only existed in attenuated forms because they remained largely isolated from African institutional supports. The acceptance by spouses of living in separate households on different plantations if they had sufficient visiting privileges undoubtedly depended more on demographic circumstances than an African past that, nonetheless, helped prepare slaves for this eventuality. Finally, an early age of eighteen at primapartum, relatively high birth intervals of thirty-five months, completed family sizes averaging eight to nine children, and smaller actual family sizes all suggest that birthing characteristics among North Carolina's slaves followed a tortuous path imposed by demography, epidemiology, a harsh labor system, and the examples, pressures, and constraints of slave owners as modified by the needs and African memories of the slaves themselves. Yet slaves did the best they could under the circumstances, constructing marriages and families that gave them nurturance, immense satisfactions, and a sense of identity—even well-being—in the midst of forced separations, pain, and heartache.

Thus, if much was in flux, change itself remained embedded in the cultural traditions of a variety of West and Central African ethnic groups. This was true with respect to slave languages, names, marriages, and families. As we will see in the next chapter, this also accurately describes how slaves in the diaspora responded to the challenges confronting their religious beliefs and practices. Slaves had to defend their heritage and themselves in these ways if they were to avoid internalizing the more nightmarish definitions that slaveowners had in store for them.

8

Slave Religiosity

Kidnapped by other Africans from his home in the southeastern portion of present-day Nigeria at the age of eleven, Olaudah Equiano passed through the hands of three or more African slaveowners before being sold to British slavers in 1756 and taken first to Barbados, then to Virginia, and finally back across the Atlantic to England as an enslaved twelve-year-old hand on a merchant vessel.[1] In each of these traumatic moves, the young Ibo lad somehow found the resources to deal with forcible and permanent separation from all he held most dear: his mother, family, friends, and village community. All slaves in the diaspora shared this disruptive, terrorizing experience, a hell that frequently resulted in death. Yet each uprooted African harbored somewhat distinctive remembrances, too often overlooked by historians primarily interested in aggregating the history of slaves. In Equiano's case, not only was he younger than most slaves separated from all kith and kin, but also by the time he reached Virginia he was denied the comfort of knowing any slave who spoke his native Ibo language or any other language he could communicate in, a situation he long remembered as being almost unbearable.[2]

It was within this numbing isolation that Equiano had to deal with the harsh and often brutal constraints of enslavement and the myriad of strange events and phenomena that bombarded his consciousness and demanded his understanding. Somehow, sense had to be made of these new experiences if disorientation and anomie were not to destroy this young African separated from the Ibo environment that had nurtured him from birth and enabled him to develop a sense of his place, his roles, and his consequent identity.

Although their actual environment and social structures were lost to enslaved Africans, memory, viewed both as conscious remembrance and as habitual response, continued intact.[3] Habitual modes of behavior and thought more often than not were viewed as categorical imperatives. Thus Ibo and other African worldviews, the "encompassing systems of meaning" that enabled them to routinize their particular ways of perceiving, thinking, and behaving, continued with Equiano as with other uprooted African slaves. Derivative from each of these worldviews were taxonomies, models, and goals that were also brought across the Atlantic at varying levels of sophistication by members of each ethnic group. These, in turn, permitted them as slaves to define reality and to choose rationally among alternate courses of action.[4]

Equiano's peculiarly severe problem was that he had to implement all this as a preadolescent isolated from older Ibo preservers and transmitters of culture. Still, his memoirs divulge several instances in which he strove to use his African past to understand new phenomena and experiences within slavery. One illustration reveals his intriguing response to the first clock he ever saw. Fascinated and menaced by this mysterious, ticking contraption that emanated from a technology and culture that he knew next to nothing about—least of all would he be prepared to understand an instrument that measured time precisely, discretely, linearly, and mechanistically—Equiano decided that the clock was a projection of his master's power that would reveal to him all of Equiano's behavior. This apparently childlike and bizarre understanding, on reflection, is neither when placed within traditional Ibo (or other African) religious belief patterns. Stressing the doctrine of *life power*, a capacity and process through which humans could manipulate lives and control events both positively and negatively, made it rational for the young Ibo to understand the clock as a particular extension of his owner's all-too-prevalent power.[5]

Similarly puzzled, Equiano explained the significance of the first portrait he saw as the means whites employed "to keep their great men when they died, and offer them libations as we used to do our friendly spirits."[6] This African sense of showing ritualistic respect to departed ancestors or great men (perhaps deified) was similar to the European use of portraits to demonstrate with pride and respect one's ancestral roots. Similarly, the African use of ritual and prayer in providing for the well-being of ancestral spirits corresponded with practices of Europeans. What was peculiarly African was the everyday behavioral, ritualistic, and prayerful interplay between living Africans and their ancestors, aided at times by specialists who could divine the causes or ways and means of alleviating or satisfying personal, interpersonal, or social problems or needs. The object of all this was to enable the living to achieve through one's ancestors a traditionally correct set of ethics, greater spirituality, and a more useful and secure life, while, by means of rituals, bestowing on ancestors the respect necessary to ensure their tranquility. It is impossible to ascertain the degree of sophistication with which an eleven-year-old Ibo comprehended all this, but as indicated by his understanding of the meaning of the portraits, many of the essentials apparently were in place.[7]

Shortly after his departure from Virginia, Equiano, who in the interim had been purchased by a British naval officer who commanded a merchant vessel, was in a severe storm while crossing the Atlantic to England. Terrified by the high waves, he concluded that the fury of the storm stemmed from the anger of the ruler of the sea toward the whites, who had not made proper sacrifice to his power. Equiano was terrified that he would be the logical choice of his white masters as a sacrifice to propitiate the wrath of the god they had offended. While in this emotional state he saw some large, fierce-looking "fish" (grampuses) that he imagined were the rulers of the sea. His fears were soon confirmed by a complete change in the weather that becalmed the vessel. Once again Equiano became desperately afraid that he would be thrown overboard by the crew to pacify the ruler of the sea.[8]

Not only is there in these recollections a stress on the necessity of exhibiting proper ritual respect to those beings who have power to affect our lives—in this case, the ruler of the seas incarnate in a large, fierce-looking "fish"—but there is also an emphasis on life power, that is, the human capacity to manipulate both natural phenomena and the deities themselves. But Olaudah Equiano's attempts to understand European artifacts and natural phenomena also suggest the possibility that the power manifested in *human* life is *the* most important. Or as others such as John S. Mbiti have contended, God or the gods in Africa seem to exist for humans. This leads Newell Booth to argue that beyond the idea of life power a second major characteristic shared by indigenous African religions, and understood by Equiano, is humanism. African religions, therefore, traditionally have been centered more on humans than on either God or nature, which, as Equiano's reactions also exemplify, suggests in turn the capacity of humans to shape their future in important ways.[9]

These few examples of Equiano's experience illustrate, at times cryptically, some of the essential qualities of African religiosity. Elsewhere in his memoirs he stresses the significance of family and community in Ibo culture (especially his close ties with his mother), whereas the instances cited above demonstrate the way humans must interrelate effectively with their total environment. All of this implies Booth's third overriding concept defining African religiosity, *wholeness*. To Africans, the sacred, that which is holy, is understood in holistic fashion. Africans find their fulfillment not as individuals but as members of families and communities. Difficulties of all kinds result from breakdowns within these relationships, and the restoration of tranquility hinges on re-establishing healthy, traditional associations. As Equiano's encounters with a clock and dangers at sea both show, humans also must interrelate with their total physical environment. Indeed, this environment at times, as was the case with the grampus, incarnates deities, and thus the African sense of wholeness transcends time and space and interconnects the living with the dead, the mortal with the immortal, the terrestrial with the celestial. It is in this sense that we can best comprehend the close, continuing ties between Africans and their ancestors, as illustrated by Equiano's comprehension of the portraiture.[10]

At this point it will be useful to examine more closely Equiano's reaction to the clock in order to gain greater insight into the African conception of time. Even if someone had tried to explain to Equiano the western meaning and uses of the clock, this explanation would have been foreign to the young Ibo's understanding. A precise measurement of a single, linear dimension of time that could be used to decide the performance and plans of people and be projected far into the future—all this would have been inconsonant with Equiano's Ibo understanding of time.[11]

Benjamin Ray delineates what he believes to be a common African approach to time. Despite variations in the creation myths adhered to by various African ethnic groups, they all emphasize the period of creation when the world came into being as a cosmogonic time that "moves from a state of cosmic eternity and perfection to a state of temporality and imperfection." Cosmogonic myth provides a model for the unification of these two time states, which are the reverse of one another: the divine, sacred, and immortal as contrasted with the human, profane, and mortal. Eternity can be joined with the transitory by repeating the gods' creative acts through ritual action. This may occur because of the special nature of ritual time, which is cyclical, not linear—"an interruption of ordinary linear time, a time out-of-time," when humans might reestablish contact with the creative occurrences of the cosmogonic period. The mythical past, then, is constantly recoverable through ritual and thus remains a constant source of ontological renewal.[12]

Traditional African thought thus turns to the past, not the future, for redemptive power. This does not mean that African religiosity lacks either a prophetic dimension or a sense of the future, as some have claimed. Divinely inspired leaders, indeed, have had visions projected to the immediate future. What African thought lacks is not a sense of the future, but that of an *indefinite* future.[13] Because of this, it is understandable, and not paradoxical, that Africans frequently call upon the services of diviners who brood about what might or must happen in the future. This is a future, however, that they conceive of with reference to the past. Or as Dominique Zahan so aptly puts it:

> "Tomorrow" is made up of elements of "yesterday" and "long ago"; it is the expression of the will of those who, though swallowed up by time, continue to testify to their presence in the multiple combinations of human destiny. In the light of this conception, can we not claim that for the African "what-will-be" blends into "what-already-was," that the future is in a certain sense the past, and that man is and will be only what he was? From this derives the diviner's profound belief in the ineluctable character of his "predictions" and, also, society's unlimited faith in the statements of its "seers."[14]

Ray, in turn, links this significantly determinate future, which Africans normally conceive as subsidiary to and defined by the past, to an African view of time as being local and foreshortened, microcosmic not macrocosmic. He then approvingly quotes Mbiti's observation: "The linear concept of time in western thought, with an indefinite past, present and future, is practically foreign to African thinking." Ray consequently asserts: "Instead of a linear, unitary conception of time, there are a variety of 'times' associated with different kinds of natural phenomena and human activities. Time is episodic and discontinuous; it is not a kind of 'thing' or commodity. There is no absolute 'clock' or single time scale. Time has multiple forms, coordinated in different ways, each having a different duration and quality, e.g., mythical time, historical time, ritual time, agricultural time, seasonal time, solar time, lunar time, and so on."[15]

If time is conceived as multiple, episodic, and discontinuous by Africans, on another level, as suggested by Booth, it nonetheless is subsumed within the African sense of wholeness. Present human communities act as links to unite the past with the present and the future, and thus with ancestors and unborn generations. The belief in reincarnation shared by some African societies is just one way to affirm this time-transcending continuity.[16]

Booth argues that the four concepts defined as life power, humanism, wholeness, and time-transcending continuity constitute the essential characteristics of African religiosity together with a fifth conception, *health*. The power to heal is an essential African religious belief understood in terms of the preservation or restoration of health to individuals and the community as a whole. Such healing power is contingent on correct human relationships and harmony with other persons and with the entire environment, including the time-transcending spirit world. This healing process involves not only following proper procedures to get something (as illustrated by the storm sequence in Equiano's memoirs), but also the celebration of what one possesses or has experienced. Persons may celebrate through ritualized or formalized expressions of appreciation such as festivals, feasts, singing, dancing, poetry, the recitation of myths, painting, and sculpture or other plastic artistic creations. These are understood as not only affirming wholeness and health, but also as contributing to them.[17]

If the eleven-year-old Olaudah Equiano managed to retain much of his African religiosity despite being isolated from his native culture, as well as significant contact with other slaves, it is hardly surprising that uprooted adult African slaves in more promising demographic circumstances retained and implemented an even greater portion of their religious past. The problem is to uncover substantiating evidence, as few colonial slaves left memoirs or letters and even fewer were interviewed by neutral observers. We thus must rely primarily on the observations of whites. The task is considerable, for we must take into account the ethnic and class-based biases that normally led them to be uninterested in as well as fearful, contemptuous, and only vaguely comprehending of the African roots and characteristics of slave religions. These attitudes, plus the Christian biases of white observers, explain their tendency to comment only on those aspects of slave religiosity that were most familiar and of greatest interest to whites: slave receptivity to conversion to Christianity, the desirability of conversion, and the quality and number of the neophytes. In short, when whites did attempt to discuss the African religious continuum among the slaves, the approach usually was ethnocentric, pejorative, and unsophisticated.

Although far too much reliance must be placed on the defective records left by whites, we still believe that the data argue persuasively that the vast majority of slaves in colonial North Carolina, and probably in the other southern mainland colonies, carried on the traditional indigenous faiths of their ancestors and made no pretense of being Christians.[18] Some slaves sought to continue traditional Muslim customs, as did Ayuba Suleiman Diallo (also known as Job ben Solomon) after arriving in Maryland in the 1730s. At times they too encountered the hostility of whites. "Job would often leave the cattle, and withdraw into the woods to pray," the white narrator of his life relates, "but a white boy frequently watched him and whilst he was at his devotion would mock him and throw dirt in his face."[19] The Reverend James Reed, Anglican minister of Craven County, testified to the presence of other Muslims in colonial North Carolina in a 1760 letter to the secretary of the Society for the Propagation of the Gospel in Foreign Parts (SPG); Reed estimated "the number of Infidels and Heathens to be about 1000" in Bladen County. Later in the same letter it becomes apparent that he considered most of the slaves to be "Heathens" and not "Infidels" (Muslims): "the greatest part of the Negroes in the whole county, may too justly be accounted heathens."[20]

Illustrative of the continuation of indigenous African religious beliefs among the slaves in North Carolina is a tantalizing interview, conducted in the 1930s by the Works Progress Administration, with Sarah Gudger, a 121-year-old former slave from North Carolina who had been born in 1816. Such interviews must be viewed with caution, as the interrogators generally were whites with whom the former slaves might be reluctant to discuss controversial matters. Aside from this problem, memory, even under the best of circumstances, is both selective and fragmentary. The interview with Gudger is especially suspect because it involves the reminiscences of an ancient ex-slave about events concerning her mother about a century before the interview. Still, her recollections are pertinent as they refer to beliefs in vogue in North Carolina during or shortly after the colonial years. In any case, Sarah Gudger's mother had noticed one night not long before she was sold to another owner that "de sta's wah fallin' jus' lak rain." Her mother was "tebble skeered" for, as Sarah explained, she believed that "evah time a sta' fall, somebuddy gonna die." The investigator who confirmed Sarah Gudger's age also corroborated that in 1833, when this event occurred, there was a spectacular shower of meteors.[21]

How does one treat this remembrance in an attempt to determine the effects of the African continuum on slave religiosity? The clearest connection is the mother's understanding that natural phenomena are causally related to human events. The falling star is seen as a manifestation of spiritual power that will cause physical death, or perhaps social death—the breakup of a family. Sarah Gudger and her mother, indeed, were separated after the meteors were seen. The mind-set is similar to Olaudah Equiano's seventy-seven years earlier. He too attempted to understand natural phenomena in typically African fashion by recognizing the power of a deity expressed through its control over the weather. Unlike Equiano's account, Sarah Gudger's recollection does not include an avatar (the grampus), nor does it discuss how humans who had failed to show proper ritualistic respect to a god could compensate for the oversight and pacify the angered deity's wrath, thus avoiding the consequences of their previous transgression.

The little information we have uncovered about the significance of stars, comets, and meteors to Africans only tangentially relates to Sarah Gudger's mother's experience with a meteor shower. Mbiti has noted that a few African societies personify such phenomena as spirits, whereas others like the Azande, Bambuti, and Chaga regard them as God's children. Some, including the Bavenda, Gikuyu, and Shona, view stars "as God's manifestations." Robert Faris Thompson, taking off on the first of Mbiti's observations, notes that in Kongo lore "shooting stars have been interpreted as spirits darting across the sky," whose special powers and insights might be creatively and permanently rendered in artifacts and invoked or used by officiants or others in the spirit manifested within the stars. He discusses how Afro-Brazilians and Afro-Cubans built on the religiosity of the Kongo by creating *minikisi* (charms or, in Cuba, *prendas*) that mystically absorbed the glitter of the falling star, "the flash of the spirit."[22] Thompson illustrates this in the case of a famous Afro-Cuban prenda: "They celebrate this prenda not in the house but in the forest . . . the stars come down to this charm. There is an hour in the night when the nkisi [singular for minikisi] is left by itself in the forest, so that the stars may come down, to enter into its power. When you see something brilliantly coming down—it is a star, entering an nkisi.[23]

In addition, because death understandably remained a fearsome although inevitable consequence of mortality, both for Africans and, as suggested by Sarah Gudger's mother's reaction to meteors, for their slave descendants, it had to be dealt with in metaphysical and ritualistic terms. For instance, we pointed out that Equiano's understanding of the first portrait he saw illustrates how Africans had to show proper respect to their deceased relatives to ensure that vengeful ancestors would not disrupt the lives of their family members and community. It follows that the death of a relative or an important person required that the mourners carefully pursue a variety of traditional observances to establish from the outset an amicable relationship with the spirit of their departed relative, who Mbiti refers to as the "living dead."[24] Culture-specific rituals and rites had to be followed to prepare the deceased properly for interment. Dahomeans, according to Melville Herskovits, saw to it that "the body of a member of a religious cult group . . . may not be touched by relatives until the priest and surviving members, employing elaborate secret rites, come and 'take the spirit' from the head of the body." Arguing that the continuation of such practices was widespread in the colonies, Herskovits cites examples in such diverse localities as Trinidad, Haiti, and South Carolina.[25]

After the corpse was properly prepared for interment, a variety of burial practices were used by different African ethnic groups. Nonetheless, a number of rituals were shared in common including, perhaps, burying the corpse without a shroud but with a variety of personal possessions and mounding and decorating the grave. Evidence for the latter two practices in the Americas exists only for the antebellum years and after.[26] Herskovits ably sums up the West African roots of such rites and burial practices and their continuation in the New World in the following passage:

> The elaborateness of funeral rites in the area is cast in terms of the role of the ancestors in the lives of their descendants, and because it is important to have the assurance of the ancestral good will, the dead are honored with extended and costly rituals. In all this region, in fact, the funeral is the true climax of life, and no belief drives deeper into the traditions of West African thought. For the problem of New World survivals this is of paramount importance, for whatever else has been lost of aboriginal custom, the attitudes toward the dead as manifested in meticulous rituals cast in the mold of West African patterns have survived.[27]

One additional survival, at least in attenuated form, that Herskovits points out was the common African practice of multiple burials. These were meant to alleviate the pain of bereavement while helping to ensure that proper ties continued between the living and the spirit of deceased relatives, "the living dead." Song, dance, and a celebratory mood seem to have typified the slaves' use of the second burial.[28] Unfortunately, the most detailed extant account of such slave behavior during the colonial years in North Carolina does not describe a slave funeral at all, but rather slave behavior at a white funeral. Janet Schaw, an aristocratic Scotswoman visiting her relatives at Cape Fear just before the outbreak of the American Revolution, describes this in her extremely interesting diary. She first notes the crass behavior of some whites at the funeral, either misunderstanding or aristocratically disdaining the social functions such occasions served among "lesser mortals." What happened after the other whites departed, however, truly intrigued her. "They were no sooner gone," Schaw reported, "than the Negroes assembled to perform their part of the funeral rites, which they did by running, jumping, crying and various exercices."[29]

Whatever the exact rites performed by the slaves that Schaw watched sympathetically, if uncomprehendingly, the dancing and singing that so fascinated her played a primary role not only in African funerals but also in many of their other celebrations. Some argue that the dance is one of the two chief nonverbal African aesthetic techniques used to understand, interrelate with, and, to some degree, capture the qualities, wisdom, and power of the ruling deities or spirits. This would be the case whether the dance was used to celebrate victory in battle, to deal with death effectively by ritually enabling the soul of the deceased to assume its spiritual roles, to ensure continued amicable relationships

The power of the African continuum among eighteenth-century slaves in North Carolina, Virginia, and South Carolina is illustrated in this watercolor by an unknown artist, found in Columbia, South Carolina, and probably painted on a plantation located somewhere between Charleston and Orangeburg in the last quarter of the eighteenth century. The musicians at right are playing a stringed instrument called a *molo* and a Yoruban drum (a *gudugudu*). The dance, presumably nonsecular, evidently is of Yoruban origin. The significance of the stick and scarves is not known. (Reproduction courtesy of the Abby Aldrich Rockefeller Folk Art Center, Williamsburg, Virginia)

between the living and their deceased ancestors, "the living dead," to give thanksgiving to the gods for their blessings of good crops and healthy children, or simply to engage in social entertainment that, in turn, contributed to good health.[30]

Schaw undoubtedly observed a limited expression by slaves of the music and dance they performed, if permitted, more usually at the second funerals of their fellow slaves. Such music was powerfully African in its insistent drum beats (when drums were allowed by slaveowners), hand clapping, and use of other traditional instruments within the framework of beautiful, at times haunting, melodies and syncopated and highly complex rhythms. The music, in turn, would be organically linked with dance, poetry, and drama.[31] Yet we have found all too little evidence of slave dances and music in colonial North Carolina beyond Schaw's comments and Elkanah Watson's account of the slave boatmen who "amused" him and other whites by "singing their plaintive African songs in cadence with the oars" while rowing across a starlit bay.

William Attmore briefly observed music and dancing in the 1780s: "I dined with Andrew Griers. After dinner saw a dance of Negroes to the Banjo in his Yard." A century and a half later, Hannah Crasson, a former slave now aged eighty-four, recalled that her aunt, who would have been born in the early nineteenth century, "waz a royal slave. She could dance all over de place wid a tumbler of water on her head without spilling it. She sho could tote herself."[32] Balancing objects on the head while dancing or as a mode of carrying burdens was a widespread skill in Africa; it remained commonplace among African Americans during and after slavery.[33] An ex-slave in Virginia, for instance, recounted how, during enslavement, she had "set a glass of water on my haid, an' de boys would bet on it. I had a great big wreaf roun' my haid an' a big ribbon bow on each side, an' didn't waste a drop of water on non of 'em."[34]

Perhaps the most fascinating examples of African-derived slave celebrations that combined costumed dancing, singing, and instrumental music were known by a variety of names: Jonkonnu in Jamaica and John Canno or John Koonering in North Carolina. Sir Hans Sloane first described this celebration in Jamaica in 1688, when he noted: "The Negros are much given to Venery" and despite being "hardwrought, will at nights or on Feast days Dance and Sing." Wearing "Rattles ty'd to their legs and wrists," the participants danced to the music of drums and banjolike instruments. Although Sloane did not give this ceremony a name, there is little doubt that it was the forerunner of increasingly elaborate ceremonies that by 1774 had come to be called Jonkonnu in Jamaica. Sometime before this date the ceremonies had been linked with the Christmas holidays, and during ensuing years they spread to other regions in the Caribbean, including St. Vincent, the Bahamas, and the Florida Keys.[35]

Just how, when, and where Jonkonnu spread to the mainland remains something of a mystery. It probably came from Jamaica but possibly directly from Africa. Except for a single description of a celebration in Suffolk, a town in southern Virginia, all accounts, strangely enough, are for North Carolina. In the earliest report, an overseer describes a "John Canno" ceremony in Edenton in 1823, "a sport common in this part of the state with slaves on Holy-days." Samuel Gregory, owner of the plantation where this ceremony was observed, explained that it had begun on Christmas Eve with the slaves "serenading & exhibiting" until late at night. The most detailed early account in North Carolina, however, was recorded about six years later by Dr. Edward Warren, who witnessed "John Koonering" while visiting Josiah Collins's plantation at Somerset Place, on the shores of Lake Scuppernong in Washington County, just south of Albemarle Sound.[36]

Internal evidence from each of these stories suggests that John Koonering had been in place for some time. The Edenton version, for instance, notes that it was "a sport" that was "common" in the region by 1824. Warren's report similarly describes a developed, formalized ceremony in which all those present—participants and observers, slaves and whites—understood their respective roles. Also indicating that the celebration was fairly long standing is the unusual manner in which the events were recorded at both Edenton and Somerset Place. In neither instance was the celebration chronicled by the owners of the plantations involved simply as a matter of curiosity. Rather, at Edenton it appeared in the testimony and depositions given at the trial and subsequent gubernatorial investigation of a slave, George, convicted of murdering an elderly white tavern keeper, Jesse Hassel, during the John Canno festivities. Although John Koonering at Somerset in 1829 was not described as an outgrowth of an extraordinary event, it was recorded by a trained observer, the physician John Warren, who fortuitously witnessed the celebration while visiting Josiah Collins's plantation.[37] This often was the manner in which various slave cultural characteristics were recorded for posterity. That is, talented itinerant observers such as John Brickell, Janet Schaw, and Edward Warren, not the slaveowners themselves, had the curiosity and acumen to document examples of bride wealth, burial rituals, and John Koonering. Slaveowners—uninterested, unsophisticated, or even hostile—either had ignored or overlooked such rituals over the years. Thus it is likely that Jonkonnu existed in North Carolina well before 1823 and that it probably was celebrated in other mainland colonies, although the actual chronology and specific locales remain a mystery.

All recent analysts agree that the roots of Jonkonnu are African, but controversy remains concerning the celebration's specific ethnic provenience. It is Sterling Stuckey's view that the festivities practiced by nineteenth-century slaves in North Carolina very likely were carryovers of Yoruban and derivative Ibo and Dahomean religious ceremonies that melded singing and dancing with other rituals. The original Yoruban harvest and fertility festival that reunited families and friends, who exchanged gifts during the festivities, eventually became syncretized with the celebration of Christmas. Its early years in the colonies undoubtedly had a more insistently African beat, with the slaves celebrating in their native or creole languages without the intervention of Christian syncretisms. Suggestive of this last is the early Jamaican example of Jonkonnu, which was not related to a Christian holiday and had, according to Sir Hans Sloane, significant sexual overtones.

The actual southern Nigerian rituals involved the use of masks, which probably represented ancestors who had returned to earth through these avatars. Occurring in June when the first fruits of the harvest had begun to come in, this principal festival sought the help of deceased ancestors to ensure both fertile fields and mothers. A possible direct linguistic tie between North Carolina's John Koonering and the African rite is that the eve of the Yoruban festival is called "Ikunle." At this time the leaders of the town would spend the entire night on their knees in a grove communing with and appealing to the prestigious ancestors of the town. According to Yoruban custom, but not a Dahomean derivative, women and children could not participate in any part of the ceremony; indeed, they were kept at a distance from the ceremonies by males carrying whips. The morning after the night in the sacred grove, the celebrants paraded to the leader of the town who saluted them and, in turn, received their blessing. Afterward a dance was held featuring traditional tunes, and during the festivities there were reunions and exchanges of gifts.[38]

Dr. Warren's account in 1829 vividly describes many ceremonies similar to those of the Yoruba. Before doing so, however, it notes that many of the slaves on Collins's plantation were old "Guinea negroes" who spoke "gibberish which was a medley of their original dialect and the English language." After trashing their creole language, Warren further berates these "antiquated darkeys" for still believing "in evil genii, charms, philters, metempsychosis [reincarnation] etc." Moreover, "they habitually indulged in an infinitude of cabalistic rites and ceremonies, in which snakes and the tails of lizards played a mysterious but very conspicuous part." He summed up by noting that they "were as uncivilized, even in their old age, as when they roamed in youthful freedom among the jungles of the dark continent."[39] As prejudiced as these comments are, they give powerful testimony to a significant African religious continuum.

This continuum becomes even more distinct when Warren depicts John Koonering. He describes a "ragman," the "leading character" of the ceremony, as wearing a costume possibly derived from the Yoruban ceremony, especially his mask and the stick (whip) he carried. His "get up" consisted of "a costume of rags, so arranged that one end of each hangs loose and dangles; two great ox horns, attached to the skin of a raccoon, which is drawn over the head and face, leaving apertures only for the eyes and mouth; sandals of the skin of some wild 'varmint; several cow or sheep bells or strings of dried goats' horns hanging about their shoulders, and so arranged as to jingle at every movement; and a short stick of seasoned wood, carried in his hands."[40]

The second most important slave in the ceremony was "the best looking darkey of the place," who accompanied the "ragman" but "wore his 'Sunday-go-to-meeting suit' and carried a small bowl or cup to collect the presents." Behind the two main characters were a half-dozen other performers "arrayed fantastically in ribbons, rags, and feathers, and bearing between them several so-called musical instruments or 'gumba boxes,' which consist of wooden frames covered over with tanned sheep-skins." These performers with their African-derived instruments were followed by slaves of all ages wearing ordinary work clothes. The entire parade made its way to the master's house. As they approached the front door, the musicians "beat their gumba-boxes violently" while the two leading characters performed "a dance of the most extraordinary character" involving "a combination of bodily contortions, flings, kicks, gyrations and antics of every imaginable description." Though they appeared to act as partners, each attempted to outdo "the other in the variety and grotesqueness of his movements." At this point, a seemingly extemporaneous song was led by the second leading character, joined in the chorus by the entire crowd "shouting and clapping their hands in the wildest glee." On completing his song the well-dressed character danced toward his master with hat in hand to receive the quarter the song called for, while the "ragman" sang at the top of his voice a song to give thanks for this Christmas gift.[41] Warren, with an eye for the continuing influence of Africa among the slaves, was convinced that this rite "was based on some festive ceremony which the Negroes had inherited from their African ancestors." Would that we could trace the earlier, perhaps colonial, antecedents in North Carolina that were still closer to their African forbears to demonstrate more precisely the correctness of his belief.[42]

Warren's observation that the older slaves of Somerset Place retained African beliefs in "evil genii, charms, [and] philters" while habitually indulging "in an infinitude of cabalistic rites and ceremonies," has even wider application to the forebears of the Somerset slaves in colonial North Carolina. Illustrative of this is Sambo's trial in nearby Pasquotank County on 2 August 1761, discussed in different contexts in previous chapters. Sambo was tried and found guilty of conspiring to poison, preparing the concoction for, and being an accessory in its administration to Mary Nash, the wife of Josiah Nash, the influential owner of a plantation situated close to where Sambo lived. The poison, "touck," the juice of a manioc root originally called "tuckahoe" by Algonquian-speaking Indians of the area, could be obtained by squeezing it out of the root. The root itself was edible after being cut and dried in the sun or before a fire and pounded into a flour for bread.[43]

Sambo's accomplice, David, who was owned by Nash, joined forces with Sambo in order to feed his mistress the touck (juice of the tuckahoe) "to make her better to him." Sambo, in turn, wanted to prevent Josiah Nash from purchasing Sambo's daughter because Mary Nash "was bad to the Negro." To this end Sambo, according to David, provided the "Touck to give his Mistress that would make her sick and if it did not do come to him and he would give him some more that could do."[44]

Sambo was a conjurer. This is evidenced by his rather peculiar sense of what would happen if Mary Nash ingested the touck. After all, there is no necessary connection between her being ill from touck with her beginning to treat David better and persuading her husband not to purchase Sambo's daughter. Without human intervention there is no reason to suppose either of these predicted consequences, and there is nothing in the court minutes to suggest that any slave tried to convince Nash that her illness should lead her to contemplate such actions. Indeed, any such communication would have been foolhardy, as the suspicions of whites almost certainly would have been aroused given their fears concerning the use of poisons by slaves. Moreover, both conjuring and the identification of Sambo as the conjurer are suggested by the leading role he played in the process. Why should David have collaborated with and deferred to Sambo? It was more dangerous to work with an off-plantation accomplice, and David almost surely knew how to make touck. Everyone commenting on touck in the court minutes appears to have been well acquainted with it. The answer is that we are not talking about a mere poison. Rather, it was a magical potion that could be prepared and administered only by a person well trained in the herbal and magical arts. Such specialists were common to a host of cultures throughout sub-Saharan Africa, and Sambo's mind-set and behavior, as well as his name, all bespeak of his close ties with these African traditions.

It is likely, therefore, that Sambo was a medicine man who, in the African tradition, would have been trained and experienced in dealing with sickness, disease, and misfortune. Because Africans believed that such adversity normally was caused or "sent" by another individual, the medicine man not only treated the malady with medicines from a variety of sources and with highly personal psychological attention and care, but he also dealt with the person who magically caused the problem. As Mbiti notes: "to combat the misfortune or ailment the cause must also be found, and either counteracted, uprooted or punished."[45] To do this, as Zahan suggests, the medicine man might have to use means similar to those who cause human misery through the dark arts of sorcery. It is hardly far fetched to assume that Sambo believed that he was dealing with a sorcerer in Mary Nash, for she fit the African pattern: most of the accused were females who supposedly directed their sorcery against relatives or neighbors, in this case, her own slaves.[46] Sambo countered Nash's penchant to cause misery by using traditional herbal and magical powers to restore the health and integrity of his family and of the surrounding slave community.

It would appear, therefore, that Sambo, in Pasquotank County on 2 August 1761, was a typical medicine man with African spiritual qualities, including herbal, social-psychological, and magical skills. He combined these special abilities to combat a force of darkness (Mary Nash) and protect, maintain, or reestablish the spiritual, psychological, physical, and social health and well-being of an African (slave) individual (David), family (his own daughter), and community (the slaves on the Nash and surrounding plantations).

This is hardly an isolated fragment of African religiosity that survived the ardors of the diaspora by remaining embedded in the memories and folkways of certain slaves. Rather, it illustrates a complex pattern of African beliefs and behavior that were integrated through the person and office of a specialist in traditional African medicine and religiosity (holistically defined), which were used to maintain the well-being and integrity of slaves, their families, and their community. Slaves were attempting to counter the enormous powers of a slav-ocracy and the terrible effects of enslavement with a typically African mind-set, worldview, and sacred cosmos that told them that they could, should, and must use available powers to protect themselves, their families, their friends, and their community. These powers were understood to embrace the now, the past, and the foreseeable future. They bridged the mortal and the immortal. And they helped to heal the sick, the infirm, and the unfortunate. There is or was nothing quixotic about either this analysis or this quest. Slaves, despite the new conditions that tormented them, tried to salvage their traditional ways of organizing and understanding their lives to ensure their continuity as a viable people. Given their tragic circumstances, their African religious dictum—that humans have the power to contest for their well-being, their health, and their future condition, mortal or immortal—served them admirably. The dream and the actuality of struggle, therefore, continued throughout slavery and after. And freedom could be grasped when the occasion arose or was created. This is not romance but reality. It was the reality that gave substance to the masters' fears, as paranoid as they, at times, might be. Sambo who lived in Pasquotank County was real. Even after this courageous medicine man's body was mutilated by his oppressors, we daresay the hatred that remained in his heart occasionally stirred a fear of retribution in the hearts of those who maimed him. And his daughter, who only comes down to us in one phrase in a county court minute, undoubtedly loved her father and hated his tormentors. This is not a victory for the slaves, far from it, but it speaks of conflict and illustrates a considerably greater humanity for the beleaguered and tormented than that exhibited by those who punished, who desecrated, who wielded the knife.

Interestingly, Job ben Soloman in his narrative of 1734 describes the poison used by Sambo to change the character of Mary Nash: "The milk, or liquor that is squeezed from the cassavi, or cassader roots (of which roots is made the bread of that name, used in Barbadoes, Jamaica, and all the Leward [sic], Caribe Islands) is so deadly a poison, that one pint of it will soon kill any creature that drinks it." Job goes on to note that "cassavi" was "native to America but widely used in West Africa as a staple food." Everywhere it was grown, including North Carolina, Native Americans and by cultural diffusion, blacks and whites, understood the uses of this parsniplike vegetable. They made bread or a porridge from it after the poisonous hydrocyanic acid of the sap had been removed and perhaps made use of the poisonous liquid, as did Sambo.[47] Unfortunately, particulars about the slaves' knowledge of the "poisons" that they brought with them from Africa or learned about in colonial North Carolina are unclear, except for the use of touck. What is certain is that slaves knew of and used poisons or "conjuring powders" to kill, hurt, or possibly transform their enemies, white or black. Records dealing with slave "crimes" make clear that Sambo's use of a poison was hardly an isolated phenomenon in colonial North Carolina.

It is equally certain that the use of touck was not an isolated instance in colonial North Carolina of the ability of slaves to assimilate Indian skills and their formidable knowledge of the natural world, and to blend these with their own vast repertoire.[48] The astute Scotswoman, Janet Schaw, more than two centuries ago recognized much of this when she observed that "the Negroes are the only people that seem to pay any attention to the various uses that the wild vegetables may be put to." To illustrate her point, she sent a friend "a paper of their vegetable pins made from the prickly pear, also molds for buttons made from the calabash, which likewise serves to hold their victuals." Recalling her grandmother, a North Carolina slave who died at the age of 110, Sarah Louise Augustus, a former slave interviewed in the 1930s, said: "She was great on curing rheumatism; she did it with herbs. She grew hops and other herbs and cured many people of this disease."[49] Except for Sambo's trial, however, the extant records say almost nothing about African integration of herbalism with religiosity.[50] As one would suspect, given the fears of masters, the documents speak loudest about the slaves' sophisticated use of poisons.[51]

If only the documents revealed more about the substance of the African religious continuum among the slaves of colonial North Carolina. They do not, at least to us. What may be presented with added effect at this juncture, however, are the reasons why we believe that the vast majority of the province's slaves remained unconverted and were only inconsequentially exposed to Christianity. Our discussion is divided into two parts: in the first, we will examine the relationships of the slaves of North Carolina to the established

Anglican Church; and in the second, we will attempt to assess how slaves responded to and affected the Great Awakening and Protestant dissenters.

The limited number of slave conversions is explained primarily by the predispositions of the slaves themselves: holding fast to their African religiosity in their slave communities, they hardly presented to European Christians minds uncommitted to another religious heritage. Thus the major reason for the successful resistance of colonial slaves to Christianization was their dependence on the traditional African religious beliefs and practices that gave meaning to their lives, helped to explain the myriad events that buffeted them in their bondage, and supported them in their attempts to withstand or counter white aggressions.

Many Anglican ministers understood the desperate adherence of slaves to their religious traditions. For instance, the Reverend Philip Reading of Delaware in a 1748 letter to England stressed, if disparagingly, the power of traditional belief patterns among slaves in the colony when he observed that one difficulty confronting would-be proselytizers was "the prejudices of Slaves themselves. Those born in Guinea are strangely prepossessed in favour of superstition and Idolatry. They have a notion, that when they die, they are translated to their own countrey, there to live in their former free condition: of this they are so fond, that many of them upon a slight affront (especially the nation called Keromantees) will lay violent hands upon themselves with great calmness and deliberation."[52]

Joseph Ottolenghe, lay catechist to the slaves in Georgia for the Society for the Propagation of the Gospel and Bray's Associates, followed a similar tack in 1754, when he noted that nothing is more difficult to remove "than Prejudices of Education, riveted by Time, & entrench'd in deep Ignorance." The Reverend Thomas Pollen of Rhode Island observed in 1755 that most slaves were not baptized and remained "in the same state of Heathen Ignorance as the Wild Indians." Ottolenghe repeated this assessment in 1758, when he complained of the difficulty of converting people who have "no idea of our holy Religion" and were "nurs'd in extravagent Idolatry."[53] That a similar situation existed in North Carolina is evidenced by the Reverend James Reed's identification in 1760 of almost all the slaves in Craven County as heathens who required considerably more attention than was possible in order to convert them to Christianity. Finally, the Reverend John Waring, secretary of Bray's Associates, wrote from London in 1770, in an overly optimistic response to messages like this, that despite the "strong attachment" of blacks "to the idolatrous Rites and Practices of their own Country," conscientious efforts by all whites in recounting the blessings of Christianity would turn most slaves from their "deep-rooted Impressions and long contracted Habits." Waring's Anglican brethren tended to disregard his blandishments, and slaves remained attached to the "Rites and Practices of their own Country."[54]

The linguistic differences and consequent communication difficulties between whites and blacks added to the obstacles confronting would-be proselytizers among blacks. Language factors together with the slaves' "deep-rooted Impressions and long contracted Habits" both shielded uprooted Africans from and made them strongly resistant to Christianization. Anglican ministers cited these very conditions to explain, rationalize, and justify failed or limited attempts to convert the slaves. Moreover, given the circumstances and the time period, it is hardly surprising that some of these same ministers succumbed to the temptation of blaming their difficulties on an alleged African biological inferiority. Rev. Philip Reading took this tack in 1748, when he observed that blacks were congenitally unable to understand the logical underpinnings of Christianity: the majority of blacks "seem to be of a species quite different from the whites, have no abstracted ideas, cannot comprehend the meaning of faith in Christ, the nature of the fall of man, the necessity of a redeemer, with other essentials of the Christian scheme." Joseph Ottolenghe, while stressing the adverse effects of the harsh treatment of Georgia's slaves, nonetheless in 1758 described blacks as being "naturally stupid." The Reverend Jonathan Boucher, an Anglican minister in Virginia, similarly wrote in 1764 about "the incorrigible Stupidity of the Majority of these wretched Creatures."[55]

As one might expect, these biases were even more pronounced among the planters. Bishop George Berkeley, after visiting America, complained to the SPG in 1731 that the chief obstacle to slave conversion was the planter's "irrational contempt of the blacks, as creatures of another species, who had no right to be admitted to the sacraments."[56] Twenty-eight years later Joseph Ottolenghe observed from Georgia that "Americans look upon their slaves, to have no Souls at all, and a favourite Dog or Horse meet with more humane treatments than they." Even Benjamin Franklin candidly acknowledged in 1764 that he only came to accept blacks as the intellectual equals of whites after observing the performance of black children in the Philadelphia school for blacks that was subsidized by Bray's Associates. He sheepishly concluded: "You will wonder perhaps that I should ever doubt it, and I will not undertake to justify all my Prejudices, nor to account for them." The remarks of the Reverend Marmaduke Browne of Rhode Island four years later suggest that many, perhaps most, northern slaveholders never underwent Franklin's conversion; Browne noted that masters did not "consider their slaves as the same species with themselves."[57]

Exasperated and somewhat incredulous at the pervasiveness of such views in the colonies, Rev. John Waring, of Bray's Associates in London, acidly asked Fielding Lewis, a wealthy and prestigious Virginia planter, if the slaveowners "ever consider that slaves have Souls" or question whether providence sent Blacks "among them merely to cultivate their Lands & do the severest Drudgery for their Masters worldly profit only without any regard to the Spiritual Welfare of the poor Slaves?" He went on to denounce the planters and proclaim that they would reap their just punishment "at the Last Day."[58] Nevertheless, Winthrop Jordan is probably correct in asserting that colonial Americans did not systematically argue black biological inferiority. Rather, they often confused and conjoined such assertions with sociocultural explanations, complacently proclaiming all this as an example of what they called black "stupidity."[59] Anglican proselytizers, indeed, emphasized sociocultural explanations, such as the commitment by slaves to traditional, African religious beliefs, more than the blacks' alleged biological inferiority to explain the paucity of slave converts to Christianity.

Clerics and others also emphasized that the harsh constraints of slavery and the poor moral examples provided by their supposedly Christian masters severely limited the desire of slaves to be converted.[60] Thus a 1715 Sabbatarian law, which forbade Sunday labor to free persons and slaves alike in North Carolina until its demise in 1741, alluded to the irreligious practices of the colony's whites. Ottolenghe in 1751 commented on the ignorance and heathenism of many whites and in 1753 typified many masters "as great Heathen as their slaves . . . a Scandal not only to human Nature but to our Holy Profession."[61] Two years later Rev. Thomas Pollen of Rhode Island complained that masters who were uninterested in Christianity were hardly likely candidates to stress its virtues to their slaves. Jonathan Boucher similarly lamented in 1762 "that several Whites, of respectable Characters, think themselves at Liberty to live totally ignorant of either of the Sacraments," many urging that baptism is "a Matter of Form" rather than of "Important Consequence." Ottolenghe had aptly summed up the problem three years earlier when he stated that it was "no Wonder that those who have so little concern for their [own] immortal Souls, should not attempt to the Salvation of those whom they believe to have no Souls at all!" As John C. Van Horne concludes from a review of all the letters he has compiled and edited: "Clergymen and catechists from Massachusetts to Georgia lamented the lack of concern [by whites] for the Church's ordinances and its effects on their attempts to convert blacks."[62]

Masters, uninterested in and uninformed about Christianity and hence hardly consumed by a desire to see their slaves converted, also generally feared the consequences of slave conversion and either strenuously opposed or refused to cooperate in the Christianization of their slaves. Perhaps the major concern of slaveowners from the seventeenth century through the first three decades of the next century was the commonly held belief that the conversion of slaves led to freedom. Such fears continued to disturb planters despite numerous assurances to the contrary by proponents of slave Christianization and the passage of laws that specified that the status of slaves would in no way be changed if they became Christians.[63] Maryland in 1664, New York in 1665, and Virginia in 1667 led the way in passing such legislation. Carolina's planters were similarly reassured in 1669 by section 107 of the Fundamental Constitutions, which attempted to provide the framework for the development of the colony's social and political organization. It reads: "Since Charity obliges us to wish well to the Souls of all Men, and Religion ought to alter nothing in any Man's Civil Estate or Right, it shall be lawful for Slaves, as well as others, to Enter themselves and be of what Church or Profession any of them shall think best, and thereof be as fully Members as any Freeman. But yet, no Slave shall hereby be exempted from that Civil Dominion his Master has over him, but be in all other things in the same State and Condition he was in before."[64]

A 1709 letter of James Adams indicates the limited impact of such assurances on North Carolina's slaveowners. The Anglican cleric complains that although a few of the 211 slaves in Pasquotank County had received religious instruction, planters would not permit them to be baptized because they had "a false notion that a Christian slave is, by law, free."[65] The provincial law of 1715, which restricted manumission, implicitly protected the planters from the feared consequences of conversion on a slave's status. That this statute too had only a limited effect is demonstrated by the lament of a Reverend Mr. Taylor in 1719:

> I was preparing 4 more of them for Baptism, and had taught one of those 4 their Catechism very perfectly, and the other 3 a good part of it, and now as I was about this good work, the enemies to the conversion and baptism of slaves, industriously and very busily buzzed into the Peoples Ears, that all slaves that were baptized were to be set free, and this silly Buckbear so greatly scared Esqur Duckenfield that he told me plainly I should Baptize no more of his slaves 'till the Society had got a Law made in England that no Baptized Slave, should be set free because he is Baptized and send it here, and many more are of the same mind, and so this good work was knocked in the head which is a grat trouble to me, because so many slaves are so very desirous to become Christians without any expectation of being set free when they are Baptized.[66]

As late as 1731 John Brickell observed that North Carolina's planters still feared that a slave's conversion would inevitably lead to freedom.[67] To offset such lingering apprehensions and to head off what were becoming more important planter misgivings about slave conversions, the Crown on 14 December 1730 instructed the newly appointed Governor George Burrington, and in subsequent years his successors, "to find out the best means to facilitate and encourage the conversion of Negroes and Indians to the Christian religion."[68]

Despite these royal instructions, planters had other fears about slave conversion that interfered with the diminution of their apprehension that Christianization necessarily led to freedom. Alarming masters, for instance, were the far-reaching implications of certain Christian tenets, such as the biblical account of a single creation with its derivative that all humans potentially are brothers and sisters in Christ who will stand, "rich and poor, bond and free," at the same level "before the Son of Man at the Last Day."[69]

Slaveowners also feared the immediate effects on slaves of such egalitarian doctrines, believing that slave behavior and attitudes demonstrably deteriorated after conversion. Converted slaves, masters often asserted, regularly became less obedient, less productive, "saucy," and more prone to run away, to commit violent crimes, or even to rise up in rebellion. Joseph Ottolenghe summarized these feelings in 1753, when he observed that owners often lamented that "a slave is ten times worse when a Christian, than in his State of Paganism." Two years later Thomas Pollen similarly concluded that the primary reason so few slaves were converted in Rhode Island was because masters believed that slaves "grow worse after Baptism." In 1770 the Reverend Thomas Baker of Virginia, where planters by law were obliged to baptize their slaves, summed up such planter misgivings: "since we got to baptizing them they are become insolent and Idle Runaways, etc."[70]

The common Anglican practice of linking conversion with education further exaggerated planter anxieties about the effects of converting slaves. Van Horne argues that fear of slave literacy was "more prevalent than the fear of Christianization itself," as planters believed that literacy had "no beneficial results" whatsoever. Slaveowners viewed it solely as a threat, fearing that it would facilitate communication among slaves and thereby increase the possibility of slave "conspiracies and insurrection." However correct Van Horne's assessment of various levels of planter misgivings, masters certainly had deep qualms about educating slaves and logically enough often joined this apprehension with their concerns about conversion. Both fears are suggested by the comments of two Virginians, Robert Carter Nicholas and William Yates, who in 1762 noted: "Another Difficulty which arises on the Part of the Owners is that an Opinion prevails amongst many of them, that it might be dangerous & impolitick to enlarge the Understandings of the Negroes, as they would probably by this Means become more impatient of their Slavery & at some future Day be more likely to rebel; they urge farther from Experience, that it is generally observable that the most sensible of our slaves are the most wicked & ungovernable."[71]

The following year the Reverend Alexander Stewart of North Carolina observed that his efforts to educate and convert blacks and Indians were hindered by whites who kept "the ignorant in distress." He hoped that the eyes of whites would finally be opened so that they would "assist the charitable design of this Pious society and do their best endeavours to increase the Kingdom of our Lord Jesus Christ." The Reverend John Barnett of Brunswick County, North Carolina, illustrated the ongoing nature of the problem when in 1767 he complained that the slaveholders of the county preferred to have "their Slaves . . . remain Ignorant as brutes."[72] "Many masters," the Reverend Mr. Baker of Virginia added three years later, "are not only averse to learning their Slaves to read but did not the Law oblige them, would not have them baptis'd."[73] Not surprisingly, these anxieties persisted despite repeated assurances by clerics that slaves would be grateful for the opportunity to become comprehending Christians and would consequently become more compliant, obedient, and productive slaves.

The loss of labor that would result from the time spent in Christianizing slaves and preventing them from backsliding once they were converted may have concerned owners most. Certainly, in 1713 masters universally felt that the slave's time on Sundays and holidays could be better spent either in the fields or, where slave gardens were significant, working "to clear ground and plant for themselves as much as will clothe and subsist them and their families." In 1758, forty-five years later, Ottolenghe of Georgia was still referring to the cost-conscious approach planters brought to slave conversion but accommodated himself by instructing slaves at night in order "to cut off their Pharoah's excuse that they cannot send their Negroes by Day because of their Labour."[74]

Secretary Waring, writing from London in 1770, attempted to make the best of the situation. He declared that slaveowners could minimize the loss of labor time by having their slaves instructed during the evening or on Sunday. Enthralled both by the potential profits available to agreeable masters and the heavenly benefits awaiting converted slaves, Waring completely overlooked the possible negative responses by slaves to a proposal that, in addition to requiring that they reject their religious heritage, interfered either with their leisure or time used to produce supplementary crops for their own consumption or for sale. Indeed, he assured owners that slaves would welcome catechism lessons and reward their masters' "Christian Compassion and Kindness . . . by a greater degree of Honesty, Fidelity, and Diligence in your Service." Although somewhat less certain of himself as surety for God's good behavior, Waring still raised the distinct possibility that in return for planter compliance with the clergy's attempts to convert the slaves, God might very well "bless your Basket and your Store, the Increase of your Kine and of your Flocks, and prosper you in all that you set your Hands unto."[75] Tempting indeed!

The temporary success of ministers of the gospel in North Carolina in obtaining the passage of a Sabbatarian law in 1715 for both slaves and freemen, consequently, was at best a mixed blessing for the slaves. As for the owners, although they originally succumbed to clerical pressure, by 1741 they allowed the law to lapse, apparently having had their fill of statutory interference with their "right" to work their slaves at pleasure.[76]

In sum, the major obstacles to slave conversion to Christianity were the continued dependence of slaves on and adherence to their African religions, their consequent resistance to conversion, and the linguistic barriers between whites and slaves. These impediments were exacerbated by the refusal of masters to cooperate with clerical attempts to convert the slaves. Moreover, Anglican ministers themselves often either ignored the slaves or made feeble attempts to reach them. Difficult circumstances and their own prejudices prevented them from developing a more effective program of outreach.

There were also institutional and doctrinal factors that interfered with Anglican efforts to Christianize the slaves. For one thing, wherever established in the colonies, the Anglican Church suffered because diocesan control rested in the hands of the bishop of London across the Atlantic. This often weakened Anglican leadership in the colonies and resulted in ineffectual establishment laws. In North Carolina workable legislation did not pass until 1764–65. These laws suffered from the absence of a bishop who could resolve the power conflict between the provincial governor and members of the parish vestries, who over the decades had competed to fill the power vacuum.

The Anglican Church had been, at least nominally, the legal or state church in North Carolina since it was so designated in the Proprietary charters, but it was not until 1701 that the Proprietary government took the initial step to establish the church. The first royal governor arrived in 1731 with instructions to set up an adequate church establishment, yet it took the Assembly nine more years to pass another weak law. Only in 1754 did an effective law finally pass during Governor Arthur Dobbs's administration, but the Crown disallowed it in 1759 because it placed control over presenting ministers in the hands of the local parish vestries. In 1762 the Crown repealed two further acts, passed in 1760. In 1764 and 1765 the legislature finally shaped strong laws, the Vestry and Orthodox Clergy Acts, that survived royal scrutiny.

Nonetheless, whatever vitality the church establishment achieved south of Virginia was largely attributable to the efforts of SPG missionaries. The Society for the Propagation of the Gospel in Foreign Parts had been organized in England in 1701 by the Reverend Thomas Bray to minister to the spiritual needs of all colonials, including blacks and Native Americans. Because proselytizing these last two groups was not the society's first priority, Bray established Bray's Associates in 1723–24 specifically to catechize and educate blacks in the colonies. But Bray's Associates proved to be unequal to the task of converting large numbers of slaves. In any case, the SPG assigned and significantly subsidized thirty-three of the forty-six ministers who served in North Carolina from 1701 to 1783. The full stipends provided by the SPG to their missionaries included annual salaries of £50 pounds sterling, a library worth £10, and a £5 yearly book allowance. Such remuneration usually equaled somewhere between one-half to two-thirds of the parochial stipends actually received by Anglican ministers in North Carolina during the period 1748–75, when laws were in place and the tax collectors properly disbursed their public monies. Whenever these conditions were absent, the missionaries relied solely on their SPG stipends; ministers without such allowances simply made it through the lean years as best they could, depending on secular sources of income.

Despite SPG missionaries, colonial North Carolina remained plagued by a severe shortage of Anglican clerics that seriously restricted its outreach to all colonials, especially to slaves and Native Americans. Although Anglicans could carry out some of their religious practices with only lay readers present, the absence of ministers severely sapped the sect's vitality because of its dependence on a learned clergy to preside over a ritualistic and sacramental church. The first Anglican minister arrived in 1705 after eight counties had been organized along the coast from the Virginia border south to Archdale County (later renamed Craven County) in the Neuse-Pamlico region. In 1732, three years after North Carolina had become a royal colony, Governor Burrington informed the bishop of London that the colony still only had three tenuously placed ministers. At the time, North Carolina had eleven counties—parishes normally being coextensive with counties. Governor Dobbs, in a letter of 29 March 1764 to the Board of Trade summarizing ecclesiastical conditions in the colony, noted that there were six Anglican clergymen in the province of whom four—headquartered in the towns of Edenton, Bath, New Bern, and Halifax—diligently attended to their duties, and two performed poorly. Shortly after enactment of the Orthodox Clergy Act of 1765, but a year after the passage of the Vestry Act of 1764, when North Carolina had fully twenty-nine counties, the number of Anglican ministers in the colony ironically had fallen to five—all but one of them SPG missionaries.[77]

The appointment of William Tryon as the new royal governor of North

Carolina on 19 July 1765 marked a turning point in the history of the Anglican Church in the province. While still governor pro tempore, he ensured passage of the Orthodox Clergy Act. Thereafter he conscientiously sought an effective church establishment up to the moment he left North Carolina on 30 June 1771 to become governor of New York. To achieve this, he strove to implement the laws of 1764 and 1765 and sought to expand their meaning while assiduously, though at times arbitrarily, using his gubernatorial power to increase the number of Anglican churches and ministers in the colony and enhance the quality of their outreach to parishioners. Thus, despite opposition from the parish vestries, Tryon interpreted the silence of the laws on who should present ministers to the parish churches as having authorized him to act. He also actively recruited clergymen for service. Bending the rules when it pleased him, he lured to North Carolina ministers who had been licensed to preach in Virginia and, at least in one instance, presented to a parish a cleric who had not been, as the rules directed, certificated and licensed by the bishop of London. On the other hand, he diligently sought certification by the bishop for a number of other individuals who had not been ordained and regularly badgered the SPG to designate and subsidize ministers already serving in the colony so as to encourage them to remain. Tryon's efforts paid off. The number of Anglican clergymen in the province jumped from five in 1765 to thirteen in 1767; seven of the new recruits had received letters of presentation to their parishes from Governor Tryon. By 1770, a year before he left the colony, the number of Anglican clerics had reached eighteen, the high point of his administration.

Despite impressive gains, Anglicanism still had problems. Sixteen of the thirty-four counties remained without Anglican clergymen in 1770. With parishes and counties usually coextensive, ministers confronted impossible situations in their attempts to cover enormous territories.[78] The existence of chapels and congregations serviced by lay readers somewhat relieved but hardly solved these problems. Parishioners in these situations only occasionally received the sacraments from either visiting or circuiting ministers.[79] Given such trying circumstances, ministers, even SPG missionaries, paid little attention to the needs of slaves, their primary responsibility being to serve their white parishioners.[80]

As the Reverend James Reed, an SPG missionary who served Christ Church Parish in Craven County, noted on 26 June 1760, ministers found it "impossible . . . in such extensive counties, to instruct them [slaves] in the principles of the Christian religion."[81] Reed followed this assessment with the oft-repeated complaint of the uncooperativeness of masters in slave conversion, concluding that he only baptized slaves "whose masters became sureties [godparents] for them."[82] In following this practice, Reed further ensured that he would have a limited impact on slaves, for masters normally were reluctant to serve as their godparents, and, conversely, blacks undoubtedly reacted negatively to being denied the right to choose godparents of their own race.

Although it is likely that slaveowners usually served as sureties for baptized slaves, black godparents were not as rare as has recently been argued.[83] It is impossible to present statistical evidence on this issue, as most accounts of slave baptisms do not specify the race of the godparents, and no systematic scholarly search has been undertaken to obtain a reliable sample. In any case, the Reverend Charles Cupples of St. John's Parish, Bute County, regularly used black sureties. In a letter to the SPG in 1768, Cupples calculated that he had "baptized 382 children, 51 of which were negro children," adding that "the engagements for some were made by their Masters and Mistresses, and others had Godfathers and Godmothers of their own color as having been previously baptized." Given the matter-of-fact way in which this was recorded, it is probable that a number of ministers who registered baptisms without noting who the sureties were may have used black godparents. Perhaps this was true for the Reverend Charles Edward Taylor of St. George's Parish, Northampton County, who recorded in 1772 that he had baptized "46 Black infants" and "55 Black adults" who seemed to be "very desirous of their instruction in their duty."[84] Whether true or not, given all the problems confronting Anglican ministers, including those of their own making, it appears that even if black Christians comprised a considerable proportion of the sureties of baptized slaves, this would not have significantly increased the number of slaves converted to Anglican Christianity.

The lackluster, inappropriate religious appeals Anglicans often made to slaves further hindered successful proselytization of slaves by the Church of England. To have any chance of success in converting slaves, ministers had to approach black adults in ways that struck responsive religious chords and to use techniques that were not offensively racist or inegalitarian. Commonly, however, Anglicans required slaves to learn the "Church Catechism by Heart and give answer to such Questions as their low Understanding will permit of." Often this would entail giving a rendition of "the Lord's Prayer, [the Apostles] Creed and Ten Commandments and such Prayers as are fitting for their wretched Conditions and Judgements." Such was the offensive and condescending approach to potential slave converts used by Joseph Ottolenghe, Georgia's leading catechist, who had been appointed by Bray's Associates expressly to educate and convert the colony's slaves. Although he represented the best Anglicans had to offer, his prejudiced assessment of the slaves' abilities to comprehend Christianity and his unappealing catechistic approach to slaves, which stressed rote learning, undoubtedly tended to be the rule rather than the exception among Anglican proselytizers.[85]

Given such unpromising situations, the wonder is not that most colonial slaves remained either untouched or unimpressed by Anglican Christianity, but that a number of slaves did offer themselves to be baptized. In North Carolina, Anglican ministers during the years 1709–72 reported to the SPG that they had baptized 18,773 whites, 1,401 blacks (6 of them free), and 6 Native Americans.[86] These figures indicate not only that a small percentage of the black population was baptized during these years (there were over 40,000 blacks in the colony in 1767 alone), but also that, compared with whites, baptism of blacks occurred in disproportionately small numbers. Blacks comprised about 22 to 25 percent of the total population from 1755 to 1771, when the bulk of the conversions occurred, but only about 7 percent of the conversions.[87]

These figures are of limited value. The baptismal figures are probably incomplete, but conversely and more important, using the number of baptisms to estimate slave conversions severely exaggerates the impact of Christianity on the slaves. Baptisms frequently did not equal true conversions to Christianity. This was the case both for child and adult baptisms, but the disproportionately large number of child baptisms among blacks reflect not only the Anglican practice of infant baptism, but also the comparative difficulties of reaching black adults as compared with children, who were more suggestible and usually spoke better English.[88] Children thus became the prime targets for baptism despite their limited understanding, their relative incapacity to convert others to Christianity, and their tendency after baptism to continue to be defined by the belief patterns of their elders. In a letter to the secretary of Bray's Associates on 30 September 1762, Robert Carter Nicholas, a prominent Williamsburg, Virginia, lawyer and the administrator of Bray's Associates Negro School in Williamsburg, and the Reverend William Yates demonstrate their awareness of the limited impact that even a Christian education had on children because of the countervailing influence of slave adults, including parents. They observe:

> There is still one greater Discouragement which we fear we shall labour under. 'Tho' the Owners of the Negro Children should chearfully close with our Proposals & submit them entirely to our Government; 'tho the Mistress of the School should be ever so diligent in her Duty, & 'tho the Scholars should make as great a Progress as could be wished, yet we fear that, notwithstanding all our Endeavours to prevent it, any good Impressions which may be made on the Children's Minds at School will be easily effaced by their mixing with other Slaves, who are mostly abandoned to every Kind of Wickedness. If evil Communications have a general Tendency to corrupt

good Manners, the Observation is never more likely to be verified than in Instances of this Sort, where the very Parents of the Children will probably much oftner, from their Intimacy, set them bad Examples than any others. Notwithstanding these & many other Difficulties, which the narrow Limits of a Letter will not permit us to particularize, stare us fully in the Face, we are resolved not to be discouraged; but hope, by the Blessing of God upon your Charity & our Endeavours, that the Undertaking will greatly prosper.[89]

Nicholas repeated his pessimistic assessment on 17 December 1765 in another letter to the secretary. He noted that those children who stayed in school for three years, the term of study he proposed to planters, generally did "learn to read pretty well, and learn their Prayers & Catechism." Nonetheless, even children who studied for this length of time lost much of what they had been taught because "I fear that most of the good Principles, which they are taught at School, are soon effaced, when they get Home, by the bad Examples set them there & for want of the Instructions necessary to confirm them in those Principles. I have a Negro Girl in my Family, who was taught at this School upwards of three Years & made as good a Progress as most, but she turns out a sad Jade, nothwithstanding all we can do to reform her."[90]

If Nicholas and Yates found this to be true of children who had been instructed in an Anglican school for three years—a period of study, Nicholas stressed, that was limited by masters to only a small minority of the slave children actually going to school, most being restricted to much shorter periods—what of the vast majority of slave children who never attended school and were baptized after little, if any, instruction and with little or no follow-up? Certainly the impact of baptism on almost all of these children was marginal.

John Van Horne, the authority on Bray's Associates, concludes that the group's Negro schools, catechists, and books reached only about two to three thousand of the nearly half-million blacks living in the colonies at the time of the Revolution. He adds that even these "few whom the Associates did reach probably did not achieve a lasting conversion or a useful degree of literacy" and concludes that "the Associates' enterprise failed to establish a permanent and effective means of carrying the gospel to and fostering education among America's blacks."[91] This assessment may confidently be projected to the vast majority of slaves who had no contact with Bray's Associates. Their "deep-rooted Impressions and long contracted Habits" had indeed shielded them from the limited and ineffectual attempts by Anglicans to convert them to Christianity.

Although Anglican exertions to convert slaves met with scant success for a wide variety of reasons, Anglicans were not the only sect to come into contact with the slaves. Quakers, German Protestants, Presbyterians, Methodists, and, above all, Baptists were also in the field, and it is to the efforts of these sects that we will now turn our attention.

Members of the Society of Friends—Quakers—were in the colony shortly after whites first came to the Albemarle Sound region. Their numbers increased, helped by the exhortations of Quaker preachers such as William Edmundson and George Fox, both of whom arrived in the early 1670s. Although the sect was well organized in North Carolina by 1676, its greatest early spurt of growth perhaps occurred during and after the gubernatorial administration of the Quaker John Archdale, who served from 1694 to 1696. Through his influence Quakers became Council members, judges, and assemblymen. Nonetheless, by 1709 they still comprised only about 10 percent of the white population. These early Friends saw nothing wrong with slavery, their main concerns during these years being requirements that they pay taxes to support the church establishment and serve in the militia.[92]

Although the percentage of Quakers in North Carolina probably never again equaled the 10 percent of the first decade of the eighteenth century, their absolute numbers did continue to grow. Some Friends moved southward from the Albemarle to the Neuse-Pamlico and Upper Cape Fear regions, establishing meetings by midcentury in Beaufort, Craven, Carteret, Dobbs, and Bladen Counties. By 1750, in addition to moving from northeastern North Carolina to the western portions of the province, Quakers in still greater numbers through the early 1770s migrated to western North Carolina from Pennsylvania, Virginia, and Nantucket, Massachusetts. Thus Orange and Rowan Counties and offshoots of these counties such as Chatham, Guilford, Randolph, and Surry became centers of Quaker settlement and activity.[93]

Not as concerned as other sects with spreading their version of Christianity among slaves after 1750, Quakers nonetheless did make some attempt to convert them. In 1758, for example, North Carolina Friends set up monthly meetings for blacks, taking care to have at least one white present "to see," as Hiram Hilty explains, "that good order was maintained." It is not clear that these instances of Quaker proselytizing met with much success: no mention of them appears in Quaker records after 1763. Perhaps the Quaker sense that the spirit of God resides in all humans tended to delimit the Friends' proselytizing zeal. The same central belief of Quakerism, no doubt, also increasingly inclined the Quakers to reject slavery during the later colonial years and even more so during the Revolution. John Woolman visited the colony in the late 1740s and began his antislavery work in Pasquotank and Perquimans Counties, where local Quakers as early as 1738 had spoken out against slavery. By the late 1760s and early 1770s Quakers in several areas of the colony had moved toward an outright prohibition on slaveholding among Friends, but they took no firm abolitionist stance until 1776, when the Standing Committee of the Yearly Meeting advised North Carolina Friends "to Cleanse their Hands" of slave ownership. Nonetheless, the prohibition merely increased the tempo of manumissions begun voluntarily in the late 1760s. This cleansing of their own house during the Revolutionary era gradually led Quakers to look beyond their own community and increasingly voice universally applicable abolitionist views. For this they gained the hostility of most of the whites in the newborn state. Yet the Quakers converted few slaves in North Carolina, as they owned relatively few slaves, manumitted these during the 1760s and 1770s, and tended to be leery of proselytizing.[94]

Even though the Moravians, who also were pacifists, owned and converted even fewer slaves than did the Quakers, we will pay considerable attention to them because their voluminous surviving records illustrate interesting interactions between slaves and masters that only infrequently are spelled out in the records left by other religious sects. The Moravians had limited impact on slaves because they were few in number and they settled in Rowan County on the North Carolina frontier, where there were very few slaves. Moravian interaction with slaves was further inhibited by the ethnic exclusiveness of these German-speaking religious enthusiasts, who were tightly bonded by their common heritage and traditions, close and extensive kinship ties, and the characteristics of gemeinschaft that peculiarly typified Moravian communities. The strangeness of African American languages, customs, and status all presented special barriers.

First settling in 1753 what they came to call Wachovia in Rowan County, the Moravians eventually confronted the issue of slave ownership in their frontier settlements. "The negro Sam, who had expressed a desire to learn to know the Savior," reads an entry in a diary left by settlers in Salem, "was bought by permission of the Lord." Sam crops up for several years in the records pertaining to Salem. On 13 November 1771, three years after being purchased, he is described as "a poor Negro, whom He had brought into the congregation and into whose heart He had placed the longing to be washed from his sins in the blood of Jesus through Holy Baptism." Led before the congregation, Sam answered questions indicating that he had undergone a period of training, was granted absolution, and was then baptized—"receiving the name Johannes Samuel. The presence of the Savior was deeply felt by the congregation, including the many friends and a few negroes; many said that the impression made upon them would never be forgotten." Three years later, an entry in the Salem

Diary on 13 November 1774 testifies to Sam's continued practice of Christianity as taught to him by the Moravians: "Our Negro, Johann Samuel, whose baptism was the first sacramental act in the consecration of our Saal three years ago was today present as a candidate for the Communion."[95]

Johannes Samuel was not the only slave influenced by the Moravians. In 1773 the Salem Diary of 17 August reports: "The little girls in Salem had their Festival. A little negro girl, ten years old, who works for Br. and Sr. Meyer, begged to attend the Lovefeast, and the little girls were told to speak a good word for Cathy to the Saviour, and pray that He would give her a tender and redeemed heart." Although Cathy may not have attended that particular festival, it is possible she participated in others. In 1774 the Salem Diary records that

> When the Mission Collection box was being taken around on Jan 6th a negress who is working in the Tavern heard of it, told two others, and all three asked that their little gifts might also be accepted. That evening she came into the Saal, dressed in white; and since then it appears that the Holy Spirit is working in her heart. One of the others was a negro who had been hired for a while, and soon after had to return to his master, leaving with many tears. Since then another negro has been bought; he worked two or three winters in Bethabara, and has been here several times, begging earnestly that we would buy him, for he wanted to find salvation, and feared to be lost.

The slave who had been hired had his wish fulfilled, for in 1775 "A negro, Jacob, who had been working in our Tavern for sometime, expressed a wish to become a Christian, and was bought from his master, Mr. Hawkings."[96]

Although the Moravians did some missionary work among slaves in Virginia and Georgia, there is no mention of such activity within North Carolina before 1775.[97] Such tendencies that may have existed to proselytize among the slaves of the western piedmont could have been dampened by the reaction to slave attempts to carve out areas of autonomy. The 11 October 1774 Minutes of the Salem Boards are suggestive of such tensions. "As there is much illicit buying and selling being done by negroes, to the disturbance of the Congregation," the Minutes read, "it was announced in Congregation Council that no one should buy from such a person unless he could show a permit from his master. In general there should be less conversation with the negroes, as that naturally has no good result."[98] How such a restriction affected further slave conversions or the instruction of slaves may be imagined.

Even when Moravians extended the right hand of religious fellowship to the few black slaves they incorporated within their community, Moravian fears persisted that blacks were potentially a destabilizing social force. The selective concentration in the records on the illicit trading of blacks not only illustrates the strict moral code of the Moravians, but also their general mistrust and fear of blacks together with their strong sense of obligation both to obey the law and to maintain the social, economic, and political status quo in the colony. This was also illustrated by their obvious antagonism to the Regulators. Thus within the Moravian community black slaves only occasionally were incorporated into the prevailing religious structure, while African Americans outside the community were kept at arms length and made accountable to the letter of the law to avoid what was believed to be their socially and economically disturbing behavior.[99]

Germans who were Lutherans and Reformed Protestants were even more numerous than Moravians in North Carolina. But they, too, played relatively insignificant roles during the colonial years both as slaveholders and as proselytizers of slaves, because most lived in the western counties where there were few slaves and they were even more hampered than were the Anglicans by a scarcity of ministers.[100]

It is likely that Presbyterians came to be the most numerous religious dissenters in North Carolina during the eighteenth century, only yielding first place at the end of the colonial period to the rapidly growing Baptists. The great majority of Presbyterian immigrants arrived in the colony during the quarter century before the Revolution. Most were either Highland Scots, who came directly from Scotland and usually settled in Bladen, Cumberland, and Anson Counties, or the even more numerous Scots-Irish, who came from Pennsylvania, Maryland, and Virginia and mostly settled in the western counties of Orange, Rowan, Anson, Mecklenburg, and Tryon. Presbyterians, therefore, like the Germans, were concentrated precisely in those areas where blacks were least numerous.

Some Presbyterian planters, their sense of responsibility toward their slaves heightened by the evangelical fervor of the Great Awakening, probably became somewhat more receptive to seeing them Christianized than had previously been the case. Indeed, by the 1770s some Presbyterians were attempting to educate blacks. Yet we do not find in the North Carolina records counterparts to the Bryans in South Carolina who, under the direct influence of George Whitefield and the heightened religious fervor of the Great Awakening, eventually left the Anglican Church to become Presbyterians and spearhead attempts to Christianize slaves in South Carolina from the 1730s to the 1750s. Without such Presbyterian evangelicals fervently committed to converting slaves to Christianity, it is hard to see Presbyterians in North Carolina playing roles much beyond that of the Anglicans in the Christianization of blacks. This was the case because Presbyterians often became part of the political establishment and were not prone to rock the boat. Also, since Presbyterians were concentrated in the western counties where slaves were least numerous in North Carolina, members of this sect had relatively few opportunities to proselytize among the slaves.

Even in South Carolina, where Presbyterians early provided the evangelical spark to reach out to the slaves, their impact appears to have been minimal. This becomes apparent on surveying the work of Harvey Jackson and Allan Gallay, who discuss how the Great Awakening in South Carolina and, to a lesser degree, Georgia affected the slaveowners' understanding and treatment of their slaves from the 1730s to the early 1750s.[101]

Unfortunately, both Jackson and Gallay analyze their stories almost exclusively from the vantage point of white planters. Neither author has found much evidence regarding the feelings or behavior of the slaves themselves. This necessarily prevents them from assessing systematically the magnitude of either the masters' outreach or the slaves' response during the Great Awakening. Jackson, however, does note that from 1745 to 1755 about thirty slaves had become members of the independent Presbyterian Stoney Creek Church. This hardly demonstrates a significant evangelical outreach to the slaves, nor does Jackson suggest otherwise. He treats these colonial evangelicals largely as forerunners of nineteenth-century evangelists whose later efforts in more fertile fields reaped considerably greater harvests for the Lord.[102]

Gallay, in attempting to show that slaves were Christianized in substantial numbers, is reduced to drawing an obvious inference from evangelical attempts to convert slaves: "Some slaves rejected Christianity while others adopted it to their own particular needs." True enough; the same undoubtedly may be said of slaves owned by more traditional Anglican masters. The question remains, how frequently did slaves respond in either direction? Unable to answer this question, but intent on demonstrating the success of the paternalistic attempts by evangelical planters to proselytize their slaves in South Carolina during the Great Awakening, Gallay baldly asserts that the slaves accepted conversion in order to receive specific rewards. Yet he mentions only two such rewards—slaves receiving Sundays off and their meeting slaves from other plantations at church or during "interplantation prayer meetings." Although Gallay only assumes that many slaves would be co-opted by such opportunities, he waxes eloquent about the supposed agreements made by slaves and masters: "Since many evangelical masters felt a moral duty to convert their slaves and to 'dispel [their] darkness,' bondspeople gained an important leverage in their relationships with slave owners. They gave their assent to their masters' religious ethic in exchange for privileges. Thus the orderliness and bounty of Jonathan Bryan's plantation was probably a result of the grant-ing of privileges that slaves on other plantations did not enjoy." With empirical verification still nowhere in sight, Gallay makes his final paternalistic points: "Christianity did not create the perfectly behaved slaves for which their mas-ters had hoped, but it did provide a basis for bargaining between the slave-holder and the enslaved. By accepting these privileges, which later bonds-people assumed were their rights, slaves confirmed their masters' claim to be moral Christian planters. This was the first step in the development of a paternalistic relationship."[103]

In assuming that slaves "gave their assent to their masters' religious ethic in exchange for privileges," Gallay does not appear to recognize that slaves had *anything* either to lose or to contribute in embracing Christianity. At best, he skirts the issue of African religiosity when he notes that some slaves did not accept Christianity, or, again, when he acknowledges the significance of back-sliding among slaves.

Moreover, both Gallay and Jackson admit that the provocative Christian message that evangelicals first brought to South Carolina slaves through mass revivals was noticeably toned down by the fierce early reactions of the local Anglican establishment and the planter elite, both of which perceived the activities of the revivalists as a threat to social order as well as to slavery. As early as 1734, South Carolina evangelicals ceased to gather slaves from several planta-tions into passionate, unstructured, cross-denominational, revival meetings. As Gallay stresses, the evangelicals acquiesced to the strictures of the planter elite and limited their efforts to convert their slaves to private meetings "on plantations and in the churches where the proceedings might be scrutinized and controlled." Such evangelizing came to emphasize, as did attempts by the more traditional Anglicans, a conversion process that hoped to produce hap-pier, more obedient, and more productive slaves. Or as Jackson concludes, "the doctrine that some had earlier feared might call their slaves to arms now called them to obedience—to God and to their masters."[104] Such was the price for evangelical acceptability and respectability in South Carolina in the 1740s and 1750s. If evangelical planters understandably often were willing to pay the going price, it remains unclear why slaves supposedly were willing to begin to bargain their birthright away for a mess of pottage.

Other historians who underscore the significance of Christianity among colonial slaves do so in relation to the Great Awakening's later offshoots or manifestations. They consequently tend to begin, not end, their analyses in the 1750s and to accentuate Baptists, and to a degree Methodists, in attempting to explain why and how colonial slaves were supposedly successfully proselytized.

Mechal Sobel, the Israeli scholar, has written the most valuable and persuasive account in this genre. She discusses the slaves' acceptance of evangelical Christianity in familiar fashion when she argues, as Jeffrey Crow has done for North Carolina, the especially appealing ways Baptists approached the slaves. In the early revivals and churches they preached the doctrine of the brotherhood of man under the Fatherhood of God and tended to accept the blacks as equal participants, and even at times as leaders. Equally appealing were the emotive qualities of Baptist religiosity that were so familiar to Africans, together with the receptiveness of the Baptists to new religious practices and beliefs and the compatibility of many of their doctrines, such as spirit possession or baptism, with African beliefs or practices. All this enabled slaves to make significant contributions to Baptist religiosity while also syncretically constructing an Afro-Baptist sacred cosmos among themselves.[105]

Although there is nothing startlingly new here, Sobel's sophisticated knowledge of African religious beliefs and practices enables her to specify how African religiosity pervaded the slaves' Afro-Christianity and to explore the way cultural diffusion resulted both in the Christianization of slaves and the incorporation of many Africanisms into white evangelical Christianity.[106] Sobel recognizes from the outset, then, the enormous significance of indigenous forms of religiosity for Africans and thereby understands that she must go beyond the special appeals or compatibility of evangelical Christianity with indigenous African beliefs to explain why large numbers of colonial slaves converted to Christianity.

She argues that traditional forms of African religiosity ceased to serve the needs of slaves adequately unless modified by many salient Christian beliefs. This was so because some central African religious tenets and institutions either could not be transplanted successfully across the ocean, or if they could be transmitted, they supposedly could not provide slaves with a coherent worldview that effectively mediated between their psychological and ethical needs and the social realities of thralldom.

Sobel's hypothesis can be effectively examined only by evaluating the particular arguments she presents on its behalf. Because she never organizes these arguments in a single statement, we will discuss some of the more significant points she makes in both of her books. In her second work, *The World They Made Together*, she correctly notes that nearly all Africans believed that the spirit or spirits of individuals lived on after death. The afterlife was similar to mortal life but different in its spirituality and relative closeness to God. The funeral was the rite of entry to a satisfying afterlife. Following proper burial rituals ensured that the spirit successfully went to the new realm and did not haunt or bother the living. Sobel adds that not all people could expect to live with the spirits. Barred were those who did not have "moral integrity," who had not lived in conformity with the rules of society, or who had died while still young or who had experienced "dishonorable deaths": deaths due to certain illnesses, "accidents, physical abnormalities, and abnormalities in behavior." Last, she notes that slaves, too, were denied honorable burials and after death could not reside with honored spirits because as slaves they had been defined as social deviants or outsiders and rejected as integral members of society.[107]

Sobel attributes her sense of traditional African beliefs in an afterlife to Zahan, but she misreads him. In the cited passage, he is not talking about the ability of persons to achieve spirituality after death. Rather, he is discussing the "illustrious" dead, those who could gain a "halo" or be the focus of a cult.[108]

According to Mbiti, all the dead become spirits. The dead "who were not in any way ancestors" such as "children, brothers, sisters, [and] barren wives" were, as much as others who died, "spirits and living dead." The last are more inclusive terms that could more properly be applied to the dead than terms that stressed ancestral ties. Mbiti does mention that "full burial rites" might only be given to those who died as adults or by "normal deaths." Such burials could be withheld from those who died as children or unmarried people, or as the result of suicides, attacks by animals, and "diseases like leprosy, smallpox, or epilepsy." The purpose here is to define proper burial rites for persons who experienced different forms of death; it is not to deny spirituality to certain less fortunate groups in society. According to traditional African beliefs, that is beyond human capacity. What living human beings may do, and at their own risk, is ignore or reject their ritualistic obligations to their dead relatives. This, more than likely, would result in discomfited, angry spirits who would cause illness, poverty, or death among their mortal relatives. Such ritualistic obligations, in any case, would cease after the last relatives who had known the deceased had died, normally after four or five generations. At this point, when the "living dead" no longer had direct ties with mortals, they became pure spirits. At whatever juncture the "living dead" actually became pure spirits, the process was inevitable and universal for all persons who died. Pure spirits were closest to God both ontologically and in their capacity to communicate directly with the supreme deity or with other deities.[109]

As to the supposed peculiar spiritual disabilities that Sobel believes slaves labored under, although separated from their families African slaves remained members of their families and lineages of origin. If they died among strangers and did not receive the proper ritualistic respect, to be sure a tragic occurrence for Africans, their spirits still eventually would enter the spirit world as full spirits without benefit of ritualistic ties with their relatives. Once again, Sobel confuses ritualistic ties between mortals and their dead relatives with spirituality itself. The latter was available to all Africans who died.

Sobel's confusion about appropriate burials and the proper ritualistic respect due to relatives or the illustrious dead with spirituality as a whole also leads her to distort the essential differences between African and Christian beliefs regarding the afterlife and spirituality. Christians, whether Anglican or evangelical, contrasted salvation with damnation, heaven with hell. With the recognition of sin and a resultant sense of contrition prodding Christians, the hope was to seek redemption through God's grace and to be glorified in His presence for eternity in heaven. Africans only occasionally accepted the possibility of being tormented spiritually in an afterlife for their sins. They accentuated their human capacities to appeal to, manipulate, or assuage the anger of deities or spirits by offering proper respect through intermediaries and rituals.[110]

The dead, then, inevitably became spirits, but traceable ties between these spirits (the "living dead") and mortal families remained binding for generations. As the years passed and memories of the departed with passing generations faded away, the living dead gradually evolved into pure spirits. This last development, however, traditionally did not mean for Africans that these spirits would finally be glorified in the presence of God. Rather, the spirit was now freed from frequent and significant responsibilities for and dependencies on mortals and had obtained an eternal, full spirituality. They were now, as full spirits, ontologically similar to God and capable of communicating directly with Her/Him along with other deities. Nonetheless, the spirits remained separate from and unequal to God, existing in an amorphous, undelineated realm of spirituality. Withal, this last, insofar as it was described, normally resembled the world of the living.[111]

Because Christian versions of salvation varied considerably over time within and among the different sects from Arminian to Calvinist—often offering little hope for salvation for many people—it is hard to see why a Christian sense of redemption mediated more effectively than did traditional African religions, as Sobel insists, between the psychological and ethical needs of African Americans and the social realities of thralldom. The slaves' African sense of self-reliance together with their complex understanding of a universally available spiritual existence after death would seem to have served the slaves very well.

Sobel further argues in *Trabelin' On* that the slaves did not presume that either their divinities or their living dead came across the ocean with them, as the slaves' extended families remained in Africa and the spirits were bound to stay with them. And they supposedly believed that it was practically impossible for spirits to cross large bodies of water. Yet Sobel, without even recognizing the contradiction, stresses that blacks believed that their souls (spirits) would return to Africa after death. If the living dead or deities could not cross the ocean westward, slave spirits somehow could travel eastward. Moreover, since both nuclear and extended families eventually developed in the colonies, a reservoir of ancestral spirits gradually was generated.

Considerable empirical evidence contradicts the notion that slaves believed that African spirits could not cross the Atlantic. To the contrary, slaves throughout the Americas incorporated African deities and spirits into their religious beliefs and practices. Indeed, even in what is now the United States the tenacious survival of African spirits is revealed in a number of ways. Slave burial ceremonies, the peculiar construction and decoration of graves, and the slaves' comprehension of healing through conjuring and herbalism all mirror an African sacred cosmos that encompasses a belief in deities, spirits, and the living dead. Slaves, as the memoirs of Olaudah Equiano suggest, simply were unaware of any logical conundrum that might deny the transference of their African deities. Their imaginative powers allowed their deities to cross the "grandywater" and exist both here and in Africa. Slaves managed this even when synthesizing various gods, for African religiosity was never so particularistic or rigid as to defy solutions to most of the difficulties presented by Sobel.[112]

Finally, we turn to a problem that indeed must have taxed the slaves' ingenuity. Sobel contends that the synthesized African sacred cosmos internalized by the slaves in the diaspora, that is, the essential core of their African worldview, which evaluated and responded to the mysterious or the inexplicable, was traditionally reflected in and closely related to definitive African social patterns and relationships. Accordingly, "the kinship structure had been an extension of the relations between spirits and living men, and the rites of passage marked the movement of an individual from birth through life to death in preparation for his continuance in the eternal order."[113] Presumably the destruction or simplification of traditional African political, social, economic, and familial structures and relationships necessarily prevented or seriously limited the transplanting of many institutional, hierarchical, and ceremonial elements of African religiosity.

Yet it does not automatically follow that the resulting effects were so destructive to the coherency of the African sacred cosmos as to cause slaves to seek a Christian replacement. The continuing significance of African definitions and forms in slave marriages, families, and naming and linguistic patterns argue against this. What remained of traditional indigenous African religiosity, along with social institutions and practices defined by the slaves' African past, satisfied the aesthetic, psychic, and social needs of slaves and provided them with the necessary moral imperatives and subsequent capacity to transcend, avoid, adjust to, or rebel against the destructive characteristics of thralldom.

Time is of the essence here. One cannot assume that because most slaves eventually became Christians, conversion substantially occurred during the colonial years. This does not jibe with the evidence describing the impact of Anglicanism or of the Great Awakening up to the 1750s. Nor is it confirmed by the bulk of the empirical evidence concerning the influence of the Baptists and Methodists on the slaves at least up to the 1790s. Let us now substantiate and attempt to quantify this last point.

Intermittent early references to Baptists—frequently referred to as Anabaptists, New Lights, New Light Baptists, and mistakenly, at times, Methodists— are found in the records, but it is not until the late 1750s that the comments of Anglican observers begin to get strident. For example, the Reverend Clement Hall on 27 February 1744 noted in a letter to the SPG that there were only a few dissenters in Chowan Parish (in the Albemarle Sound region): Quakers and some Baptists. By 1758 the Reverend Michael Smith of Johnston County wrote to the SPG more caustically, though optimistically, that the decreasing number of Anabaptists had at least served the purpose of preparing the people for a more rational religion. The next year he boasted that he had helped check the growth of the Anabaptists. However, on 26 June 1760 the Reverend James Reed of Craven County hardly suggested he was discussing a vanishing breed when he assessed the Anabaptists as "obstinate, illiterate, and grossly ignorant," while he deemed the Methodists to be "ignorant, censorious, and uncharitable."[114] By comparison, even the Quakers were beginning to look a bit more acceptable, merely drawing the comment of being "rigid." As for the Presbyterians, Reed conceded that they "are pretty moderate except here and there a bigot or rigid Calvinist." Not as inventive, the Reverend Alexander Stewart, writing to the SPG from the town of Bath in Beaufort County on 10 October 1760, simply complained of the growing number of unthinking Anabaptists in his parish.[115]

By December 1761 the Reverend Mr. Reed began to take heart, informing the SPG that "the little ground they [the Methodists, i.e., Baptists] had gained in this country, I verily believe, will in a few months be totally lost." Governor William Tryon, less optimistic, warned the Assembly at its opening session on 3 May 1765 that "in a short period of Time" dissenters might become "the Majority in all Public Assemblies." Back to his original position and once again warming to his task, Reed, in a letter of 10 July 1765 to the SPG, referred to the "Methodists" as persons whose religion was a "vile prejudice" that was simply a "pretext for their indolence and sloth."[116]

In any case, the Reverend John Barnett, in discussing conditions in the southern part of Brunswick County in a letter of 5 February 1766 to the SPG, revealed yet another reason why evangelicals—in this case, the "New Light Baptists"—were held in such disdain: the most illiterate of them were their teachers, and "even Negroes speak in their Meetings." The Reverend Charles Woodmason, in a colorful 1766 account that ends with an appeal to clean up the "Augean Stable," complained about the deplorable condition of the Anglican Church, while, among numerous other criticisms, bemoaning that the backcountry was largely peopled by scurrilous Presbyterians and Anabaptists. The sole happy note was that the two sects had a great antipathy for one another. The Reverend Charles Cupples, while not up to Woodmason's unmatched invective, nonetheless, around 26 March 1768, referred to the few dissenters in Bute County as "Ranting Anabaptists." Even Governor William Tryon began to reach top form when he noted in a letter to the SPG secretary on 20 March 1769 that only Presbyterians and Quakers were tolerated sects. The remainder were "enemies to society and a scandal to common sense." Somewhat more subdued, the Reverend James McCartney simply referred to the Baptists as great bigots in a letter to the SPG on 28 October of the same year. The Reverend Charles Edward Taylor of Northampton County grieved that his life would be happy but for the troublesome, ignorant New Light Baptists. On 24 August 1772, professing not to know what the members of the variously called Anabaptists, New Light Baptists, and Baptists actually called themselves, Taylor nevertheless concluded—whatever their correct title—that their ministers were surprisingly ignorant. By now the Quakers were almost a blessing, Taylor noting that "they are in no way troublesome." Concerning the Baptists, he somewhat selfishly thanked God that, although they remained numerous, they apparently were decreasing in his parish despite their fast-growing numbers in Virginia and other parts of North Carolina.[117]

How are we to construe the small role evangelical relationships with blacks from 1750 to the Revolution played in the comments of Anglicans fearful and critical of these all-too-numerous religious enthusiasts? There were two reasons for the relative lack of concern among these Anglicans and, we presume, the large majority of slaveholding planters. First, the link between evangelizing blacks and trying to achieve the abolition of slavery in the South, a phenomenon most significant among Methodists, did not appear with any importance until the 1780s. Any abolitionist hint aroused passions wherever it was perceived. During the colonial years, aside from the Quakers' attempts to cleanse themselves of involvement with slavery and the earlier experiment in Georgia, abolitionist tendencies in the southern colonies occurred only for a brief period in South Carolina and then were rapidly eradicated.[118]

The second reason was that evangelical conversion attempts from 1750 to the

Revolution affected relatively few blacks, as several scholars have pointed out. Unfortunately, the evidence presented often has been intermixed with data on slave conversions after the Revolution and, especially, with data for the nineteenth century. Thus, there has been a tendency to ignore the modest number of slaves converted during the pre-Revolutionary period or even to confuse them with the massive conversions of later years.

In any case, Albert J. Raboteau, in a variety of statements, argues that only a small minority of colonial slaves were either converted or significantly touched by Christianity. Lester Scherer also dates the important growth of black Baptists and Methodists from the post–Revolutionary War period. In the context of her detailed analysis of slave naming practices, Cheryl Cody notes that serious planter attempts to convert the slaves began at the earliest in the 1780s. The incidence of slave conversion, she adds, is thus consistent with slave naming patterns: the widespread slave use of biblical names occurred only during the first two decades of the nineteenth century.[119]

An analysis of the available figures concerning the number of slave converts to Methodism during the colonial years is somewhat superfluous, as this was largely a post-Revolutionary phenomenon. Still, Raboteau estimates that black Methodists in 1786 totaled about 1,890 throughout the United States, the vast majority living in the South: whites numbered around 16,900. By 1797 the number of black Methodists had risen to 12,215, and they now represented nearly one-fourth of all Methodists. The majority of black Methodists lived in three states: 5,106 in Maryland, 2,490 in Virginia, and 2,071, or 17 percent of the total, in North Carolina. South Carolina and Georgia had fewer black Methodists, 890 and 148 respectively. As late as 1787, the 790 or so black Methodists in North Carolina equaled less than .01 percent of the total black population, which by this time included some 4,500 free blacks. Figures such as these have to be taken into account when one reads that "hundreds of Negroes . . . with tears streaming down their faces" attended Methodist revivals in fourteen Virginia and two North Carolina counties conducted by the evangelical preacher, Devereux Jarratt, during the years 1773–76. The total number of blacks at such Methodist revivals was not large, and the payoff both in terms of true conversions or church membership was considerably smaller.[120]

The less centralized Baptists kept sparse records, and it is thus more difficult to estimate their black membership. Citing various estimates, Raboteau presents the following slightly divergent figures: in 1793 there were between 18,000 and 19,000 black Baptists in the United States (out of a total membership of 73,471), and in 1795 there were 17,644. The higher estimate would represent only about 2.4 percent of the total black population in the United States at this time.[121]

Charles Colcock Jones, one of the leading proponents of the establishment of plantation missions in the antebellum South, calculated that in 1793 black Baptists equaled 18,000 out of a Baptist total of 73,471. Jones, in keeping with these low figures, noted that only a small minority of blacks attended church from 1790 to 1820.[122] This, in turn, suggests that membership figures give an adequate indication of church attendance and possibly religious commitment.

Morgan Edwards, from his visits to Baptist congregations during the 1770s, has left some invaluable statistics and observations for the late colonial years. Not one to underestimate Baptist numbers, he noted that there were sixteen Baptist churches in North Carolina by 1754 and thirty-two by 1772, plus several meeting places. By the latter date he listed thirty ministers and perhaps fifteen assistants, calculating the total membership at 3,591, with a total of 7,950 families participating in these churches and meeting places. Using a multiplier of five, he arrived at a figure of 39,750 "souls" that were related to the Baptist church by 1772. It is this last figure—Morgan's attempt to calculate the number of colonists who even remotely were involved in the Baptist faith—that has erroneously been used by many historians to indicate the *actual* number of Baptists in the colony at that date. Nevertheless, it is instructive to note that Edwards found only small numbers of blacks scattered throughout the Baptist churches he visited in the South during the 1770s.[123]

Even using Edwards's highly inflated figure of about 40,000, Baptists totaled no more than one-fifth of North Carolina's population in 1770. A substantial proportion of these were New Light Baptists who had formed the Sandy Creek Church in 1755 under the evangelical preacher, Shubal Stearns. Stearns subsequently led a great revival that resulted in the establishment of many other churches, not only in North Carolina but also in Virginia and South Carolina. It is these New Lights who were especially noxious to the Anglicans. They, and Baptists in general, were concentrated in the west, especially in Orange, Guilford, and Rowan Counties, where few slaves resided. This, combined with the fact that the Baptists normally were among the least affluent whites, ensured that they owned relatively few slaves.[124] Comparatively few slaves, consequently, would have been in a position to be converted by the Baptists. This explains why Morgan Edwards observed only small numbers of blacks attending Baptist churches throughout the South.

Sobel, interestingly, cites Edwards's observation that few blacks could be seen in Baptist congregations and further observes that it was not until the 1790s that many blacks spoke English well enough to accept the Baptist invitation to participate in their church services. It is strange, then, that she still tries to demonstrate that large numbers of blacks either were members of all-black Baptist churches from the 1750s on or had joined integrated Baptist churches.

Making this contradictory effort even less convincing are her own statistics arguing that black Baptist churches were essentially a nineteenth-century phenomenon. She has uncovered only 11 black churches (6 in Virginia, 2 each in South Carolina and Georgia, and 1 in Kentucky) that were organized in the eighteenth century, compared with 194 during the nineteenth century. Only 2 and possibly 3 of these 11 churches had been established before the American Revolution: 2 in Virginia (1758 and 1776) and 1 in South Carolina (1775). North Carolina's earliest listed black church originated about 1830–31. Thus, contrary to the conclusions Sobel draws from this list, few blacks belonged to such churches before the Revolution.[125]

Nor do Sobel's figures for Virginia (where creolization among blacks was most significant in the colonial South) concerning eighteenth-century black Baptist totals, regardless of the type of Baptist churches they attended, support her contention that *most* blacks were Christianized during the late colonial period. Usually obtained from church minutes, her figures simply illustrate that *some* Virginia slaves became Baptists during the years 1750–1800. Expansively extrapolating from Sobel's data, despite the fact that about half of the years she surveys fall beyond the colonial period, yields a cumulative total of 2,500 blacks who were members of Baptist churches between 1750 and 1800.[126] We have no idea what black membership was in any given year before 1776, but it would be considerably less than 2,500. This number was insignificant when placed beside the approximately 200,000 blacks living in Virginia in 1775, even if we use a multiplier of five to seven to calculate the total number of slaves somewhat involved with the Baptist persuasion. Parenthetically, if we assume, similar to Methodist percentages, that about 20 percent of the Baptists in the United States lived in Virginia, then, using Raboteau's statistics, Virginia perhaps had 3,500 to 3,800 African American Baptists in 1793. Equaling about 1 percent of the 334,000 blacks (free and slave) living in Virginia in 1793, this roughly coincides with extrapolations from Sobel's data if we make the necessary corrections for time.[127]

Whatever the precise number of colonial blacks who converted to Christianity, there is no doubt that only a small percentage had been successfully proselytized. Most blacks constructed an Afro-Christianity only over time. During the late 1700s, but especially in the nineteenth century, as slaves developed greater skills in English, as the institutional thrust of Christianity replaced the occasional or revivalistic thrust, and as whites became more acceptant of black Christianization and more systematic in their conversion efforts, blacks, confronted by a somewhat less resilient and demanding African past, gradually developed increasing numbers of their own Christian teachers and preachers and became more receptive to conversion. Only then did Afro-

Christianity become predominant in the slave community. If eventually some Christian doctrines appeared to be superior to certain indigenous African beliefs, this was more the effect of the process of Christianization among slaves than a cause of it. The vast majority of slaves prior to the Revolution steadfastly clung to elements and syntheses of indigenous African creeds, for these beliefs continued to serve their psychological and social needs within enslavement. James Reed, Anglican minister of Craven County, understood this tenacity in 1760, when he noted that "the greatest part of the Negroes in the whole country may too justly be accounted heathens."[128]

Conclusion

Although their African past continued to define the religiosity of most slaves in colonial North Carolina, slaves had to fashion syntheses or other compromises to deal with their varied ethnic backgrounds as well as the obstacles presented by thralldom. Much was inevitably lost in this process of cultural fragmentation. The absence in America of many of the complex, traditional African political power, class, and wealth configurations that had been holistically integrated with religion was perhaps the most serious challenge to the viability of a slave religiosity largely constructed from indigenous African systems of belief and practice.

Despite such fragmentation, the bulk of the evidence still suggests that an essentially African-derived and defined religiosity continued to provide most slaves with a coherent and functional worldview that met their aesthetic, psychic, and social needs as well as the moral imperatives to direct their behavior and modes of resistance. Arguments that emphasize the strength of this con-

218

tinuum still manage to strain the credulity of scholars who emphasize the role of cultural diffusion, or even cultural hegemony, and hence the spread of Christianity to colonial slaves in British North America. Without the benefit of an institutional framework, they insist that the slaves' transplanted religion was bound to be co-opted by a supposedly more systematic, coherent, and satisfying network of ideas presented by Christianity and its churches. African religions, in their view, survived only as syncretic arrangements within Christianity or as a number of uncoordinated beliefs and practices.

At the same time, these historians choose to ignore the fact that the syncretic development of Afro-Christianity by the majority of slaves during the nineteenth century was similar to their earlier reconstruction of an African sacred cosmos in that it occurred largely without benefit of the political power, class, and wealth differentiations, or the physical mobility and elaborate institutional frameworks, that characterized and defined the growth of Christianity among whites.

In any case, the available evidence argues that few slaves in North Carolina were converted to Christianity before the Revolution, and there was little opportunity for the colony's slaves to join Christian churches, white or black. The slaves resisted conversion, and the masters overwhelmingly were either indifferent or antagonistic. Even those few ministers willing to proselytize with some vigor among colonial slaves normally lacked either or both the institutional resources and the personal and ideological qualities to have more than a limited impact.

The ability of colonial slaves to develop a functional, resilient religiosity was, as this study reveals, but one manifestation of the African American culture they created. Slaves reached into their extensive African pool of names to choose their own and their children's names. They invented pidgin and creole languages primarily from a variety of African tongues in order to converse, most frequently, among themselves. And they used African precedents painstakingly to reconstruct life-sustaining monogamous marriages and nuclear and extended families. Even bride price was continued, if less forcefully than in Africa and without its traditional ties to lineages, class, wealth, and political power.

Other aspects of slave culture, some too lightly considered in our study such as arts and crafts, medicine, poetry, dance, music, song, and folklore, were also significantly reconstituted by slaves out of their African legacies and their new situations and needs in thralldom. Still other elements of the slaves' cultural dependence on their African past including architecture and cuisine have been discussed by historians who have had access to evidence not available for colonial North Carolina.

Slaves constructed out of this complex cultural world a value system and code of conduct. This ethic supported both overt and covert methods of resistance, at times violent, to combat white domination of their lives. The massive power and control of slaveowners over legal, political, economic, and social institutions could not prevent slaves from attempting to thwart the will of masters, or even to threaten the institutional framework of slavery itself. Despite the masters' expertise in the use of terror and co-optation, they were frustrated in their designs of total dominance by their dependence on the labor of slaves, their faulty comprehension of the interior lives of these laborers, and the limited time, effort, and will that slaveowners were able to expend to achieve a thoroughgoing dominance on each plantation. Cultural hegemony was eschewed by slaveowners as much as it eluded them. Without it, their control, by definition, was limited and had to remain so.

The effort to maintain their viability and distinctiveness never ended for slaves. The rewards and victories they experienced were tragically all too limited as they mounted their challenges to slavery. But the inspiring legacy of their struggle and the abiding culture they created and passed on to their descendants will be increasingly appreciated as they are better understood.

Appendix

Table 1.1. Population Statistics for North Carolina's Regions and Counties, 1755 and 1767

Regions and Counties	1755			1767		
	Totals[1]	Whites	Blacks	Totals	Whites	Blacks
Albemarle	22,108[30]	(16,973)	(5,135)	28,517	(18,343)	(10,174)
Sound	13,393[31]	10,561	2,832	21,141	13,379	7,762
Currituck[2]	2,227	1,943	284	2,543[32]	(1,980)	(563)
Pasquotank[3]	3,000	2,308	692	4,179[33]	3,034	1,145
Perquimans[4]	3,857	(2,809)	(1,048)	4,083[34]	2,161	1,922
Chowan[5]	4,858	(3,603)	(1,255)	4,571[35]	2,526	2,045
Hertford[6]	—	—	—	4,833[36]	(2,984)	(1,849)
Bertie[7]	5,577	4,354	1,223	5,136[37]	3,223	1,913
Tyrrell[8]	2,589	1,956	633	3,172[38]	2,435	737
Neuse-	15,176	(11,302)	(3,874)	23,970	17,274	6,696
Pamlico	13,769	10,185	3,584			
Hyde[9]	1,412	1,132	280	2,341[39]	1,808	533
Beaufort-Pitt[10]	4,233	3,161	1,072	6,750[40]	4,953	1,797
Craven[11]	5,820	4,055	1,765	8,523[41]	5,650	2,873
Carteret[12]	1,407	(1,117)	(290)	2,475[42]	1,927	548
Onslow[13]	2,304	1,837	467	3,881[43]	2,936	945
Lower Cape Fear	4,308	1,624	2,684	7,942[44]	2,997	4,945
New Hanover[14]	4,308	1,624	2,684	4,973[45]	2,079	2,894
Brunswick[15]	—	—	—	2,969[46]	918	2,051
Upper Cape Fear	2,040	1,386	654	4,596	3,243	1,353
Bladen[16]	2,040	1,386	654	4,596[47]	3,243	1,353
Central Inner Plain–						
Piedmont	9,424	8,216	1,208	21,872	17,909	3,963
Dobbs[17]	—	—	—	6,533[48]	5,199	1,334
Johnston[18]	5,842	5,092	750	5,701[49]	4,629	1,072
Duplin[19]	2,204	1,886	318	5,217[50]	4,391	826
Cumberland[20]	1,378	1,238	140	4,421[51]	3,690	731

Table 1.1 (continued)

Regions and Counties	1755			1767		
	Totals[1]	Whites	Blacks	Totals	Whites	Blacks
Northern Inner Plain–				36,790	(26,352)	(10,438)
Piedmont	18,511	13,985	4,526	13,006	9,516	3,490
Northampton[21]	5,274	3,698	1,576	7,978[52]	(5,362)	(2,616)
Halifax[22]	—	—	—	8,755[53]	(6,210)	(2,545)
Edgecombe[23]	8,925	6,863	2,062	7,051[54]	(5,264)	(1,787)
Bute[24]	—	—	—	7,104[55]	5,326	1,778
Granville[25]	4,312	3,424	888	5,902[56]	4,190	1,712
				40,749	(37,677)	(3,072)
Western	12,378	11,927	451	19,208	17,503	1,705
Orange[26]	4,266	4,030	236	16,027[57]	14,649	1,378
Rowan[27]	4,678	4,576	102	13,516[58]	(12,797)	(719)
Anson[28]	3,434	3,321	113	3,181[59]	2,854	327
Mecklenburg[29]	—	—	—	8,025[60]	(7,377)	(648)

Source: Except for a few corrections, this table originally was published in Marvin L. Michael Kay and Lorin Lee Cary, "A Demographic Analysis of Colonial North Carolina with Special Emphasis upon the Slave and Black Populations," in *Black Americans in North Carolina and the South,* edited by Jeffrey J. Crow and Flora J. Hatley (Chapel Hill: University of North Carolina Press, 1984).

[1]Taxable totals may be found in the various sources listed below. White and black taxable totals were converted into population totals by using multipliers of 4.1 and 1.89, respectively. The different multipliers reflect the proportion of each population legally defined as taxables and the age distribution within each of the two populations. Because all blacks, male and female, aged twelve and over were counted as taxables, but only white males aged sixteen and over were considered taxables, it is understandable that a much greater proportion of the black population appeared on the tax lists. The smaller black multiplier primarily reflects this fact.

Because few data exist that list the black and white populations according to age, the sample used to calculate the age distribution of blacks and whites, a 1775 tax list from Pitt County, was small and insufficiently representative. Nonetheless, Pitt County in 1775 is not an outlandish choice; its comparatively immature development is offset by the late date of the sample. In any case, we believe it is the best extant sample. The 1775 Pitt County tax list may be found in Secretary of State Papers, Tax Lists, 1720–1839, (NCSA).

Special multipliers were needed to convert total listed taxables into population totals for those counties lacking racial breakdowns in the tax lists. These multipliers reflect the relative proportion of white and black taxables from the region in which the particular county is located, as well as the above multipliers of 4.1 and 1.89. The resulting multipliers, calculated for ca. 1755 and ca.1767, respectively, for each region are as follows: Albemarle—3.28, 2.86; Neuse-Pamlico—3.14, 3.09; Lower Cape Fear—2.37, 2.36; Upper Cape Fear—2.98,

Table 1.1 (continued)

3.04; Central Inner Plain–Piedmont—3.56, 3.36; Northern Inner Plain–Piedmont—3.18, 3.12; West—3.93, 3.71.

After the total population was calculated from the total number of taxables in each of the necessary instances, white and black totals were estimated for each of the relevant counties. The techniques used are described below in the appropriate notes. All such extrapolations for white and black totals are placed in parentheses.

[2]William L. Saunders, ed., *The Colonial Records of North Carolina*, 10 vols. (Raleigh: State of North Carolina, 1886–90), 5:575.

[3]Ibid.

[4]Ibid., for taxable total of 1,176. The multiplier 3.28 was used to obtain the total population of 3,857. The percentage of Perquimans County's black population in 1755 was calculated by multiplying the percentage of the Albemarle Sound region's black population in 1755 by the percentage of Perquimans County's black population in 1767 and dividing the result by the percentage of the region's black population in 1767. Black and white population totals for the county in 1755 were, in turn, calculated from the percentage obtained above.

[5]See Saunders, *Colonial Records*, 5:575, for taxable total of 1,481. See note 4 for procedures used to obtain white and black population totals. The multiplier 3.28 was used to convert the taxable total into the total population of 4,858.

[6]Hertford County was formed from Chowan, Bertie, and Northampton Counties in 1759.

[7]We used the white-black breakdown for 1751 and the taxable total for 1754 to calculate Bertie County figures for 1755. For the 1751 figures, see Colonial Court Records, Taxes and Accounts, 1679–1754, NCSA. For the 1754 totals, see Saunders, *Colonial Records*, 5:320.

[8]Saunders, *Colonial Records*, 5:575.

[9]Governors Office Papers, Lists of Taxables, Militia, and Magistrates, 1754–70 and undated, NCSA.

[10]Saunders, *Colonial Records*, 5:575. Pitt was formed from Beaufort County in 1760.

[11]Ibid.

[12]The estimated taxable total equals 448, the mean for the years 1754 and 1756. See Broadside, "Table of Taxables in the Province of North Carolina from 1748 . . . to 1770," as quoted in Evarts S. Greene and Virginia D. Harrington, *American Population before the Federal Census of 1790* (New York: Columbia University Press, 1932), 162. See note 4 for general procedures used to calculate the white and black population totals. The multiplier to obtain the population total from the taxable total in the Neuse-Pamlico region is 3.14.

[13]Saunders, *Colonial Records*, 5:575.

[14]See Treasurers and Comptrollers Papers, Tax Lists, NCSA.

[15]Brunswick County was formed from New Hanover and Bladen Counties in 1764.

[16]Governors Office Papers, Lists of Taxables, Militia, and Magistrates, 1754–70 and undated, NCSA.

[17]Dobbs County was formed from Johnston County in 1758.

[18]Governors Office Papers, Lists of Taxables, Militia, and Magistrates, 1754–70 and undated, NCSA.

[19]Saunders, *Colonial Records*, 5:575.

Table 1.1 (continued)

---

[20]Governors Office Papers, Lists of Taxables, Militia, and Magistrates, 1754–70 and undated, NCSA.

[21]Saunders, *Colonial Records*, 5:575.

[22]Halifax County was formed from Edgecombe County in 1759.

[23]Governors Office Papers, Lists of Taxables, Militia, and Magistrates, 1754–70 and undated, NCSA.

[24]Bute County was formed from Granville County in 1764.

[25]Governors Office Papers, Lists of Taxables, Militia, and Magistrates, 1754–70 and undated, NCSA.

[26]Treasurers and Comptrollers Papers, Tax Lists, NCSA.

[27]Saunders, *Colonial Records*, 5:575.

[28]Ibid.

[29]Mecklenburg County was formed from Anson County in 1762.

[30]Totals for all existing counties in the region.

[31]Totals for all existing counties in the region except for those whose estimates are in parentheses. The same pattern obtains for each region that has two totals. See note 1 above.

[32]Currituck County's total taxables were obtained from Saunders, *Colonial Records*, 7:539. The taxable total, 889, was multiplied by 2.86 to estimate the county's total 1767 population of 2,543. The percentage of Currituck County's population that was black was calculated by multiplying the percentage of the Albemarle Sound's black population in 1767 by the percentage of Currituck County's black population in 1755 and dividing the result by the percentage of the region that was black in 1753. Black and white population totals for the county in 1767 were, in turn, calculated from the percentage obtained above.

[33]Because the listing of taxables is incomplete for Pasquotank County in 1767, we used the figures for 1766. See Saunders, *Colonial Records*, 7:288–89.

[34]Saunders, *Colonial Records*, 7:288–89. The figures for Perquimans County are for 1766.

[35]Ibid. The figures for Chowan County are for 1766.

[36]Hertford County's taxable total, 1,690 was obtained from Saunders, *Colonial Records*, 7:539. Since Hertford did not exist in 1755, a procedure different from that used for Currituck had to be devised to estimate Hertford's white and black populations for 1767. This procedure consisted of taking the average distribution in the three counties from which Hertford was formed: Bertie, Chowan, and Northampton. The multiplier used to convert Hertford's taxable total into total population was 2.86.

[37]The listing of taxables for Bertie County is incomplete for 1767. We therefore extrapolated from lists for the years 1766 and 1768 to arrive at the 1767 population figures. That is, we added one-half the population differences between the two years to the totals for 1766 to calculate the 1767 population. See Bertie County Records, List of Taxables, 1765–71, NCSA.

[38]Saunders, *Colonial Records*, 7:539.

[39]Ibid.

[40]See ibid. for Beaufort County. We, however, used 1766 totals for Pitt County. Saunders, *Colonial Records*, 7:288–89.

[41]Saunders, *Colonial Records*, 7:539.

[42]Ibid.

Table 1.1 (continued)

[43]Ibid.

[44]The increases for the Lower Cape Fear are exaggerated, while those for the Upper Cape Fear are underestimated. This is so because a portion of Bladen County was incorporated into Brunswick County when it was formed in 1764. The distortions cannot be corrected.

[45]New Hanover County's totals are for 1766. See Saunders, *Colonial Records*, 7:288–89.

[46]Ibid., 539.

[47]Ibid.

[48]Ibid.

[49]Ibid.

[50]Ibid.

[51]We used Cumberland County's records for 1766 because they are more complete than those for 1767. See Saunders, *Colonial Records*, 7:288–89.

[52]See Saunders, *Colonial Records*, 7:539, for taxable totals. Northampton County's multiplier to obtain population totals is 3.12. See note 32 for the procedures used to figure the 1767 population breakdown.

[53]We averaged the percentages of blacks who lived in Northampton and Edgecombe Counties in 1767 to obtain the percentage of blacks who lived in Halifax County. We then used this percentage to calculate the county's white and black population in 1767. The total number of taxables was found in Saunders, *Colonial Records*, 7:539. Multiplier is 3.12.

[54]See Saunders, *Colonial Records*, 7:539, for taxable totals. See note 32 for procedures. Multiplier is 3.12.

[55]Saunders, *Colonial Records*, 7:539.

[56]Ibid.

[57]Ibid.

[58]Ibid., for taxable totals. See note 32 for procedures. Multiplier is 3.71.

[59]Saunders, *Colonial Records*, 7:539.

[60]Mecklenburg County's white and black totals for 1767 were calculated by averaging the percentage of blacks who lived in the other three western counties. The resulting percentage was then used for Mecklenburg County. See Saunders, *Colonial Records*, 7:539, for taxable totals. Multiplier is 3.71.

Table 1.2. Population of North Carolina and Its Regions, ca. 1755 and ca. 1767

Regions and Province	White Population Black Population Total Population	1755			
		Percentage of Province's Population in Region	Percentage of Province's White Population in Region	Percentage of Province's Black Population in Region	Percentage of Blacks within each Region and within the Province
Albemarle Sound	16,973 5,135 22,108	26.34	25.95	27.71	23.23
Neuse-Pamlico	11,302 3,874 15,176	18.08	17.28	20.90	25.53
Lower Cape Fear	1,624 2,684 4,308	5.13	2.48	14.48	62.30
Upper Cape Fear	1,386 654 2,040	2.43	2.12	3.53	32.06
Central Inner Plain–Piedmont	8,216 1,208 9,424	11.23	12.56	6.52	12.82
Northern Inner Plain–Piedmont	13,985 4,526 18,511	22.05	21.38	24.42	24.45
Western	11,927 451 12,378	14.75	18.23	2.43	3.64
North Carolina	65,413 18,532 83,945	100.00	100.00	100.00	22.08

Table 1.2 (continued)

		1767			
Regions and Province	White Population Black Population Total Population	Percentage of Province's Population in Region	Percentage of Province's White Population in Region	Percentage of Province's Black Population in Region	Percentage of Blacks within each Region and within the Province
Albemarle Sound	18,343 10,174 28,517	17.34	14.82	25.03	35.68
Neuse-Pamlico	17,274 6,696 23,970	14.58	13.95	16.48	27.93
Lower Cape Fear	2,997 4,945 7,942	4.83	2.42	12.17	62.26
Upper Cape Fear	3,243 1,353 4,596	2.80	2.62	3.33	29.44
Central Inner Plain–Piedmont	17,909 3,963 21,872	13.30	14.47	9.75	18.12
Northern Inner Plain–Piedmont	26,352 10,438 36,790	22.37	21.29	25.68	28.37
Western	37,677 3,072 40,749	24.78	30.43	7.56	7.54
North Carolina	123,795 40,641 164,436	100.00	100.00	100.00	24.72

Note: Figures in this table were calculated directly from the population figures in Table 1.1. This table was originally published in Kay and Cary, "A Demographic Analysis of Colonial North Carolina," table 3-2, pp. 82–83.

Table 1.3. Population Increases in North Carolina Regions, ca. 1755–ca. 1767

Regions and Province	Total Population Increase Percentage Increase Rate of Growth per Annum[1]	White Population Increase Percentage Increase Rate of Growth per Annum	Black Population Increase Percentage Increase Rate of Growth per Annum
Albemarle Sound	6,409 28.99 2.10	1,370 8.07 .65	5,039 98.13 5.49
Neuse-Pamlico	8,794 57.95 3.74	5,972 52.84 3.48	2,822 72.84 4.45
Lower Cape Fear[2]	3,634 84.35 4.94	1,373 84.54 4.95	2,261 84.24 4.94
Upper Cape Fear[2]	2,556 125.29 6.42	1,857 133.98 6.69	699 106.88 5.80
Central Inner Plain–Piedmont	12,448 132.09 6.63	9,693 117.98 6.18	2,755 228.06 8.88
Northern Inner Plain–Piedmont	18,279 98.75 5.51	12,367 88.43 5.11	5,912 130.62 6.58
Western	28,371 229.21 8.90	25,750 215.90 8.65	2,621 581.15 12.40
North Carolina	80,491 95.89 5.40	58,382 89.25 5.14	22,109 119.30 6.23

Source: Kay and Cary, "A Demographic Analysis of Colonial North Carolina," table 3-3, p. 84.

[1]Population increases were calculated from Table 1.2. The rate of population growth was calculated using the following approximation formula:

$$r = \frac{2(P_2 - P_1)}{n(P_1 + P_2)}$$

where r is the rate of population growth per annum; P_1 is the unit of population (total, white, or black) for a political unit (the province or a particular region) for the earlier period; P_2 is the unit of population for a political unit for the later period; n is the number of years between P_1 and P_2. See Henry S. Shryock and Jacob S. Siegel and Associates, *The Methods and Materials of Demography*, 2 vols. (Washington, D.C.: GPO, 1971), 2:380.

[2]See notes 15 and 44, Table 1.1.

Table 1.4. Black Population, Area, and Black Population Density in North Carolina, ca. 1755 and ca. 1767

Region	Black Population		Land Area (square miles)	Density of Black Population (per square mile)	
	1755	1767		1755	1767
Albemarle Sound	5,135	10,174	4,541	1.13	2.24
Neuse-Pamlico	3,874	6,696	5,129	.76	1.31
Lower Cape Fear	2,684	4,945	1,989	1.35	2.49
Upper Cape Fear	654	1,353	3,175	.21	.43
Central Inner Plain–Piedmont	1,208	3,963	7,142	.17	.55
Northern Inner Plain–Piedmont	4,526	10,438	4,268	1.06	2.45
Western	451	3,072	16,890	.03	.18
North Carolina	18,532	40,641	43,134	.43	.94
North Carolina except for Western region	18,081	37,569	26,244	.69	1.43

Sources and Methods: See Kay and Cary, "A Demographic Analysis of Colonial North Carolina," table 3-4, pp. 88–90. George Stevenson of the North Carolina State Archives computed the square mileage totals for each of the seven geographic regions as of 1767. We used the same figures for 1755. In some instances Stevenson had to assign areas to particular colonial regions arbitrarily. For all practical purposes, white settlements in 1767 stopped at the foothills; therefore the Blue Ridge counties of today were not included in the 1767 square mileage totals for the Western region. The same area used for the Western region in 1767 was also used for 1755, despite different frontiers. As a result, the 1755 population density for the actual area settled is underestimated. The population density of the Lower Cape Fear may be slightly exaggerated, that of the Upper Cape Fear slightly underestimated, because the southeastern corner of Bladen County became part of Brunswick County in 1764 when it was formed primarily from New Hanover County. Finally, some of the areas attributed to the Albemarle Sound and the Neuse-Pamlico regions were under water. The population density figures for these regions are thus somewhat deflated.

Density of population was calculated by using the following formula:

$$\frac{P_1}{a_1}$$

where P_1 is the number of persons in the county; a_1 is the number of square miles of land area in the same county. For the entire province, the same formula was applied using the total figures of population and land area.

Table 1.5. Regional and Provincial Slave Ownership Distribution Patterns (percentage of slaves owned in different numerical groupings)

Regions and Province	1748–55					1763–71				
	1–4	5–9	10–19	20+	Range	1–4	5–9	10–19	20+	Range
Albemarle Sound	32.0	23.1	36.5	8.5	27	22.9	23.0	33.0	21.1	87
Neuse-Pamlico	26.2	18.5	41.2	14.1	28	25.0	22.0	33.3	19.8	91
Lower Cape Fear	4.9	7.3	14.2	73.7	199	5.4	4.4	17.3	72.9	242
Upper Cape Fear	22.1	19.9	21.3	36.8	—	16.2	14.7	21.6	47.5	93
Central Inner Plain–Piedmont	38.5	27.3	27.1	7.1	—	32.1	23.0	33.2	11.7	47
Northern Inner Plain–Piedmont	32.3	30.0	31.1	6.7	55	13.0	12.7	42.1	32.2	64
Western	50.4	33.8	15.8	0	11	43.4	23.7	32.9	0	17
North Carolina	27.5	22.0	31.3	19.4	199	20.8	17.7	33.1	28.5	242

Sources and Methods: See Kay and Cary, "A Demographic Analysis of Colonial North Carolina," table 3-5, pp. 91–92. Slave taxable totals were converted to slave population totals in individual households by estimating that households listing 1 to 2 slave taxables owned 1 to 4 slaves; those with 3 to 4 taxables owned 5 to 9 slaves; those with 5 to 10 taxables owned 10 to 19 slaves; and those with 11 or more taxables owned 20 or more slaves. Colonial Court Records, Taxes and Accounts, 1679–1754; Bertie County Records, Lists of Taxables, 1765–71; Bute County Records, Lists of Taxables, 1771; Pasquotank County Records, Lists of Taxables, 1735–99; Treasurers and Comptrollers Papers, Tax Lists in County Settlements with the State; Secretary of State Papers, Tax Lists, 1720–1839; Legislative Papers, Tax Lists, 1771–74; all in NCSA.

The range equals the difference in the number of slaves owned by each region's largest and smallest slaveowners.

Estimates for the Upper Cape Fear region for the years 1748–55 were made by multiplying the 1763–71 percentage of slaves for the region for each category by the provincial average or the average percentage of slaves for each category within each of the five regions for which records exist from 1748 to 1755. The result was then divided by the provincial average or the average percentage of slaves for each category for all seven regions for the years 1763 to 1771. The number lower or greater than 100 was added or subtracted in accordance with the 1763–71 distribution in the Upper Cape Fear region. A similar procedure was used to obtain estimates for the Central Inner Plain–Piedmont region for the years 1748 to 1755.

Table 1.5 (continued)

Estimates for North Carolina as a whole were obtained by using the following formula for each category (1–4 slaves, etc.)

$$y = \frac{xt + x_1t_1 + x_2t_2 + x_3t_3 + x_4t_4 + x_5t_5 + x_6t_6}{100}$$

where y is the percentage of slaves within each category for each time period for the province; x, x_1, etc., is the percentage of slaves for each particular region for each category for each time period; t, t_1, etc., is the percentage of the province's slaves living within each particular region for each time period.

Data for the Albemarle Sound region for the early period consist of tax lists for Bertie County (1751) and Pasquotank County (1748). For the late period, they consist of tax lists for Bertie County (1768) and Pasquotank County (1769). These tended to be average Albemarle Sound counties. Chowan County, for example, had more pronounced slaveholding features, as may be seen in the following statistics for Chowan in 1770: 1–4 slaves, 15.7 percent; 5–9 slaves, 18.0 percent; 10–19 slaves, 36.2 percent; 20 or more slaves, 30.1 percent.

Data for the Neuse-Pamlico region for the early period consist of a tax list for Beaufort County (1755); for the later period, tax lists for Beaufort-Pitt Counties (1764) and Onslow County (1771) were used. Data for the Lower Cape Fear region consist of tax lists for New Hanover County (1755 and 1767) and Brunswick County (1769). Data for the Upper Cape Fear region consist of a tax list for Bladen County (1763). (See earlier notation for the methodology used to obtain a statement for the earlier period for this region.) Data for the Central Inner Plain–Piedmont region consist of tax lists for Pitt County (1764) and Dobbs County (1769). Data for the Northern Inner Plain–Piedmont region consist of two tax lists for Granville County (1755 and 1769) and a tax list for Bute County (1771). Data for the Western region consist of tax lists for Orange County (1755) and Anson County (1763).

Table 1.6. Proportion of Slaves on Plantations of Various Sizes in South Carolina's Lowcountry, 1760–1769, and North Carolina's Lower Cape Fear Region, 1762–1769.

Province	Years	Size of Slaveholding Unit						Number of Slaves
		1–9	10–19	20–49	50–79	80–99	100+	
South Carolina	1760–69	12%	13%	35%	21%	7%	12%	23,732
North Carolina	1762–69	14%	11%	29%	22%	3%	21%	9,087

Sources: For South Carolina, see Philip D. Morgan, "Black Society in the Lowcountry, 1610–1810," in Slavery and Freedom in the Age of the American Revolution, edited by Ira Berlin and Ronald Hoffman (Charlottesville: University Press of Virginia, 1983), 95, table 9. For North Carolina, see Treasurers and Comptrollers Papers, Tax Lists in County Settlements with the State; Secretary of State Papers, Tax Lists, 1720–1839; both in NCSA. Because the tax lists count only slave taxables, a multiplier of 1.89 was used to convert the polls to slave totals.

Table 1.7. Sample Slave Taxable Populations of North Carolina and Its Regions, with Sex Ratios, 1751–1772

	Number of Slave Taxables and Sex Ratios (Males per 100 Females)		
Region	1751–55	1761–64	1766–72
Albemarle	1,642	—	10,109
Sound[1]	163	—	134
Neuse-	1,755	—	3,238
Pamlico[2]	143	—	121
Lower	2,790	6,657	3,894
Cape Fear[3]	144	123	117
Upper	346	667	—
Cape Fear[4]	188	129	—
Central Inner	168	883	—
Plain–Piedmont[5]	182	128	—
Northern Inner	2,618	—	—
Plain–Piedmont[6]	137	—	—
Western[7]	274	68	—
	194	106	—
North Carolina (weighted estimates of ratios)	153	125	

Sources and Methods: See Kay and Cary, "A Demographic Analysis of Colonial North Carolina," table 3-6, pp. 94–96. Each extant county tax list that breaks down the county's taxable slave population by sex was used to determine the sex ratios in the above table. These tax lists are listed below. Because the slave taxable population was used to determine sex ratios, the slave population under twelve years of age has been ignored in these calculations.

Tax lists that note the sex of slaves exist for the following regions and counties: Albemarle Sound—Bertie (1751, 1754, 1761, 1763, 1766, 1768, 1769, 1770, 1772), Chowan (1768, 1771), Currituck (1752, 1754), Pasquotank (1754, 1769), Perquimans (1771, 1772); Neuse-Pamlico—Beaufort (1754), Craven (1754, 1769), Hyde (1754), Onslow (1754, 1769, 1770, 1771); Lower Cape Fear—Brunswick (1764, 1769, 1772), New Hanover (1754, 1755, 1762, 1763, 1764, 1767); Upper Cape Fear—Bladen (1754, 1763); Central Inner Plain–Piedmont—Johnston (1763), Duplin (1754, 1762), Northern Inner Plain–Piedmont—Edgecombe (1754), Granville (1754, 1755), Northampton (1754); Western—Anson (1754, 1763), Orange (1754, 1755), Rowan (1754). See notes below for sources for individual regions.

Sex ratios for each region were obtained in the following manner: The actual sex ratios for the counties where data exist were weighted in accordance with the approximate number of blacks living in the county durng the years surveyed. Thus, for the years 1751–54, estimates for 1755 were used; for 1761–64 and 1766–72, estimates for 1767 were

Table 1.7 (continued)

used. If a county had sex ratio data for more than one year, an arithmetical mean was used to determine the county's sex ratio for the period involved. Finally, we extrapolated for the Central Inner Plain–Piedmont and Western regions to achieve more representative samples. That is, we estimated mathematical trends in sex ratios for those counties where figures existed for two or more time periods and used these trends as multipliers to project probable trends in the counties for which we have actual sex ratios for at least one of the time periods.

North Carolina's sex ratios were calculated by using similar weighting techniques. To increase the sample, however, we combined the last two periods. Because there appears to have been little change in sex ratios over the years 1761–72, this process caused little distortion.

The formula used to obtain a sex ratio is: $\frac{M}{F} k$, where M is the number of males recorded in some statistical universe of persons (North Carolina or a particular region); F is the number of females in the same universe; and k is an arbitrary factor of 100. For an informative analysis of sex ratios, see George W. Barclay, *Techniques of Population Analysis* (New York: John Wiley and Sons, 1958), 21–24.

[1]Saunders, *Colonial Records*, 5:320. Colonial Court Records, Taxes and Accounts, 1679–1754; Bertie County Records, Taxables, 1755–64, 1765–71, 1772–84, and County Accounts, 1741–1860; Treasurers and Comptrollers Papers, County Settlements with the State, Tax Lists; Chowan County Records, Taxables, 1762–78; Governors Office Papers, Lists of Taxables, Militia, and Magistrates, 1754–70 and undated; Secretary of State Papers, Tax Lists, 1720–1839; Perquimans County Records, List of Taxables, 1743–1836; Legislative Papers, Tax Lists, 1771–74; all in NCSA.

[2]Saunders, *Colonial Records*, 5:320. Secretary of State Papers, Tax Lists, 1720–1839; Legislative Papers, Tax Lists, 1771–74; both in NCSA.

[3]Saunders, *Colonial Records*, 5:320. Governors Office Papers, Lists of Taxables, Militia, and Magistrates, 1754–70 and undated; Secretary of State Papers, Tax Lists, 1720–1839; Legislative Papers, Tax Lists, 1771–74; Treasurers and Comptrollers Papers, County Settlements with the State, Tax Lists; all in NCSA.

[4]Saunders, *Colonial Records*, 5:320. Secretary of State Papers, Tax Lists, 1720–1839, NCSA.

[5]Saunders, *Colonial Records*, 5:320. Governors Office Papers, Lists of Taxables, Militia, and Magistrates, 1754–70 and undated, NCSA.

[6]Saunders, *Colonial Records*, 5:320. Treasurers and Comptrollers Papers, County Settlements with the State, Tax Lists, NCSA.

[7]Saunders, *Colonial Records*, 5:320. Treasurers and Comptrollers Papers, County Settlements with the State, Tax Lists; Secretary of State Papers, Tax Lists, 1720–1839; both in NCSA.

Table 1.8. Adult Slaves Who Could Not Be Paired by Sex, Calculated from Sex Ratios and Sex Imbalance Ratios, 1748–1772 (for six of North Carolina's seven regions)

Region	Slaveholders Slaves (N)	Adult Sex Ratios	Adult Slaves Who Could Not Be Paired According to Sex Ratios	Adult Sex Imbalance Ratios	Adult Slaves Who Could Not Be Paired According to Sex Imbalance Ratios
Albemarle Sound	79 243	113.16	6.17%	53.80	30.04%
Neuse-Pamlico	23 56	124.00	10.71	43.59	39.29
Lower Cape Fear	29 104	153.66	21.15	44.44	38.46
Central Inner Plain–Piedmont	9 12	200.00	33.33	33.33	50.00
Northern Inner Plain–Piedmont	19 42	162.50	23.81	35.48	47.62
Western	59 74	60.87	24.32	23.33	62.16

We wish to thank Dr. Karl Vezner, former professor of political science, The University of Toledo, for his help in devising the formulas and computer programs necessary to implement Table 1.8.

Sources and Methods: See Kay and Cary, "A Demographic Analysis of Colonial North Carolina," table 3-7, pp. 99–101. Wills and inventories from the following counties were used to arrive at the above statistics: Albemarle Sound region—Bertie and Pasquotank Counties; Neuse-Pamlico region—Beaufort and Carteret Counties; Lower Cape Fear region—Brunswick and New Hanover Counties; Central Inner Plain–Piedmont region—Cumberland County; Northern Inner Plain–Piedmont region—Northampton and Halifax Counties; Western region—Anson, Mecklenburg, Orange, and Rowan Counties. These wills and inventories are in the following collections in NCSA: Secretary of State Records, North Carolina Wills, 1663–1789, S.S. 845–73, vols. 7–35; Chancery Proceedings and Wills, 1712–54, S.S. 878; Wills, 1738–52, 1750–58, 1755–58, 1758–73, S.S. 877, 879–81, vols. 4, 6–8; Inventories and Sales of Estates, 1714–98, S.S. 889–905; Bertie County Wills, C.R. 10.801.1–10.801.8, vols. 1–8; Bertie County Estates Papers, C.R. 10.504.1–10.504.1.15, 10.504.1, 10.504.1.114; Bertie County, Inventories of Estates, C.R. 10.507.2; Carteret County Records, Miscellaneous Papers, 1717–1844, Book A, Records of Wills and Bonds, C.R. 19.905.1; Wills, Inventories, Sales, and Settlement of Estates, C.R. 19.802.1–19.802.11, vols. 1–11; Carteret County Wills, C.R. 19.801.1, 19.905.1; New Hanover County Wills, C.R. vol. 105, C.R. 70.801.1–70.801.5; Northampton County Wills, C.R. 71.801.1, 71.802.1, 71.802.2; Cumberland County Wills, C.R. 29.801.1–29.801.4; Mecklenburg County Wills, 1749–1869, C.R. 65.009–65.027; Estate Papers, C.R. 065.508.3–C.R. 065.508.140; Orange County Estates Papers, 1758–85, C.R. 73.507.1.

Table 1.8 (continued)

The Upper Cape Fear region is omitted because of lack of data.

As we have seen in Table 1.7, to compute the sex ratio for the 218 holdings in the data under discussion, one would simply total the males and females separately across all holdings. With the resulting sum of males and sum of females, the sex ratio is easily computed.

The sex "imbalance ratio," on the other hand, takes into account not only the ratio of males to females but also the imbalance between their numbers that exists in each holding. It treats each holding as if it were a closed unit in terms of marital relationships. The sex imbalance ratio is a ratio of the number of the gender in the minority to the number of the gender in the majority in a holding. As one moves from the data for one holding to the data for another holding, the two totals that are incremented are the number in the minority and the number in the majority. In keeping with the sex ratio, the resulting ratio is multiplied by 100.

For example, suppose that there were four holdings having the following distribution of gender for adults: (1) 1 male; (2) 1 female; (3) 5 males and 3 females; and (4) 5 females and 3 males. The overall sex ratio would, of course, be 100, as there are the same number of males and females. The imbalance ratio, however, would be computed as follows:

Holding	Minority Gender	Majority Gender
1	0 (female)	1 (male)
2	0 (male)	1 (female)
3	3 (female)	5 (male)
4	3 (male)	5 (female)
Total	6	12

The imbalance ratio would be (6/12) 100, or 50, a far cry from the sex ratio of 100. To the extent that individual holdings were closed units, the imbalance ratio is much to be preferred in that it more closely approximates reality.

The same example can be used to illustrate the computation of a related statistic that is more easily grasped: the percentage of adults who cannot be paired with an adult of the opposite sex. Each of the 6 in the minority gender column can be paired with an adult of the opposity sex in the majority gender column. Thus, a total of 12 can be paired with a member of the opposite sex, leaving 6 in the majority column who cannot be paired. The 6 comprise 33.3 percent of the total of 18 slaves, which is the percentage of nonpaired adults.

The percentage of nonpaired adults can also be computed directly from the imbalance ratio using the following formula:

$$100 \; \frac{(100 - \text{Imbalance Ratio})}{(100 + \text{Imbalance Ratio})} = 100 \; \frac{(100 - 50)}{(100 + 50)} = 33.3$$

The percentage of nonpaired adults can be computed directly from the sex ratio by using the following formula when sex ratio is greater than 100:

$$\frac{\text{Sex Ratio} - 100}{\text{Sex Ratio} + 100} = \frac{113.16 - 100}{113.16 + 100} = 6.17$$

When sex ratio is less than 100, the formula would be:

$$\frac{100 - \text{Sex Ratio}}{100 + \text{Sex Ratio}} = \frac{100 - 60.87}{100 + 60.87} = 24.32$$

Table 1.9. Quantities and Estimated Values (in Pounds Sterling) of Selected Comodities Exported from the Southern Colonies to Great Britain, Ireland, Southern Europe and the Wine Islands, the West Indies, and Africa, 1768–1772

Commodity	Maryland			Virginia		
	Quantity	Value	% of Total	Quantity	Value	% of Total
Beeswax (lb)	2,554	128	.01	56,823	2,842	.08
Beef & Pork (bbl)	492	1,493	.08	28,650	60,147	1.74
Bread & Flour (tons)	20,459.49	215,759	12.15	12,258.37	129,980	3.76
Candles, Spermaceti	250	18	.00	1,075	72	.00
Cotton	—	—	—	51,911	2,586	.07
Deerskins (lb)	43,525	3,320	.19	566,778	46,962	1.36
Fish, Dried (quintals)	178	89	.01	1,129	576	.02
Flaxseed (bu)	89,703	16,981	.96	8,110	1,264	.04
Grain, Indian Corn (bu)	639,630	61,887	3.48	2,111,924	204,921	5.93
Grain, Rice (bbl)	7	24	.00	72	176	.01
Grain, Wheat (bu)	1,084,241	207,385	11.67	928,726	177,295	5.13
Hemp (tons)	9.67	247	.01	513.51	13,585	.39
Hoops (1,000)	451	840	.05	406	822	.02
Indigo	—	—	—	14,951	2,812	.08
Iron, Bar (tons)	4,155.63	61,332	3.45	1,797.32	26,207	.76
Iron, Pig (tons)	5,252.50	26,147	1.47	6,484.38	32,269	.93
Livestock, Cattle (no.)	—	—	—	—	—	—
Livestock, Horses (no.)	8	80	.01	15	150	.00
Naval Stores, Pitch (bbl)	931	343	.02	8,510	3,636	.11
Naval Stores, Tar (bbl)	1,840	690	.04	81,933	30,507	.88
Naval Stores, Turpentine (bbl)	2,194	949	.05	15,664	7,249	.21
Oil, Whale (tons)	2.87	34	.00	7.58	48	.00
Potash (tons)	6.28	150	.01	21.23	493	.01
Rum, American (gal)	2,625	198	.01	2,190	147	.00
Rum, West Indian (gal)	—	—	—	5,270	555	.02
Tobacco (cwt)	1,502,643	1,131,596	63.70	2,929,774	2,649,043	76.60
Wine (tons)	—	—	—	2	115	.00
Wood Products,						
Pine Boards (1,000 ft)	3,525	7,832	.44	4,556	10,121	.29
Staves/Headings (1,000)	12,999	38,954	2.19	17,977	53,850	1.56
Total		1,776,476	100.00		53,458,430	100.00

Source: James F. Shepherd, "Commodity Exports from the British North American Colonies to Overseas Areas, 1768–1772: Magnitudes and Patterns of Trade," Paper no. 258, October 1969, Institute for Research in the Behavioral, Economic, and Management Sciences, Purdue University, Lafayette, Ind.; 17–21, 27–28, 35–38, 47–50. The commodities Shepherd selected were "reasonably standard and homogeneous"; both

North Carolina			South Carolina			Georgia		
Quantity	Value	% of Total	Quantity	Value	% of Total	Quantity	Value	% of Total
30,425	1,522	.45	52,204	2,611	.13	9,357	468	.14
154,892	17,160	5.13	9,963	14,481	.70	4,021	5,938	1.79
475.64	4,847	1.45	934.13	9,670	.47	23.38	255	.08
1,900	130	.04	9,860	655	.03	2,150	147	.04
1,934	80	.02	6,524	295	.01	1,583	68	.02
96,873	7,843	2.34	711,324	81,808	3.98	711,200	58,722	17.67
250	122	.04	120	57	.00	115	57	.02
15,559	2,840	.85	—	—	—	—	—	—
300,992	33,825	10.11	125,132	13,552	.66	32,785	3,579	1.08
1,163	2,606	.78	781,150	1,329,667	64.63	90,273	195,391	58.79
9,740	1,836	.55	—	—	—	—	—	—
39.26	1,131	.34	82.27	2,436	.12	0.78	27	.01
196	396	.12	64	130	.01	12	24	.01
3,039	640	.19	2,632,268	542,106	26.35	84,331	16,575	4.99
1.05	22	.01	23.8	468	.02	0.03	1	.00
—	—	—	—	—	—	—	—	—
192	1,152	.34	67	402	.02	231	1,278	.38
230	2,300	.69	722	7,220	.35	1,309	13,090	3.94
9,811	3,974	1.19	32,229	12,792	.62	1,100	439	.13
294,174	108,288	32.36	16,096	5,997	.29	218	74	.02
46,284	21,497	6.42	11,535	5,399	.26	183	84	.03
15.35	184	.05	3.01	36	.00	0.12	1	.00
—	—	—	2.50	55	.00	—	—	—
3,485	306	.09	10,286	863	.04	—	—	—
1,237	127	.04	17,618	1,820	.10	420	41	.01
44,374	38,269	11.44	11,574	10,108	.49	2,190	1,849	.56
16.79	620	.19	45.85	1,523	.07	18.5	637	.19
17,075	50,203	15.00	3,393	9,889	.48	8,802	25,844	7.78
10,026	32,675	9.77	1,059	3,404	.17	2,391	7,729	2.32
	334,595	100.00		2,057,444	100.00		332,318	100.00

prices and quantities are generally available, and, depending on the particular year, they totaled from 91.71 to 92.19 percent of the value of all exports from the British North American colonies (Shepherd, "Commodity Exports," 9, 57–62, 86 [n. 19], 87 [n. 21]. The figures here represent an aggregation of the data Shepherd presents for exports to major markets, by colony, for each of the years 1768 to 1772.

Table 1.10. White Servant and Slave Populations in Some Counties and Regions and the Province, 1755–1769

Regions and Counties	Year(s)	White Servants (N)	Slaves (N)	Ratio of Slave Population to Servant Population (approximate)[1]	Servant Percentage of Unfree Population
Albemarle Sound	1763–69	1,755	5,047	3:1	26.02
Bertie	1763	660	1,656		28.50
Bertie	1768	861	1,936		30.85
Pasquotank	1769	254	1,455		14.86 22.86
Neuse-Pamlico	1755–64	844	2,575	3:1	24.69
Beaufort	1755	336	1,074		23.83
Beaufort-Pitt	1764	508	1,501		25.29
Central Inner Plain–Piedmont	1755–63	195	495	2.5:1	28.26
Cumberland	1755	107	115		48.20
Cumberland	1763	82	380		17.75
Northern Inner Plain–Piedmont					
Granville	1755	160	821	5:1	16.31
		508		1.5:1	38.22
North Carolina— Mean of Regional Means	1755–69			3.5:1	23.82
				2:1	29.30

Source: Kay and Cary, "A Demographic Analysis of Colonial North Carolina," 106–7, Table 3-9. Figures deal with population (not taxable) totals.

[1] Precise ratios for each region and the province are: Albemarle Sound region—5.05 : 1.78; Neuse-Pamlico region—2.58 : 0.84; Central Inner Plain–Piemont region—4.95 : 1.95; Northern Inner Plain–Piedmont region—5 : 1 and 1.5 : 1; North Carolina—5.2 : 1.54 and 5.2 : 2.41.

Table 1.11. Slave Price Index, 1748–1772

1748–54	1755–58	1749–64	1765–72	1748–72
Adult Males	*Adult Males*	*Adult Males*	*Adult Males*	*Adult Males*
Total cases = 24	Total cases = 2	Total cases = 47	Total cases = 53	Total cases = 126
Mean = £34:2:6.25	Mean = £33	Mean = £58:4:5.13	Mean = £89:3:7.92	Mean = £66:5:1.2
Median = £34:10:0	Median = —	Median = £60	Median = £87	Median = £60
Mode = £40	Mode = —	Mode = £60	Mode = £100	Mode = £70 & £100
Range = £5–£90	Range = £14–£52	Range = £3–£100	Range = £8–£200	Range = £3–£200
Frequency distribution:	Frequency distribution:	Frequency distribution:	Frequency distribution:	Frequency distribution:
0–£19:19:11 = 5	0–£19:19:11 = 1	0–£19:19:11 = 2	0–£19:19:11 = 3	0–£19:19:11 = 11
20– 39:19:11 = 10	20– 39:19:11 = 0	20– 39:19:11 = 7	20– 39:19:11 = 6	20– 39:19:11 = 23
40– 59:19:11 = 8	40– 59:19:11 = 1	40– 59:19:11 = 13	40– 59:19:11 = 4	40– 59:19:11 = 27
60– 79:19:11 = 0		60– 79:19:11 = 16	60– 79:19:11 = 9	60– 79:19:11 = 25
80– 99:19:11 = 1		80– 99:19:11 = 7	80– 99:19:11 = 10	80– 99:19:11 = 17
		100–119:19:11 = 2	100–119:19:11 = 8	100–119:19:11 = 10
			120–139:19:11 = 3	120–139:19:11 = 3
			140–159:19:11 = 2	140–159:19:11 = 2
			160–179:19:11 = 3	160–179:19:11 = 3
			180–199:19:11 = 1	180–199:19:11 = 1
			200–219:19:11 = 4	200–219:19:11 = 4
95.83% of the cases were not less than £60 and £80	100% of the cases were less than £60	57.45% of the cases wre £60 or less; 89.17% were £80 or less	47.19% of the cases were £80 or less	73.81% of the cases were £80 or less

continued

Table 1.11 (continued)

	1748–54	1755–58	1749–64	1765–72	1748–72
	All Males	*All Males*	*All Males*	*All Males*	*All Males*
Total cases	= 40	= 6	= 56	= 71	= 173
Mean	= £27:16:10.82	= £22:0:11.17	= £54:17:9.88	= £79:16:7.15	= £57:14:8.05
Median	= £25	= £15:17:9.5	= £55	= £75	= £52:10
Mode	= £15 & £20	= —	= £30 & £60	= £100	= £30, £40, & £100
Range	= £5–£90	= £10–£52	= £3–£100	= £4:10–£200	= £3–£200
Frequency distribution:					
0–£19:19:11	= 5	= 1	= 2	= 3	= 11
20– 39:19:11	= 10	= 0	= 7	= 6	= 23
40– 59:19:11	= 8	= 1	= 13	= 4	= 27
60– 79:19:11	= 0		= 16	= 9	= 25
80– 99:19:11	= 1		= 7	= 10	= 17
100–119:19:11			= 2	= 8	= 10
120–139:19:11				= 3	= 3
140–159:19:11				= 2	= 2
160–179:19:11				= 3	= 3
180–199:19:11				= 1	= 1
200–219:19:11				= 4	= 4
	97.5% of the cases were less than £60 and £80	100% of the cases were less than £60	62.5% of the cases were £60 or less; 89.26% were £80 or less	57.75% of the cases were £80 or less	78.16% of the cases were £80 or less

continued

Adult Females

Total cases = 17
Mean = £31:2:11.29
Median = £28
Mode = £30
Range = £7–£85
Frequency distribution:
0–£19:19:11 = 1
20– 39:19:11 = 15
40– 59:19:11 = 0
60– 79:19:11 = 0
80– 99:19:11 = 1

94.12% of the cases were less than £60 and £80

Adult Females

Total cases = 0
Mean = —
Median = —
Mode = —
Range = —
Frequency distribution:

Adult Females

Total cases = 31
Mean = £54:6:3.48
Median = £50:15
Mode = £30, £50, & £60
Range = £10–£100
Frequency distribution:
0–£19:19:11 = 2
20– 39:19:11 = 6
40– 59:19:11 = 9
60– 79:19:11 = 9
80– 99:19:11 = 3
100–119:19:11 = 2

64.52% of the cases were £60 or less; 89.17% were £80 or less

Adult Females

Total cases = 58
Mean = £60:7:1.86
Median = £60
Mode = £81:13:4
Range = £6–£150
Frequency distribution:
0–£19:19:11 = 4
20– 39:19:11 = 10
40– 59:19:11 = 13
60– 79:19:11 = 13
80– 99:19:11 = 11
100–119:19:11 = 4
120–139:19:11 = 2
140–159:19:11 = 1

74% of the cases were £80 or less

Adult Females

Total cases = 106
Mean = £53:18:1.36
Median = £50
Mode = £30
Range = £6–£150
Frequency distribution:
0–£19:19:11 = 7
20– 39:19:11 = 31
40– 59:19:11 = 22
60– 79:19:11 = 22
80– 99:19:11 = 15
100–119:19:11 = 6·
120–139:19:11 = 2
140–159:19:11 = 1

81.13% of the cases were £80 or less

Table 1.11 (continued)

	1748–54	1755–58	1749–64	1765–72	1748–72
	All Females	*All Females*	*All Females*	*All Females*	*All Females*
Total cases	= 30	= 3	= 39	= 67	= 139
Mean	= £27:1:8	= £23:17	= £50:5:7.23	= £58:2:1.12	= £49:9:5.94
Median	= £25	= £20	= £50	= £60	= £42:3.6
Mode	= £2	= —	= £30	= £60	= £30
Range	= £7–£85	= £19:1–£32:10	= £10–£100	= £5–£50	= £5–£150
Frequency distribution:					
0–£19:19:11 =	4	1	4	6	15
20– 39:19:11 =	25	2	8	11	46
40– 59:19:11 =	0		13	15	28
60– 79:19:11 =	0		9	17	26
80– 99:19:11 =	1		3	11	15
100–119:19:11 =			2	4	6
120–139:19:11 =				2	2
140–159:19:11 =				1	1
	90.67% of the cases were less than £60 and £80	100% of the cases were less than £60	71.79% of the cases were £60 or less; 89.74% were £80 or less	77.61% of the cases were £80 or less	85.61% of the cases were £80 or less

Adult Males and Females

Total cases = 41
Mean = £32:17:9.66
Median = £30
Mode = £25
Range = £5–£90
Frequency distribution:
0–£19:19:11 = 6
20– 39:19:11 = 25
40– 59:19:11 = 8
60– 79:19:11 = 0
80– 99:19:11 = 2

95.12% of the cases were less than £60 and £80

Adult Males and Females

Total cases = 2
Mean = £33
Median = —
Mode = —
Range = £14–£52
Frequency distribution:
0–£19:19:11 = 1
20– 39:19:11 = 0
40– 59:19:11 = 1

100% of the cases were less than £60

Adult Males and Females

Total cases = 87
Mean = £55:13:3.05
Median = £57
Mode = £60
Range = £3–£100
Frequency distribution:
0–£19:19:11 = 4
20– 39:19:11 = 16
40– 59:19:11 = 26
60– 79:19:11 = 27
80– 99:19:11 = 10
100–119:19:11 = 4

64.37% of the cases were £60 or less; 89.17% were £80 or less

Adult Males and Females

Total cases = 118
Mean = £71:18:6.61
Median = £70
Mode = £100
Range = £6–£200
Frequency distribution:
0–£19:19:11 = 7
20– 39:19:11 = 23
40– 59:19:11 = 17
60– 79:19:11 = 22
80– 99:19:11 = 21
100–119:19:11 = 12
120–139:19:11 = 5
140–159:19:11 = 3
160–179:19:11 = 3
180–199:19:11 = 1
200–219:19:11 = 4

63.56% of the cases were £80 or less

Adult Males and Females

Total cases = 248
Mean = £59:9:0.87
Median = £52:10
Mode = £60
Range = £3–£200
Frequency distribution:
0–£19:19:11 = 19
20– 39:19:11 = 63
40– 59:19:11 = 54
60– 79:19:11 = 48
80– 99:19:11 = 32
100–119:19:11 = 16
120–139:19:11 = 5
140–159:19:11 = 3
160–179:19:11 = 3
180–199:19:11 = 1
200–219:19:11 = 4

78.63% of the cases were £80 or less

continued

Table 1.11 (continued)

	1748–54	1755–58	1749–64	1765–72	1748–72
	All Cases	All Cases	All Cases	All Cases	All Cases
Total cases	= 83	= 9	= 112	= 153	= 357
Mean	= £27:16:2.04	= £22:11:2.67	= £51:15:1.78	= £66:0:11.5	= £51:12:7.97
Median	= £25	= £19:1	= £52:10	= £62:10	= £45
Mode	= £20	= —	= £60	= £40	= £20 & £30
Range	= £5–£90	= £10–£52	= £3–£100	= £3:10–£200	= £3–£200
Frequency distribution:					
0–£19:19:11 =	21	5	9	12	48
20– 39:19:11 =	50	3	23	32	107
40– 59:19:11 =	8	1	37	23	71
60– 79:19:11 =	1		28	34	62
80– 99:19:11 =	3		11	22	35
100–119:19:11 =			4	13	17
120–139:19:11 =				6	6
140–159:19:11 =				3	3
160–179:19:11 =				3	3
180–199:19:11 =				1	1
200–219:19:11 =				4	4

95.4% of the cases were less than £60; 96.55% were less than £80

100% of the cases were less than £60

70.54% of the cases were £60 or less; 91.07% were £80 or less

69.93% of the cases were £80 or less

83.75% of the cases were £80 or less

Sources: Anson County, Record of Wills, 1751–95; Beaufort County Court Minutes, vol. 1, 1756–61; Bertie County, County Accounts, 1741–1860; Bertie County, Individual Accounts, 1718–99; Bertie County, Inventories of Estates; Bertie County, Slave Papers, 1744–1815; Byrnes' Account Book, 1757–83; Carteret County, Wills, Inventories, Sales, and Settlement of Estates, vols. 1–11; Chowan County Estates Records; Craven County Estates Records; Edenton Superior Court Minutes, Nov. 1760–Nov. 1767; Granville County Estates Records; John and Ruth Hodges Collection; Lincoln and Tryon County Court Minutes, pt. 1, 1769–82; Mecklenburg County Estates Records; New Hanover County Estates Records; Onslow County Estates Records; Orange County Estates Papers, 1758–85; Pasquotank County, Bills of Sale (Negro), 1750–1858; Pasquotank County, 1750–1858; Pasquotank County Estates Records; Rowan County Estates Records; John Smith Collection—all in NCSA. Thomas Burke Papers, 1749–89; Loose Bennehan Papers, Cameron Papers; Coffield-Bellamy Papers; Lenoir Papers; Archibald MacLaine Commonplace Book; John Steele Papers; James Webbs Papers—all in SHC. Morris Family Papers and Simpson-Bryan Papers, both in the North Carolina Collection, University of North Carolina, Chapel Hill. Thomas Cook Papers and Negro Collection—Slavery Division, both in the Perkins Library, Duke University, Durham, N.C. Adelaide L. Fries, ed., *Records of the Moravians in North Carolina* 8 vols. (Raleigh: Edwards and Broughton Print Co.,

Table 1.12. Occupational Breakdown for North Carolina's Male and Female Slaves on Three Plantations, 1770, 1809, 1809

Gender	Occupation	Number	Percentage
Both	Field Hands	145	90.06
	Artisans	9	5.59
	Watermen (ferrymen)	1	.62
	Domestics	6	3.73
	Total	161	100.00
Males	Field Hands	70	87.50
	Artisans	8	10.00
	Watermen (ferrymen)	1	1.25
	Domestics	1	1.25
	Total	80	100.00
Females	Field Hands	75	92.60
	Artisans (weaver)	1	1.23
	Watermen	0	0
	Domestics	5	6.17
	Total	81	100.00

Note: This table was constructed from a breakdown of slave occupations on three plantations on two slaveholdings: Pollock-Mitchell (1770) and Mount Rose-Connicanary (1809). A total of 161 slaves of working age are involved. The 10.6% of the slaves in these records listed as elderly , with no indication of their occupations, were calculated as field hands, perhaps tending to increase that number disproportionately. See Pollock Papers, P.C. 31.1, NCSA.

Table 3.1. Compensation Levels, 1748–1772

Categories	Total No. of Compensations; Percentage of Total for Entire Period	Total Amount of Compensations; Percentage of Total for Entire Period	Range of Compensations	Mean	Median	Mode	Frequency Distributions
				1748–54*			
Males	7	£305:16:8	£35–£53:6:8	£43:9:2.85	£42:10:0	£40	—
Females	1 (—)	£50:0:0 (—)	—	—	—	—	—
Total	9 (10.46)	£392:10:0 (7.10)	£35–£53:6:8	£43:12:2.7	£42:10:0	£40 and £50	0–19:19:11 = 0 20–39:19:11 = 2 40–59:19:11 = 7
				1755–58			
Males	11	£715	£20–£80	£65	£70	£80	—
Females	1 (—)	£80:0:0 (—)	—	—	—	—	—
Total	12 (13.02)	£795:0:0 (14.39)	£20–£80	£66:5:0	£72:10:0	£80	0–19:19:11 = 0 20–39:19:11 = 1 40–59:19:11 = 2 60–79:19:11 = 5 80 = 4

1759–64

	Number	Total value					Distribution
Males	12	£600:0:0	£20–£60	£50	£60	£60	—
Females	1	£60:0:0	—	—	—	—	—
Total	13 15.11	£660:0:0 11.94	£20–£60	£50:15:4.6	£60	£60	0–19:19:11 = 0 20–39:19:11 = 3 40–59:19:11 = 2 60 = 8

1765–72*

	Number	Total value					Distribution
Males	44	£3,201:0:0	£50–£80	£72:15:0	£80	£80	0–19:19:11 = 0 20–39:19:11 = 0 40–59:19:11 = 5 60–79:19:11 = 12 80 = 27
Females	7	£395:0:0	£20–£80	£56:8:6.85	£65	£70	0–19:19:11 = 0 20–39:19:11 = 1 40–59:19:11 = 2 60–79:19:11 = 3 80 = 1
Total	52 60.46	£3,676:0:0 66.55	£20–£80	£70:13:10.2	£80	£80	0–19:19:11 = 0 20–39:19:11 = 1 40–59:19:11 = 7 60–79:19:11 = 15 80 = 29

continued

Table 3.1 (continued)

Categories	Total No. of Compensations; Percentage of Total for Entire Period	Total Amount of Compensations; Percentage of Total for Entire Period	Range of Compensations	Mean	Median	Mode	Frequency Distributions
			1748–72*				
Males	74 86.04	£4,821:16:8 87.3	£20–£80	£65:23:2.37	£65	£80	0–19:19:11 = 0 20–39:19:11 = 5 40–59:19:11 = 15 60–79:19:11 = 24 80 = 30
Females	10 11.63	£585:0:0 10.59	£20–£80	£56:8:6.85	£65	£50, £70, and £80	0–19:19:11 = 0 20–39:19:11 = 1 40–59:19:11 = 3 60–79:19:11 = 4 80 = 2
Total	86 100	£5,523:10:0 100	£20–£80	£64:4:6.44	£67:10:0	£80	0–19:19:11 = 0 20–39:19:11 = 7 40–59:19:11 = 18 60–79:19:11 = 28 80 = 33

Sources: See note 4 of the text for a listing of the sources used to prepare this table. An analysis of these sources reveals that, for the period through 1754, we have uncovered only one incomplete set of Committee of Claims records; eight sets are missing. Because only about 5.55% of the claims records for this period are extant, the supplementary records used for this study (primarily Treasurers and Comptrollers Papers, Secretary of State Papers—Court Records, different counties' slave papers, and various county court minutes and colonial newspapers) are the predominant sources used to obtain slave evaluations before 1754. Therefore, out of a total of nine evaluations, five came from sources other than Committee of Claims records, only three came from Committee of Claims records, and one was found in both types of source material. For the period 1755–58, we have found two complete claims records (September 1755 and November 1758) and one incomplete set (October 1756), with one set missing. The increase in surviving claims records (about 62.22% of the total have survived) is obvious in that out of a total of twelve evaluations, five are now found solely in sources other than claims records, five are found solely in claims records, and two are found in both types of records. For the period 1759–64, there are eight complete surviving sets of claims records that amount to an 88.88% to 100% survival rate. Consequently, out of a total of thirteen evaluations, none are solely found in sources other than claims records, nine are solely found in claims records, and four are found in both types of records. For the period 1765–72, four complete sets of claims records and one incomplete set survive, and two are missing—equaling about a 64.28% survival rate. As the last complete set is for December 1770, it is not surprising that out of a total of fifty-two evaluations, all five that only appear in sources other than claims records are cases from 1769 through 1772. Seventeen are found solely in claims records, and thirty are found in both types.

During the period January 1748–January 1773, the assembly held thirty-six sessions, if the April–May sessions of 1760 and the three sessions that occurred consecutively in April 1762 are counted as one each. In that time, seven legislative sessions did not appoint claims committees and therefore did not have committee meetings. In addition, the Colonial Records (William L. Saunders, ed., The Colonial Records of North Carolina, 10 vols. [Raleigh: State of North Carolina, 1886–90]) do not include the legislative journals for the November session of 1761. Consequently, there were either twenty-eight or twenty-nine Committee of Claims meetings during the period in question. However, only fourteen complete records of Committee of Claims meetings are extant. In addition, 40% of the claims of the December 1767 committee meetings have been destroyed by fire, and only a portion of the October 1751 and October 1756 records remain. Thus approximately 53% to 54% of the claims committee records are extant, and out of a total of eighty-six, fifteen appear solely in sources other than claims records, thirty-four are found solely in claims records, and thirty-seven are found in both types. Disparities in surviving Committee of Claims records are importantly offset by other materials. There is no adequate way to extrapolate for the missing data to arrive at complete estimates for compensations.

*The discrepancy between the male-female totals and the listed totals for the starred years is explained by the addition of two slaves, whose sex is not specific in the records, to the listed totals.

Table 3.2 Upper-Class and Other Slaveholders and Their Slaveholdings in Particular Counties and Regions, with the Compensations Received by Each Group

Counties and Regions	Total Slave Taxables, Regional Means	Total Number of Slave Taxables Owned by Upper Class, Regional Means	Percentage of Slave Taxables Owned by Upper Class, Regional Means	Total Number of Upper-Class Slaveholders, Regional Means	Total Number of White Taxables, Regional Means	Total Number of Households, Regional Means	Upper-Class Heads of Households, Percentage of Total White Taxables	Upper-Class Heads of Households, Percentage of Total Number of Households	Upper-Class Compensations, Number and Amount, Regional Totals	Compensations to All Other Masters, Number and Amount, Regional Totals	Percentage of Number of Compensations Awarded to Upper Class	Percentage of Money Compensations Awarded to Upper Class	Tax Lists Used for Each County
New Hanover	1,423	1,105	77.65	41	396	265	10.35	15.47	5½ £405	1 £80	84.61	83.5	1755
New Hanover	2,199	1,723	79.05	67	597	424	11.22	15.80	3½ £202:10	½ £22:10	87.50	90	1763
New Hanover & Brunswick[1]	2,749	2,034	73.95	70	744	554	9.04	12.63	11¼ £867:10	2½ £155	81.81	84.84	1767 and 1769
Lower Cape Fear region[2]	2,123.7	1,620.7	76.31	59.3	589	414.3	10.06	14.31	20¼ £1,475	4 £257:10	83.50	85.13	above
Bertie[3]	877	350	39.9	31	794	619	3.9	5	3¾ £217:10	1 £20	78.92	91.57	1763
Hertford	—	—	—	—	—	—	—	—	0	1 £60	0	0	no tax list
Chowan[4]	1,077	528	49.02	42	593	471	7.08	8.89	7½ £546	2 £140	78.94	79.59	1771
Perquimans[5]	1,086	461	42.44	44	709	524	6.2	8.39	0	1 £60	0	0	1772

Region													
Albemarle Sound region[6]	1,013	446	43.83	39	699	538	5.56	7.24	11¼ / £763:10	5 / £280	69.23	73.16	above
Onslow[7]	572	279	48.95	27	700	510	3.85	5.29	3 / £220	0	100	100	1771
Craven[8]	1,561	656	42.03	37	1,238	947	2.98	3.9	2 / £90	6 / £395	25	18.55	1769
Beaufort	563	158	28.06	15	744	579	2.01	2.59	0	2 / £86:13:4	0	0	1755
Beaufort[9]	420	125	29.78	9	355	261	2.53	3.44	4 / £235	1 / £80	80	74.6	1764
Beaufort average	491.5	141.5	28.79	12	549.5	427	2.18	2.81	4 / £235	3 / £166:13:4	57.14	58.55	1755 & 1764
Neuse-Pamlico region[10]	874.88	358.85	41.02	25	829	628	3.01	3.98	9 / £545	9 / £561:13:4	50	49.33	above
Upper Cape Fear region Bladen[11]	667	381	57.12	21	577	390	3.62	5.38	2 / £93:6:8	7 / £115	50	44.74	1763
Cumberland	63	28	44.49	5	302	195	1.65	2.56	—	—	—	—	1755
Cumberland	349	137	39.25	18	896	579	2.00	3.10	0	1 / £80	0	0	1767
Cumberland average[12]	206	82.5	40.04	11.5	599	382	1.91	3.01	—	—	—	—	1755 & 1767
Johnston	—	—	—	—	—	—	—	—	0	1 / £55	0	0	no tax list

continued

Table 3.2 (continued)

Counties and Regions	Total Slave Taxables, Regional Means	Total Number of Slave Taxables Owned by Upper Class, Regional Means	Percentage of Slave Taxables Owned by Upper Class, Regional Means	Total Number of Upper-Class Slaveholders, Regional Means	Total Number of White Taxables, Regional Means	Total Number of Households, Regional Means	Upper-Class Heads of Households, Percentage of Total White Taxables	Upper-Class Heads of Households, Percentage of Total Number of Households	Upper-Class Compensations, Number and Amount, Regional Totals	Compensations to All Other Masters, Number and Amount, Regional Totals	Percentage of Number of Compensations Awarded to Upper Class	Percentage of Money Compensations Awarded to Upper Class	Tax Lists Used for Each County
Duplin	—	—	—	—	—	—	—	—	1 £60	2 £130	33.33	31.52	no tax list
Dobbs[13]	788	332	42.13	37	1,280	946	2.89	3.91	1 £60	0	100	100	1769
Central Inner & Outer Plain—Piedmont region	497	207.25	41.7	24.25	939.5	664	2.58	3.65	2 £120	4 £265	33.33	31.17	above
Edgecombe	—	—	—	—	—	—	—	—	1 £50	0	100	100	no tax list
Halifax	—	—	—	—	—	—	—	—	0	2 £130	0	0	no tax list
Northampton	—	—	—	—	—	—	—	—	0	3 £160	0	0	no tax list
Bute[14]	1,553	610	39.27	43	1,629	1,065	2.63	4.03	0	4 £295	0	0	1771
Granville	476	184	38.65	25	836	655	2.99	3.81	1 £42:10	0	100	100	1755
Granville[15]	1,035	592	57.19	30	1,102	762	2.72	3.93	—	—	—	—	1769

												1755 & 1769
Granville average	755.5	388	51.35	27.5	969	708.5	2.83	3.88	—	—	—	—	
N. Inner & Outer Plain—Piedmont region[16]	1,014.5	397	39.13	34	1,233	860	2.75	3.95	2 £92:10	9 £585	18.18	13.65	above
N. Inner & Outer Plain—Piedmont region[17]	1,154	499	43.14	35	1,299	866.7	2.69	3.94	—	—	—	—	above
Anson[18]	73	37	48.68	6	427	320	1.4	1.87	1 £60	0	100	100	1763
Rowan	—	—	—	—	—	—	—	—	1 £35	0	100	100	no tax list
Western region	—	—	—	—	—	—	—	—	2 £95	0	100	100	above

Notes: As seen in the numbered notes for this table, a sliding scale of slaveownership was used to determine membership in the upper class for the different counties. Where tax lists or other sources were not available to determine the number of slaves held by a particular owner, he might be defined as an upper-class recipient of a compensation if he were a provincial officer or major county official: that is, a justice of the peace, sheriff, clerk, register, coroner, or high militia officer. Thus, whereas the analysis of each county's demography strictly relates to slaveholding, the class breakdown concerning the receipt of compensations supplements slaveholding with office-holding characteristics.

To achieve an adequate statistical relationship between compensations in a particular county and the county's demography, we surveyed only those tax lists from periods similar to those in which compensations were awarded. Following is a list of the sources used at the North Carolina State Archives: Secretary of State Papers, Tax Lists, 1720–1839; Treasurers and Comptrollers Papers, County Settlements with the State, Tax Lists; Legislative Papers, Tax Lists, 1771–74; Bertie County Taxables, 1755–64; Bute County, List of Taxables, 1771; Chowan County, Taxables, 1762–78; all in North Carolina State Archives (NCSA). The most important records in NCSA that aided in the compilation of offices held by individual slaveowners who received compensations for executed slaves are: Military Collection, Troop Returns (1747–1859), Militia and Continental Returns, 1770–78; Governor's Office, Lists of Taxables, Militia, and Magistrates, 1754–70; Governor's Office, Council Papers, 1761–79; Anson County Minutes, County Court of Pleas and Quarter Sessions, 1771–77; Secretary of State Papers, Election Returns and Miscellaneous, 1764–1908; Legislative Papers, 1689–1756; Legislative Papers, 1757–61; Legislative Papers, November 1764–66; Legislative Papers, 1767–November 1768; Governor's Office, Committee of Claims Reports, 1760–64; Legislative Papers, December 1768–17 December 1770; Governors Papers, Arthur Dobbs, 1754–65; Governors Papers, William Tryon, 1765–71, 1783–85; Governors Papers, Josiah Martin, 1771–75; Hillsborough District Minute Docket, 1768–88; Anson County Minute Docket, County Court, July 1771–July 1777; Beaufort County Minutes, Appearance, Prosecution, and Trial Docket, Court of Pleas and Quarter Sessions, 1756–61; Bertie County Court Minutes, 1758–72; Carteret County Court Minutes, 1745–64, 1747–77; Chowan County Court Minutes, 1740–72; Chowan County Justices of the Peace Papers, 1753–1873; Craven County Court Minutes, 1747–75; Edgecombe County Court Minutes, 1757–84; New

continued

Hanover County Court Minutes, 1738–69, 1771–98; Orange County Court Minutes, 1752–66; Pasquotank County Court Minutes, 1737–85; Rowan County, Court of Pleas and Quarter Sessions Minutes, 1753–72; Rowan County Miscellaneous; Lincoln and Tryon County Court Minutes, pt. 2, 1769–82; New Bern District, Minutes of the Superior Court, 1768–72; Edenton Superior Court Minutes, November 1760–November 1767; Wilmington District Minutes, Superior Court, October 1760–November 1783; Salisbury District Minute Docket Superior Court, 1756–70; Hillsborough District Minute Docket, 1768–88; list of members of the Assembly compiled by NCSA. Members of the council and other officers are listed in Saunders, *Colonial Records*, 4:884–917, 935–36, 945–84, 1000–10, 1032–68, 1237–74, 1314–29; 5:17–18, 29–53, 172–91, 213–31, 262–81, 439–41, 488–520, 602, 649, 653–88, 761, 787–88, 793–805, 810–43, 868–89, 965–75, 990–1039, 1085; 6:58, 75–95, 115–32, 172–84, 216–17, 243, 318–19, 330–62, 420–27, 439–69, 511–13, 558–59, 600, 628–61, 728, 744, 755–99, 804–6, 817, 819, 823, 832–92, 968, 1005–20, 1042–44, 1064–1150, 1218–57; 7:4–31, 34–39, 41–61, 118–20, 133–37, 160, 168, 187–88, 206, 225–27, 247, 258–59, 271–79, 291, 427–28, 436–37, 446–47, 449–54, 501–6, 523–29, 532–35, 545, 549–65, 595–624, 672–76, 690, 702, 720–22, 729–31, 750–52, 783–85, 792–94, 800–806, 850–51, 870–72, 875–76, 883, 890–924; 8:25–27, 36–38, 86–105, 148–50, 160–64, 191–93, 199–201, 249–55, 258–59, 262, 268–70, 272–75, 282–302, 347–84, 480–81, 490, 497–502, 536–40, 543, 549, 623–26; 9:3–4, 15–16, 24–25, 27–29, 52–53, 55–57, 66, 71–72, 75, 78, 101–36. For miscellaneous officers, see ibid., 4:1118–19, 1181–82; 5:162–63, 320, 365, 566–67, 975–86, 1046, 1084; 6:59–60, 204, 209–15, 237, 593, 897, 993; 7:262–63, 698, 707, 763–64, 821, 827, 832–33, 863–64, 888; 8:574–600, 659–77; 9:296–98, 311, 344, 572–77; Walter Clark, ed., *The State Records of North Carolina*, 16 vols., numbered 11–26 (Winston and Goldsboro: State of North Carolina, 1895–1906), 22:160–67, 305–99, 408–500, 815, 824–25, 828, 831–32, 834–35, 838; Adelaide L. Fries, ed., *Records of the Moravians in North Carolina*, 8 vols. (Raleigh: Edwards and Broughton Print Co, 1922–54), 1:288, 415–17, 469, 733.

[1] Brunswick County was formed from a portion of New Hanover County in 1764. We combined the New Hanover tax list of 1767 with the Brunswick tax list of 1769 to obtain a profile corresponding to earlier New Hanover tax lists. Some distortion occurs because Brunswick County also was formed from a small part of Bladen County.

[2] Brunswick's and New Hanover's upper-class slaveholders include all heads of households who owned 10 or more slave taxables (approximately 14 or more slaves).

[3] Bertie's upper-class slaveholders include all who owned 7 or more slave taxables. Compensations occurred in all three periods beginning in 1755.

[4] Chowan's upper-class slaveholders include all who owned 7 or more slave taxables.

[5] Perquiman's upper-class slaveholders include all who owned 7 or more slave taxables. We extrapolated to obtain total white households by using the ratio between white taxables and white households that existed in 1771.

[6] Albemarle region's demographic profile is distorted by an improper chronological distribution.

[7] Onslow's upper-class slaveholders include all who owned 6 or more slave taxables.

[8] Craven's upper-class slaveholders include all who owned 10 or more slave taxables. Craven had compensations each period from 1755.

[9] Beaufort's upper-class slaveholders include all who owned 8 or more slave taxables. The dramatic decrease in Beaufort's population is due to its losing portions of its territory in 1757, when part of the county was annexed to Craven, and in 1760, when Pitt County was formed from Beaufort. The total number of white households in 1764 was extrapolated from white taxables of that year by using the 1755 ratio between the two figures.

[10] The mean for the Neuse–Pamlico Coastal region was obtained by using the Beaufort County average together with figures for Onslow and Craven.

[11] Bladen's upper-class slaveholders include all who owned 8 or more taxables.

[12] Cumberland's upper-class slaveholders include all who owned 4 or more slave taxables in 1755 and 5 in 1767.

[13] Dobbs's upper-class slaveholders include all who owned 6 or more slave taxables.

14 The Bute tax list only includes total taxables in each household; it does not break down the taxables into whites, blacks, etc. We therefore used a rough measure to determine the number of slave taxables in each household: the subtraction of 1½ taxables from each feasible household. Assuming that this still overestimated the number of slaves, we conservatively listed the upper class as having 8½ or more slave taxables. It is impossible to calculate the number of households that owned slaves in Bute.

15 Granville's upper-class slaveholders for 1755 and 1769 include, respectively, all who owned 5 or more and 8 or more slave taxables.

16 Although population computations necessarily deal only with Bute and Granville totals, figures dealing with compensations are computed from all the region's counties. We calculated Northern Plain–Piedmont A's averages by averaging Granville County's figures for 1755 together with those from the region's other counties.

17 In this column the figures gleaned from Granville County's 1769 list are included to obtain another group of averages that more properly reflect the intensive growth of slavery in the region after 1755. In B, therefore, we have computed averages from Granville's average and Bute's figures.

18 The Anson tax list is incomplete. Anson's upper-class slaveholders include all who owned 4 or more slave taxables.

Table 4.1. Slaves Convicted by Slave Courts or Killed by the Authorities

Crime	Raw Figures	Extrapolation	Percentages Raw	Percentages Extrapolation
Murder or attempted murder	23	—	31.9	25.6
Rape	3	—	4.2	3.3
House burning	2	—	2.8	2.2
Outlaws–killed or suicides	13	—	18.1	14.4
Killed while committing a crime	2	—	2.8	2.2
Executed for second felony	1	—	1.4	1.1
Theft	18	+9	25.0	30.0
Hog stealing	4	+4	5.6	8.9
Preparation and use of poison	5	+4	6.9	10.0
Receiving and drinking liquor	1	+1	1.4	2.2
	72	90	100.1	99.9

Note: Because the data for those sentenced to corporal punishments are most severely lacking, a multiplier of 2 was used to attempt to compensate for this missing data. Because the need was minimal and the difficulties and margin of error great, no other extrapolations were made.

For sources used to construct this table, see note 18 of the text. Also see the explanatory note of Table 3.1.

Table 5.1. Frequency Distribution of Ages of Runaways in North Carolina, 1748–1775

Age in Years	Number
7.0[a]	2
10.0[b]	1
10.5	1
18[c]	6
20	5
21	1
22	3
23	3
24	2
24.5	1
25	5
26	2
27	1
27.5	2
28	4
30	8
31	1
32.5	1
35	5
37	1
37.5[d]	3
38	2
39	1
40	4
45	3
50	1
51+[e]	2

Median age = 28   N = 71

Note: The sources used for the tables in this chapter are described in the text above, in notes 7–8, and in particular citations. This table originally was published in Kay and Cary, "Slave Runaways in Colonial North Carolina, 1748–1775," *North Carolina Historical Review* 63 (January 1986): 1–39, table 1, p. 10.

[a] Two runaways were listed only as "child."
[b] This slave was listed simply as a "girl."
[c] Includes four runaways designated only as "young."
[d] These slaves were listed only as "younger than 40."
[e] These runaways were designated as "elderly" and "old."

Table 5.2. Distribution of North Carolina, South Carolina, and Virginia Runaways, by Cohort and Gender

Province and Period	Male Runaways	Female Runaways
North Carolina[a]		
1748–1775	114 (89.1%)	14 (10.9%)
South Carolina[b]		
1732–39	422 (81.9%)	93 (18.1%)
1740–49	492 (79.3%)	128 (20.7%)
1750–59	675 (77.7%)	194 (22.3%)
1760–69	1,208 (85.6%)	203 (14.4%)
1770–79	1,605 (83.8%)	310 (16.2%)
Total	4,402 (82.6%)	928 (17.4%)
South Carolina[c]		
1732–75	3,147 (82.4%)	671 (17.6%)
South Carolina[d]		
1732–74	1,360 (78.1%)	381 (21.9%)
Virginia[e]		
1730–74	659 (88.8%)	83 (11.2%)
Virginia[f]		
1736–1801	1,138 (89.0%)	141 (11.0%)

Note: This table originally was published in Kay and Cary, "Slave Runaways in Colonial North Carolina," table 2, p. 11.

[a]The gender of 6 of North Carolina's 134 runaways could not be determined.

[b]Extrapolated from table 12 in Philip D. Morgan, "Black Society in the Lowcountry, 1760–1810," in *Slavery and Freedom in the Age of the American Revolution*, edited by Ira Berlin and Ronald Hoffman (Charlottesville: University Press of Virginia, 1982), 100.

[c]Daniel C. Littlefield, *Rice and Slaves: Ethnicity and the Slave Trade in Colonial South Carolina* (Baton Rouge: Lousiana State University Press, 1981), 144. The gender of 52 slaves in Littlefield's sample could not be determined.

[d]Lathan A. Windley, "Profile of Runaway Slaves in Virginia and South Carolina from 1730 through 1787," Ph.D. diss., University of Iowa, 1974, 64. The gender of 1 slave could not be determined.

[e]Windley, "Profile of Runaway Slaves," 65. The gender of 14 slaves could not be determined.

[f]Gerald W. Mullin, *Flight and Rebellion: Slave Resistance in Eighteenth-Century Virgina* (New York: Oxford University Press, 1972), 89, 103.

Table 5.3. Slave Runaways in North Carolina, by Occupation and Sex, 1748–1775

Gender	Occupation	Number	Percentage
Both	Field hands	117	87.3
	Artisans	13	9.7
	Watermen	3	2.2
	Domestics	1	0.8
	Total	134	100.0
Males	Field hands	102	85.7
	Artisans	13	10.9
	Watermen	3	2.5
	Domestics	1	0.8
	Total	119	99.9
Females	Field hands	15	100.0
	Artisans	0	0
	Watermen	0	0
	Domestics	0	0
	Total	15	100.0

Note: The sex of 6 field hands could not be determined. They were prorated between male and female field-hand slaves in accordance with their respective percentages of the total number of field hands. This table originally was published in Kay and Cary, "Slave Runaways in Colonial North Carolina," table 3, p. 14.

Table 5.4. Male and Female Slaves on the Pollock Plantations, by Occupation, 1770–1809

Gender	Occupation	Number	Percentage
Both	Field hands	145	90.1
	Artisans	9	5.6
	Watermen (ferryman)	1	0.6
	Domestics	6	3.7
	Total	161	100.0
Males	Field hands	70	87.5
	Artisans	8	10.0
	Watermen (ferryman)	1	1.3
	Domestics	1	1.3
	Total	80	100.1
Females	Field hands	75	92.6
	Artisans	1	1.2
	Watermen (ferryman)	0	0
	Domestics	5	6.2
	Total	81	100.0

Note: This table is based on lists of slaves owned by the Pollocks, one of the oldest and wealthiest families in eastern North Carolina. These slaves worked on at least three plantations: Mount Rose, Connecanara, and Looking Glass. A total of 161 slaves of working age were included in this sample. The sample is admittedly biased for a provincewide analysis. It overestimates nonfield slaves and represents large plantations in later years. Yet it provides the most complete available data.

Sources: See List of Negroes at Mount Rose, 27 March 1809, List of Negroes at Connecanara and Looking Glass, 27 March 1809, and Inventory of "Sundry Negro Slaves" by Thomas Pollock, 27 March 1770, recorded at New Bern, 25 May 1770, Private Collections, PC 31.1, Thomas Pollock Papers, NCSA. This table originally was published in Kay and Cary, "Slave Runaways in Colonial North Carolina," table 4, p. 15.

Table 5.5. South Carolina's Male and Female Runaway Slaves, by Occupation, 1732–1779

Gender	Occupation	Number	Percentage
Both	Field hands	4,612	87.1
	Artisans	352	6.6
	Watermen	187	3.5
	Domestics	100	1.9
	Town	27	0.5
	Agriculture	8	0.2
	Miscellaneous	12	0.2
	Total	5,298	100.0
Males	Field hands	3,746	85.5
	Artisans	352	8.0
	Watermen	187	4.3
	Domestics	54	1.2
	Town	21	0.5
	Agriculture	8	0.2
	Miscellaneous	12	0.3
	Total	4,380	100.0
Females	Field hands	866	94.3
	Artisans	0	0
	Watermen	0	0
	Domestics	46	5.0
	Town	6	0.7
	Agriculture	0	0
	Miscellaneous	0	0
	Total	918	100.0

Note: This table is an extrapolation of tables 12 and 13b in Morgan, "Black Society in the Lowcountry," 100, 102. Morgan includes the category "hired slaves" (22 males and 10 females) within his "tradesmen" (artisan) grouping. Those slaves have been omitted here because it is equally possible that they were field hands. This table originally was published in Kay and Cary , "Slave Runaways in Colonial North Carolina," table 5, p. 16.

Table 5.6. South Carolina's Male and Female Inventoried Slaves, by Occupation, 1730–1779

Gender	Occupation	Number	Percentage
Both	Field hands	9,969	88.7
	Artisans	809	7.2
	Watermen	110	1.0
	Domestics	249	2.2
	Town	10	0.1
	Agriculture	88	0.8
	Miscellaneous	5	0.0
	Total	11,240	100.0
Males	Field hands	5,502	83.7
	Artisans	809	12.3
	Watermen	110	1.7
	Domestics	53	0.8
	Town	10	0.2
	Agriculture	88	1.3
	Miscellaneous	5	0.1
	Total	6,577	100.1
Females	Field hands	4,467	95.8
	Artisans	0	0
	Watermen	0	0
	Domestics	196	4.2
	Town	0	0
	Agriculture	0	0
	Miscellaneous	0	0
	Total	4,663	100.0

Source: Extrapolated from tables 11 and 13a in Morgan, "Black Society in the Lowcountry," 99, 101. This table originally was published in Kay and Cary, "Slave Runaways in Colonial North Carolina," table 6, p. 17.

Table 5.7. Slave Runaways in Virginia, by Cohort, Work, and Origin

	1730–87[a]		1736–1801[b]	
	Number	Percentage	Number	Percentage
Work				
Artisans	163	14.6	168	14.8
Watermen	58	5.2	85	7.5
Domestics	89	8.0	89	7.8
Industrial	0	0	17	1.5
Miscellaneous	9	0.8	0	0
Field	795	71.4	779	68.4
Total	1,114	100.0	1,138	100.0

	1730–74[a]		1775–87[a]		1736–1801[b]	
	Number	Percentage	Number	Percentage	Number	Percentage
Origin						
Mainland colonies	165	59.1	70	68.0	1,113	87.0
Africa	88	31.5	26	25.2	141	11.0
West Indies	26	9.3	7	6.8	25	2.0
Total	279	99.9	103	100.0	1279	100.0

Note: This table originally was published in Kay and Cary, "Slave Runaways in Colonial North Carolina," table 7, p. 19.

[a]Data adapted from Windley, "Profile of Runaway Slaves," 68, 70, 71, 138. Windley gives occupational breakdowns for males only. He could not determine the national origins of 279 and 103 slaves for the years 1730–74 and 1775–87, respectively. Moreover, for the two time periods Windley gives respective figures of 114 and 33 "noncountry"-born slaves, that is, slaves not born in the thirteen colonies. For purposes of this analysis the "noncountry" slaves have been distributed according to the relative proportions of Africans and West Indians among those runaways whose origins were specified. Windley's discussion of facility with English is not applicable to this analysis.

[b]Mullin, *Flight and Rebellion*, 94–96, 103–5, 108–9. Mullin's occupational breakdown for runaways is only for male slaves. He does not attempt to determine occupational distribution for the total slave population. His discussion of the slaves' facility with English is not applicable to this analysis.

Table 5.8. Slave Runaways in North Carolina, by Origin and Facility with English, 1748–1775

	.	Number	Percentage
Origin[a]			
Mainland colonies		26	42.6
Africa		33	54.1
West Indies		2	3.3
Total		61	100.0
Facility with English[b]			
Good		54	53.5
Some		33	32.7
None		14	13.9
Total		101	100.1

Note: This table originally was published in Kay and Cary, "Slave Runaways in Colonial North Carolina," table 8, p. 22.

[a]The national origins for 73 slaves in the sample of 134 could not be determined.

[b]The facility with English for 33 slaves in the sample of 134 could not be determined.

Table 5.9. Slave Runaways in South Carolina, by Cohort, Origin, and Facility with English

	1732–74[a]		1775–87[b]		1732–75[c]		1760–75[d]	
	Number	Percentage	Number	Percentage	Number	Percentage	Number	Percentage
Origin								
Mainland colonies	209	33.0	104	55.3	364	27.4	—	—
Africa	386	61.0	76	40.4	907	68.3	—	68.5[e]
West Indies	38	6.0	8	4.3	58	4.4	—	—
Total	633	100.0	188	100.0	1,329	100.1	—	68.5
Facility with English								
Good	—	—	—	—	348	44.6	—	—
Some	—	—	—	—	200	25.6	—	—
None	—	—	—	—	232	29.7	—	—
Total	—	—	—	—	780	99.9	—	—

Note: This table originally was published in Kay and Cary, "Slave Runaways in Colonial North Carolina," table 9, p. 23.

[a] Data from Windley, "Profile of Runaway Slaves," 68, 70, 71. Windley could not determine national origins for 1,109 and 1,603 slaves for the years 1732–74 and 1775–87, respectively. He does not deal with the slaves' facility with English.

[b] See note a above.

[c] Data from Littlefield, *Rice and Slaves*, 129–31, 151–58. Littlefield could not determine the national origins or facility with English for 2,536 and 3,090 slaves, respectively.

[d] Data from Morgan, "Black Society in the Lowcountry," 92. Morgan only gives the percentages of the runaways who were Africans and does not deal with the runaways' facility with English.

[e] Mean of means for years 1760, 1770, 1775. See Morgan, "Black Society in the Lowcountry," 92.

Table 5.10. Origin and Facility with Language among 134 North Carolina Runaways, Related to Occupation and Mode of Escape, 1748–1775

| Origin[a] | How Escaped | | | | Number and % Who Were Individual Runaways | | Number and % Who Were Group Runaways | |
| | Alone | | Group | | | | | |
	Nonfield	Field	(All Field)	Total	Including Unknown	Excluding Unknown	Including Unknown	Excluding Unknown
Mainland colonies	5	19	2	26	24	24	2	2
	19.2%	73.1%	7.7%	100%	26.7%	66.7%	4.5%	8.0%
Africa	0	11	22	33	11	11	22	22
		33.3%	66.7%	100%	12.2%	30.6%	50.0%	88.0%
Elsewhere	0	1	1	2	1	1	1	1
		50.0%	50.0%	100%	1.1%	2.8%	2.3%	4.0%
Unknown	12	42	19	73	54	—	19	—
	16.4%	57.5%	26.0%	99.9%	60.0%		43.2%	
Total	17	73	44	134	90	36	44	25
	12.7%	54.5%	32.8%	100%	100%	100.1%	100%	100%
Facility with English[b]								
Good	16	33	5	54	49	49	5	5
	29.7%	61.1%	9.2%	100%	54.4%	75.4%	11.4%	13.9%
Some	0	15	18	33	15	15	18	18
		45.5%	54.5%	100%	16.7%	23.1%	40.9%	50.0%
None	0	1	13	14	1	1	13	13
		7.1%	92.9%	100%	1.1%	1.5%	29.5%	36.1%

Unknown	1 30.0%	24 72.7%	8 24.2%	33 99.9%	25 27.7%	—	8 18.2%	—
	17	73	44	134	90	65	44	36
Total	12.7%	54.5%	32.8%	100%	99.9%	100%	100%	100%

Note: This table originally was published in Kay and Cary, "Slave Runaways in Colonial North Carolina," table 10, p. 24.

[a] This portion of the table correlates the number and percentage of slaves who escaped individually or in groups with their national origins and facility with English. The total for each category equals the full number of slaves—nonfield slaves and field hands—who escaped individually and in groups. For example, among the 26 slaves identified as being born in the mainland colonies, 5 (19.2 percent) nonfield slaves fled alone, 19 (73.1 percent) field hands escaped individually, and 2 (7.7 percent) field hands ran off together. The totals for all categories equal the percentage of field hands or nonfield slaves, regardless of their origins or facility with English, who fled as individuals or in groups. Thus, among the 134 runaways, all 17 of the nonfield slaves who ran off (12.7 percent) fled alone; 73 of the field hands fled alone (54.5 percent), but 44 field hands fled in groups (32.8 percent).

[b] This portion of the table correlates for each category the number and percentage of slaves who ran off as individuals or in groups with their national origins or facility with English. It does so both by including and excluding in the calculations those slaves who cannot be identified with respect to their national origins or facility with English. Totals here equal the number who escaped either individually or in groups for all categories. For example, among the 90 slaves who ran off individually, 49 (54.4 percent) could speak good English, 15 (16.7 percent) spoke some English, 1 (1.1) percent spoke no English, and the linguistic capabilities for 25 (27.7 percent) could not be determined. Or, calculating only for those whose linguistic ability could be discerned, 75.4 percent of the individual runaways could speak good English, 23.1 percent spoke some English, and 1.5 percent spoke no English.

Table 5.11. Dates of Flight and Capture of North Carolina Runaways

Date of Flight[a]	Number	Percentage	Date of Capture[b]	Number	Percentage
February–April	17	29.3	February–April	14	24.6
May–August	15	25.9	May–August	17	29.8
September–November	23	39.6	September–November	20	35.1
December–January	3	5.2	December–January	6	10.5
Total	58	100.0	Total	57	100.0

Note: This table originally was published in Kay and Cary, "Slave Runaways in Colonial North Carolina," table 11, p. 33.

[a]Dates of flight as given by masters.

[b]Dates of capture were determined from advertisements for captured slaves and from county court and Committee of Claims proceedings involving killed runaways. Where runaways appeared in more than one source the earliest date was used.

Table 5.12. North Carolina Runaways Compared with Those in South Carolina and Virginia, by Months of Flight

	Virginia, 1730–1787[a]		North Carolina, 1748–1775		South Carolina, 1734–1778[a]	
	Number	Percentage	Number	Percentage	Number	Percentage
February–April	218	24.2	17	29.3	217	20.3
May–August	399	44.2	15	25.9	468	43.7
September–November	178	19.8	23	39.6	215	20.1
December–January	106	11.8	3	5.2	170	15.9
Total	901	100.0	58	100.0	1,070	100.0

Note: This table originally was published in Kay and Cary, "Slave Runaways in Colonial North Carolina," table 12, p. 34.

[a]Windley, "Profile of Runaway Slaves," p. 175.

Table 6.1. Rank Order of the Most Popular Slave and Nonslave Given Names in North Carolina, 1748–1775

Rank Order	Male		Female	
	Slaves	Nonslaves	Slaves	Nonslaves
1	Jack (38)	John (164)	Phillis (32)	Mary (61)
2	Peter (28)	William (120)	Hannah (17)	Elizabeth (53)
3	Dick (20)	Thomas (68)	Jenny (16)	Sarah (43)
4	Tom (18)	James (67)	Nan/Nann (15) Rose (15) Sarah (15)	Ann/Anne (32)
5	Sam (16)	Samuel (32)	Dinah (14) Bess (14) Lucy (14)	Martha (17)
6	Caesar (15) Charles (15) Ben (15)	Frederick (26) Henry (26) Joseph (26)	Pegg (13)	Margaret (16)
7	Jo/Joe (14)	George (24) Robert (24)	Beck (12)	Jane (13)
8	Bob (13) Will (13)	David (21)	Chloe (11)	Hannah (12)
9	London (11)	Benjamin (16)	Jane (9)	Charity (9)
10	Ned (10)	Alexander (15)	Venus (8)	Catherine (8) Rachel (8)
11	George (9) Mingo (9)	Andrew (14) Richard (14)	Amy (7) Moll (7)	Rebecca (6)
12	Frank (8) Harry (8) James (8) Tony (8)	Peter (13)	Bet/Bett (6)	Agnes (5) Betty (5) Frances (5)
13	Cato (7) Jacob (7) Toby (7)	Edward (12)	Grace (5) Judith (5) Nancy (5) Pat (5) Penny (5) Silvia (5) Violet (5)	Jean (4) Nancy (4)
14	Abraham (6) Jemmy (6)	Charles (11) Jacob (11)	Flora (4) Nanny (4) Patience (4)	Eleanor (3) Grace (3) Isabel (3) Janet (3) Kaziah (3) Patience (3) Penelope (3) Ruth (3)
15	Jimmy (5) John (5)	Solomon (9)	Betty (3) Doll (3)	Amy (2) Fanny (2)

continued

Table 6.1 (continued)

Rank Order	Male		Female	
	Slaves	Nonslaves	Slaves	Nonslaves
	Quash (5)		Esther (3)	Jemima [ina] (2)
			Jean (3)	Jenny (2)
			Joan (3)	Lucy (2)
			Juda [h] (3)	Milly (2)
			Mal [1] (3)	Ollive (2)
			Maria [h] (3)	Peggy (2)
			Mary (3)	Winifred (2)
			Phebe (3)	
			Silla (3)	
			Sue (3)	
			Susan (3)	
Totals	324	713	311	347
Total N	570	975	467	429

Note: The names of all whites included to construct this table—either listed among the 15 most popular names (1,060) or just totaled (344)—were obtained from a survey of 548 estate records for the years 1748–75 for 10 geographically representative counties: Anson, Bertie, Carteret, Edgecombe, Halifax, Mecklenburg, New Hanover, Northampton, Orange, and Rowan. Ninety percent of the slaves' names (635 listed and 402 unlisted) were also obtained from these estate records. Actually, only 104 of the 548 surveyed wills and inventories had listings of slave names. All the estate records can be found in NCSA: North Carolina Wills, 1663–1789, S.S. 845–73, vols. 7–35; Chancery Proceedings and Wills, 1712–54, S.S. 878; Wills, 1738–52, 1750–58, 1755–58, 1758–73, S.S. 877, 879–81, vols. 4, 6–8; Inventories and Sales of Estates, 1714–98, S.S. 889–905; Bertie County Wills, C.R. 10.801.1–10.801.8, vols. 1–8; Bertie County Estates Papers, C.R. 10.504.1–10, 504.1.15, C. R. 10.504.1.19–10.504.1.114; Bertie County Inventories of Estates, C.R. 10.507.2; Carteret County Records, Miscellaneous Papers, 1717–1844, Book A, Records of Wills and Bonds, C.R. 19.905.1; Wills, Inventories, Sales, and Settlement of Estates, C.R. 19.802.1–19.802.11, vols. 1–11; Carteret County Wills, C.R. 19.801.1, 19.905.1; New Hanover County Wills, vols. 1–5, C.R. 70.801.1–70.802.5; Northampton County Wills, C.R. 71.801.1, CR. 71.802.1, C.R. 71.802.2; Cumberland County Wills, C.R. 29.801.1–29.801.4; Mecklenburg County Wills, 1749–1869, C.R. 65.009–65.027; Estate Papers, C.R. 065 508.3–C. R. 065 508.140; Orange County Estates Papers, 1758–85, C.R. 73.507.1.

The names of 105 North Carolina slaves (10 percent of the total number) who ran away during the years 1748–75 can be found in the following colonial newspapers and subsidiary sources. All extant issues of North Carolina's newspapers for the years 1748–75 were used: *North Carolina Magazine and Universal Intelligencer, Cape Fear Mercury, North Carolina Gazette* (New Bern), and *North Carolina Gazette* (Wilmington). In addition we examined the *South Carolina Gazette* and the various editions of the *Virginia Gazette.* Subsidiary sources used in the North Carolina State Archives to identify runaways included county court minutes, Committee of Claims records, private correspondence, and estate inventories. See Chapter 5 for a detailed listing of these sources.

Table 6.2. Distribution of First Names of Slaves (Number and Percentage), 1748–75, Categorizing Names That Possibly Could Be Either Non-African or African Derivation as Non-African

					Types of Names				
Gender	Common Anglo-American	African	Biblical	Puritanical	Classical	Descriptive	Uncommon	Place Names	Totals
Males	344 (60.4%)	78 (13.7%)	23 (4.0%)	0 (0%)	42 (7.4%)	29 (5.1%)	21 (3.7%)	33 (5.8%)	570 (100.0%)
Females	313 (67.0%)	54 (11.6%)	28 (6.0%)	19 (4.1%)	43 (9.2%)	5 (1.1%)	5 (1.1%)	0 (0%)	467 (100.0%)
All	657 (63.4%)	132 (12.7%)	51 (4.9%)	19 (1.8%)	85 (8.2%)	34 (3.3%)	26 (2.5%)	33 (3.2%)	1,037 (100.0%)

Sources: See note to Table 6.1.

Notes:

Tables 6.2 and 6.3 could not have been constructed but for the listings in the following works of African names, their meanings, and their incidence among specific African peoples: Newbell Niles Puckett, *Black Names in America: Origins and Usage* (Boston, 1975); Ogonna Chuks-orji, *Names from Africa: Their Meaning and Pronunciation* (Chicago, 1972), 4–74; Ihechuku Madubuike, *A Handbook of African Names* (Washington, D.C., 1976); J. L. Dillard, *Black English* (New York: Random House, 1972), 72–138; Dillard, *Black Names* (The Hague, The Netherlands, 1976); and Lorenzo D. Turner, *Africanisms in the Gullah Dialect* (Chicago, 1949). The etymology of the names of whites was aided considerably by Charlotte M. Yonge's *History of Christian Names* (Lonon, 1884). See also C. O. Sylvester Mawson, *International Book of Names* (New York, 1934). Puckett's work, edited posthumously by Murray Heller, builds on Puckett's seminal study, "Names of American Negro Slaves," in *Studies of the Science of Society*, edited by George Peter Murdock, 471–94 (1937; rept. Freeport, N.Y., 1969). Also see citations 3, 6–7 to the text.

Names such as James or John that could have been placed in either the biblical or common English categories were assigned to the latter. Only those obviously biblical, but uncommon, Anglo-American names were listed as biblical. These included such names as Emmanuel, Isaac, Dinah, Hagar, and Tamar.

The Puritan names used by female slaves were: Charity (2), Grace (5), Hope (2), Increase (1), and Patience (4) and its derivative, Pat (5).

Table 6.3. Distribution of First Names of Slaves (Number and Percentage), 1748–1775, Categorizing All Names as African That Possibly Could Be Traced to African Names

| | | | | Types of Names | | | | | |
Gender	Common Anglo-American	African	Biblical	Puritanical	Classical	Descriptive	Uncommon	Place Names	Totals
Males	18 (3.2%)	501 (87.9%)	5 (0.9%)	0 (0%)	10 (1.8%)	12 (2.1%)	14 (2.5%)	10 (1.8%)	570 (100.0%)
Females	10 (2.1%)	427 (91.4%)	1 (0.2%)	14 (3.0%)	5 (1.1%)	5 (1.1%)	5 (1.1%)	0 (0%)	467 (100.0%)
All	28 (2.7%)	928 (89.5%)	6 (0.6%)	14 (.4%)	15 (1.5%)	17 (1.6%)	19 (1.8%)	10 (1.0%)	1,037 (100.0%)

Note: Slave names are identified as African in this table if there are one or more like-sounding West African names for them or if they have been identified by Chuks-orji, Dillard, Joyner, Madubuike, Puckett, or Turner as being of African origin.

Table 6.4. Day Names in North Carolina, Male, 1748–1775 (N = 570)

Day	Ethnic Group	African Names	North Carolina Equivalents	Totals
Monday	Ewe	Adwo	Adam or Adem (4), Ajax (1)	
	Twi	Ajo		
	Ewe	Coujoe	Cudjoe (2), Jo (4)	
	Fante	Jojo	Joe (10), Joseph (2)	
	Akan, Ewe, Ga	Kodjo		
	Akan, Ewe	Kojo		23
Tuesday	Fante	Bobo	Bob or Bobb (13)	
	Ewe	Kobla	Wale (1), Wallis (1), Wally (1)	
	Ga	Kwabla	Willibre (1)	
	Ghana (Joyner)	Koumina		
	Akan	Kobina	Ben or Benn (15)	
	Akan-Twi	Kwabena		32
Wednesday	Ewe	Kwakou	Jack (38)	
	Fante	Kweku	Jacob (7)	
	Fante	Yoaku	Yacknee (1)	46
Thursday	Ewe	Yao	George (9)	
	Twi	Yau		
	Akan	Yaw		
	Fante	Yorkoo	York (1)	10
Friday	Hausa	Danjuma	Daniel (2)	
	Ewe	Koffi	Caff (1), Caif (1)	
	Twi, Akan, Ewe, Fante	Kofi	Catfee (1), Coti (1), Cuffee (1)	
	Ga			
	Fante	Kwefi		
	Akan	Yoofi		7
Saturday	Fante	Atu	Arthur (3)	
	Ewe	Commie	Tom (18), Tomby (1), Toney (8)	
	Akan, Twi	Kwame	Quamee (1), Quamina (1)	
	Akan, Ewe	Kwami	Quamino (1)	33
Sunday	Twi	Boseda	Boson, (2), Boston (2)	
	Yoruba	Bosede	Bosay (1)	
	Hausa	Banladi	Daniel (2)	
	Ewe	Kawsi	Kakchee (1)	
	Akan, Ewe, Twi	Kwasi	Quash (5)	
	Ewe	Quashie		

continued

Table 6.4 (continued)

Day	Ethnic Group	African Names	North Carolina Equivalents	Totals
	Akan, Fante	Kwesi	Caesar (15)	
	Fante	Sisi		28
			Total	179
			(or 31.4% of all	
			male names	
			in sample)	

Sources: See notes to Table 6.1 and Table 6.2 for the sources used to construct Tables 6.4–6.7. Because it is difficult to collate Igbo with European days of the week, we have listed them separately below:

Name	Sex	Day of the Week
Okorie	M	Born on Orie
Nworie	M	"
Adaorie	F	"
Mgborie	F	"
Okereke	M	Born on Eke
Nweke	M	"
Adaeke	F	"
Mgbeke	F	"
Okoroafo	M	Born on Afo
Okafo	M	"
Nwafo	M	"
Adafo	F	"
Mgbafo	F	"
Okoronkwo	M	Born on Nkwo
Okonkwo	M	"
Nwankwo	M	"
Adankwo	F	"
Mgbokwo	F	"

Taken from Madubuike, *Handbook of African Names,* 59.

Table 6.5. Day Names in North Carolina, Female, 1748–1775 (N = 467)

Day	Ethnic Group	African Names	North Carolina Equivalents	Totals
Monday	Akan Ewe	Adjua Ajowa	Juda (2), Judah (1), Jude (1), Judith (5), Judy (11), Jundon (1), Jubah (1)	22
Tuesday	Akan Ghana (Joyner) Akan	Abena Aminaba Benoda	Bernetta (1), Venice (1), Venus or Venis (7)	9
Wednesday	—	—	—	0
Thursday	Fante Fante Akan, Ewe	Aba Baba Yaa	Abigail (1)	1
Friday	Ewe, Twi Ewe Fante Ewe Ewe, Twi	Afi Afiba Efia Fiba Fida	Earthina (1), Finah (1), Phebe or Febe (13)	15
Saturday	Ewe Ewe Akan Fante	Alma Ami Amma Mama	Amy (7)	7
Sunday	Ewe Goun (Dahomey) Akan Fante Fante Ibo	Kwasibo Sede Asi Esi Sisi Mgbeke	Clarinda (1), Keziah (1), Qua- sheba (1), Sabeah (1), Sabia (1), Sabina (1), Saliena (1), Sally (1), Savina (1) Easter (2), Esther (3) Beck (12), Rebeccah (1)	27
			Total	81
			(or 17.3% of all female names in sample)	

Table 6.6. Positional Names in North Carolina, Female, 1748–75 (N = 467)

Position	Ethnic Group	African Names	North Carolina Equivalents	Totals
Firstborn or first daughter	Akan Hausa	Baako Danuwa	Beck (12) Rebecca (1) Dava (1)	14
Second	Igbo Akan	Ulu Manu	Lulu (1) Maniah (1)	2
Fourth	Akan Ewe Mandingo	Anan Anani Do	Nan or Nann (15) Nancy or Nance (5), Nanny (4) Doll or Dol (3), Dole (1)	24
Sixth	Akan Fante	Nsia Esia	Easter (2) Esther (3)	5
Seventh	Mandingo	Fa	Fann (2), Fanny (2)	4
Ninth	Akan	Nkruma	Kirrena (1)	1
Tenth	Akan	Badu, Baduwa, Baidoo	Bode (1), Bina (1)	2
			Total	56
			(or 12.0% of all female names in sample)	

Table 6.7. Positional Names in North Carolina, Male, 1748–1775 (N = 570)

Position	Ethnic Group	African Names	North Carolina Equivalents	Totals
Firstborn or first son	Akan	Baako	Bacit (1)	
	Ewe	Adika	Dick (20), Dicke (1)	
	Hausa	Danuwa	Daniel (4)	26
Second	Ibibio	Udok	Doc (1)	
	Mandingo	Bakari	Cary/Carry (2)	
	Hausa	Sambo	Sam (16), Sambo (3),	
			Sampson (3), Samson (3)	28
Fourth	Akan	Anan	Adam (4)	4
Sixth	Akan	Nsia	Shie (1)	1
			Total	59
			(or 10.4% of all male names in sample)	

Table 7.1. Possible Slave Marital and Familial Development in Six Regions in North Carolina, 1750–1775, as Measured by Sex and Age Distributions of Slaves Owned by Separate Masters: Calculated for Size of Plantation within Regions

Region	Total N Slaves in Household	N Slaveholds in Region's Estate Records of This Size	N Slaves in Region's Estate Records of This Size	N Slaves in Dual-Headed Families; N Families	Percentage of Slaves in Dual-Headed Families	N Slaves in Single-Headed Families; N Families	Percentage of Slaves in Single-Headed Families	Unattached Slaves on Plantations	Percentage of Unattached Slaves on Plantations	Percentage of Slaves in Single- & Dual-Headed Families
Albemarle Sound	1	25	25	0 / 0	0	0 / 0	0	25	100.00	0
	2–3	23	56	27 / 12	48.21	18 / 8	32.14	11	19.64	80.36
	4–5	10	45	26 / 8	57.78	8 / 4	17.78	11	24.45	75.55
	6–10	9	72	45 / 10	62.50	18 / 3	25.00	9	12.50	87.50
	11–15	7	90	79 / 14	87.78	0 / 0	0	11	12.22	87.78

16–20	4	69	65 / 12	94.20	0 / 0	0	4	5.80	94.20
104	1	104	98 / 29	94.23	0 / 0	0	6	5.77	94.23
Neuse-Pamlico									
1	9	9	0 / 0	0	0 / 0	0	4	100.00	0
2–3	3	7	3 / 1	42.86	0 / 0	0	4	57.14	42.86
4–5	2	9	3 / 1	33.33	5 / 1	55.56	1	11.11	88.89
6–10	7	46	32 / 6	69.57	10 / 3	21.74	4	8.70	91.30
11–15 (15)	1	15	13 / 2	86.67	0 / 0	0	2	13.33	86.67
32	1	32	31 / 7	96.88	0 / 0	0	1	3.13	96.88

continued

Table 7.1 (continued)

Region	Total N Slaves in Household	N Slaveholds in Region's Estate Records of This Size	N Slaves in Region's Estate Records of This Size	N Slaves in Dual-Headed Families; N Families	Percentage of Slaves in Dual-Headed Families	N Slaves in Single-Headed Families; N Families	Percentage of Slaves in Single-Headed Families	Unattached Slaves on Plantations	Percentage of Unattached Slaves on Plantations	Percentage of Slaves in Single- & Dual-Headed Families
Central Inner Coastal Plain—Piedmont	1	6	6	0; 0	0	0; 0	0	6	100.00	0
	2–3	1	3	0; 0	0	3; 1	100.00	0	0	100.00
	4–5	0	0	0; 0	—	0; 0	—	0	—	—
	6–10 (6, 7)	2	13	12; 3	92.31	0; 0	0	1	7.69	92.31
Western Region	1	27	27	0; 0	0	0; 0	0	27	100.00	0
	2–3	24	52	15; 7	28.85	20; 9	38.46	17	32.69	67.31

4–5	3	13	3 / 1	23.08	9 / 3	69.23	1	7.69	92.31
6–10	4	29	14 / 5	48.28	7 / 2	24.14	8	27.54	72.41
11–15 (11)	1	11	10 / 1	90.91	0 / 0	0	1	9.09	90.91
Lower Cape Fear									
1	7	7	0 / 0	0	0 / 0	0	7	100.00	0
2–3	10	26	14 / 6	56.00	3 / 1	12.00	8	32.00	68.00
4–5	5	21	4 / 1	19.05	17 / 5	80.95	0	0	100.00
6–10	3	19	18 / 5	94.74	0 / 0	0	1	5.26	94.74
11–15 (12, 14)	2	25	10 / 2	38.46	14 / 4	53.85	2	7.69	92.31
29, 66	2	95	78 / 18	82.11	0 / 0	0	17	17.89	82.11

continued

Table 7.1 (continued)

Region	Total N Slaves in Household	N Slaveholds in Region's Estate Records of This Size	N Slaves in Region's Estate Records of This Size	N Slaves in Dual-Headed Families; N Families	Percentage of Slaves in Dual-Headed Families	N Slaves in Single-Headed Families; N Families	Percentage of Slaves in Single-Headed Families	Unattached Slaves on Plantations	Percentage of Unattached Slaves on Plantations	Percentage of Slaves in Single- & Dual-Headed Families
Northern Inner Coastal Plain–Piedmont	1	6	6	0 / 0	0	0 / 0	0	6	100.00	0
	2–3	4	9	2 / 1	22.22	4 / 2	44.44	3	33.33	66.67
	4–5	2	9	4 / 1	44.44	0 / 0	0	5	55.56	44.44
	6–10	5	41	39 / 7	95.12	0 / 0	0	2	4.88	95.12
	11–15 (11, 12)	2	23	10 / 2	43.48	12 / 5	52.17	1	4.35	95.65

Sources: Wills and inventories were used to arrive at all statistics in Tables 7.1 and 7.2. All these wills and inventories are found in the North Carolina State Archives (NCSA): Secretary of State's Records: North Carolina Wills, 1663–1789, S.S. 845–73, vols. 7–35; Chancery Proceedings and Wills, 1712–54, S.S. 878;

Wills, 1738–52, 1750–58, 1755–58, 1758–73, S.S. 877, 879–81, vols. 4, 6–8; Inventories and Sales of Estates, 1714–98, S.S. 889–905; Bertie County Wills, C.R. 10.801.1–10.801.8, vols. 1–8; Bertie County Estates Papers, C.R. 10.504.1–10, 10.504.1.15, 10.504.1.19–10.504.1.114; Bertie County Inventories of Estates, C.R. 10.507.2; Carteret County Records, Miscellaneous Papers, 1717–1844, Book A, Records of Wills and Bonds, C.R. 19.905.1; Wills, Inventories, Sales, and Settlement of Estates, C.R. 19.802.1–19.802.11, vols. 1–11; Carteret County Wills, C.R. 19.801.1, 19.905.1; New Hanover County Wills, vols. 1–5, C.R. 70.801.1–70.802.5; Northampton County Wills, C.R. 71.801.1, 71.802.1, 71.802.2; Cumberland County Wills, C.R. 29.801.1–29.801.4; Mecklenburg County Wills, 1749–1869, C.R. 65.009–65.027; Estate Papers, C.R. 065 508.3–065 508.140; Orange County Estate Papers, 1758–85, C.R. 73.507.1.

In each region the N is comprised of estates that stress disproportionately slaves living on smaller plantations. The resulting distortions for the Lower Cape Fear region are serious enough to explain why the region's possibility projections in Table 7.1 are at variance with those in other regions.

Note: The algorithm used to quantify slave family relationships for Tables 7.1–7.2 was developed as follows: Two hundred and eighteen wills and inventories out of the 936 extant for twelve sample counties located in six of the seven regions of colonial North Carolina were used to extrapolate statistics for slave marriages and families during the years 1750–75 (see Tables 7.1 and 7.2). Despite the imprecise recording of age and gender in the estate records, we were able to categorize 1,014 slaves as adult males, adult females, or minors. We then devised an algorithm that enabled us to place each of these slaves within one of the three marital and familial situations: dual-headed families, single-headed families, or unattached slaves, i.e., those without family members present on the plantation. Because no algorithm could be designed without distorting actual slave relationships, we chose to use one that systematically inflated the number of slaves living in dual-headed families at the expense of those living in single-headed families. This bias would later be significantly corrected by interpolating similar findings from another statistical universe.

We identified all adult male and adult female slaves on an estate who could be paired as married couples. All nonadults on a particular estate where at least one adult male and female couple lived were also categorized as belonging to a dual-headed family. Thus, if there were three adult male slaves, three adult female slaves, and seven nonadult slaves on an estate, all would be calculated as comprising three dual-headed families. Membership in single-headed families was underestimated by the algorithm in that calculations for this group began *only* after all possible cases were categorized within dual-headed families. Slaves were identified as members of single-headed families only when no adult male or female on a plantation could be paired and when one or more nonadult slaves was also present. For instance, if four adult males, two adult females, and thirteen nonadult slaves lived on a plantation, two of each of the adult males and females plus all of the nonadults would be calculated as members of dual-headed families. The remaining two adult males would be categorized as "unattached." But if three adult female slaves plus six nonadult slaves were the slaves on an estate, they would be calculated as constituting three single-headed families with a total of nine slaves. Any estate with two adult female slaves and one nonadult slave would be counted as having one single-headed family with two slaves and one unattached adult. This method made it almost impossible to identify slaves in single-headed families on estates with sixteen or more slaves. Indeed, no single-headed families are found on estates of this size in the possibility estimates presented in Tables 7.1 and 7.2. The odds are simply too great against there not being at least one marriageable pair on plantations of this size.

continued

All slaves who could not be identified as being members of dual- or single-headed families were placed in the category "unattached slaves." Thus all slaves on estates with only one slave were placed in this category, as were all nonadult slaves present on estates without adult slaves. Finally, as noted above, adult slaves who could not be paired and who could not be assigned to families with nonadults were also categorized as unattached. For instance, an estate having two adult males, one adult female, and ten nonadult slaves was calculated as having one dual-headed family with twelve members and one adult male slave without a family. Or again, an estate with five adult male slaves and three nonadult slaves was enumerated as having three single-headed households with six slaves plus two adult male slaves without families. These procedures, interestingly, seem to have resulted in reasonably close estimates of the actual percentages of unattached slaves.

In sum, the algorithm used to determine the possible incidence of marriage and families among North Carolina's slaves, when compared with actual marital and familial formation on comparable estates, overstates the number of slaves in dual-headed families and understates those in single-headed families. On the other hand, those identified as unattached slaves probably closely correspond with their actual numbers. It follows that the sum of slaves estimated in the first two categories is close to the actual number of these slaves on the surveyed estates.

To deal with the above distortions in the estimates of slaves comprising single- and dual-headed families, respectively, it is necessary to incorporate the findings from a second data set, plantation papers. These documents list the names of married slaves and their children. Unfortunately, the sample is skewed in that papers exist for only three colonial plantations, all of them large and located in the eastern part of the province. Although statistics gleaned from this inadequate sample cannot directly be projected beyond large eastern plantations, a first step in broadening their application by interpolating them with statistics obtained from the estate records is to tabulate the specific information concerning marriages and families for the 219 slaves listed in the three extant sets of plantation papers. As these statistics will be interrelated with the possibility estimates computed from the estate records, the same categories are used to analyze the slaves in the plantation records as were used for slaves in the estate records: "dual-headed families," "single-headed families," and "unattached slaves."

Table 7.3 accordingly lists the plantations and the number of surveyed slaves on each of them. Two sets of figures are given for the *actual* number of single- and dual-headed households for each plantation because the data lent itself to two different interpretations. "Actuality A" includes, among the slaves listed in dual-headed families, all unmarried children including those who had children themselves. These grandchildren, in turn, are also included as part of the dual-headed family of origin. This system of categorization coincides with the probable extended-family inclinations of slaves. Parents normally tended to identify a child as a member of the original family until that child married and established a new nuclear family. Nevertheless, it seemed desirable to categorize unmarried slaves and their children in a second way to avoid any bias toward dual-headed families. In "Actuality B" the just-described slaves were accordingly placed in single-headed families. Finally, in order to confirm that the plantations surveyed in Table 7.3 had slaves similar to those on the estates of comparable size analyzed in the possibility tables, the algorithm used to construct the latter was also used to develop similar possibility statistics from the plantation records.

Immediately apparent when Table 7.3 is analyzed is the wide variation between the actual and the possible estimates of slaves in dual-headed families. Among Mrs. Allen's slaves, for example, either 38.6 percent ("Actuality B") or 56.14 percent ("Actuality A") of the slaves belonged to dual-headed families, while the "possibility" percentage for the plantation is 92.98 percent. Also, whereas the percentage of slaves actually in dual-headed families on the three plantations fluctuated as much as 13 percent and 25.5 perent, depending on which "actuality" was used, the possibility percentages only varied by a little more than 1 percent.

In addition, a comparison of *possibility* percentages concerning dual-headed families derived from the plantation records and those obtained from the wills and inventories are quite similar. Further analysis reveals that the most important reason for the wide variation between the actual percentage of slaves in dual-headed families in Table 7.3 and the possibility figures for dual-headed families are dual-headed families in Tables 7.1–7.3 is that the possibility figures for these families in Tables 7.1–7.3 and the possibility figures for these families are inflated primarily at the expense of the calculations for single-headed families. Thus, if estimates of possible dual- and single-headed families are combined, the resulting percentage closely approximates actuality.

These findings enabled us to devise a formula employing a proper weighting procedure that satisfactorily interpolates the statistics from both sets. To do this, we calculated ratios from the actuality and possibility statistics in Table 7.3 to convert the possibility estimates in Tables 7.1 and 7.2 (based on expansive samples) into probability estimates by correcting for the inflated and deflated figures for dual- and single-headed families, respectively.

Two ratios, accordingly, have been constructed by relating the mean percentages of dual-headed families of both Actuality A and Actuality B for all the plantations on Table 7.3 to the possibility percentages. Thus, the mean percentage of Actuality A is 61.03, while the mean possibility percentage is 92.83. The resulting ratio is .6567 to 1. Similarly, the ratio of Actuality B to possibility is .5433 to 1. The development of a ratio from data concerning dual-headed families flowed directly from the use of an algorithm that resulted in an exaggeration of the importance of these families. This made it impossible to use figures concerning single-headed families to construct the ratios, for their consequent deemphasis in the possibility calculations led to estimates of zero possibility of single-headed families for each of the three plantations in Table 7.3. Because the variations in Table 7.3 between actual and possible percentages of slaves who lived on plantations without their families was both quite low and somewhat inconsistent, we decided to treat the possibility figures for this group as consistent with reality. The results of applying the ratios may be seen in the text's analysis of Tables 7.4–7.6. Also see note 31.

Table 7.2. Possible Slave Marital and Familial Development in North Carolina, 1750–1775, as Measured by Sex and Age Distributions of Slaves Owned by Separate Masters: Calculated for Size of Estate

Total N Slaves in Household	N Slaveholds in Estates of This Size	N Slaves in Estates of This Size	N Slaves in Dual-Headed Families; N Families	Percentage of Slaves in Dual-Headed Families	N Slaves in Single-Headed Families; N Families	Percentage of Slaves in Single-Headed Families	Unattached Slaves on Plantations	Percentage of Unattached Slaves on Plantations	Percentage of Slaves in Single- & Dual-Headed Families
1	80	80	0 / 0	0	0 / 0	0	80	100.00	0
2–3	65	152	61 / 27	40.13	48 / 21	31.58	43	28.29	71.71
4–5	22	97	40 / 12	41.24	39 / 13	40.21	18	18.56	81.44
6–10	30	220	160 / 36	72.73	35 / 8	15.91	25	11.36	88.64
11–15	13	165	122 / 21	73.94	26 / 9	15.76	17	10.30	89.70

16–20	4	69	65	94.20	0	0	4	5.80	94.20
			12		0				
29, 66, 32, 104	4	201	207	89.6	0	0	24	10.39	84.60
			54		0				
Totals	218	1014	655	64.6	148	14.60	211	20.81	79.19
			162		51				

Table 7.3. Actual and Possible Slave Marital and Familial Development on Three Plantations Located in Three Eastern Regions: Two Estimates of Actual Number of Slaves in Dual- and Single-Headed Families for Each Plantation (Possibilities Measured as in Tables 7.1–7.2)

Plantation surveyed: Name of owner, county, year, region, actuality, possibility	N Slaves	N of Slaves in Dual-Headed Families; N Families	Percentage of Slaves in Dual-Headed Families	N of Slaves in Single-Headed Families; N Families	Percentage of Slaves in Single-Headed Families	N of Unattached Slaves on Plantations	Percentage of Unattached Slaves on Plantations	Percentage of Slaves in Dual- & Single-Headed Families
Mrs. Sarah Allen, New Hanover County, 1761, Lower Cape Fear region[1]								
Actuality A	57	32 5	56.14	19 4	33.33	6	10.53	89.47
Actuality B	57	22 5	38.60	29 6	50.88	6	10.53	89.45
Possibility	57	53 16	92.98	0 0	0	4	7.02	92.98

Cullen Pollock,
Tyrrell County, 1749,
Albemarle Sound region[2]

Actuality A	39	27 7	69.23	11 2	28.21	1	2.56	97.44
Actuality B	39	25 7	64.23	13 3	33.33	1	2.56	97.44
Possibility	39	36 14	92.31	0 0	0	3	7.69	92.31

Thomas Pollock–Jacob
Mitchell, Craven County,
1770, Neuse-Pamlico region[3]

Actuality A	123	71 10	57.72	45 10	36.59	7	5.69	94.31
Actuality B	123	60 10	48.78	56 13	45.53	7	5.69	94.31
Possibility	123	115 17	93.50	0 0	0	8	6.50	93.50

[1]"Negroes S[arah] Allen Their Ages in Feby—1761," New Hanover County, NCSA; James M. Robin's Papers, vol. 1, Massachusetts Historical Society.
[2]Cullen Pollock's Will, Tyrell County, 13 August 1749, proven before the June County Court, 1751, Pollock Papers, P.C. 31.1, NCSA.
[3]"Lean Made by Thomas Pollock Esqr. to Jacob Mitchell Bearing Date Twenty Seventh Day of March 1770," Pollock Papers, P.C. 31.1, NCSA.

Table 7.4. Estimates of Slave Marital and Familial Development in North Carolina, 1750–1775

Total Slaves in Household	N Slaveholds	N Slaves	Percentage of Slaves in Dual-Headed Families: Probability A & B	Percentage of Slaves in Single-Headed Families: Probability A & B	Percentage of Unattached Slaves on Plantations: Probability A & B	Percentage of Slaves in Single- & Dual-Headed Families: Probability A & B
1	80	80	A = 0 B = 0	A = 0 B = 0	A = 100.00 B = 100.00	A = 0 B = 0
2–3	65	152	A = 26.35 B = 21.80	A = 45.36 B = 49.91	A = 28.29 B = 28.29	A = 71.71 B = 71.71
4–5	22	97	A = 27.08 B = 22.41	A = 54.36 B = 59.03	A = 18.56 B = 18.56	A = 81.44 B = 81.44
6–10	30	220	A = 47.76 B = 39.51	A = 40.88 B = 49.13	A = 11.36 B = 11.36	A = 88.64 B = 88.64
11–15	13	165	A = 48.56 B = 40.17	A = 41.14 B = 49.53	A = 10.30 B = 10.30	A = 89.70 B = 89.70
16–20	4	69	A = 61.86 B = 51.18	A = 32.34 B = 43.02	A = 5.80 B = 5.80	A = 94.20 B = 94.20
29, 66, 32, 104	4	231	A = 58.84 B = 48.68	A = 30.76 B = 40.92	A = 10.39 B = 10.39	A = 89.60 B = 89.60
Totals	218	1,014	A = 42.42 B = 35.10	A = 36.77 B = 44.09	A = 20.81 B = 20.81	A = 79.19 B = 79.19

Sources: For a list of the wills, inventories, and plantation papers use to construct this table, see Sources to Table 7.1 and notes to Table 7.3.

See Table 7.1 note for an explanation of the algorithms used to extrapolate from two somewhat disparate sets of data to construct this table.

Table 7.5. Estimates of Slave Marital and Familial Development in North Carolina, 1750–1775, Albemarle Sound and Neuse-Pamlico Regions

Total Slaves in Household	N Slaveholds	N Slaves	Percentage of Slaves in Dual-Headed Families: Probability A & B	Percentage of Slaves in Single-Headed Families: Probability A & B	Percentage of Unattached Slaves on Plantations: Probability A & B	Percentage of Slaves in Single- & Dual-Headed Families: Probability A & B
1	34	34	A = 0 B = 0	A = 0 B = 0	A = 100.00 B = 100.00	A = 0 B = 0
2–3	26	63	A = 31.27 B = 25.87	A = 44.92 B = 50.32	A = 23.81 B = 23.81	A = 76.19 B = 76.19
4–5	12	54	A = 35.26 B = 29.18	A = 42.52 B = 48.60	A = 22.22 B = 22.22	A = 77.78 B = 77.78
6–10	16	118	A = 42.85 B = 35.45	A = 46.13 B = 53.53	A = 11.02 B = 11.02	A = 88.98 B = 88.98
11–15	8	105	A = 57.54 B = 47.60	A = 30.08 B = 40.02	A = 12.38 B = 12.38	A = 87.62 B = 87.62
16–20	4	69	A = 61.86 B = 51.18	A = 32.34 B = 43.02	A = 5.80 B = 5.80	A = 94.20 B = 94.20
32, 104	2	136	A = 62.29 B = 51.53	A = 32.56 B = 43.32	A = 5.15 B = 5.15	A = 94.85 B = 94.85
Totals	102	772	A = 47.86 B = 39.60	A = 35.21 B = 43.47	A = 16.93 B = 16.93	A = 83.07 B = 83.07

Sources: Secretary of State Records, North Carolina Wills, 1663–1789, S.S. 845–73, vols. 7–35; Chancery Proceedings and Wills, 1712–54, S.S. 878; Wills, 1738–52, 1750–58, 1755–58, 1758–73, S.S. 877, 879–81, vols. 4, 6–8; Inventories and Sales of Estates, 1714–98, S.S. 889–905; Bertie County Wills, C.R. 10.801.1–10.801.8, vols. 1–8; Bertie County Estates Papers, C.R. 10.502.1–10.504.1.15, 10.502.1.19–10.504.1.114; Bertie County, Inventories of Estates, C.R. 10.507.2; Carteret County Records, Miscellaneous Papers, 1717–1884, Book A, Records of Wills and Bonds, C.R. 19.905.1; Wills Inventories, Sales and Settlement of Estates, C.R. 19.802.1–19.802.11, vols. 1–11; Carteret County Wills, C.R. 19.801.1, 19.905.1; all in NCSA. Also see plantation papers listed in notes to Tables 7.3.

Table 7.6. Estimates of Slave Marital and Familial Development in North Carolina, 1750–1775, Western Region

Total Slaves in Household	N Slaveholds	N Slaves	Percentage of Slaves in Dual-Headed Families: Probability A & B	Percentage of Slaves in Single-Headed Families: Probability A & B	Percentage of Unattached Slaves on Plantations: Probability A & B	Percentage of Slaves in Single- & Dual-Headed Families: Probability A & B
1	27	27	A = 0 B = 0	A = 0 B = 0	A = 100.00 B = 100.00	A = 0 B = 0
2–3	24	52	A = 18.95 B = 15.67	A = 48.36 B = 51.64	A = 32.69 B = 32.69	A = 67.31 B = 67.31
4–5	3	13	A = 15.16 B = 12.54	A = 77.15 B = 79.77	A = 7.69 B = 7.69	A = 92.31 B = 92.31
6–10	4	29	A = 31.71 B = 26.23	A = 40.70 B = 46.18	A = 27.59 B = 27.29	A = 72.41 B = 72.41
11–15	1	11	A = 59.70 B = 49.39	A = 31.21 B = 41.52	A = 9.09 B = 9.09	A = 90.91 B = 90.91
16–20	—	—	— —	— —	— —	— —
21+	—	—	— —	— —	— —	— —
Totals	59	132	A = 20.90 B = 17.29	A = 38.19 B = 41.08	A = 40.91 B = 40.91	A = 59.09 B = 59.09

Sources: Secretary of State Records, North Carolina Wills, 1663–1789, S.S. 845–73, vols. 7–35; Chancery Proceedings and Wills, 1712–54, S.S. 878; Wills, 1738–52, 1750–58, 1755–58, 1758–73, S.S. 877, 879–81, vols. 4, 6–8; Inventories and Sales of Estates, 1714–98, S.S. 889–905; Orange County Estate Papers, 1758–85, C.R. 73.507.1; all in NCSA. Also see plantation papers listed in notes to Table 7.3.

Table 7.7. Age at First Birth and First Conception of Slave Women Born in North Carolina between 1726 and 1792

Cohort	N	Mean Age of Mothers				Median Age of Mothers				Range for Four Categories of Birth and Conception
		At Birth of Eldest Child Surviving Infancy	At Birth of First Child Calculating Infant Mortality[1]	At Conception of Eldest Child Surviving Infancy	At Conception of First Child Calculating Infant Mortality	At Birth of Eldest Child Surviving Infancy	At Birth of First Child Calculating Infant Mortality[1]	At Conception of Eldest Child Surviving Infancy	At Conception of First Child Calculating Infant Mortality	
1726–1741	6	18.40	18.01	17.65	17.26	19.08	18.69	18.33	17.94	15.17–19.75 14.78–19.36 14.42–19.00 14.03–18.61
1766–1780	15	17.43	17.04	16.68	16.29	17.50	17.11	16.75	16.36	13.5 –21.5 13.11–21.11 12.75–20.75 12.36–20.36
1781–1792	19	19.32	18.93	18.57	18.18	18.83	18.44	18.08	17.69	16.5 –23.92 16.11–23.53 15.75–23.17 15.36–22.78
Total Years	40	18.47	18.08	17.72	17.33	18.67	18.28	17.92	17.53	13.5 –23.92 13.11–23.53 12.75–23.17 12.36–22.78

continued

Table 7.7 (continued)

Sources: Six sets of plantation records were consulted for Table 7.7. See NCSA: Waightstill Avery's slaves (Rowan County) for mothers born during the years 1766–84, in Avery Family Papers, Miscellaneous, Roll Book of Slaves of the Avery Family, 1766 to 1865, P.C. 294.1; Pollock family's slaves on Mount Rose Plantation in Craven County for mothers born during the years 1779–83, in Pollock-Devereaux Papers, Inventory of Slaves in 1797 and List of Slaves, 1806, P.C. 32.1; Joseph Michaux's slaves for mothers born during the years 1785–92, in Michaux-Randolph Papers, P.C. 95.3; Major John Walker's slaves (Wilmington, New Hanover County) for mothers born during the years 1787–89, in John Walker Papers, P.C. 254.1. For Sarah Allen's slaves with mothers born during the years 1726–41, see James M. Robin's Papers, vol. 1, Massachusetts Historical Society. For Richard Bennehan's slaves with mothers born during the years 1776–92, see Gutman, *The Black Family in Slavery and Freedom, 1750–1925* (New York: Vintage Books, 1977), 169–73, 180. None of Bennehan's slaves are treated as complete families.

[1] A slight variation of Kulikoff's methods was used to convert the known figures for the mean and median ages of mothers at the conception and birth of their eldest child surviving infancy to estimates of their respective ages at the birth of their first child. This was done by making use of child mortality *estimates*. The specific method involved multiplying .25 (the estimates used for infant mortality, 250 infant deaths per 1,000 born), by x (representing N, i.e., the number of mothers) and multiplying the product by 1.55 (the time interval between the death of the infant or infants and the birth of the first living child).

With this estimate found, a new figure (the average or median age of mothers at birth or conception for a given cohort) is multiplied by N (the number of mothers in the cohort). Subtracted from the product is the above estimate concerning infant mortality. The deducted number is then divided by N, with the result equaling a rough estimate of the mean or median age of mothers at the birth of the first child. See Allan Kulikoff, "A 'Prolifick' People: Black Population Growth in the Chesapeake Colonies, 1700–1790," *Southern Studies* 16 (Winter 1977): 223–25.

Table 7.8. Maternal Age at First Birth, by Cohort, 1720–1840+, South Carolina Low Country

Cohort	N	Mean	Median	Range
1720–49	10	19.3	18.7	14.6–30.0
1750–79	32	19.6	18.3	14.5–28.1
1780–1809	113	20.1	19.4	12.6–29.6
1810–39	96	19.8	19.5	11.9–28.1
1840+	27	19.5	19.1	13.4–26.6
1720–1840+	279	19.9	19.4	11.9–30.0

Sources: Ball Family slaves reconstitution; Cheryll Ann Cody, "Slave Demography and Family Formation: A Community Study of the Ball Family Plantations, 1720–1896" (Ph.D. diss., University of Minnesota, 1982), table 3.3, p. 161.

Table 7.9. Age at First Conception of Slave Women Born between 1710 and 1759, Southern Maryland

Decade of Birth of Mother	Mean Age of Women		Total Number of Women
	At Conception of Eldest Child Living with Her	At Estimated Conception of First Child[a]	
1710s	18.4	17.8	5
1720s	18.1	17.5	8
1730s	18.8	18.1	17
1740s	19.3	18.5	71
1750s	17.9	17.6	79

Sources: Kulikoff, "Black Population Growth in the Chesapeake," 407 (see pp. 223–25 for the methods he used to minimize biases in these estimates).

[a] Allowing for the estimated impact of infant mortality.

Table 7.10. Distribution of Maternal Age at Birth of First Child, 1726–1792, North Carolina

Cohort	Less than 15		15–19		20–24		Total N
	N	%	N	%	N	%	
1726–41	1	16.66	5	83.33	0	0	6
1766–80	4	26.66	11	73.33	0	0	15
1781–92	0	0	15	78.95	4	21.05	19
Total years	5	12.5	31	77.5	4	10.0	40

Sources: See listing of sources for Table 7.7.

Table 7.11. Distribution of Maternal Age at Birth of First Child, 1720–1840, South Carolina Low Country

Cohort	Less than 15		15–19		20–24		25–29		30+		Total N
	N	%	N	%	N	%	N	%	N	%	
1720–49	1	10.0	8	80.8	0	0	0	0	1	10.0	10
1750–79	1	3.1	19	59.4	7	21.9	5	15.6	0	0	32
1780–1809	5	4.4	57	50.4	43	38.1	8	7.1	0	0	113
1810–39	5	5.2	47	49.0	38	39.6	6	6.2	0	0	96
1840+	1	3.7	16	59.3	9	33.3	1	3.7	0	0	27
1720–1840+	13	4.7	147	52.7	98	35.1	20	7.2	1	.4	279

Sources: Ball Family slaves reconstitution; Cody, "Slave Demography and Family Formation," table 3.4, p. 163.

Table 7.12. Mean and Median Birth Intervals in Months, by Cohort and Province

Cohort	Province	Birth Events	Months	
			Mean	Median
1725–60	North Carolina[1]	30	32.9	36
1766–1808	North Carolina[1]	84	36	34
1770–79	South Carolina, Lowcountry[2]	138	—	31
1724–44	King William Parish, Virginia[3]	70	28	25–29
1740–50	Chesapeake[4]	—	27	—
1760–80	Chesapeake[4]	—	25–27	—

[1] Figures obtained from papers of four plantations. See, in NCSA: Avery Family Papers, Miscellaneous, Roll Book of Slaves of the Avery Family, 1766 to 1865, P.C. 294.1; Pollock-Devereaux Papers, Inventory of Slaves in 1797 and List of Slaves, 1806, P.C. 32.1; John Walker Papers, P.C. 254.1. Also see James M. Robin's Papers, vol. 1, Massachusetts Historical Society.

[2] Cody, "Slave Demography and Family Formation," table 3.7, pp. 174–75.

[3] Joan Rezner Gunderson, "The Double Bonds of Race and Sex: Black and White Women in a Colonial Virginia Parish," *Journal of Southern History* 52 (August 1986): 354–55.

[4] Kulikoff, "Black Population Growth in the Chesapeake," 407–8.

Table 7.13. Completed Family Size in North and South Carolina, 1725–1825

Plantation	Years at Birth of First Child	Median Completed Family Size[1]	Mean Completed Family Size	Range	N Mothers
Sarah Allen—New Hanover County[2]	1725–26	8.0	8.0	7–9	2
Thos. Pollock— Craven County	?–1770 (at latest)	6.0	6.7	3–11	6
Waightstill Avery— Rowan County[4]	1766–96	11.0	10.8	8–13	6
Maj. John Walker— Wilmington, New Hanover County[5]	1781	7.0	7.0	—	1
Pollock Plantation— Mt. Rose, Craven County[6]	1781	6.0	6.0	—	1
Composite for all plantations in North Carolina	1725–96	8.5	8.4	3–13	16
South Carolina Lowcountry[7]	ca. 1740–89	10.8	12.0	5–13	8

[1]Completed families consist of all recorded families with mothers born in North Carolina, 45 years and older.

[2]James M. Robin's Papers, vol. 1, Massachusetts Historical Society.

[3]Lean by Thomas Pollock to Jacob Mitchell, Pollock Papers, P.C. 31.1, NCSA.

[4]Avery Family Papers, Miscellaneous, Roll Book of Slaves of the Avery Family, 1766–1865, P.C. 294.1, NCSA.

[5]John Walker Papers, P.C. 254.1, NCSA.

[6]Pollock-Devereaux Papers, Inventory of Slaves in 1797 and List of Slaves, 1806, P.C. 32.1, NCSA.

[7]Cody, "Slave Demography and Family Formation," table 6.2, p. 319.

Table 7.14. Family Size in Maryland and Virginia, 1739–1828

Plantation	Years of Birth of First Child	Mean Completed Family Size[a]	Mean Size All Families	Number of Women
Carroll, Md.	1739–59	7.9	—[b]	11
Jerdone, Va.	1754–75	8.0	5.8	19
Bolling, Va.	1750–95	8.3	6.0	25
Jefferson, Va.	1765–1800	7.7	—[b]	—[b]
Mt. Airy, Va.	1809–28	6.4	—[b]	—[b]

Source: Kulikoff, "Black Population Growth in the Chesapeake," 409. Kulikoff's table has been revised here to exclude two footnotes.

[a]Completed family size is defined as follows: (1) on Carroll plantation, it includes the families of all women ages 40 to 60, except for two women who had only one child; (2) on the Jerdone and Bolling plantations, it includes all women with at least seven children and all women who lived through at least fifteen childbearing years. There were ten completed families on Jerdone's plantation and fourteen on Bolling's.

[b]Data not available.

Notes

INTRODUCTION

1. Herbert G. Gutman and Ira Berlin both argue cogently the necessity of such studies. See Gutman, "Slave Culture and Slave Family and Kin Network: The Importance of Time," *South Atlantic Urban Studies* 2 (1978): 73–88; Berlin, "Time Space, and the Evolution of Afro-American Society on British Mainland North America," *American Historical Review* 85 (February 1980): 44–78. Berlin deftly synthesizes the findings of many scholars in his article, which traces the growth of slavery on the mainland of colonial British North America in three regions: the North, the Carolina low country, and the Chesapeake. His discussion of the low country, however, concentrates almost entirely on South Carolina, and he ignores slavery in other parts of the South, almost completely disregarding its occurrence, for example, in each of the different regions of North Carolina.

Three especially significant books that discuss colonial and Revolutionary slavery are Peter H. Wood, *Black Majority: Negroes in Colonial South Carolina from 1670 through the Stono Rebellion* (New York: Knopf, 1974); Gerald W. Mullin, *Flight and Rebellion: Slave Resistance in Eighteenth-Century Virginia* (New York: Oxford University Press, 1972); Gary B. Nash, *Forging Freedom: The Formation of Philadelphia's Black Community, 1720–1840* (Cambridge: Harvard University Press, 1988).

2. See, e.g., T. H. Breen and Stephen Innes, *"Myne Owne Ground": Race and Freedom on Virginia's Eastern Shore, 1640–1676* (New York: Oxford University Press, 1980); Charles B. Joyner, *Down by the Riverside: A South Carolina Slave Community* (Urbana: University of Illinois Press, 1984); Herbert S. Klein, *Slavery in the Americas: A Comparative Study of Virginia and Cuba* (Chicago: University of Chicago Press, 1967); Allan Kulikoff, *Tobacco and Slaves: The Development of Southern Cultures in the Chesapeake, 1680–1800* (Chapel Hill: Institute of Early American History and Culture, University of North Carolina Press, 1986); Ronald L. Lewis, *Coal, Iron, and Slaves: Individual Slaves in Maryland and Virginia, 1715–1865* (Westport, Conn.: Greenwood, 1979); Daniel C. Littlefield, *Rice and Slaves: Ethnicity and the Slave Trade in Colonial South Carolina* (Baton Rouge: Louisiana State University Press, 1981); Robert McColley, *Slavery and Jeffersonian Virginia* (Urbana: University of Illinois Press, 1964); Walter Minchinton, Celia King, and Peter Waite, eds., *Virginia Slave Trade Statistics, 1698–1775* (Richmond, 1984); Edmund S. Morgan, *American Slavery, American Freedom: The Ordeal of Colonial Virginia* (New York: Norton, 1975); Mullin, *Flight and Rebellion*; Philip J. Schwartz, *Twice Condemned: Slaves and the Criminal Laws of Virginia, 1705–1865* (Baton Rouge: Louisiana State University Press, 1988); Julia Floyd Smith, *Slavery and Rice Culture in Low Country Georgia, 1750–1860* (Knoxville: University of Tennessee Press, 1985); Mechal Sobel, *The World They Made Together: Black and White Values in Eighteenth-Century Virginia* (Princeton, N.J.: Princeton University Press, 1987); Thad W. Tate, *The Negro in Eighteenth-Century Williamsburg* (Williamsburg: distributed by University Press of Virginia, 1965); Betty Wood, *Slavery in Colonial Georgia, 1730–1775* (Athens: University of Georgia Press, 1984); Peter Wood, *Black Majority*.

3. Jeffrey Crow's studies of slavery in Revolutionary North Carolina are two notable exceptions. See his "Slave Rebelliousness and Social Conflict in North Carolina, 1775 to

1802," *William and Mary Quarterly*, 3d ser., 37 (January 1980): 79–102, and *The Black Experience in Revolutionary North Carolina* (Raleigh: North Carolina Department of Cultural Resources, Division of Archives and History, 1977). Two works are most helpful in gaining a better understanding of North Carolina's harsh public system of criminal justice for slaves: Don Higginbotham and William S. Price Jr., "Was It Murder for a White Man to Kill a Slave? Chief Justice Martin Howard Condemns the Peculiar Institution in North Carolina," *William and Mary Quarterly*, 3d ser., 36 (October 1979): 593–601, and Donna J. Spindel, *Crime and Society in North Carolina: 1663–1776* (Baton Rouge: Louisiana State University Press, 1989). Also very useful are John C. Inscoe's study of slave naming practices and Harry Roy Merrens's pioneering work on the historical geography of North Carolina; the latter is a treasure trove of information on the topographic, demographic, and economic characteristics of the colony's various regions. See Inscoe, "Carolina Slave Names: An Index to Acculturation," *Journal of Southern History* 49 (1983): 527–54; Merrens, *Colonial North Carolina in the Eighteenth Century: A Study in Historical Geography* (Chapel Hill: University of North Carolina Press, 1964). See also James A. Padgett, "The Status of Slaves in Colonial North Carolina," *Journal of Negro History* 14 (July 1929): 300–27; John Spencer Basset, "Slavery and Servitude in the Colony of North Carolina," *Johns Hopkins University Studies in Historical and Political Science*, ser. 14 (1896): 27–61; Alan D. Watson, "North Carolina Slave Courts, 1715–1785," *North Carolina Historical Review* 60 (January 1983): 24–36; Watson, "Impulse Toward Independence: Resistance and Rebellion among North Carolina Slaves, 1750–1775," *Journal of Negro History* 63 (Fall 1978): 317–28; Marvin L. Michael Kay and Lorin Lee Cary, "A Demographic Analysis of Colonial North Carolina with Special Emphasis upon the Slave and Black Populations," in *Black Americans in North Carolina and the South*, edited by Jeffrey J. Crow and Flora J. Hatley (Chapel Hill: University of North Carolina Press, 1984), 71–121; Kay and Cary, "Marriage and the Family among North Carolina Slaves," in *The American Family: Historical Perspectives*, edited by Jean E. Hunter and Paul T. Mason (Pittsburg, Pa.: Duquesne University Press, 1988), 58–74, 183–87; Kay and Cary, "Slave Runaways in Colonial North Carolina, 1748–1775," *North Carolina Historical Review* 63 (January 1986): 1–39; Kay and Cary, " 'The Planters Suffer Little or Nothing': North Carolina Compensations for Executed Slaves, 1748–1772," *Science and Society* 40 (Fall 1976): 288–306; Kay and Cary, " 'They Are Indeed the Constant Plague of Their Tyrants': Slave Defense of a Moral Economy in Colonial North Carolina, 1748–1772," *Slavery and Abolition* 6 (December 1985): 37–56.

4. All of this will be discussed at length in Chapter 1.

5. Ibid. See also Kay and Cary, "A Demographic Analysis," 72–93.

6. Kay and Cary, "A Demographic Analysis," 101–2; Philip D. Morgan, "Colonial South Carolina Runaways: Their Significance for Slave Culture," *Slavery and Abolition* 6 (1985): 59–61; Betty Wood, *Slavery in Colonial Georgia*, 104–5.

7. Roger Bastide argues the habitual quality of the slaves' African pasts. See his *African Civilizations in the New World* (London: C. Hurst and Co., 1971), 89.

8. See Chapters 4–8.

9. For recent analyses of the application of Gramsci's concept of cultural hegemony to problems in American history, see T. Jackson Lears, "The Concept of Cultural Hegemony: Problems and Possibilities," and John Patrick Diggins, "Comrades and Citizens: New Mythologies in American Historiography," both in *American Historical Review* 90 (1985): 567–93 and 614–38 respectively; contributions by Leon Fink, Jackson Lears, John P. Diggins,

George Lipsitz, Mari Jo Buhle, and Paul Buhle to "A Round Table: Labor, Historical Pessimism, and Hegemony," *Journal of American History* 75 (1988): 115–61; Michael Kazin, "The Historian as Populist," *New York Review of Books,* 12 May 1988, 48–50.

10. These are basic themes that run throughout much of this book.

11. We first presented a portion of this conceptual analysis at the Thirteenth Biennial Conference of the Australian and New Zealand American Studies Conference, University of Newcastle, New South Wales, Australia, 28 August–1 September 1988. The chairman of our session, Rhys Isaac, made helpful comments, as did Michael Zuckerman. Part of the paper eventually was published in Kay and Cary, "Marriage and the Family among North Carolina Slaves."

12. Berlin, "Time, Space, and the Evolution of Afro-American Society," 76–77; Gerald Mullin, *Flight and Rebellion,* 19–33, and "Obeah and Christianity: In Four Plantation Colonies in the Old British Empire" (paper, 1974), 46–49, 58–63; Michael Mullin, "British Caribbean and North American Slaves in an Era of War and Revolution, 1775–1807," in *The Southern Experience in the American Revolution,* edited by Jeffrey J. Crow and Larry E. Tise (Chapel Hill: University of North Carolina Press, 1978), 247–48; Darrett B. Rutman and Anita H. Rutman, *A Place In Time: Middlesex County, Virginia, 1650–1750* (New York: Norton, 1984), 170–73, 269 nn. 23–24; Rutman and Rutman, *A Place In Time: Explicatus* (New York: Norton, 1984), 97–103.

13. Berlin, "Time, Space, and the Evolution of Afro-American Society," 59–62, 65–67; Gerald Mullin, "Obeah and Christianity," 47–49; Michael Mullin, "British Caribbean and North American Slaves," 248–51; Philip D. Morgan, "Work and Culture: The Task System and the World of Lowcountry Blacks, 1700 to 1880," *William and Mary Quarterly,* 3d ser., 39 (October 1982): 563–99; Morgan, "Black Society in the Lowcountry, 1610–1810," in *Slavery and Freedom in the Age of the American Revolution,* edited by Ira Berlin and Ronald Hoffman (Charlottesville: University Press of Virginia, 1983), 105–8; Joyner, *Down by the Riverside,* 43–45, 51, 63.

14. See Chapter 1 and Merrens, *Colonial North Carolina in the Eighteenth Century,* 85–141.

15. See Chapter 1.

16. For examples of a blurring of reality with the rhetoric of planters, see Sobel, *The World They Made Together,* 127–68, and the works by Mullin and the Rutmans in n. 12 above.

17. See Chapters 6–8.

CHAPTER 1

1. See Ira Berlin, "Time, Space, and the Evolution of Afro-American Society on British Mainland North America," *American Historical Review* 85 (February 1980): 44–78; Harry Roy Merrens, *Colonial North Carolina in the Eighteenth Century: A Study in Historical Geography* (Chapel Hill: University of North Carolina Press, 1964), 3–15, 179; John J. McCusker and Russell R. Menard, *The Economy of British America, 1607–1789* (Chapel Hill: University of North Carolina Press, 1985), 17–34, 51–52, 86–87, 119–33.

2. Cf. A. Roger Ekirch, *"Poor Carolina": Politics and Society in Colonial North Carolina, 1729–1776* (Chapel Hill: University of North Carolina Press, 1981), 1–18, who surveys the colonial economy and stresses its immature state.

3. Little came of various improvement schemes. The province eventually marked channels and licensed pilots, but as late as the Revolution there were no lighthouses. See Charles

Christopher Crittenden, *The Commerce of North Carolina, 1763–1789* (New Haven: Yale University Press, 1936), 1–8, 43; Merrens, *Colonial North Carolina*, 92–107, 146–55; Hugh T. Lefler and William S. Powell, *Colonial North Carolina: A History* (New York: Scribner's, 1973), 81–86. Onslow County had a good river system, the New and the White Oak Rivers, but lacked a port. Boats had to go into Bogue Inlet or Sound. See Donnie D. Bellamy, "Slavery in Microcosm: Onslow County, North Carolina," *Journal of Negro History* 62 (October 1977): 240, 243. See also Edward Moseley, "A New Land Correct Map of the Province of North Carolina [1733]. . . . ," and the Bachman 1861, "Birds Eye View of North and South Carolina and Part of Georgia," both in *North Carolina in Maps*, compiled by W. P. Cumming, (Raleigh: North Carolina Department of Archives and History, 1966), plates 7, 12.

4. Crittenden, *Commerce of North Carolina*, 24–30, 34–35; Jacob Price, "Economic Function and the Growth of American Port Towns in the Eighteenth Century," in Donald Fleming and Bernard Bailyn, eds., *Perspectives in American History* 8 (1974): 161, 166, 169; Merrens, *Colonial North Carolina*, 143–67; Marvin L. Michael Kay and William S. Price Jr., "'To Ride the Wood Mare': Road Building and Militia Service in Colonial North Carolina, 1740–1775," *North Carolina Historical Review* 57 (October 1980): 361–409, 363 n. 8, 377 n. 26 (roadwork laws); Carville Earle and Ronald Hoffman, "Staple Crops and Urban Development in the Eighteenth-Century South," in Donald Fleming and Bernard Bailyn, eds., *Perspectives in American History* 10 (1976): 18; Robert W. Ramsey, *Carolina Cradle: Settlement of the Northwest Carolina Frontier, 1747–1762* (Chapel Hill: University of North Carolina Press, 1964), 173–74. The Bachman 1861 map cited in n. 3 above is especially useful for visualizing the topographic hindrances to trade.

5. See Table 1.9, which compares the official export records of all the southern colonies. See also nn. 36 and 39 of this chapter. All tables are in the Appendix.

6. Crittenden, *Commerce of North Carolina*, 97–103, 105, 110; Merrens, *Colonial North Carolina*, 15, 146; Lefler and Powell, *Colonial North Carolina*, 155–56, 165–67, 169–71; McCusker and Menard, *Economy of British America*, 35–50, 249; Kay and Price, "Road Building and Militia Service"; Marvin L. Michael Kay, "The Institutional Background to the Regulation in Colonial North Carolina" (Ph.D. diss., University of Minnesota, 1962), 261–83, 442–590. For a transcription of a portion of the "Johnston and Bennehan Account and Invoice Book, Snow Hill [Orange County], North Carolina, 1769–1773," see Kay, "Institutional Background to the Regulation," pp. 495–590. This account book may be found in the Cameron Papers, Southern Historical Collection, University of North Carolina at Chapel Hill (hereafter cited as SHC).

A series of abuses, primarily perpetrated by merchants and lawyers, combined with numerous political, fiscal, juridical, and administrative malfeasances committed over the years by colonial officials, proved to be most burdensome to and resented by farmers in the colony. Resentment was greatest in the piedmont counties, resulting in the Regulator movement of 1766–71. See Kay, "The North Carolina Regulation, 1766–1776: A Class Conflict," in *The American Revolution: Explorations in the History of American Radicalism*, edited by Alfred F. Young (De Kalb: Northern Illinois University Press, 1976), 71–123, esp. 73–76 and 116–17 n. 12.

7. William L. Saunders, ed., *The Colonial Records of North Carolina*, 10 vols. (Raleigh: State of North Carolina, 1886–90), 1:720, 722, 2:xvii, 419; Evarts B. Greene and Virginia C. Harrington, *American Population before the Federal Census of 1790* (New York: Columbia University Press, 1932), 156; Lefler and Powell, *Colonial North Carolina*, 32, 47–49; Merrens,

Colonial North Carolina, 20–24, 148; McCusker and Menard, *Economy of British America,* 170; Marvin L. Michael Kay and Lorin Lee Cary, "A Demographic Analysis of Colonial North Carolina with Special Emphasis upon the Slave and Black Populations," in *Black Americans in North Carolina and the South,* edited by Jeffrey J. Crow and Flora J. Hatley (Chapel Hill: University of North Carolina Press, 1984), 71–121 (we draw on this account here and in the following pages); Chowan County Records, Lists of Taxables, 1762–78, and List of Taxables for the Town of Edenton, 1769, in North Carolina State Archives, Raleigh (hereafter cited as NCSA); Donald R. Lennon and Ida Brooks Kellam, eds., *The Wilmington Town Book, 1743–1778* (Raleigh: North Carolina Department of Cultural Resources, Division of Archives and History, 1973), xxxiv–xxxv. The diversified economic pattern somewhat parallels what occurred during South Carolina's early history. Peter H. Wood, *Black Majority: Negroes in Colonial South Carolina from 1670 through the Stono Rebellion* (New York: Knopf, 1974), 13–30 passim. For support for our contention above that the size of the town did not necessarily determine its economic functionalism, this being primarily prompted by the availability of sufficient numbers of store owners and merchants capable of performing the roles of suppliers of goods and credit and of marketing agents, see Kay, "Institutional Background to the Regulation," 442–82; Joseph A. Ernst and H. Roy Merrens, " 'Camden's Turrets Pierce the Skies': The Urban Process in the Southern Colonies during the Eighteenth Century," *William and Mary Quarterly,* 3d ser., 30 (October 1973): 549–74.

8. Lefler and Powell, *Colonial North Carolina,* 56–65; Enoch Lawrence Lee, *The Lower Cape Fear in Colonial Days* (Chapel Hill: University of North Carolina Press, 1965), 66; Bellamy, "Slavery in Microcosm," 340, 343; Hugh Talmage Lefler and Albert Ray Newsome, *North Carolina: The History of a Southern State,* 3d ed. (Chapel Hill: University of North Carolina Press, 1973), 43–75 passim; Jeffrey J. Crow, *The Black Experience in Revolutionary North Carolina* (Raleigh: North Carolina Department of Cultural Resources, Division of Archives and History, 1977), 4; Merrens, *Colonial North Carolina,* 18–31, 143–55. The ports of entry were the administrative districts for which export records were kept by port authorities. At times the port (customs district) bore the same name as the major port in the district, as was true of the district of Port Bath Town and the port of Bath. In this case the port authorities resided in the town of Bath. At other times the customs district and the administrative authorities bore the same name as and were located in towns in the district, but these towns had ceased to be the major urban centers of their respective districts. This was true of both Port Beaufort and Port Brunswick. The authorities administering the two districts lived in the ports of Beaufort and Brunswick, but these colonial ports respectively had become much less significant than the ports of New Bern and Wilmington. In yet another variation, the customs districts of Port Currituck and Port Roanoke were simply two separate administrative units for the Albemarle Sound region. Both ports were served by the port of Edenton in Chowan County. See Merrens, *Colonial North Carolina,* 87–95. See Map 4, which denotes the jurisdictions of different customs districts and the location of the actual ports within each of these administrative units.

9. For this and the following paragraph, see Chowan County Records, Lists of Taxables, 1762–78, and List of Taxables for the Town of Edenton, 1769, NCSA; Lennon and Kellam, *Wilmington Town Book,* xxxiv–xxxv, 85; Lefler and Newsome, *North Carolina,* 72; Merrens, *Colonial North Carolina,* 27, 129, 132–33, 150–53; Lee, *Lower Cape Fear,* 97, 102, 118–19, 161; Price, "Economic Function and the Growth of American Port Towns," 166–68, 172–73; McCusker and Menard, *Economy of British America,* 170, 179–80, 184, 318; James M. Clifton,

"Golden Grains of White: Rice Planting on the Lower Cape Fear," *North Carolina Historical Review* 50 (October 1973): 365–66. On naval stores policy, see Joseph J. Malone, *Pine Trees and Politics: The Naval Stores and Forest Policy in Colonial New England, 1661–1775*, 10–46; Justin Williams, "English Mercantilism and Carolina Naval Stores, 1705–1776," *Journal of Southern History* 1 (1935): 169–85, esp. 174, 176. See also James M. Clifton, "The Rice Industry in Colonial America," *Agricultural History* 55 (1981): 266–83. For population figures of urban settlements in the colonies at large, see Carl Bridenbaugh, *Cities in Revolt: Urban Life in America, 1743–1776* (London: Oxford University Press, 1955), 4–6, 216–18.

10. The growth patterns illustrated in Tables 1.1–1.3 demonstrate that the more westerly regions' population growth was partially the result of emigration from the Albemarle Sound and Neuse-Pamlico regions. See esp. Table 1.3 and the yearly rate of growth patterns for these two regions. See also, e.g., Lefler and Newsome, *North Carolina*, 76–79. The 1730 figures cited above come from Saunders, *Colonial Records*, 2:xvii, 3:433. See also Merrens, *Colonial North Carolina*, 20–21.

11. Ekirch, *Politics and Society*, 6, 12; McCusker and Menard, *Economy of British America*, 185. In 1733 Governor George Burrington lamented the flow of goods into Virginia and pointed out "that six times more Cash is carried out of this Country into Virginia to purchase Negros and British Commoditys then is sufficient to pay the King's Quitt rents." Saunders, *Colonial Records*, 3:621–22. Items shipped overland for export from Virginia or South Carolina appear in the official records only as exports from either of these two provinces.

12. The population estimate for 1775 of 230,000 is an extrapolation made from estimates of 197,200 (1770) and 270,133 (1780) in "Estimated Population of American Colonies: 1610 to 1780," Bureau of the Census, *Historical Statistics of the United States: Colonial Times to 1957*, ser. Z 290, p. 756. For the Regulator uprising and its effect on emigration, see Kay, "The North Carolina Regulation," 73–123, but esp. 102–3, 122 n. 99. The best analysis of the Regulator migration remains Elmer D. Johnson, "The War of the Regulators: Its Place in History" (M.A. thesis, University of North Carolina, 1942), 117–23.

13. See nn. 12 above and 14 below. For ethnic immigration to North Carolina, see Ian Charles Cargill Graham, *Colonists from Scotland: Emigration to North America, 1707–1783* (Ithaca, N.Y.: Cornell University Press, 1956), 94–96, 106, 108–9, 146, 154, 156–57, 159–60; Duane Gilbert Meyer, "The Scottish Highlanders in North Carolina, 1773–1776" (Ph.D. diss., University of Iowa, 1956), 54–55, 90, 95, 97, 125, 128, 135; William K. Boyd, ed., *Some Eighteenth-Century Tracts concerning North Carolina* (Raleigh: North Carolina Historical Commission, 1927), 419–21; R. D. W. Connor, *Race Elements in the White Population of North Carolina* (Greensboro: North Carolina State Normal and Industrial College, 1920); William Herman Gehrke, "The German Element in Rowan and Cabarrus Counties" (M.A. thesis, University of North Carolina, 1934) and "The Beginnings of the Pennsylvania German Element in Rowan and Cabarrus Counties, North Carolina," *Pennsylvania Magazine of History and Biography* 58, no. 4 (1934): 342–69; Lefler and Newsome, *North Carolina*, 88–108; Kay, "Institutional Background to the Regulation," 21–68; Merrens, *Colonial North Carolina*, 53–107; American Council of Learned Societies, "Report of Committee on Linguistic and National Stocks in the Population of the United States," American Historical Association, *Annual Report for the Year 1931* (Washington, D.C., 1932), 1:107–441, esp. table on pp. 124–25; Forrest McDonald and Ellen Shapiro McDonald, "The Ethnic Origins of the American People, 1790," *William and Mary Quarterly*, 3d ser., 37 (April 1980): 179–99.

The comparative per annum increases of the white population for 1730–55 and 1755–67, respectively 3.0 and 5.1 percent, as noted above, is illustrative of the increasing significance of immigration in explaining population growth among whites. There is an underlying assumption here that natural increase among whites may have been around 2.5 percent and similar to that of blacks.

14. For population estimates for 1720 and 1730, see Saunders, *Colonial Records*, 1:720, 722, 2:xvii, 419, 3:433; Greene and Harrington, *American Population*, 156; Merrens, *Colonial North Carolina*, 20–21. Somewhat over 2,000 blacks for 1720 is a rough extrapolation from a contemporary estimate of 1,000 for 1705.

15. See the last paragraph of n. 13 above. Allan Kulikoff estimates that by the mid-eighteenth century, "one ought to expect the adult population to increase naturally by about 2.5 percent a year without further immigration from Africa. Any growth rate under 2.5 percent would indicate out-migration; any figure greatly above 2.5 percent would suggest immigration of Creoles or immigrants." A natural increase of 2.5 percent a year is probably similar to North Carolina's figure, but quite possibly a bit high. Kulikoff, "Tobacco and Slaves: Population, Economy, and Society in Eighteenth-Century Prince George's County, Maryland" (Ph.D. diss., Brandeis University, 1976), 84. See also Kulikoff, "A 'Prolifick' People: Black Population Growth in the Chesapeake Colonies, 1700–1790," *Southern Studies* 16 (Winter 1977): 412.

16. Recently Walter E. Minchinton carefully analyzed the seaborne slave trade of North Carolina during the eighteenth century. We wish to thank Jeffrey Crow for informing us of this study in time to incorporate its statistical findings into our analysis. See Minchinton, "The Seabourne Slave Trade of North Carolina," *North Carolina Historical Review* 71 (January 1994): 1–61. Because relatively few slaves appear in the state's extant port records— Minchinton states that an average of 7 per annum arrived during 1702–46, 43 during 1749– 67, 144 during 1768–72, and 113 during 1771–75—some historians have tended to downplay the significance of black immigration to North Carolina. See, e.g., John Spencer Bassett, "Slavery and Servitude in the Colony of North Carolina," *Johns Hopkins University Studies in Historical and Political Science*, ser. 14 (April–May 1896): 22–24; Merrens, *Colonial North Carolina*, 79–81, 226 n. 61. Merrens points out that the most important collection of documents about the slave trade does not include a section on North Carolina because the editor found almost no evidence of slave imports into the province. Merrens erroneously concludes, despite his acknowledgment of extremely high black growth rates, that blacks "must have increased almost entirely as a result of natural increase." See Elizabeth Donnan, ed., *Documents Illustrative of the History of the Slave Trade to America*, 4 vols. (Washington, D.C.: Carnegie Institution of Washington, 1930–35), 4:235–36.

Cf. David Galenson, *White Servitude in Colonial America: An Economic Analysis* (Cambridge: Cambridge University Press, 1981), 217–18. He estimates that net black migration into North Carolina from 1750 to 1760 totaled 7,581, rose dramatically to 24,608 from 1760 to 1770, and fell to 1,765 from 1770 to 1780. Extrapolating his figures for the years 1755–67 almost duplicates the figures we arrived at by different methods. Robert Higgins earlier shared by correspondence research findings regarding the reexport from South Carolina of many of its slave imports, primarily to Georgia and secondarily to North Carolina.

For the estimate of 179 slaves entering Port Beaufort, see *North Carolina Magazine*, 28 September–5 October 1764. For corroborative evidence, see *North Carolina Magazine*, 7–14, 21–28 September, 19–26 October 1764.

Although Minchinton does not deal with questions concerning the number of slaves coming to North Carolina by land routes and the comparative significance of immigration and natural increase in explaining slave population growth, he does agree with our belief that extant port records underestimate the actual number of slaves who reached North Carolina via the seaborne trade: "the true figure may be substantially higher." Minchinton, "Seabourne Trade," 25.

The estimate of slaves listed in the port records was lowered in the text above from 800 to 600 as the figure to be multiplied by five to calculate the number of slaves who came to North Carolina by sea routes during the period 1755–67, because an extraordinarily large cargo of 258 slaves arrived in North Carolina in 1759 directly from the Windward Coast in West Africa. Including this unique cargo in our extrapolation very likely would have resulted in a serious overestimate. See Minchinton, "Seabourne Trade," 6, 8, 10–11, 16, 26–42 (but esp. 32).

17. Saunders, *Colonial Records*, 3:430.

18. For the ethnic provenance of particular slave populations, see W. Robert Higgins, "The Geographical Origins of Negro Slaves in Colonial South Carolina," *South Atlantic Quarterly* 70 (Winter 1971): 34–47; Philip D. Curtin, *The Atlantic Slave Trade: A Census* (Madison: University of Wisconsin Press, 1969), 155–58; Darold D. Wax, "Preferences for Slaves in Colonial America," *Journal of Negro History* 58 (October 1973): 371–401; Wood, *Black Majority*, 35–62, 131–66, 333–41; Daniel C. Littlefield, *Rice and Slaves: Ethnicity and the Slave Trade in Colonial South Carolina* (Baton Rouge: University of Louisiana Press, 1981); Philip D. Morgan, "Black Society in the Lowcountry, 1610–1810," in *Slavery and Freedom in the Age of the American Revolution*, edited by Ira Berlin and Ronald Hoffman (Charlottesville: University Press of Virginia, 1983), 129–33.

19. Russell R. Menard, "The Maryland Slave Population, 1658 to 1730: A Demographic Profile of Blacks in Four Counties," *William and Mary Quarterly*, 3d ser., 32 (January 1975): 30, 49. We suspect that many of Virginia's tidewater counties would roughly correspond with the four Maryland counties but know of no other studies that calculate such rates.

20. For the economy of the Lower Cape Fear region, see n. 9 above and Merrens, *Colonial North Carolina*, 27, 85–107, 127–33, 150–53.

21. The Albemarle Sound, Neuse-Pamlico, and Northern Inner Plain–Piedmont regions exhibited these economic characteristics to varying degrees. See Merrens, *Colonial North Carolina*.

22. As North Carolina matured economically, wealth increasingly concentrated in the hands of an upper class. Heirs among this class inherited and built on their parents' legacies, over time increasing the concentration of slaves among the wealthy slaveowners. For the inequitable distribution of wealth in the colony and how wealth predicted wealth from decade to decade in the province's more mature economic regions, see Marvin L. Michael Kay and Lorin Lee Cary, "Class, Mobility, and Conflict in North Carolina on the Eve of the Revolution," in *The Southern Experience in the American Revolution*, edited by Jeffrey J. Crow and Larry E. Tise (Chapel Hill: University of North Carolina Press, 1978), 115–23. See also Tables 1.1–1.3 and 1.5.

23. See Table 1.5 and Allan Kulikoff, "The Origins of Afro-American Society in Tidewater Maryland and Virginia, 1700 to 1790," *William and Mary Quarterly*, 3d ser., 35 (April 1978): 246–49. The two Maryland counties are Prince George's and St. Mary's; York County is in Virginia. Means of means were calculated to obtain the above statistics given the limited

statistics available for Virginia and Maryland. Comparable methods had to be used to obtain statistics for North Carolina's three coastal regions. Thus the means of means were obtained from the figures for the three appropriate areas in Table 1.5. Kulikoff has published further statistics for Virginia and Maryland that do not change the above assessments. They do illustrate, however, that the Virginia piedmont's slaves were, on the average, much more concentrated on large plantations than were slaves in the North Carolina piedmont. This is not surprising given the later settlement of the latter region. See Table 1.5 and Allan Kulikoff, *Tobacco and Slaves: The Development of Southern Cultures in the Chesapeake, 1680–1800* (Chapel Hill: University of North Carolina Press, 1986), 338, table 37.

24. The slight discrepancy in the figures for the Lower Cape Fear in Tables 1.5–1.6 is explained by the different years covered by each of the surveys. For South Carolina's statistics, see Morgan, "Black Society in the Lowcountry," 93–95. It is true that some low-country parishes had higher concentrations of slaves at particular moments than those listed above. In St. James's, Goose Creek, in 1745, for instance, 97 percent of the slaves lived on units with 10 or more slaves and 93 percent, 70 percent, and 37 percent respectively on units with 20+, 50+, and 100+ slaves. These respective percentages, however, fell by 1790 to figures similar to those of the Lower Cape Fear region: 94, 83, 54, and 30. Moreover, other low-country regions in colonial South Carolina had, as one would predict from the analysis in the text, lower concentrations of slaves on large plantations than was so in the Lower Cape Fear region. In St. John's, Berkeley, in 1762, for example, 47 percent of the slaves lived on units with 50 or more slaves, and only 12 percent were owned by masters with 100 or more slaves. See Philip D. Morgan, "A Profile of a Mid-Eighteenth Century South Carolina Parish: The Tax Return of Saint James', Goose Creek," *South Carolina Historical Magazine* 81 (January 1980): 51–65, esp. 54–55.

25. For similar demographic patterns, see Menard, "Maryland Slave Population," 29–54; Allan Kulikoff, "The Beginnings of the Afro-American Family in Maryland," in *Law, Society, and Politics in Early Maryland*, edited by Aubrey C. Land, Lois Green Carr, and Edward C. Papenfuse (Baltimore: Johns Hopkins University Press, 1977), 171–96.

26. See Kulikoff, "Black Population Growth in the Chesapeake," 398–99; Kulikoff, "Origins of Afro-American Society," 231; Kulikoff, "Origins of Afro-American Society in Tidewater Maryland and Virginia"; Kay and Cary, "A Demographic Analysis," 93–96.

27. Kulikoff intelligently and persuasively develops these demographic interrelationships in "Black Population Growth in the Chesapeake." See also Kay and Cary, "A Demographic Analysis," 93.

28. Kulikoff suggests that "if the entire population [of a colonial area] were African, the sex ratio would be about 200; when a third of the adults were African-Americans, the sex ratio would drop to 156"; and if "Africans constituted only a third of the adult population, the sex ratio would decline to 125." Kulikoff, "Black Population Growth in the Chesapeake," 403. See also Kay and Cary, "A Demographic Analysis," 93–96, 101–3.

29. For Galenson's calculations, see n. 16 above. For estimates of the percentages of Africans in South Carolina's slave population, see Morgan, "Black Society in the Lowcountry," 88–92, 129–33.

30. To aggregate the actual sexual imbalances on individual plantations requires using a different universe than the one employed in Table 1.7 to develop sex ratios. Estate records (wills and inventories) for the years 1750–75 were used to construct Table 1.8 instead of the tax records that were analyzed for Table 1.7. The resulting regional sex ratios for Tables 1.7

and 1.8 are not identical, although only the ratios for the interior regions, especially the west, are significantly at variance in the two tables. One reason is that the tax records concern slave taxables (slaves twelve years and over), whereas the data gathered from wills and inventories are for adult slaves—sixteen years and older. More important perhaps, Table 1.7 is constructed from more expansive samples.

It is nonetheless questionable whether these aberrations significantly distort the differences in the sex imbalances measured by sex ratios and the actual distribution of slaves by gender on the various plantations in each region. In Table 1.8 both sex ratios and imbalance ratios were used to calculate the percentages of slaves who could not be paired in marriage. Because these percentages may be visualized more readily, the ensuing discussion will focus on them instead of the ratios from which they were derived. What is being compared and contrasted, then, are the calculated percentages of slaves who could not possibly marry because of regional sex ratios and the percentage of slaves who could not possibly marry given the sexual imbalances that actually existed on each plantation in each region. In the latter case the effects of slavery itself on the distribution of slaves by sex and age are considered. Many factors would play a role in causing the latter maldistribution, none of which can be discretely quantified: the slave trade, the length of time a region had been settled, the need for slaves with certain skills, and, of greatest importance, the inclination of owners to stress productive needs over reproductive needs. See Kay and Cary, "A Demographic Analysis," 97–101.

31. Merrens, *Colonial North Carolina*, 85–172 passim.

32. Ibid., 146–55.

33. Ibid., 155–57; Kay, "Institutional Background to the Regulation," 456–67. Farmers in the northern interior stretching westward into Granville, Orange, and Rowan Counties sent their local products through local merchants in towns or in country stores primarily to merchants at Milners, Suffolk, and Petersburg, Virginia; Halifax, North Carolina; and to Glasgow, Scotland, and Whitehaven, England. Merchants, in return, besides providing marketing services for western farmers, supplied locals with credit and a wide variety of goods for their persons, homesteads, farms, and trades, and for hunting and fishing. See also Nannie May Tilley, "Industries of Colonial Granville County," *North Carolina Historical Review* 13 (October 1936): 273–89 passim.

34. Lefler and Newsome, *North Carolina*, 80; David LeRoy Corbitt, *The Formation of the North Carolina Counties, 1763–1943* (Raleigh: North Carolina Department of Archives and History, 1950), 79; Merrens, *Colonial North Carolina*, 157–72; Kay, "Institutional Background to the Regulation," 467–75; Adelaide L. Fries, ed., *Records of Moravians in North Carolina*, 8 vols. (Raleigh: Edwards and Broughton Print Co., 1922–54), 1:28–40, 105, 112, 121, 132–33, 135, 138–39, 173, 178–81, 188, 190–91, 209, 212, 214, 229, 234–38, 241–46, 249–51, 263–64, 267, 269–70, 276–78, 281–82, 284–88, 290–91, 296, 299–301, 303, 307, 331–37, 349, 356, 358, 360–61, 373, 379–80, 387, 389, 396–98, 411–13, 417, 472, 2:539–40, 607, 614, 618, 657, 681, 688–90, 695–97, 702, 710, 731, 735–36, 741, 761–63, 778, 815–16, 820–22, 825, 835, 867–66, 868, 885, 889–93, 897–99. See also James S. Brawley, *The Rowan Story, 1753–1793* (Salisbury, N.C., 1953), 52–55.

35. See nn. 6 and 31–34 above and discussions in the text related to these notes. See also Lefler and Newsome, *North Carolina*, 78, 109–10; Corbitt, *Formation of the North Carolina Counties*, 147, 167, 185; Merrens, *Colonial North Carolina*, 120–24, 142–72; Kay, "Institutional Background to the Regulation," 261–85, 444–81; Kay and Price, "Road Building and Militia

Service," 361–409 passim; Kay, "The Payment of Provincial and Local Taxes in North Carolina, 1748–1771," *William and Mary Quarterly*, 3d ser., 26 (April 1969): 235–39; Daniel B. Thorp, "Doing Business in the Backcountry: Retail Trade in Colonial Rowan County, North Carolina," *William and Mary Quarterly*, 3d ser., 48 (July 1991): 387–407. Merchants who functioned outside the towns, but who owned or managed crucially located country stores, sought to close the interstices and to make the commercial infrastructure more serviceable, as did peddlers, the owners of gristmills and sawmills, and ferrymen and wagoners. The state provided multiple crucial services: building and maintaining the colonies' transportation, communication, military, police, and judicial systems; inspecting crops; maintaining standards of production; warehousing commodities such as tobacco; and advancing credit and increasing the supply of negotiable currency by issuing inspector's notes to farmers on stored crops.

36. James F. Shepherd, "Commodity Exports from the British North American Colonies to Overseas Areas, 1768–1772: Magnitudes and Patterns of Trade," Institute for Research in the Behavioral, Economic, and Management Sciences (Paper No. 258, October 1969), 18–20, 36–38, 48–50, 55. Figures for the increase in the value of exports for each colony are for 1768 and 1772 only and do not take into account annual fluctuations. Shepherd's calculations of export values are based on contemporary estimates of the value of selected commodities in 1768 and 1770. These include most commodities, but the percentage they represent of all exports varies somewhat from market to market. See ibid., 57–58.

37. North Carolina exports had equaled 10 percent of South Carolina's in 1736. See ibid., 6.

38. See nn. 33–34 above and Clifton, "Golden Grains of White," 368; Merrens, *Colonial North Carolina*, 114–15, 120–24, 134–38; Price, "Economic Function and the Growth of American Port Towns," 151–57. See also Charles Richard Sanders, *The Cameron Plantation in Central North Carolina (1776–1973) and Its Founder Richard Bennehan* (Durham, N.C.: Seeman Printery, 1974), 16–17. For the period after the Revolution, see Jean Bradley Anderson, *Piedmont Plantation: The Bennehan-Cameron Family and Lands in North Carolina* (Durham, N.C.: Historic Preservation Society of Durham, 1985).

39. For some further figures concerning colonial exports, see McCusker and Menard, *Economy of British America*, 130, 174, 176.

40. The bulk of North Carolina's oceanic exports, 58 percent by value, went to Great Britain. The second most important market was the West Indies, to which the colony sent 36 percent of its commodities. Southern Europe and the Wine Islands garnered 4 percent of the North Carolina trade, and 2 percent of it went to Ireland. Each of these markets had a different configuration. Thus two enumerated products, naval stores and tobacco, dominated the trade to Great Britain, accounting for 69 and 20 percent respectively. Trade to Ireland, quite small, consisted chiefly of flaxseed (40 percent), bread and flour (20 percent), wood products (18 percent), and wheat (13 percent). Southern Europe and the Wine Islands primarily received wood products (48 percent) and corn (29 percent). Wood products also dominated the list of goods sent to the West Indies (54 percent), followed by corn (24 percent) and barreled beef and pork (14 percent). Shepherd, "Commodity Exports," 19, 28, 37, 48–49.

41. Kay, "Institutional Background to the Regulation," 2:444–45, 458, 479, 491; McCusker and Menard, *Economy of British America*, 10, 297–300. The latter point out that there are two models available for explaining the characteristics and development of farming in early America. The "market model" emphasizes for the South the acquisitive, commercial thrust

of farmers bent on accumulating land and slaves. The "subsistence model," on the other hand, posits that farmers were less interested in profit than subsistence and long-term farm security, that they were suspicious of innovation and avoided risk, and that they therefore did not seek to maximize cash crop production but rather contented themselves with marketing surpluses. Both models appear to have significant explanatory power to help us to understand North Carolina's evolving farming economy and community during the late colonial years. Indeed, nearly two decades ago Marvin L. Michael Kay summarized the North Carolina Regulators' view of their social-economic condition, needs, and grievances in ways that embraced important elements of both models. On reflection, this mind-set also describes the manner in which numerous other small to middling farmers in North Carolina understood themselves. And since the Regulators realistically placed themselves within the social-economic realities of their world, their analysis could bear some attention. Kay wrote:

> While they did not reject the accumulation of land, slaves, and liquid wealth, and normally either owned, rented, or squatted on the land they worked, the Regulators saw no inconsistency in insisting that they were "labourers" and "poor peasants." As laborers, they characterized themselves and their class as the producers in society, and all others were either economic dependents or parasites. Use of the term "peasants" and the stress upon "family" suggest both their sense of community and the permanence of their economic condition. Community and family, joined with deference, were important elements of the conservative ideology of the period. However, the Regulators, in rejecting deference, were free to use their belief that they comprised a community of laboring peasants to develop a radical attack upon the ruling class. And, during this transitional period in Anglo-American history, when liberal capitalistic values were gaining acceptance, the Regulators' petty capitalistic/acquisitive thrust, though in tension with the peasant values, acted as a catalyst to deepen class tensions and further encourage Regulator demands for democracy.

> As a corollary of their view of themselves, Regulators saw their western opponents (and by extension, antagonists throughout the province) as expropriators of the fruits of "the people's" labor—"rich and powerful, . . . designing Monsters in iniquity" who (practicing "every Fraud, and . . . threats and menaces") parasitically were "dependent in their Fortunes, with great Expectations from others. . . ." Such men could be wealthy farmers or persons in other occupations. More often, Regulators saw that most of the wealth accumulated by the affluent in the western counties was gained by multiple economic pursuits: store-owning, the practice of law, land speculation, milling, tavern keeping, and money lending, all in addition to or instead of farming. Consequently, although the Regulators attacked the rich in general, they assailed in particular those they considered nonproductive, especially merchants and lawyers. The Regulators, however, never understood their enemies solely in economic terms. They believed that the wealthy also controlled the political and legal systems and used this control to aggrandize themselves further at the expense of the poor farmers. Thus, much of the Regulators' attack was concentrated upon the affluent county officers.

Thus a willingness among less affluent farmers to pursue petty capitalistic accumulation, including the purchase of slaves to help the farmers produce for a commercial market, did not preclude these same farmers from accepting and acting out some combination of peasant and yeoman values that stressed permanence of status, considerable self-sufficiency, and the production of a diversity of farm products largely for local markets.

If this were true of small to middling farmers, the wealthy planters hardly were inhibited from embracing a commercial ideal of dynamically expanding their lands and slaves. Though they very well may have been, as Gordon S. Wood has recently urged, "social leaders whose property was the source of their personal authority and independence," this did not deter their eager quest after more land and slaves and greater production. If this last does not qualify them as "risktaking entrepreneurs," as Wood correctly argues, they *were* risk-taking planters who willingly involved themselves in multiple economic pursuits.

See Kay, "The North Carolina Regulation," 74–77 (quotation, 74–75); Wood, "Equality and Social Conflict in the American Revolution," *William and Mary Quarterly*, 3d. ser., 51 (October 1994): 703–16 (quotation, 711). The best presentation of the "subsistence model" is in James Henretta, "Families and Farms: Mentalite in Pre-Industrial America," *William and Mary Quarterly*, 3d ser., 35 (January 1978): 3–32. Kay ("Institutional Background to the Regulation," 2:458) estimates that by the sixties Orange County farmers varied by devoting one-sixth to one-half of their productive time producing for the market. See his discussion of the Moravians, who were animated by a communitarian ideal but were commercially oriented, esp. pp. 468–75.

42. In the piedmont, increasing indebtedness also hindered hiring or owning additional labor. See Kay, "Institutional Background to the Regulation," 2:451–58.

43. Sometimes whites illegally enslaved free blacks to satisfy their needs. It is unclear how frequently this occurred, but a number of cases involving such blacks appear in various county court minutes. The extant records undoubtedly do not represent the sum total of such cases. See Beaufort County—Minutes, Appearances, Prosecution, and Trial Docket, Court of Pleas and Quarter Sessions, vol. 1, 1756–61; Chowan County Court Minutes, 1748–72; Craven County Court Minutes, 1750–72; Edgecombe County Court Minutes, 1757–72; New Hanover County Court Minutes, 1748–69, 1771–72; Orange County Court Minutes, 1752–66; all in NCSA. See also Kay and Cary, "A Demographic Analysis," 112–17.

44. See Kay and Cary, "A Demographic Analysis," 103–17. Galenson (*White Servitude*) provides little direct information on servitude in North Carolina. Yet his discussion of the role of the indenture system in the colonial labor market (pp. 117–40) is suggestive. Briefly, he argues that over time slaves took the place of servants in unskilled field work and that planters by the late colonial period sought servants who had the particular skills they needed. He also shows (p. 125) that the overwhelming majority of indentured servants by the late colonial period went to Pennsylvania and the Chesapeake. Incomplete evidence for the late colonial period suggests that incoming servants, particularly English ones, included, as Galenson suggests, numbers of skilled workers. See Merrens, *Colonial North Carolina*, 65. Bassett ("Slavery and Servitude," 75–86) provides the basic laws. It should be stressed, however, that indentured servitude was a status that included not only incoming immigrants but also various persons, including debtors, from within the colony. The status of apprenticeship must also be taken into account when assessing unfree labor. Free blacks were particularly susceptible to all forms of servitude. See Kay and Cary, "A Demographic Analysis," 103–17.

45. A complete list of sources used to obtain slave prices is provided in Table 1.11. See Marvin L. Michael Kay and Lorin Lee Cary, " 'The Planters Suffer Little or Nothing': North

Carolina Compensations for Executed Slaves, 1748–1772," *Science and Society* 11 (Fall 1976): 295, 298–300, 302.

46. For contemporary observations that assume a linkage between economic advancement and slave ownership, see John M. Brickell, *The Natural History of North Carolina With an Account of the Trade, Manners, and Customs of the Christian and Indian Inhabitants . . .* (1737; reprint, Murfreesboro, N.C.: Johnson Publishing Co., 1968), 43, 45, 272, 275–76; Scotus Americanus, "Informations Concerning The Province of North Carolina Addressed to Emigrants from the Highlands and Western Isles of Scotland by an Impartial Hand" (originally published in Glasgow, 1773), in Boyd, *Some Eighteenth-Century Tracts*, 445. The desire to better themselves was a strong impulse among many immigrants. See A. R. Newsome, ed., "Records of Emigrants from England and Scotland to North Carolina, 1774–1775," *North Carolina Historical Review* 11 (April 1934): 129–43. In 1716 John Urmstone, a missionary for the Society for the Propagation of the Gospel in Foreign Parts (SPG), justified his request for funds with which to purchase "3 or 4 Negroes in Guinea" this way: "there is no living without servants [,] there are none to be hired of any colour and none of the black kind to be sold good for anything under 50 or 60 pounds[,] white servants are seldom worth keeping and never stay out the time indented for." Urmstone to SPG, 15 December 1716, quoted in Saunders, *Colonial Records*, 2:260–61. On the developing reliance of the Moravians on slaves for certain jobs—animal care and tavern service, for example— see Philip Africa, "Slaveholding in the Salem Community, 1771–1851," *North Carolina Historical Review* 54 (July 1977): 271–77. On the unpredictability of white workers, see also James Millis to Sir, 25 March 1777, Chatham Furnace Papers, SHC.

47. William Attmore, "Journal of a Tour to North Carolina by William Attmore, 1787," *James Sprunt Historical Publications*, vol. 17, edited by Linda T. Rodman (1922), 44–45. By the late colonial period, there were few Indian slaves in North Carolina. See Winston Sanford, "Indian Slavery in the Carolina Region," *Journal of Negro History* 19 (1934): 431–40, a dated but informative piece.

48. See, e.g., Janet Schaw, *Journal of a Lady of Quality: Being the Narrative of a Journey from Scotland to the West Indies, North Carolina, and Portugal, in the years 1774 to 1776*, edited by Evangeline Walker Andrews and Charles M. Andrews (New Haven: Yale University Press, 1923), 147–48, 184–85, 297; Thomas Pollock to William Andrews, 2 January 1749/50, and Pollock to Malachy Slater, 2 March 1749/50, Pollock Letterbooks, NCSA; Carl Bridenbaugh, *The Colonial Craftsman* (Chicago: University of Chicago Press, 1950), 10, 21–22, 138–41; "Bishop August Gottlieb Spangenburg's Journal of Travels in North Carolina, 1752," in Fries, *Records of the Moravians*, 39. For a 1773 complaint by white pilots about slave competition, see Saunders, *Colonial Records*, 9:803–4.

49. Menard, "Maryland Slave Population," 52–53.

50. Allan Kulikoff, "Tobacco and Slaves: Population, Economy, and Society in Eighteenth-Century Prince George's County, Maryland" (Ph.D. diss., Brandeis University, 1976), 234–41. See also Kulikoff, *Development of Southern Culture in the Chesapeake*, 396–405.

51. See Morgan, "Black Society in the Lowcountry," 97–105. By the 1770s about 18 percent of the male slaves did not do field work; between 1780 and 1799 the figure rose to 30 percent. The trend remained weaker among South Carolina's female slaves, with nine out of ten still working in the fields by the 1790s.

52. James Auld, "The Journal of James Auld, 1765–1770," *Publications of the Southern History Association* 8 (July 1904): 262.

53. Harry Braverman, *Labor and Monopoly Capital: The Degradation of Work in the Twentieth Century* (New York: Monthly Review Press, 1974), 109. See also Richard S. Dunn, "A Tale of Two Plantations: Slave Life in Mesopotamia in Jamaica and Mount Airy in Virginia, 1799 to 1828," *William and Mary Quarterly*, 3d ser., 34 (January 1977): 34. Slaves in late-eighteenth-century Virginia, he suggests, "were doing much the same work as small free farmers elsewhere" in British America. For similar comments, see Menard, "Maryland Slave Population," 36; Wood, *Black Majority*, 95, 105, 196–200; Kulikoff, "Prince George's County, Maryland," 246–52, 257–58.

54. Kay and Cary, "A Demographic Analysis," 103–12; Kay and Price, "Road Building and Militia Service," 380–84.

55. Henretta, "Families and Farms," 3–32; Brickell, *Natural History*, 33; Josiah Quincy, *Memoir of the Life of Josiah Quincy, Jr. of Massachusetts* (Boston, 1825), 121; Scotus Americanus, "Informations Concerning the Province of North Carolina," 446. For a similar distinction, see "Spangenburg Journal," in Fries, *Records of the Moravians*, 1:40–41.

56. Faris to Arthur Dobbs, 7 Feb. 1749/50, Clarke Papers, SHC; Johann David Schoepf, *Travels in the Confederation, [1783–1784]*, translated and edited by Alfred J. Morrison (Philadelphia: William J. Campbell, 1911), 154; Bethabara Diary, 20 September 1773, in Fries, *Records of the Moravians*, 2:780. See also John Ferdinand Dalziel Smyth, *A Tour in the United States of America . . .* , 2 vols. (1784; reprint, New York: Arno Press, 1968), 1:213–17.

57. See, e.g., Edmund S. Morgan, *American Slavery, American Freedom: The Ordeal of Colonial Virginia* (New York: Norton, 1975); Henretta, "Farms and Families," 3–32; C. Vann Woodward, "The Southern Ethic in a Puritan World," *William and Mary Quarterly*, 3d ser., 25 (July 1968): 343–70.

58. William Byrd, *A Journey to the Land of Eden, and Other Papers* (New York, 1928), 59, 76–77, 231–32; John Lawson, *A New Voyage to Carolina* (1709; ed., Hugh Talmage Lefler, Chapel Hill: University of North Carolina Press, 1967), 74–75, 79, 83; Brickell, *Natural History*, 257; John H. Wynne, *A General History of the British Empire in America*, 2 vols. (London: Printed for W. Richardson and L. Urquhart, 1770), 2:290; Richard J. Hooker, ed., *The Carolina Backcountry on the Eve of the Revolution: The Journal and Other Writings of Charles Woodmason, Anglican Itinerant* (Chapel Hill: University of North Carolina Press, 1953), 80–81; "Journal of a French Traveler in the Colonies, 1765," *American Historical Review* 26 (1921): 733, 737; Saunders, *Colonial Records*, 1:516–17, 527, 682–83, 691; Merrens, *Colonial North Carolina*, 33; Edmund Burke, *An Account of the European Settlements in America in Six Parts* (London: Printed for R. and J. Dodsley, 1757), 2:253–54; Schaw, *Journal of a Lady of Quality*, 176–77; Attmore, "Journal of a Tour," 17; Schoepf, *Travels*, 117–18, 120–21, 126–27, 129. For a description of poor whites in the turpentine regions of North Carolina just before the Civil War, see Frederick Law Olmstead, *A Journey in the Seaboard Slave States* (1856; reprint, New York: G. P. Putnam's Sons, 1959), 348–50.

59. Harry J. Carman, ed., *American Husbandry* (1775; New York: Columbia University Press, 1939), 241, 246, 248–50. See also "Spangenburg Journal," in Fries, *Records of the Moravians*, 1:39. Assuming the validity of many of these observations for American agriculture in general rather than for just North Carolina, such practices may be explained more by American conditions than by any unique laxity of enterprise. The relative abundance and availability of land, and a limited labor supply, molded the tendency to use extensive rather than intensive agricultural methods with minimal concern for soil erosion or depletion. Plentiful land and mild climate also facilitated the open-range pasturing of livestock, as did

the growing importance of African slaves familiar with this approach in contrast with Europeans, who were not. See Wood, *Black Majority*, 28–31 and chap. 2.

60. E. P. Thompson, "Time, Work-Discipline, and Industrial Capitalism," *Past and Present*, no. 38 (December 1967): 56–97. See also Kulikoff, "Prince George's County, Maryland," 232–33; Gerald W. Mullin, *Flight and Rebellion: Slave Resistance in Eighteenth-Century Virginia* (New York: Oxford University Press, 1972), 42; George P. Rawick, *From Sunup to Sundown: The Making of the Black Community* (Westport, Conn.: Greenwood, 1972), 128; Eugene D. Genovese, *Roll, Jordon, Roll: The World the Slaves Made* (New York: Vintage Books, 1976), 289–91, 311–12.

61. James Murray to John Murray, 1759, in Murray, *Letters of James Murray, Loyalist*, edited by Nina M. Tiffany (1901; reprint, Boston: Gregg Press, 1972), 78; Penelope Dawson to Samuel Johnston, 17 July 1772, folder 63, M-324, Hayes Collection, SHC, quoted in Alan D. Watson, "Impulse Toward Independence: Resistance and Rebellion Among North Carolina Slaves, 1750–1775," *Journal of Negro History* 63 (Fall 1978): 322. See also Mrs. Burgwyn to Barbara Clark, 26 February 1755, and Murray to Richard Oswald & Co., 19 July 1756, in Murray, *Letters*, 77, 81. Kulikoff ("Prince George's County, Maryland," 255–57) discusses the difficult position of overseers in Prince George's County. It seems likely that the turnover among overseers was just as great in North Carolina and that they faced similar problems with the slaves in their charge, but the evidence is scanty. In five years Auld used three different overseers, and for two years he oversaw operations himself. Auld, "Journal," 261–62.

62. See *North Carolina Gazette*, 15 November 1751, 24 June 1768, 7 April 1775; *Virginia Gazette* (Hunter), 17 October 1755; *South Carolina Gazette*, 27 November–4 December 1755; *Virginia Gazette* (Purdie and Dixon), 7 June 1770, 10 January, 4 July 1771. See also Chapter 5.

63. Masters solved the dilemma posed by the need for punishment and the fear of destroying property by passing laws compensating masters for slaves convicted of capital crimes, for those killed during the supposed commission of a crime, or for runaways or outlawed slaves killed when apprehended. This topic is dealt with in Chapter 3.

64. Charles B. Joyner, *Down by the Riverside: A South Carolina Slave Community* (Urbana: University of Illinois Press, 1984), 43–45, 51, 63; Philip D. Morgan, "Work and Culture: The Task System and the World of Lowcountry Blacks, 1700 to 1880," *William and Mary Quarterly*, 3d ser., 39 (October 1982): 563–99; Morgan, "The Ownership of Property by Slaves in the Mid-Nineteenth Century Low Country," *Journal of Southern History* 49 (August 1983): 399–420.

65. Scotus Americanus, "Informations Concerning the Province of North Carolina," 445; Schaw, *Journal of a Lady of Quality*, 163. Donnie D. Bellamy ("Slavery in Microcosm," 344) concludes that the "task system was the predominant method of labor management in the turpentine industry, as well as with other jobs performed by slaves in Onslow. This system, however, brought best results in the forest businesses. In turpentine operations a prime hand could tap about 100 acres of pine trees." Bellamy deals chiefly with the post-Revolutionary era and neither indicates his sources for this conclusion nor provides a clue as to when tasking might have started.

66. Joyner, *Down by the Riverside*, 58–59.

67. James Millis to Sir, 25 March 1777, Chatham Furnace Papers, SHC. Payments for overwork were commonplace on Maryland and Virginia iron plantations, and the phrasing of Millis's comments implies that they were in North Carolina as well. See Ronald L. Lewis, *Coal, Iron, and Slaves: Industrial Slavery in Maryland and Virginia, 1715–1865*, esp. chap. 4,

" 'The Carrot and the Stick': Discipline and Motivation of Slave Workers," 111–45. See also Genovese, *Roll, Jordan, Roll*, 313–35.

68. Attmore, "Journal of a Tour," 26.

69. Ibid. Philip Morgan does not claim that the independent production of goods and accumulation of property by slaves was necessarily predicated on a task system, but the gist of his work for South Carolina is that garden plots and connected slave economic activities were inexorably linked with the evolution of the task system. Among the "consequences" of the task system, he suggests, were "illicit" trading in goods either stolen from masters or produced by slaves on their "own" time. Logically, the task system would allow slaves to produce more on their garden plots because presumably they would have more time to work them than under gang conditions. Yet the development of significant numbers of garden plots among slaves hinged most importantly on factors other than the presence of the task system. The persistence of slaves in the British West Indies, for example, as well as the desperate need for food and the limited number of small white producers all ensured the extensive and significant cultivation of slave garden plots on these islands well before the task system achieved importance. And no matter what labor system was used, slaves throughout the western hemisphere traded both legally and illicitly. See Morgan, "Work and Culture," esp. pp. 569–75. Michael Craton specifies the prevalence of slave garden plots while the gang system remained the prevailing slave labor technique in the British West Indies. Craton, *Testing the Chains: Resistance to Slavery in the British West Indies* (Ithaca, N.Y.: Cornell University Press, 1983), 50. See also Elsa V. Goveia, *Slave Society in the British Leeward Islands at the End of the Eighteenth Century* (New Haven: Yale University Press, 1965), 119ff, 129–31, 136–38, 160–65, 226–27, 238–39; Michael Craton, *Searching for the Invisible Man: Slaves and Plantation Life in Jamaica* (Cambridge: Harvard University Press, 1978), 56, 161–62. The illegal trade of North Carolina slaves is treated in Chapter 4.

70. Brickell, *Natural History*, 274–75; Schaw, *Journal of a Lady of Quality*, 176–77. Although slaves undoubtedly continued such economic practices, the planters still attempted to place limits on thse activities by passing provincial laws barring slaves from raising horses, cattle, or hogs, or cultivating tobacco. Walter Clark, ed., *The State Records of North Carolina*, 16 vols., numbered 11–26 (Winston and Goldsboro: State of North Carolina, 1895–1906), 23:201, 952. For an example of gardens after the Revolution, see Attmore, "Journal of a Tour," 26.

71. Schoepf, *Travels*, 147.

72. See Watson, "Impulse Toward Independence," 318; Attmore, "Journal of a Tour," 25–26, 44; n. 2, Table 1.8 above.

73. Penelope Dawson to Samuel Johnston, 6 July 1770, folder 70, M-324, Hayes Collection, SHC, quoted in Watson, "Impulse Toward Independence," 318.

74. James Millis to Sir, 25 March 1777, Chatham Furnace Papers, SHC; Sidney W. Mintz and Richard Price, *An Anthropological Approach to the Afro-American Past: A Caribbean Perspective*, Occasional Papers in Social Change, no. 2 (Philadelphia: Institute for the Study of Human Issues, 1976), 13–14; Genovese, *Roll, Jordan, Roll*, 89–91, 133–37, 142–47, 303, 313; Joyner, *Down by the Riverside*, 50–51.

75. Auld, "Journal," 262. Many studies of slavery discuss the delaying tactics slaves used. But see Kulikoff, "Prince George's County, Maryland," 215–16; Mullin, *Flight and Rebellion*, 53–57; and Genovese, *Roll, Jordan, Roll*, 309–27.

76. Schoepf, *Travels*, 117–18. Schoepf could be carried away by his thoughts of the mo-

ment without undue concern for consistency; in another context he berated masters for keeping their slaves hungry and in rags while exacting "steady work" from them. Ibid., 147.

77. David Montgomery, "Workers' Control of Machine Production in the Nineteenth Century," *Labor History* 17 (1976): 485–509, but esp. 489–91, 493–94. For similar practices among coal miners, see Carter Goodrich, *The Miners' Freedom* (1925), quoted in Herbert Gutman and Gregory S. Kealey, eds., *Many Pasts: Readings in American Social History*, 2 vols. (Englewood Cliffs, N.J., 1973), 2:293–316. The general topic of the adjustment of preindustrial work habits in an industrializing society is dealt with imaginatively and perceptively in Gutman, "Work, Culture, and Society in Industrializing America, 1815–1919," *American Historical Review* 78 (1973): 531–88.

78. Olmstead, *Journey in the Seaboard Slave States*, 99.

79. James Millis to Sir, 25 March 1777, Chatham Furnace Papers, SHC. Small quantities of pig iron were shipped to England in 1728–29 and 1734, but such products never attained the importance in North Carolina during the colonial period that they did in the Chesapeake. Although some commercial iron production got under way in the Upper Cape Fear River Valley shortly before the Revolution, the major developments were in the western region of the colony. By late 1770 two furnaces were operating in Orange County, and there were prospects for a third near Salisbury in Rowan County. By 1775 another furnace and foundry, the one discussed in the text, had opened in Chatham County. These small units contributed little to the economic development of the colony in the pre-Revolutionary era. During the period for which records are available, 1768–72, North Carolina exported about a ton and a half of bar iron, valued at £21 sterling, to the West Indies. Lester J. Cappon, "Ironmaking—A Forgotten Industry of North Carolina," *North Carolina Historical Review* 9 (October 1932): 331–33; Shepherd, "Commodity Exports," 49.

80. In Maryland, some masters paid their slaves for Sunday work. Kulikoff, "Prince George's County, Maryland," 233–34. For a lengthy discussion of how annual labor cycles patterned slave life in the South Carolina low country, see Cheryll Ann Cody, "Slave Demography and Family Formation: A Community Study of the Ball Family Plantations, 1720–1896" (Ph.D. diss., University of Minnesota, 1982), 80–143. Genovese (*Roll, Jordon, Roll*, 285–324) discusses how antebellum slaves responded to and helped shape their work routines.

81. Samuel Johnston to Thomas Barker, 10 June 1771, P.C. 40, Hayes Collection, NCSA.

82. Wood, *Black Majority*, 28–62, 95–166 passim; Berlin, "Time, Space, and the Evolution of Afro-American Society, 54–67; Joyner, *Down by the Riverside*, 58–59; Morgan, "Black Society in the Lowcountry," 98–106. For rice cultivation, see n. 88 below.

83. Schaw, *Journal of a Lady of Quality*, 176; Wood, *Black Majority*, 114–24. Many of these points are detailed in Chapters 3, 4, and 8.

84. Elkanah Watson, *Men and Times of the Revolution; or, Memoirs of Elkanah Watson, including His Journals of Travels in Europe and America, 1777–1842*, 2d ed., edited by Winslow C. Watson (New York: Dana and Co., 1857), 43. The method of using songs to express inner feelings and to set a work rhythm, which presumably was what the rowers were doing, recurred in various forms in societies throughout West Africa, and the practice continued wherever blacks congregated in America. For numerous examples of such songs among slaves in the antebellum South, see, e.g., Lawrence Levine, *Black Culture and Black Consciousness: Afro-American Folk Thought from Slavery to Freedom* (New York: Oxford University Press, 1977), 5–13, 19–20, 33, 208–15. For a similar discussion of slave rowing songs in colonial South Carolina, see Wood, *Black Majority*, 202–3.

85. For slave and Native American skills in constructing and manning these dugouts and piraguas, see Wood, *Black Majority*, 123–24, 200–203. Wood (pp. 202–3) quotes a passage from Edward McCrady, *The History of South Carolina under the Royal Government, 1719–1776* (New York, 1899), 516, that talks of slave boat hands' "plaintive, humorous, happy catches which they sang as they bent to the stroke." In this case, the songs supposedly were taught to the boat hands by the slave "naval officer" who was in charge of the boats. If this were the case, the slaves probably learned the creole lyrics to the work songs and perhaps the specific melodies. But the rhythms and harmonies undoubtedly struck familiar chords, as did the technique itself, to the presumably African rowers. Although this describes a possible way the actual songs were passed on from creole to new African generations of slaves, it does not fully explain the provenience of these songs nor the roles of Africans in passing on and adding to the folk repertoire. Also note the juxtaposition of "plaintive" with "humorous, happy catches" in the McCrady quotation. Slave languages are examined in Chapter 6 below.

86. Scotus Americanus, "Informations Concerning the Province of North Carolina," 444; Alec Martin to Col. James Madison [*sic*], Virginia, 21 September 1770, A. L. Brooks Collection, NCSA. For the cyclical pattern of slave labor, see also Dunn, "Two Plantations," 54–57; Kulikoff, "Prince George's County, Maryland," 354–55. Merrens (*Colonial North Carolina*, 123–24) argues that farmers in North Carolina did not raise tobacco and wheat conjointly. There were corn and wheat and corn and tobacco farmers, but no tobacco and wheat farmers. This was true despite both crops being raised in the same general region in the northern tier of counties.

87. Scotus Americanus, "Informations Concerning the Province of North Carolina," 444; Schaw, *Journal of a Lady of Quality*, 163. Scotus Americanus went on to observe that because each bushel of seed yielded 200–400 bushels of corn, "the sowing of 2 or 3 bushels of this grain is as much as any planter can attend to."

88. Elkanah Watson, *Men and Times of the Revolution*, 52; Cody, "Slave Demography and Family Formation," 81–84, 105–10, 121; Merrens, *Colonial North Carolina*, 125–33, 180; Berlin, "Evolution of Afro-American Society," 59–61; Morgan, "Work and Culture," 568–69; Schaw, *Journal of a Lady of Quality*, 194. Wood (*Black Majority*, 56–62) details the widespread knowledge of rice cultivation among some West Africans in South Carolina. See also Joyner, *Down by the Riverside*, 45–50, 57–59; Clifton, "Golden Grains of White," 368–70, 373–77; Clifton, "The Rice Industry in Colonial America," 276–77.

89. Carman, *American Husbandry*, 159–61; Kulikoff, "Prince George's County, Maryland," 233–34, 354. See also Berlin, "Evolution of Afro-American Society," 71.

90. Merrens, *Colonial North Carolina*, 86, 88–89; "Spangenburg Journal," in Fries, *Records of the Moravians*, 1:39.

91. John Bartram, "Diary of a Journey through the Carolinas, Georgia, and Florida," *Transactions of the American Philosophical Society* 33 (1942–44): 16; Schoepf, *Travels*, 141.

92. Schoepf, *Travels*, 141–43. J. F. D. Smyth, who toured the state at roughly the same time, reported a similar figure. Smyth, *Tour*, 2:95. See also Rosser Howard Taylor, *Slaveholding in North Carolina: An Economic View* (Chapel Hill: University of North Carolina Press, 1926), 12–13.

93. William Faris to Arthur Dobbs, 7 February 1749/50, Clarke Papers, SHC.

94. Lee, *Lower Cape Fear*, 151–52 (Moseley's quotation); James Murray to Henry McCulloh, 11 May 1741, in Murray, *Letters*, 64.

95. Merrens, *Colonial North Carolina*, 89–90, 228–29 n.

96. Schoepf, *Travels*, 140–41. Earlier accounts were often copied from yet earlier reports; all stressed that the incision cut into trees, for instance, went no higher than a man could reach. See Burke, *An Account of the European Settlements*, 2:246–47. Taylor (*Slaveholding*, 38–39) describes turpentine gathering during the nineteenth century. It does not appear that any major changes had taken place in the gathering process by that time. There is no way of evaluating the accuracy of Schoepf's production figures, although in 1765 a Frenchman in the region made similar estimates. He reported: "its said that one Negroe will tend 3000 [boxes], which will render about 100 Barls, terpentine." "Journal of a French Traveler in the American Colonies, 1765," *American Historical Review* 26 (July 1971): 726–47 (quotation, p. 726).

97. Carman, *American Husbandry*, 244–45. See also Wynne, *British Empire in America*, 2:296–97; Elkanah Watson, *Men and Times of the Revolution*, 38–39; Schoepf, *Travels*, 141–42.

98. See Brickell, *Natural History*, 275–76. The author of *American Husbandry* cited the example of a South Carolina plantation on the Pee Dee River where ten slaves produced 31 hogsheads of tobacco (not an important crop in this region), 400 bushels of Indian corn and peas, 114 barrels of tar, 4,000 shingles, and numerous skins (presumably cured). The total value amounted to £355.2.3, although in what currency is unclear, or about £33.10.0 per hand. The slaves did all this "besides making corn and other provisions for the family, cattle, poultry . . . and keeping the buildings in repair." Carman, *American Husbandry*, 245–46.

99. Schaw, *Journal of a Lady of Quality*, 185, 297. See also p. 148 for a description of another planter's "rice mills, his indigo works and timber mills." Similarly, see Richard Brownrigg's will of 7 October 1771, in Brownrigg Papers, SHC. His holdings included a fishery, a sawmill, a gristmill, and diverse tools for trades such as cooperage and bricklaying.

100. Carman, *American Husbandry*, 163–64. As the above quotation itself, together with our earlier description of tobacco, make clear, tobacco culture required attention year-round.

101. Thomas Pollock to William Andrews, 2 January 1749/50, and Pollock to Malachy Slater, 2 March 1749/50, Pollock Letterbooks, NCSA. For biographical information on the Pollock family, see Don Higginbotham, ed., *The Papers of James Iredell*, 2 vols. (Raleigh: North Carolina Department of Cultural Resources, Division of Archives and History, 1976), 1:219–20 n. 28. Cody ("Slave Demography and Family Formation," 114–16, 120) details how planting and harvesting schedules affected the work routines of skilled slaves.

102. Articles of agreement, 1 June 1747 and ca. 1748; Thomas Pollock to William Andrews, 22 June 1748, 2 January 1749/50, 17 July 1750; both in Pollock Letterbooks, NCSA. The will of Roger Moore, Brunswick County, shows that four slave carpenters and several apprentices worked at his Brices Creek sawmill. J. Bryan Grimes, *North Carolina Wills and Inventories* (Raleigh, 1912), 310.

103. James Millis to Sir, 25 March 1777, Chatham Furnace Papers, SHC. For an understanding of how comparatively tiny the North Carolina operations were, see Charles B. Dew, "David Ross and the Oxford Iron Works: A Study of Industrial Slavery in the Old South," *William and Mary Quarterly*, 3d ser., 31 (April 1974): 189–224; Lewis, *Coal, Iron, and Slaves*. See also Kulikoff, "Prince George's County, Maryland," 262–63. For slave names, see Chapter 6 of this book. For African facility in iron production, see Philip D. Curtin, Steven Feierman, Leonard Thompson, and Jan Vansina, *African History* (Boston: Little, Brown, 1978), 20–25, 33–35, 251, 266.

104. Higginbotham, *Papers of James Iredell*, 1:137, 178, 188–89, 200, 293, 451–52, including n. 1. See also Schaw, *Journal of a Lady of Quality*, 146–47, 150, 157, 177.

105. Richard Templeman to Charles Pettigrew, 10 January 1780, in Sarah McCulloh Lemon, ed., *The Pettigrew Papers* (Raleigh: North Carolina State Archives, 1971), 1:15. See also Elkanah Watson, *Men and Times of the Revolution*, 43; Schoepf, *Travels*, 153.

106. See Kay and Price, "Road Building and Militia Service," 376–84. In addition, field hands often ran off and, legally or illegally, traveled to other plantations to visit spouses, families, and friends. Except for hiring out, these opportunities are discussed in subsequent chapters.

107. The topic begs for further research. Bellamy ("Slavery in Microcosm," 345) alludes briefly to the practice. See also Sarah L. Hughes, "Slaves for Hire: The Allocation of Slave Labor in Elizabeth City County, Virginia, 1782 to 1810," *William and Mary Quarterly*, 3d ser., 35 (April 1978): 261–86; Joan Rezner Gunderson, "The Double Bonds of Race and Sex: Black and White Women in a Colonial Virginia Parish," *Journal of Southern History* 52 (August 1986): 366, 368–69, 372; Kulikoff, *Development of Southern Culture in the Chesapeake*, 139–40, 343, 405–7, 431; Joyner, *Down by the Riverside*, 86–88.

108. The earnings are listed in Alan D. Watson, "Society and Economy in Colonial Edgecombe County," *North Carolina Historical Review* 50 (Summer 1973): 248. See also Pasquotank County Court Minutes, 28 December 1756; Beaufort County Court Minutes, June 1757, September 1758; all in NCSA.

109. Samuel Johnston Sr. to Charles Eliot, 8 December 1755, Charles E. Johnston Collection, NCSA.

110. James Millis to Sir, 25 March 1777, Chatham Furnace Papers, SHC. Aside from the evidence from the ironworks, the information we have located does not sustain the conclusion—drawn by both Gunderson and Hughes about Virginia—that female slaves were more likely to be hired out than males. Gunderson, "Double Bonds of Race and Sex," 368; Hughes, "Slaves for Hire," 268–72. Except for the Chatham ironworks, the overwhelming majority of the examples we located were of males. In those instances where women were mentioned, the rates received for their outside employment were substantially lower than those for men. One black female, hired out for over a year in the early 1760s, earned 8 pence a day, or £12 per year. William Luten Ledger, 17 January 1764, NCSA. Another, her name unspecified, earned only 4 pence a day in 1765. Luten Ledger, July 1765, NCSA. "Negro Fleva" pulled in but 4 pence a day for a year of labor in the mid-1770s, or £6 for the entire year. Byrnes Account Book, 11 May 1775, NCSA. White women were not treated more favorably than slave women when it came to wages. Flors Todd earned a mere 3 pence a day for a year's hire, or £4.10.0 per year (compared to her husband's 1 shilling per day, or £18.5.0 per year). Bertie Individual Accounts, 8, 20 April 1764, NCSA. A "months hire" of an unspecified white man's "daughter" brought in 6 shillings, a little more than 2 pence per day. Bertie Individual Accounts, 1760, NCSA. In Maryland between 1747 and 1779, males represented 69 percent of those hired out, women 20 percent, and children 10 percent. See Kulikoff, *Development of Southern Culture in the Chesapeake*, 407. Joyner (*Down by the Riverside*, 86–88) implies that this was the case in antebellum South Carolina as well.

111. The cost of hiring Murray's slaves varied—£9.7.0 proclamation per year for Glasgow and £8.13.0 per year for Kelso and Berwick—probably reflecting differing skills or ages, although no information on these points is contained in the contract. Murray to James Hazel, 28 February 1743/44, in Murray, *Letters*, 67–69. Hiring-out costs rose with the passage of time, but it is doubtful that they did so as rapidly as slave sale prices.

112. The statistics concerning wages were obtained from Clark, *State Records*, 22:406, 416,

420, 450, 454, 456–57, 474, 498–99, and the following sources in the NCSA: Bertie County Individual Accounts, 1718–99; Byrnes Account Book, 1757–83 (Bladen County); William Luten Ledger, 1764–87; Edenton (Chowan County) Wills, Inventories, Sales; and Settlement of Estates, vols. 1–11, Carteret County Records. See Kay and Price, "Road Building and Militia Service," 402–3.

113. Schoepf, *Travels*, 147–48. On hiring auctions as social events, see Watson, "Society and Economy," 254.

114. The anxieties experienced by slaves as the result of being hired out are further discussed in Chapter 5, which deals with runaways. Severe reactions were less likely to occur among the numerous slaves who were hired out for short periods of time—from one to three days. Still, even such hires could disrupt an established routine and cause considerable anxiety, especially among older slaves. See also Kulikoff, *Development of Southern Culture in the Chesapeake*, 406.

115. See Hughes, "Slaves for Hire," esp. 283–86.

CHAPTER 2

1. In other studies we have identified members of the upper class for sample counties in North Carolina's different regions by estimating how personal property, especially slaves, was distributed among North Carolina's property owners. Because slave-ownership patterns varied greatly among counties and regions, we had to develop a sliding scale to determine who comprised the upper, middling, and lower classes for each county. This could be done because a small group of men owned a disproportionate share of the slaves in *all* regions and in *each* county whatever the variation in wealth totals and distributive patterns. Relating these data and findings with those concerning office holding, we have found a precise correlation between a person's wealth and the political authority and offices he was invested with.

For detailed analyses and full documentation, see Marvin L. Michael Kay, "The North Carolina Regulation, 1766–1776: A Class Conflict," in *The American Revolution: Explorations in the History of American Radicalism*, edited by Alfred F. Young (De Kalb: Northern Illinois University Press, 1976), 79–83; Kay and William S. Price Jr., " 'To Ride the Wood Mare': Road Building and Militia Service in Colonial North Carolina, 1740–1775," *North Carolina Historical Review* 57 (October 1980): 361–409 passim; Kay and Lorin Lee Cary, " 'The Planters Suffer Little or Nothing': North Carolina Compensations for Executed Slaves, 1748–1772," *Science and Society* 11 (Fall 1976): 302–6; Kay and Cary, "Class, Mobility, and Conflict in North Carolina on the Eve of the Revolution," in *The Southern Experience in the American Revolution*, edited by Jeffrey J. Crow and Larry E. Tise, 109–51 (Chapel Hill: University of North Carolina Press, 1978).

2. Several works on British history influenced this analysis. Most helpful were E. P. Thompson, "Patrician Society, Plebian Culture," *Journal of Social History* 17 (Summer 1974): 382–405; Thompson, "The Moral Economy of the English Crowd in the Eighteenth Century," *Past and Present*, no. 50 (February 1971): 76–136; Douglas Hay, Peter Linebaugh, John G. Rule, E. P. Thompson, and Cal Winslow, *Albion's Fatal Tree: Crime and Society in Eighteenth-Century England* (London: Allen Lane, 1975), esp. Hay, "Property, Authority, and the Criminal Law," 17–63; and Thompson, *Whigs and Hunters: The Origin of the Black Act* (London: Allen Lane, 1975), esp. 21–24, 219–69.

For the theory of balanced government (mixed constitution) and its applications in the colonies and the United States, see J. R. Pole, "Historians and the Problems of Early American Democracy," *American Historical Review* 167 (1962): 622–46; Bernard Bailyn, *The Ideological Origins of the American Revolution* (Cambridge: Harvard University Press, 1967), esp. 70–75; Gordon S. Wood, *The Creation of the American Republic, 1776–1787* (Chapel Hill: University of North Carolina Press, 1969), esp. 11, 18–20, 197–255.

Rhys Isaac distinguishes between patriarchy and paternalism, describing the latter as a late eighteenth-century sentimentalizing of the former. We can ignore his semantic distinction without doing violence to the substance of his analysis and still argue that no other scholar discusses planter "paternalism" (patriarchy) with greater adroitness and sophistication. Deftly weaving together well-chosen details with a highly intelligent conceptual analysis, Isaac examines why and how Virginia ceased to be a society determined by a hierarchical web of social-political relationships that were traditionally defined by a set of patriarchal (paternalistic) symbols—interlocking the authority of the king with that of individual heads of households. The Revolution replaced this with a society based on social and political contracts that stressed individual rights, needs, and aspirations. See Isaac, *The Transformation of Virginia, 1740–1790* (Chapel Hill: University of North Carolina Press, 1982) and "Preachers and Patriots: Popular Culture and the Revolution in Virginia," in Young, *The American Revolution*, 127–56.

3. William L. Saunders, ed., *The Colonial Records of North Carolina*, 10 vols. (Raleigh: State of North Carolina, 1886–90), 8:230–31; Kay, "The North Carolina Regulation," 92–93.

4. John Locke, "The Second Treatise of Government," sections 85, 94, in *Two Treatises of Government. . . .* (London, 1690), as quoted in Hay et al., *Albion's Fatal Tree*, 18–19.

5. Thompson, "Patrician Society, Plebeian Culture," 387–90.

6. Ibid., 390.

7. Lord Shaftesbury quoted in Hay, "Property, Authority, and the Criminal Law," in Hay et al., *Albion's Fatal Tree*, 19.

8. Ibid., 11, 13.

9. We have pursued these ideas in other works (cited below) and are indebted both to authors who have conceptualized the problem as we do and to scholars who have contributed analyses of planter treatment of slaves that are rich in detail and understanding. See especially the works of E. P. Thompson and Douglas Hay listed in n. 2 above. See also Jeffrey Kaplow, *The Names of Kings: The Parisian Laboring Poor in the Eighteenth Century* (New York: Basic Books, 1972).

For the use of legal terror against slaves in Virginia, South Carolina, and North Carolina, see Philip J. Schwarz, *Twice Condemned: Slaves and the Criminal Laws of Virginia, 1705–1865* (Baton Rouge: Louisiana State University Press, 1988), esp. 3–58; Darrett B. Rutman and Anita H. Rutman, *A Place in Time: Middlesex County, Virginia, 1650–1750* (New York: Norton, 1984), 170–79; Peter H. Wood, *Black Majority: Negroes in Colonial South Carolina from 1670 through the Stono Rebellion* (New York: Knopf, 1974), 271–84, 308–26; Donna J. Spindel, *Crime and Society in North Carolina, 1663–1776* (Baton Rouge: Louisiana State University Press, 1989), 20, 23–24, 54–55, 60–62, 65–66, 75–76, 133–37; Jeffrey J. Crow, *The Black Experience in Revolutionary North Carolina* (Raleigh: North Carolina Department of Cultural Resources, Division of Archives and History, 1977), 19–29; Don Higginbotham and William S. Price Jr., "Was It Murder for a White Man to Kill a Slave? Chief Justice Martin Howard Condemns the Peculiar Institution in North Carolina," *William and Mary Quar-*

terly, 3d ser., 36 (October 1979): 593–601; Marvin L. Michael Kay and Lorin Lee Cary, "Slave Runaways in Colonial North Carolina, 1748–1775," *North Carolina Historical Review* 63 (January 1986): 1–39; Kay and Cary, " 'They Are Indeed the Constant Plague of Their Tyrants': Slave Defense of a Moral Economy in Colonial North Carolina, 1748–1772," *Slavery and Abolition* 6, no. 3 (December 1985): 37–56; Kay and Cary, "North Carolina Compensations for Executed Slaves."

10. The quotations are from Kay, "The North Carolina Regulation," 75. For attempts to describe and explain the political commitments of farmers in the province's different regions, see ibid., 73–123; Jeffrey J. Crow, "Liberty Men and Loyalists: Disorder and Disaffection in the North Carolina Backcountry," in *An Uncivil War: The Southern Backcountry during the American Revolution*, edited by Ronald Hoffman, Thad W. Tate, and Peter J. Albert (Charlottesville: University Press of Virginia, 1985): 125–36; Norris W. Preyer, *Hezekiah Alexander and the Revolution in the Backcountry* (Charlotte, N.C.: Heritage Printers, 1987), 49–56.

11. Isaac, *Transformation of Virginia*, 320–21.

12. Kay, "The North Carolina Regulation," 83–84.

13. See, e.g., Gerald W. Mullin, *Flight and Rebellion: Slave Resistance in Eighteenth-Century Virginia* (New York: Oxford University Press, 1972), 3–82 passim; Darrett B. Rutman and Anita H. Rutman, *A Place in Time: Explicatus* (New York: Norton, 1984), 97–103; Rutman and Rutman, *Middlesex County, Virginia*, 170–79. Isaac (*Transformation of Virginia*, esp. 25, 299–357) refreshingly does not stress that slave culture resulted significantly from the actions of such masters.

14. This comment is not meant to be a direct criticism of Eugene Genovese's writings, for he has never argued that such a planter-slave relationship existed during the colonial years. He explicitly places it in the antebellum period. Yet Herbert Gutman's challenge of Genovese's contention that slaves internalized a modified version of planter paternalist ideology, even for these later years, remains persuasive to us. If Gutman's arguments, in the main, are convincing, he, too, errs in not questioning Genovese's analysis of the provenience of paternalism. As we have argued above, the origins and very likely the most powerful manifestations of planter paternalism occurred during the colonial years, having been brought over by immigrants as part of their English cultural baggage. We are hardly the first to point this out. A number of scholars on both sides of the Atlantic describe planter paternalism in this way, and it is surprising that Genovese and Gutman ignore this.

Even more puzzling is Allan Gallay's more recent analysis: "The Origins of Slaveholders' Paternalism: George Whitefield, the Bryan Family, and the Great Awakening in the South," *Journal of Southern History* 53 (August 1987): 369–94. He traces the roots of the planters' attempts to use paternalism as "a basis for bargaining" between slaves and slaveowners back to the evangelical planters in South Carolina during the Great Awakening of the 1730s, 1740s, and 1750s. Closely following Genovese's conceptual lead in arguing this, Gallay ignores that Genovese, with a proper sense of time, had intricately woven slaves with hegemonic masters into an organic relationship. Even less defensible, Gallay presents little documentary support for his incorporation of Genovese's hypothesis while he disregards a body of recent scholarship that traces the roots of planter paternalism to colonial sources other than those provided by evangelicals. These studies, whether concerned with slavery or not, analyze eighteenth-century paternalism essentially within the parameters set by the ways in which the elite achieved, used, and justified their wealth, status, and power. Rhys Isaac (*Transfor-*

mation of Virginia) astutely and exhaustively develops this for Virginia's ruling Anglican gentry.

Ignoring this scholarship and the problems it raises for his analysis, Gallay builds on his premise by arguing: "Christianity did not create the perfectly behaved slaves for which their masters had hoped, but it did provide a basis for bargaining between the slaveholder and the enslaved. By accepting these privileges, which later bondspeople assumed were their rights, slaves confirmed their masters' claim to be moral Christian planters. This was the first step in the development of a paternalistic relationship." Gallay, "Origins of Slaveholders' Paternalism," 394.

The inability of Gallay even to begin to exemplify or to explain satisfactorily why slaves chose to establish an organic relationship with their owners that was essentially built on the slaveowners' sense and justification of reality is discussed further in Chapter 8. Yet it should be reiterated here that, in rejecting Gallay's sense of the provenience of planter paternalism, we have not rejected the significance of the phenomenon itself. See n. 2 above and Eugene D. Genovese, *Roll, Jordan, Roll: The World the Slaves Made* (New York: Vintage Books, 1973), 3–7, 30–31, 89–93, 125, 132–33, 143, 148, 625, 658–60; Herbert Gutman, *The Black Family in Slavery and Freedom, 1750–1925* (New York: Vintage Books, 1977), 309–26. See also Gerald W. Mullin, "Obeah and Christianity: In Four Plantation Colonies in the Old British Empire" (paper, 1974); Mullin, *Flight and Rebellion*, 4–33; Michael Mullin, "British Caribbean and North American Slaves in an Era of War and Revolution, 1775–1807," in *The Southern Experience in the American Revolution*, edited by Jeffrey J. Crow and Larry E. Tise, 235–67 (Chapel Hill: University of North Carolina Press, 1978); Rutman and Rutman, *Middlesex County, Virginia*, 170–79; Marvin L. Michael Kay and Lorin Lee Cary, "Marriage and the Family among North Carolina Slaves, 1748–1775," in *The American Family: Historical Perspectives*, edited by Jean E. Hunter and Paul T. Mason, (Pittsburgh: Duquesne University Press, 1990), 58–74, but esp. 58–61.

Isaac's *Transformation of Virginia* is essential to comprehend the complementary roles of "paternalism" (patriarchy) and deference in colonial Virginia. See also in Young, *The American Revolution*: Ronald Hoffman, "The 'Disaffected' in the Revolutionary South," esp. 275–76; Dirk Hoerder, "Boston Leaders and Boston Crowds, 1765–1776," 235–71; Kay, "The North Carolina Regulation," esp. 73–77. Also helpful are Rowland Berthoff and John M. Murrin, "Feudalism, Communalism, and the Yeoman Freeholder: The American Revolution Considered as a Social Accident," in *Essays on the American Revolution*, edited by Stephen G. Kurtz and James H. Hutson, 256–88 (New York: Norton, 1973); Edward Countryman, *The American Revolution and Political Society in New York, 1760–1790* (Baltimore: Johns Hopkins University Press, 1981), 18–19, 21, 47, 114–15; Crow, "Liberty Men and Loyalists," esp. 125–29; Pole, "Problems of Early American Democracy," 622–46.

15. Isaac, *Transformation of Virginia*, 320–21.

16. For the application of Gramsci's concept of cultural hegemony to problems in American history, see T. Jackson Lears, "The Concept of Cultural Hegemony: Problems and Possibilities," and John Patrick Diggins, "Comrades and Citizens: New Mythologies in American Historiography," both in *American Historical Review* 90 (1985): 567–93, 614–38, respectively; contributions by Leon Fink, Jackson Lears, John P. Diggins, George Lipsitz, Mari Jo Buhle, and Paul Buhle to "A Round Table: Labor, Historical Pessimism, and Hegemony," *Journal of American History* 75 (1988): 115–61; Michael Kazin, "The Historian as Populist," *New York Review of Books*, 12 May 1988, 48–50.

17. Kay and Price, "Road Building and Militia Service," 361–409; Kay and Cary, "Slave Defense of a Moral Economy," 37–56, "Slave Runaways," 1–39, and "North Carolina Compensations for Executed Slaves," 288–306.

18. Higginbotham and Price, "Martin Howard Condemns the Peculiar Institution," 593–601.

19. Ibid., 598–99. The Crown was aware of the brutal treatment of "Negroes" (and Indians too). As early as 1730 in its instructions to the first royal governor, George Burrington, it admonished him to see that a law was passed ensuring "that the wilful killing of Indians and Negroes may be punished with death and that a fit penalty be imposed for the maiming of them." Saunders, *Colonial Records*, 3:112.

20. See Chapter 1 and Marvin L. Michael Kay and Lorin Lee Cary, "A Demographic Analysis of Colonial North Carolina with Special Emphasis upon the Slave and Black Populations," in *Black Americans in North Carolina and the South*, edited by Jeffrey J. Crow and Flora J. Hatley (Chapel Hill: University of North Carolina Press, 1984), 101–2; Philip D. Morgan, "Colonial South Carolina Runaways: Their Significance for Slave Culture," *Slavery and Abolition* 6 (1985): 59–61; Betty Wood, *Slavery in Colonial Georgia, 1730–1775* (Athens: University of Georgia Press, 1984), 104–5.

21. See Chapter 6.

22. See n. 1 above.

23. Especially helpful in describing the labor characteristics of the different types of producers is Martin A. Kilian and E. Lynn Tatom's "Marx, Hegel, and the Marxian of the Master Class: Eugene D. Genovese on Slavery," *Journal of Negro History* 66 (Fall 1981): 189–208.

24. The basic laws dealing with servitude and slavery passed in 1715, 1741, 1753, 1758, and 1764. See Walter Clark, ed., *The State Records of North Carolina*, 16 vols., numbered 11–26 (Winston and Goldsboro: State of North Carolina, 1895–1906), 23:62–66, 191–204, 388–90, 488–89, 656. Recent works on the legal status of slaves include Crow, *Black Experience*, esp. 1–33; William M. Wiecek, "The Statutory Law of Slavery and Race in the Thirteen Mainland Colonies of British America," *William and Mary Quarterly*, 3d. ser., 34 (April 1977): 258–80; Spindel, *Crime and Society*, 20, 23–24, 112–14, 133–34; Alan D. Watson, "North Carolina Slave Courts, 1715–1785," *North Carolina Historical Review* 60 (January 1983): 24–36; Kay and Cary, "North Carolina Compensations for Executed Slaves," 288–306 passim.

25. Major road legislation for North Carolina during the period 1741–73 may be found in Clark, *State Records*, 23:161–62, 214–15, 220–29, 238–39, 288, 367–69, 384–85, 417–19, 447–51, 489–90, 533, 607–711, 814, 851–52, 908–11, 920, 25:263–64, 330, 399–401, 463, 474–75, 478–79, 487–89. For the county administration of roads, bridges, and ferries, see the following county court minutes and road papers, all in the North Carolina State Archives, Raleigh (hereafter cited as NCSA): Bertie County—Road Papers, 1734–75; County Court Minutes, 1724–43, 1758–69, 1767–72; Chowan County—Overseers of Roads, 1725–75; Miscellaneous Court Papers; Road Papers, 1717–75; Pasquotank County—Road Papers, 1734–75; County Court Minutes, 1738–78; Perquimans County—Road Papers, 1711–75; Hyde County—Road Papers, 1767–75; Craven County—Road Papers, 1767–75; County Court Minutes, 1750–75; New Hanover County—County Court Minutes, 1738–69, 1771–75; Edgecombe County—Road Papers, 1761–75; County Court Minutes, 1757–75; Anson County—County Court Minutes, 1771–75; Orange County—County Court Minutes, 1752–66; Rowan County—Roads, 1757–75; County Court Minutes, 1753–72. See also Alan D. Watson, "Regulation and Administration of Roads and Bridges in Colonial Eastern North Carolina," *North Carolina*

Historical Review 44 (October 1968): 399–417; Kay and Price, "Road Building and Militia Service," esp. 379–91.

26. For provincial legislation concerning the North Carolina militia, see Clark, *State Records*, 23:29–31, 151, 244–47, 330–31, 518–22, 535, 585, 596–601, 760–65, 781–83, 787–88, 940–45, 25:267, 334–37, 393, 496, 511. See also E. Milton Wheeler, "Development and Organization of the North Carolina Militia," *North Carolina Historical Review* 41 (July 1964): 307–23; Kay and Price, "Road Building and Militia Service," 384–91.

27. Kay and Price, "Road Building and Militia Service," 384.

28. Robert A. Becker argues that "North Carolina's tax system was not only the most regressive in the South but also the least efficient and most corrupt." Becker, "Revolution and Reform: An Interpretation of Southern Taxation, 1763 to 1783," *William and Mary Quarterly*, 3d. ser., 32 (July 1975): 419–21. See also Marvin L. Michael Kay, "The Payment of Provincial and Local Taxes in North Carolina, 1748–1771," *William and Mary Quarterly*, 3d ser., 26 (April 1969): 218–40; Kay and Price, "Road Building and Militia Service," 390–92; R. R. Palmer, *The Age of the Democratic Revolution: The Challenge*, 2 vols. (Princeton, N.J.: Princeton University Press, 1959–64), 1:153–81. Palmer's estimates of American tax levels are far too low, but his listings of European tax levels are points of departure for a comparative analysis. See as well Robert A. Becker, *Revolution, Reform, and the Politics of American Taxation* (Baton Rouge: Louisiana State University Press, 1980), 94–99; H. James Henderson, "Taxation and Political Culture: Massachusetts and Virginia," *William and Mary Quarterly*, 3d ser., 47 (January 1990): 90–101.

29. Kay and Cary, "North Carolina Compensations for Executed Slaves." See below for a more extensive discussion.

30. For North Carolina's laws, see Clark, *State Records*, 23:62–66, 191–204, 388–90, 488–89, 656. Two thousand is a rough estimate of the black population for 1715 extrapolated from a contemporary estimate of 1,000 for 1705. See Chapter 1 and Saunders, *Colonial Records*, 1:720, 722, 2:xvii, 419; Evarts B. Greene and Virginia C. Harrington, *American Population before the Federal Census of 1790* (New York: Columbia University Press, 1932), 156. For analyses of slave codes, see Schwarz, *Twice Condemned*, 17–23; Spindel, *Crime and Society*, 20, 23–24, 54–55, 60–62, 65–66, 133–35; Watson, "North Carolina Slave Courts," 25–28; Crow, *Black Experience*, 19–29; Wood, *Black Majority*, 271–84, 323–25; Kay and Cary, "North Carolina Compensations for Executed Slaves," 290–94.

31. For the clauses in the laws of 1715 and 1741 that specify who could not be enslaved, see Clark, *State Records*, 23:62–67, 191–204 passim. The quotation from the law of 1741 is on p. 196. For the statutory clauses in the law of 1715 that prevented servants from being enslaved for life and specified their rights and duties, see ibid., 23:63. Enslavement for life probably existed in North Carolina during its first settlements in the 1660s because the slaves and their owners came from Virgina, where such slavery existed. Later in this chapter we will discuss how North Carolina denied, by law and in practice, that conversion to Christianity had any affect on the status of a slave. See above and n. 54.

The language regarding the inheritance of status through the mother is most explicit when discussing servants who had illegitimate children. Illegitimate mulatto or part–Native American children of white servant women were to become servants until thirty-one years of age. Ibid., 23:195. For a supporting analysis that practice closely followed the law, see Kay and Cary, "A Demographic Analysis," 110–12.

32. Clark, *State Records*, 23:62–66, 191–204.

33. Ibid., 62–66.

34. Ibid.

35. Ibid. The law specified that, unless "Confinement" were required, the "Labour of such Servant or Slave shall satisfy for his Imprisonment." A 1720 "Act in Explanation" clarified this point for slaves, stating that although slave courts had been granted the power to imprison slaves in lieu of corporal punishment, it had been determined that "the imprisoning [of] a Slave is an apparent Damage and Loss to the Masters" and that corporal punishments therefore "shall not be Construed to extend or include Imprisonment of the Offender." Clark, *State Records*, 23:64, 25:169–70.

36. Clark, *State Records*, 23:114.

37. Ibid., 64.

38. This belief in North Carolina's supposed leniency is apparent in various secondary works, although the emphasis is at times on the antebellum era. See, e.g., Rosser Howard Taylor, "Humanizing the Slave Code of North Carolina," *North Carolina Historical Review* 2 (July 1925): 328–29; Ernest James Clark Jr., "Aspects of the North Carolina Slave Code, 1715–1860," *North Carolina Historical Review* 39 (Spring 1962): 148–64; Alan D. Watson, "Impulse Toward Independence: Resistance and Rebellion among North Carolina Slaves, 1750–1775," *Journal of Negro History* 63 (October 1978): 318. Hugh T. Lefler and William S. Powell, in *Colonial North Carolina* (New York: Scribner's, 1973), 181, straddle the issue. Donna Spindel, in *Crime and Society*, seems to have left the hoary myth behind.

39. Clark, *State Records*, 23:191–204.

40. Ibid. A 1722 South Carolina law provided "death as a felon" for stealing slaves and taking them out of the colony. Wood, *Black Majority*, 242.

41. Clark, *State Records*, 23:64, 201–2.

42. See, e.g., Carteret County Court Minutes, 6 December 1757; Orange County Court Minutes, August 1760; Rowan County Court Minutes, July 1755, 20 January 1756, February 1769, 4 February 1772; all in NCSA. Not all provisions of the law relating to mobility of slaves, on the other hand, were adhered to consistently, for that could have disrupted the efficient working of the labor system.

43. On sadistic killings, see Chapters 3–4. On rewards, see *North Carolina Magazine*, 4–11 January 1765; *North Carolina Gazette*, 2 September 1774, 6 October, 22 December 1775. See also Lathan Algerna Windley, "A Profile of Runaway Slaves in Virginia and South Carolina from 1730 through 1787" (Ph.D. diss., University of Iowa, 1974), 49.

44. Clark, *State Records*, 23:65.

45. Ibid., 203.

46. Ibid., 65.

47. Ibid., 107.

48. Ibid., 203–4.

49. Ibid., 106–7.

50. Ibid., 106. See also Kay, "Payment of Provincial and Local Taxes," 220–21; Kay and Price, "Road Building and Militia Service," 391–92; Kay and Cary, "A Demographic Analysis," 103–17.

51. Clark, *State Records*, 23:65.

52. Ibid., 160.

53. Ibid., 23:65, 203, 25:134–35.

54. Saunders, *Colonial Records*, 1:86, 858–59, 2:332–33; John S. Bassett, "Slavery and Servi-

tude in the Colony of North Carolina," *Johns Hopkins University Studies in Historical and Political Science*, ser. 14 (1896), 56; Brickell, *Natural History*, 274. In adjoining South Carolina and Virginia, Anglican ministers reported that some slaves believed baptism would lead to freedom. See Albert J. Raboteau, *Slave Religion: The Invisible Institution in the Antebellum South* (New York: Oxford University Press, 1978), 123–24, 127. Although, as suggested above, some North Carolina slaveowners shared these sentiments, the only instances in which being a Christian actually led to freedom for slaves were those that involved free-born blacks who were citizens of a Christian nation but who had been captured and sold into slavery. One such case occurred in Craven County in 1770. Patrice "of the Island of Curracoa" had been "detained on Board a Schooner belonging to Phillemon Covington as a slave." Questioned by Craven's justices of the peace, Patrice proved that he was "a Free Born Spaniard" and thus "justly Intitled to freedom." The court unanimously ordered him "Immediately discharged and set at Liberty." When Covington's lawyer petitioned to appeal the ruling, the justices, again unanimously, ruled "that no appeal lies in this case and . . . therefore rejected" the motion. Craven County Court Minutes, June 1770, NCSA. It is less clear what happened to Joseph Derendred. In May 1752 he petitioned the Craven County Court, arguing that he was "a Freeborn Subject of the King of Portugal," had been "Imported into this Province By George Roberts Mariner" in about 1731 and "Sold here as a Slave," and was "still held and Detained as a Slave by Mrs. Mary Moore of this County Contrary to the Laws and Customs of" North Carolina. What prompted him to sue for his freedom after twenty years as a slave is not divulged in the sparse court minutes. After hearing arguments from Derendred's unnamed "Friend" and Mrs. Moore's counsel, the justices said that they would hand down a ruling in August. No further mention of the case appears in the extant records. Craven County Court Minutes, May 1752, NCSA.

55. Saunders, *Colonial Records*, 3:112, 6:265, 995–96; Bassett, "Slavery and Servitude," 49. For a general discussion of the hardships confronting the Anglican clergy in the colonies, see Raboteau, *Slave Religion*, 104–7. On planter concern about lost labor time, see Wood, *Black Majority*, 134 n. 12, 135, 138–39; Raboteau, *Slave Religion*, 99–100. These considerations are discussed and documented at greater length in Chapter 8.

56. Clark, *State Records*, 23:389.

57. Ibid., 201.

58. Ibid., 388–89. According to the 1741 act, the weapons of uncertificated slaves who had been apprehended became the property of whoever discovered them. Slave offenders were to be taken before a constable, given twenty lashes, and sent home. Their masters then had to pay the discoverer of the offense a reward. Ibid., 23:201.

The county courts authorized the arming of slaves. The few certificates issued in some county courts, within the restricted limits of the 1753 act, may mean that in practice it was permitted only under extenuating circumstances. The Bertie County Court, for instance, granted three certificates in 1758, but the only other certificates recorded were in 1766. Justices in Craven issued but three licenses, in two cases to female owners. Grace Mann explained that she was "sole and without any help," and Elizabeth Harrold, a widow, petitioned on the grounds of the "absolute necessity for one of her Negroes to Hunt & Carry a gun to kill or Destroy Varmits." In Chowan three owners received gun certificates in 1768 and 1771. And in Pasquotank only one license for a slave "to carry a gun" appears in the records. On the other hand, the limited number of certificates may simply mean that masters often chose to ignore the law, arming such slaves as they pleased.

The only county in which more than a few scattered references appear is New Hanover, where the colony's slaves constituted the highest proportion of the population and were most densely settled and most heavily concentrated on large plantations. There, between 1760 and 1772, the owners of twenty-three different slaves secured licenses permitting their slaves to be armed. The process here appears to have been regarded as a normal one, at least for the well-to-do. Most of the apparently self-confident owners who sought licenses played prominent roles in county and provincial politics and were among the leading slaveowners in the county—Frederick Gregg, Samuel Ashe, John Rutherford, Benjamin Herron, Louis De Rossett, John Ashe, James Moore, and Cornelius Harnet among them. The confidence of these wealthy slaveholders to handle this situation is further suggested by the fact that in September 1767, on the same day that three different masters received gun certificates, the clerk of court recorded: "The Court being inform'd that upwards of Twenty runaway Slaves in a body arm'd and are now in this County Order'd that the Sheriff do immediately raise the power of the County not by less than Thirty Men well Arm'd to go in pursuit of the said runaway Slaves and that the said Sheriff be impowered to Shoot to kill & destroy all such of the said runaway Slaves as shall not Surrender themselves."

All of these examples may be found in the NCSA: Bertie County Court Minutes, 24 October 1758, September 1766; Craven County Court Minutes, 13 May 1755, February 1763, October 1764; Chowan County Court Minutes, September 1768, June 1771; Pasquotank County Court Minutes, 16 June 1769; New Hanover County Court Minutes, September, 2 December 1760, 3 May 1761, 4 September, 4 December 1764, 3 September 1765, 1 September 1767, April, July 1768, 3 January, 4 April 1769, 7 April, 7 July, 6 October 1772.

59. Donald R. Lennon and Ida Brooks Kellam, eds., *The Wilmington Town Book, 1743–1778* (Raleigh: North Carolina Department of Cultural Resources, Division of Archives and History, 1973), 168.

60. Ibid., 187. Ten years later town commissioners reset the curfew at 9 P.M. between 20 March and 22 September and at 10 P.M. during the rest of the year. Ibid., 238.

61. Ibid., 205.

62. Ibid., 153–213.

CHAPTER 3

1. Don Higginbotham and William S. Price Jr., "Was It Murder for a White Man to Kill a Slave? Chief Justice Martin Howard Condemns the Peculiar Institution in North Carolina," *William and Mary Quarterly*, 3d ser., 36 (October 1979): 593–601 (quotation, p. 599).

2. The law of 1715 stipulated that the special slave court was to consist of three justices of the precinct court and four freeholders, who were also slaveholders, all from the precinct where the crime was committed. Walter Clark, ed., *The State Records of North Carolina*, 16 vols., numbered 11–26 (Winston and Goldsboro: State of North Carolina, 1895–1906), 23:64. The law of 1741 states that the court was to be comprised of at least three justices of the county court and four freeholders from the county where the crime allegedly was committed. The wording of the law is confused concerning the number of justices of the peace who were to sit on the tribunal, but almost certainly the above interpretation is correct. The three justices consisted of a justice chosen by the sheriff who granted certification of the incarceration of the slave prisoner in the county jail. This justice, in turn, was required "to issue a Summons for Two or more Justices of the said Court, and Four Freeholders, such as shall have Slaves in

the said County." The act goes on to state that the said "Three Justices and Four Freeholder Owners of Slaves" were to constitute the slave court. Thus the justices included the one chosen by the sheriff plus the two or more to whom he issued summons. Moreover, any justice of the county where the slave was tried could also join the court. Ibid., 23:202.

3. See ibid., 23:64, 202; Donna J. Spindel, *Crime and Society in North Carolina, 1663–1776* (Baton Rouge: Louisiana State University Press, 1989), 20, 112–14.

4. For the statutory clause dealing with witnesses in slave trials who were either slaves themselves or other persons of color, see the law of 1741 in Clark, *State Records*, 23:202–3. See also a law of 1746 that circumscribed the legal capacities of slaves or other persons of color to be witnesses in any cause against whites, namely: "all Negroes, Mulattoes, bond and free, to the Third Generation, and Indian Servants and Slaves, shall be deemed and taken to be Persons incapable in Law to be Witnesses in any Cause whatsoever, except against each other." Clark, *State Records*, 23:262.

The following sources in the North Carolina State Archives, Raleigh (hereafter cited as NCSA) were used to obtain data for executed slaves or those killed by authorities in accordance with statutory law (they are the basis of, for instance, the above assessment of the rare use by slaves of witnesses in their legal defense and the abolition of grand and petty juries as judicial procedures available to slaves): Treasurers and Comptrollers Papers—Payments to Masters for Executed Slaves; Secretary of State Papers—Court Records, 1702–1898; Bertie County Slave Papers, 1744–1815; Chowan County Slave Papers, 1731–1819; Slavery Papers, 1747–75, Craven County; Craven County Court Minutes, 1747–75; Cumberland County Miscellaneous Papers, 1754–1867; Edgecombe County Court Minutes, 1757–84; New Hanover County Court Minutes, 1738–67, 1771–98; Orange County Court Minutes, 1752–66; Pasquotank County Slave Papers, 1734–1860; Pasquotank County Court Minutes, 1737–85; Pasquotank County Lists of Taxables, Miscellaneous Material, 1749–1814; Perquimans County Slave Records, 1759–1864; Rowan County Court Minutes, 1753–72; Legislative Papers, 1689–1756, 1764–66, 1767–November 1768, December 1768–17 December 1770; Governor's Office, Committee of Claims Reports, 1760–64; Legislative Papers, 1689–1756, 1754–66, 1767–November 1768, December 1768–17 December 1770. See also *Virginia Gazette* (Rind), 6 September 1770; Clark, *State Records*, 22:815–66; William L. Saunders, ed., *The Colonial Records of North Carolina*, 10 vols. (Raleigh: State of North Carolina, 1886–90), 5:975–86, 6:209–15, 738–44, 8:141–43.

Two different but supplementary and complementary sets of materials supplied the basic data: trial records and claims records. The former often included extensive coverage of the testimony given at a trial. The Committee of Claims recorded and validated the specific compensations awarded the masters by the courts that had tried, sentenced, evaluated, and punished the slaves. Also recorded and validated were the payments made to slave court officers, jailers, executioners, and castrators. Usually included in both types of records were the name and sex of the slave, the owner's name (or that of an assignee) and home county, the evaluation of the slave, the county where the crime occurred, and the crime the slave was accused of. In addition, the court records normally indicated the trial, evaluation, and execution dates. The Committee of Claims records, on the other hand, might include the month and year of the trial but always listed the date when the committee validated the evaluation of the slave and thereby the master's right to compensation. They also regularly listed the dates validating other charges against the public treasury concerning the slaves' trial, apprehension, and punishments, including police, jail, trial, execution, and castration expenses.

All quoted sums of money are in terms of North Carolina currency. Although in 1748 this currency was placed at par with proclamation money, a ratio of four to three with sterling, the market exchange rate very likely reached 180 percent in 1756 and possibly 233 ⅓ percent in 1771. See Marvin L. Michael Kay, "The Payment of Provincial and Local Taxes in North Carolina, 1748–1771," *William and Mary Quarterly*, 3d ser., 26 (April 1969): 218–40, esp. 236; Kay and Lorin Lee Cary, " 'The Planters Suffer Little or Nothing': North Carolina Compensations for Executed Slaves, 1748–1772," *Science and Society* 11 (Fall 1976): 288–306.

5. Pasquotank County Court Minutes, 2 August 1761, NCSA.

6. See citations in n. 4 above, except for the various records in the Governor's Office (Committee of Claims Reports) and the Legislative Papers.

7. Ibid.

8. Alan D. Watson, "North Carolina Slave Courts, 1715–1785," *North Carolina Historical Review* 60 (January 1983): 24–36, esp. 25, 28.

9. Spindel, *Crime and Society*, 92–93. Unlike Watson, Spindel is fully appreciative of the uniquely harsh legal system slaves were subjected to. Rather than dwelling on the simplistic notion that slaves could have been treated even more harshly than they were, she stresses the comparative severity of the laws that dealt with slaves and the distinctiveness of their position.

10. Ibid., 69.

11. Ibid., 92. For sources used to obtain statistics concerning slaves, see n. 4 above and Donald R. Lennon and Ida Brooks Kellam, eds., *The Wilmington Town Book, 1743–1778* (Raleigh: North Carolina Department of Cultural Resources, Division of Archives and History, 1973), 194–239 passim.

12. See citations in n. 4 above.

13. Ibid.

14. Higginbotham and Price, "Martin Howard Condemns the Peculiar Institution," 600.

15. For the law of 1774, see Clark, *State Records*, 23:975–76. See also William M. Wiecek, "The Statutory Law of Slavery and Race in the Thirteen Mainland Colonies of British America," *William and Mary Quarterly*, 3d. ser., 34 (April 1777): 266–67.

16. Clark, *State Records*, 23:975–76; Wiecek, "Statutory Law of Slavery and Race," 266–67.

17. See citations in n. 4 above. This will be amply detailed below.

18. Spindel, *Crime and Society*, 93, 125.

19. See citations in n. 4 above.

20. New Hanover County Court Minutes, 1738–69, 1771–98; Craven County Court Minutes, 1747–75; Secretary of State Papers, Court Records, 1702–1898; all in NCSA.

21. See first note in Table 3.1.

22. See citations in n. 4 above.

23. Spindel, *Crime and Society*, 48–50, 65–66, 91–93. Slave castrations will be discussed below.

24. See citations in n. 4 above.

25. *Virginia Gazette* (Rind), 6 September 1770.

26. Ibid. See also Secretary of State Papers, Court Records, 1702–1898, NCSA; Clark, *State Records*, 22:855–63.

27. Secretary of State Papers, Court Records, 1702–1898; Legislative Papers, November 1764–66; both in NCSA; Clark, *State Records*, 22:840–47.

28. Craven County Court Minutes, 1747–75, NCSA.

29. Although only the law of 1715 specifically states that decisions were to be rendered by a simple majority of the tribunal, this provision undoubtedly was implicit in the law of 1741, because no alternative is mentioned and one would expect that a change of this magnitude would be specified. As indicated in the text, at least one trial records a split vote concerning the punishment meted out to a slave. See Sambo's case in Pasquotank County Court Minutes, 2 August 1761, NCSA. For the appropriate clauses in the laws of 1715 and 1741, see Clark, *State Records*, 23:64, 202.

Virginia's 1748 slave code, by comparison, provided that if the county court was divided on the question of guilt, then the slave would be acquitted. If execution was ordered, the law stipulated a waiting period of at least ten days "between the Time of passing Judgment, and the Day of Execution, except in Cases of Conspiracy, Insurrection, or Rebellion." See Virginia (colony), *The Acts of Assembly Now in Force* (Williamsburg, 1752), 347. A 1772 revision stipulated that four of the justices, i.e., a majority, had to concur on guilt in capital cases. *Session Laws 1772* (Williamsburg, 1772), 10. See also Philip J. Schwarz, *Twice Condemned: Slaves and the Criminal Laws of Virginia, 1705–1865* (Baton Rouge: Louisiana State University Press, 1988), 17–22.

30. For sources of slave trials, see n. 4 above. Although Spindel asserts that there were no examples of whites being decapitated after hanging and their heads displayed on poles, we have found evidence to the contrary. To obtain information about white trials, we searched all extant Superior Court Minutes and the County Court Minutes of thirteen sample counties. See the following documents in the NCSA: Bertie County Court Minutes, 1724–43, 1758–69, 1767–72; Chowan County Court Minutes, 1747–72; Pasquotank County Court Minutes, 1738–78; Beaufort County Minutes, Appearance, Prosecution, and Trial Docket; Court of Pleas and Quarter Sessions, vol. 1, 1756–61; Carteret County Court Minutes, 1747–72; Craven County Court Minutes, 1750–72; New Hanover County Court Minutes, 1738–69, 1771–72; Granville County Minutes, Court of Pleas and Quarter Sessions, 1754–70; Edgecombe County Court Minutes, 1757–72; Anson County Court Minutes, 1771–72; Orange County Court Minutes, 1752–66; Rowan County Court Minutes, 1753–72; Tryon County Court Minutes, 1768–72; New Bern District Minutes of the Superior Court, 1768–72; Edenton Superior Court Minutes, November 1760–November 1767; Wilmington District Minutes, Superior Court, October 1760–November 1772; Salisbury District Minute Docket Superior Court, 1756–70; Hillsborough District Minute Docket, 1768–88. See also Clark, *State Records*, 22:404–5, 836–47, 863–66; Saunders, *Colonial Records*, 5:975–86, 6:738–44; *Virginia Gazette* (Hunter), 10 November 1752; *North Carolina Gazette* (Davis), 14–21 September 1764; *Virginia Gazette* (Purdie and Dixon), 7 January, 28 July 1768, 28 March 1771.

31. See n. 6 above. These findings run counter to Watson's assertions in "North Carolina Slave Courts," 33. In correctly taking issue with James A. Padgett's contention "that burning was *the* common mode of execution" (emphasis added) in colonial North Carolina, Watson tends to understate burning or other especially vicious forms of execution when he notes that he has found only three executions by burning. He fails to add that he is working with an inadequate sample of executions, "11" for the years 1715–85, nor does he acknowledge that three equals 27 percent of this sample.

We have found in the records the ways in which 56 slaves were executed and peremptorily killed by the authorities during the years 1748–72. Of these, 40 were executed, including 2 who died after being castrated. Of the 40, 6, or 15 percent, were burned at the stake. The comparative significance of burning as a form of execution becomes even more evident when it is compared with the 24 hangings. Without belaboring the point, brutal forms of execution—burning, castration followed by hanging, and hanging alive in a gibbet—frequently occurred. And if one adds to this litany the sadistic public displays of mutilated slaves after death, and the horrible deaths outlawed slaves were subjected to, we come to recognize that brutal slave punishments were both common and normative forms of punishment, encouraged by statutory law in order to cow the slaves into submission.

See also James A. Padgett, "The Stakes of Slaves in Colonial North Carolina," *Journal of Negro History* 14 (July 1929): 314.

32. Secretary of State Papers, Court Records, 1702–1898; Legislative Papers, December 1768–17 December 1770; both in NCSA.

33. Craven County Court Minutes; Governor's Office, Committee of Claims Reports, 1760–64; Secretary of State Papers, Court Records, 1702–1898; Legislative Papers, November 1764–1766, December 1768–17 Dec. 1770; all in NCSA. See also *Virginia Gazette* (Rind), 6 September 1770; Saunders, *Colonial Records*, 5:975–86; Clark, *State Records*, 22:824–27, 830–35, 840–47, 855–63.

34. For Isaac, see Governor's Office, Committee of Claims Reports, 1760–64, NCSA. For Jimmy, see ibid. and Saunders, *Colonial Records*, 6:739–43.

35. For Cato, see Governor's Office, Committee of Claims Reports, 1760–64; Craven County Court Minutes, 1747–75; both in NCSA; Clark, *State Records*, 22:830–35. For Titus, see Governor's Office, Committee of Claims Reports, 1760–64, NCSA; Clark, *State Records*, 22:836–40. For Phyllis, see Legislative Papers, December 1768–17 December 1770, NCSA.

36. Secretary of State Papers, Court Records, 1702–1898; New Hanover County Court Minutes, 1738–69, 1771–98; Legislative Papers, November 1764–66, December 1768–17 December 1770; Craven County Court Minutes, 1747–75; all in NCSA; Clark, *State Records*, 22:840–47.

37. Clark, *State Records*, 22:822–23, 826–27. As explained in n. 4 above, all quoted sums of money here and in subsequent notes are in terms of North Carolina currency.

38. Castrations and other corporal punishments meted out to slaves will be documented below. For whites, see n. 30 above. See also Spindel, *Crime and Society*, 116–37, esp. 135.

39. Craven County Court Minutes, 1747–75, NCSA.

40. Pasquotank County Court Minutes, 1737–85; Slavery Papers, 1747–75, Craven County; both in NCSA.

41. For Phoebe and Mary, see Secretary of State Papers, Court Records, 1702–1898, NCSA. For Ben, whose trial took place in 1748, see Pasquotank County Court Minutes, 1747–75, NCSA.

42. For Andrew, Bob, and Simon, see Craven County Court Minutes, 1747–75, NCSA. For Dublin, see Cumberland County Miscellaneous Papers, 1754–1867, NCSA. For Dick, see Secretary of State Papers, Court Records, 1702–1898, NCSA. For Tom, see Pasquotank County Court Minutes, 1747–75, NCSA. For Ben and Sippey, see Perquimans County Slave Records, 1759–1864, folder: Slave Papers, 1759–99, Civil and Criminal Papers, NCSA. For Seller, see Bertie County Slave Papers, 1744–1815, NCSA.

43. Clark, *State Records*, 23:167.

44. Records used to obtain information about castrations in North Carolina include the following: Secretary of State Papers, Court Records, 1702–1898; Legislative Papers, 1689–1756, November 1764–66, 1767–November 1768; Governor's Office, Committee of Claims Reports, 1760–64; Craven County Court Minutes, 1747–75; Pasquotank County Court Min-

utes, 1737–85; all in NCSA; Saunders, *Colonial Records*, 6:738–44; Clark, *State Records*, 22:818–27, 830–52.

45. Clark, *State Records*, 23:489. See n. 44 above.

46. See n. 44 above and Clark, *State Records*, 23:488–89. For rape and castration as a punishment, see Winthrop D. Jordan, *White Over Black: American Attitudes toward the Negro, 1550–1812* (Chapel Hill: University of North Carolina Press, 1968), 154–58, 463–64, 473. Our own survey of the applicable laws shows no distinct regional patterns in the handling of rape and attempted rape. All colonies, with the possible exception of Rhode Island, defined rape as a capital crime punishable by death. Georgia and New York treated attempted rape in the same fashion, and four other colonies regarded this as a lesser offense and punished it in various ways—by whipping (Massachusetts), by whipping, branding, and banishment (Rhode Island and Pennsylvania), or by nailing the convicted slave's ears to a pillory and then cutting them off (Delaware). The remaining colonies, both north and south, did not specifically allude to the crime of attempted rape in their laws. As for the punishment of castration, which only four colonies besides North Carolina built into their laws at one time or another during the eighteenth century, it was primarily a southern practice and one hardly limited to expressing whites' sexual fears. Only two northern colonies, New Jersey and Pennsylvania, called for castration in their slave codes; both used it only in sex crimes—rape and attempted rape respectively—and in both cases the law was disallowed and apparently never used. In the South, as Winthrop Jordan has pointed out, castration was one punishment among many. Only two colonies specifically forbade the use of castration: New York and Georgia. For examples of some relevant legislation, see, e.g., Allen D. Candler, *Colonial Records of the State of Georgia, 1732–1782*, 26 vols. (Atlanta: C. P. Byrd, 1904–16), 18:102–44, 657, 19:209–49; James Bisset, *Abridgement and Collection of the Acts of Assembly of the Province of Maryland at Present in Force* (1759), 144–45; Lorenzo Johnston Greene, *The Negro in Colonial New England* (New York: Columbia University Press, 1942), 157–59, 191; J. H. Trumbull and C. J. Hoadly, eds., *The Public Records of the Colony of Connecticut, 1636–1776*, 15 vols. (Hartford: Lockwood and Brainard Co., 1850–90), 4–14 passim; John Russell Bartlett, ed., *Records of the Colony of Rhode Island and Providence Plantations in New England, 1636–1792*, 10 vols. (Providence: A. C. Greene and Brothers, State Printers, 1856–65), 5:72–73; *The Acts and Resolves, Public and Private, of the Province of Massachusetts Bay, 1692–1786*, 21 vols. (Boston: Wright and Potter, Printers to the State, 1869–1922), 1:2–12 passim, 578; Peter H. Wood, *Black Majority: Negroes in Colonial South Carolina from 1670 through the Stono Rebellion* (New York: Knopf, 1974), 135, 236–38, 278; *Laws of the Government of New Castle, Kent, and Sussex upon Delaware*, 1:71, 73; William W. Hening, ed., *The Statutes at Large; Being a Collection of All the Laws of Virginia, 1619–1792*, 13 vols. (Richmond, 1809–23), 3:269, 461, 4:132–33, 6:111, 356–69, 7:358; *The Colonial Laws of New York from the Year 1664 to the Revolution*, 5 vols. (Albany: J. B. Lyon, State Printer, 1894–96), 1:520, 762, 765, 1023, 2:310, 680, 684; J. T. Mitchell and Henry Flanders, eds., *Statutes at Large of Pennsylvania from 1682 to 1801* (1896–1908), 2:77–79, 235; Samuel Allinson, ed., *Acts of the General Assembly of the Province of New Jersey, 1702–1776* (1776), 27, 307–8.

47. For Tom, see Secretary of State Papers, Court Records, 1702–1898; Legislative Papers, 1689–1756; both in NCSA. For Tom and Prymus, see Governor's Office, Committee of Claims Reports, 1760–64, and Craven County Court Minutes, 1730–46, NCSA; Clark, *State Records*, 22:830–35. For Sambo, see Governor's Office, Committee of Claims Reports, 1760–

64, and Pasquotank County Court Minutes, 1737–1835, NCSA; Saunders, *Colonial Records*, 6:738–44. For Isaac, see Governor's Office, Committee of Claims Reports, 1760–64, NCSA.

48. For Isaac and Jimmy, see Governor's Office, Committee of Claims Reports, 1760–64, NCSA. For Phill, see Secretary of State Papers, Court Records, 1702–1898, NCSA.

49. See Jordan, *White Over Black*, esp. 136–78.

50. Slave marriages and families will be discussed at length in Chapter 7.

51. Spindel, *Crime and Society*, 83, 107–9.

52. Secretary of State Papers, Court Records, 1702–1898; Legislative Papers, November 1764–66; both in NCSA; Clark, *State Records*, 22:840–47, 855–63.

53. See n. 46 and Secretary of State Papers, Court Records, 1702–1898, NCSA. The documents do not reveal what happened to the women who had been raped.

54. Clark, *State Records*, 23:64, 203, 488–89, 656 (laws of 1715, 1741, 1758, and 1764); John M. Brickell, *The Natural History of North Carolina With an Account of the Trade, Manners, and Customs of the Christian and Indian Inhabitants* . . . (1737; reprint, Raleigh, N.C., 1911), 273.

55. This method of financing compensations was put in place by the law of 1741, which simply states that the legislature would directly compensate owners of executed slaves or of slaves killed by the authorities in other ways in accordance with the evaluations rendered by slave or county courts. The law of 1715, in contrast, used a more equitable system of taxation to finance the terrorizing of slaves, "a Pole-Tax on all Slaves in the Government." Clark, *State Records*, 23:64, 203.

56. The above tax and compensation figures are corrections and extrapolations of figures arrived at earlier in the following: Kay, "Payment of Provincial and Local Taxes," 239–40; Marvin L. Michael Kay and William S. Price Jr., "'To Ride the Wood Mare': Road Building and Militia Service in Colonial North Carolina, 1740–1775," *North Carolina Historical Review* 57 (October 1980): 361–409, esp. 390–93; Kay and Cary, "North Carolina Compensations for Executed Slaves," 298–300. For the sources of our statistics on compensations, see n. 4 above. See also Tables 1.11 and 3.1.

57. Clark, *State Records*, 23:64, 203, 488–89. Various factors influenced assessment levels, including market price levels, the needs of large slaveowners as a class, and events such as the French and Indian War, along with the predispositions of individual courts, personal differences among slaves (working ability, size, and strength, e.g.), the sex and occupation of the slave, and the crimes committed. Not all of these variables, or others such as recent arrival from Africa or the ability to speak English, can be weighed precisely. See Kay and Cary, "North Carolina Compensations for Executed Slaves," 288–306; Kay, "Payment of Provincial and Local Taxes," 225–28.

58. Clark, *State Records*, 23:488–89.

59. Ibid., 488.

60. Ibid., 488–89.

61. Kay, "Payment of Provincial and Local Taxes," 225–40.

62. Clark, *State Records*, 23:656.

63. Writing in 1896, John Spencer Bassett somewhat ambiguously remarked that although the precise reasons for the repeal of the castration clause could not be determined, "It would be charitable to suppose that the public mind revolted at its disgusting severity." Bassett, "Slavery and Servitude in the Colony of North Carolina," *Johns Hopkins University Studies in Historical and Political Science*, ser. 14 (1896), 32. One hundred and three years later, Donna Spindel still finds it difficult to reject this wish, or assessment, when she writes that

repeal of the castration clause in 1764 "perhaps signified a humanitarian effort or a desire to put unruly slaves to death rather than to discipline them after castration." Spindel, *Crime and Society*, 134.

64. See citations in n. 4 above and first note in Table 3.1.

65. Clark, *State Records*, 23:64.

66. Higginbotham and Price, "Martin Howard Condemns the Peculiar Institution," 600.

67. Edenton Superior Court Minutes, November 1763, NCSA.

68. Wilmington District Minutes, Superior Court, November–December 1771, NCSA.

69. Ibid., November 1771–December 1772.

70. Clark, *State Records*, 23:203.

71. Edenton Superior Court Minutes, November 1760–November 1767, NCSA.

72. Chowan County Slave Papers, 1731–1819, NCSA. See ibid. for a similar suit in October 1761.

73. Secretary of State Papers, Court Records, 1702–1898, NCSA.

74. For protections given servants, see previous chapter and Clark, *State Records*, 23:62–66, 191–204, 262, 388–90, 488–89, 656. In addition, a 1715 law prohibited the private burial of servants to prevent their being killed by unscrupulous masters. Clark, *State Records*, 23:66–67. Such protections were never accorded slaves.

75. Clark, *State Records*, 23:389–90.

CHAPTER 4

1. We discuss marriage and the family and religiosity among slaves in Chapters 7 and 8 below. See Marvin L. Michael Kay and Lorin Lee Cary, " 'They are Indeed the Constant Plague of Their Tyrants': Slave Defense of a Moral Economy in Colonial North Carolina, 1748–1772," *Slavery and Abolition* 6 (December 1985): 6.

2. *Virginia Gazette* (Rind), 6 September 1770; Secretary of State Papers, Court Records, 1702–1898, in North Carolina State Archives, Raleigh (hereafter cited as NCSA).

3. Jeffrey J. Crow, "Slave Rebelliousness and Social Conflict in North Carolina, 1775 to 1802," *William and Mary Quarterly*, 3d ser., 37 (January 1980): 93. For Nat Turner's rebellion, see Stephen B. Oates, *The Fires of Jubilee: Nat Turner's Fierce Rebellion* (New York: Harper and Row,1975); Vincent Harding, *There Is a River: The Black Struggle for Freedom in America* (New York: Vintage Books, 1983), 94–100.

4. The following critique of Eugene G. Genovese's and Gerald W. Mullin's writings is drawn from James C. Scott's recent brilliant synthesis and updating of his previous analyses of common forms of resistance practiced by Southeast Asian peasants. See his "Everyday Forms of Peasant Resistance," *Journal of Peasant Studies* 13 (1986): 5–31. For longer studies by Scott, see his *The Moral Economy of the Peasant: Rebellion and Subsistence in Southeast Asia* (New Haven: Yale University Press, 1976), but esp. see his *Weapons of the Weak: Everyday Forms of Peasant Resistance* (New Haven: Yale University Press, 1985), 28–47, 289–350. See also Mullin, *Flight and Rebellion: Slave Resistance in Eighteenth-Century Virginia* (New York: Oxford University Press, 1972), 35–37; Genovese, *Roll, Jordan, Roll: The World the Slaves Made* (New York: Vintage Books, 1973), 597–98.

5. Peter H. Wood, *Black Majority: Negroes in Colonial South Carolina from 1670 through the Stono Rebellion* (New York: Knopf, 1974), 308–17.

6. *Virginia Gazette* (Rind), 6 September 1770.

7. Wood, *Black Majority*, 318–24; Michael S. Hindus, *Prison and Plantation: Crime, Justice, and Authority in Massachusetts and South Carolina, 1767–1878* (Chapel Hill: University of North Carolina Press, 1980), 131–39.

8. New Hanover County Court Minutes, 1738–69, 1771–72, NCSA. The best work on the Cherokee and slavery is Theda Perdue, *Slavery and the Evolution of Cherokee Society, 1540–1866* (Knoxville: University of Tennessee Press, 1979), esp. 36–49. See also Perdue, "Red and Black in the Southern Appalachians," *Southern Exposure* 12 (November–December 1984), 17–24.

9. Eric Hobsbawm, *Bandits* (New York: Delacorte Press, 1969), 15; Donald Crummey, ed., *Banditry, Rebellion, and Social Protest in Africa* (London: James Currey, 1986), 6.

10. For studies of the South Carolina Regulators, see Richard J. Hooker, ed., *The Carolina Backcountry on the Eve of the Revolution: The Journal and Other Writings of Charles Woodmason, Anglican Itinerant* (Chapel Hill: University of North Carolina Press, 1953); Richard Maxwell Brown, *The South Carolina Regulators: The Story of the First Vigilante Movement* (Cambridge: Harvard University Press, 1963); Rachel N. Klein, "Ordering the Backcountry: The South Carolina Regulation," *William and Mary Quarterly*, 3d ser., 38 (October 1981): 661–80. The summary in the text most closely follows the Woodmason narration and Klein analysis. For other examples of maroons in South Carolina, see Philip D. Morgan, "Black Society in the Lowcountry, 1760–1810," in *Slavery and Freedom in the Age of the American Revolution*, edited by Ira Berlin and Ronald Hoffman (Charlottesville: University Press of Virginia, 1983), 138–39.

11. See Marvin L. Michael Kay, "The North Carolina Regulation, 1766–1776: A Class Conflict," in *The American Revolution: Explorations in History of American Radicalism*, edited by Alfred F. Young (DeKalb: Northern Illinois University Press, 1976), 72–123.

12. Jeffrey J. Crow describes maroon settlements in the Great Dismal Swamp in eighteenth-century North Carolina in *The Black Experience in Revolutionary North Carolina* (Raleigh: North Carolina Department of Cultural Resources, Division of Archives and History, 1977), 101–2.

13. J. F. D. Smyth, *A Tour in the United States of America*, 2 vols. (Dublin: Price, Moncrieffe, 1784), 1:101–2.

14. Elkanah Watson, *Men and Times of the Revolution; or, Memoirs of Elkanah Watson, including His Journals of Travels in Europe and America, 1777–1842*, 2d ed., edited by Winslow C. Watson (New York: Dana and Co., 1857), 51–52.

15. *The Interesting Narrative of the Life of Olaudah Equiano, or Gustavus Vassa, The African, Written by Himself*, Early American Imprints #23353 (New York, 1791).

16. John M. Brickell, *The Natural History of North Carolina With an Account of the Trade, Manners, and Customs of the Christian and Indian Inhabitants . . .* (1737; reprint, (1737; reprint, Murfreesboro, N.C.: Johnson Publishing Co., 1968), 272, 275.

17. Janet Schaw, *Journal of a Lady of Quality: Being the Narrative of a Journey from Scotland to the West Indies, North Carolina, and Portugal, in the years 1774 to 1776*, edited by Evangeline Walker Andrews and Charles M. Andrews (New Haven: Yale University Press, 1923), 66, 177. For reference to a similar pattern in Bermuda at this time, see Wood, *Black Majority*, 212 n. 56.

18. The sources of our data on slaves who committed crimes and their victims—in accordance with other computational needs—have been organized, by punishment, into three sets: slaves who were executed for their crimes, slaves who were castrated, and slaves

who were subjected to other corporal punishments by court order. Data for slaves who were executed for their crimes may be found in the following sources: Treasurers and Comptrollers Papers—Payments to Masters for Executed Slaves; Secretary of State Papers—Court Records, 1702–1898; Bertie County Slave Papers, 1744–1815; Chowan County Slave Papers, 1731–1819; Slavery Papers, 1747–75, Craven County; Craven County Court Minutes, 1747–75; Cumberland County Miscellaneous Papers, 1754–1867; Edgecombe County Court Minutes, 1757–84; New Hanover County Court Minutes, 1738–67, 1771–98; Orange County Court Minutes, 1752–66; Pasquotank County Slave Papers, 1734–1860; Pasquotank County Court Minutes, 1737–85; Pasquotank County Lists of Taxables, Miscellaneous Material, 1749–1814; Perquimans County Slave Records, 1759–1864; Rowan County Court Minutes, 1753–72; Legislative Papers, 1689–1756, 1764–66, 1767–November 1768, December 1768–17 December 1770; Governor's Office, Committee of Claims Reports, 1760–64; Legislative Papers, 1689–1756, 1754–66, 1767–November 1768, December 1768–17 December 1770; all in NCSA. See also *Virginia Gazette* (Rind), 6 September 1770; Walter Clark, ed., *The State Records of North Carolina*, 16 vols., numbered 11–26 (Winston and Goldsboro: State of North Carolina, 1895–1906), 22:815–66; William L. Saunders, ed., *The Colonial Records of North Carolina*, 10 vols. (Raleigh: State of North Carolina, 1886–90), 5:975–86, 6:209–15, 738–44, 8:141–43.

Data for slaves who were castrated for their crimes may be found in the following sources: Secretary of State Papers, Court Records, 1702–1898; Legislative Papers, 1689–1756, November 1764–1766, 1767–November 1768; Governor's Office, Committee of Claims Reports, 1760–64; Craven County Court Minutes, 1747–75; Pasquotank County Court Minutes, 1737–85; all in NCSA; Saunders, *Colonial Records*, 6:738–44; Clark, *State Records*, 22:818–27, 830–52.

Data for slaves who were subjected to other corporal punishments may be found in the following sources: Craven County Court Minutes, 1747–75; Pasquotank County Court Minutes, 1747–75, 1737–85; Slavery Papers, 1747–75, Craven County; Secretary of State Papers, Court Records, 1702–1898; Cumberland County Miscellaneous Papers, 1754–1867; Perquimans County Slave Records, 1759–1864, folder: Slave Papers, 1759–99, Civil and Criminal Papers; Bertie County Slave Papers, 1744–1815; all in NCSA. See Table 3.1 and notes.

19. African medical and magical practices, including herbalism, are discussed in Chapter 8.

20. Genovese, *Roll, Jordan, Roll*, 599–612, 615–17.

21. Lawrence Levine, *Black Culture and Black Consciousness: Afro-American Folk Thought from Slavery to Freedom* (New York: Oxford University Press, 1977), 123–24. Levine further argues that animal trickster tales "may have served as a convenient channel" for whatever residual guilt remained as a result of the slaves acting in ways at odds with what were "proscribed by their African heritage and their new religion" (p. 124). See Gresham M. Sykes and David Matza, "Techniques of Neutralization: A Theory of Delinquency," *American Sociological Review* 22 (December 1957): 664–70; Matza, *Delinquency and Drift* (New York: Wiley, 1964), 60–62 and passim.

22. Alex Lichtenstein, "'That Disposition To Theft, With Which They Have Been Branded': Moral Economy, Slave Management, and the Law," *Journal of Social History* 22 (Spring 1988): 414–15. He cites Ian Taylor, Paul Walton, and Jack Young, *The New Criminology: For a Social Theory of Deviance* (New York, n.d.), 184–87.

23. Lichtenstein, "Moral Economy," 414–16.

24. Ibid.

25. See E. P. Thompson, "Patrician Society, Plebeian Culture," *Journal of Social History* 7 (Summer 1974): 382–405; Thompson, "The Moral Economy of the English Crowd in the Eighteenth Century," *Past and Present* 50 (February 1971): 76–136. Lichtenstein concludes his argument by noting: "Theft in Southern slave society was similar to the 'social crime' of eighteenth-century England; it represented the slave's insistence on receiving his or her due from the master, both in terms of diet and the right to the products of labor. As such, theft fits firmly within Genovese's conception of a constant give and take between master and slave. Theft was a testing of the limits of paternalism, the claiming and reclaiming of economic rights by the slave, and the ultimate defense of what was seen by slaves as granted and legitimate." Lichtenstein, "Moral Economy," 416.

26. A "moral economy" is a peculiarly perverse model to comprehend slave actions during the colonial years, especially for colonial North Carolina, because it stresses traditional relationships between masters and slaves when so much was formative and in flux. These are strong words coming from authors who recently wrote an article entitled "Slave Defense of a Moral Economy in Colonial North Carolina."

27. As argued above, eighteenth-century African cultures and derivative African American cultures, as is the case with other cultures, defined killing, assault, and theft as either immoral or justifiable acts in accordance with the social context in which they were committed. Enslavement in America, it must be added, provided a uniquely harsh context for slaves to determine the ethical acceptability of these criminal acts. Also, to bemoan, as Genovese does, that slave criminality somehow socially determined in destructive fashion the future options of free African Americans is to project supposed legacies into the future without proper analysis of the particular modern circumstances that foster criminal responses. See Genovese, *Roll, Jordan, Roll*, 607–9.

28. For Sambo's case, see Governor's Office, Committee of Claims Reports, 1760–64; Pasquotank County Court Minutes, 1737–85; both in NCSA. See also Saunders, *Colonial Records*, 6:738–44; Kay and Cary, "Slave Defense of a Moral Economy," 37–38.

29. See Chapter 8 on religion.

30. For a few examples of such studies, see the following essays in Crummey, *Banditry, Rebellion, and Social Protest in Africa*: Crummey, Introduction: "The Great Beast," 1–29; Larry Yarak, "Murder and Theft in Early-Nineteenth-Century Elmina," 33–47; William Freund, "Theft and Social Protest among the Tin Miners of Northern Nigeria," 49–63; Ralph Austen, "Social Bandits and Other Heroic Criminals: Western Models of Resistance and Their Relevance for Africa," 89–108; Ray A. Kea, " 'I Am Here to Plunder on the General Road': Bandits and Banditry in the Pre-Nineteenth-Century Gold Coast," 109–32.

31. See n. 18 above. For an account of the gaps in the records used, see the first note in Table 3.1.

32. Our calculations suggest that roughly 47,061, 44,140, 87,576, and 184,756 slave taxables cumulatively lived in North Carolina during each of the following time spans: 1748–54, 1755–58, 1759–64, 1765–72. Using these totals to determine the weight for each period, we then projected the number of executions and castrations that would have occurred given such population totals. Distributing 115, we arrive at 14.893 for 1748–54, 13.944 for 1755–58, 27.699 for 1759–64, and 58.434 for 1765–72. These findings almost exactly correspond with the combined figures for actual executions and castrations during those periods: 13, 14, 28, and 60.

33. See n. 18 above.

34. Ibid.

35. Ibid. See Tables 6.1–6.7, esp. 6.1–6.3, concerning the origins of slave names. Almost identical breakdowns of the origin of slave names occur in analyses of both the names of slave criminals and the names of slaves that appear in wills and inventories. At the least, then, there is some indication, though hardly conclusive, that African and creole slaves committed crimes proportionate to their numbers in the slave population.

36. See n. 18 above.

37. Ibid.

38. For Henry Ormond, see Clark, *State Records*, 23:855–63; *Virginia Gazette* (Rind), 6 September 1770; Secretary of State Papers, Court Records, 1702–1898, NCSA. For Sambo and David, see Saunders, *Colonial Records*, 6:738–44; Governor's Office, Committee of Claims Reports, 1760–64; Pasquotank County Court Minutes, 1737–85; both in NCSA. For Tom and Prymus, see Clark, *State Records*, 22:830–35; Governor's Office, Committee of Claims Reports, 1760–64; Craven County Court Minutes, 1730–46; both in NCSA. For Robin, Jack and Jemmy, see Secretary of State Papers, Court Records, 1702–1898; Legislative Papers, December 1768–17 December 1770; both in NCSA. For Ned and Daniel, see Clark, *State Records*, 22: 855–63; Secretary of State Papers, Court Records, 1702–1898, NCSA.

39. Treasurers and Comptrollers Papers—Payments to Masters for Executed Slaves, NCSA. Stephen probably was an older slave, as he was evaluated at only £35.

40. Saunders, *Colonial Records*, 5:975–86; Edgecombe County Court Minutes, 1757–84, NCSA. The crimes of an additional eleven slaves who collaborated are not enumerated in the records.

41. County Records—Cumberland County, Miscellaneous Papers, 1754–1867, NCSA. The trial took place on 29 October 1764.

42. Although very likely the case, there is no indication in the trial record that Simon was a runaway slave. He is described only as "a Negroe Fellow . . . the property of Joseph Ridgway in Pennsylvania." Craven County Court Minutes, 1747–75, NCSA.

43. Pasquotank County Court Minutes, 1737–85, NCSA. For examples of phrasing that manifest upper-class disgust of lower-class whites, see, e.g., Clark, *State Records*, 23:173, 318, 435, 839. It probably was the same Moses who was convicted in 1757 of hog stealing with "Negro Tom" and sentenced to fifty lashes. Pasquotank County Court Minutes, 22 March 1757, NCSA.

44. Saunders, *Colonial Records*, 7:856–57; Clark, *State Records*, 22:847–52; Secretary of State Papers, Court Records, 1702–1898; Rowan Court of Pleas and Quarter Sessions, Minutes, 1753–72; Governor's Office, Lists of Taxables, Militia, and Magistrates, 1754, 1770; Legislative Papers, 1767–November 1768; all in NCSA.

45. For Cain, see Treasurers and Comptrollers Papers—Payments to Masters for Executed Slaves, NCSA. For Cato, see Secretary of State Papers, Court Records, 1702–1898; Legislative Papers, 1689–1756, Committee of Claims Reports beginning 30 September 1755; all in NCSA. For Peter, see Saunders, *Colonial Records*, 5:975–86. For Morrise, see Clark, *State Records*, 22:830–35; Governor's Office, Committee of Claims Reports, 1760–64, NCSA. For Cesar, see Saunders, *Colonial Records*, 6:738–44; Governor's Office, Committee of Claims Reports, 1760–64, NCSA. For Lettice, see Governor's Office, Committee of Claims Reports, 1760–64; Perquimans County Slave Records, 1759–64; both in NCSA. For Dick, see Clark, *State Records*, 22:836–40; Governor's Office, Committee of Claims Reports, 1760–64, NCSA. For Isaac, see Governor's Office, Committee of Claims Reports, 1760–64, NCSA.

For Pompey and Cato, see Clark, *State Records*, 22:840–47; Secretary of State Papers, Court Records, 1702–1898; Legislative Papers, November 1764–1766; both in NCSA. For Rose, see Clark, *State Records*, 22:840–47; Legislative Papers, November 1764–1766, NCSA. For Quash, see Clark, *State Records*, 22:847–52; Secretary of State Papers, Court Records, 1702–1898; Legislative Papers, 1767–November 1768; both in NCSA. For Dick, Simon, and Bacchus, see Clark, *State Records*, 22:847–52; Legislative Papers, 1767–November 1768, NCSA. For Jonny and Quamino, see Secretary of State Papers, Court Records, 1702–1898; Legislative Papers, December 1768–17 December 1770; both in NCSA. For Jack, see Clark, *State Records*, 22:855–63; Secretary of State Papers, Court Records, 1702–1898, NCSA.

46. For Will, see Secretary of State Papers, Court Records, 1702–1898; Legislative Papers, December 1768–17 December 1770; both in NCSA. For Harry, Jemmy, and Isaac; Jack and Jemmy; Ned and Daniel; and Jacy and Toney, see Clark, *State Records*, 22: 853–63; Secretary of State Papers, Court Records, 1702–1898; Legislative Papers, December 1768–17 December 1770; both in NCSA. For Will, Cuff, Ceasar, and George, see Clark, *State Records*, 22:855–63; Secretary of State Papers, Court Records, 1702–1898, NCSA. For Scip, see Secretary of State Papers, Court Records, 1702–1898, NCSA.

47. See n. 18 above. Lichtenstein ("Moral Economy") develops these points about theft extremely well.

48. See Brickell, *Natural History*, 272, 275; Schaw, *Journal of a Lady of Quality*, 66, 177. For ordinances for Wilmington, see Donald R. Lennon and Ida Brooks Kellam, eds., *The Wilmington Town Book, 1743–1778* (Raleigh: North Carolina Department of Cultural Resources, Division of Archives and History, 1973), 148, 164–69, 187, 197, 204–5, 209–14, 219–21, 225–29.

49. Clark, *State Records*, 23:194–95.

50. Lennon and Kellam, *Wilmington Town Book*, 164–66.

51. Ibid., 166–68.

52. Ibid., 204–5, 210–11.

53. Ibid., 209–14, 219–21, 225–29.

54. Clark, *State Records*, 23:82, 172–73.

55. *Cape Fear Mercury*, 8 December 1769; *South Carolina Gazette*, 26 February–5 March 1754; *North Carolina Gazette*, fragment, 7 January 1774.

56. Clark, *State Records*, 23:165–68. White offenders were to pay £10 plus the value of the animal and receive forty lashes; a second conviction called for branding "the left Hand, with a red hot iron, with the letter T."

57. Ibid., 201. No such provision had been included in the colony's first slave code, that of 1715. Ibid., 62–66. South Carolina, on the other hand, had barred such ownership, as well as that of boats and canoes, as early as 1722. Wood, *Black Majority*, 212–13.

58. Craven County Slavery Papers, 1747–1850, NCSA; Clark, *State Records*, 23:165–68. The law directed that both of the slave's ears were to be cut off but did not specify the number of lashes to be administered.

59. Pasquotank County Court Minutes, 22 March 1757, NCSA.

60. Craven County Court Minutes, 1747–75, NCSA.

CHAPTER 5

1. For an overview of the legal condition of blacks in the thirteen mainland British colonies, see William M. Wiecek, "The Statutory Law of Slavery and Race in the Thirteen

Mainland Colonies of British America," *William and Mary Quarterly*, 3d ser., 34 (April 1977): 258–80. For slave laws in the West Indies, see Elsa V. Goveia, "The West Indian Slave Laws of the Eighteenth Century," *Revista de Ciencias Sociales* 4 (March 1960): 75–105; Elsa V. Goveia, *Slave Society in the British Leeward Islands at the End of the Eighteenth Century* (New Haven: Yale University Press, 1965), 152–202; Orlando Patterson, *The Sociology of Slavery: An Analysis of the Origins, Development, and Structure of Negro Slave Society in Jamaica* (London: MacGibbon and Kee, 1967), 70–93.

2. North Carolina passed two basic slave and servant codes in 1715 and 1741. Five of the 21 articles in the 1715 law pertained directly to or mentioned runaways; 22 of the 58 articles of the 1741 act did so. Walter Clark, ed., *The State Records of North Carolina*, 16 vols., numbered 11–26 (Winston and Goldsboro: State of North Carolina, 1895–1906), 23:62–66, 191–204. For subsidiary laws of 1753, 1758, and 1764, see ibid., 388–90, 488–89, 656.

3. See, e.g., Peter H. Wood, *Black Majority: Negroes in Colonial South Carolina from 1670 through the Stono Rebellion* (New York: Knopf, 1974), 239–68; Gerald W. Mullin, *Flight and Rebellion: Slave Resistance in Eighteenth-Century Virginia* (New York: Oxford University Press, 1972), 34–123 and notes. For North Carolina's slaves during the Revolution, see Jeffrey J. Crow's excellent studies: *The Black Experience in Revolutionary North Carolina* (Raleigh: North Carolina Department of Cultural Resources, Division of Archives and History, 1977); "Slave Rebelliousness and Social Conflict in North Carolina, 1775 to 1802," *William and Mary Quarterly*, 3d ser. 37, (January 1980): 79–102.

4. This was discussed at length in the previous chapter.

5. See Theda Perdue's "Red and Black in the Southern Appalachians," *Southern Exposure* 12 (November–December 1984): 17–24, and her *Slavery and the Evolution of Cherokee Society, 1540–1866* (Knoxville: University of Tennessee Press, 1979), esp. 36–49.

6. For the still more expansive possibilities maroons exploited in the Caribbean and Brazil, see Eugene D. Genovese, *From Rebellion to Revolution: Afro-American Slave Revolts in the Making of the Modern World* (Baton Rouge: Louisiana State University Press, 1979), 51–81. For details on the British West Indies, see esp. Michael Craton, *Testing the Chains: Resistance to Slavery in the British West Indies* (Ithaca, N.Y.: Cornell University Press, 1982). See also Patterson, *Sociology of Slavery*, 269–83. For maroons on the mainland, see Wood, *Black Majority*, 238–326 passim; Gary B. Nash, *Red, White, and Black: The People of Early America* (Englewood Cliffs, N.J.: Prentice-Hall, 1974), 290–97; John W. Blassingame, *The Slave Community: Plantation Life in the Antebellum South* (New York: Oxford University Press, 1972), 206–15; Herbert Aptheker, *American Negro Slave Revolts* (New York: Columbia University Press, 1943), 162–292 passim; Kenneth Wiggins Porter, *The Negro on the Frontier* (New York: Arno Press, 1971); Herbert Aptheker, "Maroons within the Present Limits of the United States," *Journal of Negro History* 24 (April 1939): 167–84; Herbert Aptheker, "Additional Data on American Maroons," *Journal of Negro History* 33 (October 1947): 452–60; J. Leitch Wright, "A Note on the First Seminole Wars as Seen by the Indians, Negroes, and Their British Advisers," *Journal of Southern History* 34 (November 1968): 565–75.

7. The *North Carolina Magazine and Universal Intelligencer*, published in New Bern between 1764 and 1768, had 260 possible issues, of which 27, or 10 percent, remain. Twenty-four of the surviving issues date from 1764, 3 from 1765. The record of the *Cape Fear Mercury* is worse. Published in Wilmington between 1769 and 1775, it too had 260 issues. Only 17 unevenly dispersed issues (7 percent) have survived: 2 for 1769, 5 for 1770, 3 for 1773, 2 for 1774, and 5 for 1775. The other Wilmington paper, the *North Carolina Gazette*, appeared

between 1764 and 1766. Its last extant issue is numbered 72, and only 4 issues (6 percent) remain: 2 for 1765, 2 for 1766. The colony's major journal, the *North Carolina Gazette*, published by James Davis in New Bern between 1751 and 1759 and again between 1768 and 1778, has a similar problem. Davis published some 200 issues during the first period and over 450 in the second. Only 26 (4 percent) have survived: 1 for 1751, 2 for 1752, 2 for 1753, 1 for 1757, 1 for 1759, 2 for 1768, 1 for 1769, 1 for 1773, 5 for 1774, and 10 for 1775. In other words, 62 percent of the surviving issues of Davis's paper are for the period 1773–75. Collectively, there are 70 extant issues of North Carolina newspapers for the years under study, and 37 percent of them date from the years 1773–75.

8. The surviving issues of the *North Carolina Magazine and Universal Intelligencer* (New Bern) (hereafter cited as *North Carolina Magazine*), contain only 2 notices, both placed by masters in Craven County. Only 1 of the 6 extant advertisements and 1 proclamation of outlawry in the *Cape Fear Mercury* (Wilmington) were placed by masters who did not live in the Cape Fear counties of New Hanover, Brunswick, and Bladen. No advertisements for runaways appeared in the short-lived *North Carolina Gazette* (Wilmington), but the drawing power of James Davis's *North Carolina Gazette* (New Bern) is illustrated by the wider geographic distribution of the twenty-five masters who placed in the paper notices for runaways (19) or proclamations of outlawry (6). Of these, 10 came from Craven County and 3 from other Neuse-Pamlico counties. The remaining 12 notices were placed by masters living in a cross section of the colony's regions. North Carolina owners who put notices in South Carolina and Virginia papers exemplified the same geographic patterns as those who advertised in North Carolina papers other than the *Gazette* published by Davis. Thus masters from the Cape Fear counties closest to Charleston accounted for all 6 notices placed in the *South Carolina Gazette* (Charleston), and 13 of the 15 notices placed by North Carolina owners in the *Virginia Gazette* (Williamsburg) (hereafter cited with appropriate publishers) came from counties abutting or near the Virginia border.

9. For nonfield runaways the time lag between escape and placement of an advertisement averaged just under 4 months, the amount of elapsed time ranging from 10 days to 7 months. With field hands the lag averaged just over 4 months, and the range of elapsed time was 7 days to 2 years. See also Rosser H. Taylor, "Humanizing the Slave Code of North Carolina," *North Carolina Historical Review* 2 (July 1925): 328; Mullin, *Flight and Rebellion*, 56, 192 n. 84; Wood, *Black Majority*, 240; Daniel E. Meaders, "South Carolina Fugitives as Viewed through Local Colonial Newspapers with Emphasis on Runaway Notices, 1732–1801," *Journal of Negro History* 60 (April 1975): 290.

10. Jacob Wilkinson to Col. Alexander McAllister, November 1766, McAllister Papers, Southern Historical Collection, University of North Carolina at Chapel Hill (hereafter cited as McAllister Papers). See also *Virginia Gazette* (Rind), 6 September 1770.

11. Forty of the 134 runaways for whom records exist fled during the years 1773–75.

12. Because occupations were listed only for nonfield slaves, all slaves without listed occupations were counted as field hands. For a supportive discussion relating to the listing and nonlisting of slave occupations in inventories, see Herbert G. Gutman and Richard Sutch, "Sambo Makes Good; or, Were Slaves Imbued with the Protestant Work Ethic?" in *Reckoning with Slavery: A Critical Study in the Quantitative History of American Negro Slavery*, edited by Paul A. David, Herbert G. Gutman, Richard Sutch, Peter Temin, and Gavin Wright (New York: Oxford University Press, 1976), 78 n. 30. Only 1 percent of Virginia's and 0.7 percent of South Carolina's male runaways between 1730 and 1787 were

explicitly described by their masters as field hands. Lathan A. Windley, "Profile of Runaway Slaves in Virginia and South Carolina from 1730 through 1787" (Ph.D. diss., University of Iowa, 1974), 138.

13. See Table 5.8.

14. See Chapter 1 and Marvin L. Michael Kay and Lorin Lee Cary, "A Demographic Analysis of Colonial North Carolina with Special Emphasis upon the Slave and Black Populations," in *Black Americans in North Carolina and the South*, edited by Jeffrey J. Crow and Flora J. Hatley (Chapel Hill: University of North Carolina Press, 1984), 71–121. Herbert G. Gutman, in *The Black Family in Slavery and Freedom, 1750–1925* (New York: Random House, 1976), 265, suggests that the absence of older slaves among runaways related to the binding ties of marriage. Allan Kulikoff interprets the predominance of young males as part of a search for spouses. See his essay "The Beginnings of the Afro-American Family in Maryland" in *Law, Society, and Politics in Early Maryland*, edited by Aubrey C. Land, Lois Green Carr, and Edward C. Papenfuse (Baltimore: Johns Hopkins University Press, 1977), 187. Numerous other studies at least agree on the youthfulness of runaways, including Eugene D. Genovese, *Roll, Jordan, Roll: The World the Slaves Made* (New York: Pantheon, 1974), 798 n. 2; Blassingame, *Slave Community*, 202; Edgar J. McManus, *Black Bondage in the North* (Syracuse, N.Y.: Syracuse University Press, 1973), 111–13; Windley, "Profile of Runaway Slaves," 79–86.

15. Sex ratios in the Chesapeake, North Carolina, and the South Carolina low country probably averaged respectively during the years 1750–75 about 117, 125, and 130. Perhaps the higher sex ratios in South Carolina indirectly and paradoxically prompted a higher percentage of female slave runaways in that province. Higher sex ratios reflected higher proportions of Africans in the slave population. Because African women were more prone to run away with their husbands or friends, the greater percentage of female slave runaways in South Carolina is perhaps attributable to the colony's larger proportion of Africans. The almost identical percentages of female runaways in North Carolina and the Chesapeake, despite the former's greater percentage of African-born slaves, remains a puzzle. Clouding the issue further are the more substantial differences in sex ratios and proportions of Africans in the population between South Carolina and the Chesapeake than was the case between South Carolina and North Carolina. For sex ratios and proportions of African-born slaves in the three regions, see Chapter 1, esp. Table 1.7, and Kay and Cary, "A Demographic Analysis," 76–78, 93–103; Allan Kulikoff, "A 'Prolifick' People: Black Population Growth in the Chesapeake Colonies, 1700–1790," *Southern Studies* 16 (Winter 1977): 393–96, 403–6;

Philip D. Morgan, "Black Society in the Lowcountry, 1610–1810," in *Slavery and Freedom in the Age of the American Revolution*, edited by Ira Berlin and Ronald Hoffman (Charlottesville: University Press of Virginia, 1983), 90–92. For a contrasting view concerning the propensity of African women to run off, see n. 22 below.

16. Windley ("Profile of Runaway Slaves," 132–36) found that 22 percent of Virginia and 30 percent of South Carolina runaways had had at least one previous owner. Mullin (*Flight and Rebellion*, 89–91) points to a "correlation between multiple owners, mobility, and running away" and notes that by 1770 masters described half of all artisan runaways in Virginia as having had previous owners. Wood (*Black Majority*, 248, 253–54) singles out change of ownership as a crucial immediate reason for fleeing among all runaways, not just nonfield slaves. See also George M. Frederickson and Christopher Lasch, "Resistance to Slavery," *Civil War History* 13 (December 1967): 315–29; Gutman, *Black Family in Slavery and*

Freedom, 264–65, 318–19, 553–54 n. 33. For examples in North Carolina, see Governors Papers, Committee of Claims Reports, 1760–64, in North Carolina State Archives, Raleigh (hereafter cited as NCSA); Clark, *State Records*, 22:836–40; *North Carolina Gazette*, 24 March, 14 July 1775; *Cape Fear Mercury*, 7 August 1775; *North Carolina Magazine*, late June 1764.

17. For other colonies, see Gutman, *Black Family in Slavery and Freedom*, esp. chap. 8; Allan Kulikoff, "Tobacco and Slaves: Population, Economy, and Society in Eighteenth-Century Prince George's County, Maryland" (Ph.D. diss., Brandeis University, 1976), 226–28, 302–7; Mullin, *Flight and Rebellion*, 43, 103, 106, 109–10; Wood, *Black Majority*, 139–41, 248–49, 266. In "Profile of Runaway Slaves," Windley scarcely mentions the family.

18. *Virginia Gazette* (Purdie and Dixon), 9 July 1767, 4 July 1771, 2 April 1772; *North Carolina Gazette*, 5 May, 22 December 1775; *Virginia Gazette* (Dixon and Hunter), 24 June 1775; Jacob Wilkinson to Col. Alexander MacAllister, November 1766, McAllister Papers; *South Carolina Gazette*, 16–25 May 1748; *Virginia Gazette* (Hunter), 21 February 1751; *South Carolina Gazette*, 27 November–4 December 1775; *Virginia Gazette* (Purdie and Dixon), 5 November 1767; *North Carolina Gazette*, 10 November 1769.

19. It is also likely that owners at times carelessly neglected to mention past owners in their advertisements. The slave domestic referred to in the text was an eighteen-year-old Virginia-born waiter, George. *Virginia Gazette* (Purdie and Dixon), 5 December 1771. For the others, see *North Carolina Magazine*, early and late June 1764; *Virginia Gazette* (Purdie and Dixon), 3 November 1769, 7 August 1775.

20. For contemporary comments that suggest the frequent use of Africans as watermen, see William Attmore, *Journal of a Tour to North Carolina by William Attmore, 1787*, edited by Lida T. Rodman (Chapel Hill: University of North Carolina Press, 1922), 44–45; Elkanah Watson, *Men and Times of the Revolution; or, Memoirs of Elkanah Watson, including His Journals of Travels in Europe and America, 1777–1842*, 2d ed., edited by Winslow C. Watson (New York: Dana and Co., 1857), 43.

21. The proportion of Africans in the slave populations of North Carolina and its neighbors is discussed in Chapter 1. The techniques used to identify African-born slaves in Table 5.8 may be too conservative. In addition to the 33 slaves identifiable as Africans, 12 other field hands had African or African-derived names: 2 Mingoes, 2 Jacks, 2 Cudgoes, Jemmy, Jamey, Jem, and 3 probable variations of Quash. Jem is specifically identified as "country born," but in all of the other cases the evidence is insufficient to determine origin. Some must have been African. The same is probably true of several of the 8 field-hand runaways whose names are not cited in contemporary records. For the 12 with African names, see *South Carolina Gazette*, 15–22 January 1750, 14–21 October 1756, 1 July 1769; Governor's Office, Committee of Claims Reports, 1760–64, NCSA; Clark, *State Records*, 22:823–27, 855–63; *Virginia Gazette* (Hunter), 21 February 1751; New Hanover County Court Minutes, 4 October 1768, NCSA; *Cape Fear Mercury*, 8 December 1769, 13 January 1773; *North Carolina Gazette*, 5 May 1775. For the 8 unnamed runaways, see Rowan County Court Minutes, July 1755, Carteret County Court Minutes, 6 December 1757, and Bertie County Court Minutes, 24 July 1759; all in NCSA; *Cape Fear Mercury*, 8 December 1769; *Virginia Gazette* (Purdie and Dixon), 9 July 1767, 14 December 1769; *Virginia Gazette* (Rind), 6 September 1770, 21 October 1773; Inventory of John DuBois Estate, New Hanover County, July 1768, North Carolina Wills, 1663–1789, Secretary of State Papers, NCSA (hereafter cited as John DuBois Estate).

22. For African contributions to resistance in colonial South Carolina, see Wood, *Black Majority*, 289–92, 301–2, 314. For the prevalence of African runaways in Jamaica, see Patterson, *Sociology of Slavery*, 262–63. Daniel C. Littlefield adds a conflicting note to the issue, for he has found that African women in South Carolina were less prone to run off than "country-born" women. He also discusses which Africans were most prone to flight; the fragmentary nature of the evidence precludes such an analysis for North Carolina. See Littlefield, *Rice and Slaves: Ethnicity and the Slave Trade in Colonial South Carolina* (Baton Rouge: Louisiana State University Press, 1981), 12–33, 145.

23. See, e.g., *Virginia Gazette* (Hunter), 17 October 1755; *North Carolina Gazette*, 10 November 1769. A similar proportion of South Carolina runaways fled in groups—30 percent in the 1760s and 32 percent in the 1770s. See Morgan, "Black Society in the Lowcountry," 130.

24. *North Carolina Gazette*, 24 February, 5 May 1755. Such determination was not uncommon among newly arrived Africans. See *North Carolina Gazette*, 5 May 1775, for the case of a "short well set Negro man" about thirty years of age with "Country marks in his Temples, and his Teeth filed sharp" who fled from an unknown master, was captured and jailed in Carteret County, escaped, and then was recaptured in adjoining Craven County.

25. *Cape Fear Mercury*, 22 September 1773; *North Carolina Gazette*, 10 November 1769, 7 January 1774, 24 February, 5 May 1775; *South Carolina Gazette*, 18 March–1 April 1751; *Virginia Gazette* (Purdie and Dixon), 28 September 1769.

26. See, e.g., *South Carolina Gazette*, 2–6 October 1758, 12–19 July 1760; *Virginia Gazette* (Purdie and Dixon), 5 December 1771. On the selection of nonfield hands, a process only partially documented, see Kulikoff, "Prince George's County, Maryland," esp. chap. 7; Mullin, *Flight and Rebellion*, 83–94; and Herbert G. Gutman, *Slavery and the Numbers Game: A Critique of "Time on the Cross"* (Urbana: University of Illinois Press, 1975), 77–81.

27. See *Cape Fear Mercury*, 24 November, 8 December 1769, 7 August 1775; *North Carolina Gazette*, 13 March 1752, 5 May 1775; *North Carolina Magazine*, early and late June 1764; *South Carolina Gazette*, 26 February–5 March 1754, 2–6 October 1758, 12–19 July 1760; *Virginia Gazette* (Purdie and Dixon), 3 November 1768, 5 December 1771, 24 June 1773.

28. See Table 1.5.

29. *South Carolina Gazette*, 16–25 May 1748. The origins of the parents could not be determined. A father is listed as Jemy, an African name, but he could have been American-born. The mother's name is not given.

30. *South Carolina Gazette*, 16–25 May 1748, 22–29 November 1760, 18–25 July 1761; *North Carolina Magazine*, 4–11 January 1765; *Virginia Gazette* (Purdie and Dixon), 9 July 1767, 4 July 1771, 2 April 1772; *North Carolina Gazette*, 24 March, 5 May, 6 October 1775; *Virginia Gazette* (Dixon and Hunter), 24 June 1775. See Windley, "Profile of Runaway Slaves," 205–18. In South Carolina the percentage of runaways thought to be "visiting" friends, acquaintances, or relatives was relatively high—70 percent for 1760–69, 72 percent for 1770–79, and about the same proportion down through 1806. See Morgan, "Black Society in the Lowcountry," 129–30. Morgan does not distinguish among occupational groups in this instance.

31. *Virginia Gazette* (Purdie and Dixon), 15 August 1766, 7 June 1770; *Cape Fear Mercury*, 29 December 1773; *North Carolina Gazette*, 7 April, 22 December 1775; *Virginia Gazette* (Dixon and Hunter), 29 April, 2 December 1775; *Virginia Gazette* (Pinckney), 15 June 1775.

32. *Cape Fear Mercury*, 24 November 1769; *North Carolina Gazette*, 13 March 1752; *South Carolina Gazette*, 26 February–5 March 1754, 12–19 July 1760; *Virginia Gazette* (Purdie and

Dixon), 3 November 1768, 24 June 1773; William L. Saunders, ed., *The Colonial Records of North Carolina*, 10 vols. (Raleigh: State of North Carolina, 1886–90), 975–76. For the willingness of whites to use the labor of runaway skilled slaves, see Littlefield, *Rice and Slaves*, 165–66.

33. *North Carolina Gazette*, 24 February 1775; *South Carolina Gazette*, 17 November–4 December 1755. London and Bess fled with a slave owned by a nearby planter.

Although Snow and Batchelor's assumption that whites had stolen or "decoyed away" their slaves flowed from a common bias that denied slaves the capacity of decision making, it was not made totally without cause. The theft of slaves did occur, yet, except for the two notices cited above, no other references to this practice appear in North Carolina records before the Revolution. It is unlikely that more than a few slaves were "invegelied" away by unscrupulous whites under the pretense of helping blacks escape to freedom.

For evidence from South Carolina concerning the theft of slaves, see Wood, *Black Majority*, 242,; Windley, "Profile of Runaway Slaves," 43. A North Carolina law of 1741 provided heavy penalties for such thefts. Clark, *State Records*, 23:196–97. A 1778 act dealt specifically with the "promiscuous practice" of stealing slaves, as well as free blacks and mulattoes, and demanded the death penalty in case of conviction. Clark, *State Records*, 24:220–21. County court cases after 1741 suggest that the earlier act aimed chiefly at preventing the theft of black or mulatto servants and apprentices. In each instance, free black or mulatto servants and apprentices were the targets of whites who sought to exploit their vulnerable status and illegally enslave them. Kay and Cary, "A Demographic Analysis," 112–17, 121 n. 37.

34. Rowan County Court Minutes, August 1769, NCSA; *North Carolina Gazette*, 10 November 1769, advertisement dated 13 October. For the case of Francis Locke, see Rowan County Court Minutes, February 1769, NCSA: "Mr. Frances Lock came into Open Court & proved his property to a certain negro Wench now in the possession of the Sheriff." For an Irish servant woman and a Negro slave owned by James Davis, the colony's printer, see *North Carolina Gazette*, 15 April 1757, 24 June 1768; for a "Dutch" (German) servant and a Negro slave, see *South Carolina Gazette*, 28 May–4 June 1750, 1 June 1769; and for two white servants and a Negro slave owned by Henry Young, see *North Carolina Gazette*, 5 May 1775.

35. Thirty-four servant and apprentice runaways are recorded in newspaper advertisements and a sample of county court minutes, the sources in which such individuals appear most frequently, for the period in question. As in the case of slaves, this totally understates the number who actually ran off. Of the 34, 6 were designated as American-born (3 blacks, 1 Indian, and 2 whites), 2 as "Dutch" (German), 2 as English, 7 as Irish, and 1 as Scottish. Included among these were 2 free black and 4 Irish women. The origins of the remaining 16, all but 1 of them males, are not known. Most of the 34 were young; the average for the 17 whose ages are given was 24 years. Thirteen of the 34 had been brought to North Carolina recently. No capture notices for servants and apprentices appeared in the colony's newspapers, but county court minutes make it evident that white servants stood a better chance of escaping than did black or mulatto servants and apprentices. Fourteen cases of captured servants appear in these records, 3 involving blacks. The latter were gone relatively short periods: 11 days, 1 month, and 2 months respectively. White servants tended to be out longer before capture; the average was 6 months for the 7 for whom such information is indicated. The Native American servant who fled, Joseph Leftear, was out 8 months. In addition to the sources cited in the last two notes, see Carteret County Court Minutes, 16 September 1769; Chowan County Court Minutes, 23 July 1748; Craven County Court Minutes, May 1758,

April 1762, April 1765; Rowan County Court Minutes, October 1753, March, July 1754, July, October 1755, 20 April 1756, October 1768; all in NCSA; *Cape Fear Mercury*, 22 September, 29 December 1773; *North Carolina Gazette*, 15 April 1757; *North Carolina Magazine*, 13–20 July 1764; *South Carolina Gazette*, 28 May–4 June 1750; *Virginia Gazette* (Purdie and Dixon), 23 September 1773, 17 February 1774; *Virginia Gazette* (Rind), 14 April 1768.

36. In all, 8 of the 117 field hands who ran off bore signs of past punishments. Seven others had scars, which may or may not have been caused by maltreatment, and 2 slaves wore neck collars. See *North Carolina Gazette*, 15 November 1751, 24 June 1768, 7 April 1775; *Virginia Gazette* (Hunter), 17 October 1755; *South Carolina Gazette*, 27 November–4 December 1755; *Virginia Gazette* (Purdie and Dixon), 7 June 1770, 10 January, 4 July 1771. For a similar discussion about Virginia and South Carolina runaways, see Windley, "Profile of Runaway Slaves," 90–97. For the frequency of brands as identification among South Carolina runaways, see Littlefield, *Rice and Slaves*, 123.

37. *Virginia Gazette* (Purdie and Dixon), 3 November 1768. See also *Cape Fear Mercury*, 8 December 1769; *Virginia Gazette* (Purdie and Dixon), 24 June 1773. Three of the seventeen nonfield runaways had scars from previous punishments.

38. *Cape Fear Mercury*, 24 November, 8 December 1769; *North Carolina Gazette*, 15 November 1751, 7 April, 22 December 1775; *Virginia Gazette* (Purdie and Dixon), 3 November 1768, 7 June 1770; *Virginia Gazette* (Dixon and Hunter), 29 April 1775.

39. Mullin, *Flight and Rebellion*, 98–103; *North Carolina Gazette*, 13 March 1752; *South Carolina Gazette*, 2–6 October 1758. Mullin's (*Flight and Rebellion*, 100–101) list of stutterers includes no blacksmiths, shoemakers, or carpenters, craftsmen who "characteristically worked by themselves, at their own pace and with a minimum of direct and persistent supervision." Windley ("Profile of Runaway Slaves," 157–61) found occupations listed for 12 of the 47 stutterers in Virginia (1736–87) and 10 of the 40 stutterers in South Carolina (1732–87). Mullin's generalization that waiting men and sailors were uniquely afflicted with stuttering because of their constant and stressful contact with whites is not supported by Windley's findings for either colony.

40. *Virginia Gazette* (Hunter), 17 October 1755; *North Carolina Magazine*, early June 1764; *Virginia Gazette* (Purdie and Dixon), 5 December 1771; Kenneth Stampp, "Rebels and Sambos: The Search for the Negro's Personality in Slavery," *Journal of Southern History* 37 (August 1971): 391–92. See also Genovese, *Roll, Jordan, Roll*, 646–47; Robert W. Fogel and Stanley L. Engerman, *Time on the Cross: The Economics of American Negro Slavery*, 2 vols. (Boston: Little, Brown, 1974), 1:152–53, 2:118. Fogel and Engerman argue that slavery weighed most heavily on skilled slaves. Cf. Gutman, *Slavery and the Numbers Game*, 74–75.

41. *Virginia Gazette* (Purdie and Dixon), 3 November 1768. See also *Virginia Gazette* (Purdie and Dixon), 24 June 1773; *Cape Fear Mercury*, 8 December 1769.

42. *Virginia Gazette* (Purdie and Dixon), 26 November 1772; *North Carolina Gazette*, 10 November 1769, 2 September 1774.

43. Times of flight are based on specific data for 51 field hands, 6 nonfield runaways, and 1 whose occupation is unknown. The 57 slaves listed as "captured" include those who were killed; the dates refer to the date of the capture notices or proceedings of the county court or Committee of Claims, whichever was earlier. Only 3 nonfield hands were among those captured or killed. Although capture dates are not an accurate guide to the time of flight, as at least 17 of those captured were Africans—most of them recent imports—and over half of the remaining captured or killed slaves spoke little English, it seems plausible that most of

the captured or killed had been out a relatively short time. See Windley, "Profile of Runaway Slaves," 171–76. Cheryll Ann Cody calculates that 30.8 percent of South Carolina runaways advertised in the *South Carolina Gazette* from 1725 to 1799 fled during May, June, or July, the period of hardest labor in the rice fields. See Cody, "Slave Demography and Family Formation: A Community Study of the Ball Family Plantations, 1720–1896" (Ph.D. diss., University of Minnesota, 1982), 109.

44. *North Carolina Gazette*, 13 March 1752. See also *Cape Fear Mercury*, 24 November 1769.

45. *Virginia Gazette* (Hunter), 17 October 1755; *Virginia Gazette* (Dixon and Hunter), 29 April, 2 December 1775; *North Carolina Gazette*, November 1751; *Virginia Gazette* (Purdie and Dixon), 26 November 1772. See also *North Carolina Gazette*, 10 November 1769, 2 September 1774; *Cape Fear Mercury*, 29 December 1773; *Virginia Gazette* (Dixon and Hunter), 24 June 1775; *Virginia Gazette* (Pinckney), 15 June 1775.

46. *North Carolina Gazette*, 24 June 1768, 18 November 1769, 7 January 1774, 24 February 1775; *North Carolina Magazine*, 4–11 January 1765. See also *North Carolina Gazette*, 15 November 1751, 2 September 1774, 24 February, 5 May 1775; *South Carolina Gazette*, 14–21 October 1756; *Virginia Gazette* (Purdie and Dixon), 15 August 1766, 5 November 1767, 28 September 1769; *Cape Fear Mercury*, 13 January, 22 September 1773; *Virginia Gazette* (Dixon and Hunter), 25 February 1775.

47. *Virginia Gazette* (Hunter), 17 October 1755; *North Carolina Gazette*, 2 September 1774.

48. *Virginia Gazette* (Dixon and Hunter), 2 December 1775; *North Carolina Gazette*, 13 March 1752, 7 January 1774. Three masters did fear that their runaways might flee the colony by boat or head for port towns in Virginia. *North Carolina Gazette*, 24 June 1768; *Virginia Gazette* (Rind), 21 October 1774; *Virginia Gazette* (Dixon and Hunter), 29 April 1775. See also *North Carolina Gazette*, 24 February 1775. In Virginia 39 fled on horseback and 7 in boats, 3 percent and 0.6 percent respectively of the 1,276 runaways. In South Carolina 21 rode off and 19 used boats, 1 percent and 0.8 percent respectively of the 2,424 runaways.

49. Adelaide L. Fries, ed., *Records of the Moravians in North Carolina*, 8 vols. (Raleigh: Edwards and Broughton Print Co., 1922–54), 2:858; *North Carolina Gazette*, 7 July 1753, NCSA.

50. *North Carolina Gazette*, 24 June 1768; *Cape Fear Mercury*, 24 November 1769; *South Carolina Gazette*, 16–25 May, 25 May–1 June 1748, 18 March–1 April 1751, 26 February–5 March 1754, 14–21 October 1756, 12–19 July, 23–30 August, 22–29 November 1760, 18–25 July 1761; *Virginia Gazette* (Purdie and Dixon), 9 July 1767, 3 November 1768, 7 June 1770, 4 July 1773; *Virginia Gazette* (Rind), 21 October 1773; *Virginia Gazette* (Dixon and Hunter), 29 April, 24 June, 2 December 1775; *Virginia Gazette* (Hunter), 21 February 1751; *Virginia Gazette* (Pinckney), 13 April, 15 June 1775. Windley's data on destinations are not exactly comparable to this analysis, as he deals only with the destinations presumed by masters and considers neither where slaves were captured nor whether patterns varied by skill. Nonetheless, in Virginia prior to the Revolution, the known patterns were almost identical to those in North Carolina. Of 406 runaways for whom destinations were listed, 57 percent were thought to be staying in the colony, 37 percent to be heading out of it, and 6 percent either one or the other. In South Carolina fully 86 percent of the 677 runaways for whom destinations were given were thought to be staying in the colony, only 10 percent to be leaving, and 4 percent either one or the other. Windley, "Profile of Runaway Slaves," 205–24.

51. For slaves whose destinations were not stated, see *North Carolina Gazette*, 15 November 1751, 10 November 1769, 2 September 1774, 5 May 1775; *Virginia Gazette* (Hunter), 17

October 1755; *South Carolina Gazette*, 17 November–4 December 1755, 1 June 1769; *Virginia Gazette* (Purdie and Dixon), 9 July 1767; *Cape Fear Mercury*, 8 December 1769, 13 January 1773; *Virginia Gazette* (Rind), 6 September 1770; *Virginia Gazette* (Dixon and Hunter), 25 February 1775; James Auld, "The Journal of James Auld," *Publications of the Southern History Association* 7 (July 1904): 262; John DuBois Estate, July 1768.

For those thought to be lurking about, see *South Carolina Gazette*, 15–22 January 1750; Edgecombe County Court Minutes, 27 June 1758, NCSA; *North Carolina Magazine*, 4–11 January 1765; *North Carolina Gazette*, 2 September 1774, 24 February, 24 March, 5, 12 May, 14 July, 6 October 1775.

For those thought to be headed for other parts of North Carolina, see *North Carolina Magazine*, 4–11 January 1765; *Virginia Gazette* (Purdie and Dixon), 15 August 1766; *North Carolina Gazette*, 22 December 1775; Jacob Wilkinson to Col. Alexander McAllister, November 1766, McAllister Papers, SHC.

For those slaves caught within North Carolina but in counties other than the counties from which they fled, see *North Carolina Gazette*, 7 July 1753, 2 September 1774, 5 May 1775; *South Carolina Gazette*, 6–16 December 1760; Governors Papers—Lists of Taxables, Militia, and Magistrates, 1754–70, n.d., NCSA; Clark, *State Records*, 22, 836–40; *Virginia Gazette* (Purdie and Dixon), 28 September 1769; *Cape Fear Mercury*, 8 December 1769, 29 December 1773.

For those captured within North Carolina and whose home counties could not be determined, see Rowan County Court Minutes, July 1755, February 1772; Carteret County Court Minutes, 6 December 1757; Bertie County Court Minutes, 24 July 1759; all in NCSA; *Virginia Gazette* (Purdie and Dixon), 5 November 1767, 14 December 1769, 10 January 1771; *North Carolina Gazette*, 10 November 1769, 7 January 1774, 24 February 1775; *Cape Fear Mercury*, 22 September 1773; Stephen Blackman to Sheriff, Dobbs County, 19 September 1767, Private Collections, Colin Shaw Papers, NCSA.

52. Littlefield (*Rice and Slaves*, 128–33) notes that capture rates among slaves varied considerably. Ninety percent of the Mandingos, for example, were advertised as jailed rather than as fugitives, while under 20 percent of American-born slaves appeared in capture notices. Morgan ("Black Society in the Lowcountry," 131) makes no such distinctions, yet his figures are suggestive. Between 1760 and 1769, 36.9 percent of all advertised runaways appeared in capture notices. During the following decades, down to 1800, the percentages were 37.3, 34.9, and 22.4.

CHAPTER 6

1. Cheryll Ann Cody correctly contends that it was in the owners' interest to see that each slave be identified by a single, distinctive given name in order to simplify the allocation of tasks and provisions. She also maintains that slaveowners attempted to ensure that this came to pass by choosing names for the first generation of slaves but thereafter permitting the slaves themselves to control the naming process. We argue that the slaves normally chose their own names from their first arrival. See Cody, "There Was No 'Absalom' on the Ball Plantations: Slave-Naming Practices in the South Carolina Low Country, 1720–1865," *American Historical Review* 92 (June 1987): 572–73, 579.

2. Ogonna Chuks-orji, *Names from Africa: Their Origin, Meaning, and Pronunciation* (Chicago, 1972): 76–78.

3. For African naming practices, see ibid., 75–84; Ibechukwu Madubuike, *A Handbook of African Names* (Washington, D.C., 1976), 1–137; Lorenzo Dow Turner, *Africanisms in the Gullah Dialect* (Chicago, 1949, 1969), 31–43; John S. Mbiti, *African Religions and Philosophy*, 2d ed. (Oxford: Heinemann International, 1990), 118–20. See also John Inscoe, "Carolina Slave Names: An Index to Acculturation," *Journal of Southern History* 49 (November 1983): 531–37; Charles B. Joyner, *Down by the Riverside: A South Carolina Slave Community* (Urbana: University of Illinois Press, 1984), 217–21; Mechal Sobel, *"Trabelin On": The Slave Journey to an Afro-Baptist Faith* (Westport, Conn.: Greenwood Press, 1979), 14–15; Joey Lee Dillard, *Black English: Its History and Usage in the United States* (New York: Random House, 1972), 123–35. See as well the accounts in *African Systems of Kinship and Marriage*, edited by A. R. Radcliffe-Brown and Daryll Forde (London: Oxford University Press, 1950); A. I. Richards, "Some Types of Family Structure amongst the Central Bantu," 232; Meyer Fortes, "Kinship and Marriage among the Ashanti," 266; Daryll Forde, "Double Descent among the Yako," 296.

4. *North Carolina Gazette*, 2 September 1774.

5. When Charles ran off, for instance, his master passed along the information that he had "heard" that his slave had passed for free under the name of Benjamin Corbin and even obtained an indenture. See *Virginia Gazette* (Purdie and Dixon), 15 August 1766. See also the example of Road in the *Virginia Gazette* (Pinckney), 15 June 1775.

6. Chuks-orji (*Names from Africa*, 70) lists the names Taiwo and Thambo. The American creole names in the text derive from at least twenty ethnic groups in Africa, from Senegal and Gambia in the northwest of sub-Saharan Africa through Nigeria to the Bantu-speaking peoples as far south as Zaire and Angola. See Turner, *Africanisms in the Gullah Dialect*, 164–65, 173; Newbell Niles Puckett, "Names of American Slaves," in *Studies in the Science of Society*, edited by George Peter Murdock (New Haven, 1937; Freeport, N.Y., 1969); 451, 457. Ubaka, Ibok, and Baako are listed in Madubuike, *Handbook of African Names*, 53, 84, 105.

7. Some scholars have used slave names and naming practices effectively to study slave culture in the colonies and the United States. See Puckett, "Names of American Slaves," 471–94; Puckett, *Black Names in America: Origins and Usage* (Boston, 1975); Turner, *Africanisms in the Gullah Dialect*; Dillard, *Black English*, 123–35; Joey Lee Dillard, *Black Names* (The Hague, 1976), 17–35; Inscoe, "Carolina Slave Names," 527–54; Peter H. Wood, *Black Majority: Negroes in Colonial South Carolina from 1670 through the Stono Rebellion* (New York: Knopf, 1974), 181–86; Joyner, *Down by the Riverside*, 217–24; Cheryll Ann Cody, "Naming, Kinship, and Estate Dispersal: Notes on Slave Family Life on a South Carolina Plantation, 1786 to 1833," *William and Mary Quarterly*, 3d. ser., 39 (January 1982): 198–206; Cody, "Slave-Naming Practices," 563–96; Darrett B. Rutman and Anita H. Rutman, *A Place in Time: Middlesex County, Virginia, 1650–1750* (New York: Norton, 1984), 170–73, 260 nn. 23–24; Rutman and Rutman, *A Place in Time: Explicatus* (New York: Norton, 1984), 97–103, 105–6 nn. 17–23.

8. Rutman and Rutman, *A Place in Time: Explicatus*, 97–103, 105–6, and *A Place in Time: Middlesex County*, 170.

9. For primary and secondary sources used in this analysis, see Table 6.1 and Table 6.2 respectively. Dillard (*Black Names*, 21) identifies a common type of distortion of African names, evident in this text, that occurred in the development of a pidgin English: the "phonological reduction" of the initial letters of African words or names. Often endings of words also were omitted.

10. Inscoe reaches a similar conclusion in "Carolina Slave Names," 539–40.

11. For a paternalistic explanation of the prevalence of "familial," i.e., diminutive, names among slaves, see Rutman and Rutman, *A Place in Time: Middlesex County*, 170–73, 269 n. 23, and *A Place in Time: Explicatus*, 97–103. Gary B. Nash appears to view diminutive forms of names as primarily resulting from the derisive naming practices of whites. See his "Forging Freedom: The Emancipation Experience in the Northern Seaport Cities, 1775–1820," in *Slavery and Freedom in the Age of the American Revolution*, edited by Ira Berlin and Ronald Hoffman (Charlottesville: University Press of Virginia, 1983), 22.

12. *The Interesting Narrative of the Life of Olaudah Equiano, or Gustavus Vassa, The African, Written by Himself*, Early American Imprints #23353 (New York, 1791). For Olaudah's account and his background, see G. I. Jones, "Olaudah Equiano of the Niger Ibo," in *Africa Remembered: Narratives of West Africans from the Era of the Slave Trade*, edited by Phillip D. Curtin (Madison: University of Wisconsin Press, 1968), 60–69.

13. See Inscoe, "Carolina Slave Names," 542–44, for a demonstration of the increase in biblical names among slaves from 1770 to 1865. He probably overestimates the significance of such names during the colonial-Revolutionary period. Cody argues that significant planter attempts to convert slaves only began, at the earliest, in the 1780s and that, consistent with this, important slave use of biblical names only first began in the nineteenth century. Cody, "Slave-Naming Practices," 573, 580–81, 588.

14. Cody ("Slave-Naming Practices," 581–83) presents conflicting evidence about the continuation of the practice of giving slaves day names according to the day of the week they were born. She argues that this did not occur among slaves with actual African day names nor among slaves with like-sounding day names such as Jack for Quako. She notes, however, that eighteenth-century Ball plantation slaves with "Anglicized [translated] day-names" normally received such names based on the day they were born. It is questionable whether the Ball plantation slaves, a limited, rather rarefied sample, exemplify eighteenth-century North Carolina's slave-naming patterns.

15. To classify these languages, we primarily used William E. Welker, "African Languages: An Overview" (paper, African Studies Center, University of California at Los Angeles, 1978). Of supplementary use was George Peter Murdock, *Africa: Its Peoples and Their Culture History* (New York: McGraw-Hill, 1959). For the classification in the text, see Welker, "African Languages," 5; Murdock, *Africa*, 252–54. We wish to thank Theodore Natsoulas, professor of African history at the University of Toledo, for bringing Welker's analysis to our attention.

16. For primary and secondary sources used in this analysis, see Table 6.1 and Table 6.2 respectively.

17. Ibid.

18. For an expansive analysis of surnames from the colonial era through Reconstruction, see Inscoe, "Carolina Slave Names," 547–53. For surnames in Africa, see Madubuike, *Handbook of African Names*, 16–19. The use of surnames is still evolving in Africa. We wish to thank Professor Theodore Natsoulas for information concerning the development of surnames there.

19. John Walker Papers, P.C. 254.1, in North Carolina State Archives, Raleigh (hereafter cited as NCSA). Inscoe (Carolina Slave Names," 548) points out that "the extent to which slaves took second names is difficult to determine because of their reluctance to use them openly and their owners' refusal to acknowledge them, if indeed they were aware of them."

20. James M. Robin Papers, vol. 1, Massachusetts Historical Society, Boston; "Lean by Thomas Pollock to Jacob Mitchell," Pollock Papers, P.C. 31.1, NCSA. We have not uncovered instances of slaves acquiring the names of owners.

21. Elkanah Watson, *Men and Times of the Revolution; or, Memoirs of Elkanah Watson, including His Journals of Travels in Europe and America, 1777–1842,* 2d ed., edited by Winslow C. Watson (New York: Dana and Co., 1857), 43. Jeffrey Crow informs us that Wingran Bay is probably Winyah Bay in Georgetown, S.C. See Lester J. Capon, ed., *Atlas of Early American History: The Revolutionary Era* (Princeton, N.J.: Princeton University Press, 1976), 6. Using songs to express inner feelings and to set a work rhythm, which presumably was what the rowers were doing, recurred in various forms in societies throughout West Africa, and the practice persisted in America. See also Lawrence Levine, *Black Culture and Black Consciousness: Afro-American Folk Thought from Slavery to Freedom* (New York: Oxford University Press, 1977), 5–13, 19–20, 33, 208–15; Wood, *Black Majority.*

22. Wood quotes a passage in Edward McCrady's work that talks of slave boat hands' "plaintive, humorous, happy catches which they sang as they bent to the stroke." See McCrady, *The History of South Carolina under the Royal Government, 1719–1776* (New York, 1899), 516, as quoted in Wood, *Black Majority,* 202–3.

23. Dillard (*Black English*), who emphasizes the widespread development of pidgin-creole languages among colonial blacks, is a notable exception in this regard. Or, as he puts it within the context of analyzing black naming practices: "Like many other features of African survival, these day names serve to illustrate how absurd is the theory of Gullah's being the only repository of African practices because of its isolation" (p. 126). Although Dillard does not adequately document where and when pidgin-creole languages developed in particular colonies or regions and probably stresses too much the carryover of West African pidgin English to the colonies, his effort is nonetheless significant and we owe much to it. For his development of slave speech patterns, see pp. 73–138.

The view of Russell R. Menard more closely resembles the norm. In his article, "The Maryland Slave Population, 1658 to 1730: A Demographic Profile of Blacks in Four Counties," *William and Mary Quarterly,* 3d. ser., 32 (1975): 29–54, he denies (p. 30) the possibility of the development of a creole language in the Chesapeake. By 1730, he asserts, "The isolation that resulted from different tribal origins dissolved as English supplanted the variety of languages spoken by Africans upon arrival, as Christianity displaced African religions, and as slaves created a common culture from their diverse backgrounds in the Old World and their shared experiences in the New." The slaves' diverse African pasts, as Menard sees it, had to be dispensed with before they could establish an effective American culture out of their shared New World experiences.

In similar fashion, Ira Berlin confidently asserts that "paternalism at close quarters" ensured that blacks in the Chesapeake "developed no distinct language and rarely utilized African day names for their children." We believe Berlin to be incorrect on both counts. See Berlin, "Time, Space, and the Evolution of Afro-American Society on British Mainland North America," *American Historical Review* 85 (February 1980): 77.

24. For excellent discussions of Gullah, see Wood, *Black Majority,* 167–71; Joyner, *Down by the Riverside,* 196–224; Turner, *Africanisms in the Gullah Dialect.*

25. For the origins and linguistic patterns of slave runaways in colonial North Carolina as compared with other colonies, see Chapter 5. See also Marvin L. Michael Kay and Lorin Lee Cary, "Slave Runaways in Colonial North Carolina, 1748–1775," *North Carolina Historical*

Review 63 (January 1986): 18–27 and passim. Since masters primarily were concerned with the slaves' productivity as workers, they consonantly concentrated on the slaves' proficiency in workplace English. The term *good English*, then, normally would refer to such proficiency. See reference to Waring's letter in the text.

26. John C. Van Horne, ed., *Religious Philanthropy and Colonial Slavery: The American Correspondence of the Associates of Daniel Bray, 1717–1777* (Urbana: University of Illinois Press, 1985), 99–101. For examples of slave speech patterns and other white descriptions, see Dillard, *Black English*, 87–88.

27. Quoted in Dillard, *Black English*, 88. For the original quotation, see John Ferdinand Dalziel Smyth, *A Tour in the United States of America. . . .*, 2 vols. (1784; reprint, New York: Arno Press, 1968), 39.

28. As discussed and quoted in Sterling Stuckey, *Slave Culture: Nationalist Theory and the Foundations of Black America* (New York: Oxford University Press, 1987), 70–73. See also Edward Warren, *A Doctor's Experiences on Three Continents* (Baltimore: Cushings and Bailey Press, 1885), 200–203. We have relied heavily on Stuckey's interpretation of the physician's memoirs.

29. Van Horne, *Religious Philanthropy and Colonial Slavery*, 115–16.

30. Ibid., 129–30, 138–89.

31. Ibid., 219.

32. Ibid., 294.

33. See Dillard, *Black English*, esp. 39–77; Melville J. Herskovits, *The Myth of the Negro Past* (Boston: Beacon Press, 1958), 275–91; Joyner, *Down by the Riverside*, 196–217, 222–24.

34. See Joyner, *Down by the Riverside*, 196–97.

35. Peter Wood notes that the slaves of the Georgia Sea Islands spoke Geechee, "a roughly synonymous . . . dialect" of Gullah. He, however, is open to the proposition urged in the text that Geechee was spoken by Georgia slaves well beyond the confines of the Sea Islands. See Wood, *Black Majority*, 170–71, including nn. 7–9.

36. See n. 25 above.

CHAPTER 7

1. Nathaniel Macon Collection, P.C. 10.2, in North Carolina State Archives, Raleigh (hereafter cited as NCSA). Mourning Ivins petitioned the county court for permission to free her husband in accordance with a 1741 law that strengthened the provisions of a 1715 act restricting the power of individual owners to manumit their slaves. The later statute provided that no slave was to be freed "upon any Pretense whatsoever, except for meritorious Services, to be adjudged and allowed of by the County Court, and license thereupon first had and obtained." Walter Clark, ed., *The State Records of North Carolina*, 16 vols., numbered 11–26 (Winston and Goldsboro: State of North Carolina, 1895–1906), 23:203.

2. Johann David Schoepf, *Travels in the Confederation, 1783–1784*, 2 vols., edited and translated by Alfred J. Morrison, (Philadelphia: William J. Campbell, 1911), 2:149.

3. Elkanah Watson, *Men and Times of the Revolution; or, Memoirs of Elkanah Watson, including His Journals of Travels in Europe and America, 1777–1842*, 2d ed., edited by Winslow C. Watson (New York: Dana and Co., 1857), 58.

4. Pasquotank County Court Minutes, 1737–85, NCSA.

5. Ibid.; Governor's Office, Committee of Claims Reports, 1760–64, NCSA.

6. Eugene D. Genovese, in *Roll, Jordon, Roll: The World the Slaves Made* (New York: Pantheon, 1974), makes a distinction at odds both with the examples cited above and the interpretive analysis. He asserts, with no supporting evidence, that "slaves grieved over the sale of their children but accepted it as a fact of life; however much they suffered, they did not necessarily hate their individual masters for it. But a husband and wife who cared for each other could never accept being parted" (p. 125). Presumably the latter normally *would* hate their masters for the aggression. This distinction between marital and familial break-ups is essentially a scholastic enterprise, supported neither by the data we have reviewed, nor, as far as we are aware, by evidence provided by other scholars. All that may reasonably be said is that slaves obviously understood that they might be separated from their children, especially as they attained adolescence. To conclude that this meant that slaves would not hate their masters for such separations is, as Herbert Gutman has asserted, to confuse "the realistic expectations of slave parents about owner behavior with slave moral and social beliefs." Herbert G. Gutman, *The Black Family in Slavery and Freedom, 1750–1925* (New York: Vintage Books, 1977), 318–19. Certainly the cooper and his son, Sambo and his daughter, and the distraught slave mother and her family mentioned above were more than capable of hating whites who threatened their familial ties. Unfortunately, the voices of countless other slaves who experienced similar aggressions remain locked in the vaults of history.

7. For a similar, suggestive analysis, see Roger Bastide, *African Civilizations in the New World* (London: C. Hurst and Co., 1971), 89.

8. Michael Mullin, in "British Caribbean and North American Slaves in an Era of War and Revolution, 1775–1807," in *The Southern Experience in the American Revolution*, edited by Jeffrey J. Crow and Larry E. Tise (Chapel Hill: University of North Carolina Press, 1978), argues that particular African cultures often "may have dominated others" in the Americas (pp. 37–38). Our investigation of the way in which African bride wealth and naming practices continued in North Carolina alerted us to the incidence of slaves continuing a variety of African traditions that were not mutually exclusive.

9. For bride price, see the following essays in A. R. Radcliffe-Brown and Daryll Forde, eds., *African Systems of Kinship and Marriage* (London: Oxford University Press, 1950): Meyer Fortes, "Kinship and Marriage among the Ashanti," 279–81; Daryll Forde, "Double Descent among the Yako," 321–26; A. I. Richards, "Family Structure amongst the Central Bantu," 207–51. See also Philip D. Curtin, Steven Feierman, Leonard Thompson, and Jan Vansina, *African History* (Boston: Little, Brown, 1978), 160, 166; John S. Mbiti, *African Religions and Philosophy*, 2d ed. (Oxford: Heinemann International, 1990), 183–84; Remi Clignet, *Many Wives, Many Powers: Authority and Power in Polygynous Families* (Evanston, Ill.: Northwestern University Press, 1970), 23, 50, 250–55; George Peter Murdock, *Africa: Its Peoples and Their Culture History* (New York: McGraw-Hill, 1959), 24–25, 75, 82–83, 95, 246, 255, 262, 276–77, 282, 286, 298–99, 372, 416, 419; Oyekan Owomoyela, "The Social Signifi-cance of Gift-Giving in Yoruba Culture" (paper, n.d.), 4–6. Professor Owomoyela, a Niger-ian scholar, is a member of the English department at the University of Nebraska at Lincoln.

10. See Philip D. Curtin, "Ayuba Suleiman Diallo of Bondu" and "The Capture and Travels of Ayuba Suleiman Ibrahima," in *Africa Remembered: Narratives by West Africans from the Era of the Slave Trade*, edited by Curtin (Madison: University of Wisconsin Press, 1967), 17–59.

11. For Ayuba's account of bride wealth, see Curtin, "The Capture and Travels of Ayuba,"

49–50. Murdock (*Africa*, 413–20) discusses the Fulani; see esp. 416 and 419 regarding bride price.

12. The first two chapters of *The Interesting Narrative of Olaudah Equiano, or Gustavus Vassa, the African* (2 vols., London, 1789), together with an introduction by G. I. Jones, are published in Curtin, *Africa Remembered*, 60–98.

13. *Interesting Narrative of Olaudah Equiano*, 72.

14. Jules Chametzky and Sidney Kaplan, "History of the Amistad Captives," 9–15, in *Black and White in American Culture: An Anthology from the Massachusetts Review*, edited by Chametzky and Kaplan (Amherst: University of Massachusetts Press, 1969), 291–330. The compilation cites the tribal backgrounds of 30 of the mutineers, 29 of whom were from Sierra Leone. Eighteen were Mendi (Mende) and 11 were from five other ethnic groups in the area.

15. Ibid., 26.

16. Ibid., 12–13.

17. Murdock (*Africa*, 262), for example, notes that contemporary Kissi, Kpelle, and Mende, all of Sierra Leone, couple the practices of bride price and bride service. This also may have occurred in the 1830s.

18. The information about the Yoruba is from Owomoyela, "Social Significance of Gift-Giving," 4–6. The observation that most of the bride price served as a dowry may suggest the cultural impact of Islam on the Yoruba.

19. Fortes, "Kinship and Marriage among the Ashanti," 279–81. A further payment, *tiri sika*, could be demanded from the husband by the wife's lineage at any time during the marriage if there was an urgent need for money in the lineage. The gift, tiri sika, was in reality a loan for an indefinite period, returnable only on divorce or the death of the wife. The husband, however, could make a free gift of the tiri sika to his wife and her lineage after some years of marriage or on divorce or her death. Ibid. The ubiquitousness of bride wealth in West Africa may be further exemplified by noting that of the thirty-one or so tribes, including the Yoruba proper, that today constitute the group called Southern Nigerians, all "require a consideration in marriage. This consists primarily of bride-service and gifts among the Ekoi and Igbira and of a woman given in exchange among the Afo and some Idoma and Igbo [Ibo], but it assumes the form of a substantial bride price in all other groups." The only other variation to this is observed by the Ijaw and Kukuruku, who "permit marriages with but a minimal consideration as an alternative, but in such cases the children belong not to the father but to the mother's family." Murdock, *Africa*, 246. The Asante (Ashanti) resided seventy years ago, as now, in Ghana, located midway between Sierra Leone and the Yoruba in Nigeria.

20. Richards, "Family Structure amongst the Central Bantu," 215–17.

21. John M. Brickell, *The Natural History of North Carolina With an Account of the Trade, Manners, and Customs of the Christian and Indian Inhabitants* . . . (1737; reprint, Murfreesboro, N.C.: Johnson Publishing Co., 1968), 274.

22. The question of marital and familial development among slaves in the British West Indies, as with most important questions about slavery, has become more controversial. Both Orlando Patterson and Elsa V. Goveia have stressed the devastating impact of slavery on such development among the islands' slaves. They point out the lack of stable marital relationships and limited functions for fathers in the matriarchal families of slaves, the high incidence of slave women bearing the children of numerous males in partially polyandrous

"marital" situations, the frequency of male slaves in preferred positions having a series of women in tow in unstable, informal polygynous relationships, the high incidence of promiscuity and prostitution among slaves, the destructive impact on blacks of inadequate white marital and familial role models, the sexual aggressions of white males on black females, and the consequent insignificance among slaves of stable monogamous marriages and nuclear families. Patterson, *The Sociology of Slavery: An Analysis of the Origins, Development, and Social Structure of Negro Society in Jamaica* (Rutherford, N.J.: Fairleigh Dickinson University Press, 1969), 159–70; Goveia, *Slave Society in the British Leeward Islands at the End of the Eighteenth Century* (New Haven: Yale University Press, 1965), 234–38.

By contrast, Barry Higman attempts to demonstrate that nuclear families among slaves in Jamaica and other British West Indian societies were common, although he primarily describes the later years of slavery. Higman, "Household Structure and Fertility on Jamaican Slave Plantations: A Nineteenth-Century Example," *Population Studies* 27 (November 1973): 527–50, and "The Slave Family and Household in the British West Indies, 1800–1834," *Journal of Interdisciplinary History* 6 (Autumn 1975): 261–87. Michael Craton hedges his bets but lands closer to the Patterson-Goveia position. He too notes the predominant role females played in the family, the limited importance of monogamous nuclear families (which he apparently believes, to the degree they were manifested, were largely mimetic of European practices), and, contrastingly, the significance of extended families. Craton, *Searching for the Invisible Man: Slaves and Plantation Life in Jamaica* (Cambridge: Harvard University Press, 1978), 98, 162–67, and *Testing the Chains: Resistance to Slavery in the British West Indies* (Ithaca, N.Y.: Cornell University Press, 1982), 48–51.

Sylvia R. Frey, in *Water from the Rock: Black Resistance in a Revolutionary Age* (Princeton, N.J.: Princeton University Press, 1991), argues that polygyny remained a significant marital form among slaves throughout the South. She immediately qualifies this by noting that what she has just referred to as polygynous unions might "be more accurately described as consecutive polygyny or serial monogamy" (p. 34). If this last be so, Frey should not confuse such arrangements with polygyny. Serial monogamy, indeed, generally resulted from unstable monogamous relationships. Frey also ignores time as a factor in her analysis and gives no statistics and little evidence to support her contentions.

23. For imaginative approximations of the numerical meaning of terms such as *child, young male,* and *aged,* see Darrett B. Rutman and Anita H. Rutman in *A Place in Time: Middlesex County* (New York: Norton, 1984), 180–81, and esp. in *A Place in Time: Explicatus* (New York: Norton, 1984), 171–88. In the biographical descriptions of the monogamous *Amistad* slaves, the only indication of lack of affluence was that some had been slaves for some time in Sierra Leone. Each time a person with numerous wives is mentioned, however, as in the case of the Africans who had enslaved and sold the *Amistad* slaves to Europeans, the unusual wealth and position of that person is noted. Chametzky and Kaplan, "History of the Amistad Captives," 9–15, 26. For evaluations of the numerical significance of monogamy in some West African societies where polygyny was the preferred marital form, see Forde, "Double Descent among the Yako," 288; Fortes, "Kinship and Marriage among the Ashanti," 281; Mbiti, *African Religions and Philosophy,* 188. See also nn. 24–25 below.

24. "Extracts from the Evidence of Jno. Matthews Esqr. given to ye Committee of Privy Council," 4 March 1788, in Long's Collections, Add. MSS 18272, ff. 1–6, British Museum, London, as quoted in Daniel C. Littlefield, *Rice and Slaves: Ethnicity and the Slave Trade in Colonial South Carolina* (Baton Rouge: Louisiana State University Press, 1981), 78–79.

25. For recent ethnographic studies that make this point for different West African societies, see n. 23. Harold E. Driver similarly evaluates the practices of American Indians in his *Indians of North America* (Chicago: University of Chicago Press, 1969), 230–32.

26. Brickell, *Natural History of North Carolina*, 274–75.

27. See plantation records listed among the sources provided in Table 7.3.

28. See Chapter 1 and Marvin L. Michael Kay and Lorin Lee Cary, "A Demographic Analysis of Colonial North Carolina with Special Emphasis upon the Slave and Black Populations," in *Black Americans in North Carolina and the South*, edited by Jeffrey J. Crow and Flora J. Hatley (Chapel Hill: University of North Carolina Press, 1984), 72–93. See also Allan Kulikoff, "The Beginnings of the Afro-American Family in Maryland," in *Law, Society, and Politics in Early Maryland*, edited by Aubrey C. Land, Lois Green Carr, and Edward C. Papenfuse (Baltimore: Johns Hopkins University Press, 1977), 171–96; Russell R. Menard, "The Maryland Slave Population, 1658 to 1730: A Demographic Profile of Blacks in Four Counties," *William and Mary Quarterly*, 3d ser., 32 (January 1975): 29–54.

29. See Kay and Cary, "A Demographic Analysis," 93–97.

30. Ibid., 97–103.

31. Statistics that most closely approximate the actual number of slave marriages and families in North Carolina during the late colonial years may be obtained only through indirection and by employing a cumbersome, three-step process that incorporates two sets of relevant, if flawed data. Plantation papers cover only slaves on large plantations. Estate records are more representative but do not delineate slave marriages and families. Neither data set can be used alone to construct acceptable statistics, nor can the two data sets be directly joined into a single usable set. Thus algorithms had to be devised that quantify each data set and then mathematically join the statistical findings in ways that produce reasonably realistic statistical appraisals of marriage and the family in North Carolina from 1750 to 1775.

The results are tabulated in Tables 7.4–7.6. The tables list two different probability estimates. "Probability A" contains among the slaves listed in dual-headed families all unmarried children including those who had children themselves. These types, then, are tabulated as part of the dual-headed family of origin. Categorizing in this fashion coincides with the probable extended-family inclinations of slaves. Parents normally identified children as members of the family of origin until a child married and established a new nuclear family. To account for the possibility that such single parents and children were mature adults who constituted separate households, we have computed such slaves as single-headed families in "Probability B."

Table 7.4 analyzes the entire sample (N = 218 slaveholds and 1,014 slaves) taken from six of the province's seven regions during the years 1750–75. The sample in Table 7.5 is taken from two eastern coastal regions, the Albemarle Sound and Neuse-Pamlico; Table 7.6 is a comparable analysis of the west.

We did not follow Kulikoff's method of estimating marital and familial development among slaves on small plantations directly from available estate records for two reasons. First, we all too infrequently came upon the ages of slaves in our data and could not effectively approximate the matching procedures Kulikoff uses to reconstitute slave marriages and families. And second, even if we could have duplicated this procedure we probably would have rejected it, for we believe that extrapolating probability estimates of marriages and families directly from raw demographic data that simply list the sex and age of slaves incorporates too many distortions. The procedure we use above, despite its cumbersomeness and complexity, probably results in estimates closer to the actual marital and familial condition of slaves on small to middling plantations. See Kulikoff, "Beginnings of the Afro-American Family in Maryland," 180, table 8.2 and note. We reached this conclusion before reading the Rutmans' imaginative interpretation of terms such as *girl*, *boy*, and *young man* to determine slave ages, but we still prefer our procedure. See Rutman and Rutman, *A Place in Time: Middlesex County*, 180–81, and esp. their *A Place in Time: Explicatus*, 171–88. See note to Table 7.1 for the data and algorithm used to construct Tables 7.1–7.2 and the interpolations used to conjoin the findings in Tables 7.1–7.2 and 7.3 to construct Tables 7.4–7.6.

32. For slave attempts to maintain or establish marriages and families on individual plantations and how masters responded to these efforts, see Mary Beth Norton, Herbert Gutman, and Ira Berlin, "The Afro-American Family in the Age of Revolution," in *Slavery and Freedom in the Age of the American Revolution*, edited by Berlin and Ronald Hoffman (Charlottesville: University Press of Virginia, 1983), 184–88; Norton, *Liberty's Daughters: The Revolutionary Experience of American Women, 1750–1800* (Boston: Little, Brown, 1980), 65–70.

33. Gutman, *Black Family*, 190–94. Gutman also suggests the possibility of a slave taboo concerning the naming of children after mothers. This strains credulity, for it does not jibe with many African naming practices, and we have found a sizable number of slave children named after their mothers. Cody also rejects as untenable Gutman's hypothesis regarding a taboo. In addition, she points out that necronymic naming practices (naming children after dead siblings, some doing so in the belief that the dead child was reborn in the new infant) were virtually absent among slaves in the South Carolina low-country sample she investigated. She uses the absence of necronymic naming practices along with other slave customs—including not naming a child for up to a month after birth—as evidence of the slaves' "strong recognition of the individual identity of each child." Gutman, on the other hand, argues that slaves commonly used necronymic naming practices and that this was a major manifestation of slave cosmography, a significant example of the African continuum, and an illustration of the slaves' important control over the naming of their children. Our North Carolina sample is inconclusive concerning the incidence of necronymic naming practices among slaves. Gutman, *Black Family*, 192–94; Cheryll Ann Cody, "Naming, Kinship, and Estate Dispersal: Notes on Family Life on a South Carolina Plantation, 1786–1833," *William and Mary Quarterly*, 3d ser., 39 (January 1982): 203–6. In a more recent work, Cody reverses her 1982 assessment; she finds that about 20 percent of the Ball plantation slaves that had the opportunity to use necronyms did so. Because this occurred most often among skilled slaves who had the greatest contact with slaveowners, Cody concludes that the practice reflected either acculturation or direct owner intervention in the naming process. Cody, "There Was No 'Absalom' on the Ball Plantations: Slave-Naming Practices in the South Carolina Low Country, 1720–1865," *American Historical Review* 92 (June 1987): 595.

34. James M. Robin Papers, vol. 1, Massachusetts Historical Society, Boston (hereafter cited as Robin Papers); Pollock Papers (P.C. 31.1), John Walker Papers (P.C. 254.1), "Lean by Thomas Pollock to Jacob Mitchell," Pollock Papers (P.C. 31.1), Avery Family Papers, Miscellaneous, Roll Book of Slaves of the Avery Family, 1766–1865 (P.C. 294.1), and Pollock-Devereaux Papers, Inventory of Slaves, 1797, and List of Slaves, 1806 (P.C. 32.1); all in NCSA; Gutman, *Black Family*, 172–73, 180.

35. Clement Idun, a doctoral candidate at the University of Toledo who is a Fante and a citizen of Ghana, helped us to understand the traditional residential patterns of the Fante, Asante, and Ga. See Fortes, "Kinship and Marriage among the Ashanti," p. 261. Richards ("Family Structure amongst the Central Bantu," 248 n. 1) refers to the Ga when discussing residential patterns among the Bantu.

36. For the Ibo, see Murdock, *Africa*, 247–48. See also Richards, "Family Structure amongst the Central Bantu," 218–19.

37. Brickell, *Natural History of North Carolina*, 274–75.

38. See, e.g., James Trussell and Richard Steckel, "The Age of Slaves at Menarche and Their First Birth," *Journal of Interdisciplinary History* 8 (Winter 1978): 477–505, but esp. their conclusion on 504; Cheryll Ann Cody, "Slave Demography and Family Formation: A Community Study of the Ball Family Plantations, 1720–1896" (Ph.D. diss., University of Minnesota, 1982)," 157–71, but esp. 160–62.

39. For the influence of high sex ratios in the South Carolina low country, see Cody, "Slave Demography and Family Formation," 164–70. For the roles and functions of children in various African societies, see Fortes, "Kinship and Marriage among the Ashanti," 263–83; Richards, "Family Structure amongst the Central Bantu," 213–41; Mbiti, *African Religions and Philosophy*, 131–216.

40. See Patterson, *Sociology of Slavery*, 169.

41. For the age of white women at primapartum in the colonies and Europe, see James M. Gallman, "Determinants of Age at Marriage in Colonial Perquimans County, North Carolina," *William and Mary Quarterly*, 3d ser., 39 (January 1982): 176–82; Cody, "Slave Demography and Family Formation," 158; Gutman, *Black Family*, 50; Norton, *Liberty's Daughters*, 72; Rutman and Rutman, *A Place in Time: Explicatus*, 64–68; Philip D. Morgan, "Black Society in the Lowcountry, 1610–1810," in *Slavery and Freedom in the Age of the American Revolution*, edited by Ira Berlin and Ronald Hoffman (Charlottesville: University Press of Virginia, 1983), 88–91.

42. Trussell and Steckel, "Age of Slaves at Menarche," 504. The authors also cite what they consider to be a less reasonable estimate of the earliest average age at which slave women could bear children—eighteen.

43. See Gallman, "Determinants of Age at Marriage," 179, and n. 41 above.

44. For a detailed statistical analysis of some of these relationships in the South Carolina low country, see Cody, "Slave Demography and Family Formation," 205–49, but esp. 242–44. See also Joan R. Gundersen, "The Double Bonds of Race and Sex: Black and White Women in Colonial Virginia," *Journal of Southern History* 52 (August 1986): 362–63, and Table 7.13 below, which is taken from Allan Kulikoff, "A 'Prolifick' People: Black Population Growth in the Chesapeake Colonies, 1700–1790," *Southern Studies* 16 (Winter 1977): 409.

In comparing the size of completed families of slaves and European women, Cody found that the average family size for the two groups was almost identical, as was the average age of the wife at the birth of the last child. Significantly different was the age of the mother at primapartum: slave women were about seven years younger. Consequently, birth intervals were also at variance: they were less for European women. Slave women, therefore, bore the same number of children over a longer time period, suggesting the more destructive conditions that they had to deal with. See Cody, "Slave Demography and Family Formation," 318–23, but esp. 322, table 6.3.

See the analysis below for the different ways used to calculate "completed family size," the number of children born to a woman who lived through her childbearing years. Actual family size is calculated from the total number of slave families.

45. Cody, "Slave Demography and Family Formation," 171–89.

46. Gundersen, "Double Bonds of Race and Sex," 361–62.

47. See nn. 44–45 above and sources and notes to Tables 7.1 and 7.3. It is likely that Cody's higher estimates largely reflect both the peculiarities of her sample and her use of a technique to calculate completed family size that tends to bias her estimate upward. She designates families as complete only if both the husband and wife survived up to the wife's fiftieth year. This means that Cody's calculations are not lowered by marriages that involved husbands who died or were separated from their wives before their fiftieth birthday. We followed the more usual procedure of calculating for all females who reached the age of forty-five, whatever may have happened to their spouse, thus incorporating the possibility of lower completed family sizes brought about by marital breakups (see Table 7.13 and n. 1). See also the procedural note to Table 7.14 for Kulikoff's procedures, which differ from both Cody's and our methods.

48. For African lineages and clans and how they interrelated with other institutions, see Murdock, *Africa*, 24–32, and the following essays in Radcliffe-Brown and Forde, *African Systems of Kinship and Marriage*: Radcliffe-Brown, Introduction, 13–23, 39–43; Richards, "Family Structure amongst the Central Bantu," 207–51; Fortes, "Kinship and Marriage among the Ashanti," 252–84; Forde, "Double Descent among the Yako," 285–332. For an elegant analysis of why cognatic descent, which maximizes the number of effective kin, was much more serviceable to American slaves than traditional African unilineal descent patterns, see Sidney W. Mintz and Richard Price, *An Anthropological Approach to the Afro-American Past: A Caribbean Perspective*, Occasional Papers in Social Change, no. 2 (Philadelphia: Institute for the Study of Human Issues, 1976), 35–36.

For sources used to help develop the above and ensuing analyses, see the wills and inventories listed with the sources in Table 7.1 and the following county court minutes in the NCSA: Bertie County Court Minutes, 1724–43, 1758–69, 1767–72; Chowan County Court Minutes, 1747–72; Pasquotank County Court Minutes, 1738–78; Beaufort County Court Minutes, Appearance, Prosecution, and Trial Docket, Court of Pleas and Quarter Sessions, vol. 1, 1756–61; Carteret County Court Minutes, 1747–72; Craven County Court Minutes, 1750–72; New Hanover County Court Minutes, 1738–69, 1771–72; Granville County Minutes, Court of Pleas and Quarter Sessions, 1754–70; Edgecombe County Court Minutes, 1757–72; Anson County Court Minutes, 1771–72; Orange County Court Minutes, 1752–66; Rowan County Court Minutes, 1753–72; Tryon County Court Minutes, 1768–72. Allan Kulikoff ("Beginnings of the Afro-American Family in Maryland," 175–78) found similar conditions in Maryland.

49. Robin Papers; John Walker Papers, P.C. 254.1, NCSA.

50. "Lean by Thomas Pollock to Jacob Mitchell," Pollock Papers, P.C. 31.1, NCSA.

51. For the spread of interplantation kinship lines, see Kulikoff, "Beginnings of the Afro-American Family in Maryland," 176. Such movement is much in evidence in the estate records we have surveyed.

52. See sources and notes to Tables 7.1 and 7.3.

53. Gutman, *Black Family*, 197.

CHAPTER 8

1. *The Interesting Narrative of the Life of Olaudah Equiano, or Gustavus Vassa, The African, Written by Himself*, Early American Imprints #23353 (New York, 1791). For a discussion of Equiano's account and his background, see G. I. Jones, "Olaudah Equiano of the Niger Ibo," in *Africa Remembered: Narratives of West Africans from the Era of the Slave Trade*, edited by Phillip D. Curtin (Madison: University of Wisconsin Press, 1968), 60–69. Equiano's narrative (introduced by G. I. Jones), up to the time of his enslavement in Barbados, is included in Curtin's collection of narratives.

2. *Interesting Narrative of the Life of Olaudah Equiano.*

3. This sense of memory pervades our study. For a similar view concerning memory, see Roger Bastide, *African Civilizations in the New World* (London: Hurst and Co., 1971), 89.

4. Thomas Luckman, *The Invisible Religion: The Problem of Religion in Modern Society* (New York: Macmillan, 1967), 18–19, 52–55, 61, 70; Peter L. Berger, *The Sacred Canopy* (Garden City, N.Y.: Anchor Books, 1969); Berger and Luckman, *The Social Construction of Reality* (London: Penquin Press, 1966), as quoted and developed in Mechal Sobel, *Trabelin' On: The Slave Journey to an Afro-Baptist Faith* (Westport, Conn.: Greenwood Press, 1979), 3–4.

5. *Interesting Narrative of the Life of Olaudah Equiano.* For African concepts of time and the concept of life power, see Benjamin C. Ray, *African Religions: Symbol, Ritual, and Community* (Englewood Cliffs, N.J.: Prentice-Hall, 1976), 40–42; Dominique Zahan, *The Religion, Spirituality, and Thought of Traditional Africa* (Chicago: University of Chicago Press, 1970), 10, 34–35, 45–48, 51–52, 89; Newell S. Booth Jr., "An Approach to African Religions," in *African Religions: A Symposium*, edited by Newell S. Booth Jr. (New York: NOK Publishers, Ltd., 1977), 6–8; John S. Mbiti, *African Religions and Philosophy* (London: Heinemann Educational Books, Ltd., 1969), 15–28, 166.

6. *Interesting Narrative of the Life of Olaudah Equiano.*

7. Ray, *African Religions*, 103–6, 146–47; Zahan, *Religion . . . of Traditional Africa*, 47–52, 81–91; Mbiti, *African Religions*, 75–91, 152–61, 166–77.

8. *Interesting Narrative of the Life of Olaudah Equiano.*

9. Mbiti, *African Religions*, 92; Booth, "Approach to African Religions," 6–7; Ray, *African Religions*, 78–100; Zahan, *Religion . . . of Traditional Africa*, 66–80, 155–57.

10. Booth, "Approach to African Religions," 7–8. See also, e.g., Zahan, *Religion . . . of Traditional Africa*, 36–52; *Interesting Narrative in the Life of Olaudah Equiano.*

11. See n. 5 above.

12. Ray, *African Religions*, 40–41.

13. Ibid., 41.

14. Zahan, *Religion . . . of Traditional Africa*, 89.

15. Ray, *African Religions*, 41.

16. Booth, "Approach to African Religions," 7–8.

17. Ibid., 8–9.

18. Few pertinent ritual objects derived from or related to Africa have been found in digs around colonial slave habitations. For collateral information see Sylvia R. Frey, *Water from the Rock: Black Resistance in a Revolutionary Age* (Princeton: Princeton University Press, 1991), 36, 40–41. See also addendum to notes on p. 373.

19. "The Capture and Travels of Ayuba Suleiman Ibrahima," in Curtin, *Africa Remembered*, 41.

20. William L. Saunders, ed., *The Colonial Records of North Carolina*, 10 vols. (Raleigh: State of North Carolina, 1886–90), 6:265. As Crow notes, vestiges of Islam persisted well into the nineteenth century in North Carolina. Jeffrey J. Crow, *The Black Experience in Revolutionary North Carolina* (Raleigh: North Carolina Department of Cultural Resources, Division of Archives and History, 1977), 48. See, e.g., "Autobiography of Omar ibn Seid in North Carolina, 1831," *American Historical Review* 30 (July 1925): 791–95.

21. George P. Rawick, ed., *The American Slave: A Composite Autobiography*, 31 vols. (Westport, Conn: Greenwood Press, 1972–78), 14:350–51, 356–57.

22. Mbiti, *African Religions*, 53; Robert Faris Thompson, *Flash of the Spirit: African and Afro-American Art and Philosophy* (New York: Random House, 1983), 115–24.

23. Thompson, *Flash of the Spirit*, 124.

24. Mbiti, *African Religions*, 81–89, 152–61.

25. Melville J. Herskovits, *The Myth of the Negro Past* (Boston: Beacon Press, 1958), 203–4.

26. Frey, *Water from the Rock*, 39–41; Mbiti, *African Religions*, 154–57; Thompson, *Flash of the Spirit*, 132–45; Sterling Stuckey, *Slave Culture: Nationalist Theory and the Foundations of Black America* (New York: Oxford University Press, 1987), 11–12, 17, 22, 25, 39–43, 108–9, 361 n. 99.

27. Herskovits, *Myth of the Negro Past*, 63.

28. Ibid., 202–3; Frey, *Water from the Rock*, 41–42. Frey quotes James Murray, who wrote from the Cape Fear region of North Carolina in 1755: "The Negroes . . . are at a great loss this Christmas for want of a death to play for." James Murray, Cape Fear, to "Sister Clark," 26 December 1755, Robin Papers, Massachusetts Historical Society (Mf. CRP), typescript copy in Historical Publications Section, Division of Archives and History, Raleigh, N.C.

29. Janet Schaw, *Journal of a Lady of Quality: Being the Narrative of a Journey from Scotland to the West Indies, North Carolina, and Portugal, in the years 1774 to 1776*, edited by Evangeline Walker Andrews and Charles M. Andrews (New Haven: Yale University Press, 1923), 171.

30. Stuckey, *Slave Culture*, 25, 365 n. 59. The other most important nonverbal African aesthetic techniques used to express and incorporate religiosity were paintings, sculptures, and artifacts. Thompson's *Flash of the Spirit* is a superb analysis of the power of the African continuum in these artistic expressions by African Americans in North America, the Caribbean, and South America. For further discussion of the interrelationships between dance, song, music, and religiosity in Africa, see Zahan, *Religion . . . of Traditional Africa*, 105, 129, 131–32; Mbiti, *African Religions*, 67, 172, 175; Curtin, *Africa Remembered*, 129, 261–62, 327–28. For the continuation of various African artistic expressions in America, see also Sidney W. Mintz and Richard Price, *An Anthropological Approach to the Afro-American Past: A Caribbean Perspective*, Occasional Papers in Social Change, no. 2 (Philadelphia: Institute for the Study of Human Issues, 1976), 27; Albert J. Raboteau, *Slave Religion: The Invisible Institution in the Antebellum South* (Oxford: Oxford University Press, 1978), 15, 35–37, 61–62; Eileen Southern, *The Music of Black Americans: A History* (New York: Norton, 1971), 3–68.

31. See appropriate references in n. 30.

32. William Attmore, "Journal of a Tour to North Carolina by William Attmore, 1787," *James Sprunt Historical Publications*, vol. 17, edited by Linda T. Rodman (1922), 43; Rawick, *American Slave*, 14:191. For a general statement of the slaves' music in all of the colonies, see Southern, *Music of Black Americans*, 3–68.

33. Stuckey, *Slave Culture*, 66, 370–71 nn. 159–62.

34. Ibid., 66.

35. Elizabeth A. Fenn, "'A Perfect Equality Seemed to Reign': Slave Society and Jonkonnu," *North Carolina Historical Review* 65 (April 1988): 127–53 (quotations, 127–30).

36. Ibid., 130–33.

37. Ibid., 130–33, 148–53.

38. Stuckey, *Slave Culture*, 67–70, 371 nn. 167–69. Fenn agrees with Edward Long's view that Jonkonnu was a memorial "of John Conny, a celebrated cabocero at Tres Puntas, in Axim on the Guiney coast." See Long, *History of Jamaica* (London: T. Lowndes, 1774), 2:423–36, as quoted in Fenn, "Slave Society and Jonkonnu," 129.

39. Stuckey, *Slave Culture*, 69–73, 105; Crow, *Black Experience*, 48–49. The source of both their analyses of John Koonering is Edward Warren, *A Doctor's Experiences on Three Continents* (Baltimore: Cushings and Baily, 1885), 200–203. Although directly drawing on this source, we have relied chiefly on Stuckey's and Crow's summaries of Warren.

40. Warren, *Doctor's Experiences*, 201, as quoted in Stuckey, *Slave Culture*, 70–71. See also Fenn, "Slave Society and Jonkonnu," 132.

41. Warren, *Doctor's Experiences*, 201–2, as quoted in Stuckey, *Slave Culture*, 71–72. See also Crow, *Black Experience*, 48–49; Fenn, "Slave Society and Jonkonnu," 132–33.

42. Warren traced this celebration back to Egypt, where he had observed a ceremony by blacks "absolutely identical" to that of the slaves in North Carolina. "In Egypt they 'amused themselves,' . . . with Kunering 'at Byram—the principal feast of the Koran.'" Warren, *Doctor's Experiences*, 203, as quoted in Stuckey, *Slave Culture*, 72. See also Crow, *Black Experience*, 49.

43. For the trial, see Governor's Office, Committee of Claims Reports, 1760–64, and Pasquotank County Court Minutes, 1737–65, in North Carolina State Archives, Raleigh (hereafter cited as NCSA). See also Saunders, *Colonial Records*, 6:738–44. For descriptions of the root in question and how the poison was extracted to make the root edible, see Frederick Webb Hodge, ed., *Handbook of American Indians North of Mexico* (N.Y.: Rownian and Littlefield, 1965), 2:831–32; John R. Swanton, *The Indians of the Southeastern United States* [Smithsonian Institution, Bureau of American Ethnology, Bulletin 137] (Washington, D.C.: GPO, 1946), 270–72.

44. Pasquotank County Court Minutes, 1737–65, NCSA.

45. Mbiti, *African Religions*, 222.

46. Zahan, *Religion . . . of Traditional Africa*, 92–109. See also Mbiti, *African Religions*, 166–78; Ray, *African Religions*, 103–10. Africans here resembled Europeans and European Americans who usually identified and *punished* women as witches.

47. Curtin, *Africa Remembered*, 49 and n. 60.

48. For cultural diffusion between Indians and blacks in South Carolina, see Peter H. Wood, *Black Majority: Negroes in Colonial South Carolina from 1670 through the Stono Rebellion* (New York: Knopf, 1974), 116–17, 120–23. See also Richard Price, ed., *Maroon Societies: Rebel Slave Communities in the Americas*, 2d ed. (Baltimore: Johns Hopkins University Press, 1979), 11–12, 15–16.

49. Schaw, *Journal of a Lady of Quality*, 176; Rawick, *American Slave*, 14:54.

50. See also Eugene D. Genovese, *Roll, Jordon, Roll: The World the Slaves Made* (New York: Pantheon, 1974), 616.

51. See Chapter 4 on slave "criminality."

52. John C. Van Horne, ed., *Religious Philanthropy and Colonial Slavery: The American Correspondence of the Associates of Dr. Bray, 1717–1777* (Urbana: University of Illinois Press, 1985), 100.

53. Ibid., 116, 119, 129.

54. Saunders, *Colonial Records*, 6:265; Van Horne, *Religious Philanthropy*, 293–94 (quotations).

55. Van Horne, *Religious Philanthropy*, 100, 129, 206. Scherer argues that "even the warmest champions of Christianization" did not claim that blacks were equivalent to whites. Despite their equal capacity for immortality, they were "stupid despised black creatures." Lester B. Scherer, *Slavery and the Churches in Early America, 1619–1819* (Grand Rapids, Mich.: William B. Eeidman's Publishing Co., 1975), 92.

56. Quoted in Scherer, *Slavery and the Churches in Early America*, 91.

57. Van Horne, *Religious Philanthropy*, 138–39, 204, 271.

58. Ibid., 281. For Van Horne's assessment of the differences in attitudes between the English and the Americans, see ibid., 36–38.

59. Winthrop D. Jordan, *White Over Black: American Attitudes Toward the Negro, 1550–1812* (Chapel Hill: University of North Carolina Press, 1968), 91–98, 187–90. Jordan's analysis of colonial white attitudes about black mental capacities remains the best that has been written. Laws passed in colonial North Carolina covering the forcible removal of manumitted slaves from the colony, tax discrimination against free blacks, and black-white intermarriage—all interrelated—poignantly illustrate how the attitudes described above helped induce specific planter responses to blacks. See Walter Clark, ed., *The State Records of North Carolina*, 16 vols., numbered 11–26 (Winston and Goldsboro: State of North Carolina, 1895–1906), 23:65, 106–7, 160, 203–4. See also Scherer, *Slavery and the Churches in Early America*, 91–92; Raboteau, *Slave Religion*, 100–101.

60. For examples of ministerial condemnation of the harsh treatment of slaves by their masters and the ill effects this had on slave conversions, see Van Horne, *Religious Philanthropy*, 99–100, 116, 128–30, 134–35, 138–39, 207, 271.

61. Clark, *State Records*, 23:3–6; Van Horne, *Religious Philanthropy*, 105, 112 (Ottolenghe; see also Ottolenghe's comments in 1754, p. 116).

62. Van Horne, *Religious Philanthropy*, 119, 195, 138. Van Horne's conclusion is on p. 34. See also Raboteau, *Slave Religion*, 121–22.

63. See Scherer, *Slavery and the Churches in Early America*, 89–91; Van Horne, *Religious Philanthropy*, 25–30; Raboteau, *Slave Religion*, 98–99. Raboteau incorrectly seems to believe that this problem was solved by 1706.

64. Van Horne, *Religious Philanthropy*, 27. For the original text, see Clark, *State Records*, 25:134–35; Mattie E. Parker, ed., *North Carolina Charters and Constitutions, 1658–1698* (Raleigh: North Carolina Department of Cultural Resources, Division of Archives and History, 1963), 183.

65. Saunders, *Colonial Records*, 1:86.

66. Clark, *State Records*, 23:65 (1715 statute); Saunders, *Colonial Records*, 1:858–59, 2:332–33 (quotation).

67. John M. Brickell, *The Natural History of North Carolina With an Account of the Trade, Manners, and Customs of the Christian and Indian Inhabitants . . .* (1737; reprint, Murfreesboro, N.C.: Johnson Publishing Co., 1968), 274. Despite such widely held planter beliefs—at times shared by the slaves themselves—the only instances we have uncovered for North

Carolina in which being a Christian led to freedom for slaves were those that involved free-born blacks who were citizens of a Christian nation but who had been captured and sold into slavery. See Chapter 2, n. 54, for such instances.

68. Saunders, *Colonial Records*, 3:112; John S. Bassett, "Slavery and Servitude in the Colony of North Carolina," *Johns Hopkins University Studies in Historical and Political Science*, ser. 14 (1896), 49.

69. Van Horne, *Religious Philanthropy*, 281. See also Raboteau, *Slave Religion*, 102.

70. Van Horne, *Religions Philanthropy*, 112, 119, 289. For other examples of this fear among planters, see ibid., 124 (where Benjamin Franklin alludes to it), 186, 194, 271. Van Horne's analysis of the problem is on pp. 31–32. See also Scherer, *Slavery and the Churches in Early America*, 92–96; Raboteau, *Slave Religion*, 102–3.

71. Van Horne, *Religious Philanthropy*, 31, 112, 124, 186, 194, 271, 289, 186.

72. Saunders, *Colonial Records*, 6:995–96 (Stewart); Van Horne, *Religious Philanthropy*, 261 (Barnett). See Van Horne's analysis concerning the attempted education of slaves and the masters' reactions in his introduction, but esp. 20–25, 31–38. See also Raboteau, *Slave Religion*, 115–20.

73. Van Horne, *Religious Philanthropy*, 289.

74. The 1713 quotation is from Raboteau, *Slave Religion*, 99, as quoted in Frank J. Klingberg, *An Appraisal of the Negro in Colonial South Carolina: A Study in Americanization* (Washington, D.C.: Associated Publishers, 1941), 7; the 1758 quotation is in Van Horne, *Religious Philanthropy*, 129.

75. Van Horne, *Religious Philanthropy*, 296–97. Peter Wood (*Black Majority*, 138–39) similarly argues that Anglican ministers who urged masters to make their slaves available for religious activities on Sundays and evenings directly interfered with the brief hours Negroes had for rest and fraternization on the one hand and with their meager chance for self-sufficiency and betterment on the other.

76. Clark, *State Records*, 23:3–6.

77. Even in Virginia where the Anglican Church establishment was strongest, similar conditions ensured that nearly one-half of its parishes remained without clerics during the late colonial years. Yet Virginia and its sister Chesapeake colony, Maryland, established the Anglican Church with little outside aid. Colonies to the south of Virginia were not up to the task, and it was here that the SPG came to play its most important role.

The following secondary works proved especially useful in developing our discussion of the Anglican Church as it applies to all of the colonies: Arthur Lyon Cross, *The Anglican Episcopate and the American Colonies* (New York: Longmans, Green, 1902); Elizabeth Huey Davidson, *The Establishment of the English Church in the Continental American Colonies*, Historical Papers of Trinity College Historical Society, ser. 20 (Durham, N.C., 1936); Raboteau, *Slave Religion*, 104–5; Scherer, *Slavery and the Churches in Early America*, 82–103; Van Horne, *Religious Philanthropy*, 1–47. The most helpful secondary works on North Carolina's establishment were Gloria Beth Baker, "Dissenters in Colonial North Carolina" (Ph.D. diss., University of North Carolina at Chapel Hill, 1970), esp. 137–200; E. W. Caruthers, *A Sketch of the Life and Character of the Reverend David Caldwell, D.D.* (Greensboro, 1842), 68–70; James Ray Caldwell Jr., "The Churches of Granville County, North Carolina, in the Eighteenth Century," in *Studies in Southern History*, edited by J. Carlyle Sitterson, James Sprunt Studies in History and Political Science, vol. 39 (1959), 1–22; Paul Conkin, "The Church Establishment in North Carolina, 1765–1776," *North Carolina Historical Review* 32 (January

1955): 1–30; David Leroy Corbitt, *The Formation of the North Carolina Counties, 1663–1943* (Raleigh: North Carolina Department of Archives and History, 1950); Marvin L. Michael Kay, "The Institutional Background to the Regulation in Colonial North Carolina" (Ph.D. diss., University of Minnesota, 1962), 337–54; John Mitchell Justice, "The Work of the Society for the Propagation of the Gospel in Foreign Parts in North Carolina" (M.A. thesis, University of North Carolina, Chapel Hill, 1939), passim, but see viii–x, 114, and 151–52 for statistics about SPG missionaries in North Carolina; Sarah McCulloh Lemmon, "The Genesis of the Protestant Episcopal Diocese of North Carolina, 1701–1803," *North Carolina Historical Review* 28 (October 1951): 426–62.

For the Vestry Act of 1764 and the Orthodox Clergy Law of 1765, see Clark, *State Records*, 23:601–7, 660–62. For primary sources that document the story of the church establishment in North Carolina, see Saunders, *Colonial Records*, 1:184, 600–604, 615–16, 638, 681, 684, 686, 689, 711, 714, 719–22, 728–30, 734, 763–72, 849–51, 857–60, 884–85, 887–88, 2:17, 76–78, 116–17, 118–23, 125–28, 130–32, 180, 200–201, 207–13, 227–29, 292–95, 331–33, 373, 380–81, 430–33, 531, 573–80, 624–25, 3:342–43, 529–30, 541, 623–25, 4:10–11, 263–65, 560–62, 604–8, 621–22, 752–55, 791–97, 876, 878, 5:870, 961–62, 1014, 6:xxix–xxxiii, 10–13, 15–16, 58–59, 221–26, 230–43, 265, 312–13 (Benjamin Heron questions the Reverend Mr. Woodmason's sanity), 315–16, 537–38, 552–54, 561–62, 565, 567–68, 594–95, 709–11, 720–23, 729–30, 955, 966, 970–72, 976–80, 990–91, 994–96, 999–1000, 1020, 1026–27, 1039–41, 1047–48, 1056, 1091, 1107, 1226, 7:7–8, 35–36, 42–43, 97–99, 102–5, 131–32, 145, 150–54, 158, 162, 164, 192–93, 241–42, 252–53, 259–60, 261–65, 273–74, 284–88 (Woodmason's account), 353, 424, 432–33, 456–58, 490, 492–96, 514–15, 519–22, 540–41, 598, 689, 701, 704–5, 750, 786–87, 789–90, 856, 872, 891, 8:xliii–xlv, 12–16, 20, 23, 45, 80b, 85–86, 150–51, 154–55, 174, 179–80, 199, 219–22, 227–29, 352, 469, 481, 486–90, 502, 9:20–23, 81–84, 326, 622–23, 1015, 11:214–15; Legislative Papers—Petition of St. James Parish, 10 November 1764, Legislative Papers—Rowan County Petition, 20 December 1770, 7 January 1771, and English Records, Anglican Church Records—Letters and Orders from December 1748 to 1779 concerning Licenses Given to Anglican Ministers; all in NCSA.

78. Governor William Tryon first arrived in North Carolina as lieutenant governor and took the oath of office on 10 October 1764. His task was to relieve the aging Governor Dobbs of many of his duties and gently, or not so gently, see to his eventual retirement. On Dobbs's death, Tryon was sworn in as governor pro tempore at Wilmington on 3 April 1765; finally, after being commissioned by the Crown on 19 July 1765, he was officially sworn in as governor before the Council at Wilmington on 20 December 1765. He served in this capacity until embarking for New York on 30 June 1771 to become governor of that province. He died in London on 27 January 1788. See Saunders, *Colonial Records*, 6:1043, 1053, 1078, 1320–21, 7:xxxiv–xl, 131–32, 8:54–55; Marshall De Lancey Haywood, *Governor William Tryon and His Administration in the Province of North Carolina, 1765–1771* (Raleigh, 1903), 10, 14, 16–17, 195–208; Alonzo Thomas Dill, *Governor Tryon and His Palace* (Chapel Hill, 1955), 6; Charles Lee Raper, *North Carolina: A Study in English Colonial Government* (New York: Macmillan, 1904), 60.

For Tryon's activities on behalf of the establishment, including his recruitment, support, induction, and presentation of ministers and his attempted co-optation of Presbyterians by offering their ministers the right to perform marriages and setting up a Presbyterian school in Charlotte, Mecklenburg County, see Saunders, *Colonial Records*, 7:35–36, 42–43, 97, 102–5, 131–32, 145, 158, 241–42, 252–53, 259–63, 273–74, 424, 432–33, 456–58, 490, 492–96, 514–15,

519–22, 540–41, 689, 701, 704–5, 750, 786–87, 789–90, 891, 8:xliii–xlv, 12–16, 20, 23, 45, 80b, 85–86, 150–51, 154–55, 174, 179–80, 199, 202–10, 219–22, 352, 469, 481, 486–90, 502–7, 526–27, 622–23, 9:214–15; English Records, Anglican Church Records, and Legislative Papers, 1771–Rowan County Petition for an Anglican Minister; all in NCSA; Justice, "Society for the Propagation of the Gospel . . . in North Carolina," 73–74, 86, 151–52; Lemmon, "Protestant Episcopal Diocese of North Carolina," 429, 433–39; Conkin, "Church Establishment in North Carolina," 5–9; Caldwell, "Churches of Granville County," 4–7; Corbitt, *Formation of the North Carolina Counties.*

79. Conkin ("Church Establishment in North Carolina," 9) suggests the limited significance of such chapels and congregations.

80. Ernest Hawkins, ed., *Historical Notices of Missions of the Church of England* (London: Fellowes, 1845), 18; Van Horne, *Religious Philanthropy*, 4.

81. Saunders, *Colonial Records*, 6:265. Reed also quoted in Crow, *Black Experience*, 48.

82. Saunders, *Colonial Records*, 6:265.

83. Sobel (*Trabelin' On*, 62–63) believes that masters almost invariably refused to allow blacks to serve as godparents for their fellow slaves, as she has discovered only one colonial Anglican minister, Hugh Jones of Maryland, who used "Christian Negroes for sureties."

84. Crow, *Black Experience*, 47. See also Saunders, *Colonial Records*, 7:705, 9:326.

85. Van Horne, *Religious Philanthropy*, 138. See also Scherer, *Slavery and the Churches in Early America*, 96–103; Sobel, *Trabelin' On*, 41, 58–65.

86. Saunders, *Colonial Records*, 1:720, 858, 2:18, 153, 332–33, 4:7, 13–14, 605, 621, 791, 793–94, 924–25, 1315, 6:162, 225, 233–34, 315–16, 729, 994–95, 7:126, 424, 705, 8:553, 9:326.

87. The estimate and projection were made by relating the baptismal figures to the demographic analysis in Chapter 1. See also Marvin L. Michael Kay and Lorin Lee Cary, "A Demographic Analysis of Colonial North Carolina with Special Emphasis upon the Slave and Black Populations," in *Black Americans in North Carolina and the South*, edited by Jeffrey J. Crow and Flora J. Hatley, (Chapel Hill: University of North Carolina Press, 1984), 72–87.

88. According to the sources cited in n. 86 above, the bulk of the 1,401 blacks baptized were children, many of whom must have been born in North Carolina.

89. Van Horne, *Religious Philanthropy*, 186–87.

90. Ibid., 240–41.

91. Ibid., 38. For similar assessments of the Anglican missionary efforts among slaves, see Scherer, *Slavery and the Churches in Early America*, 96–103; Sobel, *Trabelin' On*, 41, 58–65; Allan Gallay, "The Origins of Slaveholders' Paternalism: George Whitefield, the Bryan Family, and the Great Awakening in the South," *Journal of Southern History* 53 (August 1987): 380.

92. Saunders, Colonial Records, 1:571–73, 686, 708–15, 719–22, 763–72; Elizabeth Huey Davidson, *The Establishment of the English Church in the Continental American Colonies*, Historical Papers of the Trinity College Historical Society, ser. 20 (Durham, N.C., 1936), 48; Hiram H. Hilty, "North Carolina Quakers and Slavery" (Ph.D. diss., Duke University, 1969), 19–26.

93. Rufus M. Jones, *The Quakers in the American Colonies* (London: Macmillan, 1911), 295–99; Baker, "Dissenters in Colonial North Carolina," 148.

94. Hilty, "North Carolina Quakers and Slavery," 28, 30–32, 34–36, 38–50; Raboteau, *Slave Religion*, 110–11; Baker, "Dissenters in Colonial North Carolina," 162–63, 175–76; Jeffrey J.

Crow, "Slave Rebelliousness and Social Conflict in North Carolina, 1775–1802," *William and Mary Quarterly*, 3d ser., 37 (January 1980): 91–93. Woolman did not always speak out forcefully against slavery. In a paragraph deleted in one version of his journal, he notes that although "the neglected condition of the poor slaves often affects my mind," he chose to keep silent at a June 1757 meeting, "finding by experience that to keep pace with the gentle motions of Truth, and never move but as that opens the way, is necessary for the true servants of Christ." At about this time he attended another monthly meeting, one at which Friends discussed the neglect of Negroes' education. Once again his "mind was exercised concerning the poor slaves, but did not feel my way clear to speak." Philips R. Moulton, ed., *The Journal and Major Essays of John Woolman* (New York: Oxford University Press, 1971), 38.

95. Hugh T. Lefler and William S. Powell, *Colonial North Carolina* (New York: Scribner's, 1973), 103–6; Adelaide L. Fries, ed., *Records of the Moravians in North Carolina*, 8 vols. (Raleigh: Edwards and Broughton Print Co., 1922–54), 1:385, 446, 2:821.

96. Fries, *Records of the Moravians*, 2:759, 814–15, 858.

97. Ibid., 868, 876; George Easton Simpson, *Black Religions in the New World* (New York: Columbia University Press, 1978), 215. The Moravians in North Carolina seem to have devoted more attention to missionary work among the Native Americans. Baker, "Dissenters in Colonial North Carolina," 180–81.

98. Fries, *Records of the Moravians*, 2:824.

99. Ibid., 1:432–33, 442, 450–70, 2:617–20. These pages are reprinted in *The Regulators in North Carolina: A Documentary History*, edited by William S. Powell, James K. Hupta, and Thomas J. Farnham (Raleigh: North Carolina Department of Archives and History, 1971), 304–24.

100. Our remarks about German Protestants and, below, about Presbyterians were gleaned from E. Lawrence Lee Jr., *The Lower Cape Fear in Colonial Days* (Chapel Hill: University of North Carolina Press, 1965), 223–35; Crow, *Black Experience*, 49; Caldwell, "Churches of Granville County," 1–22 passim; James Ray Caldwell Jr., "A History of Granville County, North Carolina: The Preliminary Phase, 1746–1800" (Ph.D. diss., University of North Carolina, 1950), 25, 114–34; James A. Padgett, "The Status of Slaves in Colonial North Carolina," *Journal of Negro History* 14 (July 1929): 322; Baker, "Dissenters in Colonial North Carolina," iv, 164–68, 171–74, 178–81, 187–200; Ian Charles Cargill Graham, *Colonists from Scotland: Emigration to North America, 1707–1783* (Ithaca, N.Y.: Cornell University Press, 1956), 19, 94–96, 106, 108, 146, 156–57, 159–60, 165; Duane Gilbert Meyer, "The Scottish Highlanders in North Carolina, 1773–1776" (Ph.D. diss., University of Iowa, 1956), 54–55, 71, 90, 95, 97, 108, 125, 128, 135; William K. Boyd, ed., *Some Eighteenth-Century Tracts concerning North Carolina* (Raleigh: North Carolina Historical Commission, 1927), 419–21, 425; R. D. W. Connor, *Race Elements in the White Population of North Carolina* (Greensboro: North Carolina State Normal and Industrial College, 1920), 56–57, 94–95; William Herman Gehrke, "The German Element in Rowan and Cabarrus Counties, North Carolina" (M.A. thesis, University of North Carolina, 1934); Gehrke, "The Beginnings of the Pennsylvania German Element in Rowan and Cabarrus Counties, North Carolina," *Pennsylvania Magazine of History and Biography* 58 (1934): 342–69; Hugh Talmage Lefler and Albert Ray Newsome, *North Carolina: The History of a Southern State*, 3d ed. (Chapel Hill: University of North Carolina Press, 1973), 72, 77–88; Lefler and Powell, *Colonial North Carolina*, 88–109; Kay, "Regulation in Colonial North Carolina," 43–68, 337–54; Harry Roy Merrens, *Colonial North Carolina in the Eighteenth Century: A Study in Historical Geography* (Chapel Hill:

University of North Carolina Press, 1964), 53–107; Ethel Stephens Arnett, *Greensboro, North Carolina: The County Seat of Guilford* (Chapel Hill: University of North Carolina Press, 1955), 10–11, 116; G. D. Bernheim, *History of the German Settlements and of the Lutheran Church in North and South Carolina* (Philadelphia: Lutheran Bookstore, 1872), 153, 155, 239; James S. Brawley, *The Rowan Story, 1753–1953* (Salisbury, N.C., 1953), 28–31; Albert B. Faust, *The German Element in the United States*, 2 vols. (New York: The Steuben Society of America, 1927), 1:230–31, 264, 284; Jacob L. Morgan, B. S. Brown Jr., and John Hall, eds., *History of the Lutheran Church in North Carolina* (Raleigh, 1953), 15–28, 186–350; Charles A. Hanna, *The Scotch-Irish or the Scot in North Britain, North Ireland, and North America*, 2 vols. (New York: Putnam's, 1902), 2:map, 32–38, 113–15; Saunders, *Colonial Records*, 1:686, 720, 763–72, 4:157–62, 1312, 5:24–25, 6:xxix–xxxiii, 265, 562, 1014–44, 7:241–42, 252–53, 259–60, 287–88, 422–33, 8:12–16, 20, 80b, 85–86, 144, 154–56, 179–80, 202–10, 250–52, 259, 469, 502–7, 526–27, 630–31, 727–57 (Rev. G. M. Welker, "Early German Reformed Settlement in North Carolina"), 9:622–23; Legislative Papers, 1771, NCSA. Gehrke also wrote a work specifically dealing with slaveholding among the Germans: "Negro Slavery among the Germans in North Carolina," *North Carolina Historical Review* 14 (1937): 307–12. According to him, German ministers tended to slaves' needs, but almost all his examples come from after the Revolution. See 312ff.

101. Gallay, "Origins of Slaveholders' Paternalism," 369–94; Harvey H. Jackson, "Hugh Bryan and the Evangelical Movement in Colonial South Carolina," *William and Mary Quarterly*, 3d ser., 43 (October 1986): 594–614.

102. Stoney Creek Church was first organized in 1740 by Hugh Bryan, the leading Anglican evangelical layman in South Carolina, his brothers, and a few cohorts when they became convinced they could not effectively evangelize within the Anglican establishment. The limited number of slave members in Stoney Creek Church, were almost all owned by either Bryan, his brother Jonathan, or John Hutson (their long-standing evangelical ally and the first minister of the church). See Jackson, "Evangelical Movement in Colonial South Carolina," 612–13.

103. Gallay, "Origins of Slaveholders' Paternalism," 393–94.

104. Ibid., 389, 392, 394; Jackson, "Evangelical Movement in Colonial South Carolina," 612–13.

105. In *Trabelin' On*, Sobel discusses African religiosity, Baptist beliefs and practices, and the Afro-Baptist amalgam in great depth. This analysis provides the substantive underpinning for her discussion of slave religiosity in *The World They Made Together: Black and White Values in Eighteenth-Century Virginia* (Princeton, N.J.: Princeton University Press, 1987). The latter also reviews other cultural characteristics of the slaves in Virginia. See also Crow, *Black Experience*, 50–54.

106. Sobel's emphasis on the African continuum in the slaves' dynamic structuring of their unique form of Christianity foreshadows the even stronger thrust in this direction in Stuckey's discussion of antebellum slave religiosity in his *Slave Culture*.

107. Sobel, *The World They Made Together*, 174–75.

108. Zahan, *Religion . . . of Traditional Africa*, 49–52.

109. Mbiti, *African Religions*, 74–89, 152–61.

110. Ibid.

111. Ibid., but esp. 152–61.

112. Sobel, *Trabelin' On*, 39–40. Thompson's entire book, *Flash of the Spirit*, is a magnifi-

cent analysis of the transference of African deities, spirits, charms, practices, and beliefs to various regions in the Americas including the United States. His focus is on the visual and philosophic manifestations of this African continuum. Stuckey also powerfully demonstrates the continuum throughout *Slave Culture*, but especially in his excellent first chapter. See also Herskovits, *Myth of the Negro Past*, passim, and Raboteau, *Slave Religion*, 3–92. Both demonstrate that African slaves transferred to the New World their traditional deities, spirits, charms, and religious practices and beliefs. Raboteau emphasizes, however, that slaves in the United States were less capable than many other slaves in America of maintaining their African *deities*. This does not concede Sobel's argument that African slaves were unable to transfer their spirits and deities to the New World.

113. Sobel, *Trabelin' On*, 100. We will take some literary license with her presentation of this conundrum, and thus make it more compelling, by focusing on those elements of the African sacred cosmos that she argues directly helped cause its social incoherency and necessary replacement by an Afro-Baptist sacred cosmos.

114. Saunders, *Colonial Records*, 4:752–53, 5:961–62, 6:58–59, 265. Conkin ("Church Establishment in North Carolina," 8) asserts that Reed mistakenly identified the New Light Baptists (highly evangelical and Arminian) as Methodists. See also Saunders, *Colonial Records*, 6:1060–61.

115. Saunders, *Colonial Records*, 6:265, 562.

116. Ibid., 594–95; Saunders, *Colonial Records*, 7:42–43, 97–98. In all likelihood, Reed mistakenly still used the term *Methodist* for the evangelical and Arminian New Light Baptists. See n. 114 above.

117. Saunders, *Colonial Records*, 7:194, 284–88, 704–5, 8:12–16, 85–86, 20–23, 9:326.

118. See, e.g., Scherer, *Slavery and the Churches in Early America*, 69–77, 126–41; Betty Wood, *Slavery in Colonial Georgia, 1730–1775* (Athens: University of Georgia Press, 1984), 1–87; Crow, *Black Experience*, 50; Raboteau, *Slave Religion*, 143–45. See n. 94 above.

119. Raboteau, *Slave Religion*, 128–32, 147–49, 152; Scherer, *Slavery and the Churches in Early America*, 142–46; Cheryll Ann Cody, "There Was No 'Absalom' on the Ball Plantations: Slave-Naming Practices in the South Carolina Low Country, 1720–1865," *American Historical Review* 92 (June 1987): 573, 580–81, 588. John Inscoe traces the beginning of the increased use of biblical names by North Carolina's slaves to the 1770s. See his "Carolina Slave Names: An Index to Acculturation," *Journal of Southern History* 49 (November 1983): 542–44.

120. John S. Bassett, "North Carolina Methodism and Slavery," *Trinity College Historical Society Papers*, ser. 4 (1900): 6; Crow, *Black Experience*, 50–51; Scherer, *Slavery and the Churches in Early America*, 137. Raboteau, *Slave Religion*, 131; Ira Berlin, *Slaves Without Masters: The Free Negro in the Antebellum South* (New York: Vintage Books, 1976), 46–47.

121. Raboteau, *Slave Religion*, 130–31. To arrive at the population figures for blacks, extrapolations were made from Berlin's figures in *Slaves Without Masters*, 46–47.

122. Raboteau, *Slave Religion*, 131, 149–50, 152–53.

123. George W. Paschal, ed., "From Morgan Edwards Materials," *North Carolina Historical Review* 7 (July 1930): 394–95; Sobel, *Trabelin' On*, 102. Conkin, *Church Establishment in North Carolina*, 8, is one example of the uncritical use of Morgan Edwards's figure of 39,750 Baptists in North Carolina in 1772.

124. Sobel, *Trabelin' On*, 84–87, 102, 188; Conkin, *Church Establishment in North Carolina*, 8.

125. Sobel, *Trabelin' On*, 98–102, 219–356 passim.

126. Sobel, *The World They Made Together*, 241, 188–91, 298 n. 48.

127. U.S. Bureau of the Census, *Historical Statistics of the United States, Colonial Times to 1957* (Washington, D.C., 1960), Ser. Z1-19, p. 756; Berlin, *Slaves Without Masters*, 46–47. Extrapolations were made from statistics in these two works to achieve population totals for Virginia for 1775 and 1793. These figures were then correlated with the statistics for black Baptists. See nn. 121–26 above.

128. Saunders, *Colonial Records*, 6:265.

ADDENDUM

Since 1995, an archeological find was made in an eighteenth-century Annapolis, Maryland townhouse. Items were uncovered in the slave quarters that very likely comprised "diviner's bundles" or "nlsisi," used ritualistically by conjurers and medicine men to the benefit of the slaves. If this interpretation of the findings is confirmed, it will lend powerful support to our basic contention, above, that the religiosity of colonial slaves was primarily derived from their West African beliefs and practices. This was first reported in the *Washington Post*, and reprinted in the *Cleveland Plain Dealer*, 7 September 1997, p. 2A.

Index

Acculturation: and running away, 126, 264 (Table 5.8); and surnames, 147. *See also* Cultural diffusion; Culture, slave; English language, facility for; Runaway slaves

Adams, James: on masters' fear that conversion equals freedom, 193

African beliefs and practices: concepts of work, 35; concept of time, 35, 174, 176–77; and nature, 41; and song, 41–42, 148; holistic approach to reality, 96; conjuring, herbs, and self-defense, 103, 186–88; drugs and poisons, 107, medicine men and therapeutic witchcraft, 107, 187; creation myths, 176; natural phenomena and human events, 180; music, song, dance, poetry, and drama, 182–83; religious ceremonies, 184; herbalism and religiosity, 186–89; medicine and religion, 188; worldview, 188; burials and afterlife, 208. *See also* Marriage and family, African; Marriage and Family, slave; Religiosity, African; Slaves, African-born

African peoples: linguistic affinities of, 144; shared characteristics of, 155. *See also names of specific ethnic groups and countries*

Afro-Christianity: largely post-Revolutionary development, 216–17. *See also* Baptists; Christianity; Christianity, obstacles to conversion of slaves to

Agriculture: in Albemarle Sound region, 15; in Neuse-Pamlico region, 15; techniques, 30; commercial development of, 30–31; poor reputation of North Carolina in, 35; crop schedules affect work, 42–43; models to explain development of, 311–13 (n. 41); techniques not explained by laxity, 315–16 (n. 59). *See also names of specific crops*

Albemarle Sound (Bertie, Chowan, Currituck, Hertford, Pasquotank, Perquimans, and Tyrrell counties): development, 15; exports, 15; settled with slaves, 15; population growth, 17; black percentage of population in, 22; slave sex imbalances, 26; Edenton as port, 27; percentage of slaves on large holdings, 27; Brickell on planters and serial monogamy among slaves, 160; dual-headed slave families in, 231–32; estimates of development of slave marriage and family in, 291 (Table 7.5); customs districts in, 305 (n. 8); emigration from to western counties, 306 (n. 10)

Allen plantation, slaves on: surnames of, 147; extended families of, 168

Americanus, Scotus: on immigrant work habits, 34; on task system, 36

Amistad captives: marital patterns of, 156–57, 358 (n. 23); ethnic backgrounds, 357 (n. 14); monogamy, 358 (n. 23); polygyny and wealth, 358 (n. 23)

Anabaptists. *See* Baptists

Anglicans: slaves and, 190–202; some claim biological inferiority of slaves, 191: Crown in 1730 encourages black and Indian conversion, 194; weaknesses of church, 196–99, 369 (n. 79); numbers of ministers, 197–98; weak religious appeal of to blacks, 198; baptisms of slaves and, 200; comment on Baptists, 212–13; few references to slaves in comments on evangelicals, 213–14; comparative strengths of in South, 367 (n. 77). *See also* Bray's Associates

Anson County: settlement, 19; Highland Scots in, 19, 205; slave (Dick) executed in poisoning case, 114; Scots-Irish in, 205

Archdale, John: influential Quaker, governor, 1694–96, 202

Armed slaves: authorized by county courts, 329–30 (n. 58)

Artisans, free: and ruling class, 59

Artisans, slave: work routines, 46–47; and crime, 111; characteristics of, 130; facility for English language, 130; selection of, 130; skills facilitate escape, 130; pass as free, 131; sale of father and son, 1780s, 154

Asante (Ghana): bride wealth customs, contemporary, 158, 357 (n. 19); residential patterns of spouses and children, 163

Ashe, John: obtains gun license for slave, 330 (n. 58)

Ashe, Samuel: obtains gun license for slave, 330 (n. 58)

Attmore, William: on permanence of slavery, 32; on slave diet, 37; on task system, 37; on slave music and dance, 183

Augustus, Sarah Louise: former slave, on herbs, 189

Auld, James: as small planter, 33; on slave labor, 39

Baker, Rev. Thomas: Virginia masters fear baptism of slaves, 1770, 194; Virginia masters converting slaves and teaching to read, 1770, 195

Banditry: in South Carolina, 99–100; in North Carolina, 101

Baptism: not a correct gauge of conversions, 200; of slaves by Anglicans, 200; slave children targeted for, 200, 369 (n. 88); relative frequency among slaves, 369 (n. 87). See also Christianity

Baptists: appeal of to slaves, 208; Anglican views of, 212–13; as mistakenly called Methodists, 212–13; black membership estimated, 214–15; total membership estimated, 215; in Virginia, 216

Barnett, Rev. John: blames masters for slave illiteracy, 1767, 195; disdains New Light Baptists, refers to "Negroes" speaking at meetings of, 212–13

Bassett, John Spencer: on repeal of castration clause in slave law, 336 (n. 63)

Batchelor, Edward: places ads for escaped

African slaves (Kauchee, Boohum, Ji, Sambo Pool, and Peg Manny), 129–30; assumed African runaways "invegelied" away by whites, 132

Bath Town, 15, 305 (n. 8); decline of, 11; slave (Steven) escapes from jail in, 112; Anglican minister in, 197

Baucum, Sarah: raped by slave (Phil), 85

Beaufort, 15, 305 (n. 8); decline of, 11

Beaufort County: slave trial in, 78–79; stores burglarized by slaves in, 112; Quakers in, 202; Anabaptists in, 1761, 212

Beavers, John: slave of (Prymus), castrated, 84

Becker, Robert A: on North Carolina's tax system as regressive, inefficient, corrupt, 327 (n. 28)

Bell, Joseph: slave of (Toby), poisoned by other slaves, 112

Bell, Lewis: plantation owner murdered by slave (Simon), 115

Bellamy, Donnie D: evidence on task system in Onslow County questioned, 316 (n. 65)

Benners, John: slave of (Prymus), accused of collaborating to poison, 112

Berkeley, Bishop George: on planter contempt of blacks, 191

Berlin, Ira, 301 (n. 1); analysis of slave language and naming practices critiqued, 354 (n. 23)

Bertie County: slave (Caesar) executed for murder in, 114; slave (Bacchus) executed for rape in, 115; calculation of 1755 and 1767 population figures, 223 (Table 1.1, n. 7), 224 (Table 1.1, n. 37); court of authorizes arming slaves, 329 (n. 58)

Blacks: population, 19–27; density, 22–23; migration, 26; Crown instructions to convert, 194; Methodists among, 214

Blacks, free, 214; and discriminatory poll tax, 67, 88; high proportion of are servants, 67, 313 (n. 44); slave artisans pass as, 131; wife petitions to free slave husband, 153–54, 355 (n. 1); enslavement of, 313 (n. 43), 366–67 (n. 67)

Bladen County: Highland Scots in, 19, 205; murder and attempted murder cases (Cain, Cato) in, 114; jailed slave (Will) murdered or commits suicide, 115; Muslim slaves in, 179; Quakers in, 202

Blount, Joseph: Chowan sheriff castrates slave (Isaac), 84

Boats: concern for theft of, 188

Bond, James: killed by Virginia slave (Ceasar), 115

Booth, Newell: on characteristics of African religiosity, 175, 176, 177

Boucher, Rev. Jonathan: on "biological inferiority" of Virginia slaves, 191; on religious laxity of whites in Virginia, 192

Branding: in theft case (Dick), 83, 113; mentioned by masters to identify slaves, 188

Brice, William: slave of (Bob), denies hog theft, 119–20

Bray, Rev. Thomas: organizes SPG and Bray's Associates, 197

Bray's Associates: in Georgia, 190; Rev. John Waring argues for Christianizing slaves, 1770, 195–96; and slaves, 197

Brevard, John: owner attacked by slave (Dick), 144

Brickell, John: on work habits of whites and blacks, 34; on garden plots, 37–38; on compensation system, 87; on slave theft, 102; on bride wealth, 159; on intervention of masters in slave marriage, 160, 165; as observer of slave practices, 184; on masters' fear of slave conversion, 193

Bride price (bride wealth). See Marriage and family practices, African

British West Indies, slavery in: practices inducing low birth rates, 165; gang and task systems coexist, 317 (n. 69); and garden plots, 317 (n. 69); historians disagree about impact on marriage and family, 357 (n. 22)

Brockett, Benjamin: witness in slave trial, 119

Browne, Rev. Marmaduke: on racism of slaveowners, 191

Brownrigg, Richard: diverse enterprises of, 320 (n. 99)

Brunswick, 16, 305 (n. 8)

Brunswick County: illiteracy of slaves in blamed on masters, 195; New Light Baptists in and slaves, 1766, 213; slave carpenters at saw mill in, 320 (n. 102)

Brutality: as reason to flee, 133; scars reveal, 133. See also Terror

Bryan, Hugh: South Carolina evangelical and slaves, 205

Buck, Tom: clash with master over name, 139; flees master, Joseph Hancock, 139; possible African names of, 139, 140, 141

Burnet, John: white felon, 82

Burning: of slave (Harry) in jail, 77; of slave (Morise) for murder, 114; of slave (Cato) for rape, 115

Burrington, Gov. George: on slave imports, 21; instructed to encourage conversion of Blacks and Indians, 194; reports few ministers in province, 197; laments overland trade to Virginia, 306 (n. 11)

Bute County: slaves (Ned and Daniel) hanged for poisoning a master in, 115; black godparents in, 199; slave baptisms in, 199; Anabaptists in, 1768, 213

Cape Fear Landing: and trade, 28

Cape Fear Mercury: advertisements for runaway slaves in, 344 (n. 8); extant and possible issues of, 343 (n. 7)

Cape Fear region: economic development, 15–16; and naval stores, 15–16, 32, 43–45; and lumber products, 16, 32, 45; work organization and routines on large slaveholdings, 32, 36–37; slaves at white funeral in, 181–82; Murray notes slaves and funerals in, 364 (n. 28)

Cape Fear region, Lower (Brunswick and New Hanover counties): large slaveholdings in compared to South Carolina low country, 2, 24, 161, 309 (n. 24); population growth in, 1755–67, 17; rice in, 19,

36, 43; blacks as percentage of population in, 22; percentage of slaves on large slaveholdings, 23; Wilmington as port, 27; naval stores and lumber products in, 29; settled with slaves, 31; mixed nature of workforce in, 33–34; work routines in, 36; surnames of slaves on plantation in, 147; proportion of slaves on different size holdings, 231 (Table 1.6)

Cape Fear region, Upper (Bladen County): population growth in, 1755–67, 17; black percentage of population in, 22; percentage of slaves on large slaveholdings, 23; slave sex ratios, 25; Wilmington as port, 27

Carteret County: Quakers in, 202; calculation of 1755 and 1765 black, white, and total population, 223 (Table 1.1, n. 12); runaway captured and escaped in, 347 (n. 24)

Cassava (cassavi): as poison, 188–89; as food, 189

Castration: used to punish Pasquotank slave, Sambo, in poisoning case, 80–81, 107, 154; law of 1758, 83–84, 89; ordered by slave courts as punishment, 1755–67, 83–85; substitute for execution for many slave crimes, 1758–64, 84–85, 89; ordered for second felony (Jimmy), castrated and hanged, 85; Phill, hanged and castrated, 85; used exclusively on slaves, 85; and execution in houseburning case (Isaac), 85, 114; Law of 1764 drops substitution of castration for execution, 89–90; changes in law and supposed changes in planter morality, 90; ordered in poisoning case (Tom and Prymus), 103, 112; as a punishment, 111; historians on, 336–37 (n. 63); and executions of slaves, increased according to growth of slave population, 340 (n. 32)

Celebration, slave (John Koonering). See John Koonering

Central Inner Plain–Piedmont region (Cumberland, Dobbs, Duplin, and Johnston counties): population growth in, 1755–67, 17; black percentage of population in, 22; slave sex ratios, 25; towns and trade, 27–28

Chartwright, Ezekial: white, collaborates with slaves in theft, 113–14

Chatham (Iron) Furnace, 37, 318 (n. 79); labor force at, 47; slaves hired out, 48

Chowan County: slave, Isaac, castrated and hanged, 84, 114; slave, Cato, executed for rape, 86; compensation for executed slaves, 93; white sued for attacking slaves, 93; slave, Quash, hanged for murdering slave, London, 115; white killed by Virginia slave, Ceaser, 115; calculation of population figures for 1755 and 1767, 223 (Table 1.1, n. 5), 224 (Table 1.1, n. 35); port of Edenton in, 305 (n. 8); court authorizes arming slaves, 329 (n. 58)

Chowan Parish: Baptists in, 1744, 212; dissenters in, 1744, 212; Quakers in, 1744, 212

Christianity, 6; withheld from slaves or made available in truncated form, 137; most slaves untouched by in colonial years, 189, 213–14, 219; conversion of slaves to, 190–217; blacks baptized, 199; godparents of slaves, 199; baptism not a correct gauge of conversion, 200; slave children targeted for baptism, 200, 369 (n. 88); and afterlife, 210; spread of among slaves, 216–17; effect of conversion on slave status, 327 (n. 31); enslaved Christians freed, 328–29 (n. 54); and enslavement, 366–67 (n. 67). See also Anglicans, Baptists, Moravians, Quakers

Christianity, obstacles to conversion of slaves to: whites fear conversion leads to freedom, 67–68, 192–94; linguistic differences of whites and slaves, 149–50, 191; attitudes of whites, 191–92; whites as poor model, 192; African religiosity, 190–91, 192; harshness of slavery, 192; masters fear egalitarian concepts, 194; masters fear lost labor time, 195; summarized, 196, 216–17; Anglicans, institutional and doctrinal factors, 196–201;

slave parents and education of children, 200; and Moravians, 203

Churches, black: numbers of, 216

Class, identification: based on sliding scale of slave ownership used for different counties, 322 (n. 1). *See also* Ruling class

Clayton, Francis: robbed by slave, Toney, 115

Clear, Peter: owner of slave, Isaac, castrated and hanged, 84

Cody, Cheryll Ann: on birth intervals of slave women in South Carolina, 167, 361 (n. 44); on conversion efforts after the Revolution, 314; interpretation that masters named first-generation slaves questioned, 351 (n. 1); on late development of Biblical names, 353 (n. 13); on necronymic naming practices in South Carolina, 360 (n. 33); compares South Carolina slave and European completed family size, 361 (n. 44); on age of slave women in South Carolina at prima-partum, 361 (n. 44); estimates of completed family size discussed, 362 (n. 47)

Collins, Josiah: slaves of on Albemarle Sound plantation celebrate John Koonering, 1829, 183

Committee of Claims: and compensations for killed slaves, 77; content of records of, 249 (Table 3.1, *Sources*), 331 (n. 4)

Compensation for executed and killed slaves: distributed disproportionately to wealthy owners, 59, 250–51 (Table 3.2); confirmation of to masters, 77; in murder case (Annis, Phyllis, Cuff), 79; levels of valuations, 80, 88–90, 336 (n. 57); financing of, 87–88, 336 (n. 55); increase during French and Indian War, 88; valuations not limited before 1758, 88; and slave prices, 88, 89, 90; maximum award raised in 1764, 89–90; affected by law of 1764, 90; for slave runaway (Tom), killed by owner's son, 113; levels of, by gender and time period, 246–47 (Table 3.1)

Compensation system: allows harsh criminal justice system, 61, 101, 316 (n. 63);

extends actual jurisdiction of slave courts, 74–75; when slaveowners would be compensated for slaves killed, 75; purpose of, 75, 87; provincial funds support, 87–88, 336 (n. 55)

Conditions of life, slave: compared to servants, 93–94; legal minimum of food, clothing, and housing, 99; and theft, 103; scars reveal, 133; clothing as sign of, 134–35. *See also* Laws, slave and servant; Punishments, slave criminals; Terror; Work

Conjuring: and protection of family, 107. *See also* Sambo

Conkin, Paul: and New Light Baptists misidentified as Methodists, 372 (n. 114); inadequate use of Morgan Edward's figures on Baptists, 372 (n. 123)

Cooper, Marcus: slave on Allen plantation, 147

Cooper, Tom: slave on Allen plantation, 147

Cooper, Tom: slave on Pollock plantation, 147

Coor, James: slave of (Scip), executed, 115

Corn: Indian, in Neuse-Pamlico region, 15; cultivation, 42–43; yield, 319 (n. 87)

Courts, slave: unlimited jurisdiction and plenary powers defined in laws, 70–71, 73, 75; established ca. 1715, 71; eliminate most existent procedural protections for the accused, 71–72; convictions in compared to those of whites, 72; case loads, 73; implement savage ideal of criminal justice, 73–74; and crimes against other slaves, 74; castrations, 83–84; convictions by, 256 (Table 4.1), and killings by authorities, 256 (Table 4.1); composition of, 330–31 (n. 2)

Covington, Phillemon: free-born Spanish black enslaved on schooner of, 329 (n. 54)

Craton, Michael: on gang and task systems, 317 (n. 69); on impact of slavery on marriage and family in British West Indies, 356 (n. 22)

Craven County: slaves, Tom and Prymus, castrated in, 84; slave theft case (Bob and Simon) in, 113; slave, Scip, hanged for burglary and threatening master in, 115; slave, Cato, tied for hog theft in, 119; hog theft case (Bob) in, 119–20; African slaves (Kauchee, Boohum, Ji, Sambo Pool, Peg Manny) escape in, 128–29; clothing worn by Africans captured in, 134; runaways captured in, 135 (Sam), 347 (n. 24); extended families among slaves in, 168–69; Muslim slaves in, 179; Christianity and slaves in, 190; few Anglican ministers in, 197, 198; Quakers in, 202, 212; Anabaptists in, 212; Methodists in, 212; Presbyterians in, 212; slaves in, called heathens, 217; court of, and enslaved free-born blacks in, 329 (n. 54); court of, authorizes arming slaves, 329 (n. 58)

Crime, slave: and resistance, 6–7, 96–108; illegal trade, 69, 205; criminal justice system and, 70–95 passim; execution and conviction rates compared to whites, 72, 77; within slave community, 74, 102–3; conceptualization regarding, 96–108; political dimensions of, 98; and slave values, 101–8; and defense of elemental institutions, 102; theft of alcohol, 102; whites as major targets of, 102–3, 111; theories of crime and, 104; historians and, 104–5; cultural hegemonic morality argument rejected, 104–7; problem of documenting minor crimes, 108–9; difficulty discerning incidence of major theft, 109; bearing of age on, 109; distribution of major, 109–10; bearing of gender on, 109–10; bearing of occupations on, 110–11; collaborative, 111–14; collaboration with whites, 113–14; mainly individual acts, 114; convictions for, by crime, 256 (Table 4.1); Africans and, 340 (n. 27), 341 (n. 35); Creoles and, 341 (n. 35)

Crime, white: convictions, compared to those of blacks, 72, 77; white tried for

murder of slave, 92; collaboration with slaves (Tom and Moses), 113–14

Criminal justice system for slaves: arbitrary, summary, and terroristic, 57; and ruling class, 72–73; logic of, 72–73, 74–75; two-tiered, overlapping jurisdiction of public and private, 72–74; case loads of black and white compared, 73; how two-tiered system affected severity of treatment, 76; and terror, 102. See also Crime, slave; Plantation justice

Crosby, Paul: runaway indentured servant, captured, 132

Crow, Jeffrey: on appealing ways Baptists approached slaves, 208; on maroon settlements in Great Dismal Swamp, 338 (n. 12)

Cultural diffusion, 33; and slave religion, 8; in Carolinas, 41; bidirectional nature of, 208

Culture, slave, 24–25, 58; little shared by whites and slaves, 3–4; and African heritages, 6–7, 138; song, 41–42, 182; and slaveholders, 58; slaves shape, 58; attacked by slaveowners, 137; marriage and the family, 219; names and languages, 219; variety of aspects summarized, 219–20; African American, 219–20; ethic and resistance patterns, 220; value system and code of conduct, 220. See also John Koonering

Culture, white: masters withhold from slaves, 3–4, 137, 220

Cumberland County: Highland Scots in, 19, 205; and trade, 28; slave thief whipped, 83; slave theft and murder case (Dick), 113; runaway (Jack) thought headed for former home in, 123, 124; calculations of 1767 population figures, 225 (Table 1.1, n. 51)

Cupples, Rev. Charles: on black godparents in Bute County, 199; and Anabaptists in Bute County, 213

Currituck County: calculation of 1767 population figures, 224 (Table 1.1, n. 32)

Dahomeans: burial practices of, 180–81; and John Koonering, 184

Davis, James: edits *North Carolina Gazette*, 344 (n. 7); slave and servant of flee, 348 (n. 34)

Dawson, Penelope: and harsh overseer, 36; slaves protest overseer, 38

Decapitation: in attempted murder case (Dick), 114; of slave (George) hanged for rape, 115; of slave thieves (Jonny and Quamino) in New Hanover County, 115

Delaware, slaves in: and African religions, 190; supposed incapacity to understand Christianity, 191

Derendred, Joseph: free-born Portuguese black enslaved, 329 (n. 54)

De Rossett, Louis: obtains gun license for slave, 330 (n. 58)

Dillard, Joey Lee: emphasizes extensive development of pidgin-creole languages by slaves, 354 (n. 23)

Dobbs, Gov. Arthur: and establishment law, 196; notes few ministers in province, 197

Dobbs County: slave (Dick) executed for murder in, 115; Quakers in, 202

Domestics, slave: work routines, 46; and crime, 111

Dorcas: female slave found dead in jail, 77

DuBois, John: slave of castrated for theft, 84

Dunn, John: hog stolen, 119; Coramontee slave of (Jikowife), flees, is captured, 130

Duplin County: slave (George) executed for rape, 86; slave (Morise) burned alive for murder, 114; slave (Simon) executed for murder, 115

Ear cropping, for theft: (Ben) 83, (Simon) 113, (Negro Tom) 119

Economic development, 11–17, 30–31; diversity, 2, 11; diversity and slave labor, 4, 5, 31; and slavery, 6, 23–24, 161; regional similarities of, in British North America, 10–11; and roads and rivers, 11; and natural obstacles, 11, 14; factors affecting, 14;

provincial policies and, 14; merchants and, 14, 15, 27, 310 (n. 33), 311 (n. 35); and British bounties, 14, 15–16; of Cape Fear region, 15–16; lags behind population growth, 16–17; and interior, to 1750s, 17; as infrastructure growth, 27; after 1750, 27–31; and labor demands, 31; and late maturation, 161; and limited success of internal improvements, 301–2 (n. 3)

Economy, southern: growth rate of exports, 28

Edenton: port town, 11, 27, 305 (n. 8); growth, 15; white tried for murder of slave in, 92; John Koonering celebration observed, 1823, 183; Anglican minister in, 197

Edgecombe County: series of crimes by slaves (Tom and Manger) in, 112–13; calculations of black, white, and total populations, 1767, 225 (Table 1.1, n. 54)

Education, slave: resisted by whites, 194–95; little impact of Anglicans among children in Virginia; 200–201; some Presbyterians favor, 205; Great Awakening and, 205–6

Edwards, Morgan: overestimates numbers of black Baptists, 1772, 215

English, pidgin: and "phonological reduction" of African names, 352 (n. 9)

English language, facility for: runaways and, 123; group runaways and, 129; individual runaways and, 130, 131; runaway nonfield slaves and, 130, 131; low among captured runaways, 349–50 (n. 43). *See also* Languages, slave

Equiano, Olaudah (Ibo): resists name change, 102, 143; mentions bride price, 156; captured and enslaved, 173: child isolated from other Ibo, 173–74; Ibo understanding of clock, 174; Ibo understanding of a portrait, 174-75; uses African past to fathom new environment, 174–76, 178; and view of natural phenomena, 175, 179; African religiosity retained, 178, 211; background of, 363 (n. 1)

Ethic, slave: relationship of autonomy and resistance to, 6–7; dependence on Africa, 6–7, 107; and criminality, 101–8; and moral economy, 105–7; unrestrained by hegemonic morality, 106; and limited options of, 106, 132–33, 154–55; influence of harshness of slavery and slave crimes on, 340 (n. 27). *See also* Marriage and family, slave

Evangelicals: and abolitionism, 213

Evangelicals, South Carolina: message to slaves toned down during Great Awakening, 207

Executions of slaves, 77–82, 103, 112–15; compared to those of whites, 76–78; and castrations, 77–78; for attempted murder, 112 (Dick), 114 (Cato, Pompey); for murder, 112 (Robin, Jack, Jemmy), 114 (Cain, Morise, Cesar), 115 (Dick, Will, Simon, Ceaser); for poisoning, 112 (Ned and Daniel), 114 (Lettice, Dick), 115 (Cuff, Will); for rape, 114 (Peter), 115 (Cato, Quash, George); for theft, 112 (Stephen), 115 (Jonny, Quamino, Toney, Scip); for houseburning, 115 (Rose); by authorities, 256 (Table 4.1); increased according to growth of slave population, 340 (n. 32)

Executions of whites: compared to those of slaves, 76–78

Exports, 28–30, 311 (n. 40); dairy products, 11; Indian corn, 11; livestock on hoof, 11; meat, 11; indirect, overland via other colonies, 11, 15, 17, 29; naval stores, 11, 17; tobacco, 11, 17, 29; wheat and flour, 11, 29; lumber and lumber products (other than naval stores), 11, 29, 45; from Albemarle Sound region, 15; limited before 1750, 16; economic diversity and, 17; rice, 28; growth rate of, 28–29; compared with other colonies, 28–30, 236–37 (Table 1.9); oceanic (direct), 28–30, 311 (n. 40). *See also* Economic development; *names of specific colonies*

Fanning, Col. Edmund: anti-Regulator candidate, 53; paternalism of, 53

Fante (Ghana): residential patterns of spouses and children, 163

Faris, William: on work habits of Germans, 34

Farmers: and ruling class, 58–59; trade patterns of in Western region, 310 (n. 33)

Fenn, Elizabeth A.: traces origins of John Koonering, 365 (n. 38)

Fishing: in Albemarle Sound region, 15

Flax: in Neuse-Pamlico region, 15

Francis, Patrick: slave of (Dick), charged with robbery and murder, 113

Franklin, Benjamin: admits early racist evaluation of blacks, 191

Frey, Sylvia R.: assertions on polygyny and slaves questioned, 358 (n. 22)

Fulani: bride price among, 156

Funerals: James Murray notes importance to slaves, 364 (n. 28)

Ga (Ghana): residential patterns of spouses and children, 163–64

Galenson, David: on net black migration to North Carolina, 1750–80, 26, 307 (n. 16); on slaves replacing unskilled indentured servants, 313 (n. 44)

Gallay, Allan: interpretation of Great Awakening in South Carolina and on slave religion questioned, 206–7; interpretation of planter paternalism and impact on slaves challenged, 206–7, 324–25 (n. 14)

Gang labor, slave, 5; in Chesapeake tobacco production, 4; in British West Indies, 317 (n. 69)

Gardens, slaves working in, 5; relationship to task system questioned, 317 (n. 69). *See also* Incentives, negative and positive: garden plots

Gatling, William: purchases African import (Peg Manny), 129

Genovese, Eugene: pejorative interpretation of slave crime rejected, 104, 340 (n. 27); assertions about slave distinctions of marriage and family separation rejected, 356 (n. 6)

Georgia, studies of slavery in colonial, 2; exports, 28–29; Africans in slave population, 58; African continuum helps prevent conversion to Christianity in, 190. *See also* Ottolenghe, Joseph

Germans: in western counties, 19

Goveia, Esa V.: on destructive impact of slavery on marriage and family in British West Indies, 357–58 (n. 22)

Grains and grain products, 2; production, 27; exports, 30

Gramsci, Antonio: model of cultural hegemony, 56

Great Awakening: slave education and, 205; Presbyterians and slaves, 205–6; evangelical message to slaves in South Carolina toned down, 207; Baptists and Methodists as offshoots of, 207

Great Dismal Swamp: maroons in, 99, 122; and runaways, 101, 122

Green, John (Craven County): store of broken into by slaves (Bob and Simon), 113

Green, John, Sr. (Bladen County): murdered by slave (Cain), 114

Gregg, Frederick: obtains gun license for slave, 330 (n. 58)

Gregory, Samuel: slaves of on Edenton plantation celebrate John Koonering, 1823, 183

Gudger, Sarah: WPA interview with former slave, 179, 180

Guilford County: New Light Baptists and Baptists in, 215

Gunderson, Joan: on birth intervals of slave women in Virginia, 167

Gutman, Herbert: links extended families and slave naming practices, 171; doubts slaves internalized paternalistic ethic, 324 (n. 14); interpretation of origins of planter paternalism questioned, 324 (n. 24); on slave parents and sale of children, 356 (n. 6); hypothesis on taboo of naming slaves after mothers questioned, 360 (n. 33); on necronymic naming practices, 360 (n. 33)

Halifax: midland economic center, 27–28; Anglican minister in, 197; slave (Rose) executed for house burning in, 115

Halifax County: calculations of black, white, and total population, 225 (Table 1.1, n. 53)

Hall, Rev. Clement: on dissenters in Chowan Parish, 1744, 212

Hall, Jack: free black witness for accused slave, 71

Hallow, Elizabeth: raped by slave (Cato), 86

Hancock, Joseph: clashes with slave, Tom Buck, over name, 139; Tom Buck flees, 139

Hanging: of slave for murdering master, 115; of slave (George) for rape, 115; of slave (Jack) for theft in New Hanover County, 115; of slave (Pompey) in attempted murder case, 114–15; of slave (Quash) for murdering slave (London), 115; of slave (Scip) for burglary and threatening life of owner in Craven County, 115; of slaves (Harry, Jemmy, Isaac) in Edenton, 115; of slaves (Jack and Jemmy) in Northampton County, 115; of slaves (Ned and Daniel) in Bute County, 115; of slave (Will), alive in Gibbet, in New Hanover County, 115

Harnet, Cornelius: obtains gun license for slave, 330 (n. 58)

Harrold, Elizabeth: seeks to arm slave, 329 (n. 58)

Hawkings, Mr.: sells slave to Moravians, 204

Hazel, James: hires slaves, 49

Hegemony: historians and, 104–7

Hegemony, cultural: model rejected for slaves, 2–4, 56–58; absence of, and harsh criminal justice system for slaves, 6; absence of, and African cultural continuum, 6–7, 135; and paternalism among whites, 56; terror negates impact of on slaves, 56–57; Africa and slave rejection of, 58; poor whites and criminal justice system, 72; lack of, and severity of slave courts, 72–73, 94; and interpretations

of slave criminality, 104–6; argument
of slave criminality rejected, 104–7; absence alters paternalism, 105–7; absence
prevents imposition of hegemonic
morality on slaves, 105–7; slave owners
eschew, 220. *See also* Hegemony: political and economic; Moral economy;
Paternalism; Ruling class
Hegemony, political and economic:
exerted by elite, 106
Herbs: use of by slaves, 189
Herron, Benjamin: obtains gun license for
slave, 330 (n. 58)
Herskovits, Melville: on Dahomean burial
practices, 180–81; on slave burial rites
with West African roots, 180–81
Hertford County: slave trial in, 79–80;
slave (Pompey) attempts to murder
master in, 114–15; calculation of black,
white, and total populations, 224
(Table 1.1, n. 36)
Higgins, Robert: on reexport of South Carolina slave imports to North Carolina,
307 (n. 16)
Highland Scots, 19; Presbyterians, 205
Higman, Barry: on continuation of nuclear
families among slaves in British West
Indies, 358 (n. 22)
Hilliard, Elizabeth: slaves of (Sam and
Davey), hired out, 48
Hilty, Hiram: on Quaker meeting for
blacks, 202
Hiring out slaves, 31, 34, 48–50; contracts,
48–49; wage rates, 49, 321 (nn. 110, 111);
effects upon slaves, 49–50, 322 (n. 114);
importance of, 50; ordinances about,
in Wilmington, 117; more males than
females, 321 (n. 110). *See also* Wage rates,
hires
Hog killing and stealing: few public cases,
118; cases discussed, 118–20
Houseburning: slave (Isaac) castrated and
executed for, 114; execution of slave
(Rose) for, 115
Housing: regulated for slaves in Wilmington, 117

Howard, Martin: condemns terror of
legal system for slaves, 57; denounces
slave criminal justice system, 70–71;
denounces murder of slaves, 75; on lack
of legal protection of slaves' persons,
91–92
Howeall, Edward: slave of (Jack), collaborates with Virginia slave, 112; slave of
(Jack), executed for theft, 112
Hyde County: slave (Jikowife) captured in,
130

Ibo (Nigeria): residential patterns of
spouses and children, 164; Olaudah
Equiano captured and enslaved, 173
Igbo: day names, T43 (Table 6.4, n. 1). *See
also* Ibo
Immigrants, slave: direct from Africa, 21;
and sex ratios, 25. *See also* Imports,
slave; Sex ratios, slave; Slaves, African-
born
Immigrants, white, 17, 19, 38
Imports, slave: via sea routes, 20–21, 25,
307–8 (n. 16); via overland routes, 21,
25
Incentives, negative and positive, 35–39;
punishment scars, 36; garden plots,
37–38; task system, 50–52; aim at external behavior, 57–58; and cultural hegemony, 57–58. *See also* Terror
Indentured servants. *See* Servants,
indentured
Indians: payment for scalps of, 82; use of
poison by, 186; slaves acquire knowledge
from, 189; Crown instructions to convert, 194; whites resist education of,
194–95; as slaves, few by late colonial
period, 314 (n. 47)
Indigo: Cape Fear region, 16
Inscoe, John, 372 (n. 119); overestimates
slave use of biblical names before Revolution, 353 (n. 13); argues slaves fear to
use surnames openly, 353 (n. 19)
Insurrection: roots in everyday resistance,
97–99; absence of, explained, 98–99;
potential for, in New Hanover County,

99; possibilities in South Carolina, 122; linked to slave literacy and conversion, 194. *See also* Resistance

Iredell, James: and slave servant, 47

Iron: work routines in ironworks, 47; exports of, 318 (n. 79); relative unimportance of, 318 (n. 79); in Western region, 318 (n. 79)

Isaac, Rhys: on lower-class whites and paternalism in Virginia, 55; on slaves, paternalism, and cultural hegemony in Virginia, 56, 323 (n. 2)

Islam, impact of: among eighteenth-century Maryland slaves, 178–79; in eighteenth-century North Carolina, 179; on Yoruba and dowries, 357 (n. 18); in nineteenth-century North Carolina, 364 (n. 20)

Ivins, Mourning: free black, petitions to manumit her husband Ned, 153–54

Ivins, Nat: slave husband of free black woman, 153–54

Jackson, Harvey: interpretation of Great Awakening in South Carolina and slave religion analyzed, 206–7

Jarratt, Devereux: Methodist revivalist, and slaves, 214

Jikowife: Coromantee slave flees, is captured, 130

John Canno. *See* John Koonering

John Koonering: earliest manifestations, 183, 184; African sources of 184–85; slave costumes in ceremony, 185–86; in Washington County, 185–86; Edward Warren links to Egypt, 365 (n. 42)

Johnston, Samuel: on slaves (Sam and Davey) hired out, 48; slave of (Frank), branded, 133

Johnston County: slave (Peter) executed for rape in, 114; runaway from, captured (Sam), 135; Anabaptists in 1758, 212

Jones, Charles Colcock: on numbers of black Baptists, 1733, 215

Jonkonnu: in Jamaica, 183, 184. *See also* John Koonering

Jordon, Charles: sues man who attacked his slaves, 93

Jordon, Winthrop D.: on attitudes of "black inferiority," 192, 366 (n. 59); on punishment of castration, 335 (n. 46)

Justice. *See* Criminal justice system for slaves; Plantation justice

Kate: slave murdered by white man, 92

Kelso and Berwick: slaves hired out, 49

Kendreck, Martin: hires slaves, 48

Kulikoff, Alan: calculates number of Africans in N.C., 25; on population increase, 307 (n. 15); estimates sex ratio from number of Africans, 309 (n. 28); on procedures to reconstitute slave marriages and families, 359 (n. 31)

Labor: hired, 30, 31; indentured servants, 31; free, judged unpredictable, 31, 40; mixed nature of workforce, 33–34; free, and ruling class, 59. *See also* Hiring out slaves; Wages rates, hires

Labor, slave: demography and, 4; and labor organization, small farms, 5; commercial agriculture and, 31, 32–50 passim; occupational breakdowns by gender and skill, 32–33; comparisons with other colonies, 33; incentives, positive and negative, 35–39; and iron, 40–41; skills vary by crop, 42–43; work routines, 42–48; personal servants, 47; diverse experiences of field hands, 47–48, 321 (n. 106); females and hiring out, 321 (n. 110). *See also* Hiring out slaves; Occupations; Work

Languages, slave, 3, 6, 7; slaves develop, 7, 148; diversity of, 58, 148, 151–52; linguistic affinities among enslaved Africans, 144; linguistic profile of runaways, 148; development of pidgin-creole from Delaware to Georgia, 148, 149–52; Gullah in South Carolina, 148, 151; and historians, 148, 151; evolution of, and naming as a model, 148, 151–52; as obstacle to conversion, 149–50; facility for English language limited prior to Revolution, 150, 151, 215; African syntax probable for pidgin-creole, 150–51; infusion of English language over time, 151, 215; creole, 151–52, 185; adaptive qualities of slaves evident in pidgin-creole, 152; limited geographical distribution, 354 (n. 23); Geechee in Georgia, 355 (n. 35). *See also* English language, facility for

Laws: on interracial marriage (1715, 1741), 67; on theft of boats (1715, 1741), 118; on theft of livestock (1741), 118; Sabbatarian (1715), 192, 196; Orthodox Clergy Act (1765), 196, 197; Vestry Act (1764), 196, 197; and Anglican Church, 199; on theft of slaves and free blacks (1741, 1778), 348 (n. 33)

Laws, free blacks: discriminatory poll tax (1723), 67

Laws, slave and servant: development, terms, implementation, 6, 61–69; lack of rights and protections for slaves, 61; rights and protections of servants, 61–62; enslavement exclusions (1715, 1741), 61–62, 327 (n. 31); on freedom of movement (1715, 1729), 62, 63, 328 (n. 42); armed slaves (1715), 62, (1741, 1753), 68, 329 (n. 28); on runaways (1715), 62–63, 66, 343 (n. 2), (1741), 64–65, 343 (n. 2); on runaway servants and labor time (1715), 63; right to kill outlawed slave runaways (1715, 1743), 63, 64–66; increased protection of servants (1741), 64; searchers established (1753), 66; manumission of slaves restricted (1715, 1723, 1741), 66–67, 193, 355 (n. 1); slave courts (1715, 1741), 71, 330–31 (n. 2); on hog theft (1741), 83; compensations for executed and killed slaves (1715, 1741, 1758, 1764), 87; slave castrations and evaluation limits, to save money (1758), 89; compensation and castration (1758), effects of, 89, 126; compensation maximum raised (1764), 89–90; minimal food, clothing, and housing for slaves (1753), 94; few options for slaves in, and

how slaves resisted, 101–2; and illegal trading (1741), 116; livestock and tobacco raising barred (1741), 118, 317 (n. 70); conversion to Christianity no path to freedom for slaves (1669), 193; conversion and slave status, compared to other colonies, 193; life bondage for servants prohibited, 327 (n. 31); imprisonment of slaves and lost labor time, 328 (n. 35); survey of colonial law on blacks and rape, 335 (n. 46); no private burial of servants (1715), 337 (n. 74); and racism, 366 (n. 59). *See also* Ordinances, Wilmington slave

Lee, Bryant and Mary: murdered by slave, 81, 115

Leftear, Joseph: Indian servant flees, 348 (n. 35)

Legal system: of compensation, helps maximize use of terror, 57, 91; slaves and brutality of, 333–34 (n. 31). *See also* Criminal justice system for slaves; Plantation justice

Levine, Lawrence: disagrees with Genovese on slave crime, 104; on role of trickster tales, 339 (n. 21)

Lewis, Sarah: owner of murdered slave, Kate, 92

Lichtenstein, Alex: critiques hegemonic morality argument of Genovese and Levine, 104; argues slave crime informed by counter morality embracing theft, 104–5; argument challenged, 105–6; compares slave theft and English social crime, 340 (n. 25)

Literacy: linked to slave insurrections, 194; fear of, 194–95

Livestock: in Neuse-Pamlico region, 15; production of, increases, 27; theft of, a problem, 118–19, 119–20

Locke, Francis: indentured servant (Paul Crosby) flees from, 132; three slaves of flee, 132; reclaims runaway slave, 346 (n. 34)

Lord, Peter: tried for murder of slave, 92–93

Lower Cape Fear region. *See* Cape Fear region, Lower

Lumber products, 2, 27, 45; in Cape Fear region, 16, 32, 45; exports of, 45

Luten, James: sues for damage to slave, Edenton, 1761, 93

Luten, William: tried for murder of slave, Edenton, 1763, 92

Lutherans, German: little impact on slaves, 205

McAllister, Alexander: former owner of runaway slave (Jack), 123

McCartney, Rev. James: attacks Baptists, 1769, 213

McCrady, Edward: describes slave work songs, 319 (n. 85)

Mace, William, Sr.: slaves of (Tom and Manger), commit crimes, 112

Mann, Grace: seeks to arm slave, 329 (n. 58)

Manumission: laws on, 66, 355 (n. 1); petition for, in Warren County, 153–54; Quakers and, 203

Maroons: from South Carolina, in Florida, 98; in the Great Dismal Swamp, 99; illustrate importance of setting, 122; illustrate political dimensions of flight, 122; and insurrection, 122; less important than in South Carolina, 122; location of settlements in southern colonies, 122

Marriage and family, African: West African and western Bantu, 155–60; bride service, 156; exchange marriage rare, 156; bride price (wealth), 156–59, 357 (nn. 18, 19); polygyny preferred form, 160; most marriages monogamous, 160, 358 (n. 23); and sex taboos, 163; residential patterns and marital and familial separations, 163–64; and extended families, 168–71

Marriage and family, European: age of women at primapartum, 361 (n. 44); compared to slave marriage and family, 361 (n. 44); completed family size of, 361 (n. 44)

Marriage and family, servant: legal status of, 102

Marriage and family, slave, 6, 7, 171–72; masters delegitimate, 7–8, 137–38; and slave productivity, 8; masters accept de facto marriages, 8, 137–38, 360 (n. 32); enslavement and African practices, 8, 159–60, 160–61, 163–65, 167, 168; monogamy in Africa and slavery, 8, 160–61; demography and, 8, 161–63, 278–82 (Table 7.1); and dual-headed households, 8, 162–63; sex ratios of, 25–27, 31; sex imbalances on individual plantations, 26–27; factors limiting marital opportunities, 26–27, 310 (n. 30); exogamous practices, 27; incest taboos, 27; interplantation, 27, 163–64; legal status of, 102; and running away, 124–25; importance of, and slave values, 153–55; breakups and separations of, 153–55, 155–60, 356 (n. 6); parents and sale of children, 154, 356 (n. 6); bride wealth evident in diluted form, 159; African practices diluted, 159–60; polygyny hindered by various factors, 159–60; pressures to practice monogamy, 160; incidence of serial monogamy, 160–61, 358 (n. 22); absence of family members on plantation, 162–63; children with single parents, 162–63; naming practices and, 163, 171; interplantation marriages and African practices, 163–64; extended families, 164, 168–71; nuclear family, interior life (birth intervals, completed family size), 164–68; childbearing practices of whites affect slaves, 165; on Pollock plantation, 169 (Figure 2), 170 (Figure 3); role of grandparents, 169, 171; adult children and aging parents, 171; slaves who could not marry calculated from sex imbalance ratios, 309–10 (n. 30); historians disagree on impact of slavery on, in British West Indies, 357–58 (n. 22); probability estimates explained, 359–60 (n. 31); interplantation linkages of extended families, 362 (n. 51); percentage of adults who could not be paired by sex, by region, 234 (Table 1.8); procedures for quantifying, 282–85 (Table 7.1, *Note*); development related to sex and age distribution, by region, 286 (Table 7.2); actual and possible development of, on three plantations, 288 (Table 7.3); estimates of development in N.C., 290 (Table 7.4); estimates of development, by region, 291 (Table 7.5), 292 (Table 7.6); age at first conception, 293 (Table 7.7); birth intervals, southern colonies, 297 (Table 7.12); completed family size, Carolinas, 298 (Table 7.13)

Marriage, interracial: acts of 1715, 1723, 1741, 67

Marye, Rev. James: on African languages in Virginia, 149–50

Maryland: slave demography of, compared with North Carolina, 2; studies of slavery in colonial, 2; density of slave population, 22–23; percentage of slaves on large slaveholdings, 23; growth rate of exports, 28; field and nonfield slaves, 33; Africans as percentage of adult slave population, 127; primapartum, age of slave women at, 166; completed slave families, size of, 168; Muslim customs among slaves, 178; slave family size in, compared with Virginia, 299 (Table 7.14); payment of slaves for overwork, 316 (n. 67), 318 (n. 80); hiring out slaves, by gender, 321 (n. 110)

Mayombe: matrilineal marriage and family practices of, 158; residential patterns of spouses and children, 164

Mbiti, John S.: on African gods and power of humans, 175; on religious significance of stars, comets, and meteors, 180; on afterlife, 209–10; on medicine men, 263

Mecklenberg County: settlement, 19; Scots-Irish in, 205; calculations of black, white, and total populations, 225 (Table 1.1, n. 60)

Memory, African, 156; enslavement and, 173–74; remembrance and habitual behavior and thought, 174; and retention of functional worldviews, 174; and WPA interviews, 179. *See also* Slaves, African-born

Menard, Russell: analysis of slave language critiqued, 354 (n. 23)

Merrens, Harry: estimates of natural increase in slave population questioned, 307 (n. 16)

Methodists: and abolitionism, 213; black membership estimated, 214; blacks in Maryland, Virginia, North Carolina, South Carolina, Georgia, 214

Meyer, Br. and Sr.: own slave child, Cathy, 204

Militia: benefits ruling class, 60; purpose of, 60; service as regressive tax, 60; slaves excluded from, 60; and status, 60

Millis, James: and slave labor at iron plantation, 37; on work habits in iron, whites and slaves, 39–40

Milly, Patty, and children: slaves hired out, 48

Minchinton, Walter E.: on seaborne slave trade of North Carolina, 307–8 (n. 16)

Mobility of slaves: laws restricting not always enforced, 328 (n. 42)

Moore, George: slave of (Bristol), runs off, 124

Moore, James: obtains gun license for slave, 330 (n. 58)

Moore, Mary: said to own free-born Portuguese black, 329 (n. 54)

Moore, Roger: slave of (Cato), tried for hog theft, 119; slave carpenters at his Brunswick saw mill, 320 (n. 102)

Moral economy: of slaves, 105–7; concept rejected as way to understand slave actions, 340 (n. 26). *See also* Ethic, slave; Hegemony, cultural; Paternalism

Moravians: exports to South Carolina, 28; exports via Cross Creek, 28, 205; work habits, 34; and slave runaway, Sambo, 135; and slaves, 203–5; missions among slaves, Virginia and Georgia, 204; and illicit trade by slaves, 205; reliance on slaves, 314 (n. 46); more interested in converting Indians than slaves, 370 (n. 97)

Morgan, Philip: interpretation of task system questioned, 317 (n. 69)

Mosely, Edward: on tar production and need for many slaves, 44

Mullin, Gerald W.: findings for acculturated runaways in Virginia questioned, 126. *See also* Mullin, Michael

Mullin, Michael: and predominance of particular African cultures, 356 (n. 8). *See also* Mullin, Gerald W.

Murder, by slaves: of Henry Ormond, 78–79, 97; punishments for, 84, 114–15; often starting point of slave insurrections, 97; political dimensions of, 98; as proportion of major slave crimes, 109; collaboration of slaves and, 111–12; attempted by slave (Dick), 114. *See also* Crime, slave

Murder, of slaves: not a crime before 1774, 57, 75–76, 91, 95; of slave runaways, 66; and law of 1774, 75–76

Murray, James: on slave supervision, 35–36; slaves of, hired out, 49; on slaves and funerals, 364 (n. 28)

Music, song, and dance, 41–42; African roots of, 182; and John Koonering celebration, 183–86

Names and naming patterns, African: day names, 7; positional names, 7; naming ceremonies and patterns, 138–39; differences and similarities in among ethnic groups, 138–39; multiple names, 139; examples of, 139–40; descriptive, 146–47; place, 147; surnames, 147; male day names and slave names, 273 (Table 6.4); female day names and slave names, 275 (Table 6.5); female positional names, 276 (Table 6.6); male positional names, 277, (Table 6.7)

Names and naming patterns, slave, 6; Anglicized versions of African names, 7; slave control of naming, 7, 138–40, 141–44; and African practices, 7, 138–39, 144–47; pool of African names allows diversity, 7, 141; slave defense of, 102, 139 (Tom Buck), 143 (Olaudah Equiano); affected by masters, 139, 143; homophonic transformation of African names, 139–40, 141–42; examples of African sources of, 139–40, 141–44; assumptions shape findings about origins of, 140–41; African male and female names among slaves exemplified, 141–42; rarely same as owners or immediate families, 142; African connection to diminutives of English names, 142–43; incidence of biblical tied to eventual spread of Christianity, 143–44, 353 (n. 13); naming process, 144; positional names, 144, 145–46; day names, 144–45, 146, 353 (n. 13); other African derivations, 146; surnames, 147; and evolution of slave languages, 148; after father, 163; and extended families, 171; rank order of most popular names, 269 (Table 6.1); distribution of, by possible origin, 271 (Table 6.2), 272 (Table 6.3); male day names and slave names, 273 (Table 6.4); female day names, 275 (Table 6.5); female positional names, 276 (Table 6.6); male positional names, 277 (Table 6.7); creole names derived from African names, 352 (n. 6); and naming practices scholars use to study slave culture, 352 (n. 7); African names distorted as pidgin English develops, 352 (n. 9); explanations of diminutive forms, 353 (n. 11); surnames discussed, 353 (n. 19); and masters' names, 354 (n. 20); necronymic, 360 (n. 33)

Names, white: popular, 143; those not used by slaves, 143

Nash, Josiah: slave (David) poisons Nash's wife, 80–81, 154, 186

Nash, Mary: poisoning of, 80–81; target of Sambo, a conjurer, 154, 186; seen as sorcerer, 187

Naval stores, 2, 27; province leads in production and export of, 11; British bounties on, 1705–29, 14, 15–16; in Neuse-Pamlico region, 15; in Cape Fear region, 15–16, 32; exports, 1753, 17; production, 43–45; economic appeal of, 44; slave labor in, 44

Neuse-Pamlico region (Beaufort, Carteret, Craven, Hyde, Onslow, and Pitt counties): naval stores in, 15; settlement, 15; population growth, 1755–67, 17; black percentage of population in, 22; percentage of slaves on large slaveholdings, 23; New Bern as port, 27; Anglican minister to, in 1705, 197; dual-headed slave families in, 232; estimates of development of slave marriage and family, 291 (Table 7.5); emigration from, to western counties, 306 (n. 10)

Newall, James: witness in hog theft case, 119–20

New Bern: port town, 11, 15, 27, 305 (n. 8); Anglican minister in, 197

New Hanover County: murder of master by slave (Will), 81; slaves executed in, 81; slave (Will) hanged alive in Gibbet, 81, 115; slave ("cooper") outlawed, killed, 82; slave (Phoebe) whipped, 82; slaves (Titus and Phyllis) shot dead, 82; slave (Tom) castrated for theft, 84; slave (Jimmy) castrated and hanged, 85; slave (Phill) hanged and castrated, 85; William Luten tried for murder of slave, 92–93; potential insurrection in, 99; slave (Jack) hanged for theft, 115; slaves (Jonny and Quamino) executed and decapitated for theft, 115; slave (Toney) hanged, 115; slave (Jack) runs off, 124; slave sale described, 154; extended families among slaves in, 168; calculations of population figures, 1767, 225 (Table 1.1, n. 45); court of, authorizes arming slaves, 330 (n. 58)

New Light Baptists. See Baptists, New Light

Newspapers: as source of data on runaways, 122; practices of slaveowners advertising for runaways in, 122–23

Nicholas, Robert Carter: on Virginia masters' fear of educating and Christianizing slaves, 1762, 194–95; on education of slave children in Virginia, 200

Nicholson, Thomas: theft of his hog, 119

Northampton County: murder of slave owner in, 112; slaves (Jack and Jemmy) hanged, 115; blacks baptized in, 199; New Light Baptists and Quakers in, 1772, 213; calculation of black, white, and total populations, 225 (Table 1.1, n. 52)

North Carolina: slavery in colonial era in, not studied, 2; slave demography of, compared with other southern colonies, 2, 11, 23–24; demographic characteristics of colonial slavery in, 2–3; economy and society in, compared to South Carolina, 11; growth of population, 11; diversified economy and exports, 11, 14; economy and slavery in, compared to Virginia, 11, 23–24; towns in, 14–17; black percentage of population in, 22; currency of, 31, 332 (n. 4); poor reputation of, 34–35; British models for, 52–53; banditry in, 101; square mileage of, how estimated for each region, 229 (Table 1.4, *Sources and Methods*). *See also* Population; Ruling class; Slaves; *names of specific regions and counties*

North Carolina Gazette (New Bern): extant and possible issues of, 344 (n. 7); advertisements for runaway slaves in, 344 (n. 8)

North Carolina Gazette (Wilmington): extant and possible issues of, 43–344 (n. 7)

North Carolina Magazine and Universal Intelligencer: extant and possible issues of, 343 (n. 7); advertisements for runaway slaves in, 344 (n. 8)

Northern Inner Plain–Piedmont region (Bute, Edgecombe, Granville, Halifax, and Northampton counties): population growth in, 1755, 17; black percentage of population in, 22; percentage of slaves on large slaveholdings in, 23; towns and trade in, 27–28

Norwood, John: witness in hog theft case, 120

Occupations. *See* Artisans; Domestics; Personal servants; Runaway slaves; Slaves; Watermen; Work; Work organization; Work routines

Oliver, John: slave of (Tom), castrated, 84; slave of (Tom), accused of collaborating to poison, 112

Onslow County: slave (Cuff) hanged for poisoning master, 115; river system in, 303 (n. 3); possible use of task system in, 316 (n. 65)

Orange County: settlement, 19; Quakers in, 202; Scots-Irish in, 205; New Light Baptists and Baptists in, 215: iron production in, 318 (n. 79)

Ordinances, Wilmington slave: bar congregating (1765, 1768, 1772), 69; regulate trading (1772), 69, 116–17; regulate housing (1765, 1772), 117; restrict hiring out (1765, 1772), 117

Ormond, Henry, murder of, 78–79; as resistance, 97; and slave collaboration, 111–12

Ottolenghe, Joseph: notes slave languages as obstacle to conversion in Georgia, 149–50; on slaves resisting conversion in Georgia, 190; on "biological inferiority" of Georgia slaves, 191; on planter contempt of blacks, 191; on religious laxity of whites in Georgia, 192; on planters' view of effects of conversion on slaves, 1753, 194; condescending approach of to slaves, 199–200

Outlawed slaves: laws on, 1715 and 1741, 63, 64–66; suicide of, 66, 82; and brutal treatment of, 81–82

Overseers: in South Carolina rice production, 4; harshness of, 36, 38; high turnover among, 316 (n. 61)

Pasquotank County: trial of slave (Sambo) in for use of poison, 80–81, 154, 186–87; slave (Ben) in whipped for illegal trading, 82; case of slave and white crime collaboration in (Moses, Tom), 113–14; hog theft case in (Moses, Tom), 119; masters in 1709 fear conversion equals freedom, 193; John Woolman starts antislavery work in, 202; Quaker opposition to slavery in, 202–3; calculations of population, 1767, 224 (Table 1.1, n. 33); authorizes arming slaves, 329 (n. 58)

Paternalism: and Chesapeake tobacco planters, 4, 53, 56, 323 (n. 2); claims of in Chesapeake rejected, 4, 5; and South Carolina rice planters, 4–5; in theory, 53; in England, 53–54; and terror, 53–54, 57, 106; and hegemony, 54–55; and whites of low and middling classes, 54–55; and slaves, 55–57, 69, 324–25 (n. 14); effects upon slave culture in Virginia questioned, 56; and slave culture, 56, 58; and cultural hegemony, 56–58; and absence of cultural hegemony, 105–7; and cooptation, 106; and plantation justice, 135; Gallay interpretation of challenged, 206–7; slaves and historiography, 324–25 (n. 14). *See also* Hegemony, cultural; Moral economy; Ruling class

Patterson, Orlando: on destructive impact of slavery on marriage and family in British West Indies, 357–58 (n. 22)

Peggs, Ann: owner of slave (Negro Tom) accused of hog theft, 119

Perdue, Theda: on Cherokees and black slaves, 338 (n. 8)

Perquimans County: execution of slave (Lettice) for murder in, 109, 114; theft of hog in, 119; Quaker opposition to slavery in, 202–3; calculation of black, white, and total populations, 1755 and 1767, 223 (Table 1.1, n. 4), 224 (Table 1.1, n. 34)

Person, William: describes runaway slave artisan (George), 130

Personal servants, slave: close contact with whites, 47

Pidgin-creole languages. *See* Languages, slave

Pitch: production, 44–45. *See also* Naval stores

Pitt County: calculations of population figures, 224 (Table 1.1, n. 40)

Plantation justice, 6; role of, 73–74; crimes normally dealt with, 74; evidence of, 133; and paternalism, 135

Plantation size. *See* Slaveholdings

Planters: living patterns of, in Albemarle region, 46; living patterns of, in Cape Fear region, 46; morality of, and castration of slaves, 90; "biological inferiority of blacks" and, 191–92

Poison or drug: punishment for providing, 83; slaves (Tom and Prymus) castrated for conspiring to use, 84; use of by slaves, 103, 186–89; African beliefs and practices in continued by slaves, 107, 188; incidence of among major slave crimes, 109; poisoning of master by slave (Cuff) in Onslow County, 115; trial of Sambo for use of, 154, 186–88; and conjuring, 187, 188; use of, in Caribbean, 189; from cassava roots, 189

Pollen, Rev. Thomas: on religious laxity of whites in Rhode Island, 192; on masters' fear of effect of baptism on slaves in Rhode Island, 194

Pollock, Thomas: and slave blacksmiths, 46, 47; extended families among slaves of, 168–69

Pollock plantation, surnames of slaves on, 147; occupations of slaves on, 260 (Table 5.4)

Polygyny: unsuccessful in colony, 8; significance of in southern colonies questioned, 358 (n. 22). *See also* Marriage and family, African; Marriage and family, slave

Pool, Solomon, Jr.: slave of (Moses), accused of theft, 113–14, 119

Population, 17, 19–23, 306 (n. 12); growth in interior by 1730s, 16; growth by region, 1755–67, 17; growth of after French and Indian War, 17, 19; growth of and immigration among whites, 17, 19; total by Revolution, 17, 306 (n. 12); growth rate of, 19–20; low density of, 22–23, 161; Creoles in, 25; Africans in, 25–26; unfree servants as proportion of, 31; slave crime parallels growth of, 109; and characteristics of runaways, 124; concentration on large plantations in coastal regions, 161; rapid growth of, 161; slaves, relatively low proportion of total population, 161; race totals by region and county, 1755 and 1767, 221 (Table 1.1); age distribution of blacks and whites, Pitt County 1775 list is model, 222 (Table 1.1, n. 1); conversion of white taxables to population totals, 222–23 (Table 1.1, n. 1); calculation of population by regions and counties, 222–25 (Table 1.1, nn. 1–60); regional population totals, 1755, 224 (Table 1.1, nn. 30–31); regional population, 1767, overestimated for Lower Cape Fear and underestimated for Upper Cape Fear, 225 (Table 1.1, n. 44); population statistics for province and regions, 226–27 (Table 1.2); total and per annum percentage increases by race, 1755–67, 228 (Table 1.3); approximation formula to calculate population increase per annum, 228 (Table 1.3, n. 1); density of black population, by region, 229 (Table 1.4); formula to estimate density of black population, 229 (Table 1.4, *Sources and Methods*); black population, definition of "range," 230 (Table 1.5, *Sources and Methods*); algorithm to convert slave taxables to slave totals in individual slaveholds, 230–31 (Table 1.5, *Sources and Methods*); slave taxables, 1751–72, and regional and provincial sex ratios, 232 (Table 1.7); slave and servant population compared, by regions and counties, 238 (Table 1.10); immigration and natural increase, 307 (n. 13); procedures to calculate sexual imbalances,

309–10 (n. 30); 1720, extrapolation for, 307 (n. 14)

Population, white, 19–27 passim; and immigration, 17, 19; growth rate of, 19

Presbyterians: demography of, 205; Highland Scots, 205; receptive to conversion of slaves, 205; Scots-Irish, 205; and slaves in South Carolina, 205; and slaves, 205–6; in Craven County, 1760, 212

Prices of slaves, 31, 239–40 (Table 1.11); and sex ratios, 31; compared with compensations for executed slaves, 88, 89, 90

Prinder, John: slave of (Bob), and hog theft, 119

Proclamation money. *See* North Carolina: currency of

Provisions, 2; in Neuse-Pamlico region, 15

Punishments of slave criminals: evidence of among runaways, 36, 349 (n. 36); compared to whites, 76–78, 81, 82; for burglary, 80; for murder, 81; for outlawed runaways, 81–82; whipping, 82–83; castration, 83–84; affected by compensation law of 1764, 90; corporal, for theft, 113; in capital cases, 114–15; for illegal trading, 116; and flight (Frank and Charles), 133; castration, colonial laws, and, 335 (n. 46). *See also* Branding; Burning; Castration; Decapitation; Ear cropping, for theft; Hanging; Whipping

Punishments of whites: compared to blacks, 76–78, 81, 82; decapitation after hanging, 333 (n. 30)

Quakers: establish meeting for blacks, 202; numbers of, 202; antislavery stance of, 202–3; and slaves, 202–3; manumit slaves, 203; in Craven County, 1760, 212

Quince, Richard: slave of (Frank), whipped, 133

Quincy, Josiah: on work habits of whites, 34

Raboteau, Albert J.: on slaves affected by Christianity in colonial era, 214; on number of black Methodists, 214; on number of black Baptists, 216

Racism: "biological inferiority" of slaves and, 191–92; and black-white intermarriage, 366 (n. 59); and manumission, 366 (n. 59); and tax policy regarding free blacks, 366 (n. 59)

Rape: of slave by another slave, 74; and punishment of execution, 84, 115 (Cato, Bacchus); of slave women, 85–86; punishment by race of victim, 85–87; of white women, 86–87; among major slave crimes, 109; of free woman by slave (George), 115; survey of colonial laws regarding blacks and, 335 (n. 46)

Ray, Benjamin: on African concept of time, 176, 177

Reading, Rev. Philip: describes pidgin-creole in Delaware, 149; on "biological inferiority" of blacks, 191

Reed, Rev. James, Anglican minister in Craven County, 179; on Muslim slaves, 179; on slaves as heathens, 190, 217; on lack of ministers, 198; on Anabaptists, Baptists, and Methodists in county, 212

Reformed Protestants, German: little impact on slaves, 205

Regulators, North Carolina, 19, 205; and paternalism, 54–55; reject cultural hegemony, 55; and ruling-class ideology, 55; origins of, 99–100, 304 (n. 6); and social banditry, 100–101; social-economic views, 312–13 (n. 41)

Regulators, South Carolina: banditry and social banditry, 99–100

Religiosity, African: life power, human ability to control and manipulate, 174; ritualistic respect of ancestors, 174–75; humanism, 175, 177; wholeness, 176, 177; time-transcending continuity, 176–77; health, 177–78; natural phenomena and human events, 179–80; in Brazil, 180; in Cuba, 180; death, burials, and afterlife, 180–82, 294–95, 296; music and dance, 182–83; healing, magical, and psychological skills, 187–88; medicine man and slave conjurer, 187–88; African sacred cosmos synthesized with African social customs, 211. *See also* Religiosity, slave; Slaves, African-born and hegemony, 106; sliding scale of slave ownership and, 225 (Table 3.2, nn. 1–18). *See also* Hegemony, cultural; Hegemony, political and economic; Paternalism

Runaway servants: laws of 1715 and 1741, 62; and apprentices as examples for slaves, 132; slaves as examples to, 132; and slaves from same owner, 348 (n. 34); ages of, 348 (n. 35); captured, 348 (n. 35); duration of time gone, 348 (n. 35); ethnicity of, 348 (n. 35); number of, 348 (n. 35)

Runaway slaves: in advertisements by masters, 7, 123, 139, 344 (nn. 8, 9); as social and political criminals, 62; and facility for English language, 62, 123, 129, 130, 131, 148; laws on, 62–66; outlawed, 64–66; suicides of outlawed slaves, 66, 82; and two-tiered system of criminal justice for slaves, 74; and legal system, 79–80; armed group of, 99; and Great Dismal Swamp, 101; and social banditry, 101; from Virginia, collaborate with Jack, 112; theft by, in Edgecombe County, 112–13; political dimensions of running away, 121, 122; dearth of records on, 122; importance of setting to, 122; tactics to recover, 122–23; quality and types of information about in extant records, 122–24; geographical origins of, 123; and Revolutionary crisis, 123, 344 (n. 11); not representative of slave demographic profile, 124; predominance of male, 124, 125; and multiple owners, 124, 129, 135, 345 (n. 16); ages of, 124, 257 (Table 5.1), 345 (n. 14); gender of, 124, 259 (Table 5.3); and marital and familial reasons to flee, 124–25; passing for free, 125; female, 125, 345 (n. 15); distribution by occupation, 125–27, 259 (Table 5.3); domestics among, compared to South Carolina, 126; and acculturation, 126, 264 (Table 5.8); passing for free as a goal of, 131; from masters whose indentured servants fled, 132, 348 (n. 35); options for, 132–33; reasons for flight, 132–33; rationality of, 132–35; identified by scars

(Frank, Bess), 133; conceal thoughts, 134; and timing of flight, 134, 349 (n. 43); clothing of, 134–35; goods taken by, 134–35; few take guns, 135; mode of transportation, 135; destinations of, 135–36, 352 (n. 5); difficulty of decision to flee, 136; typical advertisement for, 139; and use of own names (i.e., Tom Buck), 139; linguistic profile of, 148; distribution of compared to South Carolina and Virginia, by cohort and gender, 258 (Table 5.2); sex and occupation of, 259 (Table 5.3); origins of, 264 (Table 5.8); origin of and facility for English language among, 264 (Table 5.8); origin and language related to occupation and mode of escape, 266–67 (Table 5.10); dates of flight and capture, 268 (Table 5.11); months of flight, compared to South Carolina and Virginia runaways, 268 (Table 5.12); timing of advertisements for, 344 (n. 9); studies of stuttering among, 349 (n. 39). *See also* Maroons; *names of specific colonies*

Runaway slaves, African-born, 127–29, 134, 135, 136, 345 (n. 15); why fled, 127, 129; predominate among group runaways, 129; and sense of community, 129; determination of, 347 (n. 24). *See also* Runaway slaves captured or killed

Runaway slaves, captured or killed: vulnerability of Africans among, 134, 135, 136; groups of, outside the province, 135; facility for English language, 135, 136, 349–50 (n. 43); characteristics of, 135–36; death of in their home counties, 136; as percentage of all runaways, 136; and capture dates, 349–50 (n. 43); duration of escape time, 349–50 (n. 43)

Runaway slaves, field hands: and family reasons to flee, 124; and multiple owners, 124; almost proportionately represented, 125; number of, compared to South Carolina, 125; reasons for flight, 125–26; skills of, among individual runaways, 130–31; who try to pass for free,

131; determining number among runaways, 344–45 (n. 12); scars of punishment, 349 (n. 36)

Runaway slaves, individual: reasons to flee, 129–30, 131; and facility for language, 130, 131; African among, 129–30; Africans compared to non-Africans, 130

Runaway slaves, nonfield hands: and multiple owners, 124; almost proportionately represented, 126; number of artisans in N.C. compared to S.C., 126; proportion who were domestics, 126, 127; number of watermen among all, 126–27; watermen, special characteristics of, aid flight, 129; and facility for English language, 130; national origins of artisans, 130; artisans, salable expertise of, aids flight, 131; seek to pass as free, 131; use of waterways, 135, 350 (n. 48)

Rutherford, John: multiple enterprise of, 45; obtains gun license for slave, 330 (n. 58)

Rutman, Darret B. and Anita: argue masters controlled naming process, 140; how assumptions shape statistics on origins of slave names, 140–41; research techniques, 358 (n. 23), 360 (n. 31)

Rynchy, Jane: raped by slave (George), 86, 115

Sale of slaves: lack of legal marriage eases, 138; in Wilmington, 1778, 154; in Wilmington, 1780's, 154

Sambo: charged with preparing poison, 1761, Pasquotank County, 71–72; trial and sentencing of, 80–81, 84, 186–88; castration of, 84; and poison and African religious practices, 107; slave conjurer seeks to save daughter, 186–88

Samuel, Johannes: slave of Moravians, 203

Sandy Creek Church: Shubal Sterns forms, 215

Sawyer, Lemuel: Pasquotank sheriff castrates slave (Sambo), 84

Schaw, Janet: on corn cultivation, 36, 42; on garden plots, 38; on slave use of American flora, 40–41, 189; visits John Rutherford estate, 45; on task system, 59–60; on slave theft, 102–3; on slaves at white funeral, 181; as observer of slave practices, 184

Scherer, Lester: on slaves affected by Christianity in colonial era, 214; on advocates of Christianizing slaves believed them inferior, 366 (n. 55)

Schoepf, Johann: on conditions of slaves, 38; on poor work habits of whites and slaves, 39; on work delays by slaves, 39; on Moravian work habits, 45; on naval stores, 45; on slave auction, 154; inconsistency of, 317–18 (n. 76)

Scots-Irish: and western counties, 19; Presbyterians, 205

Scott, James C.: on Southeast Asian peasants, forms of resistance, 337 (n. 4)

Scottish Highlanders: as hired hands, 38. *See also* Highland Scots

Searchers: established 1753, 68

Senegal, 156

Servants, indentured: importance of, 31; compared to slaves, 59, 61, 62, 63; numbers, 61; legal rights and protections of, 61–62, 64, 102; runaways, 62–63, 132, 348 (n. 34), 348 (n. 35); population of, compared to slaves, 238 (Table 1.10); number replenished from within colony, 313 (n. 44); blacks among, stolen and illegally enslaved, 348 (n. 33). *See also* Laws, slave and servant; Runaway servants

Sex imbalance ratios, slave: compared to sex ratios, 26–27; causes of, 27; as tool to gauge incidence of slave marriages and families, 161–62; explained, 234 (Table 1.8, *Sources and Methods*)

Sex ratios, slave: and immigration, 25; used to calculate Africans in slave population, 25–26; among slaves, 25–27; and slave runaways, 124; polygyny, hindered by, 159; as tool to gauge incidence of slave marriages and families, 161; of slaves, calculated for province and regions from slave taxables, 1751–72, 232 (Table 1.7,

Sources and Methods); comparative, of southern colonies, 345 (n. 15)

Short, Charity: children of, slaves of John Walker, 147

Sierra Leone: bride price (wealth) in, 156–58; polygyny in, 160; bride price and bride service coupled, 357 (n. 17)

Simpson, Charles: store of in Bath Town robbed, 112

Sinclair, Malcolm: hires slaves, 48

Slave courts. *See* Courts, slave

Slaveholders: seek dominance, 4; lack control of slave ethnicity, 21; and discipline, 38; and slave courts, 72; sue for damage to slaves in civil suits, 93; claim absolute power, 106; runaways pose threat to, 121; tactics to recover runaways, 122–23, 344 (n. 9); disparage capacities of runaways, 131–32; deny European culture to slaves, 137, 220; and slave control of naming process, 138, 139–40; affect names of slaves, 139; alter African names, 141; names of slaves rarely same as, 142; slave marriages and families, 154–55; interest in monogamy among slaves, 160, 161; slave fecundity and, 160–61, 165; as poor observers of slave practices, 184, 220; resist conversion of slaves, 192–96, 198–99; resist education of slaves, 194–95; as the godparents of slaves, 199; dependence on slave labor, 220; use of terror, 220; and aspirations of whites, 314 (n. 46); refuse to acknowledge slave surnames, 353 (n. 19); concern about "workplace" English, 355 (n. 25)

Slaveholdings: in Cape Fear region, compared with South Carolina low country, 16, 309 (n. 24), 231 (Table 1.6); large, in Albemarle Sound, Neuse-Pamlico, and lower Cape Fear regions, compared to other colonies, 23–24; and occupational specialization, 32, 33; and marriage and family development, 162–63; distribution patterns of slave ownership by province and regions, 230–31 (Table 1.5); formula to obtain distribution patterns

of slave ownership for province, 230 (Table 1.5, *Sources and Methods*); compared to compensations, by selected regions and counties, 250–51 (Table 3.2); sliding scale of, and upper class, 254–55 (Table 3.2, nn. 1–18); procedures to calculate slaves in, 308–9 (n. 23)

Slave prices. *See* Prices of slaves

Slave resistance. *See* Resistance

Slavery: historiography of colonial, 1–2, 301 (n. 1); formative stages and policies of masters, 4; not conducive to cultural hegemony, 4, 56–58; differences in, among southern colonies, 4–6, 10–11, 161; growth of, compared to other southern colonies, 11, 16, 50; importance to commercial farming, 22; growth of, 1755–67, 22; and aspirations of whites, 31, 314 (n. 46); economy and demography summarized, 50–51; compared with servitude, 59; subsidized by province, 87–88, 90–91; paternalism and, 106; enslavement for life, 327 (n. 31); supposed leniency of, rejected, 328 (n. 35), 333–34 (n. 31). *See also* Slaves; *names of specific locales and colonies*

Slaves: ethnic origins unclear, 21–22, 148; diversity of experiences of, 33–34, 47–48, 130–31, 321 (n. 106); conditions of, 37–38, 57; use of flora and fauna, 40–41; comparative receptivity to Indian culture, 41; use of herbs, 41; harsh treatment of condemned, 57, 366 (n. 60); Africans as percentage of population, 58, 127; suicides of, 66, 82, 190; and weapons, 68, 329–30 (n. 58); and disturbances, 69; lack of legal protection, 75–76, 91, 92, 102; female, and rape, 85–86; pressure to bear children, 86; and terror, 91–92; as property of master protected by law of 1741, 93; armed in New Hanover County, 99, 330 (n. 58); and social banditry, 101; and multiple owners, 124; skills of, and escape, 125; stuttering as psychological scar, 133; mask selves from owners, 134; age of females at primapartum, 165–67;

age at menarche, 166; primapartum, variations in age at, significant within each colony, 166; child bearing often interrupted or prematurely ended, 166–67; age at first conception and birth, procedures, 294 (Table 7.7, n. 1); age at first conception, 295 (Table 7.9); age at first birth, distribution of, 296 (Table 7.10); inherited status through mother, 327 (n. 31); assessment levels, factor affecting, 336 (n. 57); and Islam, 364 (n. 20). *See also* Culture, slave; Delaware, slaves in; Ethic, slave; Georgia; Maryland; South Carolina, slavery in; Virginia, slavery in

Slaves, African-born: and cultural continuum, 2, 5, 364 (n. 30); percentage of adult slaves in North Carolina, 2, 25–26, 58, 127; numbers in Carolinas and Georgia, 2, 58, 127; memory and enslavement, 2, 173–74; worldviews of and enslavement, 2, 174; difficulty with English language, 3; languages of, 3; and lack of cultural hegemony, 4, 6, 58, 135; factors affecting ability to reconstruct native cultures, 6, 155–56, 159, 173–74; numbers calculated from sex ratios, 25–26; in South Carolina, 25–26, 40; and work, 36, 40, 43, 47; influence crops, 40, 43; and colonial water craft, 41; and conjuring, 103, 107, 186–88; as runaways, 123, 127–29, 130, 135, 346 (n. 21); as group runaways, 127, 129; as individual runaways, 129–30; among adult slaves in South, 127; as watermen, 127, 346 (n. 20); influence or African practices on names and languages of, 137; transformation of African names, examples, 139–40, 141–42; traumas of enslavement, 153–55; adjustment to enslavement, 155–56; from various cultures, 155–56; African practices, bride wealth persists in diluted form, 156, 159; bride service not evident in North Carolina, 159–60; polygyny not evident in North Carolina, 159–60; polygyny preferred form, 160; familial

separations and African practices, 163–64; African practices and values affect age at primapartum, 165; African practices and values affect birth rates, 165; African practices and birth intervals, 167; African religious beliefs persist, 185, 190–91; death, and return to Africa, 190; resist conversion to Christianity, 190–91; religiosity and Baptist practices, 208; Sobel view of African sacred cosmos and continuum in slavery questioned, 208–12; imports of into North Carolina, 307–8 (n. 16); and resistance, 347 (n. 22); African lineages and clans do not persist among, 362 (n. 48). *See also* Marriage and family, slave; Names and naming patterns, slave; Runaway slaves, African-born

Smith, John: witness in hog theft case, 119

Smith, Rev. Michael: on Anabaptists in Johnston County, 1758, 212

Smyth, J. F. D.: on slave runaways in Great Dismal Swamp, 101

Snow, Robert: suspects runaway slaves "decoyed away" by whites, 132

Sobel, Mechal, 371 (n. 105), 372 (n. 113); on appealing ways Baptists approached slaves, 208; on afterlife, Christian and African beliefs, 208–9; interpretation of slave religion questioned, 208–12; doubts African spirits or deities cross ocean with slaves, 210–11; errs on numbers of black Baptists, 215–16; errs on numbers of slaves Christianized, 215–16; on absence of godparents among slaves, 369 (n. 83); stresses slave role in shaping Afro-Christianity, 371 (n. 106)

Social banditry: and slave runaways, South Carolina, 99–100; and slave runaways, North Carolina, 100–101

Society for the Propagation of the Gospel in Foreign Parts (SPG), 179; in Georgia, 190; origin and purpose of, 196–97; subsidizes ministers, 197

Solomon, Job ben: bride price practices

described by, 156; on persistence of Muslim customs, 178; poison described by, 188–89

Song, slave: work chanties, 148, 318 (n. 84), 319 (n. 85), 354 (nn. 21, 22); creole lyrics, 319 (n. 85)

South Carolina, runaway slaves in: to Florida, 98; and social banditry, 99–100; males predominate, 124; field hands among, compared to North Carolina, 125; artisans underrepresented among, 126; domestics among, compared to North Carolina, 126; watermen among, 126; Africans among, 127; and timing of flight, 134; distribution of, compared to North Carolina and Virginia runaways, 258 (Table 5.2); occupation of, 261 (Table 5.5); by cohort, work, and origin, 263 (Table 5.7); by cohort, origin, and facility for English language, 265 (Table 5.9); high sex ratios and number of females runaways, 345 (n. 15); and multiple owners, 345 (n. 16); groups of, 347 (n. 23); visiting as goal, 347 (n. 30); how fled, 350 (n. 48); capture rates of, 351 (n. 52)

South Carolina, slavery in, 2, 4–5, 26, 58; studies of, 2; ethnicity of slaves, 21; percentage slaves on large slaveholdings, 24, 309 (n. 24); Africans as percentage of adults, 26, 127; and growth rate of exports, 28; field and nonfield slaves, 33; roots of Stono Rebellion in running away, marronage, and murder, 98–99; demography of, 99; banditry, 99–100; runaways, 100; maroons, 100; Gullah among slaves, 148, 151; primapartum, age of women at, 166; birth intervals, 167; completed family size, on large plantations, 168; and Presbyterians, 205; impact of Great Awakening on according to Jackson and Gallay, 206–7; occupations of runaways, 261 (Table 5.5); occupations of inventoried slaves, 262 (Table 5.6); age of females at first birth, 295 (Table 7.8); age of low country

females at first birth, 296 (Table 7.11); field hands, gender distribution, 314 (n. 51); production of skins and crops on one plantation, 320 (n. 98); necronymic naming practices, 360 (n. 33)

South Carolina Gazette: advertisements for North Carolina runaway slaves in, 344 (n. 8)

Spaight, Richard: compensated for slave executed, 81–82

Spangenburg, Bishop August Gottlieb: on naval stores, 43–44

Sparrel, William: Virginia owner of slave accused of thefts, 112

Spindel, Donna: explains high conviction rates in slave courts, 72; on case loads in criminal justice system for whites, 73; analysis of harsh criminal justice system for slaves, 332 (n. 9); on repeal of castration clause in slave law, 336–37 (n. 63)

Stearns, Shubal, and New Light Baptists, 215; in western counties, 215

Stewart, Rev. Alexander: on white resistance to educating blacks and Indians, 1763, 195; on increase in Anabaptists in Beaufort County, 1761, 212

Stokes, Drury: sued to pay damages for beating a slave, 93

Stuckey, Sterling: on African sources of John Koonering, 184; on slave culture and African continuum, 372 (n. 112)

Suicide: slaves expect to return to Africa after death, 190

Tar: production, 44–45. *See also* Naval stores

Tarboro: midland economic center, 27

Task system: in South Carolina, 4, 5, 36; in Lower Cape Fear, 5, 36–37; in North Carolina, 37; and iron production, 37, 316 (n. 67); possible use in turpentine operations, 316 (n. 65); in British West Indies, 317 (n. 69); and garden plots, 317 (n. 69). *See also* Incentives, negative and positive

Taxes: work levies, 87–88; fees, 88; liquor

Urmstone, John: SPG missionary seeks to buy slaves, 314 (n. 46)

Vail, Margaret: slave of (Bob), accused of theft, 113
Values, slave. *See* Ethic, slave
Van Horne, John C.: on converting blacks, 192; on fear of slave literacy, 194, 367 (n. 72); on limited impact of Bray's Associates, 201
Vasa, Gustavas. *See* Equiano, Olaudah
Virginia exports, 30; growth rate of, 28
Virginia, runaway slaves in: males predominate, 124; acculturation of, 126; watermen among, 126–27; timing of flight, 134; distribution of compared to North and South Carolina, by cohort and gender, 258 (Table 5.2); by cohort, work, and origin, 263 (Table 5.7); multiple owners, 345 (n. 16); how fled, 350 (n. 48)
Virginia, slavery in: demography of, compared with North Carolina, 2; studies of, 2; percentage of slaves on large slaveholdings, 23; and paternalism, 56, 323 (n. 2); birth intervals, 167; fears among whites of educating slaves, 194–95; educating children of slaves, 200–201; extensive creolization, 216; slave family size, compared to Maryland, 299 (Table 7.14); payment for overwork, 316 (n. 67); hiring out, females, 321 (n. 110); extrapolations to obtain population, 373 (n. 127)
Virginia Gazette: advertisements for North Carolina slave runaways in, 344 (n. 89)

Wachovia: slave, Sambo, runaway from, 135; Moravians settle, 203
Wage rates, of hires: slave and free compared, 49; slave women, 321 (n. 111); white women, 321 (n. 111)
Walker, John: slaves of and surnames, 147; extended families among slaves of, 168
Ward, Benjamin: murdered by slave (Cuff), 115
Waring, Rev. John: on Africans and English, 150; on overcoming slave resis-

tance to conversion, 190–91; on planter contempt of slaves, 192; on conversion and loss of labor time, 195–96
Warren, Dr. Edward: hears slave languages in Washington County, antebellum era, 149; observes John Koonering at Albemarle Sound plantation, 1829, 183, 185–86; as observer of slave practices, 184; emphasizes presence of African religious practices, 185, 186; speculates on African roots of John Koonering, 186
Warren County: free black petitions to manumit her husband, 153–54
Washington County: John Koonering described in, 185–86
Watermen, slave: work routines of, 46, 47; as runaways, 126–27; characteristics of, 127
Watson, Alan D.: understates brutality of slave punishments, 333 (n. 31)
Watson, Elkanah: observes slave work chanties, 41–42, 147–48, 182; describes slave sale, Wilmington, 1778, 154
Wealth: precisely correlated with office holding, 6, 322 (n. 1); and compensations for executed slaves, 88. *See also* Ruling class; Upper class
West, William: former slave of, manumission case, 153–54
Western region (Anson, Mecklenburg, Orange, and Rowan counties): population growth in, 1755–67, 17; slave sex ratios in, 25; towns and trade in, 27–28; black percentage of population in, 29; dual-headed slave families in, 162; estimates of development of slave marriage and family in, 292 (Table 7.6); internal migration and growth of, 306 (n. 10); trade patterns of, 310 (n. 33)
Whaling: Albemarle Sound region, 15
Wheat: not raised with tobacco, 319 (n. 86)
Wheat and flour: exports, 29
Whipping: of Phoebe, 82; in hog theft cases (Moses, Negro Tom, Cato, Bob), 82, 119, 120; for theft, 83 (Andrew, Bob, Simon,

Dublin, Dick, Tom, Ben, Sippey, Seller), 113 (Dick, Bob, Simon); evidence of, 133

Whitefield, George: influence in South Carolina on slaves, 205

Whites, poor: and criminal justice system, 72; weak models of Christianity for slaves, 192

Wiecek, William: on murder of slaves, 76

Wilkinson, Jacob: in letter seeks his runaway slave (Jack), 124, 173

Williams, Edward: slave of (Sambo), tried for poisoning, 154

Williamson, Daniel: slaveowner poisoned, 112

Wilmington: importance as port to trade, 11, 16, 27, 28, 305 (n. 8); restricts slave gatherings, 69, 116; restricts trading by slaves, 69, 116, 117; regulates slave housing, 116, 117; restricts hiring out of slaves, 117; slave owner in seeks runaway slave (Jack), 123; slave sale, 1778, described, 154; extended families among slaves in, 168

Winham, William: charged with attacking Charles Jordon's slaves, 93

Wood, Peter: on African influence on work, 40; discusses Geechee in Georgia, 355 (n. 35)

Woodmason, Rev. Charles: on Presbyterians and Anabaptists in Carolina backcountry, 1766, 213

Wood products: in Neuse-Pamlico region, 15

Woolman, John: starts antislavery work in province, 202; at times silent on slavery issue, 370 (n. 94)

Work: defining quality of, 32; whites, attitudes and habits of, 34-35, 40; habits of Africans, 35; habits of slaves, 38–40; slaves limit, 38–39, 42–43; natural interruptions, 40; seasonal patterns, 40; crops shape, 42–43; African influence on, 56; and slave songs, 354 (nn. 21–22)

Work organization: on large slaveholdings in Cape Fear region, 32; and size of slaveholding, 32, 33; discipline on small farms and plantations, 33. *See also* Gang labor, slave; Task system

Work routines: crops shape, 42–43; in rice production, 43; in tobacco production, 43; in naval stores industry, 43–45; of Cape Fear region slaves, 44–45; of domestics, 46; of riverboatmen, 46, 47; of artisans, 46–47; of slave artisans, 46–47; in iron production, 47

Yates, Richard: slave of (Pompey), attempts to murder, 114–15

Yates, Rev. William: on masters' fear of educating and Christianizing slaves in Virginia, 1762, 194–95; on education of slave children in Virginia, 200–201

Yoruba: naming practices among, 139; bride-wealth customs of, contemporary, 157–58; as source of John Koonering, 184; cultural impact of Islam on regarding dowries, 357 (n. 18)

Young, Henry: African slave of (Quamino), flees, 130, 184

Zahan, Dominique: on African concept of time, 177; on African sense of past and future, 177; on African beliefs of afterlife, 209; on medicine men, 263